Sweet & Maxwell's

Employment Law Statutes
2004/05

Th

2

AUSTRALIA
Law Book Co.
Sydney

CANADA and USA
Carswell
Toronto

HONG KONG
Sweet & Maxwell Asia

NEW ZEALAND
Brookers
Wellington

SINGAPORE and MALAYSIA
Sweet & Maxwell Asia
Singapore and Kuala Lumpur

Sweet & Maxwell's

Employment Law Statutes
2004/05

2nd Edition

Malcolm Sargeant, B.A., Ph.D.
Professor of Labour Law
Centre for Legal Research, Middlesex University

LONDON
SWEET & MAXWELL
2004

First Edition. 2003
Second Edition 2004

Published in 2004 by Sweet & Maxwell Ltd
of 100 Avenue Road, London NW3 3PF
Typeset by Sweet & Maxwell Ltd, 100 Avenue Road, London NW3 3PF
Printed in Great Britain by Ashford Colour Printers Hants

No natural forests were destroyed to make this product; only farmed timber
was used and replanted

ISBN 0 421 891 009

©
Sweet & Maxwell Limited
2004

PREFACE

This collection of employment law material is selective and is intended to provide students of the subject with the right sort of material, in a manageable form, to support their studies.

Students of employment law will be aware that there are an ever growing number of statutes and regulations and the task for this book has been to ensure that it is both completely up to date and contains all the important material that a student is likely to need. In addition there has been a need to recognise that much, but not all, of the new statute and regulation derives from the EU, often in the form of Directives.

This book is, therefore, essentially made up of three parts. First, the main statutes are included. These begin with the Equal Pay Act 1970 and conclude with the Employment Relations Bill 2004. This Bill will become an Act of Parliament after the publication date for this book, but some parts have nevertheless been included because of their importance.

The second part consists of the most important, for the employment law student, statutory instruments. These take the form of Regulations, some of which, such as the 2003 Regulations on introducing the principle of equality to employment matters concerned with sexual orientation and religion or belief, implement EU Directives and others, such as the Maternity and Parental Leave etc Regulations 1999, serve to give more detail to other statutes concerned with the subject.

The third part is the European Union section. This contains some relevant parts of the Treaty and the relevant Directives concerned with employment law, although I have tried to avoid duplication between the contents of Directives and the Regulations which implement them. By looking at this section it is possible to see just what a great impact the EU has on employment law in the United Kingdom.

One important new ACAS Code of Practice is included here. There are many more from ACAS and other statutory bodies such as the Commission for Racial Equality, the Equal Opportunities Commission and the Disability Rights Commission. These are easily available on the relevant web sites.

In all the material there are extensive footnotes which describe the source of amendments to the primary material.

Lastly I would like to dedicate this book to two great sisters, Jenny Cole and Liz Sargeant. They have been wonderful in what has been a difficult period for us all. Without them we would all be a lot worse off and the world would be a poorer place.

Malcolm Sargeant
Centre for Legal Research
Middlesex University
July 2004

CONTENTS

CHRONOLOGICAL CONTENTS

STATUTES

STATUTORY INSTRUMENTS

EC MATERIALS

CODES OF PRACTICE

ALPHABETICAL CONTENTS

STATUTES

STATUTORY INSTRUMENTS

EC MATERIALS

CODES OF PRACTICE

Equal Pay Act 1970

CHAPTER 41

1.—(1) If the terms of a contract under which a woman is employed at an establishment in Great Britain do not include (directly or by reference to a collective agreement or otherwise) an equality clause they shall be deemed to include one.

(2) An equality clause is a provision which relates to terms (whether concerned with pay or not) of a contract under which a woman is employed (the "woman's contract"), and has the effect that—

(a) where the woman is employed on like work with a man in the same employment—

  (i) if (apart from the equality clause) any term of the woman's contract is or becomes less favourable to the woman than a term of a similar kind in the contract under which that man is employed, that term of the woman's contract shall be treated as so modified as not to be less favourable, and

  (ii) if (apart from the equality clause) at any time the woman's contract does not include a term corresponding to a term benefiting that man included in the contract under which he is employed, the woman's contract shall be treated as including such a term;

(b) where the woman is employed on work rated as equivalent with that of a man in the same employment—

  (i) if (apart from the equality clause) any term of the woman's contract determined by the rating of the work is or becomes less favourable to the woman than a term of a similar kind in the contract under which that man is employed, that term of the woman's contract shall be treated as so modified as not to be less favourable, and

  (ii) if (apart from the equality clause) at any time the woman's contract does not include a term corresponding to a term benefiting that man included in the contract under which he is employed and determined by the rating of the work, the woman's contract shall be treated as including such a term.

[(c) where a woman is employed on work which, not being work in relation to which paragraph (a) or (b) above applies, is, in terms of the demands made on her (for instance under such headings as effort, skill and decision), of equal value to that of a man in the same employment—

  (i) if (apart from the equality clause) any term of the woman's contract is or becomes less favourable to the woman than a term of a similar kind in the contract under which that man is employed, that term of the woman's contract shall be treated as so modified as not to be less favourable, and

  (ii) if (apart from the equality clause) at any time the woman's contract does not include a term corresponding to a term benefiting that man included in the contract under which he is employed, the woman's contract shall be treated as including such a term.]¹

[(3) An equality clause shall not operate in relation to a variation between the woman's contract and the man's contract if the employer proves that the variation is genuinely due to a material factor which is not the difference of sex and that factor—

    (a) in the case of an equality clause falling within subsection (2)(a) or (b) above, must be a material difference between the woman's case and the man's; and

    (b) in the case of an equality clause falling within subsection (2)(c) above, may be such a material difference.]²

(4) A woman is to be regarded as employed on like work with men if, but only if, her work and theirs is of the same or a broadly similar nature, and the differences (if any) between the things she does and the things they do are not of practical importance in relation to terms and conditions of employment; and accordingly in comparing her work with theirs regard shall be had to the frequency or otherwise with which any such differences occur in practice as well as to the nature and extent of the differences.

(5) A woman is to be regarded as employed on work rated as equivalent with that of any men if, but only if, her job and their job have been given an equal value, in terms of the demand made on a worker under various headings (for instance effort, skill, decision), on a study undertaken with a view to evaluating in those terms the jobs to be done by all or any of the employees in an undertaking or group of undertakings, or would have been given an equal value but for the evaluation being made on a system setting different values for men and women on the same demand under any heading.

(6) Subject to the following subsections, for purposes of this section—

    (a) "employed" means employed under a contract of service or of apprenticeship or a contract personally to execute any work or labour, and related expressions shall be construed accordingly;

    (b) [...]³

    (c) Two employers are to be treated as associated if one is a company of which the other (directly or indirectly) has control or if both are companies of which a third person (directly or indirectly) has control,

and men shall be treated as in the same employment with a woman if they are men employed by her employer or any associated employer at the same establishment or at establishments in Great Britain which include that one and at which common terms and conditions of employment are observed either generally or for employees of the relevant classes.

Disputes as to, and enforcement of, requirement of equal treatment

1-002   **2.**—(1) Any claim in respect of the contravention of a term modified or included by virtue of an equality clause, including a claim for arrears of remuneration or damages in respect of the contravention, may be presented by way of a complaint to an [employment tribunal]⁴.

---

¹ Inserted by SI 1983/1794 reg 2 (1)
² Substituted by SI 1983/1794 reg 2 (2)
³ Repealed with saving by Armed Forces Act 1981 c.55 s 28 (2) Sch 5 Pt I Note
⁴ Words substituted by Employment Rights (Dispute Resolution) Act 1998 c.8 Pt I s 1 (2)

(1A) Where a dispute arises in relation to the effect of an equality clause the employer may apply to an [employment tribunal][1] for an order declaring the rights of the employer and the employee in relation to the matter in question.

(2) Where it appears to the Secretary of State that there may be a question whether the employer of any women is or has been contravening a term modified or included by virtue of their equality clauses, but that it is not reasonable to expect them to take steps to have the question determined, the question may be referred by him as respects all or any of them to an [employment tribunal][2] and shall be dealt with as if the reference were of a claim by the women or woman against the employer.

(3) Where it appears to the court in which any proceedings are pending that a claim or counterclaim in respect of the operation of an equality clause could more conveniently be disposed of separately by an [employment tribunal][3], the court may direct that the claim or counterclaim shall be struck out; and (without prejudice to the foregoing) where in proceedings before any court a question arises as to the operation of an equality clause, the court may on the application of any party to the proceedings or otherwise refer that question, or direct it to be referred by a party to the proceedings, to an [employment tribunal][4] for determination by the tribunal, and may stay or sist the proceedings in the meantime.

[(4) No determination may be made by an employment tribunal in the following proceedings –

  (a) on a complaint under subsection (1) above,
  (b) on an application under subsection (1A) above, or
  (c) on a reference under subsection (2) above,

unless the proceedings are instituted on or before the qualifying date (determined in accordance with section 2ZA below).][5]

[(5) A woman shall not be entitled, in proceedings brought in respect of a contravention of a term modified or included by virtue of an equality clause (including proceedings before an employment tribunal), to be awarded any payment by way of arrears of remuneration or damages –

  (a) in proceedings in England and Wales, in respect of a time earlier than the arrears date (determined in accordance with section 2ZB below), and
  (b) in proceedings in Scotland, in respect of a time before the period determined in accordance with section 2ZC below.][6]

(6) [...][7]
(7) [...][8]

[Procedure before tribunal in certain cases

2A.—(1) Where on a complaint or reference made to an employment **1-003** tribunal under section 2 above, a dispute arises as to whether any work is of equal value as mentioned in section 1(2)(c) above the tribunal
  [may either—
    (a) proceed to determine that question; or

---

[1] Words substituted by Employment Rights (Dispute Resolution) Act 1998 c.8 Pt I s 1 (2)
[2] Words substituted by Employment Rights (Dispute Resolution) Act 1998 c.8 Pt I s 1 (2)
[3] Words substituted by Employment Rights (Dispute Resolution) Act 1998 c.8 Pt I s 1 (2)
[4] Words substituted by Employment Rights (Dispute Resolution) Act 1998 c.8 Pt I s 1 (2)
[5] Substituted by SI 2003/1656 reg 3(2)
[6] Substituted by SI 2003/1656 reg 3(3)
[7] Repealed with saving by Armed Forces Act 1981 c.55 s 28 (2) Sch 5 Pt I Note
[8] Repealed with saving by Armed Forces Act 1981 c.55 s 28 (2) Sch 5 Pt I Note

(b) unless it is satisfied that there are no reasonable grounds for determining that the work is of equal value as so mentioned, require a member of the panel of independent experts to prepare a report with respect to that question;

and, if it requires the preparation of a report under paragraph (b) of this subsection, it shall not determine that question unless it has received the report.][1]

(2) Without prejudice to the generality of [...][2] subsection (1) above, there shall be taken, for the purposes of [that subsection][3], to be no reasonable grounds for determining that the work of a woman is of equal value as mentioned in section 1(2)(c) above if—

(a) that work and the work of the man in question have been given different values on a study such as is mentioned in section 1(5) above; and

(b) there are no reasonable grounds for determining that the evaluation contained in the study was (within the meaning of subsection (3) below) made on a system which discriminates on grounds of sex.

(3) An evaluation contained in a study such as is mentioned in section 1(5) above is made on a system which discriminates on grounds of sex where a difference, or coincidence, between values set by that system on different demands under the same or different headings is not justifiable irrespective of the sex of the person on whom those demands are made.

(4) In paragraph (b) of subsection (1) above the reference to a member of the panel of independent experts is a reference to a person who is for the time being designated by the Advisory, Conciliation and Arbitration Service for the purposes of that paragraph as such a member, being neither a member of the Council of that Service nor one of its officers or servants.][4]

Exclusion from ss. 1 to 5 of pensions etc

1-004   **6.**—(1) [An equality clause shall not][5] operate in relation to terms—

(a) affected by compliance with the laws regulating the employment of women, or

(b) affording special treatment to women in connection with pregnancy or childbirth.

[(1B) An equality clause shall not operate in relation to terms relating to a person's membership of, or rights under, an occupational pension scheme, being terms in relation to which, by reason only of any provision made by or under sections 62 to 64 of the Pensions Act 1995 (equal treatment), an equal treatment rule would not operate if the terms were included in the scheme.

(1C) In subsection (1B), "occupational pension scheme" has the same meaning as in the Pension Schemes Act 1993 and "equal treatment rule" has the meaning given by section 62 of the Pensions Act 1995.][6]

[Questioning of employer

1-005   **7B**—(1) For the purposes of this section—

---

[1] Substituted by SI 1996/438 reg 3 (2)
[2] Words repealed by SI 1996/438 reg 3 (3)
[3] Words substituted by SI 1996/438 reg 3 (3)
[4] Inserted by SI 1983/1794 reg 3 (1)
[5] Substituted by SI 1983/1794 reg 2 (2)
[6] Inserted by Pensions Act 1995 c.26 s 66 (1)

(a)   a person who considers that she may have a claim under section 1 above is referred to as "the complainant", and

(b)   a person against whom the complainant may decide to make, or has made, a complaint under section 2(1) or 7A(3) above is referred to as "the respondent"

(2) With a view to helping a complainant to decide whether to institute proceedings and, if she does so, to formulate and present her case in the most effective manner, the Secretary of State shall by order prescribe—

(a)   forms by which the complainant may question the respondent on any matter which is or may be relevant, and

(b)   forms by which the respondent may if he so wishes reply to any questions.

(3)   Where the complainant questions the respondent (whether in accordance with an order under subsection (2) above or not), the question and any reply by the respondent (whether in accordance with such an order or not) shall, subject to the following provisions of this section, be admissible as evidence in any proceedings under section 2(1) or 7A(3) above.

(4) If in any proceedings under section 2(1) or 7A(3) above it appears to the employment tribunal that the complainant has questioned the respondent (whether in accordance with an order under subsection (2) above or not) and that—

(a)   the respondent deliberately and without reasonable excuse omitted to reply within such period as the Secretary of State may by order prescribe, or

(b)   the respondent's reply is evasive or equivocal,

it may draw any inference which it considers it just and equitable to draw, including an inference that the respondent has contravened a term modified or included by virtue of the complainant's equality clause or corresponding term of service.

(5) Where the Secretary of State questions an employer in relation to whom he may decide to make, or has made, a reference under section 2(2) above, the question and any reply by the employer shall, subject to the following provisions of this section, be admissible as evidence in any proceedings under that provision.

(6) If in any proceedings on a reference under section 2(2) above it appears to the employment tribunal that the Secretary of State has questioned the employer to whom the reference relates and that—

(a)   the employer deliberately and without reasonable excuse omitted to reply within such period as the Secretary of State may by order prescribe, or

(b)   the employer's reply is evasive or equivocal,

it may draw any inference which it considers it just and equitable to draw, including, an inference that the employer has contravened a term modified or included by virtue of the equality clause of the woman, or women, as respects whom the reference is made.

(7) The Secretary of State may by order—

(a)   prescribe the period within which questions must be duly served in order to be admissible under subsection (3) or (5) above, and

(b)   prescribe the manner in which a question, and any reply, may be duly served.

(8) This section is without prejudice to any other enactment or rule of law regulating interlocutory and preliminary matters in proceedings before an

employment tribunal, and has effect subject to any enactment or rule of law regulating the admissibility of evidence in such proceedings.

(9) Power to make orders under this section is exercisable by statutory instrument subject to annulment in pursuance of a resolution of either House of Parliament.

(10) An order under this section may make different provision for different cases.][1]

European Communities Act 1972

CHAPTER 68

General implementation of Treaties

2-001   **2.**—(1) All such rights, powers, liabilities, obligations and restrictions from time to time created or arising by or under the Treaties, and all such remedies and procedures from time to time provided for by or under the Treaties, as in accordance with the Treaties are without further enactment to be given legal effect or used in the United Kingdom shall be recognised and available in law, and be enforced, allowed and followed accordingly; and the expression "enforceable Community right" and similar expressions shall be read as referring to one to which this subsection applies.

(2) Subject to Schedule 2 to this Act, at any time after its passing Her Majesty may by Order in Council, and any designated Minister or department may by regulations, make provision—

     (a) for the purpose of implementing any Community obligation of the United Kingdom, or enabling any such obligation to be implemented, or of enabling any rights enjoyed or to be enjoyed by the United Kingdom under or by virtue of the Treaties to be exercised; or

     (b) for the purpose of dealing with matters arising out of or related to any such obligation or rights or the coming into force, or the operation from time to time, of subsection (1) above;

and in the exercise of any statutory power or duty, including any power to give directions or to legislate by means of orders, rules, regulations or other subordinate instrument, the person entrusted with the power or duty may have regard to the objects of the Communities and to any such obligation or rights as aforesaid.

In this subsection designated Minister or department means such Minister of the Crown or government department as may from time to time be designated by Order in Council in relation to any matter or for any purpose, but subject to such restrictions or conditions (if any) as may be specified by the Order in Council.

Decisions on, and proof of, Treaties and Community instruments etc

2-002   **3.**—(1) For the purposes of all legal proceedings any question as to the meaning or effect of any of the Treaties, or as to the validity, meaning or effect of any Community instrument, shall be treated as a question of law (and, if not

---
[1] Inserted by Employment Act 2002 c.22 Pt IV s 42

referred to the European Court, be for determination as such in accordance with the principles laid down by and any relevant [decision of the European Court or any court attached thereto)][1]

(2) Judicial notice shall be taken of the Treaties, of the Official Journal of the Communities and of any decision of, or expression of opinion by, the European Court [or any court attached thereto][2] on any such question as aforesaid; and the Official Journal shall be admissible as evidence of any instrument or other act thereby communicated of any of the Communities or of any Community institution.

(3) Evidence of any instrument issued by a Community institution, including any judgment or order of the European Court [or any court attached thereto][3], or of any document in the custody of a Community institution, or any entry in or extract from such a document, may be given in any legal proceedings by production of a copy certified as a true copy by an official of that institution; and any document purporting to be such a copy shall be received in evidence without proof of the official position or handwriting of the person signing the certificate.

(4) Evidence of any Community instrument may also be given in any legal proceedings—

(a) by production of a copy purporting to be printed by the Queen's Printer;

(b) where the instrument is in the custody of a government department (including a department of the Government of Northern Ireland), by production of a copy certified on behalf of the department to be a true copy by an officer of the department generally or specially authorised so to do;

and any document purporting to be such a copy as is mentioned in paragraph (b) above of an instrument in the custody of a department shall be received in evidence without proof of the official position or handwriting of the person signing the certificate, or of his authority to do so, or of the document being in the custody of the department.

(5) In any legal proceedings in Scotland evidence of any matter given in a manner authorised by this section shall be sufficient evidence of it.

---

[1] Words substituted by European Communities (Amendment) Act 1986 c. 58 s 2 (a)
[2] Words inserted by European Communities (Amendment) Act 1986 c. 58 s 2 (b)
[3] Words inserted by European Communities (Amendment) Act 1986 c. 58 s 2 (b)

Health and Safety at Work etc. Act 1974

CHAPTER 37

PART I

HEALTH, SAFETY AND WELFARE IN CONNECTION WITH WORK,
AND CONTROL OF DANGEROUS SUBSTANCES AND CERTAIN
EMISSIONS INTO THE ATMOSPHERE

Preliminary

Preliminary

3-001   **1.**—(1) The provisions of this Part shall have effect with a view to—

    (a) securing the health, safety and welfare of persons at work;

    (b) protecting persons other than persons at work against risks to health or safety arising out of or in connection with the activities of persons at work;

    (c) controlling the keeping and use of explosive or highly flammable or otherwise dangerous substances, and generally preventing the unlawful acquisition, possession and use of such substances [...][1]

    (d) [...][2]

(2) The provisions of this Part relating to the making of health and safety regulations [...][3] and the preparation and approval of codes of practice shall in particular have effect with a view to enabling the enactments specified in the third column of Schedule 1 and the regulations, orders and other instruments in force under those enactments to be progressively replaced by a system of regulations and approved codes of practice operating in combination with the other provisions of this Part and designed to maintain or improve the standards of health, safety and welfare established by or under those enactments.

(3) For the purposes of this Part risks arising out of or in connection with the activities of persons at work shall be treated as including risks attributable to the manner of conducting an undertaking, the plant or substances used for the purposes of an undertaking and the condition of premises so used or any part of them.

(4) References in this Part to the general purposes of this Part are references to the purposes mentioned in subsection (1) above.

General duties

General duties of employers to their employees

3-002   **2.**—(1) It shall be the duty of every employer to ensure, so far as is reasonably practicable, the health, safety and welfare at work of all his employees.

(2) Without prejudice to the generality of an employer's duty under the preceding subsection, the matters to which that duty extends include in particular—

---

[1] Word repealed by Environmental Protection Act 1990 c.43 Sch 16 (I) para 1
[2] Repealed by Environmental Protection Act 1990 c.43 Sch 16 (I) para 1
[3] Words repealed by Employment Protection Act 1975 c.71 Sch 18

(a) the provision and maintenance of plant and systems of work that are, so far as is reasonably practicable, safe and without risks to health;

(b) arrangements for ensuring, so far as is reasonably practicable, safety and absence of risks to health in connection with the use, handling, storage and transport of articles and substances;

(c) the provision of such information, instruction, training and supervision as is necessary to ensure, so far as is reasonably practicable, the health and safety at work of his employees;

(d) so far as is reasonably practicable as regards any place of work under the employer's control, the maintenance of it in a condition that is safe and without risks to health and the provision and maintenance of means of access to and egress from it that are safe and without such risks;

(e) the provision and maintenance of a working environment for his employees that is, so far as is reasonably practicable, safe, without risks to health, and adequate as regards facilities and arrangements for their welfare at work.

(3) Except in such cases as may be prescribed, it shall be the duty of every employer to prepare and as often as may be appropriate revise a written statement of his general policy with respect to the health and safety at work of his employees and the organisation and arrangements for the time being in force for carrying out that policy, and to bring the statement and any revision of it to the notice of all of his employees.

(4) Regulations made by the Secretary of State may provide for the appointment in prescribed cases by recognised trade unions (within the meaning of the regulations) of safety representatives from amongst the employees, and those representatives shall represent the employees in consultations with the employers under subsection (6) below and shall have such other functions as may be prescribed.

(5) [...]¹

(6) It shall be the duty of every employer to consult any such representatives with a view to the making and maintenance of arrangements which will enable him and his employees to co-operate effectively in promoting and developing measures to ensure the health and safety at work of the employees, and in checking the effectiveness of such measures.

(7) In such cases as may be prescribed it shall be the duty of every employer, if requested to do so by the safety representatives mentioned in [subsection (4)]² above, to establish, in accordance with regulations made by the Secretary of State, a safety committee having the function of keeping under review the measures taken to ensure the health and safety at work of his employees and such other functions as may be prescribed.

General duties of employers and self-employed to persons other than their employees

3.—(1) It shall be the duty of every employer to conduct his undertaking in **3-003** such a way as to ensure, so far as is reasonably practicable, that persons not in his employment who may be affected thereby are not thereby exposed to risks to their health or safety.

(2) It shall be the duty of every self-employed person to conduct his undertaking in such a way as to ensure, so far as is reasonably practicable, that he and

---

¹ Repealed by Employment Protection Act 1975 c.71 Sch 18
² Words substituted by Employment Protection Act 1975 c.71 Sch 15 para 2

other persons (not being his employees) who may be affected thereby are not thereby exposed to risks to their health or safety.

(3) In such cases as may be prescribed, it shall be the duty of every employer and every self-employed person, in the prescribed circumstances and in the prescribed manner, to give to persons (not being his employees) who may be affected by the way in which he conducts his undertaking the prescribed information about such aspects of the way in which he conducts his undertaking as might affect their health or safety.

General duties of persons concerned with premises to persons other than their employees

3-004   **4.**—(1) This section has effect for imposing on persons duties in relation to those who—

(a) are not their employees; but

(b) use non-domestic premises made available to them as a place of work or as a place where they may use plant or substances provided for their use there,

and applies to premises so made available and other non-domestic premises used in connection with them.

(2) It shall be the duty of each person who has, to any extent, control of premises to which this section applies or of the means of access thereto or egress therefrom or of any plant or substance in such premises to take such measures as it is reasonable for a person in his position to take to ensure, so far as is reasonably practicable, that the premises, all means of access thereto or egress therefrom available for use by persons using the premises, and any plant or substance in the premises or, as the case may be, provided for use there, is or are safe and without risks to health.

(3) Where a person has, by virtue of any contract or tenancy, an obligation of any extent in relation to—

(a) the maintenance or repair of any premises to which this section applies or any means of access thereto or egress therefrom; or

(b) the safety of or the absence of risks to health arising from plant or substances in any such premises;

that person shall be treated, for the purposes of subsection (2) above, as being a person who has control of the matters to which his obligation extends.

(4) Any reference in this section to a person having control of any premises or matter is a reference to a person having control of the premises or matter in connection with the carrying on by him of a trade, business or other undertaking (whether for profit or not).

General duties of employees at work

3-005   **7.** It shall be the duty of every employee while at work—

(a) to take reasonable care for the health and safety of himself and, of other persons who may be affected by his acts or omissions at work; and

(b) as regards any duty or requirement imposed on his employer or any other person by or under any of the relevant statutory provisions, to co-operate with him so far as is necessary to enable that duty or requirement to be performed or complied with.

Sex Discrimination Act 1975

CHAPTER 65

PART I

DISCRIMINATION TO WHICH ACT APPLIES

[Direct and indirect discrimination against women

1.—(1) In any circumstances relevant for the purposes of any provision of **4-001** this Act, other than a provision to which subsection (2) applies, a person discriminates against a woman if—

    (a) on the ground of her sex he treats her less favourably than he treats or would treat a man, or

    (b) he applies to her a requirement or condition which he applies or would apply equally to a man but—

        (i) which is such that the proportion of women who can comply with it is considerably smaller than the proportion of men who can comply with it, and

        (ii) which he cannot show to be justifiable irrespective of the sex of the person to whom it is applied, and

        (iii) which is to her detriment because she cannot comply with it.

(2) In any circumstances relevant for the purposes of a provision to which this subsection applies, a person discriminates against a woman if—

    (a) on the ground of her sex, he treats her less favourably than he treats or would treat a man, or

    (b) he applies to her a provision, criterion or practice which he applies or would apply equally to a man, but—

        (i) which is such that it would be to the detriment of a considerably larger proportion of women than of men, and

        (ii) which he cannot show to be justifiable irrespective of the sex of the person to whom it is applied, and

        (iii) which is to her detriment.

(3) Subsection (2) applies to—

    (a) any provision of Part 2,

    (b) sections 35A and 35B, and

    (c) any other provision of Part 3, so far as it applies to vocational training.

(4) If a person treats or would treat a man differently according to the man's marital status, his treatment of a woman is for the purposes of subsection (1)(a) or (2)(a) to be compared to his treatment of a man having the like marital status.][1]

Sex discrimination against men

2.—(1) Section 1, and the provisions of Parts II and III relating to sex discrimi- **4-002** nation against women, are to be read as applying equally to the treatment of men, and for that purpose shall have effect with such modifications as are requisite.

(2) In the application of subsection (1) no account shall be taken of special treatment afforded to women in connection with pregnancy or childbirth.

---

[1] Substituted by SI 2001/2660 reg 3

[Discrimination on the grounds of gender reassignment

4-003   2A.—(1) A person ("A") discriminates against another person ("B") in any circumstances relevant for the purposes of—

(a) any provision of Part II,

(b) section 35A or 35B, or

(c) any other provision of Part III, so far as it applies to vocational training,

if he treats B less favourably than he treats or would treat other persons, and does so on the ground that B intends to undergo, is undergoing or has undergone gender reassignment.

(2) Subsection (3) applies to arrangements made by any person in relation to another's absence from work or from vocational training.

(3) For the purposes of subsection (1), B is treated less favourably than others under such arrangements if, in the application of the arrangements to any absence due to B undergoing gender reassignment—

(a) he is treated less favourably than he would be if the absence was due to sickness or injury, or

(b) he is treated less favourably than he would be if the absence was due to some other cause and, having regard to the circumstances of the case, it is reasonable for him to be treated no less favourably.

(4) In subsections (2) and (3) "arrangements" includes terms, conditions or arrangements on which employment, a pupillage or tenancy or vocational training is offered.

(5) For the purposes of subsection (1), a provision mentioned in that subsection framed with reference to discrimination against women shall be treated as applying equally to the treatment of men with such modifications as are requisite.][1]

[Direct and indirect discrimination against married persons in employment field

4-004   3.—(1) In any circumstances relevant for the purposes of any provision of Part 2, a person discriminates against a married person of either sex if—

(a) on the ground of his or her marital status he treats that person less favourably than he treats or would treat an unmarried person of the same sex, or

(b) he applies to that person a provision, criterion or practice which he applies or would apply equally to an unmarried person, but—

(i) which is such that it would be to the detriment of a considerably larger proportion of married persons than of unmarried persons of the same sex, and

(ii) which he cannot show to be justifiable irrespective of the marital status of the person to whom it is applied, and

(iii) which is to that person's detriment.

(2) For the purposes of subsection (1), a provision of Part 2 framed with reference to discrimination against women shall be treated as applying equally to the treatment of men, and for that purpose shall have effect with such modifications as are requisite.][2]

---

[1] Inserted by SI 1999/1102 reg 2 (1)

[2] Substituted by SI 2001/2660 reg 4

Discrimination by way of victimisation

4.—(1) A person ("the discriminator") discriminates against another person **4-005**
("the person victimised") in any circumstances relevant for the purposes of any
provision of this Act if he treats the person victimised less favourably than in
those circumstances he treats or would treat other persons, and do so by reason
that the person victimised has—

(a) brought proceedings against the discriminator or any other person
under this Act or the Equal Pay Act 1970 [or sections 62 to 65 of the
Pensions Act 1995][1], or

(b) given evidence or information in connection with proceedings brought
by any person against the discriminator or any other person under this
Act or the Equal Pay Act 1970 [or sections 62 to 65 of the Pensions Act
1995][2], or

(c) otherwise done anything under or by reference to this Act or the Equal
Pay Act 1970 [or sections 62 to 65 of the Pensions Act 1995][3] in relation
to the discriminator or any other person, or

(d) alleged that the discriminator or any other person has committed an
act which (whether or not the allegation so states) would amount to a
contravention of this Act or give rise to a claim under the Equal Pay Act
1970 [or under sections 62 to 65 of the Pensions Act 1995][4],

or by reason that the discriminator knows the person victimised intends to do
any of those things, or suspects the person victimised has done, or intends to do,
any of them.

(2) Subsection (1) does not apply to treatment of a person by reason of any
allegation made by him if the allegation was false and not made in good faith.

(3) For the purposes of subsection (1), a provision of Part II or III framed
with reference to discrimination against women shall be treated as applying
equally to the treatment of men and for that purpose shall have effect with such
modifications as are requisite.

Interpretation

5.—(1) In this Act—   **4-006**

(a) references to discrimination refer to any discrimination falling within
sections 1 to 4; and

(b) references to sex discrimination refer to any discrimination falling
within section 1 or 2,

and related expressions shall be construed accordingly.

(2) In this Act—

"woman" includes a female of any age, and

"man" includes a male of any age.

(3) A comparison of the cases of persons of different sex or marital status
under [[section 1 (1) or (2) or 3 (1)][5], or a comparison of the cases of persons
required for the purposes of section 2A,][6] must be such that the relevant circumstances in the one case are the same, or not materially different, in the other.

---

[1] Words inserted by Pensions Act 1995 c.26 Pt I s 66 (2) (a)
[2] Words inserted by Pensions Act 1995 c.26 Pt I s 66 (2) (a)
[3] Words inserted by Pensions Act 1995 c.26 Pt I s 66 (2) (a)
[4] Words inserted by Pensions Act 1995 c.26 Pt I s 66 (2) (b)
[5] Words substituted by SI 2001/2660 reg 8 (1)
[6] Words inserted by SI 1999/1102 reg 2 (2)

PART II

DISCRIMINATION IN THE EMPLOYMENT FIELD

Discrimination by employers

Discrimination against applicants and employees

4-007   **6.**—(1) It is unlawful for a person, in relation to employment by him at an establishment in Great Britain, to discriminate against a woman—
  (a) in the arrangements he makes for the purpose of determining who should be offered that employment, or
  (b) in the terms on which he offers her that employment, or
  (c) by refusing or deliberately omitting to offer her that employment.

(2) It is unlawful for a person, in the case of a woman employed by him at an establishment in Great Britain, to discriminate against her—
  (a) in the way he affords her access to opportunities for promotion, transfer or training, or to any other benefits, facilities or services, or by refusing or deliberately omitting to afford her access to them, or
  (b) by dismissing her, or subjecting her to any other detriment.

[(4) Subsections (1)(b) and (2) do not render it unlawful for a person to discriminate against a woman in relation to her membership of, or rights under, an occupational pension scheme in such a way that, were any term of the scheme to provide for discrimination in that way, then, by reason only of any provision made by or under sections 62 to 64 of the Pensions Act 1995 (equal treatment), an equal treatment rule would not operate in relation to that term.

(4A) In subsection (4), ɪoccupational pension schemeɪ has the same meaning as in the Pension Schemes Act 1993 and ɪequal treatment ruleɪ has the meaning given by section 62 of the Pensions Act 1995.][1]

(5) Subject to section 8(3), subsection (1)(b) does not apply to any provision for the payment of money which, if the woman in question were given the employment, would be included (directly [...][2] or otherwise) in the contract under which she was employed.

(6) Subsection (2) does not apply to benefits consisting of the payment of money when the provision of those benefits is regulated by the woman's contract of employment.

(7) Subsection (2) does not apply to benefits, facilities or services of any description if the employer is concerned with the provision (for payment or not) of benefits, facilities or services of that description to the public, or to a section of the public comprising the woman in question, unless—
  (a) that provision differs in a material respect from the provision of the benefits, facilities or services by the employer to his employees, or
  (b) the provision of the benefits, facilities or services to the woman in question is regulated by her contract of employment, or
  (c) the benefits, facilities or services relate to training.

[(8) In its application to any discrimination falling within section 2A, this section shall have effect with the omission of subsections (4) to (6).][3]

---

[1] Substituted by Pensions Act 1995 c.26 Pt I s 66 (3)
[2] Words repealed by Sex Discrimination Act 1986 c.59 s 9 Pt II
[3] Inserted by SI 1999/1102 reg 3 (1)

Exception where sex is a genuine occupational qualification

7.—(1) In relation to sex discrimination—

4-008

(a) section 6(1)(a) or (c) does not apply to any employment where being a man is a genuine occupational qualification for the job, and

(b) section 6(2)(a) does not apply to opportunities for promotion or transfer to, or training for, such employment.

(2) Being a man is a genuine occupational qualification for a job only where—

(a) the essential nature of the job calls for a man for reasons of physiology (excluding physical strength or stamina) or, in dramatic performances or other entertainment, for reasons of authenticity, so that the essential nature of the job would be materially different if carried out by a woman; or

(b) the job needs to be held by a man to preserve decency or privacy because—

(i) it is likely to involve physical contact with men in circumstances where they might reasonably object to its being carried out by a woman, or

(ii) the holder of the job is likely to do his work in circumstances where men might reasonably object to the presence of a woman because they are in a state of undress or are using sanitary facilities; or

[(ba) the job is likely to involve the holder of the job doing his work, or living, in a private home and needs to be held by a man because objection might reasonably be taken to allowing to a woman–

(i) the degree of physical or social contact with a person living in the home, or

(ii) the knowledge of intimate details of such a person's life,

which is likely, because of the nature or circumstances of the job or of the home, to be allowed to, or available to, the holder of the job; or]¹

(c) the nature or location of the establishment makes it impracticable for the holder of the job to live elsewhere than in premises provided by the employer, and—

(i) the only such premises which are available for persons holding that kind of job are lived in, or normally lived in, by men and are not equipped with separate sleeping accommodation for women and sanitary facilities which could be used by women in privacy from men, and

(ii) it is not reasonable to expect the employer either to equip those premises with such accommodation and facilities or to provide other premises for women; or

(d) the nature of the establishment, or of the part of it within which the work is done, requires the job to be held by a man because—

(i) it is, or is part of, a hospital, prison or other establishment for persons requiring special care, supervision or attention, and

(ii) those persons are all men (disregarding any woman whose presence is exceptional), and

(iii) it is reasonable, having regard to the essential character of the establishment or that part, that the job should not be held by a woman; or

¹ Inserted by Sex Discrimination Act 1986 c.59 s 1 (2)

   (e) the holder of the job provides individuals with personal services promoting their welfare or education, or similar personal services, and those services can most effectively be provided by a man, or

   (f) [...]¹

   (g) the job needs to be held by a man because it is likely to involve the performance of duties outside the United Kingdom in a country whose laws or customs are such that the duties could not, or could not effectively, be performed by a woman, or

   (h) the job is one of two to be held by a married couple.

(3) Subsection (2) applies where some only of the duties of the job fall within paragraphs (a) to (g) as well as where all of them do.

(4) Paragraph (a), (b), (c), (d), (e) [...]² or (g) of subsection (2) does not apply in relation to the filling of a vacancy at a time when the employer already has male employees—

   (a) who are capable of carrying out the duties falling within that paragraph, and

   (b) whom it would be reasonable to employ on those duties, and

   (c) whose numbers are sufficient to meet the employer's likely requirements in respect of those duties without undue inconvenience.

[Corresponding exception relating to gender reassignment

4-009   **7A.**—(1) In their application to discrimination falling within section 2A, subsections (1) and (2) of section 6 do not make unlawful an employer's treatment of another person if–

   (a) in relation to the employment in question–

      (i) being a man is a genuine occupational qualification for the job, or

      (ii) being a woman is a genuine occupational qualification for the job, and

   (b) the employer can show that the treatment is reasonable in view of the circumstances described in the relevant paragraph of section 7(2) and any other relevant circumstances.

(2) In subsection (1) the reference to the employment in question is a reference–

   (a) in relation to any paragraph of section 6(1), to the employment mentioned in that paragraph;

   (b) in relation to section 6(2)–

      (i) in its application to opportunities for promotion or transfer to any employment or for training for any employment, to that employment;

      (ii) otherwise, to the employment in which the person discriminated against is employed or from which that person is dismissed.

(3) In determining for the purposes of subsection (1) whether being a man or being a woman is a genuine occupational qualification for a job, section 7(4) applies in relation to dismissal from employment as it applies in relation to the filling of a vacancy.]³

[Supplementary exceptions relating to gender reassignment

4-010   **7B**—(1) In relation to discrimination falling within section 2A–

---

¹ Repealed by Employment Act 1989 c.38 ss 3 (2), 29 (4) Sch 7 Pt II (subject to a saving in Sch 9 para 1)

² Words repealed by Employment Act 1989 c.38 s 29 (4) Sch 7 Pt II

³ Inserted by SI 1999/1102 reg 4 (1)

(a) section 6(1)(a) or (c) does not apply to any employment where there is a supplementary genuine occupational qualification for the job,

(b) section 6(2)(a) does not apply to a refusal or deliberate omission to afford access to opportunities for promotion or transfer to or training for such employment, and

(c) section 6(2)(b) does not apply to dismissing an employee from, or otherwise not allowing him to continue in, such employment.

(2) Subject to subsection (3), there is a supplementary genuine occupational qualification for a job only if –

(a) the job involves the holder of the job being liable to be called upon to perform intimate physical searches pursuant to statutory powers;

(b) the job is likely to involve the holder of the job doing his work, or living, in a private home and needs to be held otherwise than by a person who is undergoing or has undergone gender reassignment, because objection might reasonably be taken to allowing to such a person –

(i) the degree of physical or social contact with a person living in the home, or

(ii) the knowledge of intimate details of such a person's life,

which is likely, because of the nature or circumstances of the job or of the home, to be allowed to, or available to, the holder of the job;

(c) the nature or location of the establishment makes it impracticable for the holder of the job to live elsewhere than in premises provided by the employer, and –

(i) the only such premises which are available for persons holding that kind of job are such that reasonable objection could be taken, for the purpose of preserving decency and privacy, to the holder of the job sharing accommodation and facilities with either sex whilst undergoing gender reassignment, and

(ii) it is not reasonable to expect the employer either to equip those premises with suitable accommodation or to make alternative arrangements; or

(d) the holder of the job provides vulnerable individuals with personal services promoting their welfare, or similar personal services, and in the reasonable view of the employer those services cannot be effectively provided by a person whilst that person is undergoing gender reassignment.

(3) Paragraphs (c) and (d) of subsection (2) apply only in relation to discrimination against a person who –

(a) intends to undergo gender reassignment, or

(b) is undergoing gender reassignment.][1]

Equal Pay Act 1970

8.—(1) [...][2]   4-011

(2) Section 1(1) of the Equal Pay Act 1970 (as set out in subsection (1) above) does not apply in determining for the purposes of section 6(1)(b) of this Act the terms on which employment is offered.

(3) Where a person offers a woman employment on certain terms, and if she accepted the offer then, by virtue of an equality clause, any of those terms would

[1] Inserted by SI 1999/1102 reg 4 (1)
[2] Substitutes new s 1 (1)-(3) in Equal Pay Act 1970 c.41

fall to be modified, or any additional term would fall to be included, the offer shall be taken to contravene section 6(1)(b).

(4) Where a person offers a woman employment on certain terms, and subsection (3) would apply but for the fact that, on her acceptance of the offer, section 1(3) of the Equal Pay Act 1970 (as set out in subsection (1) above) would prevent the equality clause from operating, the offer shall be taken not to contravene section 6(1)(b).

(5) An act does not contravene section 6(2) if—

(a) it contravenes a term modified or included by virtue of an equality clause, or

(b) it would contravene such a term but for the fact that the equality clause is prevented from operating by section 1(3) of the Equal Pay Act 1970.

(6) The Equal Pay Act 1970 is further amended as specified in Part I of Schedule 1, and accordingly has effect as set out in Part II of Schedule 1.

[(7) In its application to any discrimination falling within section 2A, this section shall have effect with the omission of subsections (3), (4) and (5)(b).][1]

Discrimination against contract workers

4-012   9.—(1) This section applies to any work for a person ("the principal") which is available for doing by individuals ("contract workers") who are employed not by the principal himself but by another person, who supplies them under a contract made with the principal.

(2) It is unlawful for the principal, in relation to work to which this section applies, to discriminate against a woman who is a contract worker—

(a) in the terms on which he allows her to do that work, or

(b) by not allowing her to do it or continue to do it, or

(c) in the way he affords her access to any benefits, facilities or services or by refusing or deliberately omitting to afford her access to them, or

(d) by subjecting her to any other detriment.

(3) [Subject to subsection (3A),][2] the principal does not contravene subsection (2)(b) by doing any act in relation to a woman at a time when if the work were to be done by a person taken into his employment being a man would be a genuine occupational qualification for the job.

[(3A) Subsection (3) does not apply in relation to discrimination falling within section 2A.

(3B) In relation to discrimination falling within section 2A, the principal does not contravene subsection (2)(a), (b), (c) or (d) by doing any act in relation to a woman if—

(a) he does it at a time when, if the work were to be done by a person taken into his employment—

(i) being a man would be a genuine occupational qualification for the job, or

(ii) being a woman would be a genuine occupational qualification for the job, and

(b) he can show that the act is reasonable in view of the circumstances relevant for the purposes of paragraph (a) and any other relevant circumstances.

(3C) In relation to discrimination falling within section 2A, the principal does not contravene subsection (2)(b) by doing any act in relation to a woman at a

---
[1] Inserted by SI 1999/1102 reg 3 (2)
[2] Words inserted by SI 1999/1102 reg 4 (2)

time when, if the work were to be done by a person taken into his employment, there would be a supplementary genuine occupational qualification for the job.]¹

(4) Subsection (2)(c) does not apply to benefits, facilities or services of any description if the principal is concerned with the provision (for payment or not) of benefits, facilities or services of that description to the public, or to a section of the public to which the woman belongs, unless that provision differs in a material respect from the provision of the benefits, facilities or services by the principal to his contract workers.

Meaning of employment at establishment in Great Britain

10.—(1) For the purposes of this Part and section 1 of the Equal Pay Act 1970 **4-013** ("the relevant purposes"), employment is to be regarded as being at an establishment in Great Britain unless the employee does his work wholly outside Great Britain [...]².

[(2) The reference to "employment" in subsection (1) includes—
  (a) employment on board a ship registered at a port of registry in Great Britain, and
  (b) employment on aircraft or hovercraft registered in the United Kingdom and operated by a person who has his principal place of business, or is ordinarily resident, in Great Britain.]³

(3) In the case of employment on board a ship registered at a port of registry in Great Britain (except where the employee does his work wholly outside Great Britain, and outside any area added under subsection (5)) the ship shall for the relevant purposes be deemed to be the establishment.

(4) Where work is not done at an establishment it shall be treated for the relevant purposes as done at the establishment from which it is done or (where it is not done from any establishment) at the establishment with which it has the closest connection.

(5) In relation to employment concerned with exploration of the sea bed or subsoil or the exploitation of their natural resources, Her Majesty may by Order in Council provide that subsections (1) and (2) shall each have effect as if the last reference to Great Britain included any area for the time being designated under section 1(7) of the Continental Shelf Act 1964, except an area or part of an area in which the law of Northern Ireland applies.

(6) An Order in Council under subsection (5) may provide that, in relation to employment to which the Order applies, this Part and section 1 of the Equal Pay Act 1970 are to have effect with such modifications as are specified in the Order.

(7) An Order in Council under subsection (5) shall be of no effect unless a draft of the Order was laid before and approved by each House of Parliament.

Discrimination by other bodies

Trade unions etc

12.—(1) This section applies to an organisation of workers, an organisation **4-014** of employers, or any other organisation whose members carry on a particular profession or trade for the purposes of which the organisation exists.

---

¹ Inserted by SI 1999/1102 reg 4 (3)
² Words repealed by SI 1999/3163 reg 2 (2)
³ Substituted by SI 1999/3163 reg 2 (3)

(2) It is unlawful for an organisation to which this section applies, in the case of a woman who is not a member of the organisation, to discriminate against her—

(a) in the terms on which it is prepared to admit her to membership, or

(b) by refusing, or deliberately omitting to accept, her application for membership.

(3) It is unlawful for an organisation to which this section applies, in the case of a woman who is a member of the organisation, to discriminate against her—

(a) in the way it affords her access to any benefits, facilities or services, or by refusing or deliberately omitting to afford her access to them, or

(b) by depriving her of membership, or varying the terms on which she is a member, or

(c) by subjecting her to any other detriment.

(4) This section does not apply to provision made in relation to the death or retirement from work of a member.

Qualifying bodies

4-015   **13.**—(1) It is unlawful for an authority or body which can confer an authorisation or qualification which is needed for, or facilitates, engagement in a particular profession or trade to discriminate against a woman—

(a) in the terms on which it is prepared to confer on her that authorisation or qualification, or

(b) by refusing or deliberately omitting to grant her application for it, or

(c) by withdrawing it from her or varying the terms on which she holds it.

(2) Where an authority or body is required by law to satisfy itself as to his good character before conferring on a person an authorisation or qualification which is needed for, or facilitates, his engagement in any profession or trade then, without prejudice to any other duty to which it is subject, that requirement shall be taken to impose on the authority or body a duty to have regard to any evidence tending to show that he, or any of his employees, or agents (whether past or present), has practised unlawful discrimination in, or in connection with, the carrying on of any profession or trade.

(3) In this section—

(a) "authorisation or qualification" includes recognition, registration, enrolment, approval and certification,

(b) "confer" includes renew or extend.

(4) Subsection (1) does not apply to discrimination which is rendered unlawful by section 22 or 23.

Persons concerned with provision of vocational training

4-016   **14.**—[(1) It is unlawful, in the case of a woman seeking or undergoing training which would help fit her for any employment, for any person who provides, or makes arrangements for the provision of, facilities for such training to discriminate against her—

(a) in the terms on which that person affords her access to any training course or other facilities concerned with such training, or

(b) by refusing or deliberately omitting to afford her such access, or

(c) by terminating her training, or

(d) by subjecting her to any detriment during the course of her training.

(2) Subsection (1) does not apply to—

(a) discrimination which is rendered unlawful by section 6(1) or (2) or section 22 or 23, or

(b) discrimination which would be rendered unlawful by any of those provisions but for the operation of any other provision of this Act.]¹

Employment agencies

15.—(1) It is unlawful for an employment agency to discriminate against a **4-017** woman—

    (a) in the terms on which the agency offers to provide any of its services, or

    (b) by refusing or deliberately omitting to provide any of its services, or

    (c) in the way it provides any of its services.

[(2) It is unlawful for a local education authority or education authority or any other person to do any act in providing services in pursuance of arrangements made, or a direction given, under section 10 of the Employment and Training Act 1973 which constitutes discrimination.]²

(3) References in subsection (1) to the services of an employment agency include guidance on careers and any other services related to employment.

(4) This section does not apply if the discrimination only concerns employment which the employer could lawfully refuse to offer the woman.

(5) An employment agency or local education authority [,education authority or other person]³ shall not be subject to any liability under this section if it proves—

    (a) that it acted in reliance on a statement made to it by the employer to the effect that, by reason of the operation of subsection (4), its action would not be unlawful, and

    (b) that it was reasonable for it to rely on the statement.

(6) A person who knowingly or recklessly makes a statement such as is referred to in subsection (5)(a) which in a material respect is false or misleading commits an offence, and shall be liable on summary conviction to a fine not exceeding level 5 on the standard scale.

[Relationships which have come to an end

20A.—(1) This section applies where– **4-018**

    (a) there has been a relevant relationship between a woman and another person ("the relevant person"), and

    (b) the relationship has come to an end (whether before or after the commencement of this section).

(2) In this section, a "relevant relationship" is a relationship during the course of which an act of discrimination by one party to the relationship against the other party to it is unlawful under any preceding provision of this Part.

(3) It is unlawful for the relevant person to discriminate against the woman by subjecting her to a detriment where the discrimination arises out of and is closely connected to the relevant relationship.]⁴

---

¹ Substituted by Employment Act 1989 c.38 s 7 (1)
² Substituted by Trade Union Reform and Employment Rights Act 1993 c.19 Sch 8 para 8
³ Words substituted by Trade Union Reform and Employment Rights Act 1993 c.19 Sch 8 para 8
⁴ Inserted by SI 2003/1657 reg 3

PART IV

OTHER UNLAWFUL ACTS

Discriminatory practices

4-019   **37.**—[(1) In this section "discriminatory practice" means—
    (a) the application of a provision, criterion or practice which results in an act of discrimination which is unlawful by virtue of any provision of Part 2 or 3 taken with section 1(2)(b) or 3(1)(b) or which would be likely to result in such an act of discrimination if the persons to whom it is applied were not all of one sex, or
    (b) the application of a requirement or condition which results in an act of discrimination which is unlawful by virtue of any provision of Part 3 taken with section 1(1)(b) or which would be likely to result in such an act of discrimination if the persons to whom it is applied were not all of one sex.][1]
    (2) A person acts in contravention of this section if and so long as—
    (a) he applies a discriminatory practice, or
    (b) he operates practices or other arrangements which in any circumstances would call for the application by him of a discriminatory practice.
    (3) Proceedings in respect of a contravention of this section shall be brought only by the Commission in accordance with sections 67 to 71.

Discriminatory advertisements

4-020   **38.**—(1) It is unlawful to publish or cause to be published an advertisement which indicates, or might reasonably be understood as indicating, an intention by a person to do any act which is or might be unlawful by virtue of Part II or III.
    (2) Subsection (1) does not apply to an advertisement if the intended act would not in fact be unlawful.
    (3) For the purposes of subsection (1), use of a job description with a sexual connotation (such as "waiter", "salesgirl", "postman" or "stewardess") shall be taken to indicate an intention to discriminate, unless the advertisement contains an indication to the contrary.
    (4) The publisher of an advertisement made unlawful by subsection (1) shall not be subject to any liability under that subsection in respect of the publication of the advertisement if he proves—
    (a) that the advertisement was published in reliance on a statement made to him by the person who caused it to be published to the effect that, by reason of the operation of subsection (2), the publication would not be unlawful, and
    (b) that it was reasonable for him to rely on the statement.
    (5) A person who knowingly or recklessly makes a statement such as is referred to in subsection (4) which in a material respect is false or misleading commits an offence, and shall be liable on summary conviction to a fine not exceeding [level 5 on the standard scale][2].

Instructions to discriminate

4-021   **39.** It is unlawful for a person—

---

[1] Substituted by SI 2001/2660 reg 8 (2)
[2] Words substituted by Criminal Justice Act 1982 c.48 ss 38, 46 and by Criminal Procedure (Scotland) Act 1975 c.21 ss 289F, 289G

(a) who has authority over another person, or
(b) in accordance with whose wishes that other person is accustomed to act,

to instruct him to do any act which is unlawful by virtue of Part II or III, or procure or attempt to procure the doing by him of any such act.

Pressure to discriminate

40.—(1) It is unlawful to induce, or attempt to induce, a person to do any act **4-022** which contravenes Part II or III by—
(a) providing or offering to provide him with any benefit, or
(b) subjecting or threatening to subject him to any detriment.

(2) An offer or threat is not prevented from falling within subsection (1) because it is not made directly to the person in question, if it is made in such a way that he is likely to hear of it.

Liability of employers and principals

41.—(1) Anything done by a person in the course of his employment shall be **4-023** treated for the purposes of this Act as done by his employer as well as by him, whether or not it was done with the employer's knowledge or approval.

(2) Anything done by a person as agent for another person with the authority (whether express or implied, and whether precedent or subsequent) of that other person shall be treated for the purposes of this Act as done by that other person as well as by him.

(3) In proceedings brought under this Act against any person in respect of an act alleged to have been done by an employee of his it shall be a defence for that person to prove that he took such steps as were reasonably practicable to prevent the employee from doing that act, or from doing in the course of his employment acts of that description.

Aiding unlawful acts

42.—(1) A person who knowingly aids another person to do an act made **4-024** unlawful by this Act shall be treated for the purposes of this Act as himself doing an unlawful act of the like description.

(2) For the purposes of subsection (1) an employee or agent for whose act the employer or principal is liable under section 41 (or would be so liable but for section 41(3)) shall be deemed to aid the doing of the act by the employer or principal.

(3) A person does not under this section knowingly aid another to do an unlawful act if—
(a) he acts in reliance on a statement made to him by that other person that, by reason of any provision of this Act, the act which he aids would not be unlawful, and
(b) it is reasonable for him to rely on the statement.

(4) A person who knowingly or recklessly makes a statement such as is referred to in subsection (3)(a) which in a material respect is false or misleading commits an offence, and shall be liable on summary conviction to a fine not exceeding [level 5 on the standard scale][1].

---
[1] Words substituted by Criminal Justice Act 1982 c.48 ss 38, 46 and by Criminal Procedure (Scotland) Act 1975 c.21 ss 289F, 289G

PART VI

EQUAL OPPORTUNITIES COMMISSION

Codes of practice

[Codes of practice

4-025 **56A.**—(1) The Commission may issue codes of practice containing such practical guidance as the Commission think fit for [one or more]¹ of the following purposes, namely—
(a) the elimination of discrimination in the field of employment;
(b) the promotion of equality of opportunity in that field between men and women.
[(ba) the promotion of equality of opportunity in that field for persons who intend to undergo, are undergoing or have undergone gender reassignment.]²
(2) When the Commission propose to issue a code of practice, they shall prepare and publish a draft of that code, shall consider any representations made to them about the draft and may modify the draft accordingly.
(3) In the course of preparing any draft code of practice for eventual publication under subsection (2) the Commission shall consult with—
(a) such organisations or associations of organisations representative of employers or of workers; and
(b) such other organisations, or bodies,
as appear to the Commission to be appropriate.
(4) If the Commission determine to proceed with the draft, they shall transmit the draft to the Secretary of State who shall—
(a) if he approves of it, lay it before both Houses of Parliament; and
(b) if he does not approve of it, publish details of his reasons for withholding approval.
(5) If, within the period of forty days beginning with the day on which a copy of a draft code of practice is laid before each House of Parliament, or, if such copies are laid on different days, with the later of the two days, either House so resolves, no further proceedings shall be taken thereon, but without prejudice to the laying before Parliament of a new draft.
(6) In reckoning the period of forty days referred to in subsection (5), no account shall be taken of any period during which Parliament is dissolved or prorogued or during which both Houses are adjourned for more than four days.
(7) If no such resolution is passed as is referred to in subsection (5), the Commission shall issue the code in the form of the draft and the code shall come into effect on such day as the Secretary of State may by order appoint.
(8) Without prejudice to section 81(4), an order under subsection (7) may contain such transitional provisions or savings as appear to the Secretary of State to be necessary or expedient in connection with the code of practice thereby brought into operation.
(9) The Commission may from time to time revise the whole or any part of a code of practice issued under this section and issue that revised code, and subsections (2) to (8) shall apply (with appropriate modifications) to such a revised code as they apply to the first issue of a code.

¹ Words substituted by SI 1999/1102 reg 7 (2) (a)
² Inserted by SI 1999/1102 reg 7 (2) (b)

(10) A failure on the part of any person to observe any provision of a code of practice shall not of itself render him liable to any proceedings; but in any proceedings under this Act [or the Equal Pay Act 1970][1] before an [employment tribunal][2] any code of practice issued under this section shall be admissible in evidence, and if any provision of such a code appears to the tribunal to be relevant to any question arising in the proceedings it shall be taken into account in determining that question.

(11) Without prejudice to subsection (1), a code of practice issued under this section may include such practical guidance as the Commission think fit as to what steps it is reasonably practicable for employers to take for the purpose of preventing their employees from doing in the course of their employment acts made unlawful by this Act.][3]

Investigations

Power to conduct formal investigations

57.—(1) Without prejudice to their general power to do anything requisite for **4-026** the performance of their duties under section 53(1), the Commission may if they think fit, and shall if required by the Secretary of State, conduct a formal investigation for any purpose connected with the carrying out of those duties.

(2) The Commission may, with the approval of the Secretary of State, appoint, on a full-time or part-time basis, one or more individuals as additional Commissioners for the purposes of a formal investigation.

(3) The Commission may nominate one or more Commissioners, with or without one or more additional Commissioners, to conduct a formal investigation on their behalf, and may delegate any of their functions in relation to the investigation to the persons so nominated.

Terms of reference

58.—(1) The Commission shall not embark on a formal investigation unless **4-027** the requirements of this section have been complied with.

(2) Terms of reference for the investigation shall be drawn up by the Commission or, if the Commission were required by the Secretary of State to conduct the investigation, by the Secretary of State after consulting the Commission.

(3) It shall be the duty of the Commission to give general notice of the holding of the investigation unless the terms of reference confine it to activities of persons named in them, but in such a case the Commission shall in the prescribed manner give those persons notice of the holding of the investigation.

[(3A) Where the terms of reference of the investigation confine it to activities of persons named in them and the Commission in the course of it propose to investigate any act made unlawful by this Act which they believe that a person so named may have done, the Commission shall—

    (a) inform that person of their belief and of their proposal to investigate the act in question; and

    (b) offer him an opportunity of making oral or written representations with regard to it (or both oral and written representations if he thinks fit);

---

[1] Words inserted by Trade Union Reform and Employment Rights Act 1993 c.19 Sch 7 para 15
[2] Words substituted by Employment Rights (Dispute Resolution) Act 1998 c.8 Pt I s 1 (2)
[3] Inserted by Race Relations Act 1976 c.74 Sch 4 para 1

and a person so named who avails himself of an opportunity under this subsection of making oral representations may be represented—

    (i) by counsel or a solicitor; or

    (ii) by some other person of his choice, not being a person to whom the Commission object on the ground that he is unsuitable.][1]

(4) The Commission or, if the Commission were required by the Secretary of State to conduct the investigation, the Secretary of State after consulting the Commission may from time to time revise the terms of reference; and subsections (1) [(3) and (3A)][2] shall apply to the revised investigation and terms of reference as they applied to the original.

Power to obtain information

4-028   **59.**—(1) For the purposes of a formal investigation the Commission, by a notice in the prescribed form served on him in the prescribed manner,—

    (a) may require any person to furnish such written information as may be described in the notice, and may specify the time at which, and the manner and form in which, the information is to be furnished;

    (b) may require any person to attend at such time and place as is specified in the notice and give oral information about, and produce all documents in his possession or control relating to, any matter specified in the notice.

(2) Except as provided by section 69, a notice shall be served under subsection (1) only where—

    (a) service of the notice was authorised by an order made by or on behalf of the Secretary of State, or

    (b) the terms of reference of the investigation state that the Commission believe that a person named in them may have done or may be doing acts of all or any of the following descriptions—

        (i) unlawful discriminatory acts,

        (ii) contraventions of section 37,

        (iii) contraventions of sections 38, 39 or 40, and

        (iv) acts in breach of a term modified or included by virtue of an equality clause,

and confine the investigation to those acts.

(3) A notice under subsection (1) shall not require a person—

    (a) to give information, or produce any documents, which he could not be compelled to give in evidence, or produce, in civil proceedings before the High Court or the Court of Session, or

    (b) to attend at any place unless the necessary expenses of his journey to and from that place are paid or tendered to him.

(4) If a person fails to comply with a notice served on him under subsection (1) or the Commission has reasonable cause to believe that he intends not to comply with it, the Commission may apply to a county court for an order requiring him to comply with it or with such directions for the like purpose as may be contained in the order; and [section 55 (penalty for neglecting or refusing to give evidence) of the County Courts Act 1984][3] shall apply to failure without reasonable excuse to comply with any such order as it applies in the cases there provided.

(5) In the application of subsection (4) to Scotland—

---

[1] Inserted by Race Relations Act 1976 c.74 Sch 4 para 2 (1)

[2] Words substituted by Race Relations Act 1976 c.74 Sch 4 para 2 (2)

[3] Words substituted by County Courts Act 1984 c.28 Sch 2 para 54

(a) for the reference to a county court there shall be substituted a reference to a sheriff court, and

(b) for the words after "order; and" to the end of the subsection there shall be substituted the words "paragraph 73 of the First Schedule to the Sheriff Courts (Scotland) Act 1907 (power of sheriff to grant second diligence for compelling the attendances of witnesses or havers) shall apply to any such order as it applies in proceedings in the sheriff court".

(6) A person commits an offence if he—

(a) wilfully alters, suppresses, conceals or destroys a document which he has been required by a notice or order under this section to produce, or

(b) in complying with such a notice or order, knowingly or recklessly makes any statement which is false in a material particular,

and shall be liable on summary conviction to a fine not exceeding [level 5 on the standard scale][1].

(7) Proceedings for an offence under subsection (6) may (without prejudice to any jurisdiction exercisable apart from this subsection) be instituted—

(a) against any person at any place at which he has an office or other place of business;

(b) against an individual at any place where he resides, or at which he is for the time being.

Recommendations and reports on formal investigations

60.—(1) If in the light of any of their findings in a formal investigation it **4-029** appears to the Commission necessary or expedient, whether during the course of the investigation or after its conclusion,—

(a) to make to any persons, with a view to promoting equality of opportunity between men and women who are affected by any of their activities, recommendations for changes in their policies or procedures, or as to any other matters, or

(b) to make to the Secretary of State any recommendations, whether for changes in the law or otherwise,

the Commission shall make those recommendations accordingly.

(2) The Commission shall prepare a report of their findings in any formal investigation conducted by them.

(3) If the formal investigation is one required by the Secretary of State—

(a) the Commission shall deliver the report to the Secretary of State, and

(b) the Secretary of State shall cause the report to be published,

and unless required by the Secretary of State the Commission shall not publish the report.

(4) If the formal investigation is not one required by the Secretary of State, the Commission shall either publish the report, or make it available for inspection in accordance with subsection (5).

(5) Where under subsection (4) a report is to be made available for inspection, any person shall be entitled, on payment of such fee (if any) as may be determined by the Commission—

(a) to inspect the report during ordinary office hours and take copies of all or any part of the report, or

---

[1] Words substituted by Criminal Justice Act 1982 c.48 ss 38, 46 and by Criminal Procedure (Scotland) Act 1975 c.21 ss 289F, 289G

(b) to obtain from the Commission a copy, certified by the Commission to be correct, of the report.

(6) The Commission may if they think fit determine that the right conferred by subsection (5)(a) shall be exercisable in relation to a copy of the report instead of, or in addition to, the original.

(7) The Commission shall give general notice of the place or places where, and the times when, reports may be inspected under subsection (5).

Restriction on disclosure of information

4-030   **61.**—(1) No information given to the Commission by any person ("the informant") in connection with a formal investigation shall be disclosed by the Commission, or by any person who is or has been a Commissioner, additional Commissioner or employee of the Commission, except—

(a) on the order of any court, or

(b) with the informant's consent, or

(c) in the form of a summary or other general statement published by the Commission which does not identify the informant or any other person to whom the information relates, or

(d) in a report of the investigation published by the Commission or made available for inspection under section 60(5), or

(e) to the Commissioners, additional Commissioners or employees of the Commission, or, so far as may be necessary for the proper performance of the functions of the Commission, to other persons, or

(f) for the purpose of any civil proceedings under this Act to which the Commission are a party, or any criminal proceedings.

(2) Any person who discloses information in contravention of subsection (1) commits an offence and shall be liable on summary conviction to a fine not exceeding [level 5 on the standard scale][1].

(3) In preparing any report for publication or for inspection the Commission shall exclude, so far as is consistent with their duties and the object of the report, any matter which relates to the private affairs of any individual or business interests of any person where the publication of that matter might, in the opinion of the Commission, prejudicially affect that individual or person.

PART VII

ENFORCEMENT

General

[Restriction of proceedings for breach of Act

4-031   **62.**—(1) Except as provided by this Act no proceedings, whether civil or criminal, shall lie against any person in respect of an act by reason that the act is unlawful by virtue of a provision of this Act.

(2) Subsection (1) does not preclude the making of an order of certiorari, mandamus or prohibition.

(3) In Scotland, subsection (1) does not preclude the exercise of the jurisdiction of the Court of Session to entertain an application for reduction or suspension of any order or determination, or otherwise to consider the validity of

---

[1] Words substituted by Criminal Justice Act 1982 c.48 ss 38, 46 and (Scotland) by Criminal Procedure (Scotland) Act 1975 c.21 ss 289F, 289G

any order or determination, or to require reasons for any order or determination to be stated.]¹

Enforcement in employment field

Jurisdiction of [employment tribunals]²

63.—(1) A complaint by any person ("the complainant") that another person **4-032** ("the respondent")—

  (a) has committed an act of discrimination against the complainant which is unlawful by virtue of Part II, or
  (b) is by virtue of section 41 or 42 to be treated as having committed such an act of discrimination against the complainant,

may be presented to an [employment tribunal]³.

(2) Subsection (1) does not apply to a complaint under section 13(1) of an act in respect of which an appeal, or proceedings in the nature of an appeal, may be brought under any enactment.

[Burden of proof: employment tribunals

63A.—(1) This section applies to any complaint presented under section 63 **4-033** to an employment tribunal.

(2) Where, on the hearing of the complaint, the complainant proves facts from which the tribunal could, apart from this section, conclude in the absence of an adequate explanation that the respondent—

  (a) has committed an act of discrimination against the complainant which is unlawful by virtue of Part 2, or
  (b) is by virtue of section 41 or 42 to be treated as having committed such an act of discrimination against the complainant,

the tribunal shall uphold the complaint unless the respondent proves that he did not commit, or, as the case may be, is not to be treated as having committed, that act.]⁴

64. [...]⁵   **4-034**

Remedies on complaint under section 63

65.—(1) Where an [employment tribunal]⁶ finds that a complaint presented **4-035** to it under section 63 is well-founded the tribunal shall make such of the following as it considers just and equitable—

  (a) an order declaring the rights of the complainant and the respondent in relation to the act to which the complaint relates;
  (b) an order requiring the respondent to pay to the complainant compensation of an amount corresponding to any damages he could have been ordered by a county court or by a sheriff court to pay to the complainant if the complaint had fallen to be dealt with under section 66;
  (c) a recommendation that the respondent take within a specified period action appearing to the tribunal to be practicable for the purpose of

---

¹ Substituted by Race Relations Act 1976 c.74 Sch 4 para 3
² Words substituted by Employment Rights (Dispute Resolution) Act 1998 c.8 Pt I s 1 (2)
³ Words substituted by Employment Rights (Dispute Resolution) Act 1998 c.8 Pt I s 1 (2)
⁴ Inserted by SI 2001/2660 reg 5
⁵ Repealed by Employment Tribunals Act 1996 c.17 Sch 3 (I) para 1
⁶ Words substituted by Employment Rights (Dispute Resolution) Act 1998 c.8 Pt I s 1 (2)

obviating or reducing the adverse effect on the complainant of any act of discrimination to which the complaint relates.

[(1A) In applying section 66 for the purposes of subsection (1)(b), no account shall be taken of subsection (3) of that section.

(1B) As respects an unlawful act of discrimination falling within [section 1(2)(b) or section 3(1)(b)][1], if the respondent proves that the [provision, criterion or practice][2] in question was not applied with the intention of treating the complainant unfavourably on the ground of his sex or marital status as the case may be, an order may be made under subsection (1)(b) only if the [employment tribunal][3]—

(a) makes such order under subsection (1)(a) and such recommendation under subsection (1)(c) (if any) as it would have made if it had no power to make an order under subsection (1)(b); and

(b) (where it makes an order under subsection (1)(a) or a recommendation under subsection (1)(c) or both) considers that it is just and equitable to make an order under subsection (1)(b) as well.][4]

(2) [...][5]

(3) If without reasonable justification the respondent to a complaint fails to comply with a recommendation made by an [employment tribunal][6] under subsection (1)(c), then, if they think it just and equitable to do so—

(a) the tribunal may increase the amount of compensation required to be paid to the complainant in respect of the complaint by an order made under subsection (1)(b), or

(b) if an order under subsection (1)(b) [was not made][7], the tribunal may make such an order.

Enforcement of Part III

Claims under Part III

4-036   **66.**—(1) A claim by any person ("the claimant") that another person ("the respondent")—

(a) has committed an act of discrimination against the claimant which is unlawful by virtue of Part III, or

(b) is by virtue of section 41 or 42 to be treated as having committed such an act of discrimination against the claimant,

may be made the subject of civil proceedings in like manner as any other claim in tort or (in Scotland) in reparation for breach of statutory duty.

(2) Proceedings under subsection (1)—

(a) shall be brought in England and Wales only in a county court, and

(b) shall be brought in Scotland only in a sheriff court,

but all such remedies shall be obtainable in such proceedings as, apart from this subsection [and section 62(1)][8], would be obtainable in the High Court or the Court of Session, as the case may be.

---

[1] Words substituted by SI 2001/2660 reg 8 (3)
[2] Words substituted by SI 2001/2660 reg 8 (3)
[3] Words substituted by Employment Rights (Dispute Resolution) Act 1998 c.8 Pt I s 1 (2)
[4] Inserted by SI 1996/438 reg 2 (2)
[5] Repealed by SI 1993/2798 reg 2
[6] Words substituted by Employment Rights (Dispute Resolution) Act 1998 c.8 Pt I s 1 (2)
[7] Words substituted by SI 1996/438 reg 2 (3)
[8] Words inserted by Race Relations Act 1976 c.74 Sch 4 para 5 (1)

(3) As respects an unlawful act of discrimination falling within section 1(1)(b) [...][1] no award of damages shall be made if the respondent proves that the requirement or condition in question was not applied with the intention of treating the claimant unfavourably on the ground of his sex [...][2].

[(3A) Subsection (3) does not affect the award of damages in respect of an unlawful act of discrimination falling within section 1(2)(b).][3]

(4) For the avoidance of doubt it is hereby declared that damages in respect of an unlawful act of discrimination may include compensation for injury to feelings whether or not they include compensation under any other head.

(5) Civil proceedings in respect of a claim by any person that he has been discriminated against in contravention of section 22 or 23 by a body to which section 25(1) applies shall not be instituted unless the claimant has given notice of the claim to the Secretary of State and either the Secretary of State has by notice informed the claimant that the Secretary of State does not require further time to consider the matter, or the period of two months has elapsed since the claimant gave notice to the Secretary of State; but nothing in this subsection applies to a counterclaim.

[(5A) In Scotland, when any proceedings are brought under this section, in addition to the service on the defender of a copy of the summons or initial writ initiating the action a copy thereof shall be sent as soon as practicable to the Commission in a manner to be prescribed by Act of Sederunt.][4]

(6) For the purposes of proceedings under subsection (1)—
  (a) [section 63(1) (assessors) of the County Courts Act 1984][5] shall apply with the omission of the words "on the application of any party", and
  (b) the remuneration of assessors appointed under the said section [63(1)][6] shall be at such rate as may be determined by the Lord Chancellor with the approval of the Minister for the Civil Service.

(7) For the purpose of proceedings before the sheriff, provision may be made by act of sederunt for the appointment of assessors by him, and the remuneration of any assessors so appointed shall be at such rate as the Lord President of the Court of Session with the approval of [the Treasury][7] may determine.

(8) A county court or sheriff court shall have jurisdiction to entertain proceedings under subsection (1) with respect to an act done on a ship, aircraft or hovercraft outside its district, including such an act done outside Great Britain.

[Burden of proof: county and sheriff courts

66A.—(1) This section applies to any claim brought under section 66(1) in a **4-037** county court in England and Wales or a sheriff court in Scotland.

(2) Where, on the hearing of the claim, the claimant proves facts from which the court could, apart from this section, conclude in the absence of an adequate explanation that the respondent—
  (a) has committed an act of discrimination against the claimant which is unlawful by virtue of—
    (i) section 35A or 35B, or
    (ii) any other provision of Part 3 so far as it applies to vocational training, or

---

[1] Words repealed by SI 1996/438 reg 2 (4)
[2] Words repealed by SI 1996/438 reg 2 (4)
[3] Inserted by SI 2001/2660 reg 7
[4] Inserted by Race Relations Act 1976 c.74 Sch 4 para 5 (2)
[5] Words substituted by County Courts Act 1984 c.28 Sch 2 para 55 (a)
[6] Words substituted by County Courts Act 1984 c.28 Sch 2 para 55 (b)
[7] Words substituted by SI 1981/1670 arts 2 (2), 3 (5)

(b) is by virtue of section 41 or 42 to be treated as having committed such
an act of discrimination against the claimant,
the court shall uphold the claim unless the respondent proves that he did not
commit, or, as the case may be, is not to be treated as having committed, that
act.][1]

Non-discrimination notices

Issue of non-discrimination notice

4-038   **67.**—(1) This section applies to—

(a) an unlawful discriminatory act, and

(b) a contravention of section 37, and

(c) a contravention of section 38, 39 or 40, and

(d) an act in breach of a term modified or included by virtue of an
equality clause,

and so applies whether or not proceedings have been brought in respect of the
act.

(2) If in the course of a formal investigation the Commission become
satisfied that a person is committing, or has committed, any such acts, the
Commission may in the prescribed manner serve on him a notice in the
prescribed form ("a non-discrimination notice") requiring him—

(a) not to commit any such acts, and

(b) where compliance with paragraph (a) involves changes in any of his
practices or other arrangements—

    (i) to inform the Commission that he has effected those changes and
what those changes are, and

    (ii) to take such steps as may be reasonably required by the notice for
the purpose of affording that information to other persons
concerned.

(3) A non-discrimination notice may also require the person on whom it is
served to furnish the Commission with such other information as may be
reasonably required by the notice in order to verify that the notice has been
complied with.

(4) The notice may specify the time at which, and the manner and form in
which, any information is to be furnished to the Commission, but the time at
which any information is to be furnished in compliance with the notice shall not
be later than five years after the notice has become final.

(5) The Commission shall not serve a non-discrimination notice in respect
of any person unless they have first—

(a) given him notice that they are minded to issue a non-discrimination
notice in his case, specifying the grounds on which they contemplate
doing so, and

(b) offered him an opportunity of making oral or written representations
in the matter (or both oral and written representations if he thinks fit)
within a period of not less than 28 days specified in the notice, and

(c) taken account of any representations so made by him.

(6) Subsection (2) does not apply to any acts in respect of which the
Secretary of State could exercise the powers conferred on him by section 25(2)
and (3); but if the Commission become aware of any such acts they shall give
notice of them to the Secretary of State.

---

[1] Inserted by SI 2001/2660 reg 6

(7) Section 59(4) shall apply to requirements under subsection (2)(b), (3) and (4) contained in a non-discrimination notice which has become final as it applies to requirements in a notice served under section 59(1).

Appeal against non-discrimination notice

68.—(1) Not later than six weeks after a non-discrimination notice is served **4-039** on any person he may appeal against any requirement of the notice—
  (a) to an [employment tribunal][1], so far as the requirement relates to acts which are within the jurisdiction of the tribunal;
  (b) to a county court or to a sheriff court so far as the requirement relates to acts which are within the jurisdiction of the court and are not within the jurisdiction of an [employment tribunal][2].

(2) Where the court or tribunal considers a requirement in respect of which an appeal is brought under subsection (1) to be unreasonable because it is based on an incorrect finding of fact or for any other reason, the court or tribunal shall quash the requirement.

(3) On quashing a requirement under subsection (2) the court or tribunal may direct that the non-discrimination notice shall be treated as if, in place of the requirement quashed, it had contained a requirement in terms specified in the direction.

(4) Subsection (1) does not apply to a requirement treated as included in a non-discrimination notice by virtue of a direction under subsection (3).

Investigation as to compliance with non-discrimination notice

69.—(1) If—   **4-040**
  (a) the terms of reference of a formal investigation state that its purpose is to determine whether any requirements of a non-discrimination notice are being or have been carried out, but section 59(2)(b) does not apply, and
  (b) section 58(3) is complied with in relation to the investigation on a date ("the commencement date") not later than the expiration of the period of five years beginning when the non-discrimination notice became final,
the Commission may within the period referred to in subsection (2) serve notices under section 59(1) for the purposes of the investigation without needing to obtain the consent of the Secretary of State.

(2) The said period begins on the commencement date and ends on the later of the following dates—
  (a) the date on which the period of five years mentioned in subsection (1)(b) expires;
  (b) the date two years after the commencement date.

Register of non-discrimination notices

70.—(1) The Commission shall establish and maintain a register ("the **4-041** register") of non-discrimination notices which have become final.

(2) Any person shall be entitled, on payment of such fee (if any) as may be determined by the Commission,—
  (a) to inspect the register during ordinary office hours and take copies of any entry, or

---

[1] Words substituted by Employment Rights (Dispute Resolution) Act 1998 c.8 Pt I s 1 (2)
[2] Words substituted by Employment Rights (Dispute Resolution) Act 1998 c.8 Pt I s 1 (2)

(b) to obtain from the Commission a copy, certified by the Commission to be correct, of any entry in the register.

(3) The Commission may, if they think fit, determine that the right conferred by subsection (2)(a) shall be exercisable in relation to a copy of the register instead of, or in addition to, the original.

(4) The Commission shall give general notice of the place or places where, and the times when, the register or a copy of it may be inspected.

Other enforcement by Commission

Persistent discrimination

4-042   **71.**—(1) If, during the period of five years beginning on the date on which either of the following became final in the case of any person, namely,—

(a) a non-discrimination notice served on him,

(b) a finding by a court or tribunal undersection 63 or 66, or section 2 of the Equal Pay Act 1970that he has done an unlawful discriminatory act or an act in breach of a term modified or included by virtue of an equality clause,

it appears to the Commission that unless restrained he is likely to do one or more acts falling within paragraph (b), or contravening section 37, the Commission may apply to a county court for an injunction, or to the sheriff court for an order, restraining him from doing so; and the court, if satisfied that the application is well-founded, may grant the injunction or order in the terms applied for or in more limited terms.

(2) In proceedings under this section the Commission shall not allege that the person to whom the proceedings relate has done an act which is within the jurisdiction of an [employment tribunal][1] unless a finding by an [employment tribunal][2] that he did that act has become final.

Enforcement of ss. 38 to 40

4-043   **72.**—(1) Proceedings in respect of a contravention of section 38, 39 or 40 shall be brought only by the Commission in accordance with the following provisions of this section.

(2) The proceedings shall be—

(a) an application for a decision whether the alleged contravention occurred, or

(b) an application under subsection (4) below,

or both.

(3) An application under subsection (2)(a) shall be made—

(a) in a case based on any provision of Part II, to an [employment tribunal][3], and

(b) in any other case to a county court or sheriff court.

(4) If it appears to the Commission—

(a) that a person has done an act which by virtue of section 38, 39 or 40 was unlawful, and

(b) that unless restrained he is likely to do further acts which by virtue of that section are unlawful,

---

[1] Words substituted by Employment Rights (Dispute Resolution) Act 1998 c.8 Pt I s 1 (2)

[2] Words substituted by Employment Rights (Dispute Resolution) Act 1998 c.8 Pt I s 1 (2)

[3] Words substituted by Employment Rights (Dispute Resolution) Act 1998 c.8 Pt I s 1 (2)

the Commission may apply to a county court for an injunction; or to a sheriff court for an order, restraining him from doing such acts; and the court, if satisfied that the application is well-founded, may grant the injunction or [...][1] order in the terms applied for or more limited terms.

(5) In proceedings under subsection (4) the Commission shall not allege that the person to whom the proceedings relate has done an act which is unlawful under this Act and within the jurisdiction of an [employment tribunal][2] unless a finding by an [employment tribunal][3] that he did that act has become final.

Preliminary action in employment cases

73.—(1) With a view to making an application under section 71(1) or 72(4) in **4-044** relation to a person the Commission may present to an [employment tribunal][4] a complaint that he has done an act within the jurisdiction of an [employment tribunal][5], and if the tribunal considers that the complaint is well-founded they shall make a finding to that effect and, if they think it just and equitable to do so in the case of an act contravening any provision of Part II may also (as if the complaint had been presented by the person discriminated against) make an order such as is referred to in section 65(1)(a), or a recommendation such as is referred to in section 65(1)(c), or both.

(2) Subsection (1) is without prejudice to the jurisdiction conferred by section 72(2).

(3) Any finding of an [employment tribunal][6] under—
   (a) this Act, or
   (b) the Equal Pay Act 1970,
in respect of any act shall, if it has become final, be treated as conclusive—
   (i) by the county court or sheriff court on an application under section 71(1) or 72(4) or in proceedings on an equality clause,
   (ii) by an [employment tribunal][7] on a complaint made by the person affected by the act under section 63 or in relation to an equality clause.

(4) In sections 71 and 72 and this section, the acts "within the jurisdiction of an [employment tribunal][8] " are those in respect of which such jurisdiction is conferred by sections 63 and 72 and by section 2 of the Equal Pay Act 1970.

Help for persons suffering discrimination

Help for aggrieved persons in obtaining information etc

74.—(1) With a view to helping a person ("the person aggrieved") who **4-045** considers he may have been discriminated against in contravention of this Act to decide whether to institute proceedings and, if he does so, to formulate and present his case in the most effective manner, the Secretary of State shall by order prescribe—
   (a) forms by which the person aggrieved may question the respondent on his reasons for doing any relevant act, or on any other matter which is or may be relevant;

---

[1] Words repealed by Race Relations Act 1976 c.74 Sch 5
[2] Words substituted by Employment Rights (Dispute Resolution) Act 1998 c.8 Pt I s 1 (2)
[3] Words substituted by Employment Rights (Dispute Resolution) Act 1998 c.8 Pt I s 1 (2)
[4] Words substituted by Employment Rights (Dispute Resolution) Act 1998 c.8 Pt I s 1 (2)
[5] Words substituted by Employment Rights (Dispute Resolution) Act 1998 c.8 Pt I s 1 (2)
[6] Words substituted by Employment Rights (Dispute Resolution) Act 1998 c.8 Pt I s 1 (2)
[7] Words substituted by Employment Rights (Dispute Resolution) Act 1998 c.8 Pt I s 1 (2)
[8] Words substituted by Employment Rights (Dispute Resolution) Act 1998 c.8 Pt I s 1 (2)

    (b) forms by which the respondent may if he so wishes reply to any questions.

(2) Where the person aggrieved questions the respondent (whether in accordance with an order under subsection (1) or not)—

    (a) the question, and any reply by the respondent (whether in accordance with such an order or not) shall, subject to the following provisions of this section, be admissible as evidence in the proceedings;

    (b) if it appears to the court or tribunal that the respondent deliberately, and without reasonable excuse, omitted to reply within a reasonable period or that his reply is evasive or equivocal, the court or tribunal may draw any inference from that fact that it considers it just and equitable to draw, including an inference that he committed an unlawful act.

(3) The Secretary of State may by order—

    (a) prescribe the period within which questions must be duly served in order to be admissible under subsection (2)(a), and

    (b) prescribe the manner in which a question, and any reply by the respondent, may be duly served.

(4) Rules may enable the court entertaining a claim under section 66 to determine, before the date fixed for the hearing of the claim, whether a question or reply is admissible under this section or not.

(5) This section is without prejudice to any other enactment or rule of law regulating interlocutory and preliminary matters in proceedings before a county court, sheriff court or industrial tribunal, and has effect subject to any enactment or rule of law regulating the admissibility of evidence in such proceedings.

(6) In this section "respondent" includes a prospective respondent and "rules"—

    (a) in relation to county court proceedings, means county court rules;

    (b) in relation to sheriff court proceedings, means sheriff court rules.

Assistance by Commission

4-046   **75.**—(1) Where, in relation to proceedings or prospective proceedings either under this Act or in respect of an equality clause, an individual who is an actual or prospective complainant or claimant applies to the Commission for assistance under this section, the Commission shall consider the application and may grant it if they think fit to do so on the ground that—

    (a) the case raises a question of principle, or

    (b) it is unreasonable, having regard to the complexity of the case or the applicant's position in relation to the respondent or another person involved or any other matter, to expect the applicant to deal with the case unaided,

or by reason of any other special consideration.

(2) Assistance by the Commission under this section may include—

    (a) giving advice;

    (b) procuring or attempting to procure the settlement of any matter in dispute;

    (c) arranging for the giving of advice or assistance by a solicitor or counsel;

    (d) arranging for representation by any person including all such assistance as is usually given by a solicitor or counsel in the steps preliminary or incidental to any proceedings, or in arriving at or giving effect to a compromise to avoid or bring to an end any proceedings, [(e) any other form of assistance which the Commission may consider appropriate][1]

but paragraph (d) shall not affect the law and practice regulating the descriptions of persons who may appear in, conduct, defend and address the court in, any proceedings.

(3) In so far as expenses are incurred by the Commission in providing the applicant with assistance under this section the recovery of those expenses (as taxed or assessed in such manner as may be prescribed by rules or regulations) shall constitute a first charge for the benefit of the Commission—

    (a) on any costs or expenses which (whether by virtue of a judgment or order of a court or tribunal or an agreement or otherwise) are payable to the applicant by any other person in respect of the matter in connection with which the assistance is given, and

    (b) so far as relates to any costs or expenses, on his rights under any compromise or settlement arrived at in connection with that matter to avoid or bring to an end any proceedings.

(4) The charge conferred by subsection (3) is subject to any charge [imposed by section 10(7) of the Access to Justice Act 1999][2], or any charge or obligation for payment in priority to other debts under the Legal Aid and Advice (Scotland) Acts 1967 and 1972 [the Legal Aid (Scotland) Act 1986][3], and is subject to any provision in [[, or made under,][4] either of those Acts for payment of any sum to the [Legal Services Commission][5] or into the Scottish Legal Aid Fund][6].

(5) In this section "respondent" includes a prospective respondent and "rules or regulations"—

    (a) in relation to county court proceedings, means county court rules;

    (b) in relation to sheriff court proceedings, means sheriff court rules;

    (c) in relation to [employment tribunal][7] proceedings, means [employment tribunal procedure regulations under][8] [Part I of the Employment Tribunals Act 1996][9]

Period within which proceedings to be brought

Period within which proceedings to be brought

76.—(1) An [employment tribunal][10] shall not consider a complaint under **4-047** section 63 unless it is presented to the tribunal before the end of [—

    (a) the period of three months beginning when the act complained of was done; or

    (b) in a case to which section 85(9A) applies, the period of six months so beginning.][11]

(2) A county court or a sheriff court shall not consider a claim under section 66 unless proceedings in respect of the claim are instituted before the end of

---

[1] Inserted by Race Relations Act 1976 c.74 Sch 4 para 7
[2] Words substituted by Access to Justice Act 1999 c.22 Sch 4 para 13 (a)
[3] Words substituted by Legal Aid (Scotland) Act 1986 c.47 s 45 Sch 3 para 5
[4] Words inserted by Access to Justice Act 1999 c.22 Sch 4 para 13 (b)
[5] Words substituted by Access to Justice Act 1999 c.22 Sch 4 para 13 (c)
[6] Words substituted by Legal Aid Act 1988 c.34 s 45 Sch 5 para 6 (b)
[7] Words substituted by Employment Rights (Dispute Resolution) Act 1998 c.8 Pt I s 1 (2)
[8] Words substituted by Employment Tribunals Act 1996 c.17 Sch 1 para 3
[9] Words substituted by Employment Rights (Dispute Resolution) Act 1998 c.8 Pt I s 1 (2) (c)
[10] Words substituted by Employment Rights (Dispute Resolution) Act 1998 c.8 Pt I s 1 (2)
[11] Words substituted by Armed Forces Act 1996 c.46 s 21 (6)

[(a) the period of six months beginning when the act complained of was done; or

(b) in a case to which section 66(5) applies, the period of eight months so beginning.][1]

[(3) An [employment tribunal][2], county court or sheriff court shall not consider an application under section 72(2)(a) unless it is made before the end of the period of six months beginning when the act to which it relates was done; and a county court or sheriff court shall not consider an application under section 72(4) unless it is made before the end of the period of five years so beginning.][3]

(4) An [employment tribunal][4] shall not consider a complaint under section 73(1) unless it is presented to the tribunal before the end of the period of six months beginning when the act complained of was done.

(5) A court or tribunal may nevertheless consider any such complaint, claim or application which is out of time if, in all the circumstances of the case, it considers that it is just and equitable to do so.

(6) For the purposes of this section—

(a) where the inclusion of any term in a contract renders the making of the contract an unlawful act that act shall be treated as extending throughout the duration of the contract, and

(b) any act extending over a period shall be treated as done at the end of that period, and

(c) a deliberate omission shall be treated as done when the person in question decided upon it,

and in the absence of evidence establishing the contrary a person shall be taken for the purposes of this section to decide upon an omission when he does an act inconsistent with doing the omitted act or, if he has done no such inconsistent act, when the period expires within which he might reasonably have been expected to do the omitted act if it was to be done.

PART VIII

SUPPLEMENTAL

Validity and revision of contracts

4-048   77.—(1) A term of a contract is void where—

(a) its inclusion renders the making of the contract unlawful by virtue of this Act, or

(b) it is included in furtherance of an act rendered unlawful by this Act, or

(c) it provides for the doing of an act which would be rendered unlawful by this Act.

(2) Subsection (1) does not apply to a term the inclusion of which constitutes, or is in furtherance of, or provides for, unlawful discrimination against a party to the contract, but the term shall be unenforceable against that party.

(3) A term in a contract which purports to exclude or limit any provision of this Act or the Equal Pay Act 1970 is unenforceable by any person in whose favour the term would operate apart from this subsection.

(4) Subsection (3) does not apply—

---

[1] Words substituted by Race Relations Act 1976 c.74 Sch 4 para 8 (a)
[2] Words substituted by Employment Rights (Dispute Resolution) Act 1998 c.8 Pt I s 1 (2)
[3] Substituted by Race Relations Act 1976 c.74 Sch 4 para 8 (b)
[4] Words substituted by Employment Rights (Dispute Resolution) Act 1998 c.8 Pt I s 1 (2)

    (a) to a contract settling a complaint to which section 63(1) of this Act or section 2 of the Equal Pay Act 1970 applies where the contract is made with the assistance of a conciliation officer;

    [(aa) to a contract settling a complaint to which section 63(1) of this Act or section 2 of the Equal Pay Act 1970 applies if the conditions regulating compromise contracts under this Act are satisfied in relation to the contract;][1]

    (b) to a contract settling a claim to which section 66 applies.

[(4A) The conditions regulating compromise contracts under this Act are that—

    (a) the contract must be in writing;

    (b) the contract must relate to the particular complaint;

    (c) the complainant must have received [advice from a relevant independent adviser][2] as to the terms and effect of the proposed contract and in particular its effect on his ability to pursue his complaint before an [employment tribunal][3];

    (d) there must be in force, when the adviser gives the advice, a [contract of insurance, or an indemnity provided for members of a profession or professional body,][4] covering the risk of a claim by the complainant in respect of loss arising in consequence of the advice;

    (e) the contract must identify the adviser; and

    (f) the contract must state that the conditions regulating compromise contracts under this Act are satisfied.][5]

[(4B) A person is a relevant independent adviser for the purposes of subsection (4A)(c)—

    (a) if he is a qualified lawyer,

    (b) if he is an officer, official, employee or member of an independent trade union who has been certified in writing by the trade union as competent to give advice and as authorised to do so on behalf of the trade union,

    (c) if he works at an advice centre (whether as an employee or a volunteer) and has been certified in writing by the centre as competent to give advice and as authorised to do so on behalf of the centre, or

    (d) if he is a person of a description specified in an order made by the Secretary of State.

(4BA) But a person is not a relevant independent adviser for the purposes of subsection (4A)(c) in relation to the complainant—

    (a) if he is, is employed by or is acting in the matter for the other party or a person who is connected with the other party,

    (b) in the case of a person within subsection (4B)(b) or (c), if the trade union or advice centre is the other party or a person who is connected with the other party,

    (c) in the case of a person within subsection (4B)(c), if the complainant makes a payment for the advice received from him, or

    (d) in the case of a person of a description specified in an order under subsection (4B)(d), if any condition specified in the order in relation to the giving of advice by persons of that description is not satisfied.

[1] Inserted by Trade Union Reform and Employment Rights Act 1993 c.19 Sch 6 para 1 (a)
[2] Words substituted by Employment Rights (Dispute Resolution) Act 1998 c.8 Pt II s 9 (2) (a)
[3] Words substituted by Employment Rights (Dispute Resolution) Act 1998 c.8 Pt I s 1 (2)
[4] Words substituted by Employment Rights (Dispute Resolution) Act 1998 c.8 Pt II s 10 (2) (a)
[5] Inserted by Trade Union Reform and Employment Rights Act 1993 c.19 Sch 6 para 1 (b)

(4BB) In subsection (4B)(a),"qualified lawyer" means—
(a) as respects England and Wales, a barrister (whether in practice as such or employed to give legal advice), a solicitor who holds a practising certificate, or a person other than a barrister or solicitor who is an authorised advocate or authorised litigator (within the meaning of the Courts and Legal Services Act 1990), and
(b) as respects Scotland, an advocate (whether in practice as such or employed to give legal advice), or a solicitor who holds a practising certificate.
(4BC) In subsection (4B)(b) "independent trade union" has the same meaning as in the Trade Union and Labour Relations (Consolidation) Act 1992.
(4C) For the purposes of subsection (4BA) any two persons are to be treated as connected—
(a) if one is a company of which the other (directly or indirectly) has control, or
(b) if both are companies of which a third person (directly or indirectly) has control.][1]
[(4D) An agreement under which the parties agree to submit a dispute to arbitration—
(a) shall be regarded for the purposes of subsection (4)(a) and (aa) as being a contract settling a complaint if—
(i) the dispute is covered by a scheme having effect by virtue of an order under section 212A of the Trade Union and Labour Relations (Consolidation) Act 1992, and
(ii) the agreement is to submit it to arbitration in accordance with the scheme, but
(b) shall be regarded for those purposes as neither being nor including such a contract in any other case.][2]
(5) On the application of any person interested in a contract to which subsection (2) applies, a county court or sheriff court may make such order as it thinks just for removing or modifying any term made unenforceable by that subsection; but such an order shall not be made unless all persons affected have been given notice of the application (except where under rules of court notice may be dispensed with) and have been afforded an opportunity to make representations to the court.
(6) An order under subsection (5) may include provision as respects any period before the making of the order.

General interpretation provisions

4-049 **82.**—(1) In this Act, unless the context otherwise requires—
"access" shall be construed in accordance with section 50;
"act" includes a deliberate omission;
"advertisement" includes every form of advertisement, whether to the public or not, and whether in a newspaper or other publication, by television or radio, by display of notices, signs, labels, showcards or goods, by distribution of samples, circulars, catalogues, price lists or other material, by exhibition of pictures, models or films, or in any other way, and references to the publishing of advertisements shall be construed accordingly;

[1] Substituted by Employment Rights (Dispute Resolution) Act 1998 c.8 Sch 1 para 2
[2] Inserted by Employment Rights (Dispute Resolution) Act 1998 c.8 Pt II s 8 (1)

"associated employer" shall be construed in accordance with subsection (2);

"the Commission" means the Equal Opportunities Commission;

"Commissioner" means a member of the Commission;

[...][1]

"designate" shall be construed in accordance with subsection (3);

"discrimination" and related terms shall be construed in accordance with section 5(1);

"employment" means employment under a contract of service or of apprenticeship or a contract personally to execute any work or labour, and related expressions shall be construed accordingly;

"employment agency" means a person who, for profit or not, provides services for the purpose of finding employment for workers or supplying employers with workers;

"equality clause" has the meaning given in section 1(2) of the Equal Pay Act 1970 (as set out in section 8(1) of this Act);

"final" shall be construed in accordance with subsection (4);

"firm" has the meaning given by section 4 of the Partnership Act 1890;

"formal investigation" means an investigation under section 57;

["gender reassignment" means a process which is undertaken under medical supervision for the purpose of reassigning a person's sex by changing physiological or other characteristics of sex, and includes any part of such a process;][2]

"general notice", in relation to any person, means a notice published by him at a time and in a manner appearing to him suitable for securing that the notice is seen within a reasonable time by persons likely to be affected by it;

"genuine occupational qualification" shall be construed in accordance with section 7(2)[, except in the expression "supplementary genuine occupational qualification", which shall be construed in accordance with section 7B(2)][3];

"Great Britain" includes such of the territorial waters of the United Kingdom as are adjacent to Great Britain;

"man" includes a male of any age;

"managers" has the same meaning for Scotland as in [section 135(1) of the Education (Scotland) Act 1980][4];

"near relative" shall be construed in accordance with subsection (5);

"non-discrimination notice" means a notice under section 67;

"notice" means a notice in writing;

"prescribed" means prescribed by regulations made by the Secretary of State by statutory instrument;

"profession" includes any vocation or occupation;

["provision, criterion or practice" includes "requirement or condition;"][5]

"retirement" includes retirement (whether voluntary or not) on grounds of age, length of service, or incapacity;

---

[1] Definition repealed by Employment Protection Act 1975 c.71 Sch 18
[2] Definition inserted by SI 1999/1102 reg 2 (3)
[3] Words inserted by SI 1999/1102 reg 4 (6)
[4] Words substituted by Education (Scotland) Act 1980 c.44 Sch 4 para 11
[5] Inserted by SI 2001/2660 reg 8 (4)

["self-governing school" has the same meaning as in the Education (Scotland) Act 1980][1];

"trade" includes any business;

"training" includes any form of education or instruction;

"woman" includes a female of any age.

Race Relations Act 1976

CHAPTER 74

PART I

DISCRIMINATION TO WHICH ACT APPLIES

Racial discrimination

5-001   **1.**—(1) A person discriminates against another in any circumstances relevant for the purposes of any provision of this Act if—

    (a) on racial grounds he treats that other less favourably than he treats or would treat other persons; or

    (b) he applies to that other a requirement or condition which he applies or would apply equally to persons not of the same racial group as that other but—

        (i) which is such that the proportion of persons of the same racial group as that other who can comply with it is considerably smaller than the proportion of persons not of that racial group who can comply with it; and

        (ii) which he cannot show to be justifiable irrespective of the colour, race, nationality or ethnic or national origins of the person to whom it is applied; and

        (iii) which is to the detriment of that other because he cannot comply with it.

[(1A) A person also discriminates against another if, in any circumstances relevant for the purposes of any provision referred to in subsection (1B), he applies to that other a provision, criterion or practice which he applies or would apply equally to persons not of the same race or ethnic or national origins as that other, but—

    (a) which puts or would put persons of the same race or ethnic or national origins as that other at a particular disadvantage when compared with other persons,

    (b) which puts that other at that disadvantage, and

    (c) which he cannot show to be a proportionate means of achieving a legitimate aim.

(1B) The provisions mentioned in subsection (1A) are—

    (a) Part II;

    (b) sections 17 to 18D;

    (c) section 19B, so far as relating to—

---

[1] Definition inserted by Self-Governing Schools etc. (Scotland) Act 1989 c.39 s 82 (1) Sch 10 para 5 (4) (b)

(i) any form of social security;
(ii) health care;
(iii) any other form of social protection; and
(iv) any form of social advantage;
which does not fall within section 20;
(d) sections 20 to 24;
(e) sections 26A and 26B;
(f) sections 76 and 76ZA; and
(g) Part IV, in its application to the provisions referred to in paragraphs (a) to (f).
(1C) Where, by virtue of subsection (1A), a person discriminates against another, subsection (1)(b) does not apply to him.]¹

(2) It is hereby declared that, for the purposes of this Act, segregating a person from other persons on racial grounds is treating him less favourably than they are treated.

Discrimination by way of victimisation

2.—(1) A person ("the discriminator") discriminates against another person **5-002** ("the person victimised") in any circumstances relevant for the purposes of any provision of this Act if he treats the person victimised less favourably than in those circumstances he treats or would treat other persons, and does so by reason that the person victimised has—
(a) brought proceedings against the discriminator or any other person under this Act; or
(b) given evidence or information in connection with proceedings brought by any person against the discriminator or any other person under this Act; or
(c) otherwise done anything under or by reference to this Act in relation to the discriminator or any other person; or
(d) alleged that the discriminator or any other person has committed an act which (whether or not the allegation so states) would amount to a contravention of this Act,
or by reason that the discriminator knows that the person victimised intends to do any of those things, or suspects that the person victimised has done, or intends to do, any of them.
(2) Subsection (1) does not apply to treatment of a person by reason of any allegation made by him if the allegation was false and not made in good faith.

Meaning of "racial grounds", "racial group" etc

3.—(1) In this Act, unless the context otherwise requires—   **5-003**
"racial grounds" means any of the following grounds, namely colour, race, nationality or ethnic or national origins;
"racial group" means a group of persons defined by reference to colour, race, nationality or ethnic or national origins, and references to a person's racial group refer to any racial group into which he falls.
(2) The fact that a racial group comprises two or more distinct racial groups does not prevent it from constituting a particular racial group for the purposes of this Act.
(3) In this Act—

---
¹ Words inserted by SI 2003/1626 reg 3

(a) references to discrimination refer to any discrimination falling within
section 1 or 2; and

(b) references to racial discrimination refer to any discrimination falling
within section 1,

and related expressions shall be construed accordingly.

(4) A comparison of the case of a person of a particular racial group with
that of a person not of that group under section 1(1) [or (1A)][1] must be such that
the relevant circumstances in the one case are the same, or not materially
different, in the other.

[Harassment

5-004   **3A**—(1) A person subjects another to harassment in any circumstances
relevant for the purposes of any provision referred to in section 1(1B) where, on
grounds of race or ethnic or national origins, he engages in unwanted conduct
which has the purpose or effect of–

(a) violating that other person's dignity, or

(b) creating an intimidating, hostile, degrading, humiliating or offensive
environment for him.

(2) Conduct shall be regarded as having the effect specified in paragraph (a)
or (b) of subsection (1) only if, having regard to all the circumstances, including in
particular the perception of that other person, it should reasonably be
considered as having that effect.][2]

PART II

DISCRIMINATION IN THE EMPLOYMENT FIELD

Discrimination by employers

[...][3] applicants and employees

5-005   **4.**—(1) It is unlawful for a person, in relation to employment by him at an
establishment in Great Britain, to discriminate against another—

(a) in the arrangements he makes for the purpose of determining who
should be offered that employment; or

(b) in the terms on which he offers him that employment; or

(c) by refusing or deliberately omitting to offer him that employment.

(2) It is unlawful for a person, in the case of a person employed by him at an
establishment in Great Britain, to discriminate against that employee—

(a) in the terms of employment which he affords him; or

(b) in the way he affords him access to opportunities for promotion,
transfer or training, or to any other benefits, facilities or services, or by
refusing or deliberately omitting to afford him access to them; or

(c) by dismissing him, or subjecting him to any other detriment.

[(2A) It is unlawful for an employer, in relation to employment by him at an
establishment in Great Britain, to subject to harassment a person whom he
employs or who has applied to him for employment.][4]

---

[1] Words inserted by SI 2003/1626 reg 4
[2] Inserted by SI 2003/1626 reg 5
[3] Words repealed by SI 2003/1626 reg 6 (1)
[4] Inserted by SI 2003/1626 reg 6 (2) (a)

(3) Except in relation to discrimination falling within section 2 [or discrimination of race or ethnic or national origins]¹, subsections (1) and (2) do not apply to employment for the purposes of a private household.

(4) Subsection (2) does not apply to benefits, facilities or services of any description if the employer is concerned with the provision (for payment or not) of benefits, facilities or services of that description to the public, or to a section of the public comprising the employee in question, unless—

  (a) that provision differs in a material respect from the provision of the benefits, facilities or services by the employer to his employees; or
  (b) the provision of the benefits, facilities or services to the employee in question is regulated by his contract of employment; or
  (c) the benefits, facilities or services relate to training.

[(4A) In subsection (2)(c) reference to the dismissal of a person from employment includes, where the discrimination is on grounds of race or ethnic or national origins, reference–

  (a) to the termination of that person's employment by the expiration of any period (including a period expiring by reference to an event or circumstance), not being a termination immediately after which the employment is renewed on the same terms; and
  (b) to the termination of that person's employment by any act of his (including the giving of notice) in circumstances such that he is entitled to terminate it without notice by reason of the conduct of the employer.]²

[Exception for genuine occupational requirement

4A.—(1) In relation to discrimination on grounds of race or ethnic or **5-006** national origins–

  (a) section 4(1)(a) or (c) does not apply to any employment; and
  (b) section 4(2)(b) does not apply to promotion or transfer to, or training for, any employment; and
  (c) section 4(2)(c) does not apply to dismissal from any employment;
where subsection (2) applies.

(2) This subsection applies where, having regard to the nature of the employment or the context in which it is carried out–

  (a) being of a particular race or of particular ethnic or national origins is a genuine and determining occupational requirement;
  (b) it is proportionate to apply that requirement in the particular case; and
  (c) either–
      (i) the person to whom that requirement is applied does not meet it, or
      (ii) the employer is not satisfied, and in all the circumstances it is reasonable for him not to be satisfied, that that person meets it.]³

Exceptions for genuine occupational qualifications

5.—(1) In relation to racial discrimination [in cases where section 4A does **5-007** not apply]⁴—

---

¹ Words inserted by SI 2003/1626 reg 6 (2) (b)
² Inserted by SI 2003/1626 reg 6 (2) (c)
³ Inserted by SI 2003/1626 reg 7
⁴ Words inserted by SI 2003/1626 reg 8

(a) section 4(1)(a) or (c) does not apply to any employment where being of a particular racial group is a genuine occupational qualification for the job; and

(b) section 4(2)(b) does not apply to opportunities for promotion or transfer to, or training for, such employment.

(2) Being of a particular racial group is a genuine occupational qualification for a job only where—

(a) the job involves participation in a dramatic performance or other entertainment in a capacity for which a person of that racial group is required for reasons of authenticity; or

(b) the job involves participation as an artist's or photographic model in the production of a work of art, visual image or sequence of visual images for which a person of that racial group is required for reasons of authenticity; or

(c) the job involves working in a place where food or drink is (for payment or not) provided to and consumed by members of the public or a section of the public in a particular setting for which, in that job, a person of that racial group is required for reasons of authenticity; or

(d) the holder of the job provides persons of that racial group with personal services promoting their welfare, and those services can most effectively be provided by a person of that racial group.

(3) Subsection (2) applies where some only of the duties of the job fall within paragraph (a), (b), (c) or (d) as well as where all of them do.

(4) Paragraph (a), (b), (c) or (d) of subsection (2) does not apply in relation to the filling of a vacancy at a time when the employer already has employees of the racial group in question—

(a) who are capable of carrying out the duties falling within that paragraph; and

(b) whom it would be reasonable to employ on those duties; and

(c) whose numbers are sufficient to meet the employer's likely requirements in respect of those duties without undue inconvenience.

Exception for employment intended to provide training in skills to be exercised outside Great Britain

5-008   **6.** Nothing in section 4 shall render unlawful any act done by an employer [,on grounds other than those of race or ethnic or national origins,][1] for the benefit of a person not ordinarily resident in Great Britain in or in connection with employing him at an establishment in Great Britain, where the purpose of that employment is to provide him with training in skills which he appears to the employer to intend to exercise wholly outside Great Britain.

[...]² contract workers

5-009   **7.**—(1) This section applies to any work for a person ("the principal") which is available for doing by individuals ("contract workers") who are employed not by the principal himself but by another person, who supplies, them under a contract made with the principal.

(2) It is unlawful for the principal, in relation to work to which this section applies, to discriminate against a contract worker—

(a) in the terms on which he allows him to do that work; or

(b) by not allowing him to do it or continue to do it; or

---

[1] Words inserted by SI 2003/1626 reg 9
[2] Words repealed by SI 2003/1626 reg 10

(c) in the way he affords him access to any benefits, facilities or services or by refusing or deliberately omitting to afford him access to them; or

(d) by subjecting him to any other detriment.

(3) The principal does not contravene subsection (2)(b) by doing any act in relation to a person not of a particular racial group [,or not of a particular race or particular ethnic or national origins,]¹ at a time when, if the work were to be done by a person taken into the principal's employment, being of that racial group [or of that race or those origins]² would be a genuine occupational qualification [or, as the case may be, that act would be lawful by virtue of section 4A]³ for the job.

[(3A) It is unlawful for the principal, in relation to work to which this section applies, to subject a contract worker to harassment.]⁴

(4) Nothing in this section shall render unlawful any act done by the principal [on grounds other than those of race or ethnic or national origins,]⁵ for the benefit of a contract worker not ordinarily resident in Great Britain in or in connection with allowing him to do work to which this section applies, where the purpose of his being allowed to do that work is to provide him with training in skills which he appears to the principal to intend to exercise wholly outside Great Britain.

(5) Subsection (2)(c) does not apply to benefits, facilities or services of any description if the principal is concerned with the provision (for payment or not) of benefits, facilities or services of that description to the public, or to a section of the public to which the contract worker in question belongs, unless that provision differs in a material respect from the provision of the benefits, facilities or services by the principal to his contract workers.

Meaning of employment at establishment in Great Britain

8.—(1) For the purposes of this Part ("the relevant purposes"), employment **5-010** is to be regarded as being at an establishment in Great Britain [if the employee –

(a) does his work wholly or partly in Great Britain; or

(b) does his work wholly outside Great Britain and subsection (1A) applies.]⁶

[(1A) This subsection applies if, in a case involving discrimination on grounds of race or ethnic or national origins, or harassment –

(a) the employer has a place of business at an establishment in Great Britain;

(b) the work is for the purposes of the business carried on at that establishment; and

(c) the employee is ordinarily resident in Great Britain –

(i) at the time when he applies for or is offered the employment, or

(ii) at any time during the course of the employment.]⁷

(2) [...]⁸

(3) In the case of employment on board a ship registered at a port of registry in Great Britain (except where the employee does his work wholly outside Great

---

¹ Words inserted by SI 2003/1626 reg 10 (2) (a) (i)
² Words inserted by SI 2003/1626 reg 10 (2) (a) (ii)
³ Words inserted by SI 2003/1626 reg 10 (2) (a) (iii)
⁴ Inserted by SI 2003/1626 reg 10 (2) (b)
⁵ Inserted by SI 2003/1626 reg 10 (2) (c)
⁶ Words inserted by SI 2003/1626 reg 11 (1)
⁷ Inserted by SI 2003/1626 reg 11 (2)
⁸ Repealed by SI 1999/3163 reg 3 (3)

Britain) the ship shall for the relevant purposes be deemed to be the establishment.

(4) Where work is not done at an establishment it shall be treated for the relevant purposes as done at the establishment from which it is done or (where it is not done from any establishment) at the establishment with which it has the closest connection.

(5) In relation to employment concerned with exploration of the sea bed or subsoil or the exploitation of their natural resources, Her Majesty may by Order in Council provide that subsections (1) to (3) shall have effect as if in both subsection (1) and subsection (3) the last reference to Great Britain included any area for the time being designated under section 1(7) of the Continental Shelf Act 1964, except an area or part of an area in which the law of Northern Ireland applies.

(6) An Order in Council under subsection (5) may provide that, in relation to employment to which the Order applies, this Part is to have effect with such modifications as are specified in the Order.

(7) An Order in Council under subsection (5) shall be of no effect unless a draft of the Order has been laid before and approved by resolution of each House of Parliament.

Discrimination by other bodies

Partnerships

5-011   **10.**—(1) It is unlawful for a firm consisting of six or more partners, in relation to a position as partner in the firm, to discriminate against a person—

 (a) in the arrangements they make for the purpose of determining who should be offered that position; or

 (b) in the terms on which they offer him that position; or

 (c) by refusing or deliberately omitting to offer him that position; or

 (d) in a case where the person already holds that position—

  (i) in the way they afford him access to any benefits, facilities or services, or by refusing or deliberately omitting to afford him access to them; or

  (ii) by expelling him from that position, or subjecting him to any other detriment.

[(1A) The limitation of subsection (1) to six or more partners does not apply in relation to discrimination on grounds of race or ethnic or national origins.

(1B) It is unlawful for a firm, in relation to a position as a partner in the firm, to subject to harassment a person who holds or has applied for that position.][1]

(2) [Subsection (1), (1A) and (1B)][2] shall apply in relation to persons proposing to form themselves into a partnership as it applies in relation to a firm.

(3) Subsection (1)(a) and (c) do not apply to a position as partner where, if it were employment, [section 4A or 5 would apply to such employment][3].

(4) In the case of a limited partnership references in this section to a partner shall be construed as references to a general partner as defined in section 3 of the Limited Partnerships Act 1907.

---

[1] Inserted by SI 2003/1626 reg 12 (a)

[2] Words substituted by SI 2003/1626 reg 12 (b)

[3] Words substituted by SI 2003/1626 reg 12 (c)

[(5) This section applies to a limited liability partnership as it applies to a firm; and, in its application to a limited liability partnership, references to a partner in a firm are references to a member of the limited liability partnership.][1]

[(6) In subsection (1)(d)(ii) reference to the expulsion of a person from a position as partner includes, where the discrimination is on grounds of race or ethnic or national origins, reference –

    (a) to the termination of that person's partnership by the expiration of any period (including a period expiring by reference to an event or circumstance), not being a termination immediately after which the partnership is renewed on the same terms; and

    (b) to the termination of that person's partnership by any act of his (including the giving of notice) in circumstances such that he is entitled to terminate it without notice by reason of the conduct of the other partners.][2]

Trade unions etc

11.—(1) This section applies to an organisation of workers, an organisation **5-012** of employers, or any other organisation whose members carry on a particular profession or trade for the purposes of which the organisation exists.

(2) It is unlawful for an organisation to which this section applies, in the case of a person who is not a member of the organisation, to discriminate against him—

    (a) in the terms on which it is prepared to admit him to membership; or

    (b) by refusing or deliberately omitting to accept, his application for membership.

(3) It is unlawful for an organisation to which this section applies, in the case of a person who is a member of the organisation, to discriminate against him—

    (a) in the way it affords him access to any benefits, facilities or services, or by refusing or deliberately omitting to afford him access to them; or

    (b) by depriving him of membership, or varying the terms on which he is a member; or

    (c) by subjecting him to any other detriment.

[(4) It is unlawful for an organisation to which this section applies, in relation to a person's membership or application for membership of that organisation, to subject him to harassment.][3]

Qualifying bodies

12.—(1) It is unlawful for an authority or body which can confer an authorisa- **5-013** tion or qualification which is needed for, or facilitates, engagement in a particular profession or trade to discriminate against a person—

    (a) in the terms on which it is prepared to confer on him that authorisation or qualification; or

    (b) by refusing, or deliberately omitting to grant, his application for it; or

    (c) by withdrawing it from him or varying the terms on which he holds it.

[(1A) It is unlawful for an authority or body to which subsection (1) applies, in relation to an authorisation or qualification conferred by it, to subject to

---

[1] Inserted by SI 2001/1090 Sch 5 para 7
[2] Inserted by SI 2003/1626 reg 12 (d)
[3] Inserted by SI 2003/1626 reg 13

harassment a person who holds or applies for such an authorisation or qualification.]¹

(2) In this section—

    (a) "authorisation or qualification" includes recognition, registration, enrolment, approval and certification;

    (b) "confer" includes renew or extend.

[(3) Subsections (1) and (1A) do not apply to discrimination or harassment which is rendered unlawful by section 17 or 18.]²

[Persons concerned with provision of vocational training

5-014   **13.**—(1) It is unlawful, in the case of an individual seeking or undergoing training which would help fit him for any employment, for any person who provides, or makes arrangements for the provision of, facilities for such training to discriminate against him—

    (a) in the terms on which that person affords him access to any training course or other facilities concerned with such training; or

    (b) by refusing or deliberately omitting to afford him such access; or

    (c) by terminating his training; or

    (d) by subjecting him to any detriment during the course of his training.

(2) Subsection (1) does not apply to—

    (a) discrimination which is rendered unlawful by section 4(1) or (2) or section 17 or 18; or

    (b) discrimination which would be rendered unlawful by any of those provisions but for the operation of any other provision of this Act.]³

[(3) It is unlawful for any person who provides, or makes arrangements for the provision of, facilities for training to which subsection (1) applies, in relation to such facilities or training, to subject to harassment a person to whom he provides such training or who is seeking to undergo such training.

(4) Subsection (3) does not apply to harassment which is rendered unlawful by section 4(2A) or by section 17 or 18.]⁴

Employment agencies

5-015   **14.**—(1) It is unlawful for an employment agency to discriminate against a person—

    (a) in the terms on which the agency offers to provide any of its services; or

    (b) by refusing or deliberately omitting to provide any of its services; or

    (c) in the way it provides any of its services.

[(1A) It is unlawful for an employment agency, in relation to the provision of its services, to subject to harassment a person to whom it provides such services or who requests the provision of such services.]⁵

[(2) It is unlawful for a local education authority or education authority or any other person to do any act in providing services in pursuance of arrangements made, or a direction given, under section 10 of the Employment and Training Act 1973 which constitutes discrimination [or harassment]⁶.]⁷

---

¹ Inserted by SI 2003/1626 reg 14 (a)
² Substituted by SI 2003/1626 reg 14 (b)
³ Substituted by Employment Act 1989 c.38 s 7 (2)
⁴ Inserted by SI 2003/1626 reg 15
⁵ Inserted by SI 2003/1626 reg 16 (a)
⁶ Words inserted by SI 2003/1626 reg 16 (b)
⁷ Substituted by Trade Union Reform and Employment Rights Act 1993 c.19 Sch 8 para 9

(3) References in [subsection (1) and (1A)]¹ to the services of an employment agency include guidance on careers and any other services related to employment.

(4) This section does not apply if the discrimination only concerns employment which the employer could lawfully refuse to offer the person in question.

(5) An employment agency or local education authority[, education authority or other person]² shall not be subject to any liability under this section if it proves—

    (a) that it acted in reliance on a statement made to it by the employer to the effect that, by reason of the operation of subsection (4), its action would not be unlawful; and

    (b) that it was reasonable for it to rely on the statement.

(6) A person who knowingly or recklessly makes a statement such as is referred to in subsection (5)(a) which in a material respect is false or misleading commits an offence, and shall be liable on summary conviction to a fine not exceeding level 5 on the standard scale.

PART IV

OTHER UNLAWFUL ACTS

[Relationships which have come to an end

27A—(1) In this section a "relevant relationship" is a relationship during the **5-016** course of which, by virtue of any provision referred to in section 1(1B), taken with section 1(1) or (1A), or (as the case may be) by virtue of section 3A–

    (a) an act of discrimination by one party to the relationship ("the relevant party") against another party to the relationship, on grounds of race or ethnic or national origins, or

    (b) harassment of another party to the relationship by the relevant party,
is unlawful.

(2) Where a relevant relationship has come to an end it is unlawful for the relevant party–

    (a) to discriminate against another party, on grounds of race or ethnic or national origins, by subjecting him to a detriment, or

    (b) to subject another party to harassment,
where the discrimination or harassment arises out of and is closely connected to that relationship.

(3) In subsection (1) reference to an act of discrimination or harassment which is unlawful includes, in the case of a relationship which has come to an end before 19th July 2003, reference to such an act which would, after that date, be unlawful.

(4) For the purposes of any proceedings in respect of an unlawful act under subsection (2), that act shall be treated as falling within circumstances relevant for the purposes of such of the provisions, or Parts, referred to in subsection (1) as determine most closely the nature of the relevant relationship.]³

Discriminatory practices

28.—(1) In this section "discriminatory practice" means   **5-017**

¹ Words substituted by SI 2003/1626 reg 16 (c)
² Substituted by Trade Union Reform and Employment Rights Act 1993 c.19 Sch 8 para 9
³ Inserted by SI 2003/1626 reg 29

[(a)]¹ the application of a requirement or condition which results in an act of discrimination which is unlawful by virtue of any provision of Part II or III taken with section 1(1)(b), or which would be likely to result in such an act of discrimination if the persons to whom it is applied included persons of any particular racial group as regards which there has been no occasion for applying it.

[or

(b) the application of a provision, criterion or practice which results in an act of discrimination which is unlawful by virtue of any provision referred to in section 1(1B), taken with section 1(1A), or which would be likely to result in such an act of discrimination, if the persons to whom it is applied included persons of any particular race or of any particular ethnic or national origins, as regards which there has been no occasion for applying it]².

(2) A person acts in contravention of this section if and so long as—

(a) he applies a discriminatory practice; or

(b) he operates practices or other arrangements which in any circumstances would call for the application by him of a discriminatory practice.

(3) Proceedings in respect of a contravention of this section shall be brought only by the Commission in accordance with sections 58 to 62.

Discriminatory advertisements

5-018 **29.**—(1) It is unlawful to publish or to cause to be published an advertisement which indicates, or might reasonably be understood as indicating, an intention by a person to do an act of discrimination, whether the doing of that act by him would be lawful or, by virtue of Part II or III, unlawful.

(2) Subsection (1) does not apply to an advertisement—

(a) if the intended act would be lawful by virtue of any of sections 5, 6, 7(3) and (4), 10(3), 26, 34(2)(b), 35 to 39 and 41; or

(b) if the advertisement relates to the services of an employment agency (within the meaning of section 14(1)) and the intended act only concerns employment which the employer could by virtue of section 5, 6 or 7(3) or (4) lawfully refuse to offer to persons against whom the advertisement indicates an intention to discriminate.

(3) Subsection (1) does not apply to an advertisement which indicates that persons of any class defined otherwise than by reference to colour, race or ethnic or national origins are required for employment outside Great Britain.

(4) The publisher of an advertisement made unlawful by subsection (1) shall not be subject to any liability under that subsection in respect of the publication of the advertisement if he proves—

(a) that the advertisement was published in reliance on a statement made to him by the person who caused it to be published to the effect that, by reason of the operation of subsection (2) or (3), the publication would not be unlawful; and

(b) that it was reasonable for him to rely on the statement.

(5) A person who knowingly or recklessly makes a statement such as is mentioned in subsection (4)(a) which in a material respect is false or misleading

---

¹ Words inserted by SI 2003/1626 reg 30 (a)
² Inserted by SI 2003/1626 reg 30 (b)

commits an offence, and shall be liable on summary conviction to a fine not exceeding [level 5 on the standard scale][1].

Instructions to [commit unlawful acts][2]

30. It is unlawful for a person—
    (a) who has authority over another person; or
    (b) in accordance with whose wishes that other person is accustomed to act,
to instruct him to do any act which is unlawful by virtue of Part II or III [section 76ZA or, where it renders an act unlawful on grounds of race or ethnic or national origins, section 76,][3] or procure or attempt to procure the doing by him of any such act.

5-019

Pressure to [commit unlawful acts][4]

31.—(1) It is unlawful to induce, or attempt to induce, a person to do any act which contravenes Part II or III [section 76ZA or, where it renders an act unlawful on grounds of race or ethnic or national origins, section 76][5].

(2) An attempted inducement is not prevented from falling within subsection (1) because it is not made directly to the person in question, if it is made in such a way that he is likely to hear of it.

5-020

Liability of employers and principals

32.—(1) Anything done by a person in the course of his employment shall be treated for the purposes of this Act (except as regards offences thereunder) as done by his employer as well as by him, whether or not it was done with the employer's knowledge or approval.

(2) Anything done by a person as agent for another person with the authority (whether express or implied, and whether precedent or subsequent) of that other person shall be treated for the purposes of this Act (except as regards offences thereunder) as done by that other person as well as by him.

(3) In proceedings brought under this Act against any person in respect of an act alleged to have been done by an employee of his it shall be a defence for that person to prove that he took such steps as were reasonably practicable to prevent the employee from doing that act, or from doing in the course of his employment acts of that description.

5-021

Aiding unlawful acts

33.—(1) A person who knowingly aids another person to do an act made unlawful by this Act shall be treated for the purposes of this Act as himself doing an unlawful act of the like description.

(2) For the purposes of subsection (1) an employee or agent for whose act the employer or principal is liable under section 32 (or would be so liable but for section 32(3)) shall be deemed to aid the doing of the act by the employer or principal.

(3) A person does not under this section knowingly aid another to do an unlawful act if—

5-022

---

[1] Words substituted by Criminal Justice Act 1982 c.48 ss 38, 46 and Criminal Procedure (Scotland) Act 1975 c.21 ss 289F, 289G
[2] Words substituted by SI 2003/1626 reg 31 (1)
[3] Words inserted by SI 2003/1626 reg 31 (2)
[4] Words substituted by SI 2003/1626 reg 32 (1)
[5] Words inserted by SI 2003/1626 reg 32 (2)

(a) he acts in reliance on a statement made to him by that other person that, by reason of any provision of this Act, the act which he aids would not be unlawful; and

(b) it is reasonable for him to rely on the statement.

(4) A person who knowingly or recklessly makes a statement such as is mentioned in subsection (3)(a) which in a material respect is false or misleading commits an offence, and shall be liable on summary conviction to a fine not exceeding [level 5 on the standard scale.][1]

PART VIII

ENFORCEMENT

Enforcement in employment field

Jurisdiction of employment tribunals

5-023   **54.**—(1) A complaint by any person ("the complainant") that another person ("the respondent")—

(a) has committed an act [...][2] against the complainant which is unlawful by virtue of Part II[, section 76ZA or, in relation to discrimination on grounds of race or ethnic or national origins, or harassment, section 26A, 26B or 76][3]; or

(b) is by virtue of section 32 or 33 to be treated as having committed such an act [...][4] against the complainant,

may be presented to an employment tribunal.

(2) Subsection (1) does not apply to a complaint under section 12(1) of an act in respect of which an appeal, or proceedings in the nature of an appeal, may be brought under any enactment [...][5].

[Burden of proof: employment tribunals

5-024   **54A**—(1) This section applies where a complaint is presented under section 54 and the complaint is that the respondent—

(a) has committed an act of discrimination, on grounds of race or ethnic or national origins, which is unlawful by virtue of any provision referred to in section 1(1B)(a), (e) or (f), or Part IV in its application to those provisions, or

(b) has committed an act of harassment.

(2) Where, on the hearing of the complaint, the complainant proves facts from which the tribunal could, apart from this section, conclude in the absence of an adequate explanation that the respondent—

(a) has committed such an act of discrimination or harassment against the complainant, or

(b) is by virtue of section 32 or 33 to be treated as having committed such an act of discrimination or harassment against the complainant,

---

[1] Words substituted by Criminal Justice Act 1982 (c.48), ss. 38, 46 and Criminal Procedure (Scotland) Act 1975 (c.21), ss. 289F, 289G
[2] Words repealed by SI 2003/1626 reg 40 (a)
[3] Words inserted by SI 2003/1626 reg 40 (b)
[4] Words repealed by SI 2003/1626 reg 40 (a)
[5] Words repealed by Armed Forces Act 1996 c.46 Sch 7 (III) para 1

the tribunal shall uphold the complaint unless the respondent proves that he did not commit or, as the case may be, is not to be treated as having committed, that act.][1]

55 [...][2]

5-025

Remedies on complaint under s. 54

56.—(1) Where an [employment tribunal][3] finds that a complaint presented 5-026 to it under section 54 is well-founded, the tribunal shall make such of the following as it considers just and equitable—

    (a) an order declaring the rights of the complainant and the respondent in relation to the act to which the complaint relates;

    (b) an order requiring the respondent to pay to the complainant compensation of an amount corresponding to any damages he could have been ordered by a county court or by a sheriff court to pay to the complainant if the complaint had fallen to be dealt with under section 57;

    (c) a recommendation that the respondent take within a specified period action appearing to the tribunal to be practicable for the purpose of obviating or reducing the adverse effect on the complainant of any act of discrimination to which the complaint relates.

    (2) [...][4]

    (3) [...][5]

    (4) If without reasonable justification the respondent to a complaint fails to comply with a recommendation made by an [employment tribunal][6] under subsection (1)(c), then, if it thinks it just and equitable to do so—

    (a) the tribunal may [...][7] increase the amount of compensation required to be paid to the complainant in respect of the complaint by an order made under subsection (1)(b); or

    (b) if an order under subsection (1)(b) could have been made but was not, the tribunal may make such an order.

    [(5) The Secretary of State may by regulations make provision—

    (a) for enabling a tribunal, where an amount of compensation falls to be awarded under subsection (1)(b), to include in the award interest on that amount; and

    (b) specifying, for cases where a tribunal decides that an award is to include an amount in respect of interest, the manner in which and the periods and rate by reference to which the interest is to be determined;

and the regulations may contain such incidental and supplementary provisions as the Secretary of State considers appropriate.

    (6) The Secretary of State may by regulations modify the operation of any order made under [section 14 of the Employment Tribunals Act 1996][8] (power to make provision as to interest on sums payable in pursuance of [employment tribunal][9] decisions) to the extent that it relates to an award of compensation under subsection (1)(b).][10]

---

[1] Inserted by SI 2003/1626 reg 41
[2] Repealed by Employment Tribunals Act 1996 c.17 Sch 3
[3] Words substituted by Employment Rights (Dispute Resolution) Act 1998 c.8 Pt I s 1 (2)
[4] Repealed by Race Relations (Remedies) Act 1994 c.10 Sch 1 Para 1
[5] Subsection repealed by SI 1993/2798 Sch 1 Para 1
[6] Words substituted by Employment Rights (Dispute Resolution) Act 1998 c.8 Pt I s 1 (2)
[7] Words omitted by Race Relations (Remedies) Act 1994 c.10 Sch 1 Para 1
[8] Words substituted by Employment Rights (Dispute Resolution) Act 1998 c.8 Pt I s 1 (2)
[9] Words substituted by Employment Rights (Dispute Resolution) Act 1998 c.8 Pt I s 1 (2)
[10] Added by Race Relations (Remedies) Act 1994 c.10 s 2 (1)

Period within which proceedings to be brought

5-027   **68.**—(1) An [employment tribunal][1] shall not consider a complaint under section 54 unless it is presented to the tribunal before the end of [—][2]

[(a) the period of three months beginning when the act complained of was done; or

(b) in a case to which section 75(8) applies, the period of six months so beginning.][3]

(2) [Subject to subsection (2A) a][4] county court or a sheriff court shall not consider a claim under section 57 unless proceedings in respect of the claim are instituted before the end of—

(a) the period of six months beginning when the act complained of was done; [...][5]

(b) [...][6]

[(2A) In relation to an immigration claim within the meaning of section 57A, the period of six months mentioned in subsection (2)(a) begins on the expiry of the period during which, by virtue of section 57A(1)(a), no proceedings may be brought under section 57(1) in respect of the claim.][7]

(3) Where, in relation to proceedings or prospective proceedings by way of a claim under section 57, an application for assistance under section 66 is made to the Commission before the end of the period of six [...][8] months mentioned in paragraph (a) [...][9] of subsection (2), the period allowed by that paragraph for instituting proceedings in respect of the claim shall be extended by two months.

(4) An [employment tribunal][10], county court or sheriff court shall not consider an application under section 63(2)(a) unless it is made before the end of the period of six months beginning when the act to which it relates was done; and a county court or sheriff court shall not consider an application under section 63(4) unless it is made before the end of the period of five years so beginning.

(5) An [employment tribunal][11] shall not consider a complaint under section 64(1) unless it is presented to the tribunal before the end of the period of six months beginning when the act complained of was done.

(6) A court or tribunal may nevertheless consider any such complaint, claim or application which is out of time if, in all the circumstances of the case, it considers that it is just and equitable to do so.

(7) For the purposes of this section—

(a) when the inclusion of any term in a contract renders the making of the contract an unlawful act, that act shall be treated as extending throughout the duration of the contract; and

(b) any act extending over a period shall be treated as done at the end of that period; and

(c) a deliberate omission shall be treated as done when the person in question decided upon it;

---

[1] Words substituted by Employment Rights (Dispute Resolution) Act 1998 c.8 Pt I s 1 (2)
[2] Substitutes subsections (a) and (b) of section 68(1) by Armed Forces Act 1996 c.46 s 23 (4)
[3] Substitutes subsections (a) and (b) of section 68(1) by Armed Forces Act 1996 c.46 s 23 (4)
[4] Words inserted by Race Relations (Amendment) Act 2000 c.34 Sch 2 Para 13
[5] Repealed by Race Relations (Amendment) Act 2000 c.34 Sch 3 Para 1
[6] Repealed by Race Relations (Amendment) Act 2000 c.34 Sch 3 Para 1
[7] Added by Race Relations (Amendment) Act 2000 c.34 Sch 2 Para 14
[8] Words repealed by Race Relations (Amendment) Act 2000 c.34 Sch 3 Para 1
[9] Words repealed by Race Relations (Amendment) Act 2000 c.34 Sch 3 Para 1
[10] Words substituted by Employment Rights (Dispute Resolution) Act 1998 c.8 Pt I s 1 (2)
[11] Words substituted by Employment Rights (Dispute Resolution) Act 1998 c.8 Pt I s 1 (2)

and in the absence of evidence establishing the contrary a person shall be taken for the purposes of this section to decide upon an omission when he does an act inconsistent with doing the omitted act or, if he has done no such inconsistent act, when the period expires within which he might reasonably have been expected to do the omitted act if it was to be done.

PART X

SUPPLEMENTAL

Collective agreements and rules of undertakings

[72A.—

—(1) This section applies to –

5-028

(a) any term of a collective agreement, including an agreement which was not intended, or is presumed not to have been intended, to be a legally enforceable contract;

(b) any rule made by an employer for application to all or any of the persons who are employed by him or who apply to be, or are, considered by him for employment;

(c) any rule made by an organisation to which section 11 (trade organisa-tions) applies, or by a body to which section 12 (qualifying bodies) applies, for application to –

(i) all or any of its members or prospective members; or

(ii) all or any of the persons on whom it has conferred authorisations or qualifications or who are seeking the authorisations or qualifi-cations which it has power to confer.

(2) Any term or rule to which this section applies is void where –

(a) the making of the collective agreement is, by reason of the inclusion of the term, unlawful on grounds of race or ethnic or national origins, by virtue of a provision referred to in section 1(1B);

(b) the term or rule is included or made in furtherance of an act which is unlawful on such grounds by virtue of such a provision; or

(c) the term or rule provides for the doing of such an act.

(3) Subsection (2) applies whether the agreement was entered into, or the rule made, before, on or after 19th July 2003; but in the case of an agreement entered into, or a rule made, before that date, that subsection does not apply in relation to any period before that date.

(4) In this section, and in section 72B, "collective agreement" means any agreement relating to one or more of the matters mentioned in section 178(2) of the Trade Union and Labour Relations (Consolidation) Act 1992 (meaning of trade dispute), being an agreement made by or on behalf of one or more employers or one or more organisations of employers or associations of such organisations with one or more organisations of workers or associations of such organisations.

72B.—(1) A person to whom this subsection applies may present a complaint to an employment tribunal that a term or rule is void by virtue of section 72A if he has reason to believe –

5-029

(a) that the term or rule may at some future time have effect in relation to him; and

(b) where he alleges that it is void by virtue of section 72A(2)(c), that –
    (i) an act for the doing of which it provides may at some such time be done in relation to him, and
    (ii) the act would be rendered unlawful on grounds of race or ethnic or national origins by a provision referred to in section 1(1B) if done in relation to him in present circumstances.

(2) In the case of a complaint about –
  (a) a term of a collective agreement made by or on behalf of –
    (i) an employer;
    (ii) an organisation of employers of which an employer is a member; or
    (iii) an association of such organisations of one of which an employer is a member; or
  (b) a rule made by an employer, within the meaning of section 72A(1)(b);
subsection (1) applies to any person who is, or is genuinely and actively seeking to become, one of his employees.

(3) In the case of a complaint about a rule made by an organisation or body to which section 72A(1)(c) applies, subsection (1) applies to any person –
  (a) who is, or is genuinely and actively seeking to become, a member of the organisation or body;
  (b) on whom the organisation or body has conferred an authorisation or qualification; or
  (c) who is genuinely and actively seeking an authorisation or qualification which the organisation or body has power to confer.

(4) When an employment tribunal finds that a complaint presented to it under subsection (1) is well-founded the tribunal shall make an order declaring that the term or rule is void.

(5) An order under subsection (4) may include provision as respects any period before the making of the order (but after 19th July 2003).

(6) The avoidance by virtue of section 72A(2) of any term or rule which provides for any person to be discriminated against shall be without prejudice to the following rights (except in so far as they enable any person to require another person to be treated less favourably than himself) namely –
  (a) such of the rights of the person to be discriminated against, and
  (b) such of the rights of any person who will be treated more favourably in direct or indirect consequence of the discrimination,
as are conferred by or in respect of a contract made or modified wholly or partly in pursuance of, or by reference to, that term or rule.][1]

Access to Medical Reports Act 1988

Chapter 28

Right of access

6-001   **1.** It shall be the right of an individual to have access, in accordance with the provisions of this Act, to any medical report relating to the individual which is to

---

[1] Inserted by SI 2003/1626 reg 49

be, or has been, supplied by a medical practitioner for employment purposes or insurance purposes.

Interpretation

2.—(1) In this Act—

"the applicant" means the person referred to in section 3(1) below;

"care" includes examination, investigation or diagnosis for the purposes of, or in connection with, any form of medical treatment;

"employment purposes", in the case of any individual, means the purposes in relation to the individual of any person by whom he is or has been, or is seeking to be, employed (whether under a contract of service or otherwise);

"health professional" has the same meaning as in the Data Protection Act 1998;

"medical practitioner" means a person registered under the Medical Act 1983;

"medical report", in the case of an individual, means a report relating to the physical or mental health of the individual prepared by a medical practitioner who is or has been responsible for the clinical care of the individual.

(2) Any reference in this Act to the supply of a medical report for employment or insurance purposes shall be construed—

(a) as a reference to the supply of such a report for employment or insurance purposes which are purposes of the person who is seeking to be supplied with it; or

(b) (in the case of a report that has already been supplied) as a reference to the supply of such a report for employment or insurance purposes which, at the time of its being supplied, were purposes of the person to whom it was supplied.

Consent to applications for medical reports for employment or insurance purposes

3.—(1) A person shall not apply to a medical practitioner for a medical report relating to any individual to be supplied to him for employment or insurance purposes unless—

(a) that person ("the applicant") has notified the individual that he proposes to make the application; and

(b) the individual has notified the applicant that he consents to the making of the application.

(2) Any notification given under subsection (1)(a) above must inform the individual of his right to withhold his consent to the making of the application, and of the following rights under this Act, namely—

(a) the rights arising under sections 4(1) to (3) and 6(2) below with respect to access to the report before or after it is supplied,

(b) the right to withhold consent under subsection (1) of section 5 below, and

(c) the right to request the amendment of the report under subsection (2) of that section,

as well as of the effect of section 7 below.

6-002

6-003

Access to reports before they are supplied

6-004   **4.**—(1) An individual who gives his consent under section 3 above to the making of an application shall be entitled, when giving his consent, to state that he wishes to have access to the report to be supplied in response to the application before it is so supplied; and, if he does so, the applicant shall—

    (a) notify the medical practitioner of that fact at the time when the application is made, and

    (b) at the same time notify the individual of the making of the application;

and each such notification shall contain a statement of the effect of subsection (2) below.

(2) Where a medical practitioner is notified by the applicant under subsection (1) above that the individual in question wishes to have access to the report before it is supplied, the practitioner shall not supply the report unless—

    (a) he has given the individual access to it and any requirements of section 5 below have been complied with, or

    (b) the period of 21 days beginning with the date of the making of the application has elapsed without his having received any communication from the individual concerning arrangements for the individual to have access to it.

(3) Where a medical practitioner—

    (a) receives an application for a medical report to be supplied for employment or insurance purposes without being notified by the applicant as mentioned in subsection (1) above, but

    (b) before supplying the report receives a notification from the individual that he wishes to have access to the report before it is supplied,

the practitioner shall not supply the report unless—

    (i) he has given the individual access to it and any requirements of section 5 below have been complied with, or

    (ii) the period of 21 days beginning with the date of that notification has elapsed without his having received (either with that notification or otherwise) any communication from the individual concerning arrangements for the individual to have access to it.

(4) References in this section and section 5 below to giving an individual access to a medical report are references to—

    (a) making the report or a copy of it available for his inspection; or

    (b) supplying him with a copy of it;

and where a copy is supplied at the request, or otherwise with the consent, of the individual the practitioner may charge a reasonable fee to cover the costs of supplying it.

Consent to supplying of report and correction of errors

6-005   **5.**—(1) Where an individual has been given access to a report under section 4 above the report shall not be supplied in response to the application in question unless the individual has notified the medical practitioner that he consents to its being so supplied.

(2) The individual shall be entitled, before giving his consent under subsection (1) above, to request the medical practitioner to amend any part of the report which the individual considers to be incorrect or misleading; and, if the individual does so, the practitioner—

    (a) if he is to any extent prepared to accede to the individual's request, shall amend the report accordingly;

(b) if he is to any extent not prepared to accede to it but the individual requests him to attach to the report a statement of the individual's views in respect of any part of the report which he is declining to amend, shall attach such a statement to the report.

(3) Any request made by an individual under subsection (2) above shall be made in writing.

Retention of reports

6.—(1) A copy of any medical report which a medical practitioner has **6-006** supplied for employment or insurance purposes shall be retained by him for at least six months from the date on which it was supplied.

(2) A medical practitioner shall, if so requested by an individual, give the individual access to any medical report relating to him which the practitioner has supplied for employment or insurance purposes in the previous six months.

(3) The reference in subsection (2) above to giving an individual access to a medical report is a reference to—

(a) making a copy of the report available for his inspection; or

(b) supplying him with a copy of it;

and where a copy is supplied at the request, or otherwise with the consent, of the individual the practitioner may charge a reasonable fee to cover the costs of supplying it.

Exemptions

7.—(1) A medical practitioner shall not be obliged to give an individual **6-007** access, in accordance with the provisions of section 4(4) or 6(3) above, to any part of a medical report whose disclosure would in the opinion of the practitioner be likely to cause serious harm to the physical or mental health of the individual or others or would indicate the intentions of the practitioner in respect of the individual.

(2) A medical practitioner shall not be obliged to give an individual access, in accordance with those provisions, to any part of a medical report whose disclosure would be likely to reveal information about another person, or to reveal the identity of another person who has supplied information to the practitioner about the individual, unless—

(a) that person has consented; or

(b) that person is a health professional who has been involved in the care of the individual and the information relates to or has been provided by the professional in that capacity.

(3) Where it appears to a medical practitioner that subsection (1) or (2) above is applicable to any part (but not the whole) of a medical report—

(a) he shall notify the individual of that fact; and

(b) references in the preceding sections of this Act to the individual being given access to the report shall be construed as references to his being given access to the remainder of it;

and other references to the report in sections 4(4),5(2) and 6(3) above shall similarly be construed as references to the remainder of the report.

(4) Where it appears to a medical practitioner that subsection (1) or (2) above is applicable to the whole of a medical report—

(a) he shall notify the individual of that fact; but

(b) he shall not supply the report unless he is notified by the individual that the individual consents to its being supplied;

and accordingly, if he is so notified by the individual, the restrictions imposed by section 4(2) and (3) above on the supply of the report shall not have effect in relation to it.

Application to the court

6-008   **8.**—(1) If a court is satisfied on the application of an individual that any person, in connection with a medical report relating to that individual, has failed or is likely to fail to comply with any requirement of this Act, the court may order that person to comply with that requirement.

(2) The jurisdiction conferred by this section shall be exercisable by a county court or, in Scotland, by the sheriff.

Notifications under this Act

6-009   **9.**—Any notification required or authorised to be given under this Act—
  (a) shall be given in writing; and
  (b) may be given by post.

Trade Union and Labour Relations (Consolidation) Act 1992

CHAPTER 52

PART I

TRADE UNIONS

CHAPTER I

INTRODUCTORY

Meaning of "trade union"

Meaning of "trade union"

7-001   **1.** In this Act a "trade union" means an organisation (whether temporary or permanent)—
  (a) which consists wholly or mainly of workers of one or more descriptions and whose principal purposes include the regulation of relations between workers of that description or those descriptions and employers or employers' associations; or
  (b) which consists wholly or mainly of—
    (i) constituent or affiliated organisations which fulfil the conditions in paragraph (a) (or themselves consist wholly or mainly of constituent or affiliated organisations which fulfil those conditions), or
    (ii) representatives of such constituent or affiliated organisations,
  and whose principal purposes include the regulation of relations between workers and employers or between workers and employers' associations, or the regulation of relations between its constituent or affiliated organisations.

The list of trade unions

2.—(1) The Certification Officer shall keep a list of trade unions containing **7-002** the names of—

    (a) the organisations whose names were, immediately before the commencement of this Act, duly entered in the list of trade unions kept by him under section 8 of the Trade Union and Labour Relations Act 1974, and

    (b) the names of the organisations entitled to have their names entered in the list in accordance with this Part.

(2) The Certification Officer shall keep copies of the list of trade unions, as for the time being in force, available for public inspection at all reasonable hours free of charge.

(3) A copy of the list shall be included in his annual report.

(4) The fact that the name of an organisation is included in the list of trade unions is evidence (in Scotland, sufficient evidence) that the organisation is a trade union.

(5) On the application of an organisation whose name is included in the list, the Certification Officer shall issue it with a certificate to that effect.

(6) A document purporting to be such a certificate is evidence (in Scotland, sufficient evidence) that the name of the organisation is entered in the list.

Application to have name entered in the list

3.—(1) An organisation of workers, whenever formed, whose name is not **7-003** entered in the list of trade unions may apply to the Certification Officer to have its name entered in the list.

(2) The application shall be made in such form and manner as the Certification Officer may require and shall be accompanied by—

    (a) a copy of the rules of the organisation,

    (b) a list of its officers,

    (c) the address of its head or main office, and

    (d) the name under which it is or is to be known,

and by the prescribed fee.

(3) If the Certification Officer is satisfied—

    (a) that the organisation is a trade union,

    (b) that subsection (2) has been complied with, and

    (c) that entry of the name in the list is not prohibited by subsection (4),

he shall enter the name of the organisation in the list of trade unions.

(4) The Certification Officer shall not enter the name of an organisation in the list of trade unions if the name is the same as that under which another organisation—

    (a) was on 30th September 1971 registered as a trade union under the Trade Union Acts 1871 to 1964,

    (b) was at any time registered as a trade union or employers' association under the Industrial Relations Act 1971, or

    (c) is for the time being entered in the list of trade unions or in the list of employers' associations kept under Part II of this Act,

or if the name is one so nearly resembling any such name as to be likely to deceive the public.

Removal of name from the list

7-004   **4.**—(1) If it appears to the Certification Officer, on application made to him or otherwise, that an organisation whose name is entered in the list of trade unions is not a trade union, he may remove its name from the list.

(2) He shall not do so without giving the organisation notice of his intention and considering any representations made to him by the organisation within such period (of not less than 28 days beginning with the date of the notice) as may be specified in the notice.

(3) The Certification Officer shall remove the name of an organisation from the list of trade unions if—

(a) he is requested by the organisation to do so, or

(b) he is satisfied that the organisation has ceased to exist.

Certification as independent trade union

Meaning of "independent trade union"

7-005   **5.** In this Act an "independent trade union" means a trade union which—

(a) is not under the domination or control of an employer or group of employers or of one or more employers' associations, and

(b) is not liable to interference by an employer or any such group or association (arising out of the provision of financial or material support or by any other means whatsoever) tending towards such control;

and references to "independence", in relation to a trade union, shall be construed accordingly.

Application for certificate of independence

7-006   **6.**—(1) A trade union whose name is entered on the list of trade unions may apply to the Certification Officer for a certificate that it is independent.

The application shall be made in such form and manner as the Certification Officer may require and shall be accompanied by the prescribed fee.

(2) The Certification Officer shall maintain a record showing details of all applications made to him under this section and shall keep it available for public inspection (free of charge) at all reasonable hours.

(3) If an application is made by a trade union whose name is not entered on the list of trade unions, the Certification Officer shall refuse a certificate of independence and shall enter that refusal on the record

(4) In any other case, he shall not come to a decision on the application before the end of the period of one month after it has been entered on the record; and before coming to his decision he shall make such enquiries as he thinks fit and shall take into account any relevant information submitted to him by any person.

(5) He shall then decide whether the applicant trade union is independent and shall enter his decision and the date of his decision on the record.

(6) If he decides that the trade union is independent he shall issue a certificate accordingly; and if he decides that it is not, he shall give reasons for his decision.

Withdrawal or cancellation of certificate

7-007   **7.**—(1) The Certification Officer may withdraw a trade union's certificate of independence if he is of the opinion that the union is no longer independent.

(2) Where he proposes to do so he shall notify the trade union and enter notice of the proposal in the record.

(3) He shall not come to a decision on the proposal before the end of the period of one month after notice of it was entered on the record; and before coming to his decision he shall make such enquiries as he thinks fit and shall take into account any relevant information submitted to him by any person.

(4) He shall then decide whether the trade union is independent and shall enter his decision and the date of his decision on the record.

(5) He shall confirm or withdraw the certificate accordingly; and if he decides to withdraw it, he shall give reasons for his decision.

(6) Where the name of an organisation is removed from the list of trade unions, the Certification Officer shall cancel any certificate of independence in force in respect of that organisation by entering on the record the fact that the organisation's name has been removed from that list and that the certificate is accordingly cancelled.

Conclusive effect of Certification Officer's decision

8.—(1) A certificate of independence which is in force is conclusive evidence **7-008** for all purposes that a trade union is independent; and a refusal, withdrawal or cancellation of a certificate of independence, entered on the record, is conclusive evidence for all purposes that a trade union is not independent.

(2) A document purporting to be a certificate of independence and to be signed by the Certification Officer, or by a person authorised to act on his behalf, shall be taken to be such a certificate unless the contrary is proved.

(3) A document purporting to be a certified copy of an entry on the record and to be signed by the Certification Officer, or by a person authorised to act on his behalf, shall be taken to be a true copy of such an entry unless the contrary is proved.

(4) If in any proceedings before a court, the Employment Appeal Tribunal, the Central Arbitration Committee, ACAS or an industrial tribunal a question arises whether a trade union is independent and there is no certificate of independence in force and no refusal, withdrawal or cancellation of a certificate recorded in relation to that trade union—

(a) that question shall not be decided in those proceedings, and
(b) the proceedings shall instead be stayed or sisted until a certificate of independence has been issued or refused by the Certification Officer.

(5) The body before whom the proceedings are stayed or sisted may refer the question of the independence of the trade union to the Certificate Officer who shall proceed in accordance with section 6 as on an application by that trade union.

Supplementary

Appeal against decision of Certification Officer

9.—(1) An organisation aggrieved by the refusal of the Certification Officer **7-009** to enter its name in the list of trade unions, or by a decision of his to remove its name from the list, may appeal to the Employment Appeal Tribunal.

(2) A trade union aggrieved by the refusal of the Certification Officer to issue it with a certificate of independence, or by a decision of his to withdraw its certificate, may appeal to the Employment Appeal Tribunal.

(3) If on appeal the Tribunal is satisfied that the organisation's name should be or remain entered in the list or, as the case may be, that the certificate should be issued or should not be withdrawn, it shall declare that fact and give directions to the Certification Officer accordingly.

(4) The rights of appeal conferred by this section extend to any question of fact or law arising in the proceedings before, or arising from the decision of, the Certification Officer.

CHAPTER II

STATUS AND PROPERTY OF TRADE UNIONS

General

Quasi-corporate status of trade unions

7-010   **10.**—(1) A trade union is not a body corporate but—
    (a) it is capable of making contracts;
    (b) it is capable of suing and being sued in its own name, whether in proceedings relating to property or founded on contract or tort or any other cause of action; and
    (c) proceedings for an offence alleged to have been committed by it or on its behalf may be brought against it in its own name.

(2) A trade union shall not be treated as if it were a body corporate except to the extent authorised by the provisions of this Part.

(3) A trade union shall not be registered—
    (a) as a company under the Companies Act 1985, or
    (b) under the Friendly Societies Act 1974 or the Industrial and Provident Societies Act 1965;
and any such registration of a trade union (whenever effected) is void.

Exclusion of common law rules as to restraint of trade

7-011   **11.**—(1) The purposes of a trade union are not, by reason only that they are in restraint of trade, unlawful so as—
    (a) to make any member of the trade union liable to criminal proceedings for conspiracy or otherwise, or
    (b) to make any agreement or trust void or voidable.

(2) No rule of a trade union is unlawful or unenforceable by reason only that it is in restraint of trade.

Liability of trade unions in proceedings in tort

Liability of trade union in certain proceedings in tort

7-012   **20.**—(1) Where proceedings in tort are brought against a trade union—
    (a) on the ground that an act—
      (i) induces another person to break a contract or interferes or induces another person to interfere with its performance, or
      (ii) consists in threatening that a contract (whether one to which the union is a party or not) will be broken or its performance interfered with, or that the union will induce another person to break a contract or interfere with its performance, or

(b) in respect of an agreement or combination by two or more persons to do or to procure the doing of an act which, if it were done without any such agreement or combination, would be actionable in tort on such a ground,

then, for the purpose of determining in those proceedings whether the union is liable in respect of the act in question, that act shall be taken to have been done by the union if, but only if, it is to be taken to have been authorised or endorsed by the trade union in accordance with the following provisions.

(2) An act shall be taken to have been authorised or endorsed by a trade union if it was done, or was authorised or endorsed—

(a) by any person empowered by the rules to do, authorise or endorse acts of the kind in question, or

(b) by the principal executive committee or the president or general secretary, or

(c) by any other committee of the union or any other official of the union (whether employed by it or not).

(3) For the purposes of paragraph (c) of subsection (2)—

(a) any group of persons constituted in accordance with the rules of the union is a committee of the union; and

(b) an act shall be taken to have been done, authorised or endorsed by an official if it was done, authorised or endorsed by, or by any member of, any group of persons of which he was at the material time a member, the purposes of which included organising or co-ordinating industrial action.

(4) The provisions of paragraphs (b) and (c) of subsection (2) apply notwithstanding anything in the rules of the union, or in any contract or rule of law, but subject to the provisions of section 21 (repudiation by union of certain acts).

(5) Where for the purposes of any proceedings an act is by virtue of this section taken to have been done by a trade union, nothing in this section shall affect the liability of any other person, in those or any other proceedings, in respect of that act.

(6) In proceedings arising out of an act which is by virtue of this section taken to have been done by a trade union, the power of the court to grant an injunction or interdict includes power to require the union to take such steps as the court considers appropriate for ensuring—

(a) that there is no, or no further, inducement of persons to take part or to continue to take part in industrial action, and

(b) that no person engages in any conduct after the granting of the injunction or interdict by virtue of having been induced before it was granted to take part or to continue to take part in industrial action.

The provisions of subsections (2) to (4) above apply in relation to proceedings for failure to comply with any such injunction or interdict as they apply in relation to the original proceedings.

(7) In this section "rules", in relation to a trade union, means the written rules of the union and any other written provision forming part of the contract between a member and the other members.

Repudiation by union of certain acts

21.—(1) An act shall not be taken to have been authorised or endorsed by a **7-013** trade union by virtue only of paragraph (c) of section 20(2) if it was repudiated by the executive, president or general secretary as soon as reasonably practicable after coming to the knowledge of any of them.

(2) Where an act is repudiated—

(a) written notice of the repudiation must be given to the committee or official in question, without delay, and

(b) the union must do its best to give individual written notice of the fact and date of repudiation, without delay—

(i) to every member of the union who the union has reason to believe is taking part, or might otherwise take part, in industrial action as a result of the act, and

(ii) to the employer of every such member.

(3) The notice given to members in accordance with paragraph (b)(i) of subsection (2) must contain the following statement—

"Your union has repudiated the call (or calls) for industrial action to which this notice relates and will give no support to unofficial industrial action taken in response to it (or them). If you are dismissed while taking unofficial industrial action, you will have no right to complain of unfair dismissal."

(4) If subsection (2) or (3) is not complied with, the repudiation shall be treated as ineffective.

(5) An act shall not be treated as repudiated if at any time after the union concerned purported to repudiate it the executive, president or general secretary has behaved in a manner which is inconsistent with the purported repudiation.

(6) The executive, president or general secretary shall be treated as so behaving if, on a request made to any of them within [three months][1] of the purported repudiation by a person who—

(a) is a party to a commercial contract whose performance has been or may be interfered with as a result of the act in question, and

(b) has not been given written notice by the union of the repudiation,

it is not forthwith confirmed in writing that the act has been repudiated.

(7) In this section "commercial contract" mean means any contract other than—

(a) a contract of employment, or

(b) any other contract under which a person agrees personally to do work or perform services for another.

Limit on damages awarded against trade unions in actions in tort

7-014   **22.**—(1) This section applies to any proceedings in tort brought against a trade union, except—

(a) proceedings for personal injury as a result of negligence, nuisance or breach of duty;

(b) proceedings for breach of duty in connection with the ownership, occupation, possession, control or use of property;

(c) proceedings brought by virtue of Part I of the Consumer Protection Act 1987 (product liability).

(2) In any proceedings in tort to which this section applies the amount which may awarded against the union by way of damages shall not exceed the following limit—

Number of members of union	Maximum award of damages
Less than 5,000	£10,000
5,000 or more but less than 25,000	£50,000

---

[1] Words substituted by Trade Union Reform and Employment Rights Act 1993 c.19 Sch 7 para 17

Number of members of union	*Maximum award of damages*
25,000 or more but less than 100,000	£125,000
100,000 or more	£250,000

(3) The Secretary of State may by order amend subsection (2) so as to vary any of the sums specified; and the order may make such transitional provision as the Secretary of State considers appropriate.

(4) Any such order shall be made by statutory instrument which shall be subject to annulment in pursuance of a resolution of either House of Parliament.

(5) In this section—

"breach of duty" means breach of a duty imposed by any rule of law or by or under any enactment;

"personal injury" includes any disease and any impairment of a person's physical or mental condition; and

"property" means any property, whether real or personal (or in Scotland, heritable or moveable).

Restriction on enforcement against certain property

Restriction on enforcement of awards against certain property

23.—(1) Where in any proceedings an amount is awarded by way of **7-015** damages, costs or expenses—

(a) against a trade union,

(b) against trustees in whom property is vested in trust for a trade union, in their capacity as such (and otherwise than in respect of a breach of trust on their part), or

(c) against members or officials of a trade union on behalf of themselves and all of the members of the union,

no part of that amount is recoverable by enforcement against any protected property.

(2) The following is protected property—

(a) property belonging to the trustees otherwise than in their capacity as such;

(b) property belonging to any member of the union otherwise than jointly or in common with the other members;

(c) property belonging to an official of the union who is neither a member nor a trustee;

(d) property comprised in the union's political fund where that fund—

(i) is subject to rules of the union which prevent property which is or has been comprised in the fund from being used for financing strikes or other industrial action, and

(ii) was so subject at the time when the act in respect of which the proceedings are brought was done;

(e) property comprised in a separate fund maintained in accordance with the rules of the union for the purpose only of providing provident benefits.

(3) For this purpose "provident benefits" includes—

(a) any payment expressly authorised by the rules of the union which is made—

    (i) to a member during sickness or incapacity from personal injury or while out of work, or

    (ii) to an aged member by way of superannuation, or

    (iii) to a member who has met with an accident or has lost his tools by fire or theft;

  (b) a payment in discharge or aid of funeral expenses on the death of a member or the wife of a member or as provision for the children of a deceased member.

CHAPTER III

TRADE UNION ADMINISTRATION

Register of members' names and addresses

Duty to maintain register of members' names and addresses

7-016   **24.**—(1) A trade union shall compile and maintain a register of the names and addresses of its members, and shall secure, so far as is reasonably practicable, that the entries in the register are accurate and are kept up-to-date.

    (2) The register may be kept by means of a computer.

    (3) A trade union shall—

  (a) allow any member, upon reasonable notice, to ascertain from the register, free of charge and at any reasonable time, whether there is an entry on it relating to him; and

  (b) if requested to do so by any member, supply him as soon as reasonably practicable, either free of charge or on payment of a reasonable fee, with a copy of any entry on the register relating to him.

    (4) [...][1]

    (5) For the purposes of this section a member's address means either his home address or another address which he has requested the union in writing to treat as his postal address.

    (6) The remedy for failure to comply with the requirements of this section is by way of application under section 25 (to the Certification Officer) or section 26 (to the court) [...][2]

[Securing confidentiality of register during ballots

7-017   **24A.**—(1) This section applies in relation to a ballot of the members of a trade union on—

  (a) an election under Chapter IV for a position to which that Chapter applies,

  (b) a political resolution under Chapter VI, and

  (c) a resolution to approve an instrument of amalgamation or transfer under Chapter VII.

    (2) Where this section applies in relation to a ballot the trade union shall impose the duty of confidentiality in relation to the register of members' names and addresses on the scrutineer appointed by the union for the purposes of the ballot and on any person appointed by the union as the independent person for the purposes of the ballot.

---

[1] Repealed by Trade Union Reform and Employment Rights Act 1993 c.19 Sch 10 para 1

[2] Words repealed by Employment Relations Act 1999 c.26 Sch 9 para 1

(3) The duty of confidentiality in relation to the register of members' names and addresses is, when imposed on a scrutineer or on an independent person, a duty—

    (a) not to disclose any name or address in the register except in permitted circumstances; and

    (b) to take all reasonable steps to secure that there is no disclosure of any such name or address by any other person except in permitted circumstances;

and any reference in this Act to "the duty of confidentiality" is a reference to the duty prescribed in this subsection.

(4) The circumstances in which disclosure of a member's name and address is permitted are—

    (a) where the member consents;

    (b) where it is requested by the Certification Officer for the purposes of the discharge of any of his functions or it is required for the purposes of the discharge of any of the functions of an inspector appointed by him;

    (c) where it is required for the purposes of the discharge of any of the functions of the scrutineer or independent person, as the case may be, under the terms of his appointment;

    (d) where it is required for the purposes of the investigation of crime or of criminal proceedings.

(5) Any provision of this Part which incorporates the duty of confidentiality as respects the register into the appointment of a scrutineer or an independent person has the effect of imposing that duty on the scrutineer or independent person as a duty owed by him to the trade union.

(6) The remedy for failure to comply with the requirements of this section is by way of application under section 25 (to the Certification Officer) or section 26 (to the court).[...][1] [2]

Remedy for failure: application to Certification Officer

25.—(1) A member of a trade union who claims that the union has failed to **7-018** comply with any of the requirements of section 24 [or 24A][3] (duties with respect to register of members' names and addresses) may apply to the Certification Officer for a declaration to that effect.

(2) On an application being made to him, the Certification Officer shall—

    (a) make such enquiries as he thinks fit, and

    (b) [...][4] give the applicant and the trade union an opportunity to be heard,

and may make or refuse the declaration asked for.

(3) If he makes a declaration he shall specify in it the provisions with which the trade union has failed to comply.

(4) Where he makes a declaration and is satisfied that steps have been taken by the union with a view to remedying the declared failure, or securing that a failure of the same or any similar kind does not occur in future, or that the union has agreed to take such steps, he shall specify those steps in the declaration.

(5) Whether he makes or refuses a declaration, he shall give reasons for his decision in writing; and the reasons may be accompanied by written observations on any matter arising from, or connected with, the proceedings.

---

[1] Words repealed by Employment Relations Act 1999 c.26 Sch 9 para 1

[2] Inserted by Trade Union Reform and Employment Rights Act 1993 c.19 Pt I s 6

[3] Words inserted by Trade Union Reform and Employment Rights Act 1993 c.19 Sch 8 para 40 (a)

[4] Words repealed by Employment Relations Act 1999 c.26 Sch 9 para 1

[(5A) Where the Certification Officer makes a declaration he shall also, unless he considers that to do so would be inappropriate, make an enforcement order, that is, an order imposing on the union one or both of the following requirements—

    (a) to take such steps to remedy the declared failure, within such period, as may be specified in the order;

    (b) to abstain from such acts as may be so specified with a view to securing that a failure of the same or a similar kind does not occur in future.

(5B) Where an enforcement order has been made, any person who is a member of the union and was a member at the time it was made is entitled to enforce obedience to the order as if he had made the application on which the order was made.]¹

(6) In exercising his functions under this section the Certification Officer shall ensure that, so far as is reasonably practicable, an application made to him is determined within six months of being made.

(7) Where he requests a person to furnish information to him in connection with enquiries made by him under this section, he shall specify the date by which that information is to be furnished and, unless he considers that it would be inappropriate to do so, shall proceed with his determination of the application notwithstanding that the information has not been furnished to him by the specified date.

[(8) The Certification Officer shall not entertain an application for a declaration as respects an alleged failure to comply with the requirements of section 24A in relation to a ballot to which that section applies unless the application is made before the end of the period of one year beginning with the last day on which votes could be cast in the ballot.]²

[(9) A declaration made by the Certification Officer under this section may be relied on as if it were a declaration made by the court.

(10) An enforcement order made by the Certification Officer under this section may be enforced in the same way as an order of the court.

(11) The following paragraphs have effect if a person applies under section 26 in relation to an alleged failure—

    (a) that person may not apply under this section in relation to that failure;

    (b) on an application by a different person under this section in relation to that failure, the Certification Officer shall have due regard to any declaration, order, observations or reasons made or given by the court regarding that failure and brought to the Certification Officer's notice.]³

Remedy for failure: application to court

7-019   **26.**—(1) A member of a trade union who claims that the union has failed to comply with any of the requirements of section 24 (duties with respect to register of members' names and addresses) may apply to the court for a declaration to that effect.

(2) [...]⁴

(3) If the court makes a declaration it shall specify in it the provisions with which the trade union has failed to comply.

---

¹ Inserted by Employment Relations Act 1999 c.26 Sch 6 para 4 (3)
² Inserted by Trade Union Reform and Employment Rights Act 1993 c.19 Sch 8 para 40 (b)
³ Inserted by Employment Relations Act 1999 c.26 Sch 6 para 4 (4)
⁴ Repealed by Employment Relations Act 1999 c.26 Sch 9 para 1

(4) Where the court makes a declaration it shall also, unless it considers that to do so would be inappropriate, make an enforcement order, that is, an order imposing on the union one or both of the following requirements—

    (a) to take such steps to remedy the declared failure, within such period, as may be specified in the order;

    (b) to abstain from such acts as may be so specified with a view to securing that a failure of the same or a similar kind does not occur in future.

(5) Where an enforcement order has been made, any person who is a member of the union and was a member at the time it was made, is entitled to enforce obedience to the order as if he had made the application on which the order was made.

(6) Without prejudice to any other power of the court, the court may on an application under this section grant such interlocutory relief (in Scotland, such interim order) as it considers appropriate.

[(7) The court shall not entertain an application for a declaration as respects an alleged failure to comply with the requirements of section 24A in relation to a ballot to which that section applies unless the application is made before the end of the period of one year beginning with the last day on which votes could be cast in the ballot.][1]

[(8) The following paragraphs have effect if a person applies under section 25 in relation to an alleged failure—

    (a) that person may not apply under this section in relation to that failure;

    (b) on an application by a different person under this section in relation to that failure, the court shall have due regard to any declaration, order, observations or reasons made or given by the Certification Officer regarding that failure and brought to the court's notice.][2]

Duty to supply copy of rules

Duty to supply copy of rules

27. A trade union shall at the request of any person supply him with a copy of **7-020** its rules either free of charge or on payment of a reasonable charge.

Chapter IV

Elections for Certain Positions

Duty to hold elections

Duty to hold elections for certain positions

46.—(1) A trade union shall secure— **7-021**

    (a) that every person who holds a position in the union to which this Chapter applies does so by virtue of having been elected to it at an election satisfying the requirements of this Chapter, and

    (b) that no person continues to hold such a position for more than five years without being re-elected at such an election.

(2) The positions to which this Chapter applies (subject as mentioned below) are—

---

[1] Inserted by Trade Union Reform and Employment Rights Act 1993 c.19 Sch 8 para 41 (b)

[2] Inserted by Employment Relations Act 1999 c.26 Sch 6 para 5 (3)

(a) member of the executive,
(b) any position by virtue of which a person is a member of the executive,
(c) president, and
(d) general secretary;

and the requirements referred to above are those set out in sections 47 to 52 below.

(3) In this Chapter "member of the executive" includes any person who, under the rules or practice of the union, may attend and speak at some or all of the meetings of the executive, otherwise than for the purpose of providing the committee with factual information or with technical or professional advice with respect to matters taken into account by the executive in carrying out its functions.

(4) This Chapter does not apply to the position of president or general secretary if the holder of that position—

(a) is not, in respect of that position, either a voting member of the executive or an employee of the union,
(b) holds that position for a period which under the rules of the union cannot end more than 13 months after he took it up, and
(c) has not held either position at any time in the period of twelve months ending with the day before he took up that position.

(5) A "voting member of the executive" means a person entitled in his own right to attend meetings of the executive and to vote on matters on which votes are taken by the executive (whether or not he is entitled to attend all such meetings or to vote on all such matters or in all circumstances).

(6) The provisions of this Chapter apply notwithstanding anything in the rules or practice of the union; and the terms and conditions on which a person is employed by the union shall be disregarded in so far as they would prevent the union from complying with the provisions of this Chapter.

Requirements to be satisfied with respect to elections

Candidates

7-022   **47.**—(1) No member of the trade union shall be unreasonably excluded from standing as a candidate.

(2) No candidate shall be required, directly or indirectly, to be a member of a political party.

(3) A member of a trade union shall not be taken to be unreasonably excluded from standing as a candidate if he is excluded on the ground that he belongs to a class of which all the members are excluded by the rules of the union.

But a rule which provides for such a class to be determined by reference to whom the union chooses to exclude shall be disregarded.

Election addresses

7-023   **48.**—(1) The trade union shall—

(a) provide every candidate with an opportunity of preparing an election address in his own words and of submitting it to the union to be distributed to the persons accorded entitlement to vote in the election; and
(b) secure that, so far as reasonably practicable, copies of every election address submitted to it in time are distributed to each of those persons by post along with the voting papers for the election.

(2) The trade union may determine the time by which an election address must be submitted to it for distribution; but the time so determined must not be earlier than the latest time at which a person may become a candidate in the election.

(3) The trade union may provide that election addresses submitted to it for distribution—

(a) must not exceed such length, not being less than one hundred words, as may be determined by the union, and

(b) may, as regards photographs and other matter not in words, incorporate only such matter as the union may determine.

(4) The trade union shall secure that no modification of an election address submitted to it is made by any person in any copy of the address to be distributed except—

(a) at the request or with the consent of the candidate, or

(b) where the modification is necessarily incidental to the method adopted for producing that copy.

(5) The trade union shall secure that the same method of producing copies is applied in the same way to every election address submitted and, so far as reasonably practicable, that no such facility or information as would enable a candidate to gain any benefit from—

(a) the method by which copies of the election addresses are produced, or

(b) the modifications which are necessarily incidental to that method, is provided to any candidate without being provided equally to all the others.

(6) The trade union shall, so far as reasonably practicable, secure that the same facilities and restrictions with respect to the preparation, submission, length or modification of an election address, and with respect to the incorporation of photographs or other matter not in words, are provided or applied equally to each of the candidates.

(7) The arrangements made by the trade union for the production of the copies to be so distributed must be such as to secure that none of the candidates is required to bear any of the expense of producing the copies.

(8) No-one other than the candidate himself shall incur any civil or criminal liability in respect of the publication of a candidate's election address or of any copy required to be made for the purposes of this section.

Entitlement to vote

50.—(1) Subject to the provisions of this section, entitlement to vote shall be **7-024** accorded equally to all members of the trade union.

(2) The rules of the union may exclude entitlement to vote in the case of all members belonging to one of the following classes, or to a class falling within one of the following—

(a) members who are not in employment;

(b) members who are in arrears in respect of any subscription or contribution due to the union;

(c) members who are apprentices, trainees or students or new members of the union.

(3) The rules of the union may restrict entitlement to vote to members who fall within—

(a) a class determined by reference to a trade or occupation,

(b) a class determined by reference to a geographical area, or

(c) a class which is by virtue of the rules of the union treated as a separate section within the union, or to members who fall within a class determined by reference to any combination of the factors mentioned in paragraphs (a), (b) and (c).

The reference in paragraph (c) to a section of a trade union includes a part of the union which is itself a trade union.

(4) Entitlement may not be restricted in accordance with subsection (3) if the effect is that any member of the union is denied entitlement to vote at all elections held for the purposes of this Chapter otherwise than by virtue of belonging to a class excluded in accordance with subsection (2).

Voting

7-025   **51.**—(1) The method of voting must be by the marking of a voting paper by the person voting.

(2) Each voting paper must—
- (a) state the name of the independent scrutineer and clearly specify the address to which, and the date by which, it is to be returned,
- (b) be given one of a series of consecutive whole numbers every one of which is used in giving a different number in that series to each voting paper printed or otherwise produced for the purposes of the election, and
- (c) be marked with its number.

(3) Every person who is entitled to vote at the election must—
- (a) be allowed to vote without interference from, or constraint imposed by, the union or any of its members, officials or employees, and
- (b) so far as is reasonably practicable, be enabled to do so without incurring any direct cost to himself.

(4) So far as is reasonably practicable, every person who is entitled to vote at the election must—
- (a) have sent to him by post, at his home address or another address which he has requested the trade union in writing to treat as his postal address, a voting paper which either lists the candidates at the election or is accompanied by a separate list of those candidates; and
- (b) be given a convenient opportunity to vote by post.

(5) The ballot shall be conducted so as to secure that—
- (a) so far as is reasonably practicable, those voting do so in secret, and
- (b) the votes given at the election are fairly and accurately counted.

For the purposes of paragraph (b) an inaccuracy in counting shall be disregarded if it is accidental and on a scale which could not affect the result of the election.

(6) The ballot shall be so conducted as to secure that the result of the election is determined solely by counting the number of votes cast directly for each candidate.

(7) Nothing in subsection (6) shall be taken to prevent the system of voting used for the election being the single transferable vote, that is, a vote capable of being given so as to indicate the voter's order of preference for the candidates and of being transferred to the next choice—
- (a) when it is not required to give a prior choice the necessary quota of votes, or
- (b) when, owing to the deficiency in the number of votes given for a prior choice, that choice is eliminated from the list of candidates.

[Counting of votes etc. by independent person

7-026   **51A.**—(1) The trade union shall ensure that—

(a) the storage and distribution of the voting papers for the purposes of the election, and

(b) the counting of the votes cast in the election,

are undertaken by one or more independent persons appointed by the union.

(2) A person is an independent person in relation to an election if—

(a) he is the scrutineer, or

(b) he is a person other than the scrutineer and the trade union has no grounds for believing either that he will carry out any functions conferred on him in relation to the election otherwise than competently or that his independence in relation to the union, or in relation to the election, might reasonably be called into question.

(3) An appointment under this section shall require the person appointed to carry out his functions so as to minimise the risk of any contravention of requirements imposed by or under any enactment or the occurrence of any unfairness or malpractice.

(4) The duty of confidentiality as respects the register is incorporated in an appointment under this section.

(5) Where the person appointed to undertake the counting of votes is not the scrutineer, his appointment shall require him to send the voting papers back to the scrutineer as soon as reasonably practicable after the counting has been completed.

(6) The trade union—

(a) shall ensure that nothing in the terms of an appointment under this section is such as to make it reasonable for any person to call into question the independence of the person appointed in relation to the union,

(b) shall ensure that a person appointed under this section duly carries out his functions and that there is no interference with his carrying out of those functions which would make it reasonable for any person to call into question the independence of the person appointed in relation to the union, and

(c) shall comply with all reasonable requests made by a person appointed under this section for the purposes of, or in connection with, the carrying out of his functions.][1]

Uncontested elections

53. Nothing in this Chapter shall be taken to require a ballot to be held at an uncontested election.   **7-027**

Remedy for failure to comply with requirements

Remedy for failure to comply with requirements: general

54.—(1) The remedy for a failure on the part of a trade union to comply with the requirements of this Chapter is by way of application under section 55 (to the Certification Officer) or section 56 (to the court).[...][2]   **7-028**

(2) An application under those sections may be made—

(a) by a person who is a member of the trade union (provided, where the election has been held, he was also a member at the time when it was held), or

[1] Inserted by Trade Union Reform and Employment Rights Act 1993 c.19 Pt I s 2 (1)
[2] Words repealed by Employment Relations Act 1999 c.26 Sch 9 para 1

(b) by a person who is or was a candidate at the election;
and the references in those sections to a person having a sufficient interest are to such a person.

(3) No such application may be made after the end of the period of one year beginning with the day on which the union announced the result of the election.

Application to Certification Officer

7-029   **55.**—(1) A person having a sufficient interest (see section 54(2)) who claims that a trade union has failed to comply with any of the requirements of this Chapter may apply to the Certification Officer for a declaration to that effect.

(2) On an application being made to him, the Certification Officer shall—

(a) make such enquiries as he thinks fit, and

(b) [...]¹ give the applicant and the trade union an opportunity to be heard,
and may make or refuse the declaration asked for.

(3) If he makes a declaration he shall specify in it the provisions with which the trade union has failed to comply.

(4) Where he makes a declaration and is satisfied that steps have been taken by the union with a view to remedying the declared failure, or securing that a failure of the same or any similar kind does not occur in future, or that the union has agreed to take such steps, he shall specify those steps in the declaration.

(5) Whether he makes or refuses a declaration, he shall give reasons for his decision in writing; and the reasons may be accompanied by written observations on any matter arising from, or connected with, the proceedings.

[(5A) Where the Certification Officer makes a declaration he shall also, unless he considers that to do so would be inappropriate, make an enforcement order, that is, an order imposing on the union one or more of the following requirements—

(a) to secure the holding of an election in accordance with the order;

(b) to take such other steps to remedy the declared failure as may be specified in the order;

(c) to abstain from such acts as may be so specified with a view to securing that a failure of the same or a similar kind does not occur in future.

The Certification Officer shall in an order imposing any such requirement as is mentioned in paragraph (a) or (b) specify the period within which the union is to comply with the requirements of the order.

(5B) Where the Certification Officer makes an order requiring the union to hold a fresh election, he shall (unless he considers that it would be inappropriate to do so in the particular circumstances of the case) require the election to be conducted in accordance with the requirements of this Chapter and such other provisions as may be made by the order.

(5C) Where an enforcement order has been made—

(a) any person who is a member of the union and was a member at the time the order was made, or

(b) any person who is or was a candidate in the election in question,

is entitled to enforce obedience to the order as if he had made the application on which the order was made.]²

(6) In exercising his functions under this section the Certification Officer shall ensure that, so far as is reasonably practicable, an application made to him is determined within six months of being made.

---

¹ Words repealed by Employment Relations Act 1999 c.26 Sch 9 para 1
² Inserted by Employment Relations Act 1999 c.26 Sch 6 para 10 (3)

(7) Where he requests a person to furnish information to him in connection with enquiries made by him under this section, he shall specify the date by which that information is to be furnished and, unless he considers that it would be inappropriate to do so, shall proceed with his determination of the application notwithstanding that the information has not been furnished to him by the specified date.

[(8) A declaration made by the Certification Officer under this section may be relied on as if it were a declaration made by the court.

(9) An enforcement order made by the Certification Officer under this section may be enforced in the same way as an order of the court.

(10) The following paragraphs have effect if a person applies under section 56 in relation to an alleged failure—

    (a) that person may not apply under this section in relation to that failure;

    (b) on an application by a different person under this section in relation to that failure, the Certification Officer shall have due regard to any declaration, order, observations or reasons made or given by the court regarding that failure and brought to the Certification Officer's notice.][1]

Application to court

56.—(1) A person having a sufficient interest (see section 54(2)) who claims **7-030** that a trade union has failed to comply with any of the requirements of this Chapter may apply to the court for a declaration to that effect.

(2) [...][2]

(3) If the court makes the declaration asked for, it shall specify in the declaration the provisions with which the trade union has failed to comply.

(4) Where the court makes a declaration it shall also, unless it considers that to do so would be inappropriate, make an enforcement order, that is, an order imposing on the union one or more of the following requirements—

    (a) to secure the holding of an election in accordance with the order;

    (b) to take such other steps to remedy the declared failure as may be specified in the order;

    (c) to abstain from such acts as may be so specified with a view to securing that a failure of the same or a similar kind does not occur in future.

The court shall in an order imposing any such requirement as is mentioned in paragraph (a) or (b) specify the period within which the union is to comply with the requirements of the order.

(5) Where the court makes an order requiring the union to hold a fresh election, the court shall (unless it considers that it would be inappropriate to do so in the particular circumstances of the case) require the election to be conducted in accordance with the requirements of this Chapter and such other provisions as may be made by the order.

(6) Where an enforcement order has been made—

    (a) any person who is a member of the union and was a member at the time the order was made, or

    (b) any person who is or was a candidate in the election in question,

is entitled to enforce obedience to the order as if he had made the application on which the order was made.

---

[1] Inserted by Employment Relations Act 1999 c.26 Sch 6 para 10 (4)
[2] Repealed by Employment Relations Act 1999 c.26 Sch 9 para 1

(7) Without prejudice to any other power of the court, the court may on an application under this section grant such interlocutory relief (in Scotland, such interim order) as it considers appropriate.

[(8) The following paragraphs have effect if a person applies under section 55 in relation to an alleged failure—

(a) that person may not apply under this section in relation to that failure;

(b) on an application by a different person under this section in relation to that failure, the court shall have due regard to any declaration, order, observations or reasons made or given by the Certification Officer regarding that failure and brought to the court's notice.][1]

[Appeals from Certification Officer

7-031   **56A.** An appeal lies to the Employment Appeal Tribunal on any question of law arising in proceedings before or arising from any decision of the Certification Officer under section 55.][2]

CHAPTER V

RIGHTS OF TRADE UNION MEMBERS

Right to a ballot before industrial action

Right to a ballot before industrial action

7-032   **62.**—(1) A member of a trade union who claims that members of the union, including himself, are likely to be or have been induced by the union to take part or to continue to take part in industrial action which does not have the support of a ballot may apply to the court for an order under this section.

[In this section "the relevant time" means the time when the application is made.][3]

(2) For this purpose industrial action shall be regarded as having the support of a ballot only if—

[(a) the union has held a ballot in respect of the action—

(i) in relation to which the requirements of section 226B so far as applicable before and during the holding of the ballot were satisfied,

(ii) in relation to which the requirements of sections 227 to 231 were satisfied, and

(iii) in which the majority voting in the ballot answered "Yes" to the question applicable in accordance with section 229(2) to industrial action of the kind which the applicant has been or is likely to be induced to take part in;

(b) such of the requirements of the following sections as have fallen to be satisfied at the relevant time have been satisfied, namely—

(i) section 226B so far as applicable after the holding of the ballot, and

(ii) section 231B; and

---

[1] Inserted by Employment Relations Act 1999 c.26 Sch 6 para 11 (3)
[2] Inserted by Employment Relations Act 1999 c.26 Sch 6 para 12
[3] Words inserted by Trade Union Reform and Employment Rights Act 1993 c.19 Sch 8 para 47 (a)

(c) the requirements of section 233 (calling of industrial action with support of ballot) are satisfied.

Any reference in this subsection to a requirement of a provision which is disapplied or modified by section 232 has effect subject to that section.][1]

(3) Where on an application under this section the court is satisfied that the claim is well-founded, it shall make such order as it considers appropriate for requiring the union to take steps for ensuring—

    (a) that there is no, or no further, inducement of members of the union to take part or to continue to take part in the industrial action to which the application relates, and

    (b) that no member engages in conduct after the making of the order by virtue of having been induced before the making of the order to take part or continue to take part in the action.

(4) Without prejudice to any other power of the court, the court may on an application under this section grant such interlocutory relief (in Scotland, such interim order) as it considers appropriate.

(5) For the purposes of this section an act shall be taken to be done by a trade union if it is authorised or endorsed by the union; and the provisions of section 20(2) to (4) apply for the purpose of determining whether an act is to be taken to be so authorised or endorsed.

Those provisions also apply in relation to proceedings for failure to comply with an order under this section as they apply in relation to the original proceedings.

(6) In this section—

    "inducement" includes an inducement which is or would be ineffective, whether because of the member's unwillingness to be influenced by it or for any other reason; and

    "industrial action" means a strike or other industrial action by persons employed under contracts of employment.

(7) Where a person holds any office or employment under the Crown on terms which do not constitute a contract of employment between that person and the Crown, those terms shall nevertheless be deemed to constitute such a contract for the purposes of this section.

(8) References in this section to a contract of employment include any contract under which one person personally does work or performs services for another; and related expressions shall be construed accordingly.

(9) Nothing in this section shall be construed as requiring a trade union to hold separate ballots for the purposes of this section and sections 226 to 234 (requirement of ballot before action by trade union).

Right not to be denied access to the courts

Right not to be denied access to the courts

63.—(1) This section applies where a matter is under the rules of a trade   **7-033** union required or allowed to be submitted for determination or conciliation in accordance with the rules of the union, but a provision of the rules purporting to provide for that to be a person's only remedy has no effect (or would have no effect if there were one).

---

[1] Substituted by Trade Union Reform and Employment Rights Act 1993 c.19 Sch 8 para 47 (b)

(2) Notwithstanding anything in the rules of the union or in the practice of any court, if a member or former member of the union begins proceedings in a court with respect to a matter to which this section applies, then if—

(a) he has previously made a valid application to the union for the matter to be submitted for determination or conciliation in accordance with the union's rules, and

(b) the court proceedings are begun after the end of the period of six months beginning with the day on which the union received the application,

the rules requiring or allowing the matter to be so submitted, and the fact that any relevant steps remain to be taken under the rules, shall be regarded for all purposes as irrelevant to any question whether the court proceedings should be dismissed, stayed or sisted, or adjourned.

(3) An application shall be deemed to be valid for the purposes of subsection (2)(a) unless the union informed the applicant, before the end of the period of 28 days beginning with the date on which the union received the application, of the respects in which the application contravened the requirements of the rules.

(4) If the court is satisfied that any delay in the taking of relevant steps under the rules is attributable to unreasonable conduct of the person who commenced the proceedings, it may treat the period specified in subsection (2)(b) as extended by such further period as it considers appropriate.

(5) In this section—

(a) references to the rules of a trade union include any arbitration or other agreement entered into in pursuance of a requirement imposed by or under the rules; and

(b) references to the relevant steps under the rules, in relation to any matter, include any steps falling to be taken in accordance with the rules for the purposes of or in connection with the determination or conciliation of the matter, or any appeal, review or reconsideration of any determination or award.

(6) This section does not affect any enactment or rule of law by virtue of which a court would apart from this section disregard any such rules of a trade union or any such fact as is mentioned in subsection (2).

Right not to be unjustifiably disciplined

Right not to be unjustifiably disciplined

7-034   **64.**—(1) An individual who is or has been a member of a trade union has the right not to be unjustifiably disciplined by the union.

(2) For this purpose an individual is "disciplined" by a trade union if a determination is made, or purportedly made, under the rules of the union or by an official of the union or a number of persons including an official that—

(a) he should be expelled from the union or a branch or section of the union,

(b) he should pay a sum to the union, to a branch or section of the union or to any other person;

(c) sums tendered by him in respect of an obligation to pay subscriptions or other sums to the union, or to a branch or section of the union, should be treated as unpaid or paid for a different purpose,

(d) he should be deprived to any extent of, or of access to, any benefits, services or facilities which would otherwise be provided or made available to him by virtue of his membership of the union, or a branch or section of the union,

(e) another trade union, or a branch or section of it, should be encouraged or advised not to accept him as a member, or

(f) he should be subjected to some other detriment;

and whether an individual is "unjustifiably disciplined" shall be determined in accordance with section 65.

(3) Where a determination made in infringement of an individual's right under this section requires the payment of a sum or the performance of an obligation, no person is entitled in any proceedings to rely on that determination for the purpose of recovering the sum or enforcing the obligation.

(4) Subject to that, the remedies for infringement of the right conferred by this section are as provided by sections 66 and 67, and not otherwise.

(5) The right not to be unjustifiably disciplined is in addition to (and not in substitution for) any right which exists apart from this section; [and, subject to section 66(4), nothing]^1 in this section or sections 65 to 67 affects any remedy for infringement of any such right.

Meaning of "unjustifiably disciplined"

65.—(1) An individual is unjustifiably disciplined by a trade union if the **7-035** actual or supposed conduct which constitutes the reason, or one of the reasons, for disciplining him is—

(a) conduct to which this section applies, or

(b) something which is believed by the union to amount to such conduct;

but subject to subsection (6) (cases of bad faith in relation to assertion of wrongdoing).

(2) This section applies to conduct which consists in—

(a) failing to participate in or support a strike or other industrial action (whether by members of the union or by others), or indicating opposition to or a lack of support for such action;

(b) failing to contravene, for a purpose connected with such a strike or other industrial action, a requirement imposed on him by or under a contract of employment;

(c) asserting (whether by bringing proceedings or otherwise) that the union, any official or representative of it or a trustee of its property has contravened, or is proposing to contravene, a requirement which is, or is thought to be, imposed by or under the rules of the union or any other agreement or by or under any enactment (whenever passed) or any rule of law;

(d) encouraging or assisting a person—

(i) to perform an obligation imposed on him by a contract of employment, or

(ii) to make or attempt to vindicate any such assertion as is mentioned in paragraph (c); [...]^2

(e) contravening a requirement imposed by or in consequence of a determination which infringes the individual's or another individual's right not to be unjustifiably disciplined.

[(f) failing to agree, or withdrawing agreement, to the making from his wages (in accordance with arrangements between his employer and the

---

^{1} Words substituted by Trade Union Reform and Employment Rights Act 1993 c.19 Sch 8 para 48

^{2} Word repealed by Trade Union Reform and Employment Rights Act 1993 c.19 Sch 10 para 1

union) of deductions representing payments to the union in respect of his membership,

(g) resigning or proposing to resign from the union or from another union, becoming or proposing to become a member of another union, refusing to become a member of another union, or being a member of another union,

(h) working with, or proposing to work with, individuals who are not members of the union or who are or are not members of another union,

(i) working for, or proposing to work for, an employer who employs or who has employed individuals who are not members of the union or who are or are not members of another union, or

(j) requiring the union to do an act which the union is, by any provision of this Act, required to do on the requisition of a member.][1]

(3) This section applies to conduct which involves [...][2] the Certification Officer being consulted or asked to provide advice or assistance with respect to any matter whatever, or which involves any person being consulted or asked to provide advice or assistance with respect to a matter which forms, or might form, the subject-matter of any such assertion as is mentioned in subsection (2)(c) above.

(4) This section also applies to conduct which consists in proposing to engage, in or doing anything preparatory or incidental to, conduct falling within subsection (2) or (3).

(5) This section does not apply to an act, omission or statement comprised in conduct falling within subsection (2), (3) or (4) above if it is shown that the act, omission or statement is one in respect of which individuals would be disciplined by the union irrespective of whether their acts, omissions or statements were in connection with conduct within subsection (2) or (3) above.

(6) An individual is not unjustifiably disciplined if it is shown—

(a) that the reason for disciplining him, or one of them, is that he made such an assertion as is mentioned in subsection (2)(c), or encouraged or assisted another person to make or attempt to vindicate such an assertion,

(b) that the assertion was false, and

(c) that he made the assertion, or encouraged or assisted another person to make or attempt to vindicate it, in the belief that it was false or otherwise in bad faith,

and that there was no other reason for disciplining him or that the only other reasons were reasons in respect of which he does not fall to be treated as unjustifiably disciplined.

(7) In this section—

"conduct" includes statements, acts and omissions;

"contract of employment" , in relation to an individual, includes any agreement between that individual and a person for whom he works or normally works; ["employer" includes such a person and related expressions shall be construed accordingly][3] [...][4]

---

[1] Inserted by Trade Union Reform and Employment Rights Act 1993 c.19 Pt I s 16 (1)

[2] Words repealed by Employment Relations Act 1999 c.26 Sch 9 para 1

[3] Words inserted by Trade Union Reform and Employment Rights Act 1993 c.19 Sch 8 para 49 (a)

[4] Word repealed by Trade Union Reform and Employment Rights Act 1993 c.19 Sch 10 para 1

"representative", in relation to a union, means a person acting or purporting to act—

(a) in his capacity as a member of the union, or

(b) on the instructions or advice of a person acting or purporting to act in that capacity or in the capacity of an official of the union.

["require" (on the part of an individual) includes request or apply for, and "requisition" shall be construed accordingly.][1]

[and

"wages" shall be construed in accordance with the definitions of "contract of employment", "employer" and related expressions.][2]

(8) Where a person holds any office or employment under the Crown on terms which do not constitute a contract of employment between him and the Crown, those terms shall nevertheless be deemed to constitute such a contract for the purposes of this section.

Complaint of infringement of right

66.—(1) An individual who claims that he has been unjustifiably disci- **7-036** plined by a trade union may present a complaint against the union to an industrial tribunal.

(2) The tribunal shall not entertain such a complaint unless it is presented—

(a) before the end of the period of three months beginning with the date of the making of the determination claimed to infringe the right, or

(b) where the tribunal is satisfied—

(i) that it was not reasonably practicable for the complaint to be presented before the end of that period, or

(ii) that any delay in making the complaint is wholly or partly attributable to a reasonable attempt to appeal against the determination or to have it reconsidered or reviewed,

within such further period as the tribunal considers reasonable.

(3) Where the tribunal finds the complaint well-founded, it shall make a declaration to that effect.

[(4) Where a complaint relating to an expulsion which is presented under this section is declared to be well-founded, no complaint in respect of the expulsion shall be presented or proceeded with under section 174 (right not to be excluded or expelled from trade union).][3]

Further remedies for infringement of right

67.—(1) An individual whose complaint under section 66 has been **7-037** declared to be well-founded may make an application for one or both of the following—

(a) an award of compensation to be paid to him by the union;

(b) an order that the union pay him an amount equal to any sum which he has paid in pursuance of any such determination as is mentioned in section 64(2)(b).

---

[1] Definition inserted by Trade Union Reform and Employment Rights Act 1993 c.19 Pt I s 16 (2)

[2] Definition inserted preceded by the word "and" by Trade Union Reform and Employment Rights Act 1993 c.19 Sch 8 para 49 (b)

[3] Substituted by Trade Union Reform and Employment Rights Act 1993 c.19 Sch 8 para 50

(2) An application under this section shall be made to the Employment Appeal Tribunal if, when it is made—

    (a) the determination infringing the applicant's right not to be unjustifiably disciplined has not been revoked, or

    (b) the union has failed to take all the steps necessary for securing the reversal of anything done for the purpose of giving effect to the determination;

and in any other case it shall be made to an [employment tribunal][1].

(3) An application under this section shall not be entertained if made before the end of the period of four weeks beginning with the date of the declaration or after the end of the period of six months beginning with that date.

(4) Where the Employment Appeal Tribunal or [employment tribunal][2] is satisfied that it would be required by virtue of subsection (2) to dismiss the application, it may instead transfer it to the tribunal to which it should have been made; and an application so transferred shall be proceeded with as if it had been made in accordance with that subsection when originally made.

(5) The amount of compensation awarded shall, subject to the following provisions, be such as the Employment Appeal Tribunal or [employment tribunal][3] considers just and equitable in all the circumstances.

(6) In determining the amount of compensation to be awarded, the same rule shall be applied concerning the duty of a person to mitigate his loss as applies to damages recoverable under the common law in England and Wales or Scotland.

(7) Where the Employment Appeal Tribunal or [employment tribunal][4] finds that the infringement complained of was to any extent caused or contributed to by the action of the applicant, it shall reduce the amount of the compensation by such proportion as it considers just and equitable having regard to that finding.

(8) The amount of compensation [calculated in accordance with subsections (5) to (7)][5] shall not exceed the aggregate of—

    (a) an amount equal to 30 times the limit for the time being imposed by [section 227(1)(a) of the Employment Rights Act 1996][6] (maximum amount of a week's pay for basic award in unfair dismissal cases), and

    (b) an amount equal to the limit for the time being imposed by [section 124(1)][7] of that Act (maximum compensatory award in such cases);

and, in the case of an award by the Employment Appeal Tribunal, shall not be less than the amount for the time being specified in [176(6) of this Act (minimum award by Employment Appeal Tribunal in cases of exclusion or expulsion from union)][8].

---

[1] Words substituted by Employment Rights (Dispute Resolution) Act 1998 c.8 Pt I s 1 (2)

[2] Words substituted by Employment Rights (Dispute Resolution) Act 1998 c.8 Pt I s 1 (2)

[3] Words substituted by Employment Rights (Dispute Resolution) Act 1998 c.8 Pt I s 1 (2)

[4] Words substituted by Employment Rights (Dispute Resolution) Act 1998 c.8 Pt I s 1 (2)

[5] Words substituted by Trade Union Reform and Employment Rights Act 1993 c.19 Sch 8 para 51 (a) (i)

[6] Words substituted by Employment Rights Act 1996 c.18 Sch 1 para 56 (2) (a)

[7] Words substituted by Employment Rights Act 1996 c.18 Sch 1 para 56 (2) (b)

[8] Substituted by Trade Union Reform and Employment Rights Act 1993 c.19 Sch 8 para 51 (a) (ii)

(9) [...]¹

Right not to suffer deduction of unauthorised or excessive
union subscriptions

[Right not to suffer deduction of unauthorised subscriptions

68.—(1) Where arrangements ("subscription deduction arrangements")   **7-038**
exist between the employer of a worker and a trade union relating to the
making from workers' wages of deductions representing payments to the
union in respect of the workers' membership of the union ("subscription
deductions"), the employer shall ensure that no subscription deduction is
made from wages payable to the worker on any day unless—

    (a) the worker has authorised in writing the making from his wages
        of subscription deductions; and

    (b) the worker has not withdrawn the authorisation.

(2) A worker withdraws an authorisation given for the purposes of
subsection (1), in relation to a subscription deduction which falls to be made
from wages payable to him on any day, if a written notice withdrawing the
authorisation has been received by the employer in time for it to be
reasonably practicable for the employer to secure that no such deduction is
made.

(3) A worker's authorisation of the making of subscription deductions
from his wages shall not give rise to any obligation on the part of the
employer to the worker to maintain or continue to maintain subscription
deduction arrangements.

(4) In this section and section 68A, "employer", "wages" and "worker"
have the same meanings as in the Employment Rights Act 1996.]²

[Complaint of infringement of rights

68A.—(1) A worker may present a complaint to an [employment   **7-039**
tribunal]³ that his employer has made a deduction from his wages in contravention of section 68—

    (a) within the period of three months beginning with the date of the
        payment of the wages from which the deduction, or (if the
        complaint relates to more than one deduction) the last of the
        deductions, was made, or

    (b) where the tribunal is satisfied that it was not reasonably practic-
        able for the complaint to be presented within that period, within
        such further period as the tribunal considers reasonable.

[(2) Where a tribunal finds that a complaint under this section is well
founded, it shall make a declaration to that effect and shall order the
employer to pay to the worker the whole amount of the deduction, less any
such part of the amount as has already been paid to the worker by the
employer.]⁴

(3) Where the making of a deduction from the wages of a worker both
contravenes section 68(1) and involves one or more of the contraventions
specified in subsection (4) of this section, the aggregate amount which may
be ordered by an [employment tribunal]⁵ or court (whether on the same

---

¹ Repealed by Trade Union Reform and Employment Rights Act 1993 c.19 Sch 8 para 51 (b)
² Substituted by SI 1998/1529 art 2 (1)
³ Words substituted by Employment Rights (Dispute Resolution) Act 1998 c.8 Pt I s 1 (2)
⁴ Substituted by SI 1998/1529 art 2 (2)
⁵ Words substituted by Employment Rights (Dispute Resolution) Act 1998 c.8 Pt I s 1 (2)

occasion or on different occasions) to be paid in respect of the contraventions shall not exceed the amount, or (where different amounts may be ordered to be paid in respect of different contraventions) the greatest amount, which may be ordered to be paid in respect of any one of them.

(4) The contraventions referred to in subsection (3) are—

(a) a contravention of the requirement not to make a deduction without having given the particulars required by section 8 (itemised pay statements) or 9(1) (standing statements of fixed deductions) of [the Employment Rights Act 1996][1],

(b) a contravention of [section 13 of that Act][2] (requirement not to make unauthorised deductions), and

(c) a contravention of section 86(1) or 90(1) of this Act (requirements not to make deductions of political fund contributions in certain circumstances).][3]

Right to terminate membership of union

Right to terminate membership of union

7-040   **69.** In every contract of membership of a trade union, whether made before or after the passing of this Act, a term conferring a right on the member, on giving reasonable notice and complying with any reasonable conditions, to terminate his membership of the union shall be implied.

Supplementary

Membership of constituent or affiliated organisation

7-041   **70.** In this Chapter "member", in relation to a trade union consisting wholly or partly of, or of representatives of, constituent or affiliated organisations, includes a member of any of the constituent or affiliated organisations.

[Recognition of trade unions

7-042   **70.A** Schedule A1 shall have effect.][4]

[Training

7-043   **70B.**—(1) This section applies where—

(a) a trade union is recognised, in accordance with Schedule A1, as entitled to conduct collective bargaining on behalf of a bargaining unit (within the meaning of Part I of that Schedule), and

(b) a method for the conduct of collective bargaining is specified by the Central Arbitration Committee under paragraph 31(3) of that Schedule (and is not the subject of an agreement under paragraph 31(5)(a) or (b)).

(2) The employer must from time to time invite the trade union to send representatives to a meeting for the purpose of—

---

[1] Words substituted by Employment Rights Act 1996 c.18 Sch 1 para 56 (4) (a)
[2] Words substituted by Employment Rights Act 1996 c.18 Sch 1 para 56 (4) (b)
[3] Inserted by Trade Union Reform and Employment Rights Act 1993 c.19 Pt I s 15
[4] Inserted by Employment Relations Act 1999 c.26 s 1 (2)

(a) consulting about the employer's policy on training for workers within the bargaining unit,

(b) consulting about his plans for training for those workers during the period of six months starting with the day of the meeting, and

(c) reporting about training provided for those workers since the previous meeting.

(3) The date set for a meeting under subsection (2) must not be later than—

(a) in the case of a first meeting, the end of the period of six months starting with the day on which this section first applies in relation to a bargaining unit, and

(b) in the case of each subsequent meeting, the end of the period of six months starting with the day of the previous meeting.

(4) The employer shall, before the period of two weeks ending with the date of a meeting, provide to the trade union any information—

(a) without which the union's representatives would be to a material extent impeded in participating in the meeting, and

(b) which it would be in accordance with good industrial relations practice to disclose for the purposes of the meeting.

(5) Section 182(1) shall apply in relation to the provision of information under subsection (4) as it applies in relation to the disclosure of information under section 181.

(6) The employer shall take account of any written representations about matters raised at a meeting which he receives from the trade union within the period of four weeks starting with the date of the meeting.

(7) Where more than one trade union is recognised as entitled to conduct collective bargaining on behalf of a bargaining unit, a reference in this section to "the trade union" is a reference to each trade union.

(8) Where at a meeting under this section (Meeting 1) an employer indicates his intention to convene a subsequent meeting (Meeting 2) before the expiry of the period of six months beginning with the date of Meeting 1, for the reference to a period of six months in subsection(2)(b) there shall be substituted a reference to the expected period between Meeting 1 and Meeting 2.

(9) The Secretary of State may by order made by statutory instrument amend any of subsections (2) to (6).

(10) No order shall be made under subsection (9) unless a draft has been laid before, and approved by resolution of, each House of Parliament.

Section 70B: complaint to employment tribunal

70C.—(1) A trade union may present a complaint to an employment **7-044** tribunal that an employer has failed to comply with his obligations under section 70B in relation to a bargaining unit.

(2) An employment tribunal shall not consider a complaint under this section unless it is presented—

(a) before the end of the period of three months beginning with the date of the alleged failure, or

(b) within such further period as the tribunal considers reasonable in a case where it is satisfied that it was not reasonably practicable for the complaint to be presented before the end of that period of three months.

(3) Where an employment tribunal finds a complaint under this section well-founded it—

    (a) shall make a declaration to that effect, and

    (b) may make an award of compensation to be paid by the employer to each person who was, at the time when the failure occurred, a member of the bargaining unit.

(4) The amount of the award shall not, in relation to each person, exceed two weeks' pay.

(5) For the purpose of subsection (4) a week's pay—

    (a) shall be calculated in accordance with Chapter II of Part XIV of the Employment Rights Act 1996 (taking the date of the employer's failure as the calculation date), and

    (b) shall be subject to the limit in section 227(1) of that Act.

(6) Proceedings for enforcement of an award of compensation under this section—

    (a) may, in relation to each person to whom compensation is payable, be commenced by that person, and

    (b) may not be commenced by a trade union.][1]

CHAPTER VIIA

BREACH OF RULES

[Right to apply to Certification Officer

7-045   **108A.**—(1) A person who claims that there has been a breach or threatened breach of the rules of a trade union relating to any of the matters mentioned in subsection (2) may apply to the Certification Officer for a declaration to that effect, subject to subsections (3) to (7).

(2) The matters are—

    (a) the appointment or election of a person to, or the removal of a person from, any office;

    (b) disciplinary proceedings by the union (including expulsion);

    (c) the balloting of members on any issue other than industrial action;

    (d) the constitution or proceedings of any executive committee or of any decision-making meeting;

    (e) such other matters as may be specified in an order made by the Secretary of State.

(3) The applicant must be a member of the union, or have been one at the time of the alleged breach or threatened breach.

(4) A person may not apply under subsection (1) in relation to a claim if he is entitled to apply under section 80 in relation to the claim.

(5) No application may be made regarding—

    (a) the dismissal of an employee of the union;

    (b) disciplinary proceedings against an employee of the union.

(6) An application must be made—

    (a) within the period of six months starting with the day on which the breach or threatened breach is alleged to have taken place, or

---

[1] Added by Employment Relations Act 1999 c.26 s 5

(b) if within that period any internal complaints procedure of the union is invoked to resolve the claim, within the period of six months starting with the earlier of the days specified in subsection (7).

(7) Those days are—

(a) the day on which the procedure is concluded, and

(b) the last day of the period of one year beginning with the day on which the procedure is invoked.

(8) The reference in subsection (1) to the rules of a union includes references to the rules of any branch or section of the union.

(9) In subsection (2)(c) "industrial action" means a strike or other industrial action by persons employed under contracts of employment.

(10) For the purposes of subsection (2)(d) a committee is an executive committee if—

(a) it is a committee of the union concerned and has power to make executive decisions on behalf of the union or on behalf of a constituent body,

(b) it is a committee of a major constituent body and has power to make executive decisions on behalf of that body, or

(c) it is a sub-committee of a committee falling within paragraph (a) or (b).

(11) For the purposes of subsection (2)(d) a decision-making meeting is—

(a) a meeting of members of the union concerned (or the representatives of such members) which has power to make a decision on any matter which, under the rules of the union, is final as regards the union or which, under the rules of the union or a constituent body, is final as regards that body, or

(b) a meeting of members of a major constituent body (or the representatives of such members) which has power to make a decision on any matter which, under the rules of the union or the body, is final as regards that body.

(12) For the purposes of subsections (10) and (11), in relation to the trade union concerned—

(a) a constituent body is any body which forms part of the union, including a branch, group, section or region;

(b) a major constituent body is such a body which has more than 1,000 members.

(13) Any order under subsection (2)(e) shall be made by statutory instrument; and no such order shall be made unless a draft of it has been laid before and approved by resolution of each House of Parliament.

(14) If a person applies to the Certification Officer under this section in relation to an alleged breach or threatened breach he may not apply to the court in relation to the breach or threatened breach; but nothing in this subsection shall prevent such a person from exercising any right to appeal against or challenge the Certification Officer's decision on the application to him.

(15) If—

(a) a person applies to the court in relation to an alleged breach or threatened breach, and

(b) the breach or threatened breach is one in relation to which he could have made an application to the Certification Officer under this section,

he may not apply to the Certification Officer under this section in relation to the breach or threatened breach.][1]

[Declarations and orders

7-046　　**108B.**—(1) The Certification Officer may refuse to accept an application under section 108A unless he is satisfied that the applicant has taken all reasonable steps to resolve the claim by the use of any internal complaints procedure of the union.

(2) If he accepts an application under section 108A the Certification Officer—

(a) shall make such enquiries as he thinks fit,

(b) shall give the applicant and the union an opportunity to be heard,

(c) shall ensure that, so far as is reasonably practicable, the application is determined within six months of being made,

(d) may make or refuse the declaration asked for, and

(e) shall, whether he makes or refuses the declaration, give reasons for his decision in writing.

(3) Where the Certification Officer makes a declaration he shall also, unless he considers that to do so would be inappropriate, make an enforcement order, that is, an order imposing on the union one or both of the following requirements—:

(a) to take such steps to remedy the breach, or withdraw the threat of a breach, as may be specified in the order;

(b) to abstain from such acts as may be so specified with a view to securing that a breach or threat of the same or a similar kind does not occur in future.

(4) The Certification Officer shall in an order imposing any such requirement as is mentioned in subsection (3)(a) specify the period within which the union is to comply with the requirement.

(5) Where the Certification Officer requests a person to furnish information to him in connection with enquiries made by him under this section, he shall specify the date by which that information is to be furnished and, unless he considers that it would be inappropriate to do so, shall proceed with his determination of the application notwithstanding that the information has not been furnished to him by the specified date.

(6) A declaration made by the Certification Officer under this section may be relied on as if it were a declaration made by the court.

(7) Where an enforcement order has been made, any person who is a member of the union and was a member at the time it was made is entitled to enforce obedience to the order as if he had made the application on which the order was made.

(8) An enforcement order made by the Certification Officer under this section may be enforced in the same way as an order of the court.

(9) An order under section 108A(2)(e) may provide that, in relation to an application under section 108A with regard to a prescribed matter, the preceding provisions of this section shall apply with such omissions or modifications as may be specified in the order; and a prescribed matter is such

---

[1] Inserted by Employment Relations Act 1999 c.26 Sch 6 para 19

matter specified under section 108A(2)(e) as is prescribed under this subsection.]¹

[Appeals from Certification Officer

108C. An appeal lies to the Employment Appeal Tribunal on any question of law arising in proceedings before or arising from any decision of the Certification Officer under this Chapter.]² 7-047

CHAPTER IX

MISCELLANEOUS AND GENERAL PROVISIONS

Interpretation

Expressions relating to trade unions

119. In this Act, in relation to a trade union— 7-048
["agent" means a banker or solicitor of, or any person employed as an auditor by, the union or any branch or section of the union;]³
"branch or section", except where the context otherwise requires, includes a branch or section which is itself a trade union;
"executive" means the principal committee of the union exercising executive functions, by whatever name it is called;
["financial affairs" means affairs of the union relating to any fund which is applicable for the purposes of the union (including any fund of a branch or section of the union which is so applicable);]⁴
"general secretary" means the official of the union who holds the office of general secretary or, where there is no such office, holds an office which is equivalent, or (except in section 14(4)) the nearest equivalent, to that of general secretary;
"officer" includes—
(a) any member of the governing body of the union, and
(b) any trustee of any fund applicable for the purposes of the union;

"official" means —
(a) an officer of the union or of a branch or section of the union, or
(b) a person elected or appointed in accordance with the rules of the union to be a representative of its members or of some of them,
and includes a person so elected or appointed who is an employee of the same employer as the members or one or more of the members whom he is to represent;

---

¹ Inserted by Employment Relations Act 1999 c.26 Sch 6 para 19
² Inserted by Employment Relations Act 1999 c.26 Sch 6 para 19
³ Definition inserted by Trade Union Reform and Employment Rights Act 1993 c.19 Sch 8 para 63 (a)
⁴ Definition inserted by Trade Union Reform and Employment Rights Act 1993 c.19 Sch 8 para 63 (b)

"president" means the official of the union who holds the office of president or, where there is no such office, who holds an office which is equivalent, or (except in section 14(4) or Chapter IV) the nearest equivalent, to that of president; and

"rules", except where the context otherwise requires, includes the rules of any branch or section of the union.

PART II

EMPLOYERS' ASSOCIATIONS

Introductory

Meaning of "employers' association"

7-049   **122.**—(1) In this Act an "employers' association" means an organisation (whether temporary or permanent)—

(a) which consists wholly or mainly of employers or individual owners of undertakings of one or more descriptions and whose principal purposes include the regulation of relations between employers of that description or those descriptions and workers or trade unions; or

(b) which consists wholly or mainly of—

(i) constituent or affiliated organisations which fulfil the conditions in paragraph (a) (or themselves consist wholly or mainly of constituent or affiliated organisations which fulfil those conditions), or

(ii) representatives of such constituent or affiliated organisations,

and whose principal purposes include the regulation of relations between employers and workers or between employers and trade unions, or the regulation of relations between its constituent or affiliated organisations.

(2) References in this Act to employers' associations include combinations of employers and employers' associations.

The list of employers' associations

The list of employers' associations

7-050   **123.**—(1) The Certification Officer shall keep a list of employers' associations containing the names of—

(a) the organisations whose names were, immediately before the commencement of this Act, duly entered in the list of employers' associations kept by him under section 8 of the Trade Union and Labour Relations Act 1974, and

(b) the names of the organisations entitled to have their names entered in the list in accordance with this Part.

(2) The Certification Officer shall keep copies of the list of employers' associations, as for the time being in force, available for public inspection at all reasonable hours free of charge.

(3) A copy of the list shall be included in his annual report.

(4) The fact that the name of an organisation is included in the list of employers' associations is evidence (in Scotland, sufficient evidence) that the organisation is an employers' association.

(5) On the application of an organisation whose name is included in the list, the Certification Officer shall issue it with a certificate to that effect.

(6) A document purporting to be such a certificate is evidence (in Scotland, sufficient evidence) that the name of the organisation is entered in the list.

PART III

RIGHTS IN RELATION TO UNION MEMBERSHIP AND ACTIVITIES

Access to employment

Refusal of employment on grounds related to union membership

137.—(1) It is unlawful to refuse a person employment—   **7-051**
  (a) because he is, or is not, a member of a trade union, or
  (b) because he is unwilling to accept a requirement—
      (i) to take steps to become or cease to be, or to remain or not to become, a member of a trade union, or
      (ii) to make payments or suffer deductions in the event of his not being a member of a trade union.

(2) A person who is thus unlawfully refused employment has a right of compliant to an [employment tribunal][1].

(3) Where an advertisement is published which indicates, or might reasonably be understood as indicating—
  (a) that employment to which the advertisement relates is open only to a person who is, or is not, a member of a trade union, or
  (b) that any such requirement as is mentioned in subsection (1)(b) will be imposed in relation to employment to which the advertisement relates,
a person who does not satisfy that condition or, as the case may be, is unwilling to accept that requirement, and who seeks and is refused employment to which the advertisement relates, shall be conclusively presumed to have been refused employment for that reason.

(4) Where there is an arrangement or practice under which employment is offered only to persons put forward or approved by a trade union, and the trade union puts forward or approves only persons who are members of the union, a person who is not a member of the union and who is refused employment in pursuance of the arrangement or practice shall be taken to have been refused employment because he is not a member of the trade union.

(5) A person shall be taken to be refused employment if he seeks employment of any description with a person and that person—
  (a) refuses or deliberately omits to entertain and process his application or enquiry, or
  (b) causes him to withdraw or cease to pursue his application or enquiry, or

---

[1] Words substituted by Employment Rights (Dispute Resolution) Act 1998 c.8 Pt I s 1 (2)

(c) refuses or deliberately omits to offer him employment of that description, or

(d) makes him an offer of such employment the terms of which are such as no reasonable employer who wished to fill the post would offer and which is not accepted, or

(e) makes him an offer of such employment but withdraws it or causes him not to accept it.

(6) Where a person is offered employment on terms which include a requirement that he is, or is not, a member of a trade union, or any such requirement as is mentioned in subsection (1)(b), and he does not accept the offer because he does not satisfy or, as the case may be, is unwilling to accept that requirement, he shall be treated as having been refused employment for that reason.

(7) Where a person may not be considered for appointment or election to an office in a trade union unless he is a member of the union, or of a particular branch or section of the union or of one of a number of particular branches or sections of the union, nothing in this section applies to anything done for the purpose of securing compliance with that condition although as holder of the office he would be employed by the union.

For this purpose an "office" means any position—

(a) by virtue of which the holder is an official of the union, or

(b) to which Chapter IV of Part I applies (duty to hold elections).

(8) The provisions of this section apply in relation to an employment agency acting, or purporting to act, on behalf of an employer as in relation to an employer.

Refusal of service of employment agency on grounds related to union membership

7-052   **138.**—(1) It is unlawful for an employment agency to refuse a person any of its services—

(a) because he is, or is not, a member of a trade union, or

(b) because he is unwilling to accept a requirement to take steps to become or cease to be, or to remain or not to become, a member of a trade union.

(2) A person who is thus unlawfully refused any service of an employment agency has a right of complaint to an industrial tribunal.

(3) Where an advertisement is published which indicates, or might reasonably be understood as indicating—

(a) that any service of an employment agency is available only to a person who is, or is not, a member of a trade union, or

(b) that any such requirement as is mentioned in subsection (1)(b) will be imposed in relation to a service to which the advertisement relates,

a person who does not satisfy that condition or, as the case may be, is unwilling to accept that requirement, and who seeks to avail himself of and is refused that service, shall be conclusively presumed to have been refused it for that reason.

(4) A person shall be taken to be refused a service if he seeks to avail himself of it and the agency—

(a) refuses or deliberately omits to make the service available to him, or

(b) causes him not to avail himself of the service or to cease to avail himself of it, or

(c) does not provide the same service, on the same terms, as is provided to others.

(5) Where a person is offered a service on terms which include a requirement that he is, or is not, a member of a trade union, or any such requirement as is mentioned in subsection (1)(b), and he does not accept the offer because he does not satisfy or, as the case may be, is unwilling to accept that requirement, he shall be treated as having been refused the service for that reason.

Time limit for proceedings

139.—(1) An [employment tribunal][1] shall not consider a complaint **7-053** under section 137 or 138 unless it is presented to the tribunal—

(a) before the end of the period of three months beginning with the date of the conduct to which the complaint relates, or

(b) where the tribunal is satisfied that it was not reasonably practicable for the complaint to be presented before the end of that period, within such further period as the tribunal considers reasonable.

(2) The date of the conduct to which a complaint under section 137 relates shall be taken to be—

(a) in the case of an actual refusal, the date of the refusal;

(b) in the case of a deliberate omission—

(i) to entertain and process the complainant's application or enquiry, or

(ii) to offer employment,

the end of the period within which it was reasonable to expect the employer to act;

(c) in the case of conduct causing the complainant to withdraw or cease to pursue his application or enquiry, the date of that conduct;

(d) in a case where an offer was made but withdrawn, the date when it was withdrawn;

(e) in any other case where an offer was made but not accepted, the date on which it was made.

(3) The date of the conduct to which a complaint under section 138 relates shall be taken to be—

(a) in the case of an actual refusal, the date of the refusal;

(b) in the case of a deliberate omission to make a service available, the end of the period within which it was reasonable to expect the employment agency to act;

(c) in the case of conduct causing the complainant not to avail himself of a service or to cease to avail himself of it, the date of that conduct;

(d) in the case of failure to provide the same service, on the same terms, as is provided to others, the date or last date on which the service in fact provided was provided.

---

[1] Words substituted by Employment Rights (Dispute Resolution) Act 1998 c.8 Pt I s 1 (2)

Remedies

7-054   **140.**—(1) Where the [employment tribunal][1] finds that a complaint under section 137 or 138 is well-founded, it shall make a declaration to that effect and may make such of the following as it considers just and equitable—

(a) an order requiring the respondent to pay compensation to the complainant of such amount as the tribunal may determine;

(b) a recommendation that the respondent take within a specified period action appearing to the tribunal to be practicable for the purpose of obviating or reducing the adverse effect on the complainant of any conduct to which the complaint relates.

(2) Compensation shall be assessed on the same basis as damages for breach of statutory duty and may include compensation for injury to feelings.

(3) If the respondent fails without reasonable justification to comply with a recommendation to take action, the tribunal may increase its award of compensation or, if it has not made such an award, make one.

(4) The total amount of compensation shall not exceed the limit for the time being imposed by [section 124(1) of the Employment Rights Act 1996][2] (limit on compensation for unfair dismissal).

Complaint against employer and employment agency

7-055   **141.**—(1) Where a person has a right of complaint against a prospective employer and against an employment agency arising out of the same facts, he may present a complaint against either of them or against them jointly.

(2) If a complaint is brought against one only, he or the complainant may request the tribunal to join or sist the other as a party to the proceedings.

The request shall be granted if it is made before the hearing of the complaint begins, but may be refused if it is made after that time; and no such request may be made after the tribunal has made its decision as to whether the complaint is well-founded.

(3) Where a complaint is brought against an employer and an employment agency jointly, or where it is brought against one and the other is joined or sisted as a party to the proceedings, and the tribunal—

(a) finds that the complaint is well-founded as against the employer and the agency, and

(b) makes an award of compensation,

it may order that the compensation shall be paid by the one or the other, or partly by one and partly by the other, as the tribunal may consider just and equitable in the circumstances.

Awards against third parties

7-056   **142.**—(1) If in proceedings on a complaint under section 137 or 138 either the complainant or the respondent claims that the respondent was induced to act in the manner complained of by pressure which a trade union or other person exercised on him by calling, organising, procuring or financing a strike or other industrial action, or by threatening to do so, the

---

[1] Words substituted by Employment Rights (Dispute Resolution) Act 1998 c.8 Pt I s 1 (2)

[2] Words substituted by Employment Rights Act 1996 c.18 Sch 1 para 56 (6)

complainant or the respondent may request the [employment tribunal]¹ to
direct that the person who he claims exercised the pressure be joined or
sisted as a party to the proceedings.

(2) The request shall be granted if it is made before the hearing of the
complaint begins, but may be refused if it is made after that time; and no
such request may be made after the tribunal has made its decision as to
whether the complaint is well-founded.

(3) Where a person has been so joined or sisted as a party to the proceedings and the tribunal—

(a) finds that the complaint is well-founded,

(b) makes an award of compensation, and

(c) also finds that the claim in subsection (1) above is well-founded,

it may order that the compensation shall be paid by the person joined
instead of by the respondent, or partly by that person and partly by the
respondent, as the tribunal may consider just and equitable in the circumstances.

(4) Where by virtue of section 141 (complaint against employer and
employment agency) there is more than one respondent, the above
provisions apply to either or both of them.

Interpretation and other supplementary provisions

143.—(1) In sections 137 to 143—   7-057

"advertisement" includes every form of advertisement or notice,
whether to the public or not, and references to publishing an
advertisement shall be construed accordingly;

"employment" means employment under a contract of employment,
and related expressions shall be construed accordingly; and

"employment agency" means a person who, for profit or not,
provides services for the purpose of finding employment for
workers or supplying employers with workers, but subject to
subsection (2) below.

(2) For the purposes of sections 137 to 143 as they apply to employment
agencies—

(a) services other than those mentioned in the definition of
"employment agency" above shall be disregarded, and

(b) a trade union shall not be regarded as an employment agency by
reason of services provided by it only for, or in relation to, its
members.

(3) References in sections 137 to 143 to being or not being a member of
a trade union are to being or not being a member of any trade union, of a
particular trade union or of one of a number of particular trade unions.

Any such reference includes a reference to being or not being a member
of a particular branch or section of a trade union or of one of a number of
particular branches or sections of a trade union.

(4) The remedy of a person for conduct which is unlawful by virtue of
section 137 or 138 is by way of a complaint to an industrial tribunal in
accordance with this Part, and not otherwise.

No other legal liability arises by reason that conduct is unlawful by
virtue of either of those sections.

---

¹ Words substituted by Employment Rights (Dispute Resolution) Act 1998 c.8 Pt I s 1 (2)

Contracts for supply of goods or services

Union membership requirement in contract for goods or services void

7-058   **144.** A term or condition of a contract for the supply of goods or services is void in so far as it purports to require that the whole, or some part, of the work done for the purposes of the contract is done only by persons who are, or are not, members of trade unions or of a particular trade union.

Refusal to deal on union membership grounds prohibited

7-059   **145.**—(1) A person shall not refuse to deal with a supplier or prospective supplier of goods or services on union membership grounds.

"Refuse to deal" and "union membership grounds" shall be construed as follows.

(2) A person refuses to deal with a person if, where he maintains (in whatever form) a list of approved suppliers of goods or services, or of persons from whom tenders for the supply of goods or services may be invited, he fails to include the name of that person in that list.

He does so on union membership grounds if the ground, or one of the grounds, for failing to include his name is that if that person were to enter into a contract with him for the supply of goods or services, work to be done for the purposes of the contract would, or would be likely to, be done by persons who were, or who were not, members of trade unions or of a particular trade union.

(3) A person refuses to deal with a person if, in relation to a proposed contract for the supply of goods or services—

  (a) he excludes that person from the group of persons from whom tenders for the supply of the goods or services are invited, or
  (b) he fails to permit that person to submit such a tender, or
  (c) he otherwise determines not to enter into a contract with that person for the supply of the goods or services.

He does so on union membership grounds if the ground, or one of the grounds, on which he does so is that if the proposed contract were entered into with that person, work to be done for the purposes of the contract would, or would be likely to, be done by persons who were, or who were not, members of trade unions or of a particular trade union.

(4) A person refuses to deal with a person if he terminates a contract with him for the supply of goods or services.

He does so on union membership grounds if the ground, or one of the grounds, on which he does so is that work done, or to be done, for the purposes of the contract has been, or is likely to be, done by persons who are or are not members of trade unions or of a particular trade union.

(5) The obligation to comply with this section is a duty owed to the person with whom there is a refusal to deal and to any other person who may be adversely affected by its contravention; and a breach of the duty is actionable accordingly (subject to the defences and other incidents applying to actions for breach of statutory duty).

Action short of dismissal

Action short of dismissal on grounds related to union membership or activities

146.—(1) An employee has the right not to [be subjected to any **7-060** detriment as an individual by any act, or any deliberate failure to act, by his employer if the act or failure takes place][1] for the purpose of—

    (a) preventing or deterring him from being or seeking to become a member of an independent trade union, or penalising him for doing so,

    (b) preventing or deterring him from taking part in the activities of an independent trade union at an appropriate time, or penalising him for doing so, or

    (c) compelling him to be or become a member of any trade union or of a particular trade union or of one of a number of particular trade unions.

(2) In subsection (1)(b) "an appropriate time" means —

    (a) a time outside the employee's working hours, or

    (b) a time within his working hours at which, in accordance with arrangements agreed with or consent given by his employer, it is permissible for him to take part in the activities of a trade union;

and for this purpose "working hours", in relation to an employee, means any time when, in accordance with his contract of employment, he is required to be at work.

(3) An employee also has the right not to [be subjected to any detriment as an individual by any act, or any deliberate failure to act, by his employer if the act or failure takes place][2] for the purpose of enforcing a requirement (whether or not imposed by his contract of employment or in writing) that, in the event of his not being a member of any trade union or of a particular trade union or of one of a number of particular trade unions, he must make one or more payments.

(4) For the purposes of subsection (3) any deduction made by an employer from the remuneration payable to an employee in respect of his employment shall, if it is attributable to his not being a member of any trade union or of a particular trade union or of one of a number of particular trade unions, be treated as [a detriment to which he has been subjected as an individual by an act of his employer taking place][3] for the purpose of enforcing a requirement of a kind mentioned in that subsection.

(5) An employee may present a complaint to an industrial tribunal on the ground that [he has been subjected to a detriment][4] by his employer in contravention of this section.

[(6) For the purposes of this section detriment is detriment short of dismissal.][5]

Time limit for proceedings

147.—[(1) An employment tribunal shall not consider a complaint **7-061** under section 146 unless it is presented—

---

[1] Words substituted by Employment Relations Act 1999 c.26 Sch 2 para 2 (2)
[2] Words substituted by Employment Relations Act 1999 c.26 Sch 2 para 2 (3)
[3] Words substituted by Employment Relations Act 1999 c.26 Sch 2 para 2 (4)
[4] Words substituted by Employment Relations Act 1999 c.26 Sch 2 para 2 (5)
[5] Inserted by Employment Relations Act 1999 c.26 Sch 2 para 2 (6)

    (a) before the end of the period of three months beginning with the date of the [act or failure to which the complaint relates or, where that act or failure is part of a series of similar acts or failures (or both) the last of them]¹, or

    (b) where the tribunal is satisfied that it was not reasonably practicable for the complaint to be presented before the end of that period, within such further period as it considers reasonable.]²

[(2) For the purposes of subsection (1)—

    (a) where an act extends over a period, the reference to the date of the act is a reference to the last day of that period;

    (b) a failure to act shall be treated as done when it was decided on.

(3) For the purposes of subsection (2), in the absence of evidence establishing the contrary an employer shall be taken to decide on a failure to act—

    (a) when he does an act inconsistent with doing the failed act, or

    (b) if he has done no such inconsistent act, when the period expires within which he might reasonably have been expected to do the failed act if it was to be done.]³

Consideration of complaint

7-062

    148.—(1) On a complaint under section 146 it shall be for the employer to show the purpose for which [he acted or failed to act]⁴.

(2) In determining any question whether [the employer acted or failed to act, or the purpose for which he did so]⁵, no account shall be taken of any pressure which was exercised on him by calling, organising, procuring or financing a strike or other industrial action, or by threatening to do so; and that question shall be determined as if no such pressure had been exercised.

[(3) In determining what was the purpose for which [the employer acted or failed to act]⁶ in a case where—

    (a) there is evidence that the employer's purpose was to further a change in his relationship with all or any class of his employees, and

    (b) there is also evidence that his purpose was one falling within section 146,

the tribunal shall regard the purpose mentioned in paragraph (a) (and not the purpose mentioned in paragraph (b)) as the purpose for which the employer [acted or failed to act, unless it considers that no reasonable employer would act or fail to act in the way concerned]⁷ having regard to the purpose mentioned in paragraph (a).

[(4) Where the tribunal determines that—

    (a) the complainant has been subjected to a detriment by an act or deliberate failure to act by his employer, and

    (b) the act or failure took place in consequence of a previous act or deliberate failure to act by the employer,

---

¹ Words substituted in what is now (1)(a) by Employment Relations Act 1999 c.26 Sch 2 para 3 (3)

² Existing s147 renumbered as s147 (1) by Employment Relations Act 1999 c.26 Sch 2 para 3 (2)

³ Inserted by Employment Relations Act 1999 c.26 Sch 2 para 3 (4)

⁴ Words substituted by Employment Relations Act 1999 c.26 Sch 2 para 4 (2)

⁵ Words substituted by Employment Relations Act 1999 c.26 Sch 2 para 4 (3)

⁶ Words substituted by Employment Relations Act 1999 c.26 Sch 2 para 4 (4) (a)

⁷ Words substituted by Employment Relations Act 1999 c.26 Sch 2 para 4 (4) (b)

paragraph (a) of subsection (3) is satisfied if the purpose mentioned in that paragraph was the purpose of the previous act or failure.][1]

(5) In subsection (3) "class", in relation to an employer and his employees, means those employed at a particular place of work, those employees of a particular grade, category or description or those of a particular grade, category or description employed at a particular place of work.][2]

Remedies

149.—(1) Where the [employment tribunal][3] finds that a complaint **7-063** under section 146 is well-founded, it shall make a declaration to that effect and may make an award of compensation to be paid by the employer to the complainant in respect of the [act or failure][4] complained of.

(2) The amount of the compensation awarded shall be such as the tribunal considers just and equitable in all the circumstances having regard to the infringement complained of and to any loss sustained by the complainant which is attributable to the [act or failure][5] which infringed his right.

(3) The loss shall be taken to include—

(a) any expenses reasonably incurred by the complainant in consequence of the [act or failure][6] complained of, and

(b) loss of any benefit which he might reasonably be expected to have had but for that [act or failure][7].

(4) In ascertaining the loss, the tribunal shall apply the same rule concerning the duty of a person to mitigate his loss as applies to damages recoverable under the common law of England and Wales or Scotland.

(5) In determining the amount of compensation to be awarded no account shall be taken of any pressure which was exercised on the employer by calling, organising, procuring or financing a strike or other industrial action, or by threatening to do so; and that question shall be determined as if no such pressure had been exercised.

(6) Where the tribunal finds that the [act or failure][8] complained of was to any extent caused or contributed to by action of the complainant, it shall reduce the amount of the compensation by such proportion as it considers just and equitable having regard to that finding.

Awards against third parties

150.—(1) If in proceedings on a complaint under section 146— **7-064**

(a) the complaint is made on the ground that [the complainant has been subjected to detriment by an act or failure by his employer taking place][9] for the purpose of compelling him to be or become a member of any trade union or of a particular trade union or of one of a number of particular trade unions, and

(b) either the complainant or the employer claims in proceedings before the tribunal that the employer was induced to [act or fail to

---

[1] Substituted by Employment Relations Act 1999 c.26 Sch 2 para 4 (5)
[2] Inserted by Trade Union Reform and Employment Rights Act 1993 c.19 Pt I s 13
[3] Words substituted by Employment Rights (Dispute Resolution) Act 1998 c.8 Pt I s 1 (2)
[4] Words substituted by Employment Relations Act 1999 c.26 Sch 2 para 5 (a)
[5] Words substituted by Employment Relations Act 1999 c.26 Sch 2 para 5 (a)
[6] Words substituted in (a) and (b) by Employment Relations Act 1999 c.26 Sch 2 para 5 (a)
[7] Words substituted in (a) and (b) by Employment Relations Act 1999 c.26 Sch 2 para 5 (a)
[8] Word substituted by Employment Relations Act 1999 c.26 Sch 2 para 5 (b)
[9] Words substituted by Employment Relations Act 1999 c.26 Sch 2 para 6 (a)

act in the way][1] complained of by pressure which a trade union or other person exercised on him by calling, organising, procuring or financing a strike or other industrial action, or by threatening to do so,

the complainant or the employer may request the tribunal to direct that the person who he claims exercised the pressure be joined or sisted as a party to the proceedings.

(2) The request shall be granted if it is made before the hearing of the complaint begins, but may be refused if it is made after that time; and no such request may be made after the tribunal has made a declaration that the complaint is well-founded.

(3) Where a person has been so joined or sisted as a party to proceedings and the tribunal—

(a) makes an award of compensation, and

(b) finds that the claim mentioned in subsection (1)(b) is well-founded,

it may order that the compensation shall be paid by the person joined instead of by the employer, or partly by that person and partly by the employer, as the tribunal may consider just and equitable in the circumstances.

Interpretation and other supplementary provisions

7-065   **151.**—(1) References in sections 146 to 150 to being, becoming or ceasing to remain a member of a trade union include references to being, becoming or ceasing to remain a member of a particular branch or section of that union and to being, becoming or ceasing to remain a member of one of a number of particular branches or sections of that union; and references to taking part in the activities of a trade union shall be similarly construed.

(2) The remedy of an employee for infringement of the right conferred on him by section 146 is by way of a complaint to an employment tribunal in accordance with this Part, and not otherwise.

Dismissal

Dismissal on grounds related to union membership or activities

7-066   **152.**—(1) For purposes of [Part X of the Employment Rights Act 1996][2] (unfair dismissal) the dismissal of an employee shall be regarded as unfair if the reason for it (or, if more than one, the principal reason) was that the employee—

(a) was, or proposed to become, a member of an independent trade union, or

(b) had taken part, or proposed to take part, in the activities of an independent trade union at an appropriate time, or

(c) was not a member of any trade union, or of a particular trade union, or of one of a number of particular trade unions, or had refused, or proposed to refuse, to become or remain a member.

(2) In subsection (1)(b) "an appropriate time" means —

(a) a time outside the employee's working hours, or

---

[1] Words substituted by Employment Relations Act 1999 c.26 Sch 2 para 6 (b)
[2] Words substituted by Employment Rights Act 1996 c.18 Sch 1 para 56 (7) (a)

(b) a time within his working hours at which, in accordance with arrangements agreed with or consent given by his employer, it is permissible for him to take part in the activities of a trade union;

and for this purpose "working hours", in relation to an employee, means any time when, in accordance with his contract of employment, he is required to be at work.

(3) Where the reason, or one of the reasons, for the dismissal was—

    (a) the employee's refusal, or proposed refusal, to comply with a requirement (whether or not imposed by his contract of employment or in writing) that, in the event of his not being a member of any trade union, or of a particular trade union, or of one of a number of particular trade unions, he must make one or more payments, or

    (b) his objection, or proposed objection, (however expressed) to the operation of a provision (whether or not forming part of his contract of employment or in writing) under which, in the event mentioned in paragraph (a), his employer is entitled to deduct one or more sums from the remuneration payable to him in respect of his employment,

the reason shall be treated as falling within subsection (1)(c).

(4) References in this section to being, becoming or ceasing to remain a member of a trade union include references to being, becoming or ceasing to remain a member of a particular branch or section of that union or of one of a number of particular branches or sections of that trade union; and references to taking part in the activities of a trade union shall be similarly construed.

Selection for redundancy on grounds related to union membership or activities

153. Where the reason or principal reason for the dismissal of an **7-067** employee was that he was redundant, but it is shown—

    (a) that the circumstances constituting the redundancy applied equally to one or more other employees in the same undertaking who held positions similar to that held by him and who have not been dismissed by the employer, and

    (b) that the reason (or, if more than one, the principal reason) why he was selected for dismissal was one of those specified in section 152(1),

the dismissal shall be regarded as unfair for the purposes of [Part X of the Employment Rights Act 1996][1] (unfair dismissal).

Exclusion of requirement as to qualifying period, &c

154.—[(1) [Sections 108 and 109 of the Employment Rights Act 1996 **7-068** (qualifying period and upper age limit for unfair dismissal protection) do][2] not apply to the dismissal of an employee if it is shown that the reason or principal reason for the dismissal [or, in a redundancy case, for selecting the employee for dismissal, was an inadmissible reason.][3]

(2) For the purposes of this section—

---

[1] Words substituted by Employment Rights Act 1996 c.18 Sch 1 para 56 (7) (b)
[2] Words substituted by Employment Rights Act 1996 c.18 Sch 1 para 56 (8)
[3] Words substituted by Trade Union Reform and Employment Rights Act 1993 c.19 Sch 7 para 1 (a)

"inadmissible", in relation to a reason, means that it is one of those specified in section 152(1); and

"a redundancy case" means a case where the reason or principal reason for the dismissal was that the employee was redundant but the equal application of the circumstances to non-dismissed employees required by section 153(a) is also shown.][1]

Matters to be disregarded in assessing contributory fault

7-069

155.—(1) Where an [employment tribunal][2] makes an award of compensation for unfair dismissal in a case where the dismissal is unfair by virtue of section 152 or 153, the tribunal shall disregard, in considering whether it would be just and equitable to reduce, or further reduce, the amount of any part of the award, any such conduct or action of the complainant as is specified below.

(2) Conduct or action of the complainant shall be disregarded in so far as it constitutes a breach or proposed breach of a requirement—

(a) to be or become a member of any trade union or of a particular trade union or of one of a number of particular trade unions,

(b) to cease to be, or refrain from becoming, a member of any trade union or of a particular trade union or of one of a number of particular trade unions, or

(c) not to take part in the activities of any trade union or of a particular trade union or of one of a number of particular trade unions.

For the purposes of this subsection a requirement means a requirement imposed on the complainant by or under an arrangement or contract of employment or other agreement.

(3) Conduct or action of the complainant shall be disregarded in so far as it constitutes a refusal, or proposed refusal, to comply with a requirement of a kind mentioned in section 152(3)(a) (payments in lieu of membership) or an objection, or proposed, objection, (however expressed) to the operation of a provision of a kind mentioned in section 152(3)(b) (deductions in lieu of membership).

Minimum basic award

7-070

156.—(1) Where a dismissal is unfair by virtue of section 152(1) or 153, the amount of the basic award of compensation, before any reduction is made under [section 122 of the Employment Rights Act 1996][3], shall be not less than [£3,600][4].

(2) But where the dismissal is unfair by virtue of section 153, [subsection (2)][5] of that section (reduction for contributory fault) applies in relation to so much of the basic award as is payable because of subsection (1) above.

---

[1] Existing text renumbered as s 154 (1) and s 154 (2) inserted by Trade Union Reform and Employment Rights Act 1993 c.19 Sch 7 para 1
[2] Words substituted by Employment Rights (Dispute Resolution) Act 1998 c.8 Pt I s 1 (2)
[3] Words substituted by Employment Rights Act 1996 c.18 Sch 1 para 56 (9) (a)
[4] Figure substituted by SI 2003/3038 Sch 1
[5] Words substituted by Employment Rights Act 1996 c.18 Sch 1 para 56 (9) (b)

Awards against third parties

160.—(1) If in proceedings before an [employment tribunal][1] on a **7-071**
complaint of unfair dismissal either the employer or the complainant
claims—

(a) that the employer was induced to dismiss the complainant by
    pressure which a trade union or other person exercised on the
    employer by calling, organising, procuring or financing a strike or
    other industrial action, or by threatening to do so, and

(b) that the pressure was exercised because the complainant was not
    a member of any trade union or of a particular trade union or of
    one of a number of particular trade unions,

the employer or the complainant may request the tribunal to direct that
the person who he claims exercised the pressure be joined or sisted as a
party to the proceedings.

(2) The request shall be granted if it is made before the hearing of the
complaint begins, but may be refused after that time; and no such request
may be made after the tribunal has made an award of compensation for
unfair dismissal or an order for reinstatement or re-engagement.

(3) Where a person has been so joined or sisted as a party to the proceedings and the tribunal—

(a) makes an award of compensation for unfair dismissal, and

(b) finds that the claim mentioned in subsection (1) is well-founded,

the tribunal may order that the compensation shall be paid by that person
instead of the employer, or partly by that person and partly by the employer,
as the tribunal may consider just and equitable.

Application for interim relief

161.—(1) An employee who presents a complaint of unfair dismissal **7-072**
alleging that the dismissal is unfair by virtue of section 152 may apply to the
tribunal for interim relief.

(2) The tribunal shall not entertain an application for interim relief
unless it is presented to the tribunal before the end of the period of seven
days immediately following the effective date of termination (whether
before, on or after that date).

(3) In a case where the employee relies on section 152(1)(a) or (b) the
tribunal shall not entertain an application for interim relief unless before
the end of that period there is also so presented a certificate in writing
signed by an authorised official of the independent trade union of which the
employee was or proposed to become a member stating—

(a) that on the date of the dismissal the employee was or proposed to
    become a member of the union, and

(b) that there appear to be reasonable grounds for supposing that the
    reason for his dismissal (or, if more than one, the principal reason)
    was one alleged in the complaint.

(4) An "authorised official" means an official of the trade union
authorised by it to act for the purposes of this section.

(5) A document purporting to be an authorisation of an official by a
trade union to act for the purposes of this section and to be signed on behalf
of the union shall be taken to be such an authorisation unless the contrary

[1] Words substituted by Employment Rights (Dispute Resolution) Act 1998 c.8 Pt I s 1 (2)

is proved; and a document purporting to be a certificate signed by such an official shall be taken to be signed by him unless the contrary is proved.

(6) For the purposes of subsection (3) the date of dismissal shall be taken to be—

(a) where the employee's contract of employment was terminated by notice (whether given by his employer or by him), the date on which the employer's notice was given, and

(b) in any other case, the effective date of termination.

Application to be promptly determined

7-073 **162.**—(1) An [employment tribunal][1] shall determine an application for interim relief as soon as practicable after receiving the application and, where appropriate, the requisite certificate.

(2) The tribunal shall give to the employer, not later than seven days before the hearing, a copy of the application and of any certificate, together with notice of the date, time and place of the hearing.

(3) If a request under section 160 (awards against third parties) is made three days or more before the date of the hearing, the tribunal shall also give to the person to whom the request relates, as soon as reasonably practicable, a copy of the application and of any certificate, together with notice of the date, time and place of the hearing.

(4) The tribunal shall not exercise any power it has of postponing the hearing of an application for interim relief except where it is satisfied that special circumstances exist which justify it in doing so.

Procedure on hearing of application and making of order

7-074 **163.**—(1) If on hearing an application for interim relief it appears to the tribunal that it is likely that on determining the complaint to which the application relates that it will find that, by virtue of section 152, the complainant has been unfairly dismissed, the following provisions apply.

(2) The tribunal shall announce its findings and explain to both parties (if present) what powers the tribunal may exercise on the application and in what circumstances it will exercise them, and shall ask the employer (if present) whether he is willing, pending the determination or settlement of the complaint—

(a) to reinstate the employee, that is to say, to treat him in all respects as if he had not been dismissed, or

(b) if not, to re-engage him in another job on terms and conditions not less favourable than those which would have been applicable to him if he had not been dismissed.

(3) For this purpose "terms and conditions not less favourable than those which would have been applicable to him if he had not been dismissed" means as regards seniority, pension rights and other similar rights that the period prior to the dismissal shall be regarded as continuous with his employment following the dismissal.

(4) If the employer states that he is willing to reinstate the employee, the tribunal shall make an order to that effect.

(5) If the employer states that he is willing to re-engage the employee in another job, and specifies the terms and conditions on which he is willing to

---

[1] Words substituted by Employment Rights (Dispute Resolution) Act 1998 c.8 Pt I s 1 (2)

do so, the tribunal shall ask the employee whether he is willing to accept the job on those terms and conditions; and—

    (a) if the employee is willing to accept the job on those terms and conditions, the tribunal shall make an order to that effect, and

    (b) if he is not, then, if the tribunal is of the opinion that the refusal is reasonable, the tribunal shall make an order for the continuation of his contract of employment, and otherwise the tribunal shall make no order.

(6) If on the hearing of an application for interim relief the employer fails to attend before the tribunal, or states that he is unwilling either to reinstate the employee or re-engage him as mentioned in subsection (2), the tribunal shall make an order for the continuation of the employee's contract of employment.

Order for continuation of contract of employment

164.—(1) An order under section 163 for the continuation of a contract **7-075** of employment is an order that the contract of employment continue in force—

    (a) for the purposes of pay or [any other benefit][1] derived from the employment, seniority, pension rights and other similar matters, and

    (b) for the purpose of determining for any purpose the period for which the employee has been continuously employed,

from the date of its termination (whether before or after the making of the order) until the determination or settlement of the complaint.

(2) Where the tribunal makes such an order it shall specify in the order the amount which is to be paid by the employer to the employee by way of pay in respect of each normal pay period, or part of any such period, falling between the date of dismissal and the determination or settlement of the complaint.

(3) Subject as follows, the amount so specified shall be that which the employee could reasonably have been expected to earn during that period, or part, and shall be paid—

    (a) in the case of payment for any such period falling wholly or partly after the making of the order, on the normal pay day for that period, and

    (b) in the case of a payment for any past period, within such time as may be specified in the order.

(4) If an amount is payable in respect only of part of a normal pay period, the amount shall be calculated by reference to the whole period and reduced proportionately.

(5) Any payment made to an employee by an employer under his contract of employment, or by way of damages for breach of that contract, in respect of a normal pay period or part of any such period shall go towards discharging the employer's liability in respect of that period under subsection (2); and conversely any payment under that subsection in respect of a period shall go towards discharging any liability of the employer under, or in respect of the breach of, the contract of employment in respect of that period.

---

[1] Words substituted by Trade Union Reform and Employment Rights Act 1993 c.19 Sch 8 para 69

(6) If an employee, on or after being dismissed by his employer, receives a lump sum which, or part of which, is in lieu of wages but is not referable to any normal pay period, the tribunal shall take the payment into account in determining the amount of pay to be payable in pursuance of any such order.

(7) For the purposes of this section the amount which an employee could reasonably have been expected to earn, his normal pay period and the normal pay day for each such period shall be determined as if he had not been dismissed.

Application for variation or revocation of order

7-076   **165.**—(1) At any time between the making of an order under section 163 and the determination or settlement of the complaint, the employer or the employee may apply to an [employment tribunal][1] for the revocation or variation of the order on the ground of a relevant change of circumstances since the making of the order.

(2) Sections 161 to 163 apply in relation to such an application as in relation to an original application for interim relief, except that—

(a) no certificate need be presented to the tribunal under section 161(3), and

(b) in the case of an application by the employer, section 162(2) (service of copy of application and notice of hearing) has effect with the substitution of a reference to the employee for the reference to the employer.

Consequences of failure to comply with order

7-077   **166.**—(1) If on the application of an employee an [employment tribunal][2] is satisfied that the employer has not complied with the terms of an order for the reinstatement or re-engagement of the employee under [section 163(4) or (5)][3], the tribunal shall—

(a) make an order for the continuation of the employee's contract of employment, and

(b) order the employer to pay the employee such compensation as the tribunal considers just and equitable in all the circumstances having regard—

(i) to the infringement of the employee's right to be reinstated or re-engaged in pursuance of the order, and

(ii) to any loss suffered by the employee in consequence of the non-compliance.

(2) Section 164 applies to an order under subsection (1)(a) as in relation to an order under section 163.

(3) If on the application of an employee an [employment tribunal][4] is satisfied that the employer has not complied with the terms of an order for the continuation of a contract of employment, the following provisions apply.

---

[1] Words substituted by Employment Rights (Dispute Resolution) Act 1998 c.8 Pt I s 1 (2)
[2] Words substituted by Employment Rights (Dispute Resolution) Act 1998 c.8 Pt I s 1 (2)
[3] Word substituted by Trade Union Reform and Employment Rights Act 1993 c.19 Sch 7 para 22
[4] Words substituted by Employment Rights (Dispute Resolution) Act 1998 c.8 Pt I s 1 (2)

(4) If the non-compliance consists of a failure to pay an amount by way of pay specified in the order, the tribunal shall determine the amount owed by the employer on the date of the determination.

If on that date the tribunal also determines the employee's complaint that he has been unfairly dismissed, it shall specify that amount separately from any other sum awarded to the employee.

(5) In any other case, the tribunal shall order the employer to pay the employee such compensation as the tribunal considers just and equitable in all the circumstances having regard to any loss suffered by the employee in consequence of the non-compliance.

Interpretation and other supplementary provisions

167.—(1) [Part X of the Employment Rights Act 1996][1] (unfair **7-078** dismissal) has effect subject to the provisions of sections 152 to 166 above.

(2) Those sections shall be construed as one with that Part; and in those sections—

"complaint of unfair dismissal" means a complaint under [section 111 of the Employment Rights Act 1996][2];

"award of compensation for unfair dismissal" means an award of compensation for unfair dismissal under [section 112(4) or 117(3)(a)][3] of that Act; and

"order for reinstatement or re-engagement" means an order for reinstatement or re-engagement under [section 113][4] of that Act.

(3) Nothing in those sections shall be construed as conferring a right to complain of unfair dismissal from employment of a description to which that Part does not otherwise apply.

Time off for trade union duties and activities

Time off for carrying out trade union duties

168.—(1) An employer shall permit an employee of his who is an **7-079** official of an independent trade union recognised by the employer to take time off during his working hours for the purpose of carrying out any duties of his, as such an official, concerned with—

(a) negotiations with the employer related to or connected with matters falling within section 178(2) (collective bargaining) in relation to which the trade union is recognised by the employer, or

(b) the performance on behalf of employees of the employer of functions related to or connected with matters falling within that provision which the employer has agreed may be so performed by the trade union.

(2) He shall also permit such an employee to take time off during his working hours for the purpose of undergoing training in aspects of industrial relations—

(a) relevant to the carrying out of such duties as are mentioned in subsection (1), and

---

[1] Words substituted by Employment Rights Act 1996 c.18 Sch 1 para 56 (12) (a)
[2] Words substituted by Employment Rights Act 1996 c.18 Sch 1 para 56 (12) (b) (i)
[3] Words substituted by Employment Rights Act 1996 c.18 Sch 1 para 56 (12) (b) (ii)
[4] Words substituted by Employment Rights Act 1996 c.18 Sch 1 para 56 (12) (b) (iii)

(b) approved by the Trades Union Congress or by the independent trade union of which he is an official.

(3) The amount of time off which an employee is to be permitted to take under this section and the purposes for which, the occasions on which and any conditions subject to which time off may be so taken are those that are reasonable in all the circumstances having regard to any relevant provisions of a Code of Practice issued by ACAS.

(4) An employee may present a complaint to an industrial tribunal that his employer has failed to permit him to take time off as required by this section.

[Time off for union learning representatives

7-080   **168A.**—(1) An employer shall permit an employee of his who is—
(a) a member of an independent trade union recognised by the employer, and
(b) a learning representative of the trade union,
to take time off during his working hours for any of the following purposes.

(2) The purposes are—
(a) carrying on any of the following activities in relation to qualifying members of the trade union—
    (i) analysing learning or training needs,
    (ii) providing information and advice about learning or training matters,
    (iii) arranging learning or training, and
    (iv) promoting the value of learning or training,
(b) consulting the employer about carrying on any such activities in relation to such members of the trade union,
(c) preparing for any of the things mentioned in paragraphs (a) and (b).

(3) Subsection (1) only applies if—
(a) the trade union has given the employer notice in writing that the employee is a learning representative of the trade union, and
(b) the training condition is met in relation to him.

(4) The training condition is met if—
(a) the employee has undergone sufficient training to enable him to carry on the activities mentioned in subsection (2), and the trade union has given the employer notice in writing of that fact,
(b) the trade union has in the last six months given the employer notice in writing that the employee will be undergoing such training, or
(c) within six months of the trade union giving the employer notice in writing that the employee will be undergoing such training, the employee has done so, and the trade union has given the employer notice of that fact.

(5) Only one notice under subsection (4)(b) may be given in respect of any one employee.

(6) References in subsection (4) to sufficient training to carry out the activities mentioned in subsection (2) are to training that is sufficient for those purposes having regard to any relevant provision of a Code of Practice issued by ACAS or the Secretary of State.

(7) If an employer is required to permit an employee to take time off under subsection (1), he shall also permit the employee to take time off during his working hours for the following purposes—

    (a) undergoing training which is relevant to his functions as a learning representative, and

    (b) where the trade union has in the last six months given the employer notice under subsection (4)(b) in relation to the employee, undergoing such training as is mentioned in subsection (4)(a).

(8) The amount of time off which an employee is to be permitted to take under this section and the purposes for which, the occasions on which and any conditions subject to which time off may be so taken are those that are reasonable in all the circumstances having regard to any relevant provision of a Code of Practice issued by ACAS or the Secretary of State.

(9) An employee may present a complaint to an employment tribunal that his employer has failed to permit him to take time off as required by this section.

(10) In subsection (2)(a), the reference to qualifying members of the trade union is to members of the trade union—

    (a) who are employees of the employer of a description in respect of which the union is recognised by the employer, and

    (b) in relation to whom it is the function of the union learning representative to act as such.

(11) For the purposes of this section, a person is a learning representative of a trade union if he is appointed or elected as such in accordance with its rules.][1]

Payment for time off under section 168

169.—(1) An employer who permits an employee to take time off under **7-081** section 168 [or 168A][2] shall pay him for the time taken off pursuant to the permission.

(2) Where the employee's remuneration for the work he would ordinarily have been doing during that time does not vary with the amount of work done, he shall be paid as if he had worked at that work for the whole of that time.

(3) Where the employee's remuneration for the work he would ordinarily have been doing during that time varies with the amount of work done, he shall be paid an amount calculated by reference to the average hourly earnings for that work.

The average hourly earnings shall be those of the employee concerned or, if no fair estimate can be made of those earnings, the average hourly earnings for work of that description of persons in comparable employment with the same employer or, if there are no such persons, a figure of average hourly earnings which is reasonable in the circumstances.

(4) A right to be paid an amount under this section does not affect any right of an employee in relation to remuneration under his contract of employment, but—

    (a) any contractual remuneration paid to an employee in respect of a period of time off to which this section applies shall go towards dis-

---

[1] Inserted by Employment Act 2002 c.22 s 43 (2)

[2] Words inserted by Employment Act 2002 c.22 s 43 (3)

charging any liability of the employer under this section in respect of that period, and

(b) any payment under this section in respect of a period shall go towards discharging any liability of the employer to pay contractual remuneration in respect of that period.

(5) An employee may present a complaint to an industrial tribunal that his employer has failed to pay him in accordance with this section.

Time off for trade union activities

7-082

170.—(1) An employer shall permit an employee of his who is a member of an independent trade union recognised by the employer in respect of that description of employee to take time off during his working hours for the purpose of taking part in—

(a) any activities of the union, and

(b) any activities in relation to which the employee is acting as a representative of the union.

(2) The right conferred by subsection (1) does not extent to activities which themselves consist of industrial action, whether or not in contemplation or furtherance of a trade dispute.

[(2A) The right conferred by subsection (1) does not extend to time off for the purpose of acting as, or having access to services provided by, a learning representative of a trade union.

(2B) An employer shall permit an employee of his who is a member of an independent trade union recognised by the employer in respect of that description of employee to take time off during his working hours for the purpose of having access to services provided by a person in his capacity as a learning representative of the trade union.

(2C) Subsection (2B) only applies if the learning representative would be entitled to time off under subsection (1) of section 168A for the purpose of carrying on in relation to the employee activities of the kind mentioned in subsection (2) of that section.][1]

(3) The amount of time off which an employee is to be permitted to take under this section and the purposes for which, the occasions on which and any conditions subject to which time off may be so taken are those that are reasonable in all the circumstances having regard to any relevant provisions of a Code of Practice issued by ACAS.

(4) An employee may present a complaint to an industrial tribunal that his employer has failed to permit him to take time off as required by this section.

[(5) For the purposes of this section—

(a) a person is a learning representative of a trade union if he is appointed or elected as such in accordance with its rules, and

(b) a person who is a learning representative of a trade union acts as such if he carries on the activities mentioned in section 168A(2) in that capacity.][2]

---

[1] Inserted by Employment Act 2002 c.22 s 43 (4)
[2] Inserted by Employment Act 2002 c.22 s 43 (5)

Time limit for proceedings

171. An [employment tribunal]¹ shall not consider a complaint under **7-083**
[section 168, 168A, 169 or 170]² unless it is presented to the tribunal—
    (a) within three months of the date when the failure occurred, or
    (b) where the tribunal is satisfied that it was not reasonably practic-
        able for the complaint to be presented within that period, within
        such further period as the tribunal considers reasonable.

Remedies

172.—(1) Where the tribunal finds a complaint under [section 168, **7-084**
168A or 170]³ is well-founded, it shall make a declaration to that effect and
may make an award of compensation to be paid by the employer to the
employee.

(2) The amount of the compensation shall be such as the tribunal
considers just and equitable in all the circumstances having regard to the
employer's default in failing to permit time off to be taken by the employee
and to any loss sustained by the employee which is attributable to the
matters complained of.

(3) Where on a complaint under section 169 the tribunal finds that the
employer has failed to pay the employee in accordance with that section, it
shall order him to pay the amount which it finds to be due.

Interpretation and other supplementary provisions

173.—(1) For the purposes of [sections 168 , 168A and 170]⁴ the working **7-085**
hours of an employee shall be taken to be any time when in accordance with
his contract of employment he is required to be at work.

(2) The remedy of an employee for infringement of the rights conferred
on him by section 168, [168A,]⁵ 169 or 170 is by way of complaint to an
[employment tribunal]⁶ in accordance with this Part, and not otherwise.

[(3) The Secretary of State may by order made by statutory instrument
amend section 168A for the purpose of changing the purposes for which an
employee may take time off under that section.

(4) No order may be made under subsection (3) unless a draft of the
order has been laid before and approved by resolution of each House of
Parliament.]⁷

*Exclusion or expulsion from trade union where employment
subject to union membership agreement*

[Right not to be excluded or expelled from union

174.—(1) An individual shall not be excluded or expelled from a trade **7-086**
union unless the exclusion or expulsion is permitted by this section.

(2) The exclusion or expulsion of an individual from a trade union is
permitted by this section if (and only if)—

---

¹ Words substituted by Employment Rights (Dispute Resolution) Act 1998 c.8 Pt I s 1 (2)
² Words inserted by Employment Rights 2002 c.22 Sch 7 para 19
³ Words inserted by Employment Act 2002 c.22 Sch 7 para 20
⁴ Words inserted by Employment Act 2002 c.22 Sch 7
⁵ Words inserted by Employment Act 2002 c.22 Sch 7
⁶ Words substituted by Employment Rights (Dispute Resolution) Act 1998 c.8 Pt I s 1 (2)
⁷ Inserted by Employment Act 2002 c.22 Pt 4 s 43

(a) he does not satisfy, or no longer satisfies, an enforceable membership requirement contained in the rules of the union,

(b) he does not qualify, or no longer qualifies, for membership of the union by reason of the union operating only in a particular part or particular parts of Great Britain,

(c) in the case of a union whose purpose is the regulation of relations between its members and one particular employer or a number of particular employers who are associated, he is not, or is no longer, employed by that employer or one of those employers, or

(d) the exclusion or expulsion is entirely attributable to his conduct.

(3) A requirement in relation to membership of a union is "enforceable" for the purposes of subsection (2)(a) if it restricts membership solely by reference to one or more of the following criteria—

(a) employment in a specified trade, industry or profession,

(b) occupational description (including grade, level or category of appointment), and

(c) possession of specified trade, industrial or professional qualifications or work experience.

(4) For the purposes of subsection (2)(d) "conduct", in relation to an individual, does not include—

(a) his being or ceasing to be, or having been or ceased to be—

(i) a member of another trade union,

(ii) employed by a particular employer or at a particular place, or

(iii) a member of a political party, or

(b) conduct to which section 65 (conduct for which an individual may not be disciplined by a trade union) applies or would apply if the references in that section to the trade union which is relevant for the purposes of that section were references to any trade union.

(5) An individual who claims that he has been excluded or expelled from a trade union in contravention of this section may present a complaint to an [employment tribunal][1].][2]

[Time limit for proceedings

7-087   **175.** An [employment tribunal][3] shall not entertain a complaint under section 174 unless it is presented—

(a) before the end of the period of six months beginning with the date of the exclusion or expulsion, or

(b) where the tribunal is satisfied that it was not reasonably practicable for the complaint to be presented before the end of that period, within such further period as the tribunal considers reasonable.][4]

[Remedies

7-088   **176.**—(1) Where the [employment tribunal][5] finds a complaint under section 174 is well-founded, it shall make a declaration to that effect.

---

[1] Words substituted by Employment Rights (Dispute Resolution) Act 1998 c.8 Pt I s 1 (2)
[2] Substituted by Trade Union Reform and Employment Rights Act 1993 c.19 Pt I s 14
[3] Words substituted by Employment Rights (Dispute Resolution) Act 1998 c.8 Pt I s 1 (2)
[4] Substituted by Trade Union Reform and Employment Rights Act 1993 c.19 Pt I s 14
[5] Words substituted by Employment Rights (Dispute Resolution) Act 1998 c.8 Pt I s 1 (2)

(2) An individual whose complaint has been declared to be well-founded may make an application for an award of compensation to be paid to him by the union.

The application shall be made to an [employment tribunal][1] if when it is made the applicant has been admitted or re-admitted to the union, and otherwise to the Employment Appeal Tribunal.

(3) The application shall not be entertained if made—

(a) before the end of the period of four weeks beginning with the date of the declaration, or

(b) after the end of the period of six months beginning with that date.

(4) The amount of compensation awarded shall, subject to the following provisions, be such as the [employment tribunal][2] or the Employment Appeal Tribunal considers just and equitable in all the circumstances.

(5) Where the [employment tribunal][3] or Employment Appeal Tribunal finds that the exclusion or expulsion complained of was to any extent caused or contributed to by the action of the applicant, it shall reduce the amount of the compensation by such proportion as it considers just and equitable having regard to that finding.

(6) The amount of compensation calculated in accordance with subsections (4) and (5) shall not exceed the aggregate of—

(a) an amount equal to thirty times the limit for the time being imposed by [section 227(1)(a) of the Employment Rights Act 1996][4] (maximum amount of a week's pay for basic award in unfair dismissal cases), and

(b) an amount equal to the limit for the time being imposed by [section 124(1)][5] of that Act (maximum compensatory award in such cases);

and, in the case of an award by the Employment Appeal Tribunal, shall not be less than [£5,900][6].

(7) [...][7]

(8) [...][8]][9]

[Interpretation and other supplementary provisions

177.—(1) For the purposes of section 174—   **7-089**

(a) "trade union" does not include an organisation falling within paragraph (b) of section 1,

(b) "conduct" includes statements, acts and omissions, and

(c) "employment" includes any relationship whereby an individual personally does work or performs services for another person (related expressions being construed accordingly).

(2) For the purposes of sections 174 to 176—

[1] Words substituted by Employment Rights (Dispute Resolution) Act 1998 c.8 Pt I s 1 (2)
[2] Words substituted by Employment Rights (Dispute Resolution) Act 1998 c.8 Pt I s 1 (2)
[3] Words substituted by Employment Rights (Dispute Resolution) Act 1998 c.8 Pt I s 1 (2)
[4] Words substituted by Employment Rights Act 1996 c.18 Sch 1 para 56 (13) (a)
[5] Words substituted by Employment Rights Act 1996 c.18 Sch 1 para 56 (13) (b)
[6] Figure substituted by SI 2003/3038 Sch 1
[7] Repealed by Employment Relations Act 1999 c.26 Sch 9 para 1
[8] Repealed by Employment Relations Act 1999 c.26 Sch 9 para 1
[9] Substituted by Trade Union Reform and Employment Rights Act 1993 c.19 Pt I s 14

    (a) if an individual's application for membership of a trade union is neither granted nor rejected before the end of the period within which it might reasonably have been expected to be granted if it was to be granted, he shall be treated as having been excluded from the union on the last day of that period, and

    (b) an individual who under the rules of a trade union ceases to be a member of the union on the happening of an event specified in the rules shall be treated as having been expelled from the union.

(3) The remedy of an individual for infringement of the rights conferred by section 174 is by way of a complaint to an [employment tribunal][1] in accordance with that section, sections 175 and 176 and this section, and not otherwise.

(4) Where a complaint relating to an expulsion which is presented under section 174 is declared to be well-founded, no complaint in respect of the expulsion shall be presented or proceeded with under section 66 (complaint of infringement of right not to be unjustifiably disciplined).

(5) The rights conferred by section 174 are in addition to, and not in substitution for, any right which exists apart from that section; and, subject to subsection (4), nothing in that section, section 175 or 176 or this section affects any remedy for infringement of any such right.][2]

PART IV

INDUSTRIAL RELATIONS

CHAPTER I

COLLECTIVE BARGAINING

Introductory

Collective agreements and collective bargaining

7-090   **178.**—(1) In this Act "collective agreement" means any agreement or arrangement made by or on behalf of one or more trade unions and one or more employers or employers' associations and relating to one or more of the matters specified below; and "collective bargaining" means negotiations relating to or connected with one or more of those matters.

(2) The matters referred to above are—

    (a) terms and conditions of employment, or the physical conditions in which any workers are required to work;

    (b) engagement or non-engagement, or termination or suspension of employment or the duties of employment, of one or more workers;

    (c) allocation of work or the duties of employment between workers or groups of workers;

    (d) matters of discipline;

    (e) a worker's membership or non-membership of a trade union;

    (f) facilities for officials of trade unions; and

---

[1] Words substituted by Employment Rights (Dispute Resolution) Act 1998 c.8 Pt I s 1 (2)
[2] Substituted by Trade Union Reform and Employment Rights Act 1993 c.19 Pt I s 14

(g) machinery for negotiation or consultation, and other procedures, relating to any of the above matters, including the recognition by employers or employers' associations of the right of a trade union to represent workers in such negotiation or consultation or in the carrying out of such procedures.

(3) In this Act "recognition", in relation to a trade union, means the recognition of the union by an employer, or two or more associated employers, to any extent, for the purpose of collective bargaining; and "recognised"and other related expressions shall be construed accordingly.

Enforceability of collective agreements

Whether agreement intended to be a legally enforceable contract

179.—(1) A collective agreement shall be conclusively presumed not to **7-091** have been intended by the parties to be a legally enforceable contract unless the agreement—
    (a) is in writing, and
    (b) contains a provision which (however expressed) states that the parties intend that the agreement shall be a legally enforceable contract.

(2) A collective agreement which does satisfy those conditions shall be conclusively presumed to have been intended by the parties to be a legally enforceable contract.

(3) If a collective agreement is in writing and contains a provision which (however expressed) states that the parties intend that one or more parts of the agreement specified in that provision, but not the whole of the agreement, shall be a legally enforceable contract, then—
    (a) the specified part or parts shall be conclusively presumed to have been intended by the parties to be a legally enforceable contract, and
    (b) the remainder of the agreement shall be conclusively presumed not to have been intended by the parties to be such a contract.

(4) A part of a collective agreement which by virtue of subsection (3)(b) is not a legally enforceable contract may be referred to for the purpose of interpretating a party of the agreement which is such a contract.

Effect of provisions restricting right to take industrial action

180.—(1) Any terms of a collective agreement which prohibit or restrict **7-092** the right of workers to engage in a strike or other industrial action, or have the effect of prohibiting or restricting that right, shall not form part of any contract between a worker and the person for whom he works unless the following conditions are met.

(2) The conditions are that the collective agreement—
    (a) is in writing,
    (b) contains a provision expressly stating that those terms shall or may be incorporated in such a contract,
    (c) is reasonably accessible at his place of work to the worker to whom it applies and is available for him to consult during working hours, and
    (d) is one where each trade union which is a party to the agreement is an independent trade union;

and that the contract with the worker expressly or impliedly incorporates those terms in the contract.

(3) The above provisions have effect notwithstanding anything in section 179 and notwithstanding any provision to the contrary in any agreement (including a collective agreement or a contract with any worker).

Disclosure of information for purposes of collective bargaining

General duty of employers to disclose information

7-093   **181.**—(1) An employer who recognises an independent trade union shall, for the purposes of all stages of collective bargaining about matters, and in relation to descriptions of workers, in respect of which the union is recognised by him, disclose to representatives of the union, on request, the information required by this section.

In this section and sections 182 to 185 "representative", in relation to a trade union, means an official or other person authorised by the union to carry on such collective bargaining.

(2) The information to be disclosed is all information relating to the employer's undertaking which is in his possession, or that of an associated employer, and is information—

    (a) without which the trade union representatives would be to a material extent impeded in carrying on collective bargaining with him, and

    (b) which it would be in accordance with good industrial relations practice that he should disclose to them for the purposes of collective bargaining.

(3) A request by trade union representatives for information under this section shall, if the employer so requests, be in writing or be confirmed in writing.

(4) In determining what would be in accordance with good industrial relations practice, regard shall be had to the relevant provisions of any Code of Practice issued by ACAS, but not so as to exclude any other evidence of what that practice is.

(5) Information which an employer is required by virtue of this section to disclose to trade union representatives shall, if they so request, be disclosed or confirmed in writing.

Restrictions on general duty

7-094   **182.**—(1) An employer is not required by section 181 to disclose information—

    (a) the disclosure of which would be against the interests of national security, or

    (b) which he could not disclose without contravening a prohibition imposed by or under an enactment, or

    (c) which has been communicated to him in confidence, or which he has otherwise obtained in consequence of the confidence reposed in him by another person, or

    (d) which relates specifically to an individual (unless that individual has consented to its being disclosed), or

(e) the disclosure of which would cause substantial injury to his under-taking for reasons other than its effect on collective bargaining, or

(f) obtained by him for the purpose of bringing, prosecuting or defending any legal proceedings.

In formulating the provisions of any Code of Practice relating to the disclosure of information, ACAS shall have regard to the provisions of this subsection.

(2) In the performance of his duty under section 181 an employer is not required—

(a) to produce, or allow inspection of, any document (other than a document prepared for the purpose of conveying or confirming the information) or to make a copy of or extracts from any document, or

(b) to compile or assemble any information where the compilation or assembly would involve an amount of work or expenditure out of reasonable proportion to the value of the information in the conduct of collective bargaining.

Complaint of failure to disclose information

183.—(1) A trade union may present a complaint to the Central Arbitra- **7-095** tion Committee that an employer has failed—

(a) to disclose to representatives of the union information which he was required to disclose to them by section 181, or

(b) to confirm such information in writing in accordance with that section.

The complaint must be in writing and in such form as the Committee may require.

(2) If on receipt of a complaint the Committee is of the opinion that it is reasonably likely to be settled by conciliation, it shall refer the complaint to ACAS and shall notify the trade union and employer accordingly, whereupon ACAS shall seek to promote a settlement of the matter.

If a complaint so referred is not settled or withdrawn and ACAS is of the opinion that further attempts at conciliation are unlikely to result in a settlement, it shall inform the Committee of its opinion.

(3) If the complaint is not referred to ACAS or, if it is so referred, on ACAS informing the Committee of its opinion that further attempts at con-ciliation are unlikely to result in a settlement, the Committee shall proceed to hear and determine the complaint and shall make a declaration stating whether it finds the complaint well-founded, wholly or in part, and stating the reasons for its findings.

(4) On the hearing of a complaint any person who the Committee considers has a proper interest in the complaint is entitled to be heard by the Committee, but a failure to accord a hearing to a person other than the trade union and employer directly concerned does not affect the validity of any decision of the Committee in those proceedings.

(5) If the Committee finds the complaint wholly or partly well-founded, the declaration shall specify—

(a) the information in respect of which the Committee finds that the complaint is well founded,

(b) the date (or, if more than one, the earliest date) on which the employer refused or failed to disclose or, as the case may be, to confirm in writing, any of the information in question, and

(c) a period (not being less than one week from the date of the declaration) within which the employer ought to disclose that information, or, as the case may be, to confirm it in writing.

(6) On a hearing of a complaint under this section a certificate signed by or on behalf of a Minister of the Crown and certifying that a particular request for information could not be complied with except by disclosing information the disclosure of which would have been against the interests of national security shall be conclusive evidence of that fact.

A document which purports to be such a certificate shall be taken to be such a certificate unless the contrary is proved.

Further complaint of failure to comply with declaration

7-096

184.—(1) After the expiration of the period specified in a declaration under section 183(5)(c) the trade union may present a further complaint to the Central Arbitration Committee that the employer has failed to disclose or, as the case may be, to confirm in writing to representatives of the union information specified in the declaration.

The complaint must be in writing and in such form as the Committee may require.

(2) On receipt of a further complaint the Committee shall proceed to hear and determine the complaint and shall make a declaration stating whether they find the complaint well-founded, wholly or in part, and stating the reasons for their finding.

(3) On the hearing of a further complaint any person who the Committee consider has a proper interest in that complaint shall be entitled to be heard by the Committee, but a failure to accord a hearing to a person other than the trade union and employer directly concerned shall not affect the validity of any decision of the Committee in those proceedings.

(4) If the Committee find the further complaint wholly or partly well-founded the declaration shall specify the information in respect of which the Committee find that that complaint is well-founded.

Determination of claim and award

7-097

185.—(1) On or after presenting a further complaint under section 184 the trade union may present to the Central Arbitration Committee a claim, in writing, in respect of one or more descriptions of employees (but not workers who are not employees) specified in the claim that their contracts should include the terms and conditions specified in the claim.

(2) The right to present a claim expires if the employer discloses or, as the case may be, confirms in writing, to representatives of the trade union the information specified in the declaration under section 183(5) or 184(4); and a claim presented shall be treated as withdrawn if the employer does so before the Committee make an award on the claim.

(3) If the Committee find, or have found, the further complaint wholly or partly well-founded, they may, after hearing the parties, make an award that in respect of any description of employees specified in the claim the employer shall, from a specified date, observe either—

(a) the terms and conditions specified in the claim; or

(b) other terms and conditions which the Committee consider appropriate.

The date specified may be earlier than that on which the award is made but not earlier than the date specified in accordance with section 183(5)(b) in the declaration made by the Committee on the original complaint.

(4) An award shall be made only in respect of a description of employees, and shall comprise only terms and conditions relating to matters in respect of which the trade union making the claim is recognised by the employer.

(5) Terms and conditions which by an award under this section an employer is required to observe in respect of an employee have effect as part of the employee's contract of employment as from the date specified in the award, except in so far as they are superseded or varied—

(a) by a subsequent award under this section,

(b) by a collective agreement between the employer and the union for the time being representing that employee, or

(c) by express or implied agreement between the employee and the employer so far as that agreement effects an improvement in terms and conditions having effect by virtue of the award.

(6) Where—

(a) by virtue of any enactment, other than one contained in this section, providing for minimum remuneration or terms and conditions, a contract of employment is to have effect as modified by an award, order or other instrument under that enactment, and

(b) by virtue of an award under this section any terms and conditions are to have effect as part of that contract,

that contract shall have effect in accordance with that award, order or other instrument or in accordance with the award under this section, whichever is the more favourable, in respect of any terms and conditions of that contract, to the employee.

(7) No award may be made under this section in respect of terms and conditions of employment which are fixed by virtue of any enactment.

Prohibition of union recognition requirements

Recognition requirement in contract for goods or services void

186. A term or condition of a contract for the supply of goods or services is void in so far as it purports to require a party to the contract— **7-098**

(a) to recognise one or more trade unions (whether or not named in the contract) for the purpose of negotiating on behalf of workers, or any class of worker, employed by him, or

(b) to negotiate or consult with, or with an official of, one or more trade unions (whether or not so named).

Refusal to deal on grounds of union exclusion prohibited

187.—(1) A person shall not refuse to deal with a supplier or prospective supplier of goods or services if the ground or one of the grounds for his action is that the person against whom it is taken does not, or is not likely to— **7-099**

(a) recognise one or more trade unions for the purpose of negotiating on behalf of workers, or any class of worker, employed by him, or

(b) negotiate or consult with, or with an official of, one or more trade unions.

(2) A person refuses to deal with a person if—

(a) where he maintains (in whatever form) a list of approved suppliers of goods or services, or of persons from whom tenders for the supply of goods or services may be invited, he fails to include the name of that person in that list; or

(b) in relation to a proposed contract for the supply of goods or services—

(i) he excludes that person from the group of persons from whom tenders for the supply of the goods or services are invited, or

(ii) he fails to permit that person to submit such a tender; or

[(iii) he otherwise determines not to enter into a contract with that person for the supply of the goods or services or][1]

[(c) he terminates a contract with that person for the supply of goods or services.][2]

(3) The obligation to comply with this section is a duty owed to the person with whom there is a refusal to deal and to any other person who may be adversely affected by its contravention; and a breach of the duty is actionable accordingly (subject to the defences and other incidents applying to actions for breach of statutory duty).

CHAPTER II

PROCEDURE FOR HANDLING REDUNDANCIES

Duty of employer to consult trade union representatives

Duty of employer to consult [...][3] representatives

7-100   **188.**—[(1) Where an employer is proposing to dismiss as redundant 20 or more employees at one establishment within a period of 90 days or less, the employer shall consult about the dismissals all the persons who are appropriate representatives of any of the employees who may be [affected by the proposed dismissals or may be affected by measures taken in connection with those dismissals][4].

(1A) The consultation shall begin in good time and in any event—

(a) where the employer is proposing to dismiss 100 or more employees as mentioned in subsection (1), at least 90 days, and

(b) otherwise, at least 30 days,

before the first of the dismissals takes effect.

[(1B) For the purposes of this section the appropriate representatives of any affected employees are—

---

[1] Existing text of paragraph (c) renumbered as paragraph (b) (iii) by Trade Union Reform and Employment Rights Act 1993 c.19 Sch 7 para 23

[2] Inserted by Trade Union Reform and Employment Rights Act 1993 c.19 Sch 7 para 23

[3] Words repealed by SI 1995/2587 reg 3 (10)

[4] Words substituted by SI 1999/1925 reg 3 (2)

    (a) if the employees are of a description in respect of which an independent trade union is recognised by their employer, representatives of the trade union, or

    (b) in any other case, whichever of the following employee representatives the employer chooses:–

        (i) employee representatives appointed re elected by the affected employees otherwise than for the purposes of this section, who (having regard to the purposes for and the method by which they were appointed or elected) have authority from those employees to receive information and to be consulted about the proposed dismissals on their behalf;

        (ii) employee representatives elected by the affected employees, for the purposes of this section, in an election satisfying the requirements of section 188A(1).][1]

(2) The consultation shall include consultation about ways of—

    (a) avoiding the dismissals,

    (b) reducing the numbers of employees to be dismissed, and

    (c) mitigating the consequences of the dismissals,

and shall be undertaken by the employer with a view to reaching agreement with the appropriate representatives.][2]

(3) In determining how many employees an employer is proposing to dismiss as redundant no account shall be taken of employees in respect of whose proposed dismissals consultation has already begun.

(4) For the purposes of the consultation the employer shall disclose in writing to the [appropriate][3] representatives—

    (a) the reasons for his proposals,

    (b) the numbers and description of employees whom it is proposed to dismiss as redundant,

    (c) the total number of employees of any such description employed by the employer at the establishment in question,

    (d) the proposed method of selecting the employees who may be dismissed, [...][4]

    (e) the proposed method of carrying out the dismissals, with due regard to any agreed procedure, including the period over which the dismissals are to take effect [and,][5]

    [(f) the proposed method of calculating the amount of any redundancy payments to be made (otherwise than in compliance with an obligation imposed by or by virtue of any enactment) to employees who may be dismissed.][6]

(5) That information shall be [given to each of the appropriate representatives by being delivered to them][7], or sent by post to an address notified by them to the employer, or [(in the case of representatives of a trade union)][8] sent by post to the union at the address of its head or main office.

---

[1] Substituted by SI 1999/1925 reg 3 (3)

[2] Subsections (1), (1A), (1B) and (2), substituted for subsections (1) and (2) by SI 1995/2587 reg 3 (2)

[3] Words substituted by SI 1995/2587 reg 3 (3)

[4] Word repealed by Trade Union Reform and Employment Rights Act 1993 c.19 Sch 10 para 1

[5] Word inserted by Trade Union Reform and Employment Rights Act 1993 c.19 Pt II s 34 (2) (a)

[6] Inserted by Trade Union Reform and Employment Rights Act 1993 c.19 Pt II s 34 (2) (a)

[7] Words substituted by SI 1995/2587 reg 3 (4) (a)

[8] Words inserted by SI 1995/2587 reg 3 (4) (b)

[(5A) The employer shall allow the appropriate representatives access to [the affected employees]¹ and shall afford to those representatives such accommodation and other facilities as may be appropriate.]² [...]³

(7) If in any case there are special circumstances which render it not reasonably practicable for the employer to comply with a requirement of subsection [(1A), (2) or (4)]⁴, the employer shall take all such steps towards compliance with that requirement as are reasonably practicable in those circumstances.

[Where the decision leading to the proposed dismissals is that of a person controlling the employer (directly or indirectly), a failure on the part of that person to provide information to the employer shall not constitute special circumstances rendering it not reasonably practicable for the employer to comply with such a requirement.]⁵

[(7A) Where—

[(a)   the employer has invited any of the affected employees to elect employee representatives, and]⁶

(b)   the invitation was issued long enough before the time when the consultation is required by subsection (1A)(a) or (b) to begin to allow them to elect representatives by that time,

the employer shall be treated as complying with the requirements of this section in relation to those employees if he complies with those requirements as soon as is reasonably practicable after the election of the representatives.]⁷

[(7B)   If, after the employer has invited affected employees to elect representatives, the affected employees fail to do so within a reasonable time, he shall give to each affected employee the information set out in subsection (4).]⁸

(8)   This section does not confer any rights on a trade union[, a representative]⁹ or an employee except as provided by sections 189 to 192 below.

7-101

[**188A.**—(1)   The requirements for the election of employee representatives under section 188(1B)(b)(ii) are that –

(a)   the employer shall make such arrangements as are reasonably practical to ensure that the election is fair;

(b)   the employer shall determine the number of representatives to be elected so that there are sufficient representatives to represent the interests of all the affected employees having regard to the number and classes of those employees;

(c)   the employer shall determine whether the affected employees should be represented either by representatives of all the affected employees or by representatives of particular classes of those employees;

(d)   before the election the employer shall determine the term of office as employee representatives so that it is of sufficient length

¹ Words substituted by SI 1999/1925 reg 3 (4)
² Inserted by SI 1995/2587 reg 3 (5)
³ Repealed by SI 1995/2587 reg 3 (6)
⁴ Words substituted by SI 1995/2587 reg 3 (7)
⁵ Words inserted by Trade Union Reform and Employment Rights Act 1993 c.19 Pt II s 34 (2) (c)
⁶ Substituted by SI 1999/1925 reg 3 (5)
⁷ Inserted by SI 1995/2587 reg 3 (8)
⁸ Inserted by SI 1999/1925 reg 3 (6)
⁹ Words inserted by SI 1995/2587 reg 3 (9)

to enable information to be given and consultations under section 188 to be completed;

(e)   the candidates for election as employee representatives are affected employees on the date of the election;

(f)   no affected employee is unreasonably excluded from standing for election;

(g)   all affected employees on the date of the election are entitled to vote for employee representatives;

(h)   the employees entitled to vote may vote for as many candidates as there are representatives to be elected to represent them or, if there are to be representatives for particular classes of employees, may vote for as many candidates as there are representatives to be elected to represent their particular class of employee;

(i)   the election is conducted so as to secure that –

    (i)   so far as is reasonably practicable, those voting do so in secret, and

    (ii) the votes given at the election are accurately counted.

(2) Where, after an election of employee representatives satisfying the requirements of subsection (1) has been held, one of those elected ceases to act as an employee representative and any of those employees are no longer represented, they shall elect another representative by an election satisfying the requirements of subsection (1)(a), (e), (f) and (i).][1]

Complaint [...][2] and protective award

189.—[(1) Where an employer has failed to comply with a requirement **7-102** of section 188 or section 188A, a complaint may be presented to an employment tribunal on that ground –

(a)   in the case of a failure relating to the election of employee representatives, by any of the affected employees or by any of the employees who have been dismissed as redundant;

(b)   in the case of any other failure relating to employee representatives, by any of the employee representatives to whom the failure related,

(c)   in the case of failure relating to representatives of a trade union, by the trade union, and

(d)   in any other case, by any of the affected employees or by any of the employees who have been dismissed as redundant.][3]

[(1A) If on a complaint under subsection (1) a question arises as to whether or not any employee representative was an appropriate representative for the purposes of section 188, it shall be for the employer to show that the employee representative had the authority to represent the affected employees.

(1B) On a complaint under subsection (1)(a) it shall be for the employer to show that the requirements in section 188A have been satisfied.][4]

(2) If the tribunal finds the complaint well-founded it shall make a declaration to that effect and may also make a protective award.

(3) A protective award is an award in respect of one or more descriptions of employees—

---

[1] Inserted by SI 1999/1925 reg 4
[2] Words repealed by SI 1995/2587 reg 4 (5)
[3] Substituted by SI 1999/1925 reg 5 (2)
[4] Inserted by SI 1999/1925 reg 5 (3)

(a) who have been dismissed as redundant, or whom it is proposed to dismiss as redundant, and

(b) in respect of whose dismissal or proposed dismissal the employer has failed to comply with a requirement of section 188,

ordering the employer to pay remuneration for the protected period.

(4) The protected period—

(a) begins with the date on which the first of the dismissals to which the complaint relates takes effect, or the date of the award, whichever is the earlier, and

(b) is of such length as the tribunal determines to be just and equitable in all the circumstances having regard to the seriousness of the employer's default in complying with any requirement of section 188;

but shall not exceed 90 days [...][1].

(5) An [employment tribunal][2] shall not consider a complaint under this section unless it is presented to the tribunal—

(a) before the [date on which the last of the dismissals to which the complaint relates][3] takes effect, or

(b) [during][4] the period of three months beginning with [that date][5], or

(c) where the tribunal is satisfied that it was not reasonably practicable for the complaint to be presented [during the][6] period of three months, within such further period as it considers reasonable.

(6) If on a complaint under this section a question arises—

(a) whether there were special circumstances which rendered it not reasonably practicable for the employer to comply with any requirement of section 188, or

(b) whether he took all such steps towards compliance with that requirement as were reasonably practicable in those circumstances,

it is for the employer to show that there were and that he did.

Entitlement under protective award

7-103   **190.**—(1) Where an [employment tribunal][7] has made a protective award, every employee of a description to which the award relates is entitled, subject to the following provisions and to section 191, to be paid remuneration by his employer for the protected period.

(2) The rate of remuneration payable is a week's pay for each week of the period; and remuneration in respect of a period less than one week shall be calculated by reducing proportionately the amount of a week's pay.

(3) [...][8]

(4) An employee is not entitled to remuneration under a protective award in respect of a period during which he is employed by the employer unless he would be entitled to be paid by the employer in respect of that period—

---

[1] Words repealed by SI 1999/1925 reg 5 (4)

[2] Words substituted by Employment Rights (Dispute Resolution) Act 1998 c.8 Pt I s 1 (2)

[3] Words substituted by SI 1995/2587 reg 4 (4) (a)

[4] Words substituted by SI 1995/2587 reg 4 (4) (b) (i)

[5] Words substituted by SI 1995/2587 reg 4 (4) (b) (ii)

[6] Words substituted by SI 1995/2587 reg 4 (4) (c)

[7] Words substituted by Employment Rights (Dispute Resolution) Act 1998 c.8 Pt I s 1 (2)

[8] Repealed by Trade Union Reform and Employment Rights Act 1993 c.19 Sch 10 para 1

(a) by virtue of his contract of employment, or

(b) by virtue of [sections 87 to 91 of the Employment Rights Act 1996][1] (rights of employee in period of notice),

if that period fell within the period of notice required to be given by [section 86(1)][2] of that Act.

(5) [Chapter II of Part XIV of the Employment Rights Act 1996][3] applies with respect to the calculation of a week's pay for the purposes of this section.

The calculation date for the purposes of [that Chapter][4] is the date on which the protective award was made or, in the case of an employee who was dismissed before the date on which the protective award was made, the date which by virtue of [section 226(5)][5] of that Schedule is the calculation date for the purpose of computing the amount of a redundancy payment in relation to that dismissal (whether or not the employee concerned is entitled to any such payment).

(6) If an employee of a description to which a protective award relates dies during the protected period, the award has effect in his case as if the protected period ended on his death.

Termination of employment during protected period

191.—(1) Where the employee is employed by the employer during the **7-104** protected period and—

(a) he is fairly dismissed by his employer [otherwise than as redundant][6], or

(b) he unreasonably terminates the contract of employment,

then, subject to the following provisions, he is not entitled to remuneration under the protective award in respect of any period during which but for that dismissal or termination he would have been employed.

(2) If an employer makes an employee an offer (whether in writing or not and whether before or after the ending of his employment under the previous contract) to renew his contract of employment, or to re-engage him under a new contract, so that the renewal or re-engagement would take effect before or during the protected period, and either—

(a) the provisions of the contract as renewed, or of the new contract, as to the capacity and place in which he would be employed, and as to the other terms and conditions of his employment, would not differ from the corresponding provisions of the previous contract, or

(b) the offer constitutes an offer of suitable employment in relation to the employee,

the following subsections have effect.

(3) If the employee unreasonably refuses the offer, he is not entitled to remuneration under the protective award in respect of a period during which but for that refusal he would have been employed.

(4) If the employee's contract of employment is renewed, or he is reengaged under a new contract of employment, in pursuance of such an

---

[1] Words substituted by Employment Rights Act 1996 c.18 Sch 1 para 56 (14) (a) (i)
[2] Words substituted by Employment Rights Act 1996 c.18 Sch 1 para 56 (14) (a) (ii)
[3] Words substituted by Employment Rights Act 1996 c.18 Sch 1 para 56 (14) (b) (i)
[4] Words substituted by Employment Rights Act 1996 c.18 Sch 1 para 56 (14) (b) (ii)
[5] Words substituted by Employment Rights Act 1996 c.18 Sch 1 para 56 (14) (b) (iii)
[6] Words substituted by Trade Union Reform and Employment Rights Act 1993 c.19 Sch 8 para 70

offer as is referred to in subsection (2)(b), there shall be a trial period in relation to the contract as renewed, or the new contract (whether or not there has been a previous trial period under this section).

(5) The trial period begins with the ending of his employment under the previous contract and ends with the expiration of the period of four weeks beginning with the date on which the he starts work under the contract as renewed, or the new contract, or such longer period as may be agreed in accordance with subsection (6) for the purpose of retraining the employee for employment under that contract.

(6) Any such agreement—

    (a) shall be made between the employer and the employee or his representative before the employee starts work under the contract as renewed or, as the case may be, the new contract,

    (b) shall be in writing,

    (c) shall specify the date of the end of the trial period, and

    (d) shall specify the terms and conditions of employment which will apply in the employee's case after the end of that period.

(7) If during the trial period—

    (a) the employee, for whatever reason, terminates the contract, or gives notice to terminate it and the contract is thereafter, in consequence, terminated, or

    (b) the employer, for a reason connected with or arising out of the change to the renewed, or new, employment, terminates the contract, or gives notice to terminate it and the contract is thereafter, in consequence, terminated,

the employee remains entitled under the protective award unless, in a case falling within paragraph (a), he acted unreasonably in terminating or giving notice to terminate the contract.

Complaint by employee to [employment tribunal][1]

7-105   **192.**—(1) An employee may present a complaint to an employment tribunal on the ground that he is an employee of a description to which a protective award relates and that his employer has failed, wholly or in part, to pay him remuneration under the award.

(2) An [employment tribunal][2] shall not entertain a complaint under this section unless it is presented to the tribunal—

    (a) before the end of the period of three months beginning with the day (or, if the complaint relates to more than one day, the last of the days) in respect of which the complaint is made of failure to pay remuneration, or

    (b) where the tribunal is satisfied that it was not reasonably practicable for the complaint to be presented within the period of three months, within such further period as it may consider reasonable.

(3) Where the tribunal finds a complaint under this section well-founded it shall order the employer to pay the complainant the amount of remuneration which it finds is due to him.

(4) The remedy of an employee for infringement of his right to remuneration under a protective award is by way of complaint under this section, and not otherwise.

---

[1] Words substituted by Employment Rights (Dispute Resolution) Act 1998 c.8 Pt I s 1 (2)
[2] Words substituted by Employment Rights (Dispute Resolution) Act 1998 c.8 Pt I s 1 (2)

Duty of employer to notify Secretary of State

Duty of employer to notify Secretary of State of certain redundancies

193.—(1) An employer proposing to dismiss as redundant 100 or more **7-106** employees at one establishment within a period of 90 days or less shall notify the Secretary of State, in writing, of his proposal at least 90 days before the first of those dismissals takes effect.

(2) An employer proposing to dismiss as redundant [20][1] or more employees at one establishment within [such a period][2] shall notify the Secretary of State, in writing, of his proposal at least 30 days before the first of those dismissals takes effect.

(3) In determining how many employees an employer is proposing to dismiss as redundant within the period mentioned in subsection (1) or (2), no account shall be taken of employees in respect of whose proposed dismissal notice has already been given to the Secretary of State.

(4) A notice under this section shall—

    (a) be given to the Secretary of State by delivery to him or by sending it by post to him, at such address as the Secretary of State may direct in relation to the establishment where the employees proposed to be dismissed are employed,

    [(b) where there are representatives to be consulted under section 188, identify them and state the date when consultation with them under that section began,][3]

    (c) be in such form and contain such particulars, in addition to those required by paragraph (b), as the Secretary of State may direct.

(5) After receiving a notice under this section from an employer the Secretary of State may by written notice require the employer to give him such further information as may be specified in the notice.

(6) [Where there are representatives to be consulted under section 188 the employer shall give to each of them a copy of any notice given under subsection (1) or (2).][4]

The copy shall be delivered to them or sent by post to an address notified by them to the employer, or [(in the case of representatives of a trade union)][5] sent by post to the union at the address of its head or main office.

(7) If in any case there are special circumstances rendering it not reasonably practicable for the employer to comply with any of the requirements of subsections (1) to (6), he shall take all such steps towards compliance with that requirement as are reasonably practicable in the circumstances.

[Where the decision leading to the proposed dismissals is that of a person controlling the employer (directly or indirectly), a failure on the part of that person to provide information to the employer shall not constitute special circumstances rendering it not reasonably practicable for the employer to comply with any of those requirements.][6]

---

[1] Word substituted by SI 1995/2587 reg 5 (2) (a)
[2] Words substituted by SI 1995/2587 reg 5 (2) (b)
[3] Substituted by SI 1995/2587 reg 5 (3)
[4] Words substituted by SI 1995/2587 reg 5 (4) (a)
[5] Words substituted by SI 1995/2587 reg 5 (4) (b)
[6] Words inserted by Trade Union Reform and Employment Rights Act 1993 c.19 Pt II s 34 (4)

Offence of failure to notify

7-107   **194.**—(1) An employer who fails to give notice to the Secretary of State in accordance with section 193 commits an offence and is liable on summary conviction to a fine not exceeding level 5 on the standard scale.

(2) Proceedings in England or Wales for such an offence shall be instituted only by or with the consent of the Secretary of State or by an officer authorised for that purpose by special or general directions of the Secretary of State.

An officer so authorised may, although not of counsel or a solicitor, prosecute or conduct proceedings for such an offence before a magistrates' court.

(3) Where an offence under this section committed by a body corporate is proved to have been committed with the consent or connivance of, or to be attributable to neglect on the part of, any director, manager, secretary or other similar officer of the body corporate, or any person purporting to act in any such capacity, he as well as the body corporate is guilty of the offence and liable to be proceeded against and punished accordingly.

(4) Where the affairs of a body corporate are managed by its members, subsection (3) applies in relation to the acts and defaults of a member in connection with his functions of management as if he were a director of the body corporate.

Supplementary provisions

[Construction of references to dismissal as redundant etc

7-108   **195.**—(1) In this Chapter references to dismissal as redundant are references to dismissal for a reason not related to the individual concerned or for a number of reasons all of which are not so related.

(2) For the purposes of any proceedings under this Chapter, where an employee is or is proposed to be dismissed it shall be presumed, unless the contrary is proved, that he is or is proposed to be dismissed as redundant.][1]

[Construction of references to representatives

7-109   **196.**—(1) For the purposes of this Chapter persons are employee representatives if—

(a) they have been elected by employees for the specific purpose of being consulted by their employer about dismissals proposed by him, or

(b) having been elected [or appointed][2] by employees (whether before or after dismissals have been proposed by their employer) otherwise than for that specific purpose, it is appropriate (having regard to the purposes for which they were elected) for the employer to consult them about dismissals proposed by him,

and (in either case) they are employed by the employer at the time when they are elected [or appointed][3].

---

[1] Substituted by Trade Union Reform and Employment Rights Act 1993 c.19 Pt II s 34 (5)
[2] Words inserted by SI 1999/1925 reg 6 (2)
[3] Words inserted by SI 1999/1925 reg 6 (3)

(2) References in this Chapter to representatives of a trade union, in relation to an employer, are to officials or other persons authorised by the trade union to carry on collective bargaining with the employer.][1]

[(3) References in this Chapter to affected employees are to employees who may be affected by the proposed dismissals ot who may be affected by measures taken in connection with such dismissals.][2]

Power to vary provisions

197.—(1) The Secretary of State may by order made by statutory **7-110** instrument vary—

(a) the provisions of sections 188(2) and 193(1) (requirements as to consultation and notification), and

(b) the periods referred to at the end of section 189(4) (maximum protected period);

but no such order shall be made which has the effect of reducing to less than 30 days the periods referred to in sections 188(2) and 193(1) as the periods which must elapse before the first of the dismissals takes effect.

(2) No such order shall be made unless a draft of the order has been laid before Parliament and approved by a resolution of each House of Parliament.

Power to adapt provisions in case of collective agreement

198.—(1) This section applies where there is in force a collective **7-111** agreement which establishes—

(a) arrangements for providing alternative employment for employees to whom the agreement relates if they are dismissed as redundant by an employer to whom it relates, or

(b) arrangements for [handling the dismissal of employees as redundant][3].

(2) On the application of all the parties to the agreement the Secretary of State may, if he is satisfied having regard to the provisions of the agreement that the arrangements are on the whole at least as favourable to those employees as the foregoing provisions of this Chapter, by order made by statutory instrument adapt, modify or exclude any of those provisions both in their application to all or any of those employees and in their application to any other employees of any such employer.

(3) The Secretary of State shall not make such an order unless the agreement—

(a) provides for procedures to be followed (whether by arbitration or otherwise) in cases where an employee to whom the agreement relates claims that any employer or other person to whom it relates has not complied with the provisions of the agreement, and

(b) provides that those procedures include a right to arbitration or adjudication by an independent referee or body in cases where (by reason of an equality of votes or otherwise) a decision cannot otherwise be reached,

---

[1] Substituted by SI 1995/2587 reg 6
[2] Inserted by SI 1999/1925 reg 6 (4)
[3] Words substituted by Trade Union Reform and Employment Rights Act 1993 c.19 Sch 8 para 71

or indicates that any such employee may present a complaint to an [employment tribunal][1] that any such employer or other person has not complied with those provisions.

(4) An order under this section may confer on an [employment tribunal][2] to whom a complaint is presented as mentioned in subsection (3) such powers and duties as the Secretary of State considers appropriate.

(5) An order under this section may be varied or revoked by a subsequent order thereunder either in pursuance of an application made by all or any of the parties to the agreement in question or without any such application.

CHAPTER III

CODES OF PRACTICE

Codes of Practice issued by ACAS

Issue of Codes of Practice by ACAS

7-112   **199.**—(1) ACAS may issue Codes of Practice containing such practical guidance as it thinks fit for the purpose of promoting the improvement of industrial relations [or for purposes connected with trade union learning representatives.][3]

(2) In particular, ACAS shall in one or more Codes of Practice provide practical guidance on the following matters—

   (a) the time off to be permitted by an employer to a trade union official in accordance with section 168 (time off for carrying out trade union duties);

   (b) the time off to be permitted by an employer to a trade union member in accordance with section 170 (time off for trade union activities); and

   (c) the information to be disclosed by employers to trade union representatives in accordance with sections 181 and 182 (disclosure of information for purposes of collective bargaining).

(3) The guidance mentioned in subsection (2)(a) shall include guidance on the circumstances in which a trade union official is to be permitted to take time off under section 168 in respect of duties connected with industrial action; and the guidance mentioned in subsection (2)(b) shall include guidance on the question whether, and the circumstances in which, a trade union member is to be permitted to take time off under section 170 for trade union activities connected with industrial action.

(4) ACAS may from time to time revise the whole or any part of a Code of Practice issued by it and issue that revised Code.

---

[1] Words substituted by Employment Rights (Dispute Resolution) Act 1998 c.8 Pt I s 1 (2)
[2] Words substituted by Employment Rights (Dispute Resolution) Act 1998 c.8 Pt I s 1 (2)
[3] Words inserted by Employment Act 2002 c. 22 Pt 4 s 43

Codes of Practice issued by the Secretary of State

Issue of Codes of Practice by the Secretary of State

203.—(1) The Secretary of State may issue Codes of Practice **7-113** containing such practical guidance as he thinks fit for the purpose [or for purposes connected with trade union learning representatives.][1]—

    (a) of promoting the improvement of industrial relations, or

    (b) of promoting what appear to him to be to be desirable practices in relation to the conduct by trade unions of ballots and elections.

(2) The Secretary of State may from time to time revise the whole or any part of a Code of Practice issued by him and issue that revised Code.

Procedure for issue of Code by Secretary of State

204.—(1) When the Secretary of State proposes to issue a Code of **7-114** Practice, or a revised Code, he shall after consultation with ACAS prepare and publish a draft of the Code, shall consider any representations made to him about the draft and may modify the draft accordingly.

(2) If he determines to proceed with the draft, he shall lay it before both Houses of Parliament and, if it is approved by resolution of each House, shall issue the Code in the form of the draft.

(3) A Code issued under this section shall come into effect on such day as the Secretary of State may by order appoint.

The order may contain such transitional provisions or savings as appear to him to be necessary or expedient.

(4) An order under subsection (3) shall be made by statutory instrument, which shall be subject to annulment in pursuance of a resolution of either House of Parliament.

Consequential revision of Code issued by Secretary of State

205.—(1) A Code of Practice issued by the Secretary of State may be **7-115** revised by him in accordance with this section for the purpose of bringing it into conformity with subsequent statutory provisions by the making of consequential amendments and the omission of obsolete passages.

"Subsequent statutory provisions" means provisions made by or under an Act of Parliament and coming into force after the Code was issued (whether before or after the commencement of this Act).

(2) Where the Secretary of State proposes to revise a Code under this section, he shall lay a draft of the revised Code before each House of Parliament.

(3) If within the period of 40 days beginning with the day on which the draft is laid before Parliament, or, if copies are laid before the two Houses on different days, with the later of the two days, either House so resolves, no further proceedings shall be taken thereon, but without prejudice to the laying before Parliament of a new draft.

In reckoning the period of 40 days no account shall be taken of any period during which Parliament is dissolved or prorogued or during which both Houses are adjourned for more than four days.

---

[1] Words inserted by Employment Act 2002 c. 22 Pt 4 s 43

(4) If no such resolution is passed the Secretary of State shall issue the Code in the form of the draft and it shall come into effect on such day as he may appoint by order made by statutory instrument.

The order may contain such transitional provisions and savings as appear to him to be appropriate.

Revocation of Code issued by Secretary of State

7-116

206.—(1) A Code of Practice issued by the Secretary of State may be revoked by him by order made by statutory instrument.

The order may contain such transitional provisions and savings as appear to him to be appropriate.

(2) An order shall not be made under this section unless a draft of it has been laid before and approved by resolution of each House of Parliament.

Supplementary provisions

Effect of failure to comply with Code

7-117

207.—(1) A failure on the part of any person to observe any provision of a Code of Practice issued under this Chapter shall not of itself render him liable to any proceedings.

(2) In any proceedings before an [employment tribunal][1] or the Central Arbitration Committee any Code of Practice issued under this Chapter by ACAS shall be admissible in evidence, and any provision of the Code which appears to the tribunal or Committee to be relevant to any question arising in the proceedings shall be taken into account in determining that question.

(3) In any proceedings before a court or [employment tribunal][2] or the Central Arbitration Committee any Code of Practice issued under this Chapter by the Secretary of State shall be admissible in evidence, and any provision of the Code which appears to the court, tribunal or Committee to be relevant to any question arising in the proceedings shall be taken into account in determining that question.

Provisions of earlier Code superseded by later

7-118

208.—(1) If ACAS is of the opinion that the provisions of a Code of Practice to be issued by it under this Chapter will supersede the whole or part of a Code previously issued under this Chapter, by it or by the Secretary of State, it shall in the new Code state that on the day on which the new Code comes into effect the old Code or a specified part of it shall cease to have effect.

(2) If the Secretary of State is of the opinion that the provisions of a Code of Practice to be issued by him under this Chapter will supersede the whole or part of a Code previously issued under this Chapter by him or by ACAS, he shall in the new Code state that on the day on which the new Code comes into effect the old Code or a specified part of it shall cease to have effect.

---

[1] Words substituted by Employment Rights (Dispute Resolution) Act 1998 c.8 Pt I s 1 (2)
[2] Words substituted by Employment Rights (Dispute Resolution) Act 1998 c.8 Pt I s 1 (2)

(3) The above provisions do not affect any transitional provisions or savings made by the order bringing the new Code into effect.

CHAPTER IV

GENERAL

Functions of ACAS

General duty to promote improvement of industrial relations

209. It is the general duty of ACAS to promote the improvement of industrial relations [...][1]. **7-119**

Conciliation

210.—(1) Where a trade dispute exists or is apprehended ACAS may, at **7-120** the request of one or more parties to the dispute or otherwise, offer the parties to the dispute its assistance with a view to bringing about a settlement.

(2) The assistance may be by way of conciliation or by other means, and may include the appointment of a person other than an officer or servant of ACAS to offer assistance to the parties to the dispute with a view to bringing about a settlement.

(3) In exercising its functions under this section ACAS shall have regard to the desirability of encouraging the parties to a dispute to use any appropriate agreed procedures for negotiation or the settlement of disputes.

Conciliation officers

211.—(1) ACAS shall designate some of its officers to perform the **7-121** functions of conciliation officers under any enactment (whenever passed) relating to matters which are or could be the subject of proceedings before an [employment tribunal][2].

(2) References in any such enactment to a conciliation officer are to an officer designated under this section.

Arbitration

212.—(1) Where a trade dispute exists or is apprehended ACAS may, at **7-122** the request of one or more of the parties to the dispute and with the consent of all the parties to the dispute, refer all or any of the matters to which the dispute relates for settlement to the arbitration of—

    (a) one or more persons appointed by ACAS for that purpose (not being officers or employees of ACAS), or

    (b) the Central Arbitration Committee.

(2) In exercising its functions under this section ACAS shall consider the likelihood of the dispute being settled by conciliation.

(3) Where there exist appropriate agreed procedures for negotiation or the settlement of disputes, ACAS shall not refer a matter for settlement to arbitration under this section unless—

---

[1] Words repealed by Employment Relations Act 1999 c.26 Sch 9 para 1
[2] Words substituted by Employment Rights (Dispute Resolution) Act 1998 c.8 Pt I s 1 (2)

(a) those procedures have been used and have failed to result in a settlement, or

(b) there is, in ACAS's opinion, a special reason which justifies arbitration under this section as an alternative to those procedures.

(4) Where a matter is referred to arbitration under subsection (1)(a)—

(a) if more than one arbitrator or arbiter is appointed, ACAS shall appoint one of them to act as chairman; and

(b) the award may be published if ACAS so decides and all the parties consent.

(5) [Part I of the Arbitration Act 1996][1] (general provisions as to arbitration) does not apply to an arbitration under this section.

[Arbitration scheme for unfair dismissal cases etc

7-123

212A.—(1) ACAS may prepare a scheme providing for arbitration in the case of disputes involving proceedings, or claims which could be the subject of proceedings, before an employment tribunal [under, or][2] arising out of a contravention or alleged contravention of—

[(za) section 80G(1) or 80H(1)(b) of the Employment Rights Act 1996 (flexible working),][3]

(a) Part X of [that Act][4] (unfair dismissal), or

(b) any enactment specified in an order made by the Secretary of State.

(2) When ACAS has prepared such a scheme it shall submit a draft of the scheme to the Secretary of State who, if he approves it, shall make an order—

(a) setting out the scheme, and

(b) making provision for it to come into effect.

(3) ACAS may from time to time prepare a revised version of such a scheme and, when it has done so, shall submit a draft of the revised scheme to the Secretary of State who, if he approves it, shall make an order—

(a) setting out the revised scheme, and

(b) making provision for it to come into effect.

(4) ACAS may take any steps appropriate for promoting awareness of a scheme prepared under this section.

(5) Where the parties to any dispute within subsection (1) agree in writing to submit the dispute to arbitration in accordance with a scheme having effect by virtue of an order under this section, ACAS shall refer the dispute to the arbitration of a person appointed by ACAS for the purpose (not being an officer or employee of ACAS).

(6) Nothing in the Arbitration Act 1996 shall apply to an arbitration conducted in accordance with a scheme having effect by virtue of an order under this section except to the extent that the order provides for any provision of Part I of that Act so to apply; and the order may provide for any such provision so to apply subject to modifications.

(7) A scheme set out in an order under this section may, in relation to an arbitration conducted in accordance with the law of Scotland, make provision—

(a) that a reference on a preliminary point may be made, or

---

[1] Words substituted by Arbitration Act 1996 c.23 Sch 3 para 56
[2] Words inserted by Employment Act 2002 c.22 Sch 7 para 22 (a)
[3] Inserted by Employment Act 2002 c.22 Sch 7 para 22 (b)
[4] Words substituted by Employment Act 2002 c.22 Sch 7 para 22 (c)

(b) conferring a right of appeal which shall lie,

to the relevant court on such grounds and in respect of such matters as may be specified in the scheme; and in this subsection "relevant court" means such court, being the Court of Session or the Employment Appeal Tribunal, as may be specified in the scheme, and a different court may be specified as regards different grounds or matters.

(8) Where a scheme set out in an order under this section includes provision for the making of re-employment orders in arbitrations conducted in accordance with the scheme, the order setting out the scheme may require employment tribunals to enforce such orders—

(a) in accordance with section 117 of the Employment Rights Act 1996 (enforcement by award of compensation), or

(b) in accordance with that section as modified by the order.

For this purpose "re-employment orders" means orders requiring that persons found to have been unfairly dismissed be reinstated, re-engaged or otherwise re-employed.

(9) An order under this section setting out a scheme may provide that, in the case of disputes within subsection (1)(a), such part of an award made in accordance with the scheme as is specified by the order shall be treated as a basic award of compensation for unfair dismissal for the purposes of section 184(1)(d) of the Employment Rights Act 1996 (which specifies such an award as a debt which the Secretary of State must satisfy if the employer has become insolvent).

(10) An order under this section shall be made by statutory instrument.

(11) No order shall be made under subsection (1)(b) unless a draft of the statutory instrument containing it has been laid before Parliament and approved by a resolution of each House.

(12) A statutory instrument containing an order under this section (other than one of which a draft has been approved by resolution of each House of Parliament) shall be subject to annulment in pursuance of a resolution of either House of Parliament.][1]

[Dismissal procedures agreements

212B. ACAS may, in accordance with any dismissal procedures **7-124** agreement (within the meaning of the Employment Rights Act 1996), refer any matter to the arbitration of a person appointed by ACAS for the purpose (not being an officer or employee of ACAS).][2]

[Advice

213.—(1) ACAS may, on request or otherwise, give employers, **7-125** employers' associations, workers and trade unions such advice as it thinks appropriate on matters concerned with or affecting or likely to affect industrial relations.

(2) ACAS may also publish general advice on matters concerned with or affecting or likely to affect industrial relations.][3]

---

[1] Inserted by Employment Rights (Dispute Resolution) Act 1998 c.8 Pt II s 7
[2] Inserted by Employment Rights (Dispute Resolution) Act 1998 c.8 Sch 1 para 7
[3] Substituted by Trade Union Reform and Employment Rights Act 1993 c.19 Pt III s 43 (2)

Inquiry

7-126   **214.**—(1) ACAS may, if it thinks fit, inquire into any question relating to industrial relations generally or to industrial relations in any particular industry or in any particular undertaking or part of an undertaking.

(2) The findings of an inquiry under this section, together with any advice given by ACAS in connection with those findings, may be published by ACAS if—

(a) it appears to ACAS that publication is desirable for the improvement of industrial relations, either generally or in relation to the specific question inquired into, and

(b) after sending a draft of the findings to all parties appearing to to be concerned and taking account of their views, it thinks fit.

Courts of inquiry

Inquiry and report by court of inquiry

7-127   **215.**—(1) Where a trade dispute exists or is apprehended, the Secretary of State may inquire into the causes and circumstances of the dispute, and, if he thinks fit, appoint a court of inquiry and refer to it any matters appearing to him to be connected with or relevant to the dispute.

(2) The court shall inquire into the matters referred to it and report on them to the Secretary of State; and it may make interim reports if it thinks fit.

(3) Any report of the court, and any minority report, shall be laid before both Houses of Parliament as soon as possible.

(4) The Secretary of State may, before or after the report has been laid before Parliament, publish or cause to be published from time to time, in such manner as he thinks fit, any information obtained or conclusions arrived at by the court as the result or in the course of its inquiry.

(5) No report or publication made or authorised by the court or the Secretary of State shall include any information obtained by the court of inquiry in the course of its inquiry—

(a) as to any trade union, or

(b) as to any individual business (whether carried on by a person, firm, or company),

which is not available otherwise than through evidence given at the inquiry, except with the consent of the secretary of the trade union or of the person, firm, or company in question.

Nor shall any individual member of the court or any person concerned in the inquiry disclose such information without such consent.

(6) The Secretary of State shall from time to time present to Parliament a report of his proceedings under this section.

Supplementary provisions

Meaning of "trade dispute" in Part IV

7-128   **218.**—(1) In this Part "trade dispute" means a dispute between employers and workers, or between workers and workers, which is connected with one or more of the following matters—

(a) terms and conditions of employment, or the physical conditions in which any workers are required to work;

(b) engagement or non-engagement, or termination or suspension of employment or the duties of employment, of one or more workers;

(c) allocation of work or the duties of employment as between workers or groups of workers;

(d) matters of discipline;

(e) the membership or non-membership of a trade union on the part of a worker;

(f) facilities for officials of trade unions; and

(g) machinery for negotiation or consultation, and other procedures, relating to any of the foregoing matters, including the recognition by employers or employers' associations of the right of a trade union to represent workers in any such negotiation or consultation or in the carrying out of such procedures.

(2) A dispute between a Minister of the Crown and any workers shall, notwithstanding that he is not the employer of those workers, be treated for the purposes of this Part as a dispute between an employer and those workers if the dispute relates—

(a) to matters which have been referred for consideration by a joint body on which, by virtue of any provision made by or under any enactment, that Minister is represented, or

(b) to matters which cannot be settled without that Minister exercising a power conferred on him by or under an enactment.

(3) There is a trade dispute for the purpose of this Part even though it relates to matters occurring outside Great Britain.

(4) A dispute to which a trade union or employer's association is a party shall be treated for the purposes of this Part as a dispute to which workers or, as the case may be, employers are parties.

(5) In this section—

"employment" includes any relationship whereby one person personally does work or performs services for another; and

"worker", in relation to a dispute to which an employer is a party, includes any workers even if not employed by that employer.

PART V

INDUSTRIAL ACTION

Protection of acts in contemplation or furtherance of trade dispute

Protection from certain tort liabilities

219.—(1) An act done by a person in contemplation or furtherance of a **7-129** trade dispute is not actionable in tort on the ground only—

(a) that it induces another person to break a contract or interferes or induces another person to interfere with its performance, or

(b) that it consists in his threatening that a contract (whether one to which he is a party or not) will be broken or its performance interfered with, or that he will induce another person to break a contract or interfere with its performance.

(2) An agreement or combination by two or more persons to do or procure the doing of an act in contemplation or furtherance of a trade dispute is not actionable in tort if the act is one which if done without any such agreement or combination would not be actionable in tort.

(3) Nothing in subsections (1) and (2) prevents an act done in the course of picketing from being actionable in tort unless it is done in the course of attendance declared lawful by section 220 (peaceful picketing)

(4) Subsections (1) and (2) have effect subject to sections 222 to 225 (action excluded from protection) and to [sections 226 (requirement of ballot before action by trade union) and 234A (requirement of notice to employer of industrial action); and in those sections "not protected" means excluded from the protection afforded by this section or, where the expression is used with reference to a particular person, excluded from that protection as respects that person.][1]

Peaceful picketing

7-130   **220.**—(1) It is lawful for a person in contemplation or furtherance of a trade dispute to attend—

(a) at or near his own place of work, or

(b) if he is an official of a trade union, at or near the place of work of a member of the union whom he is accompanying and whom he represents,

for the purpose only of peacefully obtaining or communicating information, or peacefully persuading any person to work or abstain from working.

(2) If a person works or normally works—

(a) otherwise than at any one place, or

(b) at a place the location of which is such that attendance there for a purpose mentioned in subsection (1) is impracticable,

his place of work for the purposes of that subsection shall be any premises of his employer from which he works or from which his work is administered.

(3) In the case of a worker not in employment where—

(a) his last employment was terminated in connection with a trade dispute, or

(b) the termination of his employment was one of the circumstances giving rise to a trade dispute,

in relation to that dispute his former place of work shall be treated for the purposes of subsection (1) as being his place of work.

(4) A person who is an official of a trade union by virtue only of having been elected or appointed to be a representative of some of the members of the union shall be regarded for the purposes of subsection (1) as representing only those members; but otherwise an official of a union shall be regarded for those purposes as representing all its members.

Restrictions on grant of injunctions and interdicts

7-131   **221.**—(1) Where—

(a) an application for an injunction or interdict is made to a court in the absence of the party against whom it is sought or any representative of his, and

---

[1] Words substituted by Trade Union Reform and Employment Rights Act 1993 c.19 Sch 8 para 72

(b) he claims, or in the opinion of the court would be likely to claim, that he acted in contemplation or furtherance of a trade dispute,

the court shall not grant the injunction or interdict unless satisfied that all steps which in the circumstances were reasonable have been taken with a view to securing that notice of the application and an opportunity of being heard with respect to the application have been given to him.

(2) Where—

(a) an application for an interlocutory injunction is made to a court pending the trial of an action, and

(b) the party against whom it is sought claims that he acted in contemplation or furtherance of a trade dispute,

the court shall, in exercising its discretion whether or not to grant the injunction, have regard to the likelihood of that party's succeeding at the trial of the action in establishing any matter which would afford a defence to the action under section 219 (protection from certain tort liabilities) or section 220 (peaceful picketing).

This subsection does not extend to Scotland.

Action excluded from protection

Action to enforce trade union membership

222.—(1) An act is not protected if the reason, or one of the reasons, **7-132** for which it is done is the fact or belief that a particular employer—

(a) is employing, has employed or might employ a person who is not a member of a trade union, or

(b) is failing, has failed or might fail to discriminate against such a person.

(2) For the purposes of subsection (1)(b) an employer discriminates against a person if, but only if, he ensures that his conduct in relation to—

(a) persons, or persons of any description, employed by him, or who apply to be, or are, considered by him for employment, or

(b) the provision of employment for such persons,

is different, in some or all cases, according to whether or not they are members of a trade union, and is more favourable to those who are.

(3) An act is not protected if it constitutes, or is one of a number of acts which together constitute, an inducement or attempted inducement of a person—

(a) to incorporate in a contract to which that person is a party, or a proposed contract to which he intends to be a party, a term or condition which is or would be void by virtue of section 144 (union membership requirement in contract for goods or services), or

(b) to contravene section 145 (refusal to deal with person on grounds relating to union membership).

(4) References in this section to an employer employing a person are to a person acting in the capacity of the person for whom a worker works or normally works.

(5) References in this section to not being a member of a trade union are to not being a member of any trade union, of a particular trade union or of one of a number of particular trade unions.

Any such reference includes a reference to not being a member of a particular branch or section of a trade union or of one of a number of particular branches or sections of a trade union.

Action taken because of dismissal for taking unofficial action

7-133   **223.** An act is not protected if the reason, or one of the reasons, for doing it is the fact or belief that an employer has dismissed one or more employees in circumstances such that by virtue of section 237 (dismissal in connection with unofficial action) they have no right to complain of unfair dismissal.

Secondary action

7-134   **224.**—(1) An act is not protected if one of the facts relied on for the purpose of establishing liability is that there has been secondary action which is not lawful picketing.

(2) There is secondary action in relation to a trade dispute when, and only when, a person—

(a) induces another to break a contract of employment or interferes or induces another to interfere with its performance, or

(b) threatens that a contract of employment under which he or another is employed will be broken or its performance interfered with, or that he will induce another to break a contract of employment or to interfere with its performance,

and the employer under the contract of employment is not the employer party to the dispute.

(3) Lawful picketing means acts done in the course of such attendance as is declared lawful by section 220 (peaceful picketing)—

(a) by a worker employed (or, in the case of a worker not in employment, last employed) by the employer party to the dispute, or

(b) by a trade union official whose attendance is lawful by virtue of subsection (1)(b) of that section.

(4) For the purposes of this section an employer shall not be treated as party to a dispute between another employer and workers of that employer; and where more than one employer is in dispute with his workers, the dispute between each employer and his workers shall be treated as a separate dispute.

In this subsection "worker" has the same meaning as in section 244 (meaning of "trade dispute").

(5) An act in contemplation or furtherance of a trade dispute which is primary action in relation to that dispute may not be relied on as secondary action in relation to another trade dispute.

Primary action means such action as is mentioned in paragraph (a) or (b) of subsection (2) where the employer under the contract of employment is the employer party to the dispute.

(6) In this section "contract of employment" includes any contract under which one person personally does work or performs services for another, and related expressions shall be construed accordingly.

Pressure to impose union recognition requirement

7-135   **225.**—(1) An act is not protected if it constitutes, or is one of a number of acts which together constitute, an inducement or attempted inducement of a person—

(a) to incorporate in a contract to which that person is a party, or a proposed contract to which he intends to be a party, a term or condition which is or would be void by virtue of section 186 (recognition requirement in contract for goods or services), or

    (b) to contravene section 187 (refusal to deal with person on grounds of union exclusion).

(2) An act is not protected if—

    (a) it interferes with the supply (whether or not under a contract) of goods or services, or can reasonably be expected to have that effect, and

    (b) one of the facts relied upon for the purpose of establishing liability is that a person has—

        (i) induced another to break a contract of employment or interfered or induced another to interfere with its performance, or

        (ii) threatened that a contract of employment under which he or another is employed will be broken or its performance interfered with, or that he will induce another to break a contract of employment or to interfere with its performance, and

    (c) the reason, or one of the reasons, for doing the act is the fact or belief that the supplier (not being the employer under the contract of employment mentioned in paragraph (b)) does not, or might not—

        (i) recognise one or more trade unions for the purpose of negotiating on behalf of workers, or any class of worker, employed by him, or

        (ii) negotiate or consult with, or with an official of, one or more trade unions.

Requirement of ballot before action by trade union

Requirement of ballot before action by trade union

226.—(1) An act done by a trade union to induce a person to take part, **7-136** or continue to take part, in industrial action

    [(a) is not protected unless the industrial action has the support of a ballot, and

    (b) where section 226A falls to be complied with in relation to the person's employer, is not protected as respects the employer unless the trade union has complied with section 226A in relation to him.][1]

[In this section "the relevant time", in relation to an act by a trade union to induce a person to take part, or continue to take part, in industrial action, means the time at which proceedings are commenced in respect of the act.][2]

(2) Industrial action shall be regarded as having the support of a ballot only if—

    [(a) the union has held a ballot in respect of the action—

---

[1] Subsections (a) and (b) substituted for words "is not protected" to the end in section 226 (1) by Trade Union Reform and Employment Rights Act 1993 c.19 Pt I s 18 (1)

[2] Words inserted by Trade Union Reform and Employment Rights Act 1993 c.19 Sch 8 para 73 (a)

(i) in relation to which the requirements of section 226B so far as applicable before and during the holding of the ballot were satisfied,

(ii) in relation to which the requirements of [sections 227 to 231][1] were satisfied, and

(iii) in which the majority voting in the ballot answered "Yes" to the question applicable in accordance with section 229(2) to industrial action of the kind to which the act of inducement relates;

(b) such of the requirements of the following sections as have fallen to be satisfied at the relevant time have been satisfied, namely—

(i) section 226B so far as applicable after the holding of the ballot, and

(ii) section 231B;

[(bb) section 232A does not prevent the industrial action from being regarded as having the support of the ballot; and][2]

(c) the requirements of section 233 (calling of industrial action with support of ballot) are satisfied.

Any reference in this subsection to a requirement of a provision which is disapplied or modified by section 232 has effect subject to that section.][3]

(3) [Where separate workplace ballots are held by virtue of section 228(1)—

(a) industrial action shall be regarded as having the support of a ballot if the conditions specified in subsection (2) are satisfied, and

(b) the trade union shall be taken to have complied with the requirements relating to a ballot imposed by section 226A if those requirements are complied with,

in relation to the ballot for the place of work of the person induced to take part, or continue to take part, in the industrial action.][4]

[(3A) If the requirements of section 231A fall to be satisfied in relation to an employer, as respects that employer industrial action shall not be regarded as having the support of a ballot unless those requirements are satisfied in relation to that employer.][5]

(4) For the purposes of this section an inducement, in relation to a person, includes an inducement which is or would be ineffective, whether because of his unwillingness to be influenced by it or for any other reason.

[Notice of ballot and sample voting paper for employers

7-137   **226A.**—(1) The trade union must take such steps as are reasonably necessary to ensure that—

(a) not later than the seventh day before the opening day of the ballot, the notice specified in subsection (2), and

(b) not later than the third day before the opening day of the ballot, the sample voting paper specified in subsection (3),

---

[1] Word substituted by Employment Relations Act 1999 c.26 Sch 3 para 2 (2)
[2] Inserted by Employment Relations Act 1999 c.26 Sch 3 para 2 (2)
[3] Substituted by Trade Union Reform and Employment Rights Act 1993 c.19 Sch 8 para 73 (b)
[4] Substituted by Trade Union Reform and Employment Rights Act 1993 c.19 Sch 8 para 73 (c)
[5] Inserted by Employment Relations Act 1999 c.26 Sch 3 para 2 (3)

is received by every person who it is reasonable for the union to believe (at the latest time when steps could be taken to comply with paragraph (a)) will be the employer of persons who will be entitled to vote in the ballot.

(2) The notice referred to in paragraph (a) of subsection (1) is a notice in writing—

(a) stating that the union intends to hold the ballot,

(b) specifying the date which the union reasonably believes will be the opening day of the ballot, and

(c) [containing such information in the union's possession as would help the employer to make plans and bring information to the attention of those of his employees]¹ who it is reasonable for the union to believe (at the time when the steps to comply with that paragraph are taken) will be entitled to vote in the ballot.

(3) The sample voting paper referred to in paragraph (b) of subsection (1) is—

(a) a sample of the form of voting paper which is to be sent to the employees who it is reasonable for the trade union to believe (at the time when the steps to comply with paragraph (a) of that subsection are taken) will be entitled to vote in the ballot, or

(b) where they are not all to be sent the same form of voting paper, a sample of each form of voting paper which is to be sent to any of them.

[(3A) These rules apply for the purposes of paragraph (c) of subsection (2)—

(a) if the union possesses information as to the number, category or work-place of the employees concerned, a notice must contain that information (at least);

(b) if a notice does not name any employees, that fact shall not be a ground for holding that it does not comply with paragraph (c) of subsection (2).

(3B) In subsection (3) references to employees are to employees of the employer concerned.]²

(4) In this section references to the opening day of the ballot are references to the first day when a voting paper is sent to any person entitled to vote in the ballot.

(5) This section, in its application to a ballot in which merchant seamen to whom section 230(2A) applies are entitled to vote, shall have effect with the substitution in subsection (3), for references to the voting paper which is to be sent to the employees, of references to the voting paper which is to be sent or otherwise provided to them.]³

[Appointment of scrutineer

226B.—(1) The trade union shall, before the ballot in respect of the **7-138** industrial action is held, appoint a qualified person ("the scrutineer") whose terms of appointment shall require him to carry out in relation to the ballot the functions of—

(a) taking such steps as appear to him to be appropriate for the purpose of enabling him to make a report to the trade union (see section 231B); and

---

¹ Words substituted by Employment Relations Act 1999 c.26 Sch 3 para 3 (2)
² Inserted by Employment Relations Act 1999 c.26 Sch 3 para 3 (3)
³ Inserted by Trade Union Reform and Employment Rights Act 1993 c.19 Pt I s 18 (2)

(b) making the report as soon as reasonably practicable after the date of the ballot and, in any event, not later than the end of the period of four weeks beginning with that date.

(2) A person is a qualified person in relation to a ballot if—

(a) he satisfies such conditions as may be specified for the purposes of this section by order of the Secretary of State or is himself so specified; and

(b) the trade union has no grounds for believing either that he will carry out the functions conferred on him under subsection (1) otherwise than competently or that his independence in relation to the union, or in relation to the ballot, might reasonably be called into question.

An order under paragraph (a) shall be made by statutory instrument which shall be subject to annulment in pursuance of a resolution of either House of Parliament.

(3) The trade union shall ensure that the scrutineer duly carries out the functions conferred on him under subsection (1) and that there is no interference with the carrying out of those functions from the union or any of its members, officials or employees.

(4) The trade union shall comply with all reasonable requests made by the scrutineer for the purposes of, or in connection with, the carrying out of those functions.][1]

[Exclusion for small ballots

7-139   **226C.** Nothing in section 226B, section 229(1A)(a) or section 231B shall impose a requirement on a trade union unless—

(a) the number of members entitled to vote in the ballot, or

(b) where separate workplace ballots are held in accordance with section 228(1), the aggregate of the number of members entitled to vote in each of them,

exceeds 50.][2]

Entitlement to vote in ballot

7-140   **227.**—(1) Entitlement to vote in the ballot must be accorded equally to all the members of the trade union who it is reasonable at the time of the ballot for the union to believe will be induced to take part or, as the case may be, to continue to take part in the industrial action in question, and to no others.

[Separate workplace ballots

7-141   **228.**—(1) Subject to subsection (2), this section applies if the members entitled to vote in a ballot by virtue of section 227 do not all have the same workplace.

(2) This section does not apply if the union reasonably believes that all those members have the same workplace.

(3) Subject to section 228A, a separate ballot shall be held for each workplace; and entitlement to vote in each ballot shall be accorded equally to, and restricted to, members of the union who—

(a) are entitled to vote by virtue of section 227, and

(b) have that workplace.

---

[1] Inserted by Trade Union Reform and Employment Rights Act 1993 c.19 Pt I s 20 (1)

[2] Inserted by Trade Union Reform and Employment Rights Act 1993 c.19 Pt I s 20 (4)

(4) In this section and section 228A "workplace" in relation to a person who is employed means—

(a) if the person works at or from a single set of premises, those premises, and

(b) in any other case, the premises with which the person's employment has the closest connection.][1]

[Separate workplaces: single and aggregate ballots

228A.—(1) Where section 228(3) would require separate ballots to be **7-142** held for each workplace, a ballot may be held in place of some or all of the separate ballots if one of subsections (2) to (4) is satisfied in relation to it.

(2) This subsection is satisfied in relation to a ballot if the workplace of each member entitled to vote in the ballot is the workplace of at least one member of the union who is affected by the dispute.

(3) This subsection is satisfied in relation to a ballot if entitlement to vote is accorded to, and limited to, all the members of the union who—

(a) according to the union's reasonable belief have an occupation of a particular kind or have any of a number of particular kinds of occupation, and

(b) are employed by a particular employer, or by any of a number of particular employers, with whom the union is in dispute.

(4) This subsection is satisfied in relation to a ballot if entitlement to vote is accorded to, and limited to, all the members of the union who are employed by a particular employer, or by any of a number of particular employers, with whom the union is in dispute.

(5) For the purposes of subsection (2) the following are members of the union affected by a dispute—

(a) if the dispute relates (wholly or partly) to a decision which the union reasonably believes the employer has made or will make concerning a matter specified in subsection (1)(a), (b) or (c) of section 244 (meaning of "trade dispute"), members whom the decision directly affects,

(b) if the dispute relates (wholly or partly) to a matter specified in subsection (1)(d) of that section, members whom the matter directly affects,

(c) if the dispute relates (wholly or partly) to a matter specified in subsection (1)(e) of that section, persons whose membership or non-membership is in dispute,

(d) if the dispute relates (wholly or partly) to a matter specified in subsection (1)(f) of that section, officials of the union who have used or would use the facilities concerned in the dispute.][2]

Voting paper

229.—(1) The method of voting in a ballot must be by the marking of a **7-143** voting paper by the person voting.

[(1A) Each voting paper must—

(a) state the name of the independent scrutineer,

(b) clearly specify the address to which, and the date by which, it is to be returned,

---

[1] Substituted by Employment Relations Act 1999 c.26 Sch 3 para 5
[2] Substituted by Employment Relations Act 1999 c.26 Sch 3 para 5

(c) be given one of a series of consecutive whole numbers every one of which is used in giving a different number in that series to each voting paper printed or otherwise produced for the purposes of the ballot, and

(d) be marked with its number.

This subsection, in its application to a ballot in which merchant seamen to whom section 230(2A) applies are entitled to vote, shall have effect with the substitution, for the reference to the address to which the voting paper is to be returned, of a reference to the ship to which the seamen belong.][1]

(2) The voting paper must contain at least one of the following questions—

(a) a question (however framed) which requires the person answering it to say, by answering "Yes" or "No", whether he is prepared to take part or, as the case may be, to continue to take part in a strike;

(b) a question (however framed) which requires the person answering it to say, by answering "Yes" or "No", whether he is prepared to take part or, as the case may be, to continue to take part in industrial action short of a strike.

[(2A) For the purposes of subsection (2) an overtime ban and a call-out ban constitute industrial action short of a strike][2]

(3) The voting paper must specify who, in the event of a vote in favour of industrial action, is authorised for the purposes of section 233 to call upon members to take part or continue to take part in the industrial action.

The person or description of persons so specified need not be authorised under the rules of the union but must be within [section 20(2)][3] (persons for whose acts the union is taken to be responsible).

(4) The following statement must (without being qualified or commented upon by anything else on the voting paper) appear on every voting paper—

"If you take part in a strike or other industrial action, you may be in breach of your contract of employment. [However, if you are dismissed for taking part in strike or other industrial action which is called officially and is otherwise lawful, the dismissal will be unfair if it takes place fewer than eight weeks after you started taking part in the action, and depending on the circumstances may be unfair if it takes place later.][4]"

Conduct of ballot

7-144

230.—(1) Every person who is entitled to vote in the ballot must—

(a) be allowed to vote without interference from, or constraint imposed by, the union or any of its members, officials or employees, and

(b) so far as is reasonably practicable, be enabled to do so without incurring any direct cost to himself.

[(2) Except as regards persons falling within subsection (2A), so far as is reasonably practicable, every person who is entitled to vote in the ballot must—

---

[1] Inserted by Trade Union Reform and Employment Rights Act 1993 c.19 Pt I s 20 (2)

[2] Inserted by Employment Relations Act 1999 c.26

[3] Word substituted by Trade Union Reform and Employment Rights Act 1993 c.19 Sch 7 para 25

[4] Words inserted by Employment Relations Act 1999 c.26 s 4 Sch 3 para 6 (3)

(a) have a voting paper sent to him by post at his home address or any other address which he has requested the trade union in writing to treat as his postal address; and

(b) be given a convenient opportunity to vote by post.

[(2A) Subsection (2B) applies to a merchant seaman if the trade union reasonably believes that—

(a) he will be employed in a ship either at sea or at a place outside Great Britain at some time in the period during which votes may be cast, and

(b) it will be convenient for him to receive a voting paper and to vote while on the ship or while at a place where the ship is rather than in accordance with subsection (2).

(2B) Where this subsection applies to a merchant seaman he shall, if it is reasonably practicable—

(a) have a voting paper made available to him while on the ship or while at a place where the ship is, and

(b) be given an opportunity to vote while on the ship or while at a place where the ship is.][1]

(2C) In subsections (2A) and (2B) "merchant seaman" means a person whose employment, or the greater part of it, is carried out on board sea-going ships.][2]

(4) A ballot shall be conducted so as to secure that—

(a) so far as is reasonably practicable, those voting do so in secret, and

(b) the votes given in the ballot are fairly and accurately counted.

For the purposes of paragraph (b) an inaccuracy in counting shall be disregarded if it is accidental and on a scale which could not affect the result of the ballot.

Information as to result of ballot

231. As soon as is reasonably practicable after the holding of the ballot, **7-145** the trade union shall take such steps as are reasonably necessary to ensure that all persons entitled to vote in the ballot are informed of the number of—

(a) votes cast in the ballot,

(b) individuals answering "Yes" to the question, or as the case may be, to each question,

(c) individuals answering "No" to the question, or, as the case may be, to each question, and

(d) spoiled voting papers.

[Employers to be informed of ballot result

231A.—(1) As soon as reasonably practicable after the holding of the **7-146** ballot, the trade union shall take such steps as are reasonably necessary to ensure that every relevant employer is informed of the matters mentioned in section 231.

(2) In subsection (1) "relevant employer" means a person who it is reasonable for the trade union to believe (at the time when the steps are

---

[1] Inserted by Employment Relations Act 1999 c.26 Sch 3 para 7
[2] Substituted by Trade Union Reform and Employment Rights Act 1993 c.19 Pt I s 17

taken) was at the time of the ballot the employer of any persons entitled to vote.][1]

[Scrutineer's report

7-147   **231B.**—(1) The scrutineer's report on the ballot shall state whether the scrutineer is satisfied—

(a) that there are no reasonable grounds for believing that there was any contravention of a requirement imposed by or under any enactment in relation to the ballot,

(b) that the arrangements made with respect to the production, storage, distribution, return or other handling of the voting papers used in the ballot, and the arrangements for the counting of the votes, included all such security arrangements as were reasonably practicable for the purpose of minimising the risk that any unfairness or malpractice might occur, and

(c) that he has been able to carry out the functions conferred on him under section 226B(1) without any interference from the trade union or any of its members, officials or employees;

and if he is not satisfied as to any of those matters, the report shall give particulars of his reason for not being satisfied as to that matter.

(2) If at any time within six months from the date of the ballot—

(a) any person entitled to vote in the ballot, or

(b) the employer of any such person,

requests a copy of the scrutineer's report, the trade union must, as soon as practicable, provide him with one either free of charge or on payment of such reasonable fee as may be specified by the trade union.][2]

[Inducement of member denied entitlement to vote

7-148   **232A.** Industrial action shall not be regarded as having the support of a ballot if the following conditions apply in the case of any person—

(a) he was a member of the trade union at the time when the ballot was held,

(b) it was reasonable at that time for the trade union to believe he would be induced to take part or, as the case may be, to continue to take part in the industrial action,

(c) he was not accorded entitlement to vote in the ballot, and

(d) he was induced by the trade union to take part or, as the case may be, to continue to take part in the industrial action.][3]

[Small accidental failures to be disregarded

7-149   **232B.**—(1) If—

(a) in relation to a ballot there is a failure (or there are failures) to comply with a provision mentioned in subsection (2) or with more than one of those provisions, and

(b) the failure is accidental and on a scale which is unlikely to affect the result of the ballot or, as the case may be, the failures are accidental and taken together are on a scale which is unlikely to affect the result of the ballot,

the failure (or failures) shall be disregarded.

[1] Inserted by Trade Union Reform and Employment Rights Act 1993 c.19 Pt I s 19
[2] Inserted by Trade Union Reform and Employment Rights Act 1993 c.19 Pt I s 20 (3)
[3] Inserted by Employment Relations Act 1999 c.26 Sch 3 para 8

(2) The provisions are section 227(1), section 230(2) and section 230(2A).][1]

Calling of industrial action with support of ballot

233.—(1) Industrial action shall not be regarded as having the support **7-150** of a ballot unless it is called by a specified person and the conditions specified below are satisfied.

(2) A "specified person" means a person specified or of a description specified in the voting paper for the ballot in accordance with section 229(3).

(3) The conditions are that—

(a) there must have been no call by the trade union to take part or continue to take part in industrial action to which the ballot relates, or any authorisation or endorsement by the union of any such industrial action, before the date of the ballot;

(b) there must be a call for industrial action by a specified person, and industrial action to which it relates must take place, before the ballot ceases to be effective in accordance with section 234.

(4) For the purposes of this section a call shall be taken to have been made by a trade union if it was authorised or endorsed by the union; and the provisions of section 20(2) to (4) apply for the purpose of determining whether a call, or industrial action, is to be taken to have been so authorised or endorsed.

Period after which ballot ceases to be effective

234.—[(1) Subject to the following provisions, a ballot ceases to be **7-151** effective for the purposes of section 233(3)(b) in relation to industrial action by members of a trade union at the end of the period, beginning with the date of the ballot—

(a) of four weeks, or

(b) of such longer duration not exceeding eight weeks as is agreed between the union and the members' employer.][2]

(2) Where for the whole or part of that period the calling or organising of industrial action is prohibited—

(a) by virtue of a court order which subsequently lapses or is discharged, recalled or set aside, or

(b) by virtue of an undertaking given to a court by any person from which he is subsequently released or by which he ceases to be bound,

the trade union may apply to the court for an order that the period during which the prohibition had effect shall not count towards the period referred to in subsection (1).

(3) The application must be made forthwith upon the prohibition ceasing to have effect—

(a) to the court by virtue of whose decision it ceases to have effect, or

(b) where an order lapses or an undertaking ceases to bind without any such decision, to the court by which the order was made or to which the undertaking was given;

and no application may be made after the end of the period of eight weeks beginning with the date of the ballot.

---

[1] Inserted by Employment Relations Act 1999 c.26 Sch 3 para 9
[2] Substituted by Employment Relations Act 1999 c.26 Sch 3 para 10

(4) The court shall not make an order if it appears to the court—
  (a) that the result of the ballot no longer represents the views of the union members concerned, or
  (b) that an event is likely to occur as a result of which those members would vote against industrial action if another ballot were to be held.

(5) No appeal lies from the decision of the court to make or refuse an order under this section.

(6) The period between the making of an application under this section and its determination does not count towards the period referred to in subsection (1).

But a ballot shall not by virtue of this subsection (together with any order of the court) be regarded as effective for the purposes of section 233(3)(b) after the end of the period of twelve weeks beginning with the date of the ballot.

[Notice to employers of industrial action

7-152

234A.—(1) An act done by a trade union to induce a person to take part, or continue to take part, in industrial action is not protected as respects his employer unless the union has taken or takes such steps as are reasonably necessary to ensure that the employer receives within the appropriate period a relevant notice covering the act.

(2) Subsection (1) imposes a requirement in the case of an employer only if it is reasonable for the union to believe, at the latest time when steps could be taken to ensure that he receives such a notice, that he is the employer of persons who will be or have been induced to take part, or continue to take part, in the industrial action.

(3) For the purposes of this section a relevant notice is a notice in writing which—
  (a) [contains such information in the union's possession as would help the employer to make plans and bring information to the attention of those of his employees whom][1] the union intends to induce or has induced to take part, or continue to take part, in the industrial action ("the affected employees"),
  (b) states whether industrial action is intended to be continuous or discontinuous and specifies—
    (i) where it is to be continuous, the intended date for any of the affected employees to begin to take part in the action,
    (ii) where it is to be discontinuous, the intended dates for any of the affected employees to take part in the action, and
  (c) states that it is given for the purposes of this section.

(4) For the purposes of subsection (1) the appropriate period is the period—
  (a) beginning with the day when the union satisfies the requirement of section 231A in relation to the ballot in respect of the industrial action, and
  (b) ending with the seventh day before the day, or before the first of the days, specified in the relevant notice.

(5) For the purposes of subsection (1) a relevant notice covers an act done by the union if the person induced is one of the affected employees and—

---

[1] Words substituted by Employment Relations Act 1999 c.26 Sch 3 para 11 (2)

(a) where he is induced to take part or continue to take part in industrial action which the union intends to be continuous, if—
    (i) the notice states that the union intends the industrial action to be continuous, and
    (ii) there is no participation by him in the industrial action before the date specified in the notice in consequence of any inducement by the union not covered by a relevant notice; and
(b) where he is induced to take part or continue to take part in industrial action which the union intends to be discontinuous, if there is no participation by him in the industrial action on a day not so specified in consequence of any inducement by the union not covered by a relevant notice.

[(5A) These rules apply for the purposes of paragraph (a) of subsection (3)—
(a) if the union possesses information as to the number, category or work-place of the employees concerned, a notice must contain that information (at least);
(b) if a notice does not name any employees, that fact shall not be a ground for holding that it does not comply with paragraph (a) of subsection (3).][1]

(6) For the purposes of this section—
(a) a union intends industrial action to be discontinuous if it intends it to take place only on some days on which there is an opportunity to take the action, and
(b) a union intends industrial action to be continuous if it intends it to be not so restricted.

(7) [Subject to subsections (7A) and (7B) where][2]—
(a) continuous industrial action which has been authorised or endorsed by a union ceases to be so authorised or endorsed otherwise than to enable the union to comply with a court order or an undertaking given to a court, and
(b) the industrial action has at a later date again been authorised or endorsed by the union (whether as continuous or discontinuous action),

no relevant notice covering acts done to induce persons to take part in the earlier action shall operate to cover acts done to induce persons to take part in the action authorised or endorsed at the later date and this section shall apply in relation to an act to induce a person to take part, or continue to take part, in the industrial action after that date as if the references in subsection (3)(b)(i) to the industrial action were to the industrial action taking place after that date.

[(7A) Subsection (7) shall not apply where industrial action ceases to be authorised or endorsed in order to enable the union to comply with a court order or an undertaking given to a court.

(7B) Subsection (7) shall not apply where—
(a) a union agrees with an employer, before industrial action ceases to be authorised or endorsed, that it will cease to be authorised or endorsed with effect from a date specified in the agreement ("the suspension date") and that it may again be authorised or endorsed

[1] Inserted by Employment Relations Act 1999 c.26 Sch 3 para 11 (3)
[2] Words inserted by Employment Relations Act 1999 c.26 Sch 3 para 11 (4) (a)

with effect from a date not earlier than a date specified in the
agreement ("the resumption date"),

(b) the action ceases to be authorised or endorsed with effect from
the suspension date, and

(c) the action is again authorised or endorsed with effect from a date
which is not earlier than the resumption date or such later date as
may be agreed between the union and the employer.][1]

(8) The requirement imposed on a trade union by subsection (1) shall
be treated as having been complied with if the steps were taken by other
relevant persons or committees whose acts were authorised or endorsed by
the union and references to the belief or intention of the union in subsection
(2) or, as the case may be, subsections (3), (5) and (6) shall be construed as
references to the belief or the intention of the person or committee taking
the steps.

(9) The provisions of section 20(2) to (4) apply for the purpose of determining for the purposes of subsection (1) who are relevant persons or
committees and whether the trade union is to be taken to have authorised or
endorsed the steps the person or committee took and for the purposes of
[subsections (7) to (7B)][2] whether the trade union is to be taken to have
authorised or endorsed the industrial action.][3]

Construction of references to contract of employment

7-153   **235.** In [sections 226 to 234A][4] (requirement of ballot before action by
trade union) references to a contract of employment include any contract
under which one person personally does work or performs services for
another; [and "employer" and other related expressions][5] shall be construed
accordingly.

Industrial action affecting supply of goods or services to an individual

[Industrial action affecting supply of goods or services to an individual

7-154   **235A.**—(1) Where an individual claims that—

(a) any trade union or other person has done, or is likely to do, an
unlawful act to induce any person to take part, or to continue to
take part, in industrial action, and

(b) an effect, or a likely effect, of the industrial action is or will be
to—

(i) prevent or delay the supply of goods or services, or

(ii) reduce the quality of goods or services supplied,

to the individual making the claim,

he may apply to the High Court or the Court of Session for an order
under this section.

(2) For the purposes of this section an act to induce any person to take
part, or to continue to take part, in industrial action is unlawful—

(a) if it is actionable in tort by any one or more persons, or

---

[1] Inserted by Employment Relations Act 1999 c.26 Sch 3 para 11 (5)
[2] Words substituted by Employment Relations Act 1999 c.26 Sch 3 para 11 (6)
[3] Inserted by Trade Union Reform and Employment Rights Act 1993 c.19 Pt I s 21
[4] Word substituted by Trade Union Reform and Employment Rights Act 1993 c.19 Sch 8 para
75 (a)
[5] Words substituted by Trade Union Reform and Employment Rights Act 1993 c.19 Sch 8 para
75 (b)

(b) (where it is or would be the act of a trade union) if it could form the basis of an application by a member under section 62.

(3) In determining whether an individual may make an application under this section it is immaterial whether or not the individual is entitled to be supplied with the goods or services in question.

(4) Where on an application under this section the court is satisfied that the claim is well-founded, it shall make such order as it considers appropriate for requiring the person by whom the act of inducement has been, or is likely to be, done to take steps for ensuring—

(a) that no, or no further, act is done by him to induce any persons to take part or to continue to take part in the industrial action, and

(b) that no person engages in conduct after the making of the order by virtue of having been induced by him before the making of the order to take part or continue to take part in the industrial action.

(5) Without prejudice to any other power of the court, the court may on an application under this section grant such interlocutory relief (in Scotland, such interim order) as it considers appropriate.

(6) For the purposes of this section an act of inducement shall be taken to be done by a trade union if it is authorised or endorsed by the union; and the provisions of section 20(2) to (4) apply for the purposes of determining whether such an act is to be taken to be so authorised or endorsed.

Those provisions also apply in relation to proceedings for failure to comply with an order under this section as they apply in relation to the original proceedings.
[...]¹]²

No compulsion to work

No compulsion to work

236. No court shall, whether by way of—   **7-155**

(a) an order for specific performance or specific implement of a contract of employment, or

(b) an injunction or interdict restraining a breach or threatened breach of such a contract,

compel an employee to do any work or attend at any place for the doing of any work.

Loss of unfair dismissal protection

Dismissal of those taking part in unofficial industrial action

237.—(1) An employee has no right to complain of unfair dismissal if at **7-156** the time of dismissal he was taking part in an unofficial strike or other unofficial industrial action.

(1A) Subsection (1) does not apply to the dismissal of the employee if it is shown that the reason (or, if more than one, the principal reason) for the dismissal or, in a redundancy case, for selecting the employee for dismissal was one of those specified in [or under—

---
¹ Repealed by Employment Relations Act 1999 c.26 Sch 9 para 1
² Inserted by Trade Union Reform and Employment Rights Act 1993 c.19 Pt I s 22

(a) section 99, 100, 101A(d), 103 or 103A of the Employment Rights Act 1996 (dismissal in family, health and safety, working time, employee representative and protected disclosure cases),

(b) section 104 of that Act in its application in relation to time off under section 57A of that Act (dependants).][1]

In this subsection "redundancy case" has the meaning given in section 105(9) of that Act; [and a reference to a specified reason for dismissal includes a reference to specified circumstances of dismissal.][2]

(2) A strike or other industrial action is unofficial in relation to an employee unless—

(a) he is a member of a trade union and the action is authorised or endorsed by that union, or

(b) he is not a member of a trade union but there are among those taking part in the industrial action members of a trade union by which the action has been authorised or endorsed.

Provided that, a strike or other industrial action shall not be regarded as unofficial if none of those taking part in it are members of a trade union.

(3) The provisions of section 20(2) apply for the purpose of determining whether industrial action is to be taken to have been authorised or endorsed by a trade union.

(4) The question whether industrial action is to be so taken in any case shall be determined by reference to the facts as at the time of dismissal.

Provided that, where an act is repudiated as mentioned in section 21, industrial action shall not thereby be treated as unofficial before the end of the next working day after the day on which the repudiation takes place.

(5) In this section the "time of dismissal" means —

(a) where the employee's contract of employment is terminated by notice, when the notice is given,

(b) where the employee's contract of employment is terminated without notice, when the termination takes effect, and

(c) where the employee is employed under a contract for a fixed term which expires without being renewed under the same contract, when that term expires;

and a "working day" means any day which is not a Saturday or Sunday, Christmas Day, Good Friday or a bank holiday under the Banking and Financial Dealings Act 1971.

(6) For the purposes of this section membership of a trade union for purposes unconnected with the employment in question shall be disregarded; but an employee who was a member of a trade union when he began to take part in industrial action shall continue to be treated as a member for the purpose of determining whether that action is unofficial in relation to him or another notwithstanding that he may in fact have ceased to be a member.

Dismissals in connection with other industrial action

7-157   **238.**—(1) This section applies in relation to an employee who has a right to complain of unfair dismissal (the "complainant") and who claims to have been unfairly dismissed, where at the date of the dismissal—

(a) the employer was conducting or instituting a lock-out, or

---

[1] Words substituted by Employment Relations Act 1999 c.26 Sch 4 (III) para 2 (a)
[2] Substituted by Employment Relations Act 1999 c.26 Sch 4 (III) para 2 (a)

(b) the complainant was taking part in a strike or other industrial action.

(2) In such a case an [employment tribunal][1] shall not determine whether the dismissal was fair or unfair unless it is shown—

    (a) that one or more relevant employees of the same employer have not been dismissed, or

    (b) that a relevant employee has before the expiry of the period of three months beginning with the date of his dismissal been offered re-engagement and that the complainant has not been offered re-engagement.

[(2A) Subsection (2) does not apply to the dismissal of the employee if it is shown that the reason (or, if more than one, the principal reason) for the dismissal or, in a redundancy case, for selecting the employee for dismissal was one of those specified in [or under—][2]

    [(a) section 99, 100, 101A(d) or 103 of the Employment Rights Act 1996 (dismissal in family, health and safety, working time and employee representative cases),

    (b) section 104 of that Act in its application in relation to time off under section 57A of that Act (dependants);][3]

[In this subsection ɪredundancy caseɪ has the meaning given in section 105(9) of that Act; and a reference to a specified reason for dismissal includes a reference to specified circumstances of dismissal.][4]][5]

[(2B) Subsection (2) does not apply in relation to an employee who is regarded as unfairly dismissed by virtue of section 238A below.][6]

(3) For this purpose "relevant employees" means —

    (a) in relation to a lock-out, employees who were directly interested in the dispute in contemplation or furtherance of which the lock-out occurred, and

    (b) in relation to a strike or other industrial action, those employees at the establishment of the employer at or from which the complainant works who at the date of his dismissal were taking part in the action.

Nothing in section 237 (dismissal of those taking part in unofficial industrial action) affects the question who are relevant employees for the purposes of this section.

(4) An offer of re-engagement means an offer (made either by the original employer or by a successor of that employer or an associated employer) to re-engage an employee, either in the job which he held immediately before the date of dismissal or in a different job which would be reasonably suitable in his case.

(5) In this section "date of dismissal" means—

    (a) where the employee's contract of employment was terminated by notice, the date on which the employer's notice was given, and

    (b) in any other case, the effective date of termination.

---

[1] Words substituted by Employment Rights (Dispute Resolution) Act 1998 c.8 Pt I s 1 (2)
[2] Words substituted by Employment Relations Act 1999 c.26 Sch 4 (III) para 3 (a)
[3] Words substituted by Employment Relations Act 1999 c.26 Sch 4 (III) para 3 (a)
[4] Words substituted by Employment Relations Act 1999 c.26 Sch 4 (III) para 3 (a)
[5] Inserted by Trade Union Reform and Employment Rights Act 1993 c.19 Sch 8 para 77
[6] Inserted by Employment Relations Act 1999 c.26 Sch 5 para 2

[Participation in official industrial action

7-158

238A.—(1) For the purposes of this section an employee takes protected industrial action if he commits an act which, or a series of acts each of which, he is induced to commit by an act which by virtue of section 219 is not actionable in tort.

(2) An employee who is dismissed shall be regarded for the purposes of Part X of the Employment Rights Act 1996 (unfair dismissal) as unfairly dismissed if—

    (a) the reason (or, if more than one, the principal reason) for the dismissal is that the employee took protected industrial action, and

    (b) subsection (3), (4) or (5) applies to the dismissal.

(3) This subsection applies to a dismissal if it takes place within the period of eight weeks beginning with the day on which the employee started to take protected industrial action.

(4) This subsection applies to a dismissal if—

    (a) it takes place after the end of that period, and

    (b) the employee had stopped taking protected industrial action before the end of that period.

(5) This subsection applies to a dismissal if—

    (a) it takes place after the end of that period,

    (b) the employee had not stopped taking protected industrial action before the end of that period, and

    (c) the employer had not taken such procedural steps as would have been reasonable for the purposes of resolving the dispute to which the protected industrial action relates.

(6) In determining whether an employer has taken those steps regard shall be had, in particular, to—

    (a) whether the employer or a union had complied with procedures established by any applicable collective or other agreement;

    (b) whether the employer or a union offered or agreed to commence or resume negotiations after the start of the protected industrial action;

    (c) whether the employer or a union unreasonably refused, after the start of the protected industrial action, a request that conciliation services be used;

    (d) whether the employer or a union unreasonably refused, after the start of the protected industrial action, a request that mediation services be used in relation to procedures to be adopted for the purposes of resolving the dispute.

(7) In determining whether an employer has taken those steps no regard shall be had to the merits of the dispute.

(8) For the purposes of this section no account shall be taken of the repudiation of any act by a trade union as mentioned in section 21 in relation to anything which occurs before the end of the next working day (within the meaning of section 237) after the day on which the repudiation takes place.][1]

---

[1] Inserted by Employment Relations Act 1999 c.26 Sch 5 para 3

Supplementary provisions relating to unfair dismissal

239.—(1) [Sections 237 to 238A][1] (loss of unfair dismissal protection in **7-159** connection with industrial action) shall be construed as one with [Part X of the Employment Rights Act 1996][2] (unfair dismissal)[; but sections 108 and 109 of that Act (qualifying period and age limit) shall not apply in relation to section 238A of this Act][3].

(2) In relation to a complaint to which [section 238 or 238A][4] applies, [section 111(2)][5] of that Act (time limit for complaint) does not apply, but an [employment tribunal][6] shall not consider the complaint unless it is presented to the tribunal—

    (a) before the end of the period of six months beginning with the date of the complainant's dismissal (as defined by section 238(5)), or

    (b) where the tribunal is satisfied that it was not reasonably practicable for the complaint to be presented before the end of that period, within such further period as the tribunal considers reasonable.

(3) Where it is shown that the condition referred to in section 238(2)(b) is fulfilled (discriminatory re-engagement), the references in—

    (a) [sections 98 to 106 of the Employment Rights Act 1996][7], and

    (b) sections 152 and 153 of this Act,

to the reason or principal reason for which the complainant was dismissed shall be read as references to the reason or principal reason he has not been offered re-engagement.

[(4) In relation to a complaint under section 111 of the 1996 Act (unfair dismissal: complaint to employment tribunal) that a dismissal was unfair by virtue of section 238A of this Act—

    (a) no order shall be made under section 113 of the 1996 Act (reinstatement or re-engagement) until after the conclusion of protected industrial action by any employee in relation to the relevant dispute,

    (b) regulations under section 7 of the Employment Tribunals Act 1996 may make provision about the adjournment and renewal of applications (including provision requiring adjournment in specified circumstances), and

    (c) regulations under section 9 of that Act may require a pre-hearing review to be carried out in specified circumstances.][8]

Criminal offences

Breach of contract involving injury to persons or property

240.—(1) A person commits an offence who wilfully and maliciously **7-160** breaks a contract of service or hiring, knowing or having reasonable cause

---

[1] Words substituted by Employment Relations Act 1999 c.26 Sch 5 para 4 (2)

[2] Words substituted by Employment Rights Act 1996 c.18 Sch 1 para 56 (16) (a)

[3] Words inserted by Employment Relations Act 1999 c.26 Sch 5 para 4 (3)

[4] Words inserted by Employment Relations Act 1999 c.26 Sch 5 para 4 (4)

[5] Words substituted by Employment Rights Act 1996 c.18 Sch 1 para 56 (16) (b)

[6] Words substituted by Employment Rights (Dispute Resolution) Act 1998 c.8 Pt I s 1 (2)

[7] Words substituted by Employment Rights Act 1996 c.18 Sch 1 para 56 (16) (c)

[8] Inserted by Employment Relations Act 1999 c.26 Sch 5 para 4 (5)

to believe that the probable consequences of his so doing, either alone or in combination with others, will be—

(a) to endanger human life or cause serious bodily injury, or

(b) to expose valuable property, whether real or personal, to destruction or serious injury.

(2) Subsection (1) applies equally whether the offence is committed from malice conceived against the person endangered or injured or, as the case may be, the owner of the property destroyed, or otherwise.

(3) A person guilty of an offence under this section is liable on summary conviction to imprisonment for a term not exceeding three months or to a fine not exceeding level 2 on the standard scale or both.

(4) This section does not apply to seamen.

Intimidation or annoyance by violence or otherwise

7-161   **241.**—(1) A person commits an offence who, with a view to compelling another person to abstain from doing or to do any act which that person has a legal right to do or abstain from doing, wrongfully and without legal authority—

(a) uses violence to or intimidates that person or his wife or children, or injures his property,

(b) persistently follows that person about from place to place,

(c) hides any tools, clothes or other property owned or used by that person, or deprives him of or hinders him in the use thereof,

(d) watches or besets the house or other place where that person resides, works, carries on business or happens to be, or the approach to any such house or place, or

(e) follows that person with two or more other persons in a disorderly manner in or through any street or road.

(2) A person guilty of an offence under this section is liable on summary conviction to imprisonment for a term not exceeding six months or a fine not exceeding level 5 on the standard scale, or both.

(3) A constable may arrest without warrant anyone he reasonably suspects is committing an offence under this section.

Restriction of offence of conspiracy: England and Wales

7-162   **242.**—(1) Where in pursuance of any such agreement as is mentioned in section 1(1) of the Criminal Law Act 1977 (which provides for the offence of conspiracy) the acts in question in relation to an offence are to be done in contemplation or furtherance of a trade dispute, the offence shall be disregarded for the purposes of that subsection if it is a summary offence which is not punishable with imprisonment.

(2) This section.extends to England and Wales only.

Restriction of offence of conspiracy: Scotland

7-163   **243.**—(1) An agreement or combination by two or more persons to do or procure to be done an act in contemplation or furtherance of a trade dispute is not indictable as a conspiracy if that act committed by one person would not be punishable as a crime.

(2) A crime for this purpose means an offence punishable on indictment, or an offence punishable on summary conviction, and for the commission of which the offender is liable under the statute making the

offence punishable to be imprisoned either absolutely or at the discretion of the court as an alternative for some other punishment.

(3) Where a person is convicted of any such agreement or combination as is mentioned above to do or procure to be done an act which is punishable only on summary conviction, and is sentenced to imprisonment, the imprisonment shall not exceed three months or such longer time as may be prescribed by the statute for the punishment of the act when committed by one person.

(4) Nothing in this section—

    (a) exempts from punishment a person guilty of a conspiracy for which a punishment is awarded by an Act of Parliament, or

    (b) affects the law relating to riot, unlawful assembly, breach of the peace, or sedition or any offence against the State or the Sovereign.

(5) This section extends to Scotland only.

Supplementary

Meaning of "trade dispute" in Part V

244.—(1) In this Part a "trade dispute" means a dispute between **7-164** workers and their employer which relates wholly or mainly to one or more of the following—

    (a) terms and conditions of employment, or the physical conditions in which any workers are required to work;

    (b) engagement or non-engagement, or termination or suspension of employment or the duties of employment, of one or more workers;

    (c) allocation of work or the duties of employment between workers or groups of workers;

    (d) matters of discipline;

    (e) a worker's membership or non-membership of a trade union;

    (f) facilities for officials of trade unions; and

    (g) machinery for negotiation or consultation, and other procedures, relating to any of the above matters, including the recognition by employers or employers' associations of the right of a trade union to represent workers in such negotiation or consultation or in the carrying out of such procedures.

(2) A dispute between a Minister of the Crown and any workers shall, notwithstanding that he is not the employer of those workers, be treated as a dispute between those workers and their employer if the dispute relates to matters which—

    (a) have been referred for consideration by a joint body on which, by virtue of provision made by or under any enactment, he is represented, or

    (b) cannot be settled without him exercising a power conferred on him by or under an enactment.

(3) There is a trade dispute even though it relates to matters occurring outside the United Kingdom, so long as the person or persons whose actions in the United Kingdom are said to be in contemplation or furtherance of a trade dispute relating to matters occurring outside the United Kingdom are likely to be affected in respect of one or more of the matters specified in subsection (1) by the outcome of the dispute.

(4) An act, threat or demand done or made by one person or organisation against another which, if resisted, would have led to a trade dispute with that other, shall be treated as being done or made in contemplation of a trade dispute with that other, notwithstanding that because that other submits to the act or threat or accedes to the demand no dispute arises.

(5) In this section—

"employment" includes any relationship whereby one person personally does work or performs services for another; and

"worker", in relation to a dispute with an employer, means —

(a) a worker employed by that employer; or

(b) a person who has ceased to be so employed if his employment was terminated in connection with the dispute or if the termination of his employment was one of the circumstances giving rise to the dispute.

Crown employees and contracts

7-165   **245.** Where a person holds any office or employment under the Crown on terms which do not constitute a contract of employment between that person and the Crown, those terms shall nevertheless be deemed to constitute such a contract for the purposes of—

(a) the law relating to liability in tort of a person who commits an act which—

(i) induces another person to break a contract, interferes with the performance of a contract or induces another person to interfere with its performance, or

(ii) consists in a threat that a contract will be broken or its performance interfered with, or that any person will be induced to break a contract or interfere with its performance, and

(b) the provisions of this or any other Act which refer (whether in relation to contracts generally or only in relation to contracts of employment) to such an act.

Minor definitions

7-166   **246.** In this Part—

"date of the ballot" means , in the case of a ballot in which votes may be cast on more than one day, the last of those days;

[...]¹

"strike" means any concerted stoppage of work;

"working hours", in relation to a person, means any time when under his contract of employment, or other contract personally to do work or perform services, he is required to be at work.

---

¹ Definition repealed by Trade Union Reform and Employment Rights Act 1993 c.19 Sch 10 para 1

PART VI

ADMINISTRATIVE PROVISIONS

ACAS

ACAS

247.—(1) There shall continue to be a body called the Advisory, Conci- **7-167** liation and Arbitration Service (referred to in this Act as "ACAS").

(2) ACAS is a body corporate of which the corporators are the members of its Council.

(3) Its functions, and those of its officers and servants, shall be performed on behalf of the Crown, but not so as to make it subject to directions of any kind from any Minister of the Crown as to the manner in which it is to exercise its functions under any enactment.

(4) For the purposes of civil proceedings arising out of those functions the Crown Proceedings Act 1947 applies to ACAS as if it were a government department and the Crown Suits (Scotland) Act 1857 applies to it as if it were a public department.

(5) Nothing in section 9 of the Statistics of Trade Act 1947 (restriction on disclosure of information obtained under that Act) shall prevent or penalise the disclosure to ACAS, for the purposes of the exercise of any of its functions, of information obtained under that Act by a government department.

(6) ACAS shall maintain offices in such of the major centres of employment in Great Britain as it thinks fit for the purposes of discharging its functions under any enactment.

The Certification Officer

The Certification Officer

254.—(1) There shall continue to be an officer called the Certification **7-168** Officer.

(2) The Certification Officer shall be appointed by the Secretary of State after consultation with ACAS.

(3) The Certification Officer may appoint one or more assistant certification officers and shall appoint an assistant certification officer for Scotland.

(4) The Certification Officer may delegate to an assistant certification officer such functions as he thinks appropriate, and in particular may delegate to the assistant certification officer for Scotland such functions as he thinks appropriate in relation to organisations whose principal office is in Scotland.

References to the Certification Officer in enactments relating to his functions shall be construed accordingly.

(5) ACAS shall provide for the Certification Officer the requisite staff (from among the officers and servants of ACAS) and the requisite accommodation, equipment and other facilities.

[(5A) Subject to subsection (6), ACAS shall pay to the Certification Officer such sums as he may require for the performance of any of his functions.][1]

(6) The Secretary of State shall pay to the Certification Officer such sums as he may require for making payments under the scheme under section 115 (payments towards expenditure in connection with secret ballots).

Remuneration, &c. of Certification Officer and assistants

7-169

255.—(1) ACAS shall pay to the Certification Officer and any assistant certification officer such remuneration and travelling and other allowances as may be determined by the Secretary of State.

(2) The Secretary of State may pay, or make provision for payment, to or in respect of the Certification Officer and any assistant certification officer such pension, allowance or gratuity on death or retirement as he may determine.

(3) Where a person ceases to be the Certification Officer or an assistant certification officer otherwise than on the expiry of his term of office and it appears to the Secretary of State that there are special circumstances which make it right for him to receive compensation, he may make him a payment of such amount he may determine.

(4) The approval of the Treasury is required for any determination by the Secretary of State under this section.

References to the Certification Officer in enactments relating to his functions shall be construed accordingly.

Procedure before the Certification Officer

7-170

256.—(1) Except in relation to matters as to which express provision is made by or under an enactment, the Certification Officer may regulate the procedure to be followed—

(a) on any application or complaint made to him, or

(b) where his approval is sought with respect to any matter.

[(2) He shall in particular make provision about the disclosure, and restriction of the disclosure, of the identity of an individual who has made or is proposing to make any such application or complaint.

(2A) Provision under subsection (2) shall be such that if the application or complaint relates to a trade union—

(a) the individual's identity is disclosed to the union unless the Certification Officer thinks the circumstances are such that it should not be so disclosed;

(b) the individual's identity is disclosed to such other persons (if any) as the Certification Officer thinks fit.][2]

(3) The Secretary of State may, with the consent of the Treasury, make a scheme providing for the payment by the Certification Officer to persons of such sums as may be specified in or determined under the scheme in respect of expenses incurred by them for the purposes of, or in connection with, their attendance at hearings held by him in the course of carrying out his functions.

---

[1] Inserted by Trade Union Reform and Employment Rights Act 1993 c.19 Sch 8 para 78
[2] Substituted by Employment Relations Act 1999 c.26 Sch6 para 22

[Vexatious litigants

256A.—(1) The Certification Officer may refuse to entertain any application or complaint made to him under a provision of Chapters III to VIIA of Part I by a vexatious litigant. **7-171**

(2) The Certification Officer must give reasons for such a refusal.

(3) Subsection (1) does not apply to a complaint under section 37E(1)(b) or to an application under section 41.

(4) For the purposes of subsection (1) a vexatious litigant is a person who is the subject of—

(a) an order which is made under section 33(1) of the Employment Tribunals Act 1996 and which remains in force,

(b) a civil proceedings order or an all proceedings order which is made under section 42(1) of the Supreme Court Act 1981 and which remains in force;

(c) an order which is made under section 1 of the Vexatious Actions (Scotland) Act 1898, or

(d) an order which is made under section 32 of the Judicature (Northern Ireland) Act 1978.

Vexatious litigants: applications disregarded

256B.—(1) For the purposes of a relevant enactment an application to the Certification Officer shall be disregarded if— **7-172**

(a) it was made under a provision mentioned in the relevant enactment, and

(b) it was refused by the Certification Officer under section 256A(1).

(2) The relevant enactments are sections 26(8), 31(7), 45C(5B), 56(8), 72A(10), 81(8) and 108A(13).][1]

Custody of documents submitted under earlier legislation

257.—(1) The Certification Officer shall continue to have custody of the annual returns, accounts, copies of rules and other documents submitted for the purposes of— **7-173**

(a) the Trade Union Acts 1871 to 1964,

(b) the Industrial Relations Act 1971, or

(c) the Trade Union and Labour Relations Act 1974,

of which he took custody under section 9 of the Employment Protection Act 1975.

(2) He shall keep available for public inspection (either free of charge or on payment of a reasonable charge) at all reasonable hours such of those documents as were available for public inspection in pursuance of any of those Acts.

Annual report and accounts

258.—(1) The Certification Officer shall, as soon as practicable after the end of each [financial year][2], make a report of his activities during that year to ACAS and to the Secretary of State. **7-174**

The Secretary of State shall lay a copy of the report before each House of Parliament and arrange for it to be published.

[1] Inserted by Employment Relations Act 1999 c.26 Sch 6 para 23
[2] Words substituted by Employment Relations Act 1999 c.26 Sch 6 para 24

(2) The accounts prepared by ACAS in respect of any financial year shall show separately any sums disbursed to or on behalf of the Certification Officer in consequence of the provisions of this Part.

Central Arbitration Committee

The Central Arbitration Committee

7-175   **259.**—(1) There shall continue to be a body called the Central Arbitration Committee.

(2) The functions of the Committee shall be performed on behalf of the Crown, but not so as to make it subject to directions of any kind from any Minister of the Crown as to the manner in which it is to exercise its functions.

(3) ACAS shall provide for the Committee the requisite staff (from among the officers and servants of ACAS) and the requisite accommodation, equipment and other facilities.

Excluded classes of employment

Short-term employment

7-176   **282.**—(1) The provisions of Chapter II of Part IV (procedure for handling redundancies) do not apply to employment—

    (a) under a contract for a fixed term of three months or less, or

    (b) under a contract made in contemplation of the performance of a specific task which is not expected to last for more than three months,

where the employee has not been continuously employed for a period of more than three months.

[(2) Chapter I of Part XIV of the Employment Rights Act 1996 (computation of period of continuous employment), and any provision modifying or supplementing that Chapter for the purposes of that Act, apply for the purposes of this section.][1]

PART VII

MISCELLANEOUS AND GENERAL

Contracting out, &c

Restriction on contracting out

7-177   **288.**—(1) Any provision in an agreement (whether a contract of employment or not) is void in so far as it purports—

    (a) to exclude or limit the operation of any provision of this Act, or

    (b) to preclude a person from bringing—

        (i) proceedings before an [employment tribunal][2] or the Central Arbitration Committee under any provision of this Act, or

        (ii) an application to the Employment Appeal Tribunal under section 67(remedy for infringement of right not to be unjusti-

---

[1] Words substituted by Employment Relations Act 1996 c.18 Sch 1 para 56 (18)

[2] Words substituted by Employment Rights (Dispute Resolution) Act 1998 c.8 Pt I s 1 (2)

fiably disciplined) or section 176 (compensation for [...][1] exclusion or expulsion).

(2) Subsection (1) does not apply to an agreement to refrain from instituting or continuing proceedings where a conciliation officer has taken action under—

[[section 18 of the Employment Tribunals Act 1996][2] (conciliation)][3]

[(2A) Subsection (1) does not apply to an agreement to refrain from instituting or continuing any proceedings, other than excepted proceedings, specified in [subsection (1)(b) of that section][4] before an [employment tribunal][5] if the conditions regulating compromise agreements under this Act are satisfied in relation to the agreement.

(2B) The conditions regulating compromise agreements under this Act are that—

(a) the agreement must be in writing;

(b) the agreement must relate to the particular [proceedings][6];

(c) the complainant must have received [advice from a relevant independent advisor][7] as to the terms and effect of the proposed agreement and in particular its effect on his ability to pursue his rights before an [employment tribunal][8];

(d) there must be in force, when the adviser gives the advice, [contract of insurance, or an indemnity provided for members of a profession or professional body,][9] covering the risk of a claim by the complainant in respect of loss arising in consequence of the advice;

(e) the agreement must identify the adviser; and

(f) the agreement must state that the conditions regulating compromise agreements under this Act are satisfied.

(2C) The proceedings excepted from subsection (2A) are proceedings on a complaint of non-compliance with section 188.][10]

(3) Subsection (1) does not apply—

(a) to such an agreement as is referred to in section 185(5)(b) or (c) to the extent that it varies or supersedes an award under that section;

(b) to any provision in a collective agreement excluding rights under Chapter II of Part IV (procedure for handling redundancies), if an order under section 198 is in force in respect of it.

[(4) A person is a relevant independent adviser for the purposes of subsection (2B)(c)—

(a) if he is a qualified lawyer,

(b) if he is an officer, official, employee or member of an independent trade union who has been certified in writing by the trade union as competent to give advice and as authorised to do so on behalf of the trade union,

---

[1] Word repealed by Trade Union Reform and Employment Rights Act 1993 c.19 Sch 10 para 1
[2] Words substituted by Employment Rights (Dispute Resolution) Act 1998 c.8 Pt I s 1 (2) (c)
[3] Words substituted by Industrial Tribunals Act 1996 c.17 Sch 1 para 8 (a)
[4] Words substituted by Industrial Tribunals Act 1996 c.17 Sch 1 para 8 (b)
[5] Words substituted by Employment Rights (Dispute Resolution) Act 1998 c.8 Pt I s 1 (2)
[6] Word substituted by Employment Rights (Dispute Resolution) Act 1998 c.8 Sch 1 para 9 (2)
[7] Words substituted by Employment Rights (Dispute Resolution) Act 1998 c.8 Pt II s 9 (2) (c)
[8] Words substituted by Employment Rights (Dispute Resolution) Act 1998 c.8 Pt I s 1 (2)
[9] Words substituted by Employment Rights (Dispute Resolution) Act 1998 c.8 Pt II s 10 (2) (c)
[10] Inserted by Trade Union Reform and Employment Rights Act 1993 c.19 Sch 6 para 4 (a)

(c) if he works at an advice centre (whether as an employee or a volunteer) and has been certified in writing by the centre as competent to give advice and as authorised to do so on behalf of the centre, or

(d) if he is a person of a description specified in an order made by the Secretary of State.

(4A) But a person is not a relevant independent adviser for the purposes of subsection (2B)(c) in relation to the complainant—

(a) if he is, is employed by or is acting in the matter for the other party or a person who is connected with the other party,

(b) in the case of a person within subsection (4)(b) or (c), if the trade union or advice centre is the other party or a person who is connected with the other party,

(c) in the case of a person within subsection (4)(c), if the complainant makes a payment for the advice received from him, or

(d) in the case of a person of a description specified in an order under subsection (4)(d), if any condition specified in the order in relation to the giving of advice by persons of that description is not satisfied.

(4B) In subsection (4)(a) "qualified lawyer" means—

(a) as respects England and Wales, a barrister (whether in practice as such or employed to give legal advice), a solicitor who holds a practising certificate, or a person other than a barrister or solicitor who is an authorised advocate or authorised litigator (within the meaning of the Courts and Legal Services Act 1990), and

(b) as respects Scotland, an advocate (whether in practice as such or employed to give legal advice), or a solicitor who holds a practising certificate.

(4C) An order under subsection (4)(d) shall be made by statutory instrument which shall be subject to annulment in pursuance of a resolution of either House of Parliament.

(5) For the purposes of subsection (4A) any two persons are to be treated as connected—

(a) if one is a company of which the other (directly or indirectly) has control, or

(b) if both are companies of which a third person (directly or indirectly) has control.][1]

[(6) An agreement under which the parties agree to submit a dispute to arbitration—

(a) shall be regarded for the purposes of subsections (2) and (2A) as being an agreement to refrain from instituting or continuing proceedings if—

(i) the dispute is covered by a scheme having effect by virtue of an order under section 212A, and

(ii) the agreement is to submit it to arbitration in accordance with the scheme, but

(b) shall be regarded for those purposes as neither being nor including such an agreement in any other case.][2]

---

[1] Substituted by Employment Rights (Dispute Resolution) Act 1998 c.8 Sch 1 para 9 (3)
[2] Inserted by Employment Rights (Dispute Resolution) Act 1998 c.8 Pt II s 8 (3)

Employment governed by foreign law

289.—For the purposes of this Act it is immaterial whether the law **7-178** which (apart from this Act) governs any person's employment is the law of the United Kingdom, or of a part of the United Kingdom, or not.

Other supplementary provisions

Death of employee or employer

292.—(1) This section has effect in relation to the following provisions **7-179** so far as they confer rights on employees or make provision in connection therewith—

(a) sections 146 to 151 (action short of dismissal taken on grounds related to union membership or activities);

(b) sections 168 to 173 (time off for trade union duties and activities);

(c) sections 188 to 198 (procedure for handling redundancies).

(2) Where the employee or employer dies, tribunal proceedings may be instituted or continued by a personal representative of the deceased employee or, as the case may be, defended by a personal representative of the deceased employer.

(3) If there is no personal representative of a deceased employee, tribunal proceedings or proceedings to enforce a tribunal award may be instituted or continued on behalf of his estate by such other person as the industrial tribunal may appoint, being either—

(a) a person authorised by the employee to act in connection with the proceedings before his death, or

(b) the widower, widow, child, father, mother, brother or sister of the employee.

In such a case any award made by the [employment tribunal][1] shall be in such terms and shall be enforceable in such manner as may be prescribed.

(4) Any right arising under any of the provisions mentioned in subsection (1) which by virtue of this section accrues after the death of the employee in question shall devolve as if it had accrued before his death.

(5) Any liability arising under any of those provisions which by virtue of this section accrues after the death of the employer in question shall be treated for all purposes as if it had accrued immediately before his death.

Interpretation

Meaning of "employee" and related expressions

295.—(1) In this Act— **7-180**

"contract of employment" means a contract of service or of apprenticeship,

"employee" means an individual who has entered into or works under (or, where the employment has ceased, worked under) a contract of employment, and

"employer", in relation to an employee, means the person by whom the employee is (or, where the employment has ceased, was) employed.

---

[1] Words substituted by Employment Rights (Dispute Resolution) Act 1998 c.8 Pt I s 1 (2)

(2) Subsection (1) has effect subject to section 235 and other provisions conferring a wider meaning on "contract of employment" or related expressions.

Meaning of "worker" and related expressions

7-181   **296.**—(1) In this Act "worker" means an individual who works, or normally works or seeks to work—

(a) under a contract of employment, or

(b) under any other contract whereby he undertakes to do or perform personally any work or services for another party to the contract who is not a professional client of his, or

(c) in employment under or for the purposes of a government department (otherwise than as a member of the naval, military or air forces of the Crown) in so far as such employment does not fall within paragraph (a) or (b) above.

(2) In this Act "employer", in relation to a worker, means a person for whom one or more workers work, or have worked or normally work or seek to work.

[(3) This section has effect subject to section 68(11).][1]

Associated employers

7-182   **297.** For the purposes of this Act any two employers shall be treated as associated if—

(a) one is a company of which the other (directly or indirectly) has control, or

(b) both are companies of which a third person (directly or indirectly) has control;

and "associated employer" shall be construed accordingly.

Minor definitions: general

7-183   **298.** In this Act, unless the context otherwise requires—

"act" and "action" each includes omission, and references to doing an act or taking action shall be construed accordingly;

"contravention" includes a failure to comply, and cognate expressions shall be construed accordingly; ·

"dismiss", "dismissal" and "effective date of termination", in relation to an employee, shall be construed in accordance with [Part X of the Employment Rights Act 1996][2];

[...][3]

"tort", as respects Scotland, means delict, and cognate expressions shall be construed accordingly.

---

[1] Inserted by Trade Union Reform and Employment Rights Act 1993 c.19 Sch 8 para 88
[2] Words substituted by Employment Rights Act 1996 c.18 Sch 1 para 56 (19)
[3] Definition repealed by SI 2001/1149 Sch 2 para 1

SCHEDULES

Schedule A1

COLLECTIVE BARGAINING: RECOGNITION

RECOGNITION

Introduction

[**1.** A trade union (or trade unions) seeking recognition to be entitled to conduct collective bargaining on behalf of a group or groups of workers may make a request in accordance with this Part of this Schedule.]¹   **7-184**

[**2.**— (1) This paragraph applies for the purposes of this Part of this Schedule.   **7-185**

(2) References to the bargaining unit are to the group of workers concerned (or the groups taken together).

(3) References to the proposed bargaining unit are to the bargaining unit proposed in the request for recognition.

(4) References to the employer are to the employer of the workers constituting the bargaining unit concerned.

(5) References to the parties are to the union (or unions) and the employer.]²

[**3.**— (1) This paragraph applies for the purposes of this Part of this Schedule.   **7-186**

(2) The meaning of collective bargaining given by section 178(1) shall not apply.

(3) References to collective bargaining are to negotiations relating to pay, hours and holidays; but this has effect subject to sub-paragraph (4).

(4) If the parties agree matters as the subject of collective bargaining, references to collective bargaining are to negotiations relating to the agreed matters; and this is the case whether the agreement is made before or after the time when the CAC issues a declaration, or the parties agree, that the union is (or unions are) entitled to conduct collective bargaining on behalf of a bargaining unit.

(5) Sub-paragraph (4) does not apply in construing paragraph 31(3).

(6) Sub-paragraphs (2) to (5) do not apply in construing paragraph 35 or 44.]³

Request for recognition

[**4.**— (1) The union or unions seeking recognition must make a request for recognition to the employer.   **7-187**

(2) Paragraphs 5 to 9 apply to the request.]⁴

[**5.** The request is not valid unless it is received by the employer.]⁵   **7-188**

[**6.** The request is not valid unless the union (or each of the unions) has a certificate under section 6 that it is independent.]⁶   **7-189**

[**7.**— (1) The request is not valid unless the employer, taken with any associated employer or employers, employs—   **7-190**

(a) at least 21 workers on the day the employer receives the request, or

(b) an average of at least 21 workers in the 13 weeks ending with that day.

(2) To find the average under sub-paragraph (1)(b)—

(a) take the number of workers employed in each of the 13 weeks (including workers not employed for the whole of the week);

(b) aggregate the 13 numbers;

(c) divide the aggregate by 13.

---

¹ Inserted by Employment Relations Act 1999 c.26 Sch 1 para 1
² Inserted by Employment Relations Act 1999 c.26 Sch 1 para 1
³ Inserted by Employment Relations Act 1999 c.26 Sch 1 para 1
⁴ Inserted by Employment Relations Act 1999 c.26 Sch 1 para 1
⁵ Inserted by Employment Relations Act 1999 c.26 Sch 1 para 1
⁶ Inserted by Employment Relations Act 1999 c.26 Sch 1 para 1

(3) For the purposes of sub-paragraph (1)(a) any worker employed by an associated company incorporated outside Great Britain must be ignored unless the day the request was made fell within a period during which he ordinarily worked in Great Britain.

(4) For the purposes of sub-paragraph (1)(b) any worker employed by an associated company incorporated outside Great Britain must be ignored in relation to a week unless the whole or any part of that week fell within a period during which he ordinarily worked in Great Britain.

(5) For the purposes of sub-paragraphs (3) and (4) a worker who is employed on board a ship registered in the register maintained under section 8 of the Merchant Shipping Act 1995 shall be treated as ordinarily working in Great Britain unless—

    (a) the ship's entry in the register specifies a port outside Great Britain as the port to which the vessel is to be treated as belonging,

    (b) the employment is wholly outside Great Britain, or

    (c) the worker is not ordinarily resident in Great Britain.

(6) The Secretary of State may by order—

    (a) provide that sub-paragraphs (1) to (5) are not to apply, or are not to apply in specified circumstances, or

    (b) vary the number of workers for the time being specified in sub-paragraph (1);

and different provision may be made for different circumstances.

(7) An order under sub-paragraph (6)—

    (a) shall be made by statutory instrument, and

    (b) may include supplementary, incidental, saving or transitional provisions.

(8) No such order shall be made unless a draft of it has been laid before Parliament and approved by a resolution of each House of Parliament.][1]

7-191   [**8.** The request is not valid unless it—

    (a) is in writing,

    (b) identifies the union or unions and the bargaining unit, and

    (c) states that it is made under this Schedule.][2]

7-192   [**9.** The Secretary of State may by order made by statutory instrument prescribe the form of requests and the procedure for making them; and if he does so the request is not valid unless it complies with the order.][3]

Parties agree

7-193   [**10.**— (1) If before the end of the first period the parties agree a bargaining unit and that the union is (or unions are) to be recognised as entitled to conduct collective bargaining on behalf of the unit, no further steps are to be taken under this Part of this Schedule.

(2) If before the end of the first period the employer informs the union (or unions) that the employer does not accept the request but is willing to negotiate, sub-paragraph (3) applies

(3) The parties may conduct negotiations with a view to agreeing a bargaining unit and that the union is (or unions are) to be recognised as entitled to conduct collective bargaining on behalf of the unit.

(4) If such an agreement is made before the end of the second period no further steps are to be taken under this Part of this Schedule.

(5) The employer and the union (or unions) may request ACAS to assist in conducting the negotiations.

(6) The first period is the period of 10 working days starting with the day after that on which the employer receives the request for recognition.

(7) The second period is—

    (a) the period of 20 working days starting with the day after that on which the first period ends, or

    (b) such longer period (so starting) as the parties may from time to time agree.][4]

Employer rejects request

7-194   [**11.**— (1) This paragraph applies if—

    (a) before the end of the first period the employer fails to respond to the request, or

---

[1] Inserted by Employment Relations Act 1999 c.26 Sch 1 para 1

[2] Inserted by Employment Relations Act 1999 c.26 Sch 1 para 1

[3] Inserted by Employment Relations Act 1999 c.26 Sch 1 para 1

[4] Inserted by Employment Relations Act 1999 c.26 Sch 1 para 1

(b) before the end of the first period the employer informs the union (or unions) that the employer does not accept the request (without indicating a willingness to negotiate).

(2) The union (or unions) may apply to the CAC to decide both these questions—

(a) whether the proposed bargaining unit is appropriate or some other bargaining unit is appropriate;

(b) whether the union has (or unions have) the support of a majority of the workers constituting the appropriate bargaining unit.]¹

Negotiations fail

[**12.**— (1) Sub-paragraph (2) applies if—   **7-195**

(a) the employer informs the union (or unions) under paragraph 10(2), and

(b) no agreement is made before the end of the second period.

(2) The union (or unions) may apply to the CAC to decide both these questions—

(a) whether the proposed bargaining unit is appropriate or some other bargaining unit is appropriate;

(b) whether the union has (or unions have) the support of a majority of the workers constituting the appropriate bargaining unit.

(3) Sub-paragraph (4) applies if—

(a) the employer informs the union (or unions) under paragraph 10(2), and

(b) before the end of the second period the parties agree a bargaining unit but not that the union is (or unions are) to be recognised as entitled to conduct collective bargaining on behalf of the unit.

(4) The union (or unions) may apply to the CAC to decide the question whether the union has (or unions have) the support of a majority of the workers constituting the bargaining unit.

(5) But no application may be made under this paragraph if within the period of 10 working days starting with the day after that on which the employer informs the union (or unions) under paragraph 10(2) the employer proposes that ACAS be requested to assist in conducting the negotiations and—

(a) the union rejects (or unions reject) the proposal, or

(b) the union fails (or unions fail) to accept the proposal within the period of 10 working days starting with the day after that on which the employer makes the proposal.]²

Acceptance of applications

[**13.** The CAC must give notice to the parties of receipt of an application under 11 or 12.]³   **7-196**

[**14.**— (1) This paragraph applies if—   **7-197**

(a) two or more relevant applications are made,

(b) at least one worker falling within one of the relevant bargaining units also falls within the other relevant bargaining unit (or units), and

(c) the CAC has not accepted any of the applications.

(2) A relevant application is an application under paragraph 11 or 12.

(3) In relation to a relevant application, the relevant bargaining unit is—

(a) the proposed bargaining unit, where the application is under paragraph 11(2) or 12(2);

(b) the agreed bargaining unit, where the application is under paragraph 12(4).

(4) Within the acceptance period the CAC must decide, with regard to each relevant application, whether the 10 per cent test is satisfied.

(5) The 10 per cent test is satisfied if members of the union (or unions) constitute at least 10 per cent of the workers constituting the relevant bargaining unit.

(6) The acceptance period is—

(a) the period of 10 working days starting with the day after that on which the CAC receives the last relevant application, or

(b) such longer period (so starting) as the CAC may specify to the parties by notice containing reasons for the extension.

(7) If the CAC decides that—

(a) the 10 per cent test is satisfied with regard to more than one of the relevant applications, or

(b) the 10 per cent test is satisfied with regard to none of the relevant applications,

---

¹ Inserted by Employment Relations Act 1999 c.26 Sch 1 para 1
² Inserted by Employment Relations Act 1999 c.26 Sch 1 para 1
³ Inserted by Employment Relations Act 1999 c.26 Sch 1 para 1

the CAC must not accept any of the relevant applications.

(8) If the CAC decides that the 10 per cent test is satisfied with regard to one only of the relevant applications the CAC—

    (a) must proceed under paragraph 15 with regard to that application, and

    (b) must not accept any of the other relevant applications.

(9) The CAC must give notice of its decision to the parties.

(10) If by virtue of this paragraph the CAC does not accept an application, no further steps are to be taken under this Part of this Schedule in relation to that application.][1]

7-198

[**15.**— (1) This paragraph applies to these applications—

    (a) any application with regard to which no decision has to be made under paragraph 14;

    (b) any application with regard to which the CAC must proceed under this paragraph by virtue of paragraph 14.

(2) Within the acceptance period the CAC must decide whether—

    (a) the request for recognition to which the application relates is valid within the terms of paragraphs 5 to 9, and

    (b) the application is made in accordance with paragraph 11 or 12 and admissible within the terms of paragraphs 33 to 42.

(3) In deciding those questions the CAC must consider any evidence which it has been given by the employer or the union (or unions).

(4) If the CAC decides that the request is not valid or the application is not made in accordance with paragraph 11 or 12 or is not admissible—

    (a) the CAC must give notice of its decision to the parties,

    (b) the CAC must not accept the application, and

    (c) no further steps are to be taken under this Part of this Schedule.

(5) If the CAC decides that the request is valid and the application is made in accordance with paragraph 11 or 12 and is admissible it must—

    (a) accept the application, and

    (b) give notice of the acceptance to the parties.

(6) The acceptance period is—

    (a) the period of 10 working days starting with the day after that on which the CAC receives the application, or

    (b) such longer period (so starting) as the CAC may specify to the parties by notice containing reasons for the extension.][2]

Withdrawal of application

7-199

[**16.**— (1) If an application under paragraph 11 or 12 is accepted by the CAC, the union (or unions) may not withdraw the application—

    (a) after the CAC issues a declaration under paragraph 22(2), or

    (b) after the union (or the last of the unions) receives notice under paragraph 22(3) or 23(2).

(2) If an application is withdrawn by the union (or unions)—

    (a) the CAC must give notice of the withdrawal to the employer, and

    (b) no further steps are to be taken under this Part of this Schedule.][3]

Notice to cease consideration of application

7-200

[**17.**— (1) This paragraph applies if the CAC has received an application under paragraph 11 or 12 and—

    (a) it has not decided whether the application is admissible, or

    (b) it has decided that the application is admissible.

(2) No further steps are to be taken under this Part of this Schedule if, before the final event occurs, the parties give notice to the CAC that they want no further steps to be taken.

(3) The final event occurs when the first of the following occurs—

    (a) the CAC issues a declaration under paragraph 22(2) in consequence of the application;

    (b) the last day of the notification period ends;

and the notification period is that defined by paragraph 24(5) and arising from the application.][4]

---

[1] Inserted by Employment Relations Act 1999 c.26 Sch 1 para 1
[2] Inserted by Employment Relations Act 1999 c.26 Sch 1 para 1
[3] Inserted by Employment Relations Act 1999 c.26 Sch 1 para 1
[4] Inserted by Employment Relations Act 1999 c.26 Sch 1 para 1

Appropriate bargaining unit

[**18.**— (1) If the CAC accepts an application under paragraph 11(2) or 12(2) it must try to **7-201** help the parties to reach within the appropriate period an agreement as to what the appropriate bargaining unit is.

(2) The appropriate period is—
    (a) the period of 20 working days starting with the day after that on which the CAC gives notice of acceptance of the application, or
    (b) such longer period (so starting) as the CAC may specify to the parties by notice containing reasons for the extension.][1]

[**19.**— (1) This paragraph applies if— **7-202**
    (a) the CAC accepts an application under paragraph 11(2) or 12(2), and
    (b) the parties have not agreed an appropriate bargaining unit at the end of the appropriate period.

(2) The CAC must decide the appropriate bargaining unit within—
    (a) the period of 10 working days starting with the day after that on which the appropriate period ends, or
    (b) such longer period (so starting) as the CAC may specify to the parties by notice containing reasons for the extension.

(3) In deciding the appropriate bargaining unit the CAC must take these matters into account—
    (a) the need for the unit to be compatible with effective management;
    (b) the matters listed in sub-paragraph (4), so far as they do not conflict with that need.

(4) The matters are—
    (a) the views of the employer and of the union (or unions);
    (b) existing national and local bargaining arrangements;
    (c) the desirability of avoiding small fragmented bargaining units within an undertaking;
    (d) the characteristics of workers falling within the proposed bargaining unit and of any other employees of the employer whom the CAC considers relevant;
    (e) the location of workers.

(5) The CAC must give notice of its decision to the parties.][2]

Union recognition

[**20.**— (1) This paragraph applies if— **7-203**
    (a) the CAC accepts an application under paragraph 11(2) or 12(2),
    (b) the parties have agreed an appropriate bargaining unit at the end of the appropriate period, or the CAC has decided an appropriate bargaining unit, and
    (c) that bargaining unit differs from the proposed bargaining unit.

(2) Within the decision period the CAC must decide whether the application is invalid within the terms of paragraphs 43 to 50.

(3) In deciding whether the application is invalid, the CAC must consider any evidence which it has been given by the employer or the union (or unions).

(4) If the CAC decides that the application is invalid—
    (a) the CAC must give notice of its decision to the parties,
    (b) the CAC must not proceed with the application, and
    (c) no further steps are to be taken under this Part of this Schedule.

(5) If the CAC decides that the application is not invalid it must—
    (a) proceed with the application, and
    (b) give notice to the parties that it is so proceeding.

(6) The decision period is—
    (a) the period of 10 working days starting with the day after that on which the parties agree an appropriate bargaining unit or the CAC decides an appropriate bargaining unit, or
    (b) such longer period (so starting) as the CAC may specify to the parties by notice containing reasons for the extension.][3]

[**21.**— (1) This paragraph applies if— **7-204**
    (a) the CAC accepts an application under paragraph 11(2) or 12(2),

---

[1] Inserted by Employment Relations Act 1999 c.26 Sch 1 para 1
[2] Inserted by Employment Relations Act 1999 c.26 Sch 1 para 1
[3] Inserted by Employment Relations Act 1999 c.26 Sch 1 para 1

(b) the parties have agreed an appropriate bargaining unit at the end of the appropriate period, or the CAC has decided an appropriate bargaining unit, and

(c) that bargaining unit is the same as the proposed bargaining unit.

(2) This paragraph also applies if the CAC accepts an application under paragraph 12(4).

(3) The CAC must proceed with the application.][1]

7-205   [**22.**— (1) This paragraph applies if—

(a) the CAC proceeds with an application in accordance with paragraph 20 or 21, and

(b) the CAC is satisfied that a majority of the workers constituting the bargaining unit are members of the union (or unions).

(2) The CAC must issue a declaration that the union is (or unions are) recognised as entitled to conduct collective bargaining on behalf of the workers constituting the bargaining unit.

(3) But if any of the three qualifying conditions is fulfilled, instead of issuing a declaration under sub-paragraph (2) the CAC must give notice to the parties that it intends to arrange for the holding of a secret ballot in which the workers constituting the bargaining unit are asked whether they want the union (or unions) to conduct collective bargaining on their behalf.

(4) These are the three qualifying conditions—

(a) the CAC is satisfied that a ballot should be held in the interests of good industrial relations;

(b) a significant number of the union members within the bargaining unit inform the CAC that they do not want the union (or unions) to conduct collective bargaining on their behalf;

(c) membership evidence is produced which leads the CAC to conclude that there are doubts whether a significant number of the union members within the bargaining unit want the union (or unions) to conduct collective bargaining on their behalf.

(5) For the purposes of sub-paragraph (4)(c) membership evidence is—

(a) evidence about the circumstances in which union members became members;

(b) evidence about the length of time for which union members have been members, in a case where the CAC is satisfied that such evidence should be taken into account.][2]

7-206   [**23.**— (1) This paragraph applies if—

(a) the CAC proceeds with an application in accordance with paragraph 20 or 21, and

(b) the CAC is not satisfied that a majority of the workers constituting the bargaining unit are members of the union (or unions).

(2) The CAC must give notice to the parties that it intends to arrange for the holding of a secret ballot in which the workers constituting the bargaining unit are asked whether they want the union (or unions) to conduct collective bargaining on their behalf.][3]

7-207   [**24.**— (1) This paragraph applies if the CAC gives notice under paragraph 22(3) or 23(2).

(2) Within the notification period—

(a) the union (or unions), or

(b) the union (or unions) and the employer,

may notify the CAC that the party making the notification does not (or the parties making the notification do not) want the CAC to arrange for the holding of the ballot.

(3) If the CAC is so notified—

(a) it must not arrange for the holding of the ballot,

(b) it must inform the parties that it will not arrange for the holding of the ballot, and why, and

(c) no further steps are to be taken under this Part of this Schedule.

(4) If the CAC is not so notified it must arrange for the holding of the ballot.

(5) The notification period is the period of 10 working days starting—

(a) for the purposes of sub-paragraph (2)(a), with the day on which the union (or last of the unions)receives the CAC's notice under paragraph 22(3) or 23(2), or

(b) for the purposes of sub-paragraph (2)(b), with that day or (if later) the day on which the employer receives the CAC's notice under paragraph 22(3) or 23(2).][4]

---

[1] Inserted by Employment Relations Act 1999 c.26 Sch 1 para 1
[2] Inserted by Employment Relations Act 1999 c.26 Sch 1 para 1
[3] Inserted by Employment Relations Act 1999 c.26 Sch 1 para 1
[4] Inserted by Employment Relations Act 1999 c.26 Sch 1 para 1

[**25.**— (1) This paragraph applies if the CAC arranges under paragraph 24 for the holding of **7-208** a ballot.

(2) The ballot must be conducted by a qualified independent person appointed by the CAC.

(3) The ballot must be conducted within—

    (a) the period of 20 working days starting with the day after that on which the qualified independent person is appointed, or

    (b) such longer period (so starting) as the CAC may decide.

(4) The ballot must be conducted—

    (a) at a workplace or workplaces decided by the CAC,

    (b) by post, or

    (c) by a combination of the methods described in sub-paragraphs (a) and (b),

depending on the CAC's preference.

(5) In deciding how the ballot is to be conducted the CAC must take into account—

    (a) the likelihood of the ballot being affected by unfairness or malpractice if it were conducted at a workplace or workplaces;

    (b) costs and practicality;

    (c) such other matters as the CAC considers appropriate.

(6) The CAC may not decide that the ballot is to be conducted as mentioned in sub-paragraph (4)(c) unless there are special factors making such a decision appropriate; and special factors include—

    (a) factors arising from the location of workers or the nature of their employment;

    (b) factors put to the CAC by the employer or the union (or unions).

(7) A person is a qualified independent person if—

    (a) he satisfies such conditions as may be specified for the purposes of this paragraph by order of the Secretary of State or is himself so specified, and

    (b) there are no grounds for believing either that he will carry out any functions conferred on him in relation to the ballot otherwise than competently or that his independence in relation to the ballot might reasonably be called into question.

(8) An order under sub-paragraph (7)(a) shall be made by statutory instrument subject to annulment in pursuance of a resolution of either House of Parliament.

(9) As soon as is reasonably practicable after the CAC is required under paragraph 24 to arrange for the holding of a ballot it must inform the parties—

    (a) that it is so required;

    (b) of the name of the person appointed to conduct the ballot and the date of his appointment;

    (c) of the period within which the ballot must be conducted;

    (d) whether the ballot is to be conducted by post or at a workplace or workplaces;

    (e) of the workplace or workplaces concerned (if the ballot is to be conducted at a workplace or workplaces).][1]

[**26.**— (1) An employer who is informed by the CAC under paragraph 25(9) must comply **7-209** with the following three duties.

(2) The first duty is to co-operate generally, in connection with the ballot, with the union (or unions) and the person appointed to conduct the ballot; and the second and third duties are not to prejudice the generality of this.

(3) The second duty is to give to the union (or unions) such access to the workers constituting the bargaining unit as is reasonable to enable the union (or unions) to inform the workers of the object of the ballot and to seek their support and their opinions on the issues involved.

(4) The third duty is to do the following (so far as it is reasonable to expect the employer to do so)—

    (a) to give to the CAC, within the period of 10 working days starting with the day after that on which the employer is informed under paragraph 25(9), the names and home address of the workers constituting the bargaining unit;

    (b) to give to the CAC, as soon as is reasonably practicable, the name and home address of any worker who joins the unit after the employer has complied with paragraph (a);

    (c) to inform the CAC, as soon as is reasonably practicable, of any worker whose name has been given to the CAC under paragraph (a) or (b) but who ceases to be within the unit.

(5) As soon as is reasonably practicable after the CAC receives any information under sub-paragraph (4) it must pass it on to the person appointed to conduct the ballot.

---

[1] Inserted by Employment Relations Act 1999 c.26 Sch 1 para 1

(6) If asked to do so by the union (or unions) the person appointed to conduct the ballot must send to any worker—

(a) whose name and home address have been given under sub-paragraph (5), and

(b) who is still within the unit (so far as the person so appointed is aware),

any information supplied by the union (or unions) to the person so appointed.

(7) The duty under sub-paragraph (6) does not apply unless the union bears (or unions bear) the cost of sending the information.

(8) Each of the following powers shall be taken to include power to issue Codes of Practice about reasonable access for the purposes of sub-paragraph (3)—

(a) the power of ACAS under section 199(1);

(b) the power of the Secretary of State under section 203(1)(a).][1]

7-210

[**27.**— (1) If the CAC is satisfied that the employer has failed to fulfil any of the three duties imposed by paragraph 26, and the ballot has not been held, the CAC may order the employer—

(a) to take such steps to remedy the failure as the CAC considers reasonable and specifies in the order, and

(b) to do so within such period as the CAC considers reasonable and specifies in the order.

(2) If the CAC is satisfied that the employer has failed to comply with an order under sub-paragraph (1), and the ballot has not been held, the CAC may issue a declaration that the union is (or unions are) recognised as entitled to conduct collective bargaining on behalf of the bargaining unit.

(3) If the CAC issues a declaration under sub-paragraph (2) it shall take steps to cancel the holding of the ballot; and if the ballot is held it shall have no effect.][2]

7-211

[**28.**— (1) This paragraph applies if the holding of a ballot has been arranged under paragraph 24 whether or not it has been cancelled.

(2) The gross costs of the ballot shall be borne—

(a) as to half, by the employer, and

(b) as to half, by the union (or unions).

(3) If there is more than one union they shall bear their half of the gross costs—

(a) in such proportions as they jointly indicate to the person appointed to conduct the ballot, or

(b) in the absence of such an indication, in equal shares.

(4) The person appointed to conduct the ballot may send to the employer and the union (or each of the unions) a demand stating—

(a) the gross costs of the ballot, and

(b) the amount of the gross costs to be borne by the recipient.

(5) In such a case the recipient must pay the amount stated to the person sending the demand, and must do so within the period of 15 working days starting with the day after that on which the demand is received.

(6) In England and Wales, if the amount stated is not paid in accordance with sub-paragraph (5) it shall, if a county court so orders, be recoverable by execution issued from that court or otherwise as if it were payable under an order of that court.

(7) References to the costs of the ballot are to—

(a) the costs wholly, exclusively and necessarily incurred in connection with the ballot by the person appointed to conduct it,

(b) such reasonable amount as the person appointed to conduct the ballot charges for his services, and

(c) such other costs as the employer and the union (or unions) agree.][3]

7-212

[**29.**— (1) As soon as is reasonably practicable after the CAC is informed of the result of a ballot by the person conducting it, the CAC must act under this paragraph.

(2) The CAC must inform the employer and the union (or unions) of the result of the ballot.

(3) If the result is that the union is (or unions are) supported by—

(a) a majority of the workers voting, and

(b) at least 40 per cent of the workers constituting the bargaining unit,

the CAC must issue a declaration that the union is (or unions are) recognised as entitled to conduct collective bargaining on behalf of the bargaining unit.

---

[1] Inserted by Employment Relations Act 1999 c.26 Sch 1 para 1
[2] Inserted by Employment Relations Act 1999 c.26 Sch 1 para 1
[3] Inserted by Employment Relations Act 1999 c.26 Sch 1 para 1

(4) If the result is otherwise the CAC must issue a declaration that the union is (or unions are) not entitled to be so recognised.

(5) The Secretary of State may by order amend sub-paragraph (3) so as to specify a different degree of support; and different provision may be made for different circumstances.

(6) An order under sub-paragraph (5) shall be made by statutory instrument.

(7) No such order shall be made unless a draft of it has been laid before Parliament and approved by a resolution of each House of Parliament.][1]

[*Consequences of recognition*

30.— (1) This paragraph applies if the CAC issues a declaration under this Part of this **7-213** Schedule that the union is (or unions are) recognised as entitled to conduct collective bargaining on behalf of a bargaining unit.

(2) The parties may in the negotiation period conduct negotiations with a view to agreeing a method by which they will conduct collective bargaining.

(3) If no agreement is made in the negotiation period the employer or the union (or unions) may apply to the CAC for assistance.

(4) The negotiation period is—
    (a) the period of 30 working days starting with the start day, or
    (b) such longer period (so starting) as the parties may from time to time agree.

(5) The start day is the day after that on which the parties are notified of the declaration.][2]

Pensions Act 1995

CHAPTER 26

PART I

OCCUPATIONAL PENSIONS

Equal treatment

The equal treatment rule

62.—(1) An occupational pension scheme which does not contain an equal **8-001** treatment rule shall be treated as including one.

(2) An equal treatment rule is a rule which relates to the terms on which—
    (a) persons become members of the scheme, and
    (b) members of the scheme are treated.

(3) Subject to subsection (6), an equal treatment rule has the effect that where—
    (a) a woman is employed on like work with a man in the same employment,
    (b) a woman is employed on work rated as equivalent with that of a man in the same employment, or
    (c) a woman is employed on work which, not being work in relation to which paragraph (a) or (b) applies, is, in terms of the demands made on her (for instance under such headings as effort, skill and decision) of equal value to that of a man in the same employment,

---

[1] Inserted by Employment Relations Act 1999 c.26 Sch 1 para 1
[2] Inserted by Employment Relations Act 1999 c.26 Sch 1 para 1

but (apart from the rule) any of the terms referred to in subsection (2) is or becomes less favourable to the woman than it is to the man, the term shall be treated as so modified as not to be less favourable.

(4) An equal treatment rule does not operate in relation to any difference as between a woman and a man in the operation of any of the terms referred to in subsection (2) if the trustees or managers of the scheme prove that the difference is genuinely due to a material factor which—

    (a) is not the difference of sex, but

    (b) is a material difference between the woman's case and the man's case.

(5) References in subsection (4) and sections 63 to 65 to the terms referred to in subsection (2), or the effect of any of those terms, include—

    (a) a term which confers on the trustees or managers of an occupational pension scheme, or any other person, a discretion which, in a case within any of paragraphs (a) to (c) of subsection (3)—

        (i) may be exercised so as to affect the way in which persons become members of the scheme, or members of the scheme are treated, and

        (ii) may (apart from the equal treatment rule) be so exercised in a way less favourable to the woman than to the man, and

    (b) the effect of any exercise of such a discretion;

and references to the terms on which members of the scheme are treated are to be read accordingly.

(6) In the case of a term within subsection (5)(a) the effect of an equal treatment rule is that the term shall be treated as so modified as not to permit the discretion to be exercised in a way less favourable to the woman than to the man.

Equal treatment rule: supplementary

8-002   **63.**—(1) The reference in section 62(2) to the terms on which members of a scheme are treated includes those terms as they have effect for the benefit of dependants of members, and the reference in section 62(5) to the way in which members of a scheme are treated includes the way they are treated as it has effect for the benefit of dependants of members.

(2) Where the effect of any of the terms referred to in section 62(2) on persons of the same sex differs according to their family or marital status, the effect of the term is to be compared for the purposes of section 62 with its effect on persons of the other sex who have the same status.

(3) An equal treatment rule has effect subject to paragraphs 5 and 6 of Schedule 5 to the Social Security Act 1989 (employment-related benefit schemes: maternity and family leave provisions).

(4) Section 62 shall be construed as one with section 1 of the Equal Pay Act 1970 (requirement of equal treatment for men and women in the same employment); and sections 2 and 2A of that Act (disputes and enforcement) shall have effect for the purposes of section 62 as if—

    (a) references to an equality clause were to an equal treatment rule,

    (b) references to employers and employees were to the trustees or managers of the scheme (on the one hand) and the members, or prospective members, of the scheme (on the other),

    (c) for section 2(4) there were substituted—

        "(4) No claim in respect of the operation of an equal treatment rule in respect of an occupational pension scheme shall be referred to an [employment tribunal][1] otherwise than by virtue of

---

[1] Words substituted by Employment Rights (Dispute Resolution) Act 1998 c.8 Pt I s 1 (2)

subsection (3) above unless the woman concerned has been employed in a description or category of employment to which the scheme relates within the six months preceding the date of the reference"

, and

(d) references to section 1(2)(c) of the Equal Pay Act 1970 were to section 62(3)(c) of this Act.

(5) Regulations may make provision for the Equal Pay Act 1970 to have effect, in relation to an equal treatment rule, with prescribed modifications; and subsection (4) shall have effect subject to any regulations made by virtue of this subsection.

(6) Section 62, so far as it relates to the terms on which members of a scheme are treated, is to be treated as having had effect in relation to any pensionable service on or after 17th May 1990.

Equal treatment rule: exceptions

64.—(1) An equal treatment rule does not operate in relation to any **8-003** variation as between a woman and a man in the effect of any of the terms referred to in section 62(2) if the variation is permitted by or under any of the provisions of this section.

(2) Where a man and a woman are eligible, in prescribed circumstances, to receive different amounts by way of pension, the variation is permitted by this subsection if, in prescribed circumstances, the differences are attributable only to differences between men and women in the benefits under sections 43 to 55 of the Social Security Contributions and Benefits Act 1992 (State retirement pensions) to which, in prescribed circumstances, they are or would be entitled.

(3) A variation is permitted by this subsection if—

(a) the variation consists of the application of actuarial factors which differ for men and women to the calculation of contributions to a scheme by employers, being factors which fall within a prescribed class or description, or

(b) the variation consists of the application of actuarial factors which differ for men and women to the determination of benefits falling within a prescribed class or description;

and in this subsection "benefits" include any payment or other benefit made to or in respect of a person as a member of the scheme.

(4) Regulations may—

(a) permit further variations, or

(b) amend or repeal subsection (2) or (3);

and regulations made by virtue of this subsection may have effect in relation to pensionable service on or after 17th May 1990 and before the date on which the regulations are made.

Disability Discrimination Act 1995

CHAPTER 50

PART I

DISABILITY

Meaning of "disability" and "disabled person"

9-001   **1.**—(1) Subject to the provisions of Schedule 1, a person has a disability for the purposes of this Act if he has a physical or mental impairment which has a substantial and long-term adverse effect on his ability to carry out normal day-to-day activities.

(2) In this Act "disabled person" means a person who has a disability.

Past disabilities

9-002   **2.**—(1) The provisions of this Part and [Parts II to IV][1] apply in relation to a person who has had a disability as they apply in relation to a person who has that disability.

(2) Those provisions are subject to the modifications made by Schedule 2

(3) Any regulations or order made under this Act may include provision with respect to persons who have had a disability.

[(3A) "Adjudicating body" means –

(a) a court;

(b) a tribunal; and

(c) any other person who, or body which, may decide a claim under Part IV.][2]

(4) In any proceedings under [Part II, III or IV][3] of this Act, the question whether a person had a disability at a particular time ("the relevant time") shall be determined, for the purposes of this section, as if the provisions of, or under, this Act in force when the act complained of was done had been in force at the relevant time.

(5) The relevant time may be a time before the passing of this Act.

Guidance

9-003   **3.**—(1) The Secretary of State may issue guidance about the matters to be taken into account in determining—

(a) whether an impairment has a substantial adverse effect on a person's ability to carry out normal day-to-day activities; or

(b) whether such an impairment has a long-term effect.

(2) The guidance may, among other things, give examples of—

(a) effects which it would be reasonable, in relation to particular activities, to regard for purposes of this Act as substantial adverse effects;

(b) effects which it would not be reasonable, in relation to particular activities, to regard for such purposes as substantial adverse effects;

---

[1] Words substituted by Special Educational Needs and Disability Act 2001 c.10 Pt II c 3 s 38 (2) (a)

[2] Inserted by Special Educational Needs and Disability Act 2001 c.10 Pt II c 3 s 38 (4)

[3] Words substituted by Special Educational Needs and Disability Act 2001 c.10 Pt II c 3 s 38 (2) (b)

(c) substantial adverse effects which it would be reasonable to regard, for such purposes, as long-term;

(d) substantial adverse effects which it would not be reasonable to regard, for such purposes, as long-term.

(3) [An adjudicating body][1] determining, for any purpose of this Act, whether an impairment has a substantial and long-term adverse effect on a person's ability to carry out normal day-to-day activities, shall take into account any guidance which appears to it to be relevant.

PART II

[THE EMPLOYMENT FIELD][2]

[Meaning of "discrimination" and "harassment"

Meaning of "discrimination"

3A.—(1) For the purposes of this Part, a person discriminates against a **9-004** disabled person if –
(a) for a reason which relates to the disabled person's disability, he treats him less favourably than he treats or would treat others to whom that reason does not or would not apply, and
(b) he cannot show that the treatment in question is justified.

(2) For the purposes of this Part, a person also discriminates against a disabled person if he fails to comply with a duty to make reasonable adjustments imposed on him in relation to the disabled person.

(3) Treatment is justified for the purposes of subsection (1)(b) if, but only if, the reason for it is both material to the circumstances of the particular case and substantial.

(4) But treatment of a disabled person cannot be justified under subsection (3) if it amounts to direct discrimination falling within subsection (5).

(5) A person directly discriminates against a disabled person if, on the ground of the disabled person's disability, he treats the disabled person less favourably than he treats or would treat a person not having that particular disability whose relevant circumstances, including his abilities, are the same as, or not materially different from, those of the disabled person.

(6) If, in a case falling within subsection (1), a person is under a duty to make reasonable adjustments in relation to a disabled person but fails to comply with that duty, his treatment of that person cannot be justified under subsection (3) unless it would have been justified even if he had complied with that duty.

Meaning of "harassment"

3B.—(1) For the purposes of this Part, a person subjects a disabled person to **9-005** harassment where, for a reason which relates to the disabled person's disability, he engages in unwanted conduct which has the purpose or effect of –
(a) violating the disabled person's dignity, or
(b) creating an intimidating, hostile, degrading, humiliating or offensive environment for him.

(2) Conduct shall be regarded as having the effect referred to in paragraph (a) or (b) of subsection (1) only if, having regard to all the circumstances,

---
[1] Words substituted by Special Educational Needs and Disability Act 2001 c.10 Pt II c 3 s 38 (3)
[2] Words substituted by SI 2003/1673 reg 4 (1), with effect October 1 2004

including in particular the perception of the disabled person, it should reasonably be considered as having that effect.]¹

[Employment

Employers: discrimination and harassment

9-006   **4.**—(1) It is unlawful for an employer to discriminate against a disabled person—

    (a) in the arrangements which he makes for the purpose of determining to whom he should offer employment;

    (b) in the terms on which he offers that person employment; or

    (c) by refusing to offer, or deliberately not offering, him employment.

(2) It is unlawful for an employer to discriminate against a disabled person whom he employs—

    (a) in the terms of employment which he affords him;

    (b) in the opportunities which he affords him for promotion, a transfer, training or receiving any other benefit;

    (c) by refusing to afford him, or deliberately not affording him, any such opportunity; or

    (d) by dismissing him, or subjecting him to any other detriment.

(3) It is also unlawful for an employer, in relation to employment by him, to subject to harassment—

    (a) a disabled person whom he employs; or

    (b) a disabled person who has applied to him for employment.

(4) Subsection (2) does not apply to benefits of any description if the employer is concerned with the provision (whether or not for payment) of benefits of that description to the public, or to a section of the public which includes the employee in question, unless—

    (a) that provision differs in a material respect from the provision of the benefits by the employer to his employees;

    (b) the provision of the benefits to the employee in question is regulated by his contract of employment; or

    (c) the benefits relate to training.

(5) The reference in subsection (2)(d) to the dismissal of a person includes a reference—

    (a) to the termination of that person's employment by the expiration of any period (including a period expiring by reference to an event or circumstance), not being a termination immediately after which the employment is renewed on the same terms; and

    (b) to the termination of that person's employment by any act of his (including the giving of notice) in circumstances such that he is entitled to terminate it without notice by reason of the conduct of the employer.

(6) This section applies only in relation to employment at an establishment in Great Britain.

Employers: duty to make adjustments

9-007   **4A.**—(1) Where—

---

¹ Inserted by SI 2003/1673 reg 4 (2), with effect October 1 2004

    (a) a provision, criterion or practice applied by or on behalf of an
        employer, or
    (b) any physical feature of premises occupied by the employer,
places the disabled person concerned at a substantial disadvantage in
comparison with persons who are not disabled, it is the duty of the employer to
take such steps as it is reasonable, in all the circumstances of the case, for him to
have to take in order to prevent the provision, criterion or practice, or feature,
having that effect.

    (2) In subsection (1), "the disabled person concerned" means –
    (a) in the case of a provision, criterion or practice for determining to
        whom employment should be offered, any disabled person who is, or has
        notified the employer that he may be, an applicant for that
        employment;
    (b) in any other case, a disabled person who is –
        (i) an applicant for the employment concerned, or
        (ii) an employee of the employer concerned.

    (3) Nothing in this section imposes any duty on an employer in relation to a
disabled person if the employer does not know, and could not reasonably be
expected to know –
    (a) in the case of an applicant or potential applicant, that the disabled
        person concerned is, or may be, an applicant for the employment; or
    (b) in any case, that that person has a disability and is likely to be affected
        in the way mentioned in subsection (1).

Contract workers

Contract workers

    4B.—(1) It is unlawful for a principal, in relation to contract work, to discrimi- **9-008**
nate against a disabled person who is a contract worker (a "disabled contract
worker")–
    (a) in the terms on which he allows him to do that work;
    (b) by not allowing him to do it or continue to do it;
    (c) in the way he affords him access to any benefits or by refusing or deliber-
        ately omitting to afford him access to them; or
    (d) by subjecting him to any other detriment.

    (2) It is also unlawful for a principal, in relation to contract work, to subject
a disabled contract worker to harassment.

    (3) Subsection (1) does not apply to benefits of any description if the
principal is concerned with the provision (whether or not for payment) of
benefits of that description to the public, or to a section of the public which
includes the contract worker in question, unless that provision differs in a
material respect from the provision of the benefits by the principal to contract
workers.

    (4) This subsection applies to a disabled contract worker where, by virtue of–
    (a) a provision, criterion or practice applied by or on behalf of all or most
        of the principals to whom he is or might be supplied, or
    (b) a physical feature of premises occupied by such persons,
he is likely, on each occasion when he is supplied to a principal to do contract
work, to be placed at a substantial disadvantage in comparison with persons who
are not disabled which is the same or similar in each case.

    (5) Where subsection (4) applies to a disabled contract worker, his employer
must take such steps as he would have to take under section 4A if the provision,

criterion or practice were applied by him or on his behalf or (as the case may be) if the premises were occupied by him.

(6) Section 4A applies to any principal, in relation to contract work, as if he were, or would be, the employer of the disabled contract worker and as if any contract worker supplied to do work for him were an employee of his.

(7) However, for the purposes of section 4A as applied by subsection (6), a principal is not required to take a step in relation to a disabled contract worker if under that section the disabled contract worker's employer is required to take the step in relation to him.

(8) This section applies only in relation to contract work done at an establishment in Great Britain (the provisions of section 68 about the meaning of "employment at an establishment in Great Britain" applying for the purposes of this subsection with the appropriate modifications).

(9) In this section—
  "principal" means a person ("A") who makes work available for doing by individuals who are employed by another person who supplies them under a contract made with A;
  "contract work" means work so made available; and
  "contract worker" means any individual who is supplied to the principal under such a contract.

Office-holders

Office-holders: introductory

9-009   **4C.**—(1) Subject to subsection (5), sections 4D and 4E apply to an office or post if—
  (a) no relevant provision of this Part applies in relation to an appointment to the office or post; and
  (b) one or more of the conditions specified in subsection (3) is satisfied.

(2) The following are relevant provisions of this Part for the purposes of subsection (1)(a): section 4, section 4B, section 6A, section 7A, section 7C and section 14C.

(3) The conditions specified in this subsection are that—
  (a) the office or post is one to which persons are appointed to discharge functions personally under the direction of another person, and in respect of which they are entitled to remuneration;
  (b) the office or post is one to which appointments are made by a Minister of the Crown, a government department, the National Assembly for Wales or any part of the Scottish Administration;
  (c) the office or post is one to which appointments are made on the recommendation of, or subject to the approval of, a person referred to in paragraph (b).

(4) For the purposes of subsection (3)(a) the holder of an office or post—
  (a) is to be regarded as discharging his functions under the direction of another person if that other person is entitled to direct him as to when and where he discharges those functions;
  (b) is not to be regarded as entitled to remuneration merely because he is entitled to payments—
    (i) in respect of expenses incurred by him in carrying out the functions of the office or post, or

(ii) by way of compensation for the loss of income or benefits he would or might have received from any person had he not been carrying out the functions of the office or post.

(5) Sections 4D and 4E do not apply to–

(a) any office of the House of Commons held by a member of it,

(b) a life peerage within the meaning of the Life Peerages Act 1958, or any office of the House of Lords held by a member of it,

(c) any office mentioned in Schedule 2 (Ministerial offices) to the House of Commons Disqualification Act 1975,

(d) the offices of Leader of the Opposition, Chief Opposition Whip or Assistant Opposition Whip within the meaning of the Ministerial and other Salaries Act 1975,

(e) any office of the Scottish Parliament held by a member of it,

(f) a member of the Scottish Executive within the meaning of section 44 of the Scotland Act 1998, or a junior Scottish Minister within the meaning of section 49 of that Act,

(g) any office of the National Assembly for Wales held by a member of it,

(h) in England, any office of a county council, a London borough council, a district council or a parish council held by a member of it,

(i) in Wales, any office of a county council, a county borough council or a community council held by a member of it,

(j) in relation to a council constituted under section 2 of the Local Government etc. (Scotland) Act 1994 or a community council established under section 51 of the Local Government (Scotland) Act 1973, any office of such a council held by a member of it,

(k) any office of the Greater London Authority held by a member of it,

(l) any office of the Common Council of the City of London held by a member of it,

(m) any office of the Council of the Isles of Scilly held by a member of it, or

(n) any office of a political party.

Office-holders: discrimination and harassment

4D.—(1) It is unlawful for a relevant person, in relation to an appointment to **9-010** an office or post to which this section applies, to discriminate against a disabled person–

(a) in the arrangements which he makes for the purpose of determining who should be offered the appointment;

(b) in the terms on which he offers him the appointment; or

(c) by refusing to offer him the appointment.

(2) It is unlawful for a relevant person, in relation to an appointment to an office or post to which this section applies and which satisfies the condition set out in section 4C(3)(c), to discriminate against a disabled person–

(a) in the arrangements which he makes for the purpose of determining who should be recommended or approved in relation to the appointment; or

(b) in making or refusing to make a recommendation, or giving or refusing to give an approval, in relation to the appointment.

(3) It is unlawful for a relevant person, in relation to a disabled person who has been appointed to an office or post to which this section applies, to discriminate against him–

(a) in the terms of the appointment;

(b) in the opportunities which he affords him for promotion, a transfer, training or receiving any other benefit, or by refusing to afford him any such opportunity;

(c) by terminating the appointment; or

(d) by subjecting him to any other detriment in relation to the appointment.

(4) It is also unlawful for a relevant person, in relation to an office or post to which this section applies, to subject to harassment a disabled person –

(a) who has been appointed to the office or post;

(b) who is seeking or being considered for appointment to the office or post; or

(c) who is seeking or being considered for a recommendation or approval in relation to an appointment to an office or post satisfying the condition set out in section 4C(3)(c).

(5) Subsection (3) does not apply to benefits of any description if the relevant person is concerned with the provision (for payment or not) of benefits of that description to the public, or a section of the public to which the disabled person belongs, unless –

(a) that provision differs in a material respect from the provision of the benefits to persons appointed to offices or posts which are the same as, or not materially different from, that to which the disabled person has been appointed;

(b) the provision of the benefits to the person appointed is regulated by the terms and conditions of his appointment; or

(c) the benefits relate to training.

(6) In subsection (3)(c) the reference to the termination of the appointment includes a reference –

(a) to the termination of the appointment by the expiration of any period (including a period expiring by reference to an event or circumstance), not being a termination immediately after which the appointment is renewed on the same terms and conditions; and

(b) to the termination of the appointment by any act of the person appointed (including the giving of notice) in circumstances such that he is entitled to terminate the appointment by reason of the conduct of the relevant person.

(7) In this section –

(a) references to making a recommendation include references to making a negative recommendation; and

(b) references to refusal include references to deliberate omission.

Office-holders: duty to make adjustments

9-011   **4E.**—(1) Where –

(a) a provision, criterion or practice applied by or on behalf of a relevant person, or

(b) any physical feature of premises –

(i) under the control of a relevant person, and

(ii) at or from which the functions of an office or post to which this section applies are performed,

places the disabled person concerned at a substantial disadvantage in comparison with persons who are not disabled, it is the duty of the relevant person to take such steps as it is reasonable, in all the circumstances of the case, for him to have to take in order to prevent the provision, criterion or practice, or feature, having that effect.

(2) In this section, "the disabled person concerned" means –

    (a) in the case of a provision, criterion or practice for determining who should be appointed to, or recommended or approved in relation to, an office or post to which this section applies, any disabled person who –

        (i) is, or has notified the relevant person that he may be, seeking appointment to, or (as the case may be) seeking a recommendation or approval in relation to, that office or post, or

        (ii) is being considered for appointment to, or (as the case may be) for a recommendation or approval in relation to, that office or post;

    (b) in any other case, a disabled person –

        (i) who is seeking or being considered for appointment to, or a recommendation or approval in relation to, the office or post concerned, or

        (ii) who has been appointed to the office or post concerned.

(3) Nothing in this section imposes any duty on the relevant person in relation to a disabled person if the relevant person does not know, and could not reasonably be expected to know –

    (a) in the case of a person who is being considered for, or is or may be seeking, appointment to, or a recommendation or approval in relation to, an office or post, that the disabled person concerned –

        (i) is, or may be, seeking appointment to, or (as the case may be) seeking a recommendation or approval in relation to, that office or post, or

        (ii) is being considered for appointment to, or (as the case may be) for a recommendation or approval in relation to, that office or post; or

    (b) in any case, that that person has a disability and is likely to be affected in the way mentioned in subsection (1).

Office-holders: supplementary

4F.—(1) In sections 4C to 4E, appointment to an office or post does not **9-012** include election to an office or post.

(2) In sections 4D and 4E, "relevant person" means –

    (a) in a case relating to an appointment to an office or post, the person with power to make that appointment;

    (b) in a case relating to the making of a recommendation or the giving of an approval in relation to an appointment, a person or body referred to in section 4C(3)(b) with power to make that recommendation or (as the case may be) to give that approval;

    (c) in a case relating to a term of an appointment, the person with power to determine that term;

    (d) in a case relating to a working condition afforded in relation to an appointment –

        (i) the person with power to determine that working condition; or

        (ii) where there is no such person, the person with power to make the appointment;

    (e) in a case relating to the termination of an appointment, the person with power to terminate the appointment;

    (f) in a case relating to the subjection of a disabled person to any other detriment or to harassment, any person or body falling within one or more of paragraphs (a) to (e) in relation to such cases as are there mentioned.

(3) In subsection (2)(d), "working condition" includes–

(a) any opportunity for promotion, a transfer, training or receiving any other benefit; and

(b) any physical feature of premises at or from which the functions of an office or post are performed.]¹

[Partnerships

Partnerships: discrimination and harassment

9-013   **6A.**—(1) It is unlawful for a firm, in relation to a position as partner in the firm, to discriminate against a disabled person–

(a) in the arrangements which they make for the purpose of determining who should be offered that position;

(b) in the terms on which they offer him that position;

(c) by refusing or deliberately omitting to offer him that position; or

(d) in a case where the person already holds that position–

(i) in the way they afford him access to any benefits or by refusing or deliberately omitting to afford him access to them; or

(ii) by expelling him from that position, or subjecting him to any other detriment.

(2) It is also unlawful for a firm, in relation to a position as partner in the firm, to subject to harassment a disabled person who holds or has applied for that position.

(3) Subsection (1) does not apply to benefits of any description if the firm are concerned with the provision (whether or not for payment) of benefits of that description to the public, or to a section of the public which includes the partner in question, unless that provision differs in a material respect from the provision of the benefits to other partners.

(4) The reference in subsection (1)(d)(ii) to the expulsion of a person from a position as partner includes a reference–

(a) to the termination of that person's partnership by the expiration of any period (including a period expiring by reference to an event or circumstance), not being a termination immediately after which the partnership is renewed on the same terms; and

(b) to the termination of that person's partnership by any act of his (including the giving of notice) in circumstances such that he is entitled to terminate it without notice by reason of the conduct of the other partners.

Partnerships: duty to make adjustments

9-014   **6B.**—(1) Where–

(a) a provision, criterion or practice applied by or on behalf of a firm, or

(b) any physical feature of premises occupied by the firm,

places the disabled person concerned at a substantial disadvantage in comparison with persons who are not disabled, it is the duty of the firm to take such steps as it is reasonable, in all the circumstances of the case, for them to have to take in order to prevent the provision, criterion or practice, or feature, having that effect.

---

¹ Sections 4, 4A–4F substituted for sections 4–6 by SI 2003/1673 reg 5, with effect October 1 2004

(2) In this section, "the disabled person concerned" means –

    (a) in the case of a provision, criterion or practice for determining to whom the position of partner should be offered, any disabled person who is, or has notified the firm that he may be, a candidate for that position;

    (b) in any other case, a disabled person who is –

        (i) a partner, or

        (ii) a candidate for the position of partner.

(3) Nothing in this section imposes any duty on a firm in relation to a disabled person if the firm do not know, and could not reasonably be expected to know –

    (a) in the case of a candidate or potential candidate, that the disabled person concerned is, or may be, a candidate for the position of partner; or

    (b) in any case, that that person has a disability and is likely to be affected in the way mentioned in subsection (1).

(4) Where a firm are required by this section to take any steps in relation to the disabled person concerned, the cost of taking those steps shall be treated as an expense of the firm; and the extent to which such cost should be borne by that person, where he is or becomes a partner in the firm, shall not exceed such amount as is reasonable, having regard in particular to the proportion in which he is entitled to share in the firm's profits.

Partnerships: supplementary

6C.—(1) Sections 6A(1)(a) to (c) and (2) and section 6B apply in relation to **9-015** persons proposing to form themselves into a partnership as they apply in relation to a firm.

(2) Sections 6A and 6B apply to a limited liability partnership as they apply to a firm; and, in the application of those sections to a limited liability partnership, references to a partner in a firm are references to a member of the limited liability partnership.

(3) In the case of a limited partnership, references in sections 6A and 6B to a partner shall be construed as references to a general partner as defined in section 3 of the Limited Partnerships Act 1907.

(4) In sections 6A and 6B and in this section, "firm" has the meaning given by section 4 of the Partnership Act 1890.][1]

    7.— [...][2]   **9-016**

[Barristers and advocates

Barristers: discrimination and harassment

7A.—(1) It is unlawful for a barrister or a barrister's clerk, in relation to any **9-017** offer of a pupillage or tenancy, to discriminate against a disabled person –

    (a) in the arrangements which are made for the purpose of determining to whom it should be offered;

    (b) in respect of any terms on which it is offered; or

    (c) by refusing, or deliberately omitting, to offer it to him.

(2) It is unlawful for a barrister or a barrister's clerk, in relation to a disabled pupil or tenant in the set of chambers in question, to discriminate against him –

---

[1] Inserted by SI 2003/1673 reg 6, with effect October 1 2004
[2] Repealed by SI 2003/1673 reg 7, with effect October 1 2004

(a) in respect of any terms applicable to him as a pupil or tenant;

(b) in the opportunities for training, or gaining experience, which are afforded or denied to him;

(c) in the benefits which are afforded or denied to him;

(d) by terminating his pupillage or by subjecting him to any pressure to leave the chambers; or

(e) by subjecting him to any other detriment.

(3) It is unlawful for a barrister or barrister's clerk, in relation to a pupillage or tenancy, to subject to harassment a disabled person who is, or has applied to be, a pupil or tenant in the set of chambers in question.

(4) It is also unlawful for any person, in relation to the giving, withholding or acceptance of instructions to a barrister, to discriminate against a disabled person or to subject him to harassment.

(5) In this section and in section 7B—

"barrister's clerk" includes any person carrying out any of the functions of a barrister's clerk;

"pupil", "pupillage" and "set of chambers" have the meanings commonly associated with their use in the context of barristers practising in independent practice; and

"tenancy" and "tenant" have the meanings commonly associated with their use in the context of barristers practising in independent practice, but they also include reference to any barrister permitted to practise from a set of chambers.

Barristers: duty to make adjustments

9-018   **7B**—(1) Where—

(a) a provision, criterion or practice applied by or on behalf of a barrister or barrister's clerk, or

(b) any physical feature of premises occupied by a barrister or a barrister's clerk,

places the disabled person concerned at a substantial disadvantage in comparison with persons who are not disabled, it is the duty of the barrister or barrister's clerk to take such steps as it is reasonable, in all the circumstances of the case, for him to have to take in order to prevent the provision, criterion or practice, or feature, having that effect.

(2) In a case where subsection (1) applies in relation to two or more barristers in a set of chambers, the duty in that subsection is a duty on each of them to take such steps as it is reasonable, in all of the circumstances of the case, for him to have to take.

(3) In this section, "the disabled person concerned" means—

(a) in the case of a provision, criterion or practice for determining to whom a pupillage or tenancy should be offered, any disabled person who is, or has notified the barrister or the barrister's clerk concerned that he may be, an applicant for a pupillage or tenancy;

(b) in any other case, a disabled person who is—

(i) a tenant;

(ii) a pupil; or

(iii) an applicant for a pupillage or tenancy.

(4) Nothing in this section imposes any duty on a barrister or a barrister's clerk in relation to a disabled person if he does not know, and could not reasonably be expected to know—

    (a) in the case of an applicant or potential applicant, that the disabled person concerned is, or may be, an applicant for a pupillage or tenancy; or

    (b) in any case, that that person has a disability and is likely to be affected in the way mentioned in subsection (1).

Advocates: discrimination and harassment

7C—(1) It is unlawful for an advocate, in relation to taking any person as his pupil, to discriminate against a disabled person–   **9-019**

    (a) in the arrangements which he makes for the purpose of determining whom he will take as his pupil;

    (b) in respect of any terms on which he offers to take the disabled person as his pupil; or

    (c) by refusing, or deliberately omitting, to take the disabled person as his pupil.

(2) It is unlawful for an advocate, in relation to a disabled person who is a pupil, to discriminate against him–

    (a) in respect of any terms applicable to him as a pupil;

    (b) in the opportunities for training, or gaining experience, which are afforded or denied to him;

    (c) in the benefits which are afforded or denied to him;

    (d) by terminating the relationship or by subjecting him to any pressure to leave; or

    (e) by subjecting him to any other detriment.

(3) It is unlawful for an advocate, in relation to taking any person as his pupil, to subject to harassment a disabled person who is, or has applied to be taken as, his pupil.

(4) It is also unlawful for any person, in relation to the giving, withholding or acceptance of instructions to an advocate, to discriminate against a disabled person or to subject him to harassment.

(5) In this section and section 7D–

    "advocate" means a member of the Faculty of Advocates practising as such; and

    "pupil" has the meaning commonly associated with its use in the context of a person training to be an advocate.

Advocates: duty to make adjustments

7D—(1) Where–   **9-020**

    (a) a provision, criterion or practice applied by or on behalf of an advocate, or

    (b) any physical feature of premises occupied by, and under the control of, an advocate,

places the disabled person concerned at a substantial disadvantage in comparison with persons who are not disabled, it is the duty of the advocate to take such steps as it is reasonable, in all the circumstances of the case, for him to have to take in order to prevent the provision, criterion or practice, or feature, having that effect.

(2) In this section, "the disabled person concerned" means–

    (a) in the case of a provision, criterion or practice for determining whom he will take as his pupil, any disabled person who has applied, or has notified the advocate that he may apply, to be taken as a pupil;

    (b) in any other case, a disabled person who is–

(i) an applicant to be taken as the advocate's pupil, or

(ii) a pupil.

(3) Nothing in this section imposes any duty on an advocate in relation to a disabled person if he does not know, and could not reasonably be expected to know—

(a) in the case of an applicant or potential applicant, that the disabled person concerned is, or may be, applying to be taken as his pupil; or

(b) in any case, that that person has a disability and is likely to be affected in the way mentioned in subsection (1).][1]

9-021   **9.**—[...][2]

9-022   **11.**—[...][3]

Discrimination by other persons

9-023   **12.**—[...][4]

[Trade and professional bodies

Trade organisations: discrimination and harassment

9-024   **13.**—(1) It is unlawful for a trade organisation to discriminate against a disabled person—

(a) in the arrangements which it makes for the purpose of determining who should be offered membership of the organisation;

(b) in the terms on which it is prepared to admit him to membership of the organisation; or

(c) by refusing to accept, or deliberately not accepting, his application for membership.

(2) It is unlawful for a trade organisation, in the case of a disabled person who is a member of the organisation, to discriminate against him—

(a) in the way it affords him access to any benefits or by refusing or deliberately omitting to afford him access to them;

(b) by depriving him of membership, or varying the terms on which he is a member; or

(c) by subjecting him to any other detriment.

(3) It is also unlawful for a trade organisation, in relation to membership of that organisation, to subject to harassment a disabled person who—

(a) is a member of the organisation; or

(b) has applied for membership of the organisation.

(4) In this section and section 14 "trade organisation" means—

(a) an organisation of workers;

(b) an organisation of employers; or

(c) any other organisation whose members carry on a particular profession or trade for the purposes of which the organisation exists.

Trade organisations: duty to make adjustments

9-025   **14.**—(1) Where—

---

[1] Inserted by SI 2003/1673 reg 8, with effect October 1 2004
[2] Repealed by SI 2003/1673 reg 9, with effect October 1 2004
[3] Repealed by SI 2003/1673 reg 12, with effect October 1 2004
[4] Repealed by SI 2003/1673 reg 12, with effect October 1 2004

    (a) a provision, criterion or practice applied by or on behalf of a trade organisation, or

    (b) any physical feature of premises occupied by the organisation,

places the disabled person concerned at a substantial disadvantage in comparison with persons who are not disabled, it is the duty of the organisation to take such steps as it is reasonable, in all the circumstances of the case, for it to have to take in order to prevent the provision, criterion or practice, or feature, having that effect.

    (2) In this section "the disabled person concerned" means –

    (a) in the case of a provision, criterion or practice for determining to whom membership should be offered, any disabled person who is, or has notified the organisation that he may be, an applicant for membership;

    (b) in any other case, a disabled person who is –

       (i) a member of the organisation, or

       (ii) an applicant for membership of the organisation.

    (3) Nothing in this section imposes any duty on an organisation in relation to a disabled person if the organisation does not know, and could not reasonably be expected to know –

    (a) in the case of an applicant or potential applicant, that the disabled person concerned is, or may be, an applicant for membership of the organisation; or

    (b) in any case, that that person has a disability and is likely to be affected in the way mentioned in subsection (1).

Qualifications bodies: discrimination and harassment

    14A—(1) It is unlawful for a qualifications body to discriminate against a **9-026** disabled person –

    (a) in the arrangements which it makes for the purpose of determining upon whom to confer a professional or trade qualification;

    (b) in the terms on which it is prepared to confer a professional or trade qualification on him;

    (c) by refusing or deliberately omitting to grant any application by him for such a qualification; or

    (d) by withdrawing such a qualification from him or varying the terms on which he holds it.

    (2) It is also unlawful for a qualifications body, in relation to a professional or trade qualification conferred by it, to subject to harassment a disabled person who holds or applies for such a qualification.

    (3) In determining for the purposes of subsection (1) whether the application by a qualifications body of a competence standard to a disabled person constitutes discrimination within the meaning of section 3A, the application of the standard is justified for the purposes of section 3A(1)(b) if, but only if, the qualifications body can show that –

    (a) the standard is, or would be, applied equally to persons who do not have his particular disability; and

    (b) its application is a proportionate means of achieving a legitimate aim.

    (4) For the purposes of subsection (3)–

    (a) section 3A(2) (and (6)) does not apply; and

    (b) section 3A(4) has effect as if the reference to section 3A(3) were a reference to subsection (3) of this section.

    (5) In this section and section 14B–

"qualifications body" means any authority or body which can confer a professional or trade qualification, but it does not include –

    (a) a responsible body (within the meaning of Chapter 1 or 2 of Part 4),

    (b) a local education authority in England or Wales, or

    (c) an education authority (within the meaning of section 135(1) of the Education (Scotland) Act 1980);

"confer" includes renew or extend;

"professional or trade qualification" means an authorisation, qualification, recognition, registration, enrolment, approval or certification which is needed for, or facilitates engagement in, a particular profession or trade;

"competence standard" means an academic, medical or other standard applied by or on behalf of a qualifications body for the purpose of determining whether or not a person has a particular level of competence or ability.

Qualifications bodies: duty to make adjustments

9-027   **14B**—(1) Where –

    (a) a provision, criterion or practice, other than a competence standard, applied by or on behalf of a qualifications body; or

    (b) any physical feature of premises occupied by a qualifications body,

places the disabled person concerned at a substantial disadvantage in comparison with persons who are not disabled, it is the duty of the qualifications body to take such steps as it is reasonable, in all the circumstances of the case, for it to have to take in order to prevent the provision, criterion or practice, or feature, having that effect.

    (2) In this section "the disabled person concerned" means –

    (a) in the case of a provision, criterion or practice for determining on whom a professional or trade qualification is to be conferred, any disabled person who is, or has notified the qualifications body that he may be, an applicant for the conferment of that qualification;

    (b) in any other case, a disabled person who –

        (i) holds a professional or trade qualification conferred by the qualifications body, or

        (ii) applies for a professional or trade qualification which it confers.

    (3) Nothing in this section imposes a duty on a qualifications body in relation to a disabled person if the body does not know, and could not reasonably be expected to know –

    (a) in the case of an applicant or potential applicant, that the disabled person concerned is, or may be, an applicant for the conferment of a professional or trade qualification; or

    (b) in any case, that that person has a disability and is likely to be affected in the way mentioned in subsection (1).

Practical work experience

Practical work experience: discrimination and harassment

9-028   **14C**—(1) It is unlawful, in the case of a disabled person seeking or undertaking a work placement, for a placement provider to discriminate against him –

    (a) in the arrangements which he makes for the purpose of determining who should be offered a work placement;

(b) in the terms on which he affords him access to any work placement or any facilities concerned with such a placement;

(c) by refusing or deliberately omitting to afford him such access;

(d) by terminating the placement; or

(e) by subjecting him to any other detriment in relation to the placement.

(2) It is also unlawful for a placement provider, in relation to a work placement, to subject to harassment–

(a) a disabled person to whom he is providing a placement; or

(b) a disabled person who has applied to him for a placement.

(3) This section and section 14D do not apply to–

(a) anything made unlawful by section 4 or any provision of Part 3 or 4; or

(b) anything which would be unlawful under that section or any such provision but for the operation of any other provision of this Act.

(4) In this section and section 14D–

"work placement" means practical work experience undertaken for a limited period for the purposes of a person's vocational training;

"placement provider" means any person who provides a work placement to a person whom he does not employ.

(5) This section and section 14D do not apply to a work placement undertaken in any of the naval, military and air forces of the Crown.

Practical work experience: duty to make adjustments

14D—(1) Where–   9-029

(a) a provision, criterion or practice applied by or on behalf of a placement provider, or

(b) any physical feature of premises occupied by the placement provider,

places the disabled person concerned at a substantial disadvantage in comparison with persons who are not disabled, it is the duty of the placement provider to take such steps as it is reasonable, in all the circumstances of the case, for him to have to take in order to prevent the provision, criterion or practice, or feature, having that effect.

(2) In this section, "the disabled person concerned" means–

(a) in the case of a provision, criterion or practice for determining to whom a work placement should be offered, any disabled person who is, or has notified the placement provider that he may be, an applicant for that work placement;

(b) in any other case, a disabled person who is–

(i) an applicant for the work placement concerned, or

(ii) undertaking a work placement with the placement provider.

(3) Nothing in this section imposes any duty on a placement provider in relation to the disabled person concerned if he does not know, and could not reasonably be expected to know–

(a) in the case of an applicant or potential applicant, that the disabled person concerned is, or may be, an applicant for the work placement; or

(b) in any case, that that person has a disability and is likely to be affected in the way mentioned in subsection (1).]¹

---

¹ Substituted by SI 2003/1673 reg 13, with effect October 1 2004

[Other unlawful acts

Relationships which have come to an end

9-030   **16A**—(1) This section applies where–
(a) there has been a relevant relationship between a disabled person and another person ("the relevant person"), and
(b) the relationship has come to an end.
(2) In this section a "relevant relationship" is–
(a) a relationship during the course of which an act of discrimination against, or harassment of, one party to the relationship by the other party to it is unlawful under any preceding provision of this Part; or
(b) a relationship between a person providing employment services (within the meaning of Part 3) and a person receiving such services.
(3) It is unlawful for the relevant person–
(a) to discriminate against the disabled person by subjecting him to a detriment, or
(b) to subject the disabled person to harassment,
where the discrimination or harassment arises out of and is closely connected to the relevant relationship.
(4) This subsection applies where–
(a) a provision, criterion or practice applied by the relevant person to the disabled person in relation to any matter arising out of the relevant relationship, or
(b) a physical feature of premises which are occupied by the relevant person,
places the disabled person at a substantial disadvantage in comparison with persons who are not disabled, but are in the same position as the disabled person in relation to the relevant person.
(5) Where subsection (4) applies, it is the duty of the relevant person to take such steps as it is reasonable, in all the circumstances of the case, for him to have to take in order to prevent the provision, practice or criterion, or feature, having that effect.
(6) Nothing in subsection (5) imposes any duty on the relevant person if he does not know, and could not reasonably be expected to know, that the disabled person has a disability and is likely to be affected in the way mentioned in that subsection.
(7) In subsection (2), reference to an act of discrimination or harassment which is unlawful includes, in the case of a relationship which has come to an end before the commencement of this section, reference to such an act which would, after the commencement of this section, be unlawful.

Discriminatory advertisements

9-031   **16B**—(1) It is unlawful for a person, in relation to a relevant appointment or benefit which he intends to make or confer, to publish or cause to be published an advertisement which–
(a) invites applications for that appointment or benefit; and
(b) indicates, or might reasonably be understood to indicate, that an application will or may be determined to any extent by reference to–
(i) the applicant not having any disability, or any particular disability, or

(ii) any reluctance of the person determining the application to comply with a duty to make reasonable adjustments or (in relation to employment services) with the duty imposed by section 21(1) as modified by section 21A(6).

(2) Subsection (1) does not apply where it would not in fact be unlawful under this Part or, to the extent that it relates to the provision of employment services, Part 3 for an application to be determined in the manner indicated (or understood to be indicated) in the advertisement.

(3) In subsection (1), "relevant appointment or benefit" means—

(a) any employment, promotion or transfer of employment;

(b) membership of, or a benefit under, an occupational pension scheme;

(c) an appointment to any office or post to which section 4D applies;

(d) any partnership in a firm (within the meaning of section 6A);

(e) any tenancy or pupillage (within the meaning of section 7A or 7C);

(f) any membership of a trade organisation (within the meaning of section 13);

(g) any professional or trade qualification (within the meaning of section 14A);

(h) any work placement (within the meaning of section 14C);

(i) any employment services (within the meaning of Part 3).

(4) In this section, "advertisement" includes every form of advertisement or notice, whether to the public or not.

Instructions and pressure to discriminate

16C—(1) It is unlawful for a person— **9-032**

(a) who has authority over another person, or

(b) in accordance with whose wishes that other person is accustomed to act,

to instruct him to do any act which is unlawful under this Part or, to the extent that it relates to the provision of employment services, Part 3, or to procure or attempt to procure the doing by him of any such act.

(2) It is also unlawful to induce, or attempt to induce, a person to do any act which contravenes this Part or, to the extent that it relates to the provision of employment services, Part 3 by—

(a) providing or offering to provide him with any benefit, or

(b) subjecting or threatening to subject him to any detriment.

(3) An attempted inducement is not prevented from falling within subsection (2) because it is not made directly to the person in question, if it is made in such a way that he is likely to hear of it.][1]

Occupational pension schemes [...][2]

Occupational pension schemes

17.—(1) Every occupational pension scheme shall be taken to include a **9-033** provision ("a non-discrimination rule")—

(a) relating to the terms on which—

(i) persons become members of the scheme; and

(ii) members of the scheme are treated; and

---

[1] Inserted by SI 2003/1673 reg 15 (1), with effect October 1 2004

[2] Words repealed by SI 2003/1673 reg 15 (2), with effect October 1 2004

(b) requiring the trustees or managers of the scheme to refrain from any act or omission which, if done in relation to a person by an employer, would amount to unlawful discrimination against that person for the purposes of this Part.

(2) The other provisions of the scheme are to have effect subject to the non-discrimination rule.

(3) Without prejudice to section 67, regulations under this Part may—

(a) with respect to trustees or managers of occupational pension schemes make different provision from that made with respect to employers; or

(b) make provision modifying the application to such trustees or managers of any regulations made under this Part, or of any provisions of this Part so far as they apply to employers.

(4) In determining, for the purposes of this section, whether an act or omission would amount to unlawful discrimination if done by an employer, any provision made under subsection (3) shall be applied as if it applied in relation to the notional employer.

Enforcement etc

Enforcement, remedies and procedure

9-034 17A.—(1) A complaint by any person that another person—

(a) has discriminated against him [, or subjected him to harassment,]¹ in a way which is unlawful under this Part, or

(b) is, by virtue of section 57 or 58, to be treated as having [done so]²,

may be presented to an [employment tribunal]³.

[(1A) Subsection (1) does not apply to a complaint under section 14A (1) or (2) of an act in respect of which an appeal, or proceedings in the nature of an appeal, may be brought under any enactment.

(1B) In subsection (1A), "enactment" includes an enactment comprised in, or in an instrument made under, an Act of the Scottish Parliament.

(1C) Where, on the hearing of a complaint under subsection (1), the complainant proves facts from which the tribunal could, apart from this subsection, conclude in the absence of an adequate explanation that the respondent has acted in a way which is unlawful under this Part, the tribunal shall uphold the complaint unless the respondent proves that he did not so act.]⁴

(2) Where an [employment tribunal]⁵ finds that a complaint presented to it under this section is well-founded, it shall take such of the following steps as it considers just and equitable—

(a) making a declaration as to the rights of the complainant and the respondent in relation to the matters to which the complaint relates;

(b) ordering the respondent to pay compensation to the complainant;

(c) recommending that the respondent take, within a specified period, action appearing to the tribunal to be reasonable, in all the circumstances of the case, for the purpose of obviating or reducing the adverse effect on the complainant of any matter to which the complaint relates.

(3) Where a tribunal orders compensation under subsection (2)(b), the amount of the compensation shall be calculated by applying the principles

---

¹ Words inserted by SI 2003/1673 reg 9 (2) (a), with effect October 1 2004
² Words substituted by SI 2003/1673 reg 9 (2) (b), with effect October 1 2004
³ Words substituted by Employment Rights (Dispute Resolution) Act 1998 c.8 Pt I s 1 (2)
⁴ Inserted by SI 2003/1673 reg 9 (2) (c), with effect October 1 2004
⁵ Words substituted by Employment Rights (Dispute Resolution) Act 1998 c.8 Pt I s 1 (2)

applicable to the calculation of damages in claims in tort or (in Scotland) in reparation for breach of statutory duty.

(4) For the avoidance of doubt it is hereby declared that compensation in respect of discrimination in a way which is unlawful under this Part may include compensation for injury to feelings whether or not it includes compensation under any other head.

(5) If the respondent to a complaint fails, without reasonable justification, to comply with a recommendation made by an [employment tribunal][1] under subsection (2)(c) the tribunal may, if it thinks it just and equitable to do so—

(a) increase the amount of compensation required to be paid to the complainant in respect of the complaint, where an order was made under subsection (2)(b); or

(b) make an order under subsection (2)(b).

(6) Regulations may make provision—

(a) for enabling a tribunal, where an amount of compensation falls to be awarded under subsection (2)(b), to include in the award interest on that amount; and

(b) specifying, for cases where a tribunal decides that an award is to include an amount in respect of interest, the manner in which and the periods and rate by reference to which the interest is to be determined.

(7) Regulations may modify the operation of any order made under [section 14 of the Employment Tribunals Act 1996][2] (power to make provision as to interest on sums payable in pursuance of [employment tribunal][3] decisions) to the extent that it relates to an award of compensation under subsection (2)(b).

(8) Part I of Schedule 3 makes further provision about the enforcement of this Part and about procedure.

[Enforcement of sections 16B and 16C

17B.—(1) Only the Disability Rights Commission may bring proceedings in **9-035** respect of a contravention of section 16B (discriminatory advertisements) or section 16C (instructions and pressure to discriminate).

(2) The Commission shall bring any such proceedings in accordance with subsection (3) or (4).

(3) The Commission may present to an employment tribunal a complaint that a person has done an act which is unlawful under section 16B or 16C; and if the tribunal finds that the complaint is well-founded it shall make a declaration to that effect.

(4) Where–

(a) a tribunal has made a finding pursuant to subsection (3) that a person has done an act which is unlawful under section 16B or 16C,

(b) that finding has become final, and

(c) it appears to the Commission that, unless restrained, he is likely to do a further act which is unlawful under that section,

the Commission may apply to a county court for an injunction, or (in Scotland) to a sheriff court for an interdict, restraining him from doing such an act; and the court, if satisfied that the application is well-founded, may grant the injunction or interdict in the terms applied for or in more limited terms.

---

[1] Words substituted by Employment Rights (Dispute Resolution) Act 1998 c.8 Pt I s 1 (2)

[2] Words "Industrial Tribunals Act" substituted with "Employment Tribunals Act" by virtue of an amendment already made by 1996 c.17 Sch.1 para 12 (2) by Employment Rights (Dispute Resolution) Act 1998 c.8 Pt I s 1 (2) (c)

[3] Words substituted by Employment Rights (Dispute Resolution) Act 1998 c.8 Pt I s 1 (2)

(5) A finding of a tribunal under subsection (3) in respect of any act shall, if it has become final, be treated as conclusive by a county court or sheriff court upon an application under subsection (4).

(6) A finding of a tribunal becomes final for the purposes of this section when an appeal against it is dismissed, withdrawn or abandoned or when the time for appealing expires without an appeal having been brought.

(7) An employment tribunal shall not consider a complaint under subsection (3) unless it is presented before the end of the period of six months beginning when the act to which it relates was done; and a county court or sheriff court shall not consider an application under subsection (4) unless it is made before the end of the period of five years so beginning.

(8) A court or tribunal may consider any such complaint or application which is out of time if, in all the circumstances of the case, it considers that it is just and equitable to do so.

(9) The provisions of paragraph 3(3) and (4) of Schedule 3 apply for the purposes of subsection (7) as they apply for the purposes of paragraph 3(1) of that Schedule.

Validity of contracts, collective agreements and rules of undertakings

9-036   **17C.** Schedule 3A shall have effect.][1]

[Supplementary and general][2]

Insurance services

9-037   **18.**—(1) This section applies where a provider of insurance services ("the insurer") enters into arrangements with an employer under which the employer's employees, or a class of his employees—

  (a) receive insurance services provided by the insurer; or

  (b) are given an opportunity to receive such services.

(2) The insurer is to be taken, for the purposes of this Part, to discriminate unlawfully against a disabled person who is a relevant employee if he acts in relation to that employee in a way which would be unlawful discrimination for the purposes of Part III if—

  (a) he were providing the service in question to members of the public; and

  (b) the employee was provided with, or was trying to secure the provision of, that service as a member of the public.

(3) In this section—

  "insurance services" means services of a prescribed description for the provision of benefits in respect of—

      (a) termination of service;

      (b) retirement, old age or death;

      (c) accident, injury, sickness or invalidity; or

      (d) any other prescribed matter; and

  "relevant employee" means—

      (a) in the case of an arrangement which applies to employees of the employer in question, an employee of his;

---

[1] Words inserted by SI 2003/1673 reg 16 (1), with effect October 1 2004
[2] Words inserted by SI 2003/1673 reg 17 (1), with effect October 1 2004

(b) in the case of an arrangement which applies to a class of employees of the employer, an employee who is in that class.

(4) For the purposes of the definition of "relevant employee" in subsection (3), "employee", in relation to an employer, includes a person who has applied for, or is contemplating applying for, employment by that employer or (as the case may be) employment by him in the class in question.

18A.—(1) This section applies where— **9-038**
- (a) [a person to whom a duty to make reasonable adjustments applies][1] ("the occupier") occupies premises under a lease;
- (b) but for this section, the occupier would not be entitled to make a particular alteration to the premises; and
- (c) the alteration is one which the occupier proposes to make in order to comply with [that duty][2].

(2) Except to the extent to which it expressly so provides, the lease shall have effect by virtue of this subsection as if it provided—
- (a) for the occupier to be entitled to make the alteration with the written consent of the lessor;
- (b) for the occupier to have to make a written application to the lessor for consent if he wishes to make the alteration;
- (c) if such an application is made, for the lessor not to withhold his consent unreasonably; and
- (d) for the lessor to be entitled to make his consent subject to reasonable conditions.

(3) In this section—
"lease" includes a tenancy, sub-lease or sub-tenancy and an agreement for a lease, tenancy, sub-lease or sub-tenancy; and
"sub-lease" and "sub-tenancy" have such meaning as may be prescribed.

(4) If the terms and conditions of a lease—
- (a) impose conditions which are to apply if the occupier alters the premises, or
- (b) entitle the lessor to impose conditions when consenting to the occupier's altering the premises,

the occupier is to be treated for the purposes of subsection (1) as not being entitled to make the alteration.

(5) Part I of Schedule 4 supplements the provisions of this section.

[Reasonable adjustments: supplementary

18B.—(1) In determining whether it is reasonable for a person to have to take **9-039** a particular step in order to comply with a duty to make reasonable adjustments, regard shall be had, in particular, to–
- (a) the extent to which taking the step would prevent the effect in relation to which the duty is imposed;
- (b) the extent to which it is practicable for him to take the step;
- (c) the financial and other costs which would be incurred by him in taking the step and the extent to which taking it would disrupt any of his activities;
- (d) the extent of his financial and other resources;
- (e) the availability to him of financial or other assistance with respect to taking the step;

---

[1] Words substituted by SI 2003/1673 reg 14 (3) (a), with effect October 1 2004
[2] Words substituted by SI 2003/1673 reg 14 (3) (b), with effect October 1 2004

(f) the nature of his activities and the size of his undertaking;

(g) where the step would be taken in relation to a private household, the extent to which taking it would–
   (i) disrupt that household, or
   (ii) disturb any person residing there.

(2) The following are examples of steps which a person may need to take in relation to a disabled person in order to comply with a duty to make reasonable adjustments–

(a) making adjustments to premises;

(b) allocating some of the disabled person's duties to another person;

(c) transferring him to fill an existing vacancy;

(d) altering his hours of working or training;

(e) assigning him to a different place of work or training;

(f) allowing him to be absent during working or training hours for rehabilitation, assessment or treatment;

(g) giving, or arranging for, training or mentoring (whether for the disabled person or any other person);

(h) acquiring or modifying equipment;

(i) modifying instructions or reference manuals;

(j) modifying procedures for testing or assessment;

(k) providing a reader or interpreter;

(l) providing supervision or other support.

(3) For the purposes of a duty to make reasonable adjustments, where under any binding obligation a person is required to obtain the consent of another person to any alteration of the premises occupied by him–

(a) it is always reasonable for him to have to take steps to obtain that consent; and

(b) it is never reasonable for him to have to make that alteration before that consent is obtained.

(4) The steps referred to in subsection (3)(a) shall not be taken to include an application to a court or tribunal.

(5) In subsection (3), "binding obligation" means a legally binding obligation (not contained in a lease (within the meaning of section 18A(3)) in relation to the premises, whether arising from an agreement or otherwise.

(6) A provision of this Part imposing a duty to make reasonable adjustments applies only for the purpose of determining whether a person has discriminated against a disabled person; and accordingly a breach of any such duty is not actionable as such.][1]

[Charities and support for particular groups of persons

9-040   **18C.**—(1) Nothing in this Part—

(a) affects any charitable instrument which provides for conferring benefits on one or more categories of person determined by reference to any physical or mental capacity; or

(b) makes unlawful any act done by a charity or recognised body in pursuance of any of its charitable purposes, so far as those purposes are connected with persons so determined.

(2) Nothing in this Part prevents—

(a) a person who provides supported employment from treating members of a particular group of disabled persons more favourably than other persons in providing such employment; or

---

[1] Inserted by SI 2003/1673 reg 17 (2), with effect October 1 2004

(b) the Secretary of State from agreeing to arrangements for the provision of supported employment which will, or may, have that effect.

(3) In this section—

"charitable instrument" means an enactment or other instrument (whenever taking effect) so far as it relates to charitable purposes;

"charity" has the same meaning as in the Charities Act 1993;

"recognised body" means a body which is a recognised body for the purposes of Part I of the Law Reform (Miscellaneous Provisions) (Scotland) Act 1990; and

"supported employment" means facilities provided, or in respect of which payments are made, under section 15 of the Disabled Persons (Employment) Act 1944.

(4) In the application of this section to England and Wales, "charitable purposes" means purposes which are exclusively charitable according to the law of England and Wales.

(5) In the application of this section to Scotland, "charitable purposes" shall be construed in the same way as if it were contained in the Income Tax Acts.][1]

[Interpretation of Part 2

18D.—(1) Subject to any duty to make reasonable adjustments, nothing in **9-041** this Part is to be taken to require a person to treat a disabled person more favourably than he treats or would treat others.

(2) In this Part–

"benefits" includes facilities and services;

"detriment", except in section 16C(2)(b), does not include conduct of the nature referred to in section 3B (harassment);

"discriminate", "discrimination" and other related expressions are to be construed in accordance with section 3A;

"duty to make reasonable adjustments" means a duty imposed by or under section 4A, 4B(5) or (6), 4E, 6B, 7B, 7D, 14, 14B, 14D or 16A(5);

"employer" includes a person who has no employees but is seeking to employ another person;

"harassment" is to be construed in accordance with section 3B;

"physical feature", in relation to any premises, includes any of the following (whether permanent or temporary)–

(a) any feature arising from the design or construction of a building on the premises,

(b) any feature on the premises of any approach to, exit from or access to such a building,

(c) any fixtures, fittings, furnishings, furniture, equipment or material in or on the premises,

(d) any other physical element or quality of any land comprised in the premises;

"provision, criterion or practice" includes any arrangements.][2]

---

[1] Existing s 10 moved to follow s 18B and renumbered as s 18C by SI 2003/1673 reg 11
[2] Inserted by SI 2003/1673 reg 18, with effect October 1 2004

PART VII

SUPPLEMENTAL

[Codes of practice

9-042   **53A.**—[(1) The Disability Rights Commission may prepare and issue codes of practice giving practical guidance on how to avoid [acts which are unlawful under Part 2, 3 or 4][1], or on any other matter relating to the operation of any provision of [those Parts][2], to—

   (a) employers;
   (b) service providers;
   (c) bodies which are responsible bodies for the purposes of Chapter 1 or 2 of Part 4; or
   (d) other persons to whom the provisions of Parts 2 or 3 or Chapter 2 of Part 4 apply.

(1A) The Commission may also prepare and issue codes of practice giving practical guidance to any persons on any other matter with a view to—

   (a) promoting the equalisation of opportunities for disabled persons and persons who have had a disability; or
   (b) encouraging good practice in the way such persons are treated,

in any field of activity regulated by any provision of Part 2, 3 or 4.][3]][4]

(1B) Neither subsection (1) nor (1A) applies in relation to any duty imposed by or under sections 28D or 28E.

(2) The Commission shall, when requested to do so by the Secretary of State, prepare a code of practice dealing with the matters specified in the request.

(3) In preparing a code of practice the Commission shall carry out such consultations as it considers appropriate (which shall include the publication for public consultation of proposals relating to the code).

(4) The Commission may not issue a code of practice unless—

   (a) a draft of it has been submitted to and approved by the Secretary of State and laid by him before both Houses of Parliament; and
   (b) the 40 day period has elapsed without either House resolving not to approve the draft.

(5) If the Secretary of State does not approve a draft code of practice submitted to him he shall give the Commission a written statement of his reasons.

(6) A code of practice issued by the Commission—

   (a) shall come into effect on such day as the Secretary of State may by order appoint;
   (b) may be revised in whole or part, and re-issued, by the Commission; and
   (c) may be revoked by an order made by the Secretary of State at the request of the Commission.

(7) Where the Commission proposes to revise a code of practice—

   (a) it shall comply with subsection (3) in relation to the revisions; and
   (b) the other provisions of this section apply to the revised code of practice as they apply to a new code of practice.

---

[1] Words substituted by SI 2003/1673 reg 20 (a) (i), with effect October 1 2004
[2] Words substituted by SI 2003/1673 reg 20 (a) (ii), with effect October 1 2004
[3] Substituted by Special Educational Needs and Disability Act 2001 c.10 Pt II c 3 s 36 (2)
[4] Inserted by Disability Rights Commission Act 1999 c.17 s 9 (1)

(8) Failure to observe any provision of a code of practice does not of itself make a person liable to any proceedings.

(8A) But if a provision of a code of practice appears to a court, tribunal or other body hearing any proceedings under Part 2, 3 or 4 to be relevant, it must take that provision into account.

(9) In this section—

"code of practice" means a code of practice under this section; [and][1]

[...][2]

"40 day period" has the same meaning in relation to a draft code of practice as it has in section 3 in relation to draft guidance.

Further provision about codes issued under section 53

54.—(8) The Secretary of State may by order revoke a code.   **9-043**

[...][3]

Victimisation

55.—(1) For the purposes of [Part II, Part 3 or Part 4][4], a person ("A") discri- **9-044** minates against another person ("B") if—

    (a) he treats B less favourably than he treats or would treat other persons whose circumstances are the same as B's; and

    (b) he does so for a reason mentioned in subsection (2).

(2) The reasons are that—

    (a) B has—

        (i) brought proceedings against A or any other person under this Act; or

        (ii) given evidence or information in connection with such proceedings brought by any person; or

        (iii) otherwise done anything under this Act in relation to A or any other person; or

        (iv) alleged that A or any other person has (whether or not the allegation so states) contravened this Act; or

    (b) A believes or suspects that B has done or intends to do any of those things.

(3) Where B is a disabled person, or a person who has had a disability, the disability in question shall be disregarded in comparing his circumstances with those of any other person for the purposes of subsection (1)(a).

[(3A) For the purposes of Chapter 1 of Part 4–

    (a) references in subsection (2) to B include references to–

        (i) a person who is, for the purposes of that Chapter, B's parent; and

        (ii) a sibling of B; and

    (b) references in that subsection to this Act are, as respects a person mentioned in sub-paragraph (i) or (ii) of paragraph (a), restricted to that Chapter.][5]

(4) Subsection (1) does not apply to treatment of a person because of an allegation made by him if the allegation was false and not made in good faith.

---

[1] Word inserted by SI 2003/1673 Pt II reg 20 (b), with effect October 1 2004

[2] Definition repealed by SI 2003/1673 Pt II reg 20 (b), with effect October 1 2004

[3] Subsections (1)-(7) and (9) repealed by Disability Rights Commission Act 1999 c.17 Sch 5

[4] Words substituted by Special Educational Needs and Disability Act 2001 c.10 Pt II c 3 s 38 (7)

[5] Inserted by Special Educational Needs and Disability Act 2001 c.10 Pt II c 3 s 38 (8)

(5) In the case of an act which constitutes discrimination by virtue of this section, sections 4, 4B, 4D, 6A, 7A, 7C, 13, 14A, 14C and 16A also apply to discrimination against a person who is not disabled.

(6) For the purposes of Part 2 and, to the extent that it relates to the provision of employment services, Part 3, subsection (2)(a) (iii) has effect as if there were inserted after "under" "or by reference to".

Help for persons suffering discrimination

9-045   **56.**—(1) For the purposes of this section—

  (a) a person who considers that he may have been discriminated against [or subjected to harassment][1], in contravention of any provision of Part II [or, to the extent that it relates to the provision of employment services, Part 3][2], is referred to as "the complainant"; and

  (b) a person against whom the complainant may decide to make, or has made, a complaint under Part II [or, to the extent that it relates to the provision of employment services, Part 3][3] is referred to as "the respondent".

(2) The Secretary of State shall, with a view to helping the complainant to decide whether to make a complainant against the respondent and, if he does so, to formulate and present his case in the most effective manner, by order prescribe—

  (a) forms by which the complainant may question the respondent on his reasons for doing any relevant act, or on any other matter which is or may be relevant; and

  (b) forms by which the respondent may if he so wishes reply to any questions.

(3) Where the complainant questions the respondent in accordance with forms prescribed by an order under subsection (2)—

  (a) the question, and any reply by the respondent (whether in accordance with such an order or not), shall be admissible as evidence in any proceedings under Part II [or, to the extent that it relates to the provision of employment services, Part 3][4];

  (b) if it appears to the tribunal in any such proceedings—

    (i) that the respondent deliberately, and without reasonable excuse, omitted to reply within [the period of eight weeks beginning with the day on which the question was served on him][5], or

    (ii) that the respondent's reply is evasive or equivocal, it may draw any inference which it considers it just and equitable to draw, including an inference that the respondent has contravened a provision of Part II [or, to the extent that it relates to the provision of employment services, Part 3][6].

(4) The Secretary of State may by order prescribe—

  (a) the period within which questions must be duly served in order to be admissible under subsection (3)(a); and

  (b) the manner in which a question, and any reply by the respondent, may be duly served.

---

[1] Words inserted by SI 2003/1673 reg 22 (b), with effect October 1 2004
[2] Words inserted by SI 2003/1673 reg 22 (a), with effect October 1 2004
[3] Words inserted by SI 2003/1673 reg 22 (a), with effect October 1 2004
[4] Words inserted by SI 2003/1673 reg 22 (a), with effect October 1 2004
[5] Words substituted by SI 2003/1673 reg 22 (c), with effect October 1 2004
[6] Words inserted by SI 2003/1673 reg 22 (a), with effect October 1 2004

(5) This section is without prejudice to any other enactment or rule of law regulating interlocutory and preliminary matters in proceedings before an [employment tribunal][1], and has effect subject to any enactment or rule of law regulating the admissibility of evidence in such proceedings.

Aiding unlawful acts

57.—(1) A person who knowingly aids another person to do an [unlawful **9-046** act][2] is to be treated for the purposes of this Act as himself doing the same kind of unlawful act.

(2) For the purposes of subsection (1), an employee or agent for whose act the employer or principal is liable under section 58 (or would be so liable but for section 58(5)) shall be taken to have aided the employer or principal to do the act.

(3) For the purposes of this section, a person does not knowingly aid another to do an unlawful act if—

(a) he acts in reliance on a statement made to him by that other person that, because of any provision of this Act, the act would not be unlawful; and

(b) it is reasonable for him to rely on the statement.

(4) A person who knowingly or recklessly makes such a statement which is false or misleading in a material respect is guilty of an offence.

(5) Any person guilty of an offence under subsection (4) shall be liable on summary conviction to a fine not exceeding level 5 on the standard scale.

[(6) "Unlawful act" means an act made unlawful by any provision of this Act other than a provision contained in Chapter 1 of Part 4.][3]

Liability of employers and principals

58.—(1) Anything done by a person in the course of his employment shall be **9-047** treated for the purposes of this Act as also done by his employer, whether or not it was done with the employer's knowledge or approval.

(2) Anything done by a person as agent for another person with the authority of that other person shall be treated for the purposes of this Act as also done by that other person.

(3) Subsection (2) applies whether the authority was—

(a) express or implied; or

(b) given before or after the act in question was done.

(4) Subsections (1) and (2) do not apply in relation to an offence under section 57(4).

(5) In proceedings under this Act against any person in respect of an act alleged to have been done by an employee of his, it shall be a defence for that person to prove that he took such steps as were reasonably practicable to prevent the employee from—

(a) doing that act; or

(b) doing, in the course of his employment, acts of that description.

---

[1] Words substituted by Employment Rights (Dispute Resolution) Act 1998 c.8 Pt I s 1 (2)
[2] Words substituted by Special Educational Needs and Disability Act 2001 c.10 Pt II c 3 s 38 (9)
[3] Inserted by Special Educational Needs and Disability Act 2001 c.10 Pt II c 3 s 38 (10)

PART VIII

MISCELLANEOUS

Interpretation

9-048   **68.**—(1) In this Act—

"accessibility certificate" means a certificate issued under section 41(1)(a);

"act"includes a deliberate omission;

"approval certificate" means a certificate issued under section 42(4);

[...][1]

"conciliation officer" means a person designated under section 211 of the Trade Union and Labor Relations (Consolidated) Act 1992;

"employment" means , subject to any prescribed provision, employment under a contract of service or of apprenticeship or a contract personally to do any work, and related expressions are to be construed accordingly;

["employment at an establishment in Great Britain" is to be construed in accordance with subsections (2) to (4A)][2];

"enactment" includes subordinate legislation and any Order in Council;

["Great Britain" includes such of the territorial waters of the United Kingdom as are adjacent to Great Britain;][3]

"licensing authority" means —

(a) in relation to the area to which the Metropolitan Public Carriage Act 1869 applies, the Secretary of State or the holder of any office for the time being designated by the Secretary of State; or

(b) in relation to any other area in England and Wales, the authority responsible for licensing taxis in that area;

"mental impairment" does not have the same meaning as in the Mental Health Act 1983 or the Mental Health (Scotland) Act 1984 but the fact that an impairment would be a mental impairment for the purposes of either of those Acts does not prevent it from being a mental impairment for the purposes of this Act;

["Minister of the Crown" includes the Treasury and the Defence Council][4];

"occupational pension scheme" has the same meaning as in the Pension Schemes Act 1993;

"Premises" includes land of any description;

"prescribed" means prescribed by regulations;

"profession" includes any vocation or occupation;

"provider of services" has the meaning given in section 19(2)(b);

"public service vehicle" and "regulated public service vehicle" have the meaning given in section 40;

"PSV accessibility regulations" means regulations made under section 40(1);

"rail vehicle" and "regulated rail vehicle" have the meaning given in section 46;

"rails vehicle accessibility regulations" means regulations made under section 46(1);

---

[1] Definition repealed by SI 2003/1673 reg 27 (a) (i), with effect October 1 2004
[2] Definition substituted by SI 2003/1673 reg 27 (a) (ii), with effect October 1 2004
[3] Definition inserted by SI 2003/1673 reg 27 (a) (iii), with effect October 1 2004
[4] Definition inserted by SI 2003/1673 reg 27 (a) (iv), with effect October 1 2004

"regulations" means regulations made by the Secretary of State;

[...]¹

[...]²

"section 21 duty" means any duty imposed by or under section 21;

"subordinate legislation" has the same meaning as in section 21 of the Interpretation Act 1978;

"taxi" and "regulated taxi" have the meaning given in section 32;

"taxi accessibility regulations" means regulations made under section 32(1);

"trade" includes any business;

"trade organisation" has the meaning given in section 13;

"vehicle examiner" means an examiner appointed under section 66A of the Road Traffic Act 1988.

[(2) Employment (including employment on board a ship to which subsection (2B) applies or on an aircraft or hovercraft to which subsection (2C) applies) is to be regarded as being employment at an establishment in Great Britain if the employee –

(a) does his work wholly or partly in Great Britain; or

(b) does his work wholly outside Great Britain and subsection (2A) applies.

(2A) This subsection applies if –

(a) the employer has a place of business at an establishment in Great Britain;

(b) the work is for the purposes of the business carried on at the establishment; and

(c) the employee is ordinarily resident in Great Britain –

(i) at the time when he applies for or is offered the employment, or

(ii) at any time during the course of the employment.

(2B) This subsection applies to a ship if –

(a) it is registered at a port of registry in Great Britain; or

(b) it belongs to or is possessed by Her Majesty in right of the Government of the United Kingdom.

(2C) This subsection applies to an aircraft or hovercraft if –

(a) it is –

(i) registered in the United Kingdom, and

(ii) operated by a person who has his principal place of business, or is ordinarily resident, in Great Britain; or

(b) it belongs to or is possessed by Her Majesty in right of the Government of the United Kingdom.

(2D) The following are not to be regarded as being employment at an establishment in Great Britain –

(a) employment on board a ship to which subsection (2B) does not apply;

(b) employment on an aircraft or hovercraft to which subsection (2C) does not apply.]³

(4) Employment of a prescribed kind, or in prescribed circumstances, is to be regarded as not being employment at an establishment in Great Britain.

[(4A) For the purposes of determining if employment concerned with the exploration of the sea bed or sub-soil or the exploitation of their natural resources is outside Great Britain, subsections (2)(a) and (b), (2A) and (2C) of this section

---

¹ Definition repealed by SI 2003/1673 reg 27 (a) (i), with effect October 1 2004
² Definition repealed by SI 2003/1673 reg 27 (a) (i), with effect October 1 2004
³ Substituted by SI 2003/1673 reg 27 (b), with effect October 1 2004

each have effect as if "Great Britain" had the same meaning as that given to the last reference to Great Britain in section 10(1) of the Sex Discrimination Act 1975 by section 10(5) of that Act read with the Sex Discrimination and Equal Pay (Offshore Employment) Order 1987.][1]

(5) [...][2]

SCHEDULES

Section 1(1)   Schedule 1

PROVISIONS SUPPLEMENTING SECTION 1

Impairment

9-049   **1.**— (1) "Mental impairment"includes an impairment resulting from or consisting of a mental illness only if the illness is a clinically well-recognised illness.

(2) Regulations may make provision, for the purposes of this Act—

(a) for conditions of a prescribed description to be treated as amounting to impairments;

(b) for conditions of a prescribed description to be treated as not amounting to impairments.

(3) Regulations made under sub-paragraph (2) may make provision as to the meaning of "condition" for the purposes of those regulations.

Long-term effects

9-050   **2.**— [(1) The effect of an impairment is a long-term effect if it has lasted for at least 12 months.

(2) Where an impairment ceases to have a substantial adverse effect on a person's ability to carry out normal day-to-day activities, it is to be treated as continuing to have that effect if that effect recurs.

(3) For the purposes of sub-paragraph (2), the recurrence of an effect shall be disregarded in prescribed circumstances.][3]

(4) Regulations may prescribe circumstances in which, for the purposes of this Act—

(a) an effect which would not otherwise be a long-term effect is to be treated as such an effect; or

(b) an effect which would otherwise be a long-term effect is to be treated as not being such an effect.

Severe disfigurement

9-051   **3.**— (1) An impairment which consists of a severe disfigurement is to be treated as having a substantial adverse effect on the ability of the person concerned to carry out normal day-to-day activities.

(2) Regulations may provide that in prescribed circumstances a severe disfigurement is not to be treated as having that effect.

(3) Regulations under sub-paragraph (2) may, in particular, make provision with respect to deliberately acquired disfigurements.

Normal day-to-day activities

9-052   **4.**— (1) An impairment is to be taken to affect the ability of the person concerned to carry out normal day-to-day activities only if it affects one of the following—

(a) mobility;

(b) manual dexterity;

(c) physical co-ordination;

(d) continence;

(e) ability to life, carry or otherwise move everyday objects;

(f) speech, hearing or eyesight;

(g) memory or ability to concentrate, learn or understand; or

(h) perception of the risk of physical danger.

---

[1] Inserted by SI 2003/1673 reg 27 (c), with effect October 1 2004
[2] Repealed by SI 2003/1673 reg 27 (d), with effect October 1 2004
[3] Substituted by Disability Discrimination Act 1995 c.50 Sch 2 para 5

(2) Regulations may prescribe—
    (a) circumstances in which an impairment which does not have an effect falling within sub-paragraph (1) is to be taken to affect the ability of the person concerned to scary out normal day-to-day activities;
    (b) circumstances in which an impairment which has an effect falling within sub-paragraph (1) is to be taken not to affect the ability of the person concerned to carry out normal day-to-day activities.

Substantial adverse effects

5. Regulations may make provisions for the purposes of this Act—   **9-053**
    (a) for an effect of a prescribed kind on the ability of a person to carry out normal day-to-day activities to be treated as a substantial adverse effect;
    (b) for an effect of a prescribed kind on the ability of a person to carry out normal day-to-day activities to be treated as not being a substantial adverse effect.

Effect of medical treatment

6.— (1) An impairment which would be likely to have a substantial adverse effect on the ability **9-054** of the person concerned to carry out normal day-to-day activities, but for the fact that measures are being taken to treat or correct it, is to be treated as having that effect.
    (2) In sub-paragraph (1) "measures"includes, in particular, medical treatment and the use of a prosthesis or other aid.
    (3) Sub-paragraph (1) does not apply—
    (a) in relation to the impairment of a person's sight, to the extent that the impairment is, in his case, correctable by spectacles or contact lenses or in such other ways as may be prescribed; or
    (b) in relation to such other impairments as may be prescribed, in such circumstances as may be prescribed.

Persons deemed to be disabled

7.— (1) Sub-paragraph (2) applies to any person whose name is, both on 12th January 1995 and **9-055** on the date when this paragraph comes into force, in the register of disabled persons maintained under section 6 of the Disabled Persons (Employment) Act 1944.
    (2) That person is to be deemed—
    (a) during the initial period, to have disability, and hence to be a disabled person; and
    (b) afterwards, to have had a disability and hence to have been a disabled person during that period.
    (3) A certificate of registration shall be conclusive evidence, in relation to the person with respect to whom it was issued, of the matters certified.
    (4) Unless the contrary is shown, any document purporting to be a certificate of registration shall be taken to be such a certificate and to have been validly issued.
    (5) Regulations may provide for prescribed descriptions of person to be deemed to have disabilities, and hence to be disabled persons, for the purpose of this Act.
    (6) Regulations may prescribe circumstances in which a person who has been deemed to be a disabled person by the provisions of sub-paragraph (1) or regulations made under sub-paragraph (5) is to be treated as no longer being deemed to be such a person.
    (7) In this paragraph—
    "certificate of registration" means a certificate issued under regulations made under regulations made under section 6 of the Act of 1944; and
    "initial period" means the period of three years beginning with the date on which this paragraph comes into force.

Progressive conditions

8.— (1) Where—   **9-056**
    (a) a person has a progressive condition (such as cancer, multiple sclerosis or muscular dystrophy or infection by the human immunodeficiency virus),
    (b) as a result of that condition, he has an impairment which has (or had) an effect on his ability to carry out normal day-to-day activities, but
    (c) that effect is not (or was not) a substantial adverse effect,
he shall be taken to have an impairment which has such a substantial adverse effect if the condition is likely to result in his having such an impairment.
    (2) Regulations may make provision, for the purpose of this paragraph—
    (a) for conditions of a prescribed description to be treated as being progressive;
    (b) for conditions of a prescribed description to be treated as not being progressive.

Section 2(2)   Schedule 2

PAST DISABILITIES

9-057   **1.** The modifications referred to in section 2 are as follows.

9-058   **2.** References in [Parts II to 4][1] to a disabled person are to be read as references to a person who has had a disability.

9-059   [**2A.** References in Chapter 1 of Part 4 to a disabled pupil are to be read as references to a pupil who has had a disability.][2]

9-060   [**2B.** References in Chapter 2 of Part 4 to a disabled student are to be read as references to a student who has had a disability.][3]

9-061   [**2C.** In section 3A(5), after "not having that particular disability" insert "and who has not had that particular disability.][4]

9-062   [**3.** In sections 4A(1), 4B(4), 4E(1), 6B(1), 7B(1), 7D(1), 14(1), 14B(1), 14D(1) and 16A(4), section 21A(4)(a) (in the words to be read as section 19(1)(aa)) and section 21A(6)(a) (in the words to be substituted in section 21(1)), after "not disabled" (in each place it occurs) insert "and who have not had a disability.][5]

9-063   [**4.** In sections 4A(3)(b), 4E(3)(b), 6B(3)(b), 7B(4)(b), 7D(3)(b), 14(3)(b), 14B(3)(b), 14D(3)(b) and 16A(6), for "has" (in each place it occurs) substitute "has had".][6]

9-064   [**4A.** In section 28B(3)(a) and (4), after "disabled" insert "or that he had had a disability".][7]

9-065   [**4B.** In section 28C(1), in paragraphs (a) and (b), after "not disabled" insert "and who have not had a disability".][8]

9-066   [**4C.** In section 28S(3)(a) and (4), after "disabled" insert "or that he had had a disability".][9]

9-067   [**4D.** In subsection (1) of section 28T, after "not disabled" insert "and who have not had a disability".][10]

9-068   [**4E.** In that subsection as substituted by paragraphs 2 and 6 of Schedule 4C, after "not disabled" insert "and who have not had a disability".][11]

9-069   **5.** For paragraph 2(1) to (3) of Schedule 1, substitute—
        "(1) The effect of an impairment is a long-term effect if it has lasted for at least 12 months.
        (2) Where an impairment ceases to have a substantial adverse effect on a person's ability to carry out normal day-to-day activities, it is to be treated as continuing to have that effect if that effect recurs.
        (3) For the purposes of sub-paragraph (2), the recurrence of an effect shall be disregarded in prescribed circumstances."

---

[1] Words substituted by Special Educational Needs and Disability Act 2001 c.10 Pt II c 3 s 38 (11)
[2] Inserted by Special Educational Needs and Disability Act 2001 c.10 Pt II c 3 s 38 (12)
[3] Inserted by Special Educational Needs and Disability Act 2001 c.10 Pt II c 3 s 38 (12)
[4] Inserted by SI 2003/1673 reg 29 (1) (a), with effect October 1 2004
[5] Substituted by SI 2003/1673 reg 29 (1) (b), with effect October 1 2004
[6] Substituted by SI 2003/1673 reg 29 (1) (c), with effect October 1 2004
[7] Inserted by Special Educational Needs and Disability Act 2001 c.10 Pt II c 3 s 38 (13)
[8] Inserted by Special Educational Needs and Disability Act 2001 c.10 Pt II c 3 s 38 (13)
[9] Inserted by Special Educational Needs and Disability Act 2001 c.10 Pt II c 3 s 38 (13)
[10] Inserted by Special Educational Needs and Disability Act 2001 c.10 Pt II c 3 s 38 (13)
[11] Inserted by Special Educational Needs and Disability Act 2001 c.10 Pt II c 3 s 38 (13)

ENFORCEMENT AND PROCEDURE

EMPLOYMENT

Conciliation

1.— [...]¹   **9-070**

Restriction on proceedings for breach of Part II

2.— [(1) Except as provided by Part 2, no civil or criminal proceedings may be brought against **9-071**
any person in respect of an act merely because the act is unlawful under that Part]².

(2) Sub-paragraph (1) does not prevent the making of an application for judicial review.

Period within which proceedings must be brought

3.— (1) An [employment tribunal]³ shall not consider a complaint under [section 17A or 25(8)]⁴ **9-072**
unless it presented before the end of the period of three months beginning when the act complained of
was done.

(2) A tribunal may consider any such complaint which is out of time if, in all the circumstances
of the case, if considers that it is just and equitable to do so.

(3) For the purpose of sub-paragraph (1)—

(a) where an unlawful act [...]⁵ is attributable to a term in a contract, that act is to be treated
as extending throughout the duration of the contract;

(b) any act extending over a period shall be treated as done at the end of that period; and

(c) a deliberate omission shall be treated as done when the person in question decided upon
it.

(4) In the absence of evidence establishing the contrary, a person shall be taken for the purpose
of this paragraph to decide upon an omission—

(a) when he does an act inconsistent with doing the omitted act; or

(b) if he has done no such inconsistent act, when the period expires within which he might
reasonably have been expected to do the omitted act if it was to be done.

Evidence

4.— (1) In any proceedings under [section 17A or 25(8)]⁶, a certificate signed by or on behalf of a **9-073**
Minister of the Crown and certifying—

(a) that any conditions or requirements specified in the certificate were imposed by a
Minister of the Crown and were in operation at a time or throughout a time so specified,
[...]⁷

(b) [...]⁸ shall be conclusive evidence of the matters certified.

(2) A document purporting to be such a certificate shall be received in evidence and, unless the
contrary is proved, be deemed to be such a certificate.

---

¹ Repealed by Industrial Tribunals Act 1996 c.17 Sch 3 Pt I para 1
² Words substituted by SI 2003/1673 reg 29 (2) (b), with effect October 1 2004
³ Words substituted by Employment Rights (Dispute Resolution) Act 1998 c.8 Pt I s 1 (2)
⁴ Words substituted by SI 2003/1673 reg 29 (2) (c), with effect October 1 2004
⁵ Words repealed by SI 2003/1673 reg 29 (2) (d), with effect October 1 2004
⁶ Words substituted by SI 2003/1673 reg 29 (2) (e), with effect October 1 2004
⁷ Repealed by Employment Relations Act 1999 c.26 Sch 9 para 1
⁸ Repealed by Employment Relations Act 1999 c.26 Sch 9 para 1

[Employment Tribunals Act 1996][1]

CHAPTER 17

PART I

[EMPLOYMENT TRIBUNALS][2]

Introductory

[Employment tribunals][3]

10-001   **1.**—(1) The Secretary of State may by regulations make provision for the establishment of tribunals to be known as [employment tribunals][4].

(2) Regulations made wholly or partly under section 128(1) of the Employment Protection (Consolidation) Act 1978 and in force immediately before this Act comes into force shall, so far as made under that provision, continue to have effect (until revoked) as if made under subsection (1) [...][5].

Jurisdiction

Enactments conferring jurisdiction on [employment tribunals][6]

10-002   **2.** [Employment tribunals][7] shall exercise the jurisdiction conferred on them by or by virtue of this Act or any other Act, whether passed before or after this Act.

Power to confer further jurisdiction on [employment tribunals][8]

10-003   **3.**—(1) The appropriate Minister may by order provide that proceedings in respect of—

    (a) any claim to which this section applies, or

    (b) any claim to which this section applies and which is of a description specified in the order.

may, subject to such exceptions (if any) as may be so specified, be brought before an [employment tribunal][9].

    (2) Subject to subsection (3), this section applies to—

    (a) a claim for damages for breach of a contract of employment or other contract connected with employment,

    (b) a claim for a sum due under such a contract, and

    (c) a claim for the recovery of a sum in pursuance of any enactment relating to the terms or performance of such a contract.

---

[1] Title substituted by Employment Rights (Dispute Resolution) Act 1998 c.8 Pt I s 1 (2)
[2] Words substituted by Employment Rights (Dispute Resolution) Act 1998 c.8 Pt I s 1 (2)
[3] Words substituted by Employment Rights (Dispute Resolution) Act 1998 c.8 Pt I s 1 (2)
[4] Words substituted by Employment Rights (Dispute Resolution) Act 1998 c.8 Pt I s 1 (2)
[5] Words repealed by Employment Rights (Dispute Resolution) Act 1998 c.8 Sch 2 para 1
[6] Words substituted by Employment Rights (Dispute Resolution) Act 1998 c.8 Pt I s 1 (2)
[7] Words substituted by Employment Rights (Dispute Resolution) Act 1998 c.8 Pt I s 1 (2)
[8] Words substituted by Employment Rights (Dispute Resolution) Act 1998 c.8 Pt I s 1 (2)
[9] Words substituted by Employment Rights (Dispute Resolution) Act 1998 c.8 Pt I s 1 (2)

if the claim is such that a court in England and Wales or Scotland would under the law for the time being in force have jurisdiction to hear and determine an action in respect of the claim.

(3) This section does not apply to a claim for damages, or for a sum due, in respect of personal injuries.

(4) Any jurisdiction conferred on an [employment tribunal][1] by virtue of this section in respect of any claim is exercisable concurrently with any court in England and Wales or in Scotland which has jurisdiction to hear and determine an action in respect of the claim.

(5) In this section—

"appropriate Minister", as respects a claim in respect of which an action could be heard and determined by a court in England and Wales, means the Lord Chancellor and, as respects a claim in respect of which an action could be heard and determined by a court in Scotland, means the Lord Advocate, and

"personal injuries" includes any disease and any impairment of a person's physical or mental condition.

(6) In this section a reference to breach of a contract includes a reference to breach of—

(a) a term implied in a contract by or under any enactment or otherwise,

(b) a term of a contract as modified by or under any enactment or otherwise, and

(c) a term which, although not contained in a contract, is incorporated in the contract by another term of the contract.

Membership etc

Composition of a tribunal

4.—(1) Subject to the following provisions of this section [and to section **10-004** 7(3A)][2], proceedings before an [employment tribunal][3] shall be heard by—

(a) the person who in accordance with regulations made under section 1(1), is the chairman, and

(b) two other members, or (with the consent of the parties) one other member, selected as the other members (or member) in accordance with regulations so made.

(2) Subject to subsection (5), the proceedings specified in subsection (3) shall be heard by the person mentioned in subsection (1)(a) alone.

(3) The proceedings referred to in subsection (2) are—

(a) proceedings [on a complaint under [section 68A, 87 or 192 of the Trade Union and Labour Relations (Consolidation) Act 1992][4] or][5] on an application under section 161, 165 or 166 of [that Act][6].

(b) proceedings on a complaint under section 126 of the Pension Schemes Act 1993.

(c) proceedings [on a reference under section 11, 163 or 170 of the Employment Rights Act 1996,][7] on a complaint under [section 23, 34 or

---

[1] Words substituted by Employment Rights (Dispute Resolution) Act 1998 c.8 Pt I s 1 (2)

[2] Words inserted by Employment Rights (Dispute Resolution) Act 1998 c.8 Sch 1 para 12 (2)

[3] Words substituted by Employment Rights (Dispute Resolution) Act 1998 c.8 Pt I s 1 (2)

[4] Words inserted by Employment Rights (Dispute Resolution) Act 1998 c.8 Sch 1 para 12 (3)

[5] Words inserted by Employment Rights (Dispute Resolution) Act 1998 c.8 Pt I s 3 (2) (a)

[6] Words substituted by Employment Rights (Dispute Resolution) Act 1998 c.8 Pt I s 3 (2) (b)

[7] Words inserted by Employment Rights (Dispute Resolution) Act 1998 c.8 Pt I s 3 (3) (a)

188 of]^1 [that Act, on a complaint under section 70(1) of that Act relating to section 64 of that Act,]^2 on an application under section 128, 131 or 132 of that [Act or for an appointment under section 206(4) of that]^3 Act,

[(ca) proceedings on a complaint under regulation 11(5) of the Transfer of Undertakings (Protection of Employment) Regulations 1981,]^4

[(cc) proceedings on a complaint under section 11 of the National Minimum Wage Act 1998;

(cd) proceedings on an appeal under section 19 or 22 of the National Minimum Wage Act 1998;]^5

(d) proceedings in respect of which an [employment tribunal]^6 has jurisdiction by virtue of section 3 of this Act,

(e) proceedings in which the parties have given their written consent to the proceedings being heard in accordance with subsection (2) (whether or not they have subsequently withdrawn it).

(f) [...]^7 and

(g) proceedings in which the person (or, where more than one, each of the persons) against whom the proceedings are brought does not, or has ceased to, contest the case.

(4) The Secretary of State may by order amend the provisions of subsection (3).

(5) Proceedings specified in subsection (3) shall be heard in accordance with subsection (1) if a person who, in accordance with regulations made under section 1(1), may be the chairman of an [employment tribunal]^8, having regard to—

(a) whether there is a likelihood of a dispute arising on the facts which makes it desirable for the proceedings to be heard in accordance with subsection (1),

(b) whether there is a likelihood of an issue of law arising which would make it desirable for the proceedings to be heard in accordance with subsection (2),

(c) any views of any of the parties as to whether or not the proceedings ought to be heard in accordance with either of those subsections, and

(d) whether there are other proceedings which might be heard concurrently but which are not proceedings specified in subsection (3),

decides at any stage of the proceedings that the proceedings are to be heard in accordance with subsection (1),

Remuneration, fees and allowances

10-005   **5.**—(1) The Secretary of State may pay to—

(a) the [President of the Employment Tribunals (England and Wales)]^9,

(b) the [President of the Employment Tribunals (Scotland)]^{10},

---

^{1} Words inserted by Employment Rights (Dispute Resolution) Act 1998 c.8 Pt I s 3 (3) (b)
^{2} Words substituted by Employment Rights (Dispute Resolution) Act 1998 c.8 Pt I s 3 (3) (c)
^{3} Words inserted by Employment Rights (Dispute Resolution) Act 1998 c.8 Pt I s 3 (3) (d)
^{4} Inserted by Employment Rights (Dispute Resolution) Act 1998 c.8 Pt I s 3 (4)
^{5} Inserted by National Minimum Wage Act 1998 c.39 s 27 (1)
^{6} Words substituted by Employment Rights (Dispute Resolution) Act 1998 c.8 Pt I s 1 (2)
^{7} Words repealed by Employment Rights (Dispute Resolution) Act 1998 c.8 Sch 2 para 1
^{8} Words substituted by Employment Rights (Dispute Resolution) Act 1998 c.8 Pt I s 1 (2)
^{9} Words substituted by Employment Rights (Dispute Resolution) Act 1998 c.8 Pt I s 1 (2)
^{10} Words substituted by Employment Rights (Dispute Resolution) Act 1998 c.8 Pt I s 1 (2)

(c) any person who is a member on a full-time basis of a panel of chairmen of tribunals which is appointed in accordance with regulations made under section 1(1), and

(d) any person who is a legal officer appointed in accordance with such regulations,

such remuneration as he may with the consent of the Treasury determine.

(2) The Secretary of State may pay to—

(a) members of [employment tribunals][1],

(b) any assessors appointed for the purposes of proceedings before [employment tribunals][2], and

(c) any persons required for the purposes of section 2A(1)(b) of the Equal Pay Act 1970 to prepare reports,

(3) The Secretary of State may pay to any other persons such allowances as he may with the consent of the Treasury determine for the purposes of, or in connection with, their attendance at [employment tribunals][3].

Conduct of hearings

6.—(1) A person may appear before an [employment tribunal][4] in person or **10-006** be represented by—

(a) counsel or a solicitor,

(b) a representative of a trade union or an employers' association, or

(c) any other person whom he desires to represent him.

(2) The Part I of the Arbitration Act 1996 does not apply to any proceedings before an [employment tribunal][5].

Procedure

[Employment Tribunal][6] procedure regulations

7.—(1) The Secretary of State may by regulations ("[employment tribunal][7] **10-007** procedure regulations") make such provision as appears to him to be necessary or expedient with respect to proceedings before [employment tribunals][8].

(2) Proceedings before [employment tribunals][9] shall be instituted in accordance with [employment tribunal][10] procedure regulations.

(3) [Employment tribunal][11] procedure regulations may, in particular, include provision—

(a) for determining by which tribunal any proceedings are to be determined,

(b) for enabling an [employment tribunal][12] to hear and determine proceedings brought by virtue of section 3 concurrently with proceedings brought before the tribunal otherwise than by virtue of that section,

[1] Words substituted by Employment Rights (Dispute Resolution) Act 1998 c.8 Pt I s 1 (2)
[2] Words substituted by Employment Rights (Dispute Resolution) Act 1998 c.8 Pt I s 1 (2)
[3] Words substituted by Employment Rights (Dispute Resolution) Act 1998 c.8 Pt I s 1 (2)
[4] Words substituted by Employment Rights (Dispute Resolution) Act 1998 c.8 Pt I s 1 (2)
[5] Words substituted by Employment Rights (Dispute Resolution) Act 1998 c.8 Pt I s 1 (2)
[6] Words substituted by Employment Rights (Dispute Resolution) Act 1998 c.8 Pt I s 1 (2)
[7] Words substituted by Employment Rights (Dispute Resolution) Act 1998 c.8 Pt I s 1 (2)
[8] Words substituted by Employment Rights (Dispute Resolution) Act 1998 c.8 Pt I s 1 (2)
[9] Words substituted by Employment Rights (Dispute Resolution) Act 1998 c.8 Pt I s 1 (2)
[10] Words substituted by Employment Rights (Dispute Resolution) Act 1998 c.8 Pt I s 1 (2)
[11] Words substituted by Employment Rights (Dispute Resolution) Act 1998 c.8 Pt I s 1 (2)
[12] Words substituted by Employment Rights (Dispute Resolution) Act 1998 c.8 Pt I s 1 (2)

(c) for treating the Secretary of State (either generally or in such circumstances as may be prescribed by the regulations) as a party to any proceedings before an [employment tribunal][1] (where he would not otherwise be a party to them) and entitling him to appear and to be heard accordingly.

(d) for requiring persons to attend to give evidence and produce documents and for authorising the administration of oaths to witnesses,

(e) for enabling an [employment tribunal][2], on the application of any party to the proceedings before it or of its own motion, to order—
   (i) in England and Wales, such discovery or inspection of documents, or the furnishing of such further particulars, as might be ordered by a county court on application by a party to proceedings before it, or
   (ii) in Scotland, such recovery or inspection of documents as might be ordered by a sheriff,

(f) for prescribing the procedure to be followed in any proceedings before an [employment tribunal][3], including provision—
   (i) [...][4]
   (ii) for enabling an [employment tribunal][5] to review its decisions, and revoke or vary its orders and awards, in such circumstances as may be determined in accordance with the regulations,

(g) for the appointment of one or more assessors for the purposes of any proceedings before an [employment tribunal][6], where the proceedings are brought under an enactment which provides for one or more assessors to be appointed,

(h) for authorising an [employment tribunal][7] to require persons to furnish information and produce documents to a person required for the purposes of section 2A(1)(b) of the Equal Pay Act 1970 to prepare a report, and

(j) for the registration and proof of decisions, orders and awards of [employment tribunals][8].

[(3A) Employment tribunal procedure regulations may authorise the determination of proceedings without any hearing (and in private) where the parties have given their written consent (whether or not they have subsequently withdrawn it).

(3B) Employment tribunal procedure regulations may authorise the determination of proceedings without hearing anyone other than the person or persons by whom the proceedings are brought (or his or their representatives) where—

(a) the person (or, where more than one, each of the persons) against whom the proceedings are brought has done nothing to contest the case, or

(b) it appears from the application made by the person (or, where more than one, each of the persons) bringing the proceedings that he is not (or they are not) seeking any relief which an employment tribunal has

---

[1] Words substituted by Employment Rights (Dispute Resolution) Act 1998 c.8 Pt I s 1 (2)
[2] Words substituted by Employment Rights (Dispute Resolution) Act 1998 c.8 Pt I s 1 (2)
[3] Words substituted by Employment Rights (Dispute Resolution) Act 1998 c.8 Pt I s 1 (2)
[4] Repealed by Employment Rights (Dispute Resolution) Act 1998 c.8 Sch 2 para 1
[5] Words substituted by Employment Rights (Dispute Resolution) Act 1998 c.8 Pt I s 1 (2)
[6] Words substituted by Employment Rights (Dispute Resolution) Act 1998 c.8 Pt I s 1 (2)
[7] Words substituted by Employment Rights (Dispute Resolution) Act 1998 c.8 Pt I s 1 (2)
[8] Words substituted by Employment Rights (Dispute Resolution) Act 1998 c.8 Pt I s 1 (2)

power to give or that he is not (or they are not) entitled to any such relief.

(3C) Employment tribunal procedure regulations may authorise the determination of proceedings without hearing anyone other than the person or persons by whom, and the person or persons against whom, the proceedings are brought (or his or their representatives) where—

    (a) an employment tribunal is on undisputed facts bound by the decision of a court in another case to dismiss the case of the person or persons by whom, or of the person or persons against whom, the proceedings are brought, or

    (b) the proceedings relate only to a preliminary issue which may be heard and determined in accordance with regulations under section 9(4).][1]

(4) A person who without reasonable excuse fails to comply with—

    (a) any requirement imposed by virtue of subsection (3)(d) or (h), or

    (b) any requirement with respect to the discovery, recovery or inspection of documents imposed by virtue of subsection (3)(e), [or][2]

    [(c) any requirement imposed by virtue of employment tribunal procedure regulations to give written answers for the purpose of facilitating the determination of proceedings as mentioned in subsection (3A), (3B) or (3C),][3]

is guilty of an offence and liable on summary conviction to a fine not exceeding level 3 on the standard scale.

(5) Subject to any regulations under section 11(1)(a), [employment tribunal][4] procedure regulations may include provision authorising or requiring an [employment tribunal][5], in circumstances specified in the regulations, to send notice or a copy of—

    (a) any document specified in the regulations which relates to any proceedings before the tribunal, or

    (b) any decision, order or award of the tribunal,

to any government department or other person or body so specified.

(6) Where in accordance with [employment tribunal][6] procedure regulations an [employment tribunal][7] determines in the same proceedings—

    (a) a complaint presented under section 111 of the Employment Rights Act 1996, and

    (b) a question referred under section 163 of that Act,

subsection (2) of that section has no effect for the purposes of the proceedings in so far as they relate to the complaint under section 111.

Practice directions

7A.—(1) Employment tribunal procedure regulations may include **10-008** provision—

    (a) enabling the President to make directions about the procedure of employment tribunals, including directions about the exercise by tribunals of powers under such regulations,

    (b) for securing compliance with such directions, and

    (c) about the publication of such directions.

[1] Inserted by Employment Rights (Dispute Resolution) Act 1998 c.8 Pt I s 2
[2] Word inserted by Employment Rights (Dispute Resolution) Act 1998 c.8 Sch 1 para 14 (3)
[3] Inserted by Employment Rights (Dispute Resolution) Act 1998 c.8 Sch 1 para 14 (3)
[4] Words substituted by Employment Rights (Dispute Resolution) Act 1998 c.8 Pt I s 1 (2)
[5] Words substituted by Employment Rights (Dispute Resolution) Act 1998 c.8 Pt I s 1 (2)
[6] Words substituted by Employment Rights (Dispute Resolution) Act 1998 c.8 Pt I s 1 (2)
[7] Words substituted by Employment Rights (Dispute Resolution) Act 1998 c.8 Pt I s 1 (2)

(2) Employment tribunal procedure regulations may, instead of providing for any matter, refer to provision made or to be made about that matter by directions made by the President.

(3) In this section, references to the President are to a person appointed in accordance with regulations under section 1(1) as—

    (a) President of the Employment Tribunals (England and Wales), or

    (b) President of the Employment Tribunals (Scotland).

Procedure in contract cases

10-009   **8.**—(1) Where in proceedings brought by virtue of section 3 an [employment tribunal][1] finds that the whole or part of a sum claimed in the proceedings is due, the tribunal shall order the respondent to the proceedings to pay the amount which it finds due.

(2) An order under section 3 may provide that an [employment tribunal][2] shall not in proceedings in respect of a claim, or a number of claims relating to the same contract, order the payment of an amount exceeding such sum as may be specified in the order as the maximum amount which an [employment tribunal][3] may order to be paid in relation to a claim or in relation to a contract.

(3) An order under section 3 may include provisions—

    (a) as to the manner in which and time within which proceedings are to be brought by virtue of that section, and

    (b) modifying any other enactment.

(4) An order under that section may make different provision in relation to proceedings in respect of different descriptions of claims.

Conciliation

Conciliation

10-010   **18.**—(1) This section applies in the case of [employment tribunal][4] proceedings and claims which could be the subject of [employment tribunal][5] proceedings—

    (a) under—

        (i) section 2(1) of the Equal Pay Act 1970,

        (ii) section 63 of the Sex Discrimination Act 1975, or

        (iii) section 54 of the Race Relations Act 1976,

    (b) arising out of a contravention, or alleged contravention, of section 64, [68][6], 137, 138, 146, 168, [168A,][7] 169, 170, 174, 188 or 190 of the Trade Union and Labour Relations (Consolidation) Act 1992,

    (c) under section 8 of the Disability Discrimination Act 1995,

    (d) under, or arising out of a contravention, or alleged contravention, of [section 8, 13, 15, 18(1), 21(1), 28, [80G(1), 80H(1)(b),][8] 80(1), 92 or 135, or of Part V,VI,VII or X, of the Employment Rights Act 1996][9],

---

[1] Words substituted by Employment Rights (Dispute Resolution) Act 1998 c.8 Pt I s 1 (2)
[2] Words substituted by Employment Rights (Dispute Resolution) Act 1998 c.8 Pt I s 1 (2)
[3] Words substituted by Employment Rights (Dispute Resolution) Act 1998 c.8 Pt I s 1 (2)
[4] Words substituted by Employment Rights (Dispute Resolution) Act 1998 c.8 Pt I s 1 (2)
[5] Words substituted by Employment Rights (Dispute Resolution) Act 1998 c.8 Pt I s 1 (2)
[6] Words inserted by Employment Rights (Dispute Resolution) Act 1998 c.8 Sch 1 para 16
[7] Inserted by Employment Act 2002 c.22 Sch 7 para 23
[8] Inserted by Employment Act 2002 c.22 Sch 7 para 23
[9] Word inserted by SI 2000/1337 art 2

[(dd) under or by virtue of section 11, 18, 20(1)(a) or 24 of the National Minimum Wage Act 1998;][1]

(e) which are proceedings in respect of which an [employment tribunal][2] has jurisdiction by virtue of section 3 of this Act, [...][3]

(f) under, or arising out of a contravention, or alleged contravention, of a provision specified by an order under subsection (8)(b) as a provision to which this paragraph applies.

[(ff) under regulation 30 of the Working Time Regulations 1998.][4] [...][5]

[(g) under regulation 27 or 32 of the Transnational Information and Consultation of Employees Regulations 1999.][6] [...][7]

[(h) arising out of a contravention, or alleged contravention of [regulation 5(1) or 7(2) of the Part-time Workers (Prevention of Less Favourable Treatment) Regulations 2000][8].][9]

[(i) arising out of a contravention, or alleged contravention of regulation 3 or 6(2) of the Fixed-term Employees (Prevention of Less Favourable Treatment) Regulations 2002; or

(j) under regulation 9 of those Regulations.][10]

(2) Where an application has been presented to an [employment tribunal][11], and a copy of it has been sent to a conciliation officer, it is the duty of the conciliation officer—

(a) if he is requested to do so by the person by whom and the person against whom the proceedings are brought, or

(b) if, in the absence of any such request, the conciliation officer considers that he could act under this subsection with a reasonable prospect of success,

to endeavour to promote a settlement of the proceedings without their being determined by an [employment tribunal][12].

(3) Where at any time—

(a) a person claims that action has been taken in respect of which proceedings could be brought by him before an [employment tribunal][13], but

(b) before any application relating to that action has been presented by him a request is made to a conciliation officer (whether by that person or by the person against whom the proceedings could be instituted) to make his services available to them,

the conciliation officer shall act in accordance with subsection (2) as if an application had been presented to an [employment tribunal][14].

(4) Where a person who has presented a complaint to an [employment tribunal][15] under section 111 of the Employment Rights Act 1996 has ceased to be employed by the employer against whom the complaint was made, the concilia-

---

[1] Inserted by National Minimum Wage Act 1998 c.39 s 30 (1)
[2] Words substituted by Employment Rights (Dispute Resolution) Act 1998 c.8 Pt I s 1 (2)
[3] Word repealed by SI 1998/1833 Pt IV reg 33 (a)
[4] Inserted by SI 1998/1833 Pt IV reg 33 (b)
[5] Word repealed by SI 2000/1551 Sch 1 para 1 (a) (i)
[6] Inserted by SI 1999/3323 Pt VII reg 33 (1) (b)
[7] Word repealed by SI 2002/2034 Sch 2 (1) para 2 (a) (i)
[8] Words inserted by SI 2001/1107 reg 2
[9] Inserted by SI 2000/1551 Sch 1 para 1 (a) (ii)
[10] Inserted by SI 2002/2034 Sch 2 (1) para 2 (a) (ii)
[11] Words substituted by Employment Rights (Dispute Resolution) Act 1998 c.8 Pt I s 1 (2)
[12] Words substituted by Employment Rights (Dispute Resolution) Act 1998 c.8 Pt I s 1 (2)
[13] Words substituted by Employment Rights (Dispute Resolution) Act 1998 c.8 Pt I s 1 (2)
[14] Words substituted by Employment Rights (Dispute Resolution) Act 1998 c.8 Pt I s 1 (2)
[15] Words substituted by Employment Rights (Dispute Resolution) Act 1998 c.8 Pt I s 1 (2)

tion officer shall (for the purpose of promoting a settlement of the complaint in accordance with subsection (2) in particular—

    (a) seek to promote the reinstatement or re-engagement of the complainant by the employer, or by a successor of the employer or by an associated employer, on terms appearing to the conciliation officer to be equitable, or

    (b) where the complainant does not wish to be reinstated or reengaged, or where reinstatement or re-engagement is not practicable, and the parties desire the conciliation officer to act, seek to promote agreement between them as to a sum by way of compensation to be paid by the employer to the complainant.

  (5) Where at any time—

    (a) a person claims that action has been taken in respect of which a complaint could be presented by him to an [employment tribunal][1] under section 111 of the Employment Rights Act 1996, but

    (b) before any complaint relating to that action has been presented by him a request is made to a conciliation officer (whether by that person or by the employer) to make his services available to them,

the conciliation officer shall act in accordance with subsection (4) as if a complaint had been presented to an [employment tribunal][2] under section 111.

  (6) In proceeding under this section a conciliation officer shall, where appropriate, have regard to the desirability of encouraging the use of other procedures available for the settlement of grievances.

  (7) Anything communicated to a conciliation officer in connection with the performance of his functions under this section shall not be admissible in evidence in any proceedings before an [employment tribunal][3], except with the consent of the person who communicated it to that officer.

  (8) The Secretary of State may by order—

    (a) direct that further provisions of the Employment Rights Act 1996 be added to the list in subsection (1)(d), or

    (b) specify a provision of any other Act as a provision to which subsection (1)(f) applies.

Conciliation procedure

10-011   **19.**—Employment tribunal procedure regulations shall include in relation to employment tribunal proceedings in the case of which any enactment makes provision for conciliation—

  (a) provisions requiring a copy of the application by which the proceedings are instituted, and a copy of any notice relating to it which is lodged by or on behalf of the person against whom the proceedings are brought, to be sent to a conciliation officer,

  (b) provisions securing that the applicant and the person against whom the proceedings are brought are notified that the services of a conciliation officer are available to them [...][4]

---

[1] Words substituted by Employment Rights (Dispute Resolution) Act 1998 c.8 Pt I s 1 (2)
[2] Words substituted by Employment Rights (Dispute Resolution) Act 1998 c.8 Pt I s 1 (2)
[3] Words substituted by Employment Rights (Dispute Resolution) Act 1998 c.8 Pt I s 1 (2)
[4] Words repealed by Employment Act 2002 c.22 Sch 8

PART II

THE EMPLOYMENT APPEAL TRIBUNAL

Introductory

The Appeal Tribunal

20.—(1) The Employment Appeal Tribunal ("the Appeal Tribunal") shall **10-012** continue in existence.

(2) The Appeal Tribunal shall have a central office in London but may sit at any time and in any place in Great Britain.

(3) The Appeal Tribunal shall be a superior court of record and shall have an official seal which shall be judicially noticed.

[(4) Subsection (2) is subject to regulation 34 of the Transnational Information and Consultation of Employees Regulations 1999.][1]

Jurisdiction

Jurisdiction of Appeal Tribunal

21.—(1) An appeal lies to the Appeal Tribunal on any question of law arising **10-013** from any decision of, or arising in any proceedings before, an [employment tribunal][2] under or by virtue of—

    (a) the Equal Pay Act 1970,

    (b) the Sex Discrimination Act 1975,

    (c) the Race Relations Act 1976,

    (d) the Trade Union and Labour Relations (Consolidation) Act 1992,

    (e) the Disability Discrimination Act 1995, [...][3]

    (f) the Employment Rights Act 1996[, [...][4]

    [(ff) the National Minimum Wage Act 1998,][5]

    [(fg) the Tax Credits Act 1999, or][6]

    (g) this Act[,][7]][8]

    [(h) the Working Time Regulations 1998, [...][9]

    (i) the Transnational Information and Consultation of Employees Regulations 1999, [...][10]][11]

    [(j) the Part-time Workers (Prevention of Less Favourable Treatment) Regulations 2000[, or][12]][13]

    [(k) the Fixed-term Employees (Prevention of Less Favourable Treatment) Regulations 2002.][14]

---

[1] Inserted by SI 1999/3323 Pt VIII reg 35 (2)

[2] Words substituted by Employment Rights (Dispute Resolution) Act 1998 c.8 Pt I s 1 (2)

[3] Word repealed by Employment Rights (Dispute Resolution) Act 1998 c.8 Sch 2 para 1

[4] Word repealed by National Minimum Wage Act 1998 c.39 Sch 3 para 1

[5] Inserted by National Minimum Wage Act 1998 c.39 s 29

[6] Inserted by Tax Credits Act 1999 c.10 Sch 3 para 5

[7] Words substituted and (h) and (i) inserted by SI 1999/3323 Pt VIII reg 35 (3) (b)

[8] Inserted by Employment Rights (Dispute Resolution) Act 1998 c.8 Sch 1 para 17 (2)

[9] Word repealed by SI 2000/1551 Sch 1 para 1 (b) (i)

[10] Word repealed by SI 2002/2034 Sch 2 (1) para 2 (b) (i)

[11] Inserted by SI 1999/3323 Pt VIII reg 35 (3) (b)

[12] Inserted by SI 2002/2034 Sch 2 (1) para 2 (b) (ii)

[13] Inserted by SI 2000/1551 Sch 1 para 1 (b) (ii)

[14] Inserted by SI 2002/2034 Sch 2 (1) para 2 (b) (ii)

(2) No appeal shall lie except to the Appeal Tribunal from any decision of an [employment tribunal][1] under or by virtue of the Acts listed [or the Regulations referred to][2] in subsection (1).

(3) Subsection (1) does not affect any provision contained in, or made under, any Act which provides for an appeal to lie to the Appeal Tribunal (whether from an [employment tribunal][3], the Certification Officer or any other person or body) otherwise than on a question to which that subsection applies.

[(4) The Appeal Tribunal also has any jurisdiction in respect of matters other than appeals which is conferred on it by or under—

(a) the Trade Union and Labour Relations (Consolidation) Act 1992,
(b) this Act, or
(c) any other Act.][4]

Membership etc

Membership of Appeal Tribunal

10-014 **22.**—(1) The Appeal Tribunal shall consist of—

(a) such number of judges as may be nominated from time to time by the Lord Chancellor from the judges (other than the Lord Chancellor) of the High Court and the Court of Appeal.
(b) at least one judge of the Court of Session nominated from time to time by the Lord President of the Court of Session, and
(c) such number of other members as may be appointed from time to time by Her Majesty on the joint recommendation of the Lord Chancellor and the Secretary of State ("appointed members").

(2) The appointed members shall be persons who appear to the Lord Chancellor and the Secretary of State to have special knowledge or experience of industrial relations either—

(a) as representatives of employers, or
(b) as representatives of workers (within the meaning of the Trade Union and Labour Relations (Consolidation) Act 1992).

(3) The Lord Chancellor shall, after consultation with the Lord President of the Court of Session, appoint one of the judges nominated under subsection (1) to be the President of the Appeal Tribunal.

(4) No judge shall be nominated a member of the Appeal Tribunal except with his consent.

PART III

SUPPLEMENTARY

Interpretation

10-015 **42.**—(1) In this Act—

"the Appeal Tribunal" means the Employment Appeal Tribunal.
"Appeal Tribunal procedure rules" shall be construed in accordance with section 30(1),

---

[1] Words substituted by Employment Rights (Dispute Resolution) Act 1998 c.8 Pt I s 1 (2)
[2] Words inserted by SI 1998/1833 Pt IV reg 34 (b)
[3] Words substituted by Employment Rights (Dispute Resolution) Act 1998 c.8 Pt I s 1 (2)
[4] Inserted by Employment Rights (Dispute Resolution) Act 1998 c.8 Sch 1 para 17 (3)

"appointed member" shall be construed in accordance with section 22(1)(c),

"conciliation officer" means an officer designated by the Advisory, Conciliation and Arbitration Service under section 211 of the Trade Union and Labour Relations (Consolidation) Act 1992,

"contract of employment" means a contract of service or apprenticeship, whether express or implied, and (if it is express) whether oral or in writing,

"employee" means an individual who has entered into or works under (or, where the employment has ceased, worked under) a contract of employment,

"employer", in relation to an employee, means the person by whom the employee is (or, where the employment has ceased, was) employed,

"employers' association" has the same meaning as in the Trade Union and Labour Relations (Consolidation) Act 1992,

"employment" means employment under a contract of employment and "employed" shall be construed accordingly.

"employment tribunal procedure regulations" shall be construed in accordance with section 7(1),

"statutory provision" means a provision, whether of a general or a special nature, contained in, or in any document made or issued under, any Act, whether of a general or special nature,

"successor", in relation to the employer of an employee, means (subject to subsection (2)) a person who in consequence of a change occurring (whether by virtue of a sale or other disposition or by operation of law) in the ownership of the undertaking, or of the part of the undertaking, for the purposes of which the employee was employed, has become the owner of the undertaking or part, and

"trade union" has the meaning given by section 1 of the Trade Union and Labour Relations (Consolidation) Act 1992.

(2) The definition of "successor" in subsection (1) has effect (subject to the necessary modifications) in relation to a case where—

(a) the person by whom an undertaking or part of an undertaking is owned immediately before a change is one of the persons by whom (whether as partners, trustees or otherwise) it is owned immediately after the change, or

(b) the persons by whom an undertaking or part of an undertaking is owned immediately before a change (whether as partners, trustees or otherwise) include the persons by whom, or include one or more of the persons by whom, it is owned immediately after the change,

as it has effect where the previous owner and the new owner are wholly different persons.

(3) For the purposes of this Act any two employers shall be treated as associated if—

(a) one is a company of which the other (directly or indirectly) has control, or

(b) both are companies of which a third person (directly or indirectly) has control;

and "associated employer" shall be construed accordingly.

Employment Rights Act 1996

CHAPTER 18

PART I

EMPLOYMENT PARTICULARS

Right to statements of employment particulars

Statement of initial employment particulars

11-001   **1.**—(1) Where an employee begins employment with an employer, the employer shall give to the employee a written statement of particulars of employment.

(2) The statement may (subject to section 2(4)) be given in instalments and (whether or not given in instalments) shall be given not later than two months after the beginning of the employment.

(3) The statement shall contain particulars of—

    (a) the names of the employer and employee,

    (b) the date when the employment began, and

    (c) the date on which the employee's period of continuous employment began (taking into account any employment with a previous employer which counts towards that period).

(4) The statement shall also contain particulars, as at a specified date not more than seven days before the statement (or the instalment containing them) is given, of—

    (a) the scale or rate of remuneration or the method of calculating remuneration,

    (b) the intervals at which remuneration is paid (that is, weekly, monthly or other specified intervals),

    (c) any terms and conditions relating to hours of work (including any terms and conditions relating to normal working hours),

    (d) any terms and conditions relating to any of the following—

        (i) entitlement to holidays, including public holidays, and holiday pay (the particulars given being sufficient to enable the employee's entitlement, including any entitlement to accrued holiday pay on the termination of employment, to be precisely calculated),

        (ii) incapacity for work due to sickness or injury, including any provision for sick pay, and

        (iii) pensions and pension schemes,

    (e) the length of notice which the employee is obliged to give and entitled to receive to terminate his contract of employment,

    (f) the title of the job which the employee is employed to do or a brief description of the work for which he is employed,

    (g) where the employment is not intended to be permanent, the period for which it is expected to continue or, if it is for a fixed term, the date when it is to end,

(h) either the place of work or, where the employee is required or permitted to work at various places, an indication of that and of the address of the employer,

(j) any collective agreements which directly affect the terms and conditions of the employment including, where the employer is not a party, the persons by whom they were made, and

(k) where the employee is required to work outside the United Kingdom for a period of more than one month—

    (i) the period for which he is to work outside the United Kingdom,

    (ii) the currency in which remuneration is to be paid while he is working outside the United Kingdom,

    (iii) any additional remuneration payable to him, and any benefits to be provided to or in respect of him, by reason of his being required to work outside the United Kingdom, and

    (iv) any terms and conditions relating to his return to the United Kingdom.

(5) Subsection (4)(d)(iii) does not apply to an employee of a body or authority if—

(a) the employee's pension rights depend on the terms of a pension scheme established under any provision contained in or having effect under any Act, and

(b) any such provision requires the body or authority to give to a new employee information concerning the employee's pension rights or the determination of questions affecting those rights.

Statement of initial particulars: supplementary

2.—(1) If, in the case of a statement under section 1, there are no particulars **11-002** to be entered under any of the heads of paragraph (d) or (k) of subsection (4) of that section, or under any of the other paragraphs of subsection (3) or (4) of that section, that fact shall be stated.

(2) A statement under section 1 may refer the employee for particulars of any of the matters specified in subsection (4)(d)(ii) and (iii) of that section to the provisions of some other document which is reasonably accessible to the employee.

(3) A statement under section 1 may refer the employee for particulars of either of the matters specified in subsection (4)(e) of that section to the law or to the provisions of any collective agreement directly affecting the terms and conditions of the employment which is reasonably accessible to the employee.

(4) The particulars required by section 1(3) and (4)(a) to (c), (d)(i), (f) and (h) shall be included in a single document.

(5) Where before the end of the period of two months after the beginning of an employee's employment the employee is to begin to work outside the United Kingdom for a period of more than one month, the statement under section 1 shall be given to him not later than the time when he leaves the United Kingdom in order to begin so to work.

(6) A statement shall be given to a person under section 1 even if his employment ends before the end of the period within which the statement is required to be given.

Note about disciplinary procedures and pensions

3.—(1) A statement under section 1 shall include a note— **11-003**

(a) specifying any disciplinary rules applicable to the employee or referring the employee to the provisions of a document specifying such rules which is reasonably accessible to the employee,

[(aa) specifying any procedure applicable to the taking of disciplinary decisions relating to the employee, or to a decision to dismiss the employee, or referring the employee to the provisions of a document specifying such a procedure which is reasonably accessible to the employee,][1]

(b) specifying (by description or otherwise)—

  (i) a person to whom the employee can apply if dissatisfied with any disciplinary decision relating to him [or any decision to dismiss him][2], and

  (ii) a person to whom the employee can apply for the purpose of seeking redress of any grievance relating to his employment,

and the manner in which any such application should be made, and

(c) where there are further steps consequent on any such application, explaining those steps or referring to the provisions of a document explaining them which is reasonably accessible to the employee.

(2) Subsection (1) does not apply to rules, disciplinary decisions, [decisions to dismiss][3] grievances or procedures relating to health or safety at work.

(3) [...][4]

(4) [...][5]

Statement of changes

11-004   **4.**—(1) If, after the material date, there is a change in any of the matters particulars of which are required by sections 1 to 3 to be included or referred to in a statement under section 1, the employer shall give to the employee a written statement containing particulars of the change.

(2) For the purposes of subsection (1)—

(a) in relation to a matter particulars of which are included or referred to in a statement given under section 1 otherwise than in instalments, the material date is the date to which the statement relates,

(b) in relation to a matter particulars of which—

  (i) are included or referred to in an instalment of a statement given under section 1, or

  (ii) are required by section 2(4) to be included in a single document but are not included in an instalment of a statement given under section 1 which does include other particulars to which that provision applies,

the material date is the date to which the instalment relates, and

(c) in relation to any other matter, the material date is the date by which a statement under section 1 is required to be given.

(3) A statement under subsection (1) shall be given at the earliest opportunity and, in any event, not later than—

(a) one month after the change in question, or

(b) where that change results from the employee being required to work outside the United Kingdom for a period of more than one month, the

---

[1] Inserted by Employment Act 2002 c.22 s 35 (2)

[2] Words inserted by Employment Act 2002 c.22 s 35 (3)

[3] Words inserted by Employment Act 2002 c.22 s 35 (4)

[4] Repealed by Employment Act 2002 c 22 s 36

[5] Repealed by Employment Act 2002 c 22 s 36

time when he leaves the United Kingdom in order to begin so to work, if that is earlier.

(4) A statement under subsection (1) may refer the employee to the provisions of some other document which is reasonably accessible to the employee for a change in any of the matters specified in sections 1(4)(d)(ii) and (iii) and 3(1)(a) and (c).

(5) A statement under subsection (1) may refer the employee for a change in either of the matters specified in section 1(4)(e) to the law or to the provisions of any collective agreement directly affecting the terms and conditions of the employment which is reasonably accessible to the employee.

(6) Where, after an employer has given to an employee a statement under section 1, either—

(a) the name of the employer (whether an individual or a body corporate or partnership) is changed without any change in the identity of the employer, or

(b) the identity of the employer is changed in circumstances in which the continuity of the employee's period of employment is not broken,

and subsection (7) applies in relation to the change, the person who is the employer immediately after the change is not required to give to the employee a statement under section 1; but the change shall be treated as a change falling within subsection (1) of this section.

(7) This subsection applies in relation to a change if it does not involve any change in any of the matters (other than the names of the parties) particulars of which are required by sections 1 to 3 to be included or referred to in the statement under section 1.

(8) A statement under subsection (1) which informs an employee of a change such as is referred to in subsection (6)(b) shall specify the date on which the employee's period of continuous employment began.

Exclusion from rights to statements

5.—(1) Sections 1 to 4 apply to an employee who at any time comes or ceases **11-005** to come within the exceptions from those sections provided by [section][1] 199, and under section 209, as if his employment with his employer terminated or began at that time.

(2) The fact that section 1 is directed by subsection (1) to apply to an employee as if his employment began on his ceasing to come within the exceptions referred to in that subsection does not affect the obligation under section 1(3)(b) to specify the date on which his employment actually began.

Reasonably accessible document or collective agreement

6. In sections 2 to 4 references to a document or collective agreement which **11-006** is reasonably accessible to an employee are references to a document or collective agreement which—

(a) the employee has reasonable opportunities of reading in the course of his employment, or

(b) is made reasonably accessible to the employee in some other way.

Power to require particulars of further matters

7. The Secretary of State may by order provide that section 1 shall have effect **11-007** as if particulars of such further matters as may be specified in the order were

---

[1] Word substituted by Employment Relations Act 1999 c.26 s 32 (3)

included in the particulars required by that section; and, for that purpose, the order may include such provisions amending that section as appear to the Secretary of State to be expedient.

[Use of alternative documents to give particulars

11-008   **7A**—(1) Subsections (2) and (3) apply where—
    (a) an employer gives an employee a document in writing in the form of a contract of employment or letter of engagement,
    (b) the document contains information which, were the document in the form of a statement under section 1, would meet the employer's obligation under that section in relation to the matters mentioned in subsections (3) and (4)(a) to (c), (d)(i), (f) and (h) of that section, and
    (c) the document is given after the beginning of the employment and before the end of the period for giving a statement under that section.

(2) The employer's duty under section 1 in relation to any matter shall be treated as met if the document given to the employee contains information which, were the document in the form of a statement under that section, would meet the employer's obligation under that section in relation to that matter.

(3) The employer's duty under section 3 shall be treated as met if the document given to the employee contains information which, were the document in the form of a statement under section 1 and the information included in the form of a note, would meet the employer's obligation under section 3.

(4) For the purposes of this section a document to which subsection (1)(a) applies shall be treated, in relation to information in respect of any of the matters mentioned in section 1(4), as specifying the date on which the document is given to the employee as the date as at which the information applies.

(5) Where subsection (2) applies in relation to any matter, the date on which the document by virtue of which that subsection applies is given to the employee shall be the material date in relation to that matter for the purposes of section 4(1).

(6) Where subsection (3) applies, the date on which the document by virtue of which that subsection applies is given to the employee shall be the material date for the purposes of section 4(1) in relation to the matters of which particulars are required to be given under section 3.

(7) The reference in section 4(6) to an employer having given a statement under section 1 shall be treated as including his having given a document by virtue of which his duty to give such a statement is treated as met.

Giving of alternative documents before start of employment

11-009   **7B.** A document in the form of a contract of employment or letter of engagement given by an employer to an employee before the beginning of the employee's employment with the employer shall, when the employment begins, be treated for the purposes of section 7A as having been given at that time.][1]

Right to itemised pay statement

Itemised pay statement

11-010   **8.**—(1) An employee has the right to be given by his employer, at or before the time at which any payment of wages or salary is made to him, a written itemised pay statement.

---

[1] Inserted by Employment Act 2002 c.22 s 37

(2) The statement shall contain particulars of—

(a) the gross amount of the wages or salary,

(b) the amounts of any variable, and (subject to section 9) any fixed, deductions from that gross amount and the purposes for which they are made,

(c) the net amount of wages or salary payable, and

(d) where different parts of the net amount are paid in different ways, the amount and method of payment of each part-payment.

Standing statement of fixed deductions

9.—(1) A pay statement given in accordance with section 8 need not contain **11-011** separate particulars of a fixed deduction if—

(a) it contains instead an aggregate amount of fixed deductions, including that deduction, and

(b) the employer has given to the employee, at or before the time at which the pay statement is given, a standing statement of fixed deductions which satisfies subsection (2).

(2) A standing statement of fixed deductions satisfies this subsection if—

(a) it is in writing,

(b) it contains, in relation to each deduction comprised in the aggregate amount of deductions, particulars of—

(i) the amount of the deduction,

(ii) the intervals at which the deduction is to be made, and

(iii) the purpose for which it is made, and

(c) it is (in accordance with subsection (5)) effective at the date on which the pay statement is given.

(3) A standing statement of fixed deductions may be amended, whether by—

(a) addition of a new deduction,

(b) a change in the particulars, or

(c) cancellation of an existing deduction,

by notice in writing, containing particulars of the amendment, given by the employer to the employee.

(4) An employer who has given to an employee a standing statement of fixed deductions shall—

(a) within the period of twelve months beginning with the date on which the first standing statement was given, and

(b) at intervals of not more than twelve months afterwards,

re-issue it in a consolidated form incorporating any amendments notified in accordance with subsection (3).

(5) For the purposes of subsection (2)(c) a standing statement of fixed deductions—

(a) becomes effective on the date on which it is given to the employee, and

(b) ceases to be effective at the end of the period of twelve months beginning with that date or, where it is re-issued in accordance with subsection (4), with the end of the period of twelve months beginning with the date of the last re-issue.

Power to amend provisions about pay and standing statements

10. The Secretary of State may by order— **11-012**

(a) vary the provisions of sections 8 and 9 as to the particulars which must be included in a pay statement or a standing statement of fixed deductions by adding items to, or removing items from, the particulars listed in those sections or by amending any such particulars, and

(b) vary the provisions of subsection (4) and (5) of section 9 so as to shorten or extend the periods of twelve months referred to in those sub-sections, or those periods as varied from time to time under this section.

Enforcement

References to [employment tribunals][1]

11-013   **11.**—(1) Where an employer does not give an employee a statement as required by section 1, 4 or 8 (either because he gives him no statement or because the statement he gives does not comply with what is required), the employee may require a reference to be made to an [employment tribunal][2] to determine what particulars ought to have been included or referred to in a statement so as to comply with the requirements of the section concerned.

(2) Where—

(a) a statement purporting to be a statement under section 1 or 4, or a pay statement or a standing statement of fixed deductions purporting to comply with section 8 or 9, has been given to an employee, and

(b) a question arises as to the particulars which ought to have been included or referred to in the statement so as to comply with the requirements of this Part,

either the employer or the employee may require the question to be referred to and determined by an [employment tribunal][3].

(3) For the purposes of this section—

(a) a question as to the particulars which ought to have been included in the note required by section 3 to be included in the statement under section 1 does not include any question whether the employment is, has been or will be contracted-out employment (for the purposes of Part III of the Pension Schemes Act 1993), and

(b) a question as to the particulars which ought to have been included in a pay statement or standing statement of fixed deductions does not include a question solely as to the accuracy of an amount stated in any such particulars.

(4) An [employment tribunal][4] shall not consider a reference under this section in a case where the employment to which the reference relates has ceased unless an application requiring the reference to be made was made—

(a) before the end of the period of three months beginning with the date on which the employment ceased, or

(b) within such further period as the tribunal considers reasonable in a case where it is satisfied that it was not reasonably practicable for the application to be made before the end of that period of three months.

Determination of references

11-014   **12.**—(1) Where, on a reference under section 11(1), an [employment tribunal][5] determines particulars as being those which ought to have been

[1] Words substituted by Employment Rights (Dispute Resolution) Act 1998 c.8 Pt I s 1 (2)
[2] Words substituted by Employment Rights (Dispute Resolution) Act 1998 c.8 Pt I s 1 (2)
[3] Words substituted by Employment Rights (Dispute Resolution) Act 1998 c.8 Pt I s 1 (2)
[4] Words substituted by Employment Rights (Dispute Resolution) Act 1998 c.8 Pt I s 1 (2)
[5] Words substituted by Employment Rights (Dispute Resolution) Act 1998 c.8 Pt I s 1 (2)

included or referred to in a statement given under section 1 or 4, the employer shall be deemed to have given to the employee a statement in which those particulars were included, or referred to, as specified in the decision of the tribunal.

(2) On determining a reference under section 11(2) relating to a statement purporting to be a statement under section 1 or 4, an [employment tribunal][1] may—

    (a) confirm the particulars as included or referred to in the statement given by the employer,

    (b) amend those particulars, or

    (c) substitute other particulars for them,

as the tribunal may determine to be appropriate; and the statement shall be deemed to have been given by the employer to the employee in accordance with the decision of the tribunal.

(3) Where on a reference under section 11 an [employment tribunal][2] finds—

    (a) that an employer has failed to give an employee any pay statement in accordance with section 8, or

    (b) that a pay statement or standing statement of fixed deductions does not, in relation to a deduction, contain the particulars required to be included in that statement by that section or section 9,

the tribunal shall make a declaration to that effect.

(4) Where on a reference in the case of which subsection (3) applies the tribunal further finds that any unnotified deductions have been made from the pay of the employee during the period of thirteen weeks immediately preceding the date of the application for the reference (whether or not the deductions were made in breach of the contract of employment), the tribunal may order the employer to pay the employee a sum not exceeding the aggregate of the unnotified deductions so made.

(5) For the purposes of subsection (4) a deduction is an unnotified deduction if it is made without the employer giving the employee, in any pay statement or standing statement of fixed deductions, the particulars of the deduction required by section 8 or 9.

PART II

PROTECTION OF WAGES

Deductions by employer

Right not to suffer unauthorised deductions

13.—(1) An employer shall not make a deduction from wages of a worker **11-015** employed by him unless—

    (a) the deduction is required or authorised to be made by virtue of a statutory provision or a relevant provision of the worker's contract, or

    (b) the worker has previously signified in writing his agreement or consent to the making of the deduction.

(2) In this section "relevant provision", in relation to a worker's contract, means a provision of the contract comprised—

---

[1] Words substituted by Employment Rights (Dispute Resolution) Act 1998 c.8 Pt I s 1 (2)

[2] Words substituted by Employment Rights (Dispute Resolution) Act 1998 c.8 Pt I s 1 (2)

(a) in one or more written terms of the contract of which the employer has given the worker a copy on an occasion prior to the employer making the deduction in question, or

(b) in one or more terms of the contract (whether express or implied and, if express, whether oral or in writing) the existence and effect, or combined effect, of which in relation to the worker the employer has notified to the worker in writing on such an occasion.

(3) Where the total amount of wages paid on any occasion by an employer to a worker employed by him is less than the total amount of the wages properly payable by him to the worker on that occasion (after deductions), the amount of the deficiency shall be treated for the purposes of this Part as a deduction made by the employer from the worker's wages on that occasion.

(4) Subsection (3) does not apply in so far as the deficiency is attributable to an error of any description on the part of the employer affecting the computation by him of the gross amount of the wages properly payable by him to the worker on that occasion.

(5) For the purposes of this section a relevant provision of a worker's contract having effect by virtue of a variation of the contract does not operate to authorise the making of a deduction on account of any conduct of the worker, or any other event occurring, before the variation took effect.

(6) For the purposes of this section an agreement or consent signified by a worker does not operate to authorise the making of a deduction on account of any conduct of the worker, or any other event occurring, before the agreement or consent was signified.

(7) This section does not affect any other statutory provision by virtue of which a sum payable to a worker by his employer but not constituting "wages" within the meaning of this Part is not to be subject to a deduction at the instance of the employer.

Excepted deductions

11-016   **14.**—(1) Section 13 does not apply to a deduction from a worker's wages made by his employer where the purpose of the deduction is the reimbursement of the employer in respect of—

(a) an overpayment of wages, or

(b) an overpayment in respect of expenses incurred by the worker in carrying out his employment,

made (for any reason) by the employer to the worker.

(2) Section 13 does not apply to a deduction from a worker's wages made by his employer in consequence of any disciplinary proceedings if those proceedings were held by virtue of a statutory provision.

(3) Section 13 does not apply to a deduction from a worker's wages made by his employer in pursuance of a requirement imposed on the employer by a statutory provision to deduct and pay over to a public authority amounts determined by that authority as being due to it from the worker if the deduction is made in accordance with the relevant determination of that authority.

(4) Section 13 does not apply to a deduction from a worker's wages made by his employer in pursuance of any arrangements which have been established—

(a) in accordance with a relevant provision of his contract to the inclusion of which in the contract the worker has signified his agreement or consent in writing, or

(b) otherwise with the prior agreement or consent of the worker signified in writing, and under which the employer is to deduct and pay over to a third person amounts notified to the employer by that person as being due to him from the worker, if the deduction is made in accordance with the relevant notification by that person.

(5) Section 13 does not apply to a deduction from a worker's wages made by his employer where the worker has taken part in a strike or other industrial action and the deduction is made by the employer on account of the worker's having taken part in that strike or other action.

(6) Section 13 does not apply to a deduction from a worker's wages made by his employer with his prior agreement or consent signified in writing where the purpose of the deduction is the satisfaction (whether wholly or in part) of an order of a court or tribunal requiring the payment of an amount by the worker to the employer.

Payments to employer

Right not to have to make payments to employer

15.—(1) An employer shall not receive a payment from a worker employed **11-017** by him unless—
  (a) the payment is required or authorised to be made by virtue of a statutory provision or a relevant provision of the worker's contract, or
  (b) the worker has previously signified in writing his agreement or consent to the making of the payment.

(2) In this section "relevant provision", in relation to a worker's contract, means a provision of the contract comprised—
  (a) in one or more written terms of the contract of which the employer has given the worker a copy on an occasion prior to the employer receiving the payment in question, or
  (b) in one or more terms of the contract (whether express or implied and, if express, whether oral or in writing) the existence and effect, or combined effect, of which in relation to the worker the employer has notified to the worker in writing on such an occasion.

(3) For the purposes of this section a relevant provision of a worker's contract having effect by virtue of a variation of the contract does not operate to authorise the receipt of a payment on account of any conduct of the worker, or any other event occurring, before the variation took effect.

(4) For the purposes of this section an agreement or consent signified by a worker does not operate to authorise the receipt of a payment on account of any conduct of the worker, or any other event occurring, before the agreement or consent was signified.

(5) Any reference in this Part to an employer receiving a payment from a worker employed by him is a reference to his receiving such a payment in his capacity as the worker's employer.

Excepted payments

16.—(1) Section 15 does not apply to a payment received from a worker by **11-018** his employer where the purpose of the payment is the reimbursement of the employer in respect of—
  (a) an overpayment of wages, or
  (b) an overpayment in respect of expenses incurred by the worker in carrying out his employment,

made (for any reason) by the employer to the worker.

(2) Section 15 does not apply to a payment received from a worker by his employer in consequence of any disciplinary proceedings if those proceedings were held by virtue of a statutory provision.

(3) Section 15 does not apply to a payment received from a worker by his employer where the worker has taken part in a strike or other industrial action and the payment has been required by the employer on account of the worker's having taken part in that strike or other action.

(4) Section 15 does not apply to a payment received from a worker by his employer where the purpose of the payment is the satisfaction (whether wholly or in part) of an order of a court or tribunal requiring the payment of an amount by the worker to the employer.

Enforcement

Complaints to [employment tribunals][1]

11-019   **23.**—(1) A worker may present a complaint to an [employment tribunal][2]—

    (a) that his employer has made a deduction from his wages in contravention of section 13 (including a deduction made in contravention of that section as it applies by virtue of section 18(2)),

    (b) that his employer has received from him a payment in contravention of section 15 (including a payment received in contravention of that section as it applies by virtue of section 20(1)),

    (c) that his employer has recovered from his wages by means of one or more deductions falling within section 18(1) an amount or aggregate amount exceeding the limit applying to the deduction or deductions under that provision, or

    (d) that his employer has received from him in pursuance of one or more demands for payment made (in accordance with section 20) on a particular pay day, a payment or payments of an amount or aggregate amount exceeding the limit applying to the demands or demands under section 21(1).

(2) Subject to subsection (4), an [employment tribunal][3] shall not consider a complaint under this section unless it is presented before the end of the period of three months beginning with—

    (a) in the case of a complaint relating to a deduction by the employer, the date of payment of the wages from which the deduction was made, or

    (b) in the case of a complaint relating to a payment received by the employer, the date when the payment was received.

(3) Where a complaint is brought under this section in respect of—

    (a) a series of deductions or payments, or

    (b) a number of payments falling within subsection (1)(d) and made in pursuance of demands for payment subject to the same limit under section 21(1) but received by the employer on different dates,

the references in subsection (2) to the deduction or payment are to the last deduction or payment in the series or to the last of the payments so received.

(4) Where the [employment tribunal][4] is satisfied that it was not reasonably practicable for a complaint under this section to be presented before the end of

---

[1] Words substituted by Employment Rights (Dispute Resolution) Act 1998 c.8 Pt I s 1 (2)

[2] Words substituted by Employment Rights (Dispute Resolution) Act 1998 c.8 Pt I s 1 (2)

[3] Words substituted by Employment Rights (Dispute Resolution) Act 1998 c.8 Pt I s 1 (2)

[4] Words substituted by Employment Rights (Dispute Resolution) Act 1998 c.8 Pt I s 1 (2)

the relevant period of three months, the tribunal may consider the complaint if it is presented within such further period as the tribunal considers reasonable.

[(5) No complaint shall be presented under this section in respect of any deduction made in contravention of section 86 of the Trade Union and Labour Relations (Consolidation) Act 1992 (deduction of political fund contribution where certificate of exemption or objection has been given).][1]

Determination of complaints

24. Where a tribunal finds a complaint under section 23 well-founded, it **11-020** shall make a declaration to that effect and shall order the employer—
  (a) in the case of a complaint under section 23(1)(a), to pay to the worker the amount of any deduction made in contravention of section 13,
  (b) in the case of a complaint under section 23(1)(b), to repay to the worker the amount of any payment received in contravention of section 15,
  (c) in the case of a complaint under section 23(1)(c), to pay to the worker any amount recovered from him in excess of the limit mentioned in that provision, and
  (d) in the case of a complaint under section 23(1)(d), to repay to the worker any amount received from him in excess of the limit mentioned in that provision.

Determinations: supplementary

25.—(1) Where, in the case of any complaint under section 23(1)(a), a **11-021** tribunal finds that, although neither of the conditions set out in section 13(1)(a) and (b) was satisfied with respect to the whole amount of the deduction, one of those conditions was satisfied with respect to any lesser amount, the amount of the deduction shall for the purposes of section 24(a) be treated as reduced by the amount with respect to which that condition was satisfied.

(2) Where, in the case of any complaint under section 23(1)(b), a tribunal finds that, although neither of the conditions set out in section 15(1)(a) and (b) was satisfied with respect to the whole amount of the payment, one of those conditions was satisfied with respect to any lesser amount, the amount of the payment shall for the purposes of section 24(b) be treated as reduced by the amount with respect to which that condition was satisfied.

(3) An employer shall not under section 24 be ordered by a tribunal to pay or repay to a worker any amount in respect of a deduction or payment, or in respect of any combination of deductions or payments, in so far as it appears to the tribunal that he has already paid or repaid any such amount to the worker.

(4) Where a tribunal has under section 24 ordered an employer to pay or repay to a worker any amount in respect of a particular deduction or payment falling within section 23(1)(a) to (d), the amount which the employer is entitled to recover (by whatever means) in respect of the matter in relation to which the deduction or payment was originally made or received shall be treated as reduced by that amount.

(5) Where a tribunal has under section 24 ordered an employer to pay or repay to a worker any amount in respect of any combination of deductions or payments falling within section 23(1)(c) or (d), the aggregate amount which the employer is entitled to recover (by whatever means) in respect of the cash shortages or stock deficiencies in relation to which the deductions or payments

---

[1] Inserted by Employment Rights (Dispute Resolution) Act 1998 c.8 Sch 1 para 18

were originally made or required to be made shall be treated as reduced by that amount.

Complaints and other remedies

11-022 **26.** Section 23 does not affect the jurisdiction of an [employment tribunal][1] to consider a reference under section 11 in relation to any deduction from the wages of a worker; but the aggregate of any amounts ordered by an [employment tribunal][2] to be paid under section 12(4) and under section 24 (whether on the same or different occasions) in respect of a particular deduction shall not exceed the amount of the deduction.

Supplementary

Meaning of "wages" etc

11-023 **27.**—(1) In this Part "wages", in relation to a worker, means any sums payable to the worker in connection with his employment, including—

    (a) any fee, bonus, commission, holiday pay or other emolument referable to his employment, whether payable under his contract or otherwise,

    (b) statutory sick pay under Part XI of the Social Security Contributions and Benefits Act 1992,

    (c) statutory maternity pay under Part XII of that Act,

    [(ca) statutory paternity pay under Part 12ZA of that Act,

    (cb) statutory adoption pay under Part 12ZB of that Act,][3]

    (d) a guarantee payment (under section 28 of this Act),

    (e) any payment for time off under Part VI of this Act or section 169 of the Trade Union and Labour Relations (Consolidation) Act 1992 (payment for time off for carrying out trade union duties etc.),

    (f) remuneration on suspension on medical grounds under section 64 of this Act and remuneration on suspension on maternity grounds under section 68 of this Act,

    (g) any sum payable in pursuance of an order for reinstatement or re-engagement under section 113 of this Act,

    (h) any sum payable in pursuance of an order for the continuation of a contract of employment under section 130 of this Act or section 164 of the Trade Union and Labour Relations (Consolidation) Act 1992, and

    (j) remuneration under a protective award under section 189 of that Act,

but excluding any payments within subsection (2).

    (2) Those payments are—

    (a) any payment by way of an advance under an agreement for a loan or by way of an advance of wages (but without prejudice to the application of section 13 to any deduction made from the worker's wages in respect of any such advance),

    (b) any payment in respect of expenses incurred by the worker in carrying out his employment,

    (c) any payment by way of a pension, allowance or gratuity in connection with the worker's retirement or as compensation for loss of office,

    (d) any payment referable to the worker's redundancy, and

    (e) any payment to the worker otherwise than in his capacity as a worker.

---

[1] Words substituted by Employment Rights (Dispute Resolution) Act 1998 c.8 Pt I s 1 (2)

[2] Words substituted by Employment Rights (Dispute Resolution) Act 1998 c.8 Pt I s 1 (2)

[3] Inserted by Employment Act 2002 c.22 Sch 7 para 25

(3) Where any payment in the nature of a non-contractual bonus is (for any reason) made to a worker by his employer, the amount of the payment shall for the purposes of this Part—

(a) be treated as wages of the worker, and

(b) be treated as payable to him as such on the day on which the payment is made.

(4) In this Part "gross amount", means in relation to any wages payable to a worker, the total amount of those wages before deductions of whatever nature.

(5) For the purposes of this Part any monetary value attaching to any payment or benefit in kind furnished to a worker by his employer shall not be treated as wages of the worker except in the case of any voucher, stamp or similar document which is—

(a) of a fixed value expressed in monetary terms, and

(b) capable of being exchanged (whether on its own or together with other vouchers, stamps or documents, and whether immediately or only after a time) for money, goods or services (or for any combination of two or more of those things).

PART III

GUARANTEE PAYMENTS

Right to guarantee payment

28.—(1) Where throughout a day during any part of which an employee **11-024** would normally be required to work in accordance with his contract of employment the employee is not provided with work by his employer by reason of—

(a) a diminution in the requirements of the employer's business for work of the kind which the employee is employed to do, or

(b) any other occurrence affecting the normal working of the employer's business in relation to work of the kind which the employee is employed to do,

the employee is entitled to be paid by his employer an amount in respect of that day.

(2) In this Act a payment to which an employee is entitled under subsection (1) is referred to as a guarantee payment.

(3) In this Part—

(a) a day falling within subsection (1) is referred to as a "workless day", and

(b) "workless period" has a corresponding meaning.

(4) In this Part "day" means the period of twenty-four hours from midnight to midnight.

(5) Where a period of employment begun on any day extends, or would normally extend, over midnight into the following day—

(a) if the employment before midnight is, or would normally be, of longer duration than that after midnight, the period of employment shall be treated as falling wholly on the first day, and

(b) in any other case, the period of employment shall be treated as falling wholly on the second day.

Exclusions from right to guarantee payment

11-025   **29.**—(1) An employee is not entitled to a guarantee payment unless he has been continuously employed for a period of not less than one month ending with the day before that in respect of which the guarantee payment is claimed.

(2) [...][1]

(3) An employee is not entitled to a guarantee payment in respect of a workless day if the failure to provide him with work for that day occurs in consequence of a strike, lock-out or other industrial action involving any employee of his employer or of an associated employer.

(4) An employee is not entitled to a guarantee payment in respect of a workless day if—

(a) his employer has offered to provide alternative work for that day which is suitable in all the circumstances (whether or not it is work which the employee is under his contract employed to perform), and

(b) the employee has unreasonably refused that offer.

(5) An employee is not entitled to a guarantee payment if he does not comply with reasonable requirements imposed by his employer with a view to ensuring that his services are available.

Calculation of guarantee payment

11-026   **30.**—(1) Subject to section 31, the amount of a guarantee payment payable to an employee in respect of any day is the sum produced by multiplying the number of normal working hours on the day by the guaranteed hourly rate; and, accordingly, no guarantee payment is payable to an employee in whose case there are no normal working hours on the day in question.

(2) The guaranteed hourly rate, in relation to an employee, is the amount of one week's pay divided by the number of normal working hours in a week for that employee when employed under the contract of employment in force on the day in respect of which the guarantee payment is payable.

(3) But where the number of normal working hours differs from week to week or over a longer period, the amount of one week's pay shall be divided instead by—

(a) the average number of normal working hours calculated by dividing by twelve the total number of the employee's normal working hours during the period of twelve weeks ending with the last complete week before the day in respect of which the guarantee payment is payable, or

(b) where the employee has not been employed for a sufficient period to enable the calculation to be made under paragraph (a), a number which fairly represents the number of normal working hours in a week having regard to such of the considerations specified in subsection (4) as are appropriate in the circumstances.

(4) The considerations referred to in subsection (3)(b) are—

(a) the average number of normal working hours in a week which the employee could expect in accordance with the terms of his contract, and

(b) the average number of normal working hours of other employees engaged in relevant comparable employment with the same employer.

(5) If in any case an employee's contract has been varied, or a new contract has been entered into, in connection with a period of short-time working, subsection (2) and (3) have effect as if for the references to the day in respect of

---

[1] Repealed by SI 2002/2034 Sch 2 (1) para 3 (2)

which the guarantee payment is payable there were substituted references to the last day on which the original contract was in force.

Limits on amount of and entitlement to guarantee payment

31.—(1) The amount of a guarantee payment payable to an employee in respect of any day shall not exceed [£17.80][1]. **11-027**

(2) An employee is not entitled to guarantee payments in respect of more than the specified number of days in any period of three months.

(3) The specified number of days for the purposes of subsection (2) is the number of days, not exceeding five, on which the employee normally works in a week under the contract of employment in force on the day in respect of which the guarantee payment is claimed.

(4) But where that number of days varies from week to week or over a longer period, the specified number of days is instead—

  (a) the average number of such days, not exceeding five, calculated by dividing by twelve the total number of such days during the period of twelve weeks ending with the last complete week before the day in respect of which the guarantee payment is claimed, and rounding up the resulting figure to the next whole number, or

  (b) where the employee has not been employed for a sufficient period to enable the calculation to be made under paragraph (a), a number which fairly represents the number of the employee's normal working days in a week, not exceeding five, having regard to such of the considerations specified in subsection (5) as are appropriate in the circumstances.

(5) The considerations referred to in subsection (4)(b) are—

  (a) the average number of normal working days in a week which the employee could expect in accordance with the terms of his contract, and

  (b) the average number of such days of other employees engaged in relevant comparable employment with the same employer.

(6) If in any case an employee's contract has been varied, or a new contract has been entered into, in connection with a period of short-time working, subsections (3) and (4) have effect as if for the references to the day in respect of which the guarantee payment is claimed there were substituted references to the last day on which the original contract was in force.

[(7) The Secretary of State may by order vary—

  (a) the length of the period specified in subsection (2);

  (b) a limit specified in subsection (3) or (4).][2]

Contractual remuneration

32.—(1) A right to a guarantee payment does not affect any right of an employee in relation to remuneration under his contract of employment ("contractual remuneration"). **11-028**

(2) Any contractual remuneration paid to an employee in respect of a workless day goes towards discharging any liability of the employer to pay a guarantee payment in respect of that day; and, conversely, any guarantee payment paid in respect of a day goes towards discharging any liability of the employer to pay contractual remuneration in respect of that day.

(3) For the purposes of subsection (2), contractual remuneration shall be treated as paid in respect of a workless day—

---

[1] Figure substituted by SI 2003/3038 Sch 1

[2] Substituted by Employment Relations Act 1999 c.26 s 35

(a) where it is expressed to be calculated or payable by reference to that day or any part of that day, to the extent that it is so expressed, and

(b) in any other case, to the extent that it represents guaranteed remuneration, rather than remuneration for work actually done, and is referable to that day when apportioned rateably between that day and any other workless period falling within the period in respect of which the remuneration is paid.

Power to modify provisions about guarantee payments

11-029   **33.** The Secretary of State may by order provide that in relation to any description of employees the provisions of—

(a) sections 28(4) and (5), 30, 31(3) to (5) (as originally enacted or as varied under section 31(7)) and 32, and

(b) so far as they apply for the purposes of those provisions, Chapter II of Part XIVand section 234,

shall have effect subject to such modifications and adaptations as may be prescribed by the order.

Complaints to [employment tribunals][1]

11-030   **34.**—(1) An employee may present a complaint to an [employment tribunal][2] that his employer has failed to pay the whole or any part of a guarantee payment to which the employee is entitled.

(2) An [employment tribunal][3] shall not consider a complaint relating to a guarantee payment in respect of any unless the complaint is presented to the tribunal—

(a) before the end of the period of three months beginning with that day, or

(b) within such further period as the tribunal considers reasonable in a case where it is satisfied that it was not reasonably practicable for the complaint to be presented before the end of that period of three months.

(3) Where an [employment tribunal][4] finds a complaint under this section well-founded, the tribunal shall order the employer to pay to the employee the amount of guarantee payment which it finds is due to him.

Exemption orders

11-031   **35.**—(1) Where—

(a) at any time there is in force a collective agreement, or an agricultural wages order, under which employees to whom the agreement or order relates have a right to guaranteed remuneration, and

(b) on the application of all the parties to the agreement, or of the Board making the order, the appropriate Minister (having regard to the provisions of the agreement or order) is satisfied that section 28 should not apply to those employees,

he may make an order under this section excluding those employees from the operation of that section.

(2) In subsection (1) "agricultural wages order" means an order made under—

---

[1] Words substituted by Employment Rights (Dispute Resolution) Act 1998 c.8 Pt I s 1 (2)
[2] Words substituted by Employment Rights (Dispute Resolution) Act 1998 c.8 Pt I s 1 (2)
[3] Words substituted by Employment Rights (Dispute Resolution) Act 1998 c.8 Pt I s 1 (2)
[4] Words substituted by Employment Rights (Dispute Resolution) Act 1998 c.8 Pt I s 1 (2)

(a) section 3 of the Agricultural Wages Act 1948, or

(b) section 3 of the Agricultural Wages (Scotland) Act 1949.

(3) In subsection (1) "the appropriate Minister" means—

(a) in relation to a collective agreement or to an order such as is referred to in subsection (2)(b), the Secretary of State, and

(b) in relation to an order such as is referred to in subsection (2)(a), the [Secretary of State][1].

(4) The Secretary of State shall not make an order under this section in respect of an agreement unless—

(a) the agreement provides for procedures to be followed (whether by arbitration or otherwise) in cases where an employee claims that his employer has failed to pay the whole or any part of any guaranteed remuneration to which the employee is entitled under the agreement and those procedures include a right to arbitration or adjudication by an independent referee or body in cases where (by reason of an equality of votes or otherwise) a decision cannot otherwise be reached, or

(b) the agreement indicates that an employee to whom the agreement relates may present a complaint to an [employment tribunal][2] that his employer has failed to pay the whole or any part of any guaranteed remuneration to which the employee is entitled under the agreement.

(5) Where an order under this section is in force in respect of an agreement indicating as described in paragraph (b) of subsection (4) an [employment tribunal][3] shall have jurisdiction over a complaint such as is mentioned in that paragraph as if it were a complaint falling within section 34.

(6) An order varying or revoking an earlier order under this section may be made in pursuance of an application by all or any of the parties to the agreement in question, or the Board which made the order in question, or in the absence of such an application.

PART IVA

PROTECTED DISCLOSURES

[Meaning of "protected disclosure"

43A. In this Act a "protected disclosure" means a qualifying disclosure (as **11-032** defined by section 43B) which is made by a worker in accordance with any of sections 43C to 43H.][4]

[Disclosures qualifying for protection

43B.—(1) In this Part a "qualifying disclosure" means any disclosure of infor- **11-033** mation which, in the reasonable belief of the worker making the disclosure, tends to show one or more of the following—

(a) that a criminal offence has been committed, is being committed or is likely to be committed,

(b) that a person has failed, is failing or is likely to fail to comply with any legal obligation to which he is subject,

(c) that a miscarriage of justice has occurred, is occurring or is likely to occur,

---

[1] Words substituted by SI 2002/794 Sch 1 para 37
[2] Words substituted by Employment Rights (Dispute Resolution) Act 1998 c.8 Pt I s 1 (2)
[3] Words substituted by Employment Rights (Dispute Resolution) Act 1998 c.8 Pt I s 1 (2)
[4] Inserted by Public Interest Disclosure Act 1998 c.23 s 1

   (d) that the health or safety of any individual has been, is being or is likely to be endangered,

   (e) that the environment has been, is being or is likely to be damaged, or

   (f) that information tending to show any matter falling within any one of the preceding paragraphs has been, is being or is likely to be deliberately concealed.

(2) For the purposes of subsection (1), it is immaterial whether the relevant failure occurred, occurs or would occur in the United Kingdom or elsewhere, and whether the law applying to it is that of the United Kingdom or of any other country or territory.

(3) A disclosure of information is not a qualifying disclosure if the person making the disclosure commits an offence by making it.

(4) A disclosure of information in respect of which a claim to legal professional privilege (or, in Scotland, to confidentiality as between client and professional legal adviser) could be maintained in legal proceedings is not a qualifying disclosure if it is made by a person to whom the information had been disclosed in the course of obtaining legal advice.

(5) In this Part "the relevant failure", in relation to a qualifying disclosure, means the matter falling within paragraphs (a) to (f) of subsection (1).][1]

[Disclosure to employer or other responsible person

11-034   **43C.**—(1) A qualifying disclosure is made in accordance with this section if the worker makes the disclosure in good faith—

   (a) to his employer, or

   (b) where the worker reasonably, believes that the relevant failure relates solely or mainly to—

      (i) the conduct of a person other than his employer, or

      (ii) any other matter for which a person other than his employer has legal responsibility,

to that other person.

(2) A worker who, in accordance with a procedure whose use by him is authorised by his employer, makes a qualifying disclosure to a person other than his employer, is to be treated for the purposes of this Part as making the qualifying disclosure to his employer.][2]

[Disclosure to legal adviser

11-035   **43D.** A qualifying disclosure is made in accordance with this section if it is made in the course of obtaining legal advice.][3]

[Disclosure to Minister of the Crown

11-036   **43E.** A qualifying disclosure is made in accordance with this section if—

   (a) the worker's employer is—

      (i) an individual appointed under any enactment [(including any enactment comprised in, or in an instrument made under, an Act of the Scottish Parliament)][4] by a Minister of the Crown [or a member of the Scottish Executive][5], or

      (ii) a body any of whose members are so appointed, and

---

[1] Inserted by Public Interest Disclosure Act 1998 c.23 s 1
[2] Inserted by Public Interest Disclosure Act 1998 c.23 s 1
[3] Inserted by Public Interest Disclosure Act 1998 c.23 s 1
[4] Words inserted by SI 2000/2040 Sch 1 (I) para 19 (2)
[5] Words inserted by SI 2000/2040 Sch 1 (I) para 19 (3)

(b) the disclosure is made in good faith to a Minister of the Crown [or a member of the Scottish Executive]^1.]^2

[Disclosure to prescribed person

43F.—(1) A qualifying disclosure is made in accordance with this section if **11-037** the worker—
- (a) makes the disclosure in good faith to a person prescribed by an order made by the Secretary of State for the purposes of this section, and
- (b) reasonably believes—
  - (i) that the relevant failure falls within any description of matters in respect of which that person is so prescribed, and
  - (ii) that the information disclosed, and any allegation contained in it, are substantially true.

(2) An order prescribing persons for the purposes of this section may specify persons or descriptions of persons, and shall specify the descriptions of matters in respect of which each person, or persons of each description, is or are prescribed.]^3

[Disclosure in other cases

43G.—(1) A qualifying disclosure is made in accordance with this section **11-038** if—
- (a) the worker makes the disclosure in good faith,
- (b) he reasonably believes that the information disclosed, and any allegation contained in it, are substantially true,
- (c) he does not make the disclosure for purposes of personal gain,
- (d) any of the conditions in subsection (2) is met, and
- (e) in all the circumstances of the case, it is reasonable for him to make the disclosure.

(2) The conditions referred to in subsection (1)(d) are—
- (a) that, at the time he makes the disclosure, the worker reasonably believes that he will be subjected to a detriment by his employer if he makes a disclosure to his employer or in accordance with section 43F,
- (b) that, in a case where no person is prescribed for the purposes of section 43F in relation to the relevant failure, the worker reasonably believes that it is likely that evidence relating to the relevant failure will be concealed or destroyed if he makes a disclosure to his employer, or
- (c) that the worker has previously made a disclosure of substantially the same information—
  - (i) to his employer, or
  - (ii) in accordance with section 43F.

(3) In determining for the purposes of subsection (1)(e) whether it is reasonable for the worker to make the disclosure, regard shall be had, in particular, to—
- (a) the identity of the person to whom the disclosure is made,
- (b) the seriousness of the relevant failure,
- (c) whether the relevant failure is continuing or is likely to occur in the future,
- (d) whether the disclosure is made in breach of a duty of confidentiality owed by the employer to any other person,

---

^{1} Words inserted by SI 2000/2040 Sch 1 (I) para 19 (3)
^{2} Inserted by Public Interest Disclosure Act 1998 c.23 s 1
^{3} Inserted by Public Interest Disclosure Act 1998 c.23 s 1

(e) in a case falling within subsection (2)(c)(i) or (ii), any action which the employer or the person to whom the previous disclosure in accordance with section 43F was made has taken or might reasonably be expected to have taken as a result of the previous disclosure, and

(f) in a case falling within subsection (2)(c)(i), whether in making the disclosure to the employer the worker complied with any procedure whose use by him was authorised by the employer.

(4) For the purposes of this section a subsequent disclosure may be regarded as a disclosure of substantially the same information as that disclosed by a previous disclosure as mentioned in subsection (2)(c) even though the subsequent disclosure extends to information about action taken or not taken by any person as a result of the previous disclosure.][1]

[Disclosure of exceptionally serious failure

11-039   **43H.**—(1) A qualifying disclosure is made in accordance with this section if—

(a) the worker makes the disclosure in good faith,

(b) he reasonably believes that the information disclosed, and any allegation contained in it, are substantially true,

(c) he does not make the disclosure for purposes of personal gain,

(d) the relevant failure is of an exceptionally serious nature, and

(e) in all the circumstances of the case, it is reasonable for him to make the disclosure.

(2) In determining for the purposes of subsection (1)(e) whether it is reasonable for the worker to make the disclosure, regard shall be had, in particular, to the identity of the person to whom the disclosure is made.][2]

[Contractual duties of confidentiality

11-040   **43J.**—(1) Any provision in an agreement to which this section applies is void in so far as it purports to preclude the worker from making a protected disclosure.

(2) This section applies to any agreement between a worker and his employer (whether a worker's contract or not), including an agreement to refrain from instituting or continuing any proceedings under this Act or any proceedings for breach of contract.][3]

[Extension of meaning of "worker" etc. for Part IVA

11-041   **43K.**—(1) For the purposes of this Part "worker" includes an individual who is not a worker as defined by section 230(3) but who—

(a) works or worked for a person in circumstances in which—

(i) he is or was introduced or supplied to do that work by a third person, and

(ii) the terms on which he is or was engaged to do the work are or were in practice substantially determined not by him but by the person for whom he works or worked, by the third person or by both of them,

(b) contracts or contracted with a person, for the purposes of that person's business, for the execution of work to be done in a place not under the control or management of that person and would fall within section

---

[1] Inserted by Public Interest Disclosure Act 1998 c.23 s 1
[2] Inserted by Public Interest Disclosure Act 1998 c.23 s 1
[3] Inserted by Public Interest Disclosure Act 1998 c.23 s 1

230(3)(b) if for "personally" in that provision there were substituted "(whether personally or otherwise)",

[(ba) works or worked as a person performing services under a contract entered into by him with a Primary Care Trust or Local Health Board under section 28K or 28Q of the National Health Service Act 1977,][1]

[(bb) works or worked as a person performing services under a contract entered into by him with a Health Board under section 17J of the National Health Service (Scotland) Act 1978,][2]

(c) works or worked as a person providing [...][3] general dental services, general ophthalmic services or pharmaceutical services in accordance with arrangements made—

   (i) by a [Primary Care Trust or][4] Health Authority under section [...][5] 38 or 41 of the National Health Service Act 1977, or

   (ii) by a Health Board under section [...][6] 25, 26 or 27 of the National Health Service (Scotland) Act 1978, or

(d) is or was provided with work experience provided pursuant to a training course or programme or with training for employment (or with both) otherwise than—

   (i) under a contract of employment, or

   (ii) by an educational establishment on a course run by that establishment;

and any reference to a worker's contract, to employment or to a worker being "employed" shall be construed accordingly.

(2) For the purposes of this Part "employer" includes—

(a) in relation to a worker falling within paragraph (a) of subsection (1), the person who substantially determines or determined the terms on which he is or was engaged,

[(aa) in relation to a worker falling within paragraph (ba) of that subsection, the Primary Care Trust or Local Health Board referred to in that paragraph,][7]

[(ab) in relation to a worker falling within paragraph (bb) of that subsection, the Health Board referred to in that paragraph,][8]

(b) in relation to a worker falling within paragraph (c) of that subsection, the authority or board referred to in that paragraph, and

(c) in relation to a worker falling within paragraph (d) of that subsection, the person providing the work experience or training.

(3) In this section "educational establishment" includes any university, college, school or other educational establishment,][9]

[Application of this Part and related provisions to police

43KA.—(1) For the purposes of—

11-042

---

[1] Inserted by Health and Social Care (Community Health and Standards) Act 2003 c.43 Sch 11 para 65 (2)

[2] Inserted by SI 2004/957 Sch 1 para 8 (a) (i)

[3] Words repealed by SI 2004/957 Sch 1 para 8 (a) (ii)

[4] Words inserted by National Health Service Reform and Health Care Professions Act 2002 c.17 Sch 2 (2) para 63

[5] Words repealed by Health and Social Care (Community Health and Standards) Act 2003 c.43 Sch 14

[6] Words repealed by SI 2004/957 Sch 1 para 8 (a) (iii)

[7] Inserted by Health and Social Care (Community Health and Standards) Act 2003 c.43 Sch 11 para 65 (3)

[8] Inserted by SI 2004/957 Sch 1 para 8 (b)

[9] Inserted by Public Interest Disclosure Act 1998 c.23 s 1

(a) this Part,

(b) section 47B and sections 48 and 49 so far as relating to that section, and

(c) section 103A and the other provisions of Part 10 so far as relating to the right not to be unfairly dismissed in a case where the dismissal is unfair by virtue of section 103A,

a person who holds, otherwise than under a contract of employment, the office of constable or an appointment as a police cadet shall be treated as an employee employed by the relevant officer under a contract of employment; and any reference to a worker being 'employed' and to his 'employer' shall be construed accordingly.

(2) In this section 'the relevant officer' means—

(a) in relation to a member of a police force or a special constable appointed for a police area, the chief officer of police;

(b) in relation to a person appointed as a police member of the NCIS, the Director General of NCIS;

(c) in relation to a person appointed as a police member of the NCS, the Director General of NCS;

(d) in relation to any other person holding the office of constable or an appointment as police cadet, the person who has the direction and control of the body of constables or cadets in question.][1]

[Other interpretative provisions

11-043   **43L.**—(1) In this Part—

"qualifying disclosure" has the meaning given by section 43B;

"the relevant failure", in relation to a qualifying disclosure, has the meaning given by section 43B(5).

(2) In determining for the purposes of this Part whether a person makes a disclosure for purposes of personal gain, there shall be disregarded any reward payable by or under any enactment.

(3) Any reference in this Part to the disclosure of information shall have effect, in relation to any case where the person receiving the information is already aware of it, as a reference to bringing the information to his attention.][2]

PART V

PROTECTION FROM SUFFERING DETRIMENT IN EMPLOYMENT

Rights not to suffer detriment

Health and safety cases

11-044   **44.**—(1) An employee has the right not to be subjected to any detriment by any act, or any deliberate failure to act, by his employer done on the ground that—

(a) having been designated by the employer to carry out activities in connection with preventing or reducing risks to health and safety at work, the employee carried out (or proposed to carry out) any such activities,

---

[1] Inserted by Police Reform Act 2002 c.30 s 37 (1)

[2] Inserted by Public Interest Disclosure Act 1998 c.23 s 1

(b) being a representative of workers on matters of health and safety at work or member of a safety committee—
  (i) in accordance with arrangements established under or by virtue of any enactment, or
  (ii) by reason of being acknowledged as such by the employer,
the employee performed (or proposed to perform) any functions as such a representative or a member of such a committee,

[(ba) the employee took part (or proposed to take part) in consultation with the employer pursuant to the Health and Safety (Consultation with Employees) Regulations 1996 or in an election of representatives of employee safety within the meaning of those Regulations (whether as a candidate or otherwise),][1]

(c) being an employee at a place where—
  (i) there was no such representative or safety committee, or
  (ii) there was such a representative or safety committee but it was not reasonably practicable for the employee to raise the matter by those means,
he brought to his employer's attention, by reasonable means, circumstances connected with his work which he reasonably believed were harmful or potentially harmful to health or safety,

(d) in circumstances of danger which the employee reasonably believed to be serious and imminent and which he could not reasonably have been expected to avert, he left (or proposed to leave) or (while the danger persisted) refused to return to his place of work or any dangerous part of his place of work, or

(e) in circumstances of danger which the employee reasonably believed to be serious and imminent, he took (or proposed to take) appropriate steps to protect himself or other persons from the danger.

(2) For the purposes of subsection (1)(e) whether steps which an employee took (or proposed to take) were appropriate is to be judged by reference to all the circumstances including, in particular, his knowledge and the facilities and advice available to him at the time.

(3) An employee is not to be regarded as having been subjected to any detriment on the ground specified in subsection (1)(e) if the employer shows that it was (or would have been) so negligent for the employee to take the steps which he took (or proposed to take) that a reasonable employer might have treated him as the employer did.

(4) [...][2] This section does not apply where the detriment in question amounts to dismissal (within the meaning of [Part X][3]).

Sunday working for shop and betting workers

45.—(1) An employee who is—   **11-045**
  (a) a protected shop worker or an opted-out shop worker, or
  (b) a protected betting worker or an opted-out betting worker,
has the right not to be subjected to any detriment by any act, or any deliberate failure to act, by his employer done on the ground that the employee refused (or proposed to refuse) to do shop work, or betting work, on Sunday or on a particular Sunday.

---

[1] Inserted by SI 1996/1513 reg 8
[2] Words repealed by Employment Relations Act 1999 c.26 Sch 9 para 1
[3] Words substituted by Employment Relations Act 1999 c.26 s 18 (2) (b)

(2) Subsection (1) does not apply to anything done in relation to an opted-out shop worker or an opted-out betting worker on the ground that he refused (or proposed to refuse) to do shop work, or betting work, on any Sunday or Sundays falling before the end of the notice period.

(3) An employee who is a shop worker or a betting worker has the right not to be subjected to any detriment by any act, or any deliberate failure to act, by his employer done on the ground that the employee gave (or proposed to give) an opting-out notice to his employer.

(4) Subsections (1) and (3) do not apply where the detriment in question amounts to dismissal (within the meaning of Part X).

(5) For the purposes of this section a shop worker or betting worker who does not work on Sunday or on a particular Sunday is not to be regarded as having been subjected to any detriment by—

> (a) a failure to pay remuneration in respect of shop work, or betting work, on a Sunday which he has not done,
>
> (b) a failure to provide him with any other benefit, where that failure results from the application (in relation to a Sunday on which the employee has not done shop work, or betting work) of a contractual term under which the extent of that benefit varies according to the number of hours worked by the employee or the remuneration of the employee, or
>
> (c) a failure to provide him with any work, remuneration or other benefit which by virtue of section 38 or 39 the employer is not obliged to provide.

(6) Where an employer offers to pay a sum specified in the offer to any one or more employees—

> (a) who are protected shop workers or opted-out shop workers or protected betting workers or opted-out betting workers, or
>
> (b) who under their contracts of employment are not obliged to do shop work, or betting work, on Sunday,

if they agree to do shop work, or betting work, on Sunday or on a particular Sunday subsections (7) and (8) apply.

(7) An employee to whom the offer is not made is not to be regarded for the purposes of this section as having been subjected to any detriment by any failure to make the offer to him or to pay him the sum specified in the offer.

(8) An employee who does not accept the offer is not to be regarded for the purposes of this section as having been subjected to any detriment by any failure to pay him the sum specified in the offer.

(9) For the purposes of section 36(2)(b) or 41(1)(b), the appropriate date in relation to this section is the date of the act or failure to act.

(10) For the purposes of subsection (9)—

> (a) where an act extends over a period, the "date of the act" means the first day of that period, and
>
> (b) a deliberate failure to act shall be treated as done when it was decided on;

and, in the absence of evidence establishing the contrary, an employer shall be taken to decide on a failure to act when he does an act inconsistent with doing the failed act or, if he has done no such inconsistent act, when the period expires within which he might reasonably have been expected to do the failed act if it was to be done.

[Working time cases

45A.—(1) A worker has the right not to be subjected to any detriment by any **11-046**
Act, or any deliberate failure to act, by his employer done on the ground that the
worker –

    (a) refused (or proposed to refuse) to comply with a requirement which the
        employer imposed (or proposed to impose) in contravention of the
        Working Time Regulations 1998,

    (b) refused (or proposed to refuse) to forgo a right conferred on him by
        those Regulations,

    (c) failed to sign a workforce agreement for the purposes of those Regula-
        tions, or to enter into, or agree to vary or extend, any other agreement
        with his employer which is provided for in those Regulations,

    (d) being –
        (i) a representative of members of the workforce for the purposes of
            Schedule 1 to those Regulations, or
        (ii) a candidate in an election in which any person elected will, on
            being elected, be such a representative,

performed (or proposed to perform) any functions or activities as such a
representative or candidate,

    (e) brought proceedings against the employer to enforce a right conferred
        on him by those Regulations, or

    (f) alleged that the employer had infringed such a right.

(2) It is immaterial for the purposes of subsection (1)(e) or (f)–

    (a) whether or not the worker has the right, or

    (b) whether or not the right has been infringed,

but, for those provisions to apply, the claim to the right and that it has been
infringed must be made in good faith.

(3) It is sufficient for subsection (1)(f) to apply that the worker, without
specifying the right, made it reasonably clear to the employer what the right
claimed to have been infringed was.

(4) This section does not apply where a worker is an employee and the
detriment in question amounts to dismissal within the meaning of Part X [...]¹.

[(5) A reference in this section to the Working Time Regulations 1998
includes a reference to the Merchant Shipping (Working Time: Inland
Waterways) Regulations 2003.]²]³

Trustees of occupational pension schemes

46.—(1) An employee has the right not to be subjected to any detriment by **11-047**
any act, or any deliberate failure to act, by his employer done on the ground that,
being a trustee of a relevant occupational pension scheme which relates to his
employment, the employee performed (or proposed to perform) any functions as
such a trustee.

(2) [...]⁴ This section does not apply where the detriment in question
amounts to dismissal (within the meaning of [Part X]⁵).

[(2A) This section applies to an employee who is a director of a company
which is a trustee of a relevant occupational pension scheme as it applies to an

---

¹ Words repealed by Employment Relations Act 1999 c.26 Sch 9
² Inserted by SI 2003/3049 Sch 2 para 3 (2)
³ Inserted by SI 1998/1833 reg 31 (1)
⁴ Words repealed by Employment Relations Act 1999 c.26 Sch 9 para 1
⁵ Words substituted by Employment Relations Act 1999 c.26 s 18 (2) (b)

employee who is a trustee of such a scheme (references to such a trustee being read for this purpose as references to such a director).][1]

(3) In this section "relevant occupational pension scheme" means an occupational pension scheme (as defined in section 1 of the Pension Schemes Act 1993) established under a trust.

Employee representatives

11-048   **47.**—(1) An employee has the right not to be subjected to any detriment by any act, or any deliberate failure to act, by his employer done on the ground that, being—

  (a) an employee representative for the purposes of Chapter II of Part IV of the Trade Union and Labour Relations (Consolidation) Act 1992 (redundancies) or Regulations 10 and 11 of the Transfer of Undertakings (Protection of Employment) Regulations 1981, or

  (b) a candidate in an election in which any person elected will, on being elected, be such an employee representative,

he performed (or proposed to perform) any functions or activities as such an employee representative or candidate.

[(1A) An employee has the right not to be subjected to any detriment by any act, or by any deliberate failure to act, by his employer done on the ground of his participation in an election of employee representatives for the purposes of Chapter II of Part IV of the Trade Union and Labour Relations (Consolidation) Act 1992 (redundancies) or Regulations 10 and 11 of the Transfer of Undertakings (Protection of Employment) Regulations 1981.][2]

(2) [...][3] This section does not apply where the detriment in question amounts to a dismissal (within the meaning of [Part X][4]).

[Employees exercising right to time off work for study or training

11-049   **47A.**—(1) An employee has the right not to be subjected to any detriment by any act, or any deliberate failure to act, by his employer or the principal (within the meaning of section 63A(3)) done on the ground that, being a person entitled to—

  (a) time off under section 63A(1) or (3), and

  (b) remuneration under section 63B(1) in respect of that time taken off,

the employee exercised (or proposed to exercise) that right or received (or sought to receive) such remuneration.

(2) [...][5] This section does not apply where the detriment in question amounts to dismissal (within the meaning of [Part X][6]).][7]

[Protected disclosures

11-050   **47B.**—(1) A worker has the right not to be subjected to any detriment by any act, or any deliberate failure to act, by his employer done on the ground that the worker has made a protected disclosure.

(2) [...][8] This section does not apply where—

  (a) the worker is an employee, and

---

[1] Words inserted by Welfare Reform and Pensions Act 1999 c.30 Sch 2 para 19 (2)
[2] Words inserted by SI 1999/1925 reg 12
[3] Words repealed by Employment Relations Act 1999 c.26 Sch 9 para 1
[4] Words substituted by Employment Relations Act 1999 c.26 s 18 (2) (b)
[5] Words repealed by Employment Relations Act 1999 c.26 Sch 9 para 1
[6] Words substituted by Employment Relations Act 1999 c.26 s 18 (2) (b)
[7] Inserted by Teaching and Higher Education Act 1998 c.30 Sch 3 para 10
[8] Words repealed by Employment Relations Act 1999 c.26 Sch 9 para 1

(b) the detriment in question amounts to dismissal (within the meaning of [Part X][1]).

(3) For the purposes of this section, and of sections 48 and 49 so far as relating to this section, "worker" "worker's contract", "employment" and "employer" have the extended meaning given by section 43K.][2]

[Leave for family and domestic reasons

47C.—(1) An employee has the right not to be subjected to any detriment by any act, or any deliberate failure to act, by his employer done for a prescribed reason.

(2) A prescribed reason is one which is prescribed by regulations made by the Secretary of State and which relates to—

(a) pregnancy, childbirth or maternity,

(b) ordinary, compulsory or additional maternity leave,

[(ba) ordinary or additional adoption leave,][3]

(c) parental leave,

[(ca) paternity leave, or][4]

(d) time off under section 57A.

(3) A reason prescribed under this section in relation to parental leave may relate to action which an employee takes, agrees to take or refuses to take under or in respect of a collective or workforce agreement.

(4) Regulations under this section may make different provision for different cases or circumstances.][5]

11-051

[Tax credits

47D—(1) An employee has the right not to be subjected to any detriment by any act, or any deliberate failure to act, by his employer, done on the ground that—

(a) any action was taken, or was proposed to be taken, by or on behalf of the employee with a view to enforcing, or otherwise securing the benefit of, a right conferred on the employee by regulations under section 25 of the Tax Credits Act 2002,

(b) a penalty was imposed on the employer, or proceedings for a penalty were brought against him, under that Act, as a result of action taken by or on behalf of the employee for the purpose of enforcing, or otherwise securing the benefit of, such a right, or

(c) the employee is entitled, or will or may be entitled, to working tax credit.

(2) It is immaterial for the purposes of subsection (1)(a) or (b)—

(a) whether or not the employee has the right, or

(b) whether or not the right has been infringed,

but, for those provisions to apply, the claim to the right and (if applicable) the claim that it has been infringed must be made in good faith.

(3) Subsections (1) and (2) apply to a person who is not an employee within the meaning of this Act but who is an employee within the meaning of section 25 of the Tax Credits Act 2002, with references to his employer in those subsections

11-052

---

[1] Words substituted by Employment Relations Act 1999 c.26 s 18 (2) (b)

[2] Inserted by Public Interest Disclosure Act 1998 c.23 s 2

[3] Inserted by Employment Act 2002 c.22 Sch 7 para 26 (2)

[4] Substituted by Employment Act 2002 c.22 Sch 7 para 26 (3)

[5] Inserted by Employment Relations Act 1999 c.26 Sch 4 (III) para 8

(and sections 48(2) and (4) and 49(1)) being construed in accordance with that section.

(4) Subsections (1) and (2) do not apply to an employee if the detriment in question amounts to dismissal (within the meaning of Part 10).][1]

[Flexible working

11-053   **47E**—(1) An employee has the right not to be subjected to any detriment by any act, or any deliberate failure to act, by his employer done on the ground that the employee—

(a) made (or proposed to make) an application under section 80F,

(b) exercised (or proposed to exercise) a right conferred on him under section 80G,

(c) brought proceedings against the employer under section 80H, or

(d) alleged the existence of any circumstance which would constitute a ground for bringing such proceedings.

(2) This section does not apply where the detriment in question amounts to dismissal within the meaning of Part 10.][2]

Enforcement

Complaints to [employment tribunals][3]

11-054   **48.**—(1) An employee may present a complaint to an [employment tribunal][4] that he has been subjected to a detriment in contravention of [section 44, 45, 46, 47, 47A, [47C or 47D][5]][6].

[[(1A) A worker may present a complaint to an employment tribunal that he has been subjected to a detriment in contravention of section 47B.][7]

[(1B) A person may present a complaint to an employment tribunal that he has been subjected to a detriment in contravention of section 47D.][8]

(1ZA) A worker may present a complaint to an employment tribunal that he has been subjected to a detriment in contravention of section 45A.][9]

(2) On such a complaint it is for the employer to show the ground on which any act, or deliberate failure to act, was done.

(3) An [employment tribunal][10] shall not consider a complaint under this section unless it is presented—

(a) before the end of the period of three months beginning with the date of the act or failure to act to which the complaint relates or, where that act or failure is part of a series of similar acts or failures, the last of them, or

(b) within such further period as the tribunal considers reasonable in a case where it is satisfied that it was not reasonably practicable for the complaint to be presented before the end of that period of three months.

(4) For the purposes of subsection (3)—

---

[1] Inserted by Tax Credits Act 2002 c.21 Sch 1 para 1 (2)
[2] Inserted by Employment Act 2002 c.22 s 47 (3)
[3] Words substituted by Employment Rights (Dispute Resolution) Act 1998 c.8 Pt I s 1 (2)
[4] Words substituted by Employment Rights (Dispute Resolution) Act 1998 c.8 Pt I s 1 (2)
[5] Words substituted by Employment Act 2002 c.22 Sch 7 para 27
[6] Words substituted by Employment Relations Act 1999 c.26 Sch 4 (III) para 9
[7] Inserted by Public Interest Disclosure Act 1998 c.23 s 3
[8] Inserted by Tax Credits Act 2002 c.21 Sch 1 para 1 (3)
[9] Inserted by SI 1998/1833 Pt IV reg 31 (2)
[10] Words substituted by Employment Rights (Dispute Resolution) Act 1998 c.8 Pt I s 1 (2)

(a) where an act extends over a period, the "date of the act" means the last day of that period, and

(b) a deliberate failure to act shall be treated as done when it was decided on;

and, in the absence of evidence establishing the contrary, an employer shall be taken to decide on a failure to act when he does an act inconsistent with doing the failed act or, if he has done no such inconsistent act, when the period expires within which he might reasonably have been expected to do the failed act if it was to be done.

[(5) In this section and section 49 any reference to the employer includes, where a person complains that he has been subjected to a detriment in contravention of section 47A, the principal (within the meaning of section 63A(3)).][1]

Remedies

49.—(1) Where an [employment tribunal][2] finds a complaint under section 48 well-founded, the tribunal— **11-055**

(a) shall make a declaration to that effect, and

(b) may make an award of compensation to be paid by the employer to the complainant in respect of the act or failure to act to which the complaint relates.

(2) [[Subject to subsections (5A)][3] and (6)][4] the amount of the compensation awarded shall be such as the tribunal considers just and equitable in all the circumstances having regard to—

(a) the infringement to which the complaint relates, and

(b) any loss which is attributable to the act, or failure to act, which infringed the complainant's right.

(3) The loss shall be taken to include—

(a) any expenses reasonably incurred by the complainant in consequence of the act, or failure to act, to which the complaint relates, and

(b) loss of any benefit which he might reasonably be expected to have had but for that act or failure to act.

(4) In ascertaining the loss the tribunal shall apply the same rule concerning the duty of a person to mitigate his loss as applies to damages recoverable under the common law of England and Wales or (as the case may be) Scotland.

(5) Where the tribunal finds that the act, or failure to act, to which the complaint relates was to any extent caused or contributed to by action of the complainant, it shall reduce the amount of the compensation by such proportion as it considers just and equitable having regard to that finding.

[(5A) Where–

(a) the complaint is made under section 48 (1ZA),

(b) the detriment to which the worker is subjected is the termination of his worker's contract, and

(c) that contract is not a contract of employment,

any compensation must not exceed the compensation that would be payable under Chapter II of Part X if the worker had been an employee and had been dismissed for the reason specified in section 101A.][5]

[(6) Where—

---

[1] Inserted by Teaching and Higher Education Act 1998 c.30 Sch 3 para 11 (b)

[2] Words substituted by Employment Rights (Dispute Resolution) Act 1998 c.8 Pt I s 1 (2)

[3] Words substituted by SI 1998/1833 Pt IV reg 31 (3) (a)

[4] Words inserted by Public Interest Disclosure Act 1998 c.23 s 4 (2)

[5] Inserted by SI 1998/1833 Pt IV reg 31 (3) (b)

(a) the complaint is made under section 48(1A),
(b) the detriment to which the worker is subjected is the termination of his worker's contract, and
(c) that contract is not a contract of employment,

any compensation must not exceed the compensation that would be payable under Chapter II of Part X if the worker had been an employee and had been dismissed for the reason specified in section 103A.][1]

[(7) Where—

(a) the complaint is made under section 48(1B) by a person who is not an employee, and
(b) the detriment to which he is subjected is the termination of his contract with the person who is his employer for the purposes of section 25 of the Tax Credits Act 2002,

any compensation must not exceed the compensation that would be payable under Chapter 2 of Part 10 if the complainant had been an employee and had been dismissed for the reason specified in section 104B.][2]

PART VI

TIME OFF WORK

Public duties

Right to time off for public duties

11-056   **50.**—(1) An employer shall permit an employee of his who is a justice of the peace to take time off during the employee's working hours for the purpose of performing any of the duties of his office.

(2) An employer shall permit an employee of his who is a member of—

(a) a local authority,
(b) a statutory tribunal,
(c) a police authority,
[(ca) the Service Authority for the National Criminal Intelligence Service or the Service Authority for the National Crime Squad,][3]
(d) a board of prison visitors or a prison visiting committee,
(e) a relevant health body,
(f) a relevant education body, [...][4]
(g) the Environment Agency or the Scottish Environment Protection Agency, [or][5]

to take time off during the employee's working hours for the purposes specified in subsection (3).

(3) The purposes referred to in subsection (2) are—

(a) attendance at a meeting of the body or any of its committees or sub-committees, and
(b) the doing of any other thing approved by the body, or anything of a class so approved, for the purpose of the discharge of the functions of the body or of any of its committees or sub-committees[, and][6]

---

[1] Inserted by Public Interest Disclosure Act 1998 c.23 s 4 (3)
[2] Inserted by Tax Credits Act 2002 c.21 Sch 1 para 1 (4)
[3] Inserted by Police Act 1997 c.50 Sch 9 para 88
[4] Word repealed by SI 2000/1737 art 2 (a)
[5] Word inserted by SI 2000/1737 art 2 (b)
[6] Inserted by SI 2002/808 art 29

[(c) in the case of a local authority which are operating executive arrangements—

    (i) attendance at a meeting of the executive of that local authority or committee of that executive; and

    (ii) the doing of any other thing, by an individual member of that executive, for the purposes of the discharge of any function which is to any extent the responsibility of that executive.][1]

(4) The amount of time off which an employee is to be permitted to take under this section, and the occasions on which and any conditions subject to which time off may be so taken, are those that are reasonable in all the circumstances having regard, in particular, to—

(a) how much time off is required for the performance of the duties of the office or as a member of the body in question, and how much time off is required for the performance of the particular duty,

(b) how much time off the employee has already been permitted under this section or sections 168 and 170 of the Trade Union and Labour Relations (Consolidation) Act 1992 (time off for trade union duties and activities), and

(c) the circumstances of the employer's business and the effect of the employee's absence on the running of that business.

(5) In subsection (2)(a) "a local authority" means—

(a) a local authority within the meaning of the Local Government Act 1972,

(b) a council constituted under section 2 of the Local Government etc. (Scotland) Act 1994,

(c) the Common Council of the City of London,

(d) a National Park authority, or

(e) the Broads Authority.

(6) The reference in subsection (2) to a member of a police authority is to a person appointed as such a member under Schedule 2 to the Police Act 1996.

(7) In subsection (2)(d)—

(a) "a board of prison visitors" means a board of visitors appointed under section 6(2) of the Prison Act 1952, and

(b) "a prison visiting committee" means a visiting committee appointed under section 19(3) of the Prisons (Scotland) Act 1989 or constituted by virtue of rules made under section 39 (as read with section 8(1) of that Act.

(8) In subsection (2)(e) "a relevant health body" means—

(a) a National Health Service trust established under Part I of the National Health Service and Community Care Act 1990 or the National Health Service (Scotland) Act 1978,

[(ab) an NHS foundation trust,][2]

(b) a [Strategic Health Authority or][3] Health Authority established under section 8 of the National Health Service Act 1977[, a Special Health Authority established under section 11 of that Act or a Primary Care Trust established under section 16A of that Act][4], or

---

[1] Inserted by SI 2002/808 art 29

[2] Words inserted by Health and Social Care (Community Health and Standards) Act 2003 c.43 Sch 4 para 100

[3] Words inserted by SI 2002/2469 Sch 1 (1) para 22 (2)

[4] Words substituted by SI 2000/90 Sch 1 para 30 (2)

(c) a Health Board constituted under section 2 of the National Health Service (Scotland) Act 1978.

(9) In subsection (2)(f) "a relevant education body" means—

(a) a managing or governing body of an educational establishment maintained by a local education authority,

(b) a governing body of a [...]¹ further education corporation or higher education corporation,

(c) a school council appointed under section 125(1) of the Local Government (Scotland) Act 1973,

(d) a school board within the meaning of section 1(1) of the School Boards (Scotland) Act 1988,

(e) a board of management of a self-governing school within the meaning of section 135(1) of the Education (Scotland) Act 1980,

(f) a board of management of a college of further education within the meaning of section 36(1) of the Further and Higher Education (Scotland) Act 1992,

(g) a governing body of a central institution within the meaning of section 135(1) of the Education (Scotland) Act 1980, [...]²

(h) a governing body of a designated institution within the meaning of Part II of the Further and Higher Education (Scotland) Act 1992.

[(i) the General Teaching Council for England, or

(j) the General Teaching Council for Wales.]³

[(9A) In subsection (3)(c) of this section "executive" and "executive arrangements" have the same meaning as in Part II of the Local Government Act 2000.]⁴

(10) The Secretary of State may by order—

(a) modify the provisions of subsections (1) and (2) and (5) to (9) by adding any office or body, removing any office or body or altering the description of any office or body, or

(b) modify the provisions of subsection (3).

(11) For the purposes of this section the working hours of an employee shall be taken to be any time when, in accordance with his contract of employment, the employee is required to be at work.

Complaints to [employment tribunals]⁵

11-057   **51.**—(1) An employee may present a complaint to an [employment tribunal]⁶ that his employer has failed to permit him to take time off as required by section 50.

(2) An [employment tribunal]⁷ shall not consider a complaint under this section that an employer has failed to permit an employee to take time off unless it is presented—

(a) before the end of the period of three months beginning with the date on which the failure occurred, or

(b) within such further period as the tribunal considers reasonable in a case where it is satisfied that it was not reasonably practicable for the

¹ Words repealed by School Standards and Framework Act 1998 c.31 Sch 31 para 1
² Word repealed by SI 2000/2463 art 2 (2)
³ Inserted by SI 2000/2463 art 2 (3)
⁴ Inserted by SI 2002/808 art 29
⁵ Words substituted by Employment Rights (Dispute Resolution) Act 1998 c.8 Pt I s 1 (2)
⁶ Words substituted by Employment Rights (Dispute Resolution) Act 1998 c.8 Pt I s 1 (2)
⁷ Words substituted by Employment Rights (Dispute Resolution) Act 1998 c.8 Pt I s 1 (2)

complaint to be presented before the end of that period of three months.

(3) Where an [employment tribunal][1] finds a complaint under this section well-founded, the tribunal—

(a) shall make a declaration to that effect, and

(b) may make an award of compensation to be paid by the employer to the employee.

(4) The amount of the compensation shall be such as the tribunal considers just and equitable in all the circumstances having regard to—

(a) the employer's default in failing to permit time off to be taken by the employee, and

(b) any loss sustained by the employee which is attributable to the matters to which the complaint relates.

Looking for work and making arrangements for training

Right to time off to look for work or arrange training

52.—(1) An employee who is given notice of dismissal by reason of **11-058** redundancy is entitled to be permitted by his employer to take reasonable time off during the employee's working hours before the end of his notice in order to—

(a) look for new employment, or

(b) make arrangements for training for future employment.

(2) An employee is not entitled to take time off under this section unless, on whichever is the later of—

(a) the date on which the notice is due to expire, and

(b) the date on which it would expire were it the notice required to be given by section 86(1),

he will have been (or would have been) continuously employed for a period of two years or more.

(3) For the purposes of this section the working hours of an employee shall be taken to be any time when, in accordance with his contract of employment, the employee is required to be at work.

Right to remuneration for time off under section 52

53.—(1) An employee who is permitted to take time off under section 52 is **11-059** entitled to be paid remuneration by his employer for the period of absence at the appropriate hourly rate.

(2) The appropriate hourly rate, in relation to an employee, is the amount of one week's pay divided by the number of normal working hours in a week for that employee when employed under the contract of employment in force on the day when the notice of dismissal was given.

(3) But where the number of normal working hours differs from week to week or over a longer period, the amount of one week's pay shall be divided instead by the average number of normal working hours calculated by dividing by twelve the total number of the employee's normal working hours during the period of twelve weeks ending with the last complete week before the day on which the notice was given.

(4) If an employer unreasonably refuses to permit an employee to take time off from work as required by section 52, the employee is entitled to be paid an

---

[1] Words substituted by Employment Rights (Dispute Resolution) Act 1998 c.8 Pt I s 1 (2)

amount equal to the remuneration to which he would have been entitled under subsection (1) if he had been permitted to take the time off.

(5) The amount of an employer's liability to pay remuneration under subsection (1) shall not exceed, in respect of the notice period of any employee, forty per cent. of a week's pay of that employee.

(6) A right to any amount under subsection (1) or (4) does not affect any right of an employee in relation to remuneration under his contract of employment ("contractual remuneration").

(7) Any contractual remuneration paid to an employee in respect of a period of time off under section 52 goes towards discharging any liability of the employer to pay remuneration under subsection (1) in respect of that period; and, conversely, any payment of remuneration under subsection (1) in respect of a period goes towards discharging any liability of the employer to pay contractual remuneration in respect of that period.

Complaints to [employment tribunals][1]

11-060   **54.**—(1) An employee may present a complaint to an [employment tribunal][2] that his employer—

    (a) has unreasonably refused to permit him to take time off as required by section 52, or

    (b) has failed to pay the whole or any part of any amount to which the employee is entitled under section 53(1) or (4).

(2) An [employment tribunal][3] shall not consider a complaint under this section unless it is presented—

    (a) before the end of the period of three months beginning with the date on which it is alleged that the time off should have been permitted, or

    (b) within such further period as the tribunal considers reasonable in a case where it is satisfied that it was not reasonably practicable for the complaint to be presented before the end of that period of three months.

(3) Where an [employment tribunal][4] finds a complaint under this section well-founded, the tribunal shall—

    (a) make a declaration to that effect, and

    (b) order the employer to pay to the employee the amount which it finds due to him.

(4) The amount which may be ordered by a tribunal to be paid by an employer under subsection (3) (or, where the employer is liable to pay remuneration under section 53, the aggregate of that amount and the amount of that liability) shall not exceed, in respect of the notice period of any employee, forty per cent. of a week's pay of that employee.

Ante-natal care

Right to time off for ante-natal care

11-061   **55.**—(1) An employee who—

    (a) is pregnant, and

---

[1] Words substituted by Employment Rights (Dispute Resolution) Act 1998 c.8 Pt I s 1 (2)
[2] Words substituted by Employment Rights (Dispute Resolution) Act 1998 c.8 Pt I s 1 (2)
[3] Words substituted by Employment Rights (Dispute Resolution) Act 1998 c.8 Pt I s 1 (2)
[4] Words substituted by Employment Rights (Dispute Resolution) Act 1998 c.8 Pt I s 1 (2)

(b) has, on the advice of a registered medical practitioner, registered midwife or [registered nurse][1], made an appointment to attend at any place for the purpose of receiving ante-natal care,

is entitled to be permitted by her employer to take time off during the employee's working hours in order to enable her to keep the appointment.

(2) An employee is not entitled to take time off under this section to keep an appointment unless, if her employer requests her to do so, she produces for his inspection—

(a) a certificate from a registered medical practitioner, registered midwife or [registered nurse][2] stating that the employee is pregnant, and

(b) an appointment card or some other document showing that the appointment has been made.

(3) Subsection (2) does not apply where the employee's appointment is the first appointment during her pregnancy for which she seeks permission to take time off in accordance with subsection (1).

(4) For the purposes of this section the working hours of an employee shall be taken to be any time when, in accordance with her contract of employment, the employee is required to be at work.

Right to remuneration for time off under section 55

56.—(1) An employee who is permitted to take time off under section 55 is **11-062** entitled to be paid remuneration by her employer for the period of absence at the appropriate hourly rate.

(2) The appropriate hourly rate, in relation to an employee, is the amount of one week's pay divided by the number of normal working hours in a week for that employee when employed under the contract of employment in force on the day when the time off is taken.

(3) But where the number of normal working hours differs from week to week or over a longer period, the amount of one week's pay shall be divided instead by—

(a) the average number of normal working hours calculated by dividing by twelve the total number of the employee's normal working hours during the period of twelve weeks ending with the last complete week before the day on which the time off is taken, or

(b) where the employee has not been employed for a sufficient period to enable the calculation to be made under paragraph (a), a number which fairly represents the number of normal working hours in a week having regard to such of the considerations specified in subsection (4) as are appropriate in the circumstances.

(4) The considerations referred to in subsection (3)(b) are—

(a) the average number of normal working hours in a week which the employee could expect in accordance with the terms of her contract, and

(b) the average number of normal working hours of other employees engaged in relevant comparable employment with the same employer.

(5) A right to any amount under subsection (1) does not affect any right of an employee in relation to remuneration under her contract of employment ("contractual remuneration").

(6) Any contractual remuneration paid to an employee in respect of a period of time off under section 55 goes towards discharging any liability of the employer

---

[1] Words substituted by SI 2002/253 Sch 5 para 13
[2] Words substituted by SI 2002/253 Sch 5 para 13

to pay remuneration under subsection (1) in respect of that period; and, conversely, any payment of remuneration under subsection (1) in respect of a period goes towards discharging any liability of the employer to pay contractual remuneration in respect of that period.

Complaints to [employment tribunals][1]

11-063   **57.**—(1) An employee may present a complaint to an [employment tribunal][2] that her employer—

(a) has unreasonably refused to permit her to take time off as required by section 55, or

(b) has failed to pay the whole or any part of any amount to which the employee is entitled under section 56.

(2) An [employment tribunal][3] shall not consider a complaint under this section unless it is presented—

(a) before the end of the period of three months beginning with the date of the appointment concerned, or

(b) within such further period as the tribunal considers reasonable in a case where it is satisfied that it was not reasonably practicable for the complaint to be presented before the end of that period of three months.

(3) Where an [employment tribunal][4] finds a complaint under this section well-founded, the tribunal shall make a declaration to that effect.

(4) If the complaint is that the employer has unreasonably refused to permit the employee to take time off, the tribunal shall also order the employer to pay to the employee an amount equal to the remuneration to which she would have been entitled under section 56 if the employer had not refused.

(5) If the complaint is that the employer has failed to pay the employee the whole or part of any amount to which she is entitled under section 56, the tribunal shall also order the employer to pay to the employee the amount which it finds due to her.

Dependants

[Time off for dependants

11-064   **57A.**—(1) An employee is entitled to be permitted by his employer to take a reasonable amount of time off during the employee's working hours in order to take action which is necessary—

(a) to provide assistance on an occasion when a dependant falls ill, gives birth or is injured or assaulted,

(b) to make arrangements for the provision of care for a dependant who is ill or injured,

(c) in consequence of the death of a dependant,

(d) because of the unexpected disruption or termination of arrangements for the care of a dependant, or

(e) to deal with an incident which involves a child of the employee and which occurs unexpectedly in a period during which an educational establishment which the child attends is responsible for him.

(2) Subsection (1) does not apply unless the employee—

---

[1] Words substituted by Employment Rights (Dispute Resolution) Act 1998 c.8 Pt I s 1 (2)
[2] Words substituted by Employment Rights (Dispute Resolution) Act 1998 c.8 Pt I s 1 (2)
[3] Words substituted by Employment Rights (Dispute Resolution) Act 1998 c.8 Pt I s 1 (2)
[4] Words substituted by Employment Rights (Dispute Resolution) Act 1998 c.8 Pt I s 1 (2)

(a) tells his employer the reason for his absence as soon as reasonably practicable, and

(b) except where paragraph (a) cannot be complied with until after the employee has returned to work, tells his employer for how long he expects to be absent.

(3) Subject to subsections (4) and (5), for the purposes of this section "dependant" means, in relation to an employee—

(a) a spouse,

(b) a child,

(c) a parent,

(d) a person who lives in the same household as the employee, otherwise than by reason of being his employee, tenant, lodger or boarder.

(4) For the purposes of subsection (1)(a) or (b) "dependant" includes, in addition to the persons mentioned in subsection (3), any person who reasonably relies on the employee—

(a) for assistance on an occasion when the person falls ill or is injured or assaulted, or

(b) to make arrangements for the provision of care in the event of illness or injury.

(5) For the purposes of subsection (1)(d) "dependant" includes, in addition to the persons mentioned in subsection (3), any person who reasonably relies on the employee to make arrangements for the provision of care.

(6) A reference in this section to illness or injury includes a reference to mental illness or injury.][1]

[Complaint to employment tribunal

57B.—(1) An employee may present a complaint to an employment tribunal **11-065** that his employer has unreasonably refused to permit him to take time off as required by section 57A.

(2) An employment tribunal shall not consider a complaint under this section unless it is presented—

(a) before the end of the period of three months beginning with the date when the refusal occurred, or

(b) within such further period as the tribunal considers reasonable in a case where it is satisfied that it was not reasonably practicable for the complaint to be presented before the end of that period of three months.

(3) Where an employment tribunal finds a complaint under subsection (1) well-founded, it—

(a) shall make a declaration to that effect, and

(b) may make an award of compensation to be paid by the employer to the employee.

(4) The amount of compensation shall be such as the tribunal considers just and equitable in all the circumstances having regard to—

(a) the employer's default in refusing to permit time off to be taken by the employee, and

(b) any loss sustained by the employee which is attributable to the matters complained of.][2]

---

[1] Inserted by Employment Relations Act 1999 c.26 Sch 4 (II) para 1
[2] Inserted by Employment Relations Act 1999 c.26 Sch 4 (II) para 1

Occupational pension scheme trustees

Right to time off for pension scheme trustees

11-066 **58.**—(1) The employer in relation to a relevant occupational pension scheme shall permit an employee of his who is a trustee of the scheme to take time off during the employee's working hours for the purpose of—
(a) performing any of his duties as such a trustee, or
(b) undergoing training relevant to the performance of those duties.
(2) The amount of time off which an employee is to be permitted to take under this section and the purposes for which, the occasions on which and any conditions subject to which time off may be so taken are those that are reasonable in all the circumstances having regard, in particular, to—
(a) how much time off is required for the performance of the duties of a trustee of the scheme and the undergoing of relevant training, and how much time off is required for performing the particular duty or for undergoing the particular training, and
(b) the circumstances of the employer's business and the effect of the employee's absence on the running of that business.
[(2A) This section applies to an employee who is a director of a company which is a trustee of a relevant occupational pension scheme as it applies to an employee who is a trustee of such a scheme (references to such a trustee being read for this purpose as references to such a director).][1]
(3) In this section—
(a) "relevant occupational pension scheme" means an occupational pension scheme (as defined in section 1 of the Pension Schemes Act 1993) established under a trust, and
(b) references to the employer, in relation to such a scheme, are to an employer of persons in the description or category of employment to which the scheme relates[, and][2]
[(c) references to training are to training on the employer's premises or elsewhere.][3]
(4) For the purposes of this section the working hours of an employee shall be taken to be any time when, in accordance with his contract of employment, the employee is required to be at work.

Right to payment for time off under section 58

11-067 **59.**—(1) An employer who permits an employee to take time off under section 58 shall pay him for the time taken off pursuant to the permission.
(2) Where the employee's remuneration for the work he would ordinarily have been doing during that time does not vary with the amount of work done, he must be paid as if he had worked at that work for the whole of that time.
(3) Where the employee's remuneration for the work he would ordinarily have been doing during that time varies with the amount of work done, he must be paid an amount calculated by reference to the average hourly earnings for that work.
(4) The average hourly earnings mentioned in subsection (3) are—
(a) those of the employee concerned, or

[1] Inserted by Welfare Reform and Pensions Act 1999 c.30 Sch 2 para 19 (3)
[2] Word inserted by Teaching and Higher Education Act 1998 c.30 Sch 3 para 12
[3] Inserted by Teaching and Higher Education Act 1998 c.30 Sch 3 para 12

(b) if no fair estimate can be made of those earnings, the average hourly earnings for work of that description of persons in comparable employment with the same employer or, if there are no such persons, a figure of average hourly earnings which is reasonable in the circumstances.

(5) A right to be paid an amount under subsection (1) does not affect any right of an employee in relation to remuneration under his contract of employment ("contractual remuneration").

(6) Any contractual remuneration paid to an employee in respect of a period of time off under section 58 goes towards discharging any liability of the employer under subsection (1) in respect of that period; and, conversely, any payment under subsection (1) in respect of a period goes towards discharging any liability of the employer to pay contractual remuneration in respect of that period.

Complaints to [employment tribunals][1]

60.—(1) An employee may present a complaint to an [employment tribunal][2] **11-068**
that his employer—
    (a) has failed to permit him to take time off as required by section 58, or
    (b) has failed to pay him in accordance with section 59.

(2) An [employment tribunal][3] shall not consider a complaint under this section unless it is presented—
    (a) before the end of the period of three months beginning with the date when the failure occurred, or
    (b) within such further period as the tribunal considers reasonable in a case where it is satisfied that it was not reasonably practicable for the complaint to be presented before the end of that period of three months.

(3) Where an [employment tribunal][4] finds a complaint under subsection (1)(a) well-founded, the tribunal—
    (a) shall make a declaration to that effect, and
    (b) may make an award of compensation to be paid by the employer to the employee.

(4) The amount of the compensation shall be such as the tribunal considers just and equitable in all the circumstances having regard to—
    (a) the employer's default in failing to permit time off to be taken by the employee, and
    (b) any loss sustained by the employee which is attributable to the matters complained of.

(5) Where on a complaint under subsection (1)(b) an [employment tribunal][5] finds that an employer has failed to pay an employee in accordance with section 59, it shall order the employer to pay the amount which it finds to be due.

Employee representatives

Right to time off for employee representatives

61.—(1) An employee who is—   **11-069**

---

[1] Words substituted by Employment Rights (Dispute Resolution) Act 1998 c.8 Pt I s 1 (2)
[2] Words substituted by Employment Rights (Dispute Resolution) Act 1998 c.8 Pt I s 1 (2)
[3] Words substituted by Employment Rights (Dispute Resolution) Act 1998 c.8 Pt I s 1 (2)
[4] Words substituted by Employment Rights (Dispute Resolution) Act 1998 c.8 Pt I s 1 (2)
[5] Words substituted by Employment Rights (Dispute Resolution) Act 1998 c.8 Pt I s 1 (2)

(a) an employee representative for the purposes of Chapter II of Part IV of the Trade Union and Labour Relations (Consolidation) Act 1992 (redundancies) or Regulations 10 and 11 of the Transfer of Undertakings (Protection of Employment) Regulations 1981, or

(b) a candidate in an election in which any person elected will, on being elected, be such an employee representative,

is entitled to be permitted by his employer to take reasonable time off during the employee's working hours in order to perform his functions as such an employee representative or candidate [or in order to undergo training to perform such functions][1].

(2) For the purposes of this section the working hours of an employee shall be taken to be any time when, in accordance with his contract of employment, the employee is required to be at work.

Right to remuneration for time off under section 61

11-070   **62.**—(1) An employee who is permitted to take time off under section 61 is entitled to be paid remuneration by his employer for the time taken off at the appropriate hourly rate.

(2) The appropriate hourly rate, in relation to an employee, is the amount of one week's pay divided by the number of normal working hours in a week for that employee when employed under the contract of employment in force on the day when the time off is taken.

(3) But where the number of normal working hours differs from week to week or over a longer period, the amount of one week's pay shall be divided instead by—

(a) the average number of normal working hours calculated by dividing by twelve the total number of the employee's normal working hours during the period of twelve weeks ending with the last complete week before the day on which the time off is taken, or

(b) where the employee has not been employed for a sufficient period to enable the calculation to be made under paragraph (a), a number which fairly represents the number of normal working hours in a week having regard to such of the considerations specified in subsection (4) as are appropriate in the circumstances.

(4) The considerations referred to in subsection (3)(b) are—

(a) the average number of normal working hours in a week which the employee could expect in accordance with the terms of his contract, and

(b) the average number of normal working hours of other employees engaged in relevant comparable employment with the same employer.

(5) A right to any amount under subsection (1) does not affect any right of an employee in relation to remuneration under his contract of employment ("contractual remuneration").

(6) Any contractual remuneration paid to an employee in respect of a period of time off under section 61 goes towards discharging any liability of the employer to pay remuneration under subsection (1) in respect of that period; and, conversely, any payment of remuneration under subsection (1) in respect of a period goes towards discharging any liability of the employer to pay contractual remuneration in respect of that period.

---

[1] Words inserted by SI 1999/1925 reg 15

Complaints to [employment tribunals][1]

63.—(1) An employee may present a complaint to an [employment tribunal][2] **11-071**
that his employer—
    (a) has unreasonably refused to permit him to take time off as required by
        section 61, or
    (b) has failed to pay the whole or any part of any amount to which the
        employee is entitled under section 62.

(2) An [employment tribunal][3] shall not consider a complaint under this
section unless it is presented—
    (a) before the end of the period of three months beginning with the day on
        which the time off was taken or on which it is alleged the time off should
        have been permitted, or
    (b) within such further period as the tribunal considers reasonable in a
        case where it is satisfied that it was not reasonably practicable for the
        complaint to be presented before the end of that period of three
        months.

(3) Where an [employment tribunal][4] finds a complaint under this section
well-founded, the tribunal shall make a declaration to that effect.

(4) If the complaint is that the employer has unreasonably refused to permit
the employee to take time off, the tribunal shall also order the employer to pay to
the employee an amount equal to the remuneration to which he would have been
entitled under section 62 if the employer had not refused.

(5) If the complaint is that the employer has failed to pay the employee the
whole or part of any amount to which he is entitled under section 62, the tribunal
shall also order the employer to pay to the employee the amount which it finds
due to him.

[Right to time off for young person for study or training

63A.—(1) An employee who— **11-072**
    (a) is aged 16 or 17,
    (b) is not receiving full-time secondary or further education, and
    (c) has not attained such standard of achievement as is prescribed by regu-
        lations made by the Secretary of State,
is entitled to be permitted by his employer to take time off during the employee's
working hours in order to undertake study or training leading to a relevant qualification.

(2) In this section—
    (a) "secondary education" —
        (i) in relation to England and Wales, has the same meaning as in the
            Education Act 1996, and
        (ii) in relation to Scotland, has the same meaning as in section
            135(2)(b) of the Education (Scotland) Act 1980;
    (b) "further education"—
        (i) in relation to England and Wales, [has the same meaning as in the
            Education Act 1996,][5] and
        (ii) in relation to Scotland, has the same meaning as in section 1(3) of
            the Further and Higher Education (Scotland) Act 1992;

---

[1] Words substituted by Employment Rights (Dispute Resolution) Act 1998 c.8 Pt I s 1 (2)
[2] Words substituted by Employment Rights (Dispute Resolution) Act 1998 c.8 Pt I s 1 (2)
[3] Words substituted by Employment Rights (Dispute Resolution) Act 1998 c.8 Pt I s 1 (2)
[4] Words substituted by Employment Rights (Dispute Resolution) Act 1998 c.8 Pt I s 1 (2)
[5] Words substituted by Learning and Skills Act 2000 c.21 Sch 9 para 50

and
(c) "relevant qualification" means an external qualification the attainment of which—
  (i) would contribute to the attainment of the standard prescribed for the purposes of subsection (1)(c), and
  (ii) would be likely to enhance the employee's employment prospects (whether with his employer or otherwise);
and for the purposes of paragraph (c) "external qualification" means an academic or vocational qualification awarded or authenticated by such person or body as may be specified in or under regulations made by the Secretary of State.

(3) An employee who—
(a) satisfies the requirements of paragraphs (a) to (c) of subsection (1), and
(b) is for the time being supplied by his employer to another person ("the principal") to perform work in accordance with a contract made between the employer and the principal,
is entitled to be permitted by the principal to take time off during the employee's working hours in order to undertake study or training leading to a relevant qualification.

(4) Where an employee—
(a) is aged 18,
(b) is undertaking study or training leading to a relevant qualification, and
(c) began such study or training before attaining that age,
subsections (1) and (3) shall apply to the employee, in relation to that study or training, as if "or 18" were inserted at the end of subsection (1)(a).

(5) The amount of time off which an employee is to be permitted to take under this section, and the occasions on which and any conditions subject to which time off may be so taken, are those that are reasonable in all the circumstances having regard, in particular, to—
(a) the requirements of the employee's study or training, and
(b) the circumstances of the business of the employer or the principal and the effect of the employee's time off on the running of that business.

(6) Regulations made for the purposes of subsections (1)(c) and (2) may make different provision for different cases, and in particular may make different provision in relation to England, Wales and Scotland respectively.

(7) References in this section to study or training are references to study or training on the premises of the employer or (as the case may be) principal or elsewhere.

(8) For the purposes of this section the working hours of an employee shall be taken to be any time when, in accordance with his contract of employment, the employee is required to be at work.][1]

[Right to remuneration for time off under section 63A

11-073   **63B.**—(1) An employee who is permitted to take time off under section 63A is entitled to be paid remuneration by his employer for the time taken off at the appropriate hourly rate.

(2) The appropriate hourly rate, in relation to an employee, is the amount of one week's pay divided by the number of normal working hours in a week for that employee when employed under the contract of employment in force on the day when the time off is taken.

---

[1] Inserted by Teaching and Higher Education Act 1998 c.30 Pt III s 32

(3) But where the number of normal working hours differs from week to week or over a longer period, the amount of one week's pay shall be divided instead by—

    (a) the average number of normal working hours calculated by dividing by twelve the total number of the employee's working hours during the period of twelve weeks ending with the last complete week before the day on which the time off is taken, or

    (b) where the employee has not been employed for a sufficient period to enable the calculation to be made under paragraph (a), a number which fairly represents the number of normal working hours in a week having regard to such of the considerations specified in subsection (4) as are appropriate in the circumstances.

(4) The considerations referred to in subsection (3)(b) are—

    (a) the average number of normal working hours in a week which the employee could except in accordance with the terms of his contract, and

    (b) the average number of normal working hours of other employees engaged in relevant comparable employment with the same employer.

(5) A right to any amount under subsection (1) does not affect any right of an employee in relation to remuneration under his contract of employment ("contractual remuneration").

(6) Any contractual remuneration paid to an employee in respect of a period of time off under section 63A goes towards discharging any liability of the employer to pay remuneration under subsection (1) in respect of that period; and, conversely, any payment of remuneration under subsection (1) in respect of a period goes towards discharging any liability of the employer to pay contractual remuneration in respect of that period.][1]

[Complaints to employment tribunals

63C.—(1) An employee may present a complaint to an employment tribunal **11-074** that—

    (a) his employer, or the principal referred to in subsection (3) of section 63A, has unreasonably refused to permit him to take time off as required by that section, or

    (b) his employer has failed to pay the whole or any part of any amount to which the employee is entitled under section 63B.

(2) An employment tribunal shall not consider a complaint under this section unless it is presented—

    (a) before the end of the period of three months beginning with the day on which the time off was taken or on which it is alleged the time off should have been permitted, or

    (b) within such further period as the tribunal considers reasonable in a case where it is satisfied that it was not reasonably practicable for the complaint to be presented before the end of that period of three months.

(3) Where an employment tribunal finds a complaint under this section well-founded, the tribunal shall make a declaration to that effect.

(4) If the complaint is that the employer or the principal has unreasonably refused to permit the employee to take time off, the tribunal shall also order the employer or the principal, as the case may be, to pay to the employee an amount

---

[1] Inserted by Teaching and Higher Education Act 1998 c.30 Pt III s 33

equal to the remuneration to which he would have been entitled under section 63B if the employer or the principal had not refused.

(5) If the complaint is that the employer has failed to pay the employee the whole or part of any amount to which he is entitled under section 63B, the tribunal shall also order the employer to pay to the employee the amount which it finds due to him.][1]

PART VII

SUSPENSION FROM WORK

Suspension on medical grounds

Right to remuneration on suspension on medical grounds

11-075   **64.**—(1) An employee who is suspended from work by his employer on medical grounds is entitled to be paid by his employer remuneration while he is so suspended for a period not exceeding twenty-six weeks.

(2) For the purposes of this Part an employee is suspended from work on medical grounds if he is suspended from work in consequence of—

    (a) a requirement imposed by or under a provision of an enactment or of an instrument made under an enactment, or

    (b) a recommendation in a provision of a code of practice issued or approved under section 16 of the Health and Safety at Work etc. Act 1974,

and the provision is for the time being specified in subsection (3).

(3) The provisions referred to in subsection (2) are—

Regulation 16 of the Control of Lead at Work Regulations 1980,

[Regulation 24 of the Ionising Radiations Regulations 1999 [SI 1999/3232]][2], and

Regulation 11 of the Control of Substances Hazardous to Health Regulations 1988.

(4) The Secretary of State may by order add provisions to or remove provisions from the list of provisions specified in subsection (3).

(5) For the purposes of this Part an employee shall be regarded as suspended from work on medical grounds only if and for so long as he—

    (a) continues to be employed by his employer, but

    (b) is not provided with work or does not perform the work he normally performed before the suspension.

Exclusions from right to remuneration

11-076   **65.**—(1) An employee is not entitled to remuneration under section 64 unless he has been continuously employed for a period of not less than one month ending with the day before that on which the suspension begins.

(2) [...][3]

(3) An employee is not entitled to remuneration under section 64 in respect of any period during which he is incapable of work by reason of disease or bodily or mental disablement.

---

[1] Inserted by Teaching and Higher Education Act 1998 c.30 Pt III s 33
[2] Words substituted by SI 1999/3232 Sch 9 para 2
[3] Repealed by SI 2002/2034 Sch 2 (1) para 3 (3)

(4) An employee is not entitled to remuneration under section 64 in respect of any period if—

    (a) his employer has offered to provide him with suitable alternative work during the period (whether or not it is work which the employee is under his contract, or was under the contract in force before the suspension, employed to perform) and the employee has unreasonably refused to perform that work, or

    (b) he does not comply with reasonable requirements imposed by his employer with a view to ensuring that his services are available.

Suspension on maternity grounds

Meaning of suspension on maternity grounds

66.—(1) For the purposes of this Part an employee is suspended from work **11-077** on maternity grounds if, in consequence of any relevant requirement or relevant recommendation, she is suspended from work by her employer on the ground that she is pregnant, has recently given birth or is breastfeeding a child.

(2) In subsection (1)—

    "relevant requirement" means a requirement imposed by or under a specified provision of an enactment or of an instrument made under an enactment, and

    "relevant recommendation" means a recommendation in a specified provision of a code of practice issued or approved under section 16 of the Health and Safety at Work etc. Act 1974;

and in this subsection "specified provision" means a provision for the time being specified in an order made by the Secretary of State under this subsection.

(3) For the purposes of this Part an employee shall be regarded as suspended from work on maternity grounds only if and for so long as she—

    (a) continues to be employed by her employer, but

    (b) is not provided with work or (disregarding alternative work for the purposes of section 67) does not perform the work she normally performed before the suspension.

Right to offer of alternative work

67.—(1) Where an employer has available suitable alternative work for an **11-078** employee, the employee has a right to be offered to be provided with the alternative work before being suspended from work on maternity grounds.

(2) For alternative work to be suitable for an employee for the purposes of this section—

    (a) the work must be of a kind which is both suitable in relation to her and appropriate for her to do in the circumstances, and

    (b) the terms and conditions applicable to her for performing the work, if they differ from the corresponding terms and conditions applicable to her for performing the work she normally performs under her contract of employment, must not be substantially less favourable to her than those corresponding terms and conditions.

Right to remuneration

68.—(1) An employee who is suspended from work on maternity grounds is **11-079** entitled to be paid remuneration by her employer while she is so suspended.

(2) An employee is not entitled to remuneration under this section in respect of any period if—

(a) her employer has offered to provide her during the period with work which is suitable alternative work for her for the purposes of section 67, and

(b) the employee has unreasonably refused to perform that work.

General

Calculation of remuneration

11-080   **69.**—(1) The amount of remuneration payable by an employer to an employee under section 64 or 68 is a week's pay in respect of each week of the period of suspension; and if in any week remuneration is payable in respect of only part of that week the amount of a week's pay shall be reduced proportionately.

(2) A right to remuneration under section 64 or 68 does not affect any right of an employee in relation to remuneration under the employee's contract of employment ("contractual remuneration").

(3) Any contractual remuneration paid by an employer to an employee in respect of any period goes towards discharging the employer's liability under section 64 or 68 in respect of that period; and, conversely, any payment of remuneration in discharge of an employer's liability under section 64 or 68 in respect of any period goes towards discharging any obligation of the employer to pay contractual remuneration in respect of that period.

Complaints to [employment tribunals][1]

11-081   **70.**—(1) An employee may present a complaint to an [employment tribunal][2] that his or her employer has failed to pay the whole or any part of remuneration to which the employee is entitled under section 64 or 68.

(2) An [employment tribunal][3] shall not consider a complaint under subsection (1) relating to remuneration in respect of any day unless it is presented—

(a) before the end of the period of three months beginning with that day, or

(b) within such further period as the tribunal considers reasonable in a case where it is satisfied that it was not reasonably practicable for the complaint to be presented within that period of three months.

(3) Where an [employment tribunal][4] finds a complaint under subsection (1) well-founded, the tribunal shall order the employer to pay the employee the amount of remuneration which it finds is due to him or her.

(4) An employee may present a complaint to an [employment tribunal][5] that in contravention of section 67 her employer has failed to offer to provide her with work.

(5) An [employment tribunal][6] shall not consider a complaint under subsection (4) unless it is presented—

[1] Words substituted by Employment Rights (Dispute Resolution) Act 1998 c.8 Pt I s 1 (2)
[2] Words substituted by Employment Rights (Dispute Resolution) Act 1998 c.8 Pt I s 1 (2)
[3] Words substituted by Employment Rights (Dispute Resolution) Act 1998 c.8 Pt I s 1 (2)
[4] Words substituted by Employment Rights (Dispute Resolution) Act 1998 c.8 Pt I s 1 (2)
[5] Words substituted by Employment Rights (Dispute Resolution) Act 1998 c.8 Pt I s 1 (2)
[6] Words substituted by Employment Rights (Dispute Resolution) Act 1998 c.8 Pt I s 1 (2)

(a) before the end of the period of three months beginning with the first day of the suspension, or

(b) within such further period as the tribunal considers reasonable in a case where it is satisfied that it was not reasonably practicable for the complaint to be presented within that period of three months.

(6) Where an [employment tribunal]¹ finds a complaint under subsection (4) well-founded, the tribunal may make an award of compensation to be paid by the employer to the employee.

(7) The amount of the compensation shall be such as the tribunal considers just and equitable in all the circumstances having regard to—

(a) the infringement of the employee's right under section 67 by the failure on the part of the employer to which the complaint relates, and

(b) any loss sustained by the employee which is attributable to that failure.

PART VIII

CHAPTER I

MATERNITY LEAVE

[Ordinary maternity leave

71.—(1) An employee may, provided that she satisfies any conditions which **11-082** may be prescribed, be absent from work at any time during an ordinary maternity leave period.

(2) An ordinary maternity leave period is a period calculated in accordance with regulations made by the Secretary of State.

(3) Regulations under subsection (2)—

(a) shall secure that no ordinary maternity leave period is less than 18 weeks;

(b) may allow an employee to choose, subject to any prescribed restrictions, the date on which an ordinary maternity leave period starts.

(4) Subject to section 74, an employee who exercises her right under subsection (1)—

(a) is entitled[, for such purposes and to such extent as may be prescribed,]² to the benefit of the terms and conditions of employment which would have applied if she had not been absent,

(b) is bound[, for such purposes and to such extent as may be prescribed]³ by any obligations arising under those terms and conditions (except in so far as they are inconsistent with subsection (1)), and

[(c) is entitled to return from leave to a job of a prescribed kind.]⁴

(5) In subsection (4)(a) "terms and conditions of employment"—

(a) includes matters connected with an employee's employment whether or not they arise under her contract of employment, but

(b) does not include terms and conditions about remuneration.

(6) The Secretary of State may make regulations specifying matters which are, or are not, to be treated as remuneration for the purposes of this section.

---

¹ Words substituted by Employment Rights (Dispute Resolution) Act 1998 c.8 Pt I s 1 (2)
² Words inserted by Employment Act 2002 c.22 Pt 1 c 2 s 17 (2) (a)
³ Words inserted by Employment Act 2002 c.22 Pt 1 c 2 s 17 (2) (b)
⁴ Substituted by Employment Act 2002 c.22 Pt 1 c 2 s 17 (2) (c)

[(7) The Secretary of State may make regulations making provision, in relation to the right to return under subsection (4)(c) above, about—

(a) seniority, pension rights and similar rights;

(b) terms and conditions of employment on return.][1]][2]

[Compulsory maternity leave

11-083   **72.**—(1) An employer shall not permit an employee who satisfies prescribed conditions to work during a compulsory maternity leave period.

(2) A compulsory maternity leave period is a period calculated in accordance with regulations made by the Secretary of State.

(3) Regulations under subsection (2) shall secure—

(a) that no compulsory leave period is less than two weeks, and

(b) that every compulsory maternity leave period falls within an ordinary maternity leave period.

(4) Subject to subsection (5), any provision of or made under the Health and Safety at Work etc. Act 1974 shall apply in relation to the prohibition under subsection (1) as if it were imposed by regulations under section 15 of that Act.

(5) Section 33(1)(c) of the 1974 Act shall not apply in relation to the prohibition under subsection (1); and an employer who contravenes that subsection shall be—

(a) guilty of an offence, and

(b) liable on summary conviction to a fine not exceeding level 2 on the standard scale.][3]

[Additional maternity leave

11-084   **73.**—(1) An employee who satisfies prescribed conditions may be absent from work at any time during an additional maternity leave period.

(2) An additional maternity leave period is a period calculated in accordance with regulations made by the Secretary of State.

(3) Regulations under subsection (2) may allow an employee to choose, subject to prescribed restrictions, the date on which an additional maternity leave period ends.

(4) Subject to section 74, an employee who exercises her right under subsection (1)—

(a) is entitled, for such purposes and to such extent as may be prescribed, to the benefit of the terms and conditions of employment which would have applied if she had not been absent,

(b) is bound, for such purposes and to such extent as may be prescribed, by obligations arising under those terms and conditions (except in so far as they are inconsistent with subsection (1)), and

(c) is entitled to return from leave to a job of a prescribed kind.

(5) In subsection (4)(a) "terms and conditions of employment"—

(a) includes matters connected with an employee's employment whether or not they arise under her contract of employment, but

(b) does not include terms and conditions about remuneration.

[(5A) In subsection (4)(c), the reference to return from leave includes, where appropriate, a reference to a continuous period of absence attributable partly to additional maternity leave and partly to ordinary maternity leave.][4]

---

[1] Substituted by Employment Act 2002 c.22 Pt 1 c 2 s 17 (3)

[2] Substituted by Employment Relations Act 1999 c.26 Sch 4 (I) para 1

[3] Substituted by Employment Relations Act 1999 c.26 Sch 4 (I) para 1

[4] Inserted by Employment Act 2002 c.22 Pt 1 c 2 s 17 (4)

(6) The Secretary of State may make regulations specifying matters which are, or are not, to be treated as remuneration for the purposes of this section.

(7) The Secretary of State may make regulations making provision, in relation to the right to return under subsection (4)(c), about—

 (a) seniority, pension rights and similar rights;

 (b) terms and conditions of employment on return.][1]

[Redundancy and dismissal

74.—(1) Regulations under section 71 or 73 may make provision about **11-085** redundancy during an ordinary or additional maternity leave period.

(2) Regulations under section 71 or 73 may make provision about dismissal (other than by reason of redundancy) during an ordinary or additional maternity leave period.

(3) Regulations made by virtue of subsection (1) or (2) may include—

 (a) provision requiring an employer to offer alternative employment;

 (b) provision for the consequences of failure to comply with the regulations (which may include provision for a dismissal to be treated as unfair for the purposes of Part X).

(4) Regulations under [section 71 or 73][2] may make provision—

 (a) for [section 71(4)(c) or 73(4)(c)][3] not to apply in specified cases, and

 (b) about dismissal at the conclusion of an [ordinary or][4] additional maternity leave period.][5]

CHAPTER IA

ADOPTION LEAVE

[Ordinary adoption leave

75A—(1) An employee who satisfies prescribed conditions may be absent **11-086** from work at any time during an ordinary adoption leave period.

(2) An ordinary adoption leave period is a period calculated in accordance with regulations made by the Secretary of State.

(3) Subject to section 75C, an employee who exercises his right under subsection (1)—

 (a) is entitled, for such purposes and to such extent as may be prescribed, to the benefit of the terms and conditions of employment which would have applied if he had not been absent,

 (b) is bound, for such purposes and to such extent as may be prescribed, by any obligations arising under those terms and conditions (except in so far as they are inconsistent with subsection (1)), and

 (c) is entitled to return from leave to a job of a prescribed kind.

(4) In subsection (3)(a) "terms and conditions of employment"—

 (a) includes matters connected with an employee's employment whether or not they arise under his contract of employment, but

 (b) does not include terms and conditions about remuneration.

---

[1] Substituted by Employment Relations Act 1999 c.26 Sch 4 (I) para 1
[2] Words inserted by Employment Act 2002 c.22 Pt 1 c 2 s 17 (5) (a)
[3] Words inserted by Employment Act 2002 c.22 Pt 1 c 2 s 17 (5) (b)
[4] Words inserted by Employment Act 2002 c.22 Pt 1 c 2 s 17 (5) (c)
[5] Substituted by Employment Relations Act 1999 c.26 Sch 4 (I) para 1

(5) In subsection (3)(c), the reference to return from leave includes, where appropriate, a reference to a continuous period of absence attributable partly to ordinary adoption leave and partly to maternity leave.

(6) The Secretary of State may make regulations specifying matters which are, or are not, to be treated as remuneration for the purposes of this section.

(7) The Secretary of State may make regulations making provision, in relation to the right to return under subsection (3)(c), about—

    (a) seniority, pension rights and similar rights;

    (b) terms and conditions of employment on return.][1]

[Additional adoption leave

11-087 **75B**—(1) An employee who satisfies prescribed conditions may be absent from work at any time during an additional adoption leave period.

(2) An additional adoption leave period is a period calculated in accordance with regulations made by the Secretary of State.

(3) Regulations under subsection (2) may allow an employee to choose, subject to prescribed restrictions, the date on which an additional adoption leave period ends.

(4) Subject to section 75C, an employee who exercises his right under subsection (1)—

    (a) is entitled, for such purposes and to such extent as may be prescribed, to the benefit of the terms and conditions of employment which would have applied if he had not been absent,

    (b) is bound, for such purposes and to such extent as may be prescribed, by obligations arising under those terms and conditions (except in so far as they are inconsistent with subsection (1)), and

    (c) is entitled to return from leave to a job of a prescribed kind.

(5) In subsection (4)(a) "terms and conditions of employment"—

    (a) includes matters connected with an employee's employment whether or not they arise under his contract of employment, but

    (b) does not include terms and conditions about remuneration.

(6) In subsection (4)(c), the reference to return from leave includes, where appropriate, a reference to a continuous period of absence attributable partly to additional adoption leave and partly to—

    (a) maternity leave, or

    (b) ordinary adoption leave,

or to both.

(7) The Secretary of State may make regulations specifying matters which are, or are not, to be treated as remuneration for the purposes of this section.

(8) The Secretary of State may make regulations making provision, in relation to the right to return under subsection (4)(c), about—

    (a) seniority, pension rights and similar rights;

    (b) terms and conditions of employment on return.][2]

[Redundancy and dismissal

11-088 **75C**—(1) Regulations under section 75A or 75B may make provision about—

    (a) redundancy, or

    (b) dismissal (other than by reason of redundancy),

during an ordinary or additional adoption leave period.

(2) Regulations made by virtue of subsection (1) may include—

---

[1] Inserted by Employment Act 2002 c.22 Pt 1 c 1 s 3
[2] Inserted by Employment Act 2002 c.22 Pt 1 c 1 s 3

    (a) provision requiring an employer to offer alternative employment;

    (b) provision for the consequences of failure to comply with the regulations (which may include provision for a dismissal to be treated as unfair for the purposes of Part 10).

  (3) Regulations under section 75A or 75B may make provision—

    (a) for section 75A(3)(c) or 75B(4)(c) not to apply in specified cases, and

    (b) about dismissal at the conclusion of an ordinary or additional adoption leave period.]¹

[Chapter 1A: supplemental

75D—(1) Regulations under section 75A or 75B may—   **11-089**

    (a) make provision about notices to be given, evidence to be produced and other procedures to be followed by employees and employers;

    (b) make provision requiring employers or employees to keep records;

    (c) make provision for the consequences of failure to give notices, to produce evidence, to keep records or to comply with other procedural requirements;

    (d) make provision for the consequences of failure to act in accordance with a notice given by virtue of paragraph (a);

    (e) make special provision for cases where an employee has a right which corresponds to a right under this Chapter and which arises under his contract of employment or otherwise;

    (f) make provision modifying the effect of Chapter 2 of Part 14 (calculation of a week's pay) in relation to an employee who is or has been absent from work on ordinary or additional adoption leave;

    (g) make provision applying, modifying or excluding an enactment, in such circumstances as may be specified and subject to any conditions specified, in relation to a person entitled to ordinary or additional adoption leave;

    (h) make different provision for different cases or circumstances.

  (2) In sections 75A and 75B "prescribed" means prescribed by regulations made by the Secretary of State.]²

CHAPTER II

PARENTAL LEAVE

[Entitlement to parental leave

76.—(1) The Secretary of State shall make regulations entitling an employee **11-090** who satisfies specified conditions—

    (a) as to duration of employment, and

    (b) as to having, or expecting to have, responsibility for a child,

to be absent from work on parental leave for the purpose of caring for a child.

  (2) The regulations shall include provision for determining—

    (a) the extent of an employee's entitlement to parental leave in respect of a child;

    (b) when parental leave may be taken.

  (3) Provision under subsection (2)(a) shall secure that where an employee is entitled to parental leave in respect of a child he is entitled to a period or total

---

¹ Inserted by Employment Act 2002 c.22 Pt 1 c 1 s 3
² Inserted by Employment Act 2002 c.22 Pt 1 c 1 s 3

period of leave of at least three months; but this subsection is without prejudice to any provision which may be made by the regulations for cases in which—

 (a) a person ceases to satisfy conditions under subsection (1);

 (b) an entitlement to parental leave is transferred.

 (4) Provision under subsection (2)(b) may, in particular, refer to—

 (a) a child's age, or

 (b) a specified period of time starting from a specified event.

 (5) Regulations under subsection (1) may—

 (a) specify things which are, or are not, to be taken as done for the purpose of caring for a child;

 (b) require parental leave to be taken as a single period of absence in all cases or in specified cases;

 (c) require parental leave to be taken as a series of periods of absence in all cases or in specified cases;

 (d) require all or specified parts of a period of parental leave to be taken at or by specified times;

 (e) make provision about the postponement by an employer of a period of parental leave which an employee wishes to take;

 (f) specify a minimum or maximum period of absence which may be taken as part of a period of parental leave.

 (g) specify a maximum aggregate of periods of parental leave which may be taken during a specified period of time.]¹

[Rights during and after parental leave

11-091 **77.**—(1) Regulations under section 76 shall provide—

 (a) that an employee who is absent on parental leave is entitled, for such purposes and to such extent as may be prescribed, to the benefit of the terms and conditions of employment which would have applied if he had not been absent,

 (b) that an employee who is absent on parental leave is bound, for such purposes and to such extent as may be prescribed, by any obligations arising under those terms and conditions (except in so far as they are inconsistent with section 76(1)), and

 (c) that an employee who is absent on parental leave is entitled, subject to section 78(1), to return from leave to a job of such kind as the regulations may specify.

 (2) In subsection (1)(a) "terms and conditions of employment"—

 (a) includes matters connected with an employee's employment whether or not they arise under a contract of employment, but

 (b) does not include terms and conditions about remuneration.

 (3) Regulations under section 76 may specify matters which are, or are not, to be treated as remuneration for the purposes of subsection (2)(b) above.

 (4) The regulations may make provision, in relation to the right to return mentioned in subsection (1)(c), about—

 (a) seniority, pension rights and similar rights;

 (b) terms and conditions of employment on return.]²**Special cases**

11-092 **78.**—(1) Regulations under section 76 may make provision—

 (a) about redundancy during a period of parental leave;

---

¹ Substituted by Employment Relations Act 1999 c.26 Sch 4 (I) para 1
² Substituted by Employment Relations Act 1999 c.26 Sch 4 (I) para 1

(b) about dismissal (other than by reason of redundancy) during a period of parental leave.

(2) Provision by virtue of subsection (1) may include—

    (a) provision requiring an employer to offer alternative employment;

    (b) provision for the consequences of failure to comply with the regulations (which may include provision for a dismissal to be treated as unfair for the purposes of Part X).

(3) Regulations under section 76 may provide for an employee to be entitled to choose to exercise all or part of his entitlement to parental leave—

    (a) by varying the terms of his contract of employment as to hours of work, or

    (b) by varying his normal working practice as to hours of work,

in a way specified in or permitted by the regulations for a period specified in the regulations.

(4) Provision by virtue of subsection (3)—

    (a) may restrict an entitlement to specified circumstances;

    (b) may make an entitlement subject to specified conditions (which may include conditions relating to obtaining the employer's consent);

    (c) may include consequential and incidental provision.

(5) Regulations under section 76 may make provision permitting all or part of an employee's entitlement to parental leave in respect of a child to be transferred to another employee in specified circumstances.

(6) The reference in section 77(1)(c) to absence on parental leave includes, where appropriate, a reference to a continuous period of absence attributable partly [to parental leave and partly to—

    (a) maternity leave, or

    (b) adoption leave,

or to both.][1]

(7) Regulations under section 76 may provide for specified provisions of the regulations not to apply in relation to an employee if any provision of his contract of employment—

    (a) confers an entitlement to absence from work for the purpose of caring for a child, and

    (b) incorporates or operates by reference to all or part of a collective agreement, or workforce agreement, of a kind specified in the regulations.

[Supplemental

79.—(1) Regulations under section 76 may, in particular—   **11-093**

    (a) make provision about notices to be given and evidence to be produced by employees to employers, by employers to employees, and by employers to other employers;

    (b) make provision requiring employers or employees to keep records;

    (c) make provision about other procedures to be followed by employees and employers;

    (d) make provision (including provision creating criminal offences) specifying the consequences of failure to give notices, to produce evidence, to keep records or to comply with other procedural requirements;

    (e) make provision specifying the consequences of failure to act in accordance with a notice given by virtue of paragraph (a);

---

[1] Words substituted by Employment Act 2002 c.22 Sch 7 para 28

(f) make special provision for cases where an employee has a right which corresponds to a right conferred by the regulations and which arises under his contract of employment or otherwise;

(g) make provision applying, modifying or excluding an enactment, in such circumstances as may be specified and subject to any conditions specified, in relation to a person entitled to parental leave;

(h) make different provision for different cases or circumstances.

(2) The regulations may make provision modifying the effect of Chapter II of Part XIV (calculation of a week's pay) in relation to an employee who is or has been absent from work on parental leave.

(3) Without prejudice to the generality of section 76, the regulations may make any provision which appears to the Secretary of State to be necessary or expedient—

(a) for the purpose of implementing Council Directive 96/34/EC on the framework agreement on parental leave, or

(b) for the purpose of dealing with any matter arising out of or related to the United Kingdom's obligations under that Directive.][1]

[Complaint to employment tribunal

11-094   **80.**—(1) An employee may present a complaint to an employment tribunal that his employer—

(a) has unreasonably postponed a period of parental leave requested by the employee, or

(b) has prevented or attempted to prevent the employee from taking parental leave.

(2) An employment tribunal shall not consider a complaint under this section unless it is presented—

(a) before the end of the period of three months beginning with the date (or last date) of the matters complained of, or

(b) within such further period as the tribunal considers reasonable in a case where it is satisfied that it was not reasonably practicable for the complaint to be presented before the end of that period of three months.

(3) Where an employment tribunal finds a complaint under this section well-founded it—

(a) shall make a declaration to that effect, and

(b) may make an award of compensation to be paid by the employer to the employee.

(4) The amount of compensation shall be such as the tribunal considers just and equitable in all the circumstances having regard to—

(a) the employer's behaviour, and

(b) any loss sustained by the employee which is attributable to the matters complained of.][2]

---

[1] Substituted by Employment Act 1999 c.26 Sch 4
[2] Substituted by Employment Relations Act 1999 c.26 Sch 4 (I) para 1

CHAPTER 3

PATERNITY LEAVE

[Entitlement to paternity leave: birth

80A—(1) The Secretary of State shall make regulations entitling an **11-095** employee who satisfies specified conditions—
- (a) as to duration of employment,
- (b) as to relationship with a newborn, or expected, child, and
- (c) as to relationship with the child's mother,

to be absent from work on leave under this section for the purpose of caring for the child or supporting the mother.

(2) The regulations shall include provision for determining—
- (a) the extent of an employee's entitlement to leave under this section in respect of a child;
- (b) when leave under this section may be taken.

(3) Provision under subsection (2)(a) shall secure that where an employee is entitled to leave under this section in respect of a child he is entitled to at least two weeks' leave.

(4) Provision under subsection (2)(b) shall secure that leave under this section must be taken before the end of a period of at least 56 days beginning with the date of the child's birth.

(5) Regulations under subsection (1) may—
- (a) specify things which are, or are not, to be taken as done for the purpose of caring for a child or supporting the child's mother;
- (b) make provision excluding the right to be absent on leave under this section in respect of a child where more than one child is born as a result of the same pregnancy;
- (c) make provision about how leave under this section may be taken.

(6) Where more than one child is born as a result of the same pregnancy, the reference in subsection (4) to the date of the child's birth shall be read as a reference to the date of birth of the first child born as a result of the pregnancy.

(7) In this section—

"newborn child" includes a child stillborn after twenty-four weeks of pregnancy;

"week" means any period of seven days.][1]

[Entitlement to paternity leave: adoption

80B—(1) The Secretary of State shall make regulations entitling an employee **11-096** who satisfies specified conditions—
- (a) as to duration of employment,
- (b) as to relationship with a child placed, or expected to be placed, for adoption under the law of any part of the United Kingdom, and
- (c) as to relationship with a person with whom the child is, or is expected to be, so placed for adoption,

to be absent from work on leave under this section for the purpose of caring for the child or supporting the person by reference to whom he satisfies the condition under paragraph (c).

(2) The regulations shall include provision for determining—

[1] Inserted by Employment Act 2002 c.22 Pt 1 c 1 s 1

(a) the extent of an employee's entitlement to leave under this section in respect of a child;

(b) when leave under this section may be taken.

(3) Provision under subsection (2)(a) shall secure that where an employee is entitled to leave under this section in respect of a child he is entitled to at least two weeks' leave.

(4) Provision under subsection (2)(b) shall secure that leave under this section must be taken before the end of a period of at least 56 days beginning with the date of the child's placement for adoption.

(5) Regulations under subsection (1) may—

(a) specify things which are, or are not, to be taken as done for the purpose of caring for a child or supporting a person with whom a child is placed for adoption;

(b) make provision excluding the right to be absent on leave under this section in the case of an employee who exercises a right to be absent from work on adoption leave;

(c) make provision excluding the right to be absent on leave under this section in respect of a child where more than one child is placed for adoption as part of the same arrangement;

(d) make provision about how leave under this section may be taken.

(6) Where more than one child is placed for adoption as part of the same arrangement, the reference in subsection (4) to the date of the child's placement shall be read as a reference to the date of placement of the first child to be placed as part of the arrangement.

(7) In this section, "week" means any period of seven days.

(8) The Secretary of State may by regulations provide for this section to have effect in relation to cases which involve adoption, but not the placement of a child for adoption under the law of any part of the United Kingdom, with such modifications as the regulations may prescribe.][1]

[Rights during and after paternity leave

11-097   **80C**—(1) Regulations under section 80A shall provide—

(a) that an employee who is absent on leave under that section is entitled, for such purposes and to such extent as the regulations may prescribe, to the benefit of the terms and conditions of employment which would have applied if he had not been absent;

(b) that an employee who is absent on leave under that section is bound, for such purposes and to such extent as the regulations may prescribe, by obligations arising under those terms and conditions (except in so far as they are inconsistent with subsection (1) of that section), and

(c) that an employee who is absent on leave under that section is entitled to return from leave to a job of a kind prescribed by regulations, subject to section 80D(1).

(2) The reference in subsection (1)(c) to absence on leave under section 80A includes, where appropriate, a reference to a continuous period of absence attributable partly to leave under that section and partly to any one or more of the following—

(a) maternity leave,

(b) adoption leave, and

(c) parental leave.

---

[1] Inserted by Employment Act 2002 c.22 Pt 1 c 1 s 1

(3) Subsection (1) shall apply to regulations under section 80B as it applies to regulations under section 80A.

(4) In the application of subsection (1)(c) to regulations under section 80B, the reference to absence on leave under that section includes, where appropriate, a reference to a continuous period of absence attributable partly to leave under that section and partly to any one or more of the following—

(a) maternity leave,
(b) adoption leave,
(c) parental leave, and
(d) leave under section 80A.

(5) In subsection (1)(a), "terms and conditions of employment"—

(a) includes matters connected with an employee's employment whether or not they arise under his contract of employment, but
(b) does not include terms and conditions about remuneration.

(6) Regulations under section 80A or 80B may specify matters which are, or are not, to be treated as remuneration for the purposes of this section.

(7) Regulations under section 80A or 80B may make provision, in relation to the right to return mentioned in subsection (1)(c), about—

(a) seniority, pension rights and similar rights;
(b) terms and conditions of employment on return.][1]

[Special cases

80D—(1) Regulations under section 80A or 80B may make provision **11-098** about—

(a) redundancy, or
(b) dismissal (other than by reason of redundancy),

during a period of leave under that section.

(2) Provision by virtue of subsection (1) may include—

(a) provision requiring an employer to offer alternative employment;
(b) provision for the consequences of failure to comply with the regulations (which may include provision for a dismissal to be treated as unfair for the purposes of Part 10).][2]

PART VIIIA

FLEXIBLE WORKING

[Statutory right to request contract variation

80F—(1) A qualifying employee may apply to his employer for a change in **11-099** his terms and conditions of employment if—

(a) the change relates to—
    (i) the hours he is required to work,
    (ii) the times when he is required to work,
    (iii) where, as between his home and a place of business of his employer, he is required to work, or
    (iv) such other aspect of his terms and conditions of employment as the Secretary of State may specify by regulations, and
(b) his purpose in applying for the change is to enable him to care for someone who, at the time of application, is a child in respect of whom

---

[1] Inserted by Employment Act 2002 c.22 Pt 1 c 1 s 1
[2] Inserted by Employment Act 2002 c.22 Pt 1 c 1 s 1

he satisfies such conditions as to relationship as the Secretary of State may specify by regulations.

(2) An application under this section must—

    (a) state that it is such an application,

    (b) specify the change applied for and the date on which it is proposed the change should become effective,

    (c) explain what effect, if any, the employee thinks making the change applied for would have on his employer and how, in his opinion, any such effect might be dealt with, and

    (d) explain how the employee meets, in respect of the child concerned, the conditions as to relationship mentioned in subsection (1)(b).

(3) An application under this section must be made before the fourteenth day before the day on which the child concerned reaches the age of six or, if disabled, eighteen.

(4) If an employee has made an application under this section, he may not make a further application under this section to the same employer before the end of the period of twelve months beginning with the date on which the previous application was made.

(5) The Secretary of State may by regulations make provision about—

    (a) the form of applications under this section, and

    (b) when such an application is to be taken as made.

(6) The Secretary of State may by order substitute a different age for the first of the ages specified in subsection (3).

(7) In subsection (3), the reference to a disabled child is to a child who is entitled to a disability living allowance within the meaning of section 71 of the Social Security Contributions and Benefits Act 1992 (c. 4).

(8) For the purposes of this section, an employee is—

    (a) a qualifying employee if he—

        (i) satisfies such conditions as to duration of employment as the Secretary of State may specify by regulations, and

        (ii) is not an agency worker;

    (b) an agency worker if he is supplied by a person ("the agent") to do work for another ("the principal") under a contract or other arrangement made between the agent and the principal.][1]

[Employer's duties in relation to application under section 80F

11-100   **80G**—(1) An employer to whom an application under section 80F is made—

    (a) shall deal with the application in accordance with regulations made by the Secretary of State, and

    (b) shall only refuse the application because he considers that one or more of the following grounds applies—

        (i) the burden of additional costs,

        (ii) detrimental effect on ability to meet customer demand,

        (iii) inability to re-organise work among existing staff,

        (iv) inability to recruit additional staff,

        (v) detrimental impact on quality,

        (vi) detrimental impact on performance,

        (vii) insufficiency of work during the periods the employee proposes to work,

        (viii) planned structural changes, and

---

[1] Inserted by Employment Act 2002 c.22 Pt IV s 47 (2)

(ix) such other grounds as the Secretary of State may specify by regulations.

(2) Regulations under subsection (1)(a) shall include—

(a) provision for the holding of a meeting between the employer and the employee to discuss an application under section 80F within twenty eight days after the date the application is made;

(b) provision for the giving by the employer to the employee of notice of his decision on the application within fourteen days after the date of the meeting under paragraph (a);

(c) provision for notice under paragraph (b) of a decision to refuse the application to state the grounds for the decision;

(d) provision for the employee to have a right, if he is dissatisfied with the employer's decision, to appeal against it within fourteen days after the date on which notice under paragraph (b) is given;

(e) provision about the procedure for exercising the right of appeal under paragraph (d), including provision requiring the employee to set out the grounds of appeal;

(f) provision for notice under paragraph (b) to include such information as the regulations may specify relating to the right of appeal under paragraph (d);

(g) provision for the holding, within fourteen days after the date on which notice of appeal is given by the employee, of a meeting between the employer and the employee to discuss the appeal;

(h) provision for the employer to give the employee notice of his decision on any appeal within fourteen days after the date of the meeting under paragraph (g);

(i) provision for notice under paragraph (h) of a decision to dismiss an appeal to state the grounds for the decision;

(j) provision for a statement under paragraph (c) or (i) to contain a sufficient explanation of the grounds for the decision;

(k) provision for the employee to have a right to be accompanied at meetings under paragraph (a) or (g) by a person of such description as the regulations may specify;

(l) provision for postponement in relation to any meeting under paragraph (a) or (g) which a companion under paragraph (k) is not available to attend;

(m) provision in relation to companions under paragraph (k) corresponding to section 10(6) and (7) of the Employment Relations Act 1999 (c. 26) (right to paid time off to act as companion, etc.);

(n) provision, in relation to the rights under paragraphs (k) and (l), for the application (with or without modification) of sections 11 to 13 of the Employment Relations Act 1999 (provisions ancillary to right to be accompanied under section 10 of that Act).

(3) Regulations under subsection (1)(a) may include—

(a) provision for any requirement of the regulations not to apply where an application is disposed of by agreement or withdrawn;

(b) provision for extension of a time limit where the employer and employee agree, or in such other circumstances as the regulations may specify;

(c) provision for applications to be treated as withdrawn in specified circumstances;

and may make different provision for different cases.

(4) The Secretary of State may by order amend subsection (2).]¹

[**Complaints to employment tribunals**

11-101   **80H**—(1) An employee who makes an application under section 80F may present a complaint to an employment tribunal—

(a) that his employer has failed in relation to the application to comply with section 80G(1), or

(b) that a decision by his employer to reject the application was based on incorrect facts.

(2) No complaint under this section may be made in respect of an application which has been disposed of by agreement or withdrawn.

(3) In the case of an application which has not been disposed of by agreement or withdrawn, no complaint under this section may be made until the employer—

(a) notifies the employee of a decision to reject the application on appeal, or

(b) commits a breach of regulations under section 80G(1)(a) of such description as the Secretary of State may specify by regulations.

(4) No complaint under this section may be made in respect of failure to comply with provision included in regulations under subsection (1)(a) of section 80G because of subsection (2)(k), (l) or (m) of that section.

(5) An employment tribunal shall not consider a complaint under this section unless it is presented—

(a) before the end of the period of three months beginning with the relevant date, or

(b) within such further period as the tribunal considers reasonable in a case where it is satisfied that it was not reasonably practicable for the complaint to be presented before the end of that period of three months.

(6) In subsection (5)(a), the reference to the relevant date is—

(a) in the case of a complaint permitted by subsection (3)(a), the date on which the employee is notified of the decision on the appeal, and

(b) in the case of a complaint permitted by subsection (3)(b), the date on which the breach concerned was committed.]²

[**Remedies**

11-102   **80I**—(1) Where an employment tribunal finds a complaint under section 80H well-founded it shall make a declaration to that effect and may—

(a) make an order for reconsideration of the application, and

(b) make an award of compensation to be paid by the employer to the employee.

(2) The amount of compensation shall be such amount, not exceeding the permitted maximum, as the tribunal considers just and equitable in all the circumstances.

(3) For the purposes of subsection (2), the permitted maximum is such number of weeks' pay as the Secretary of State may specify by regulations.

(4) Where an employment tribunal makes an order under subsection (1)(a), section 80G, and the regulations under that section, shall apply as if the application had been made on the date of the order.]³

---

¹ Inserted by Employment Act 2002 c.22 Pt IV s 47 (2)
² Inserted by Employment Act 2002 c.22 Pt IV s 47 (2)
³ Inserted by Employment Act 2002 c.22 Pt IV s 47 (2)

PART IX

TERMINATION OF EMPLOYMENT

Minimum period of notice

Rights of employer and employee to minimum notice

86.—(1) The notice required to be given by an employer to terminate the **11-103** contract of employment of a person who has been continuously employed for one month or more—

(a) is not less than one week's notice if his period of continuous employment is less than two years,

(b) is not less than one week's notice for each year of continuous employment if his period of continuous employment is two years or more but less than twelve years, and

(c) is not less than twelve weeks' notice if his period of continuous employment is twelve years or more.

(2) The notice required to be given by an employee who has been continuously employed for one month or more to terminate his contract of employment is not less than one week.

(3) Any provision for shorter notice in any contract of employment with a person who has been continuously employed for one month or more has effect subject to subsections (1) and (2); but this section does not prevent either party from waiving his right to notice on any occasion or from accepting a payment in lieu of notice.

(4) Any contract of employment of a person who has been continuously employed for three months or more which is a contract for a term certain of one month or less shall have effect as if it were for an indefinite period; and, accordingly, subsections (1) and (2) apply to the contract.

(5) [...][1]

(6) This section does not affect any right of either party to a contract of employment to treat the contract as terminable without notice by reason of the conduct of the other party.

Rights of employee in period of notice

87.—(1) If an employer gives notice to terminate the contract of employment **11-104** of a person who has been continuously employed for one month or more, the provisions of sections 88 to 91 have effect as respects the liability of the employer for the period of notice required by section 86(1).

(2) If an employee who has been continuously employed for one month or more gives notice to terminate his contract of employment, the provisions of sections 88 to 91 have effect as respects the liability of the employer for the period of notice required by section 86(2).

(3) In sections 88 to 91 "period of notice" means—

(a) where notice is given by an employer, the period of notice required by section 86(1), and

(b) where notice is given by an employee, the period of notice required by section 86(2).

---

[1] Repealed by SI 2002/2034 Sch 2 (1) para 3 (4)

(4) This section does not apply in relation to a notice given by the employer or the employee if the notice to be given by the employer to terminate the contract must be at least one week more than the notice required by section 86(1).

Employments with normal working hours

11-105   **88.**—(1) If an employee has normal working hours under the contract of employment in force during the period of notice and during any part of those normal working hours—

(a) the employee is ready and willing to work but no work is provided for him by his employer,

(b) the employee is incapable of work because of sickness or injury,

(c) the employee is absent from work wholly or partly because of pregnancy or childbirth [or on]¹ [adoption leave, parental leave or paternity leave]², or

(d) the employee is absent from work in accordance with the terms of his employment relating to holidays,

the employer is liable to pay the employee for the part of normal working hours covered by any of paragraphs (a), (b), (c) and (d) a sum not less than the amount of remuneration for that part of normal working hours calculated at the average hourly rate of remuneration produced by dividing a week's pay by the number of normal working hours.

(2) Any payments made to the employee by his employer in respect of the relevant part of the period of notice (whether by way of sick pay, statutory sick pay, maternity pay, statutory maternity pay, [paternity pay, statutory paternity pay, adoption pay, statutory adoption pay,]³ holiday pay or otherwise) go towards meeting the employer's liability under this section.

(3) Where notice was given by the employee, the employer's liability under this section does not arise unless and until the employee leaves the service of the employer in pursuance of the notice.

Employments without normal working hours

11-106   **89.**—(1) If an employee does not have normal working hours under the contract of employment in force in the period of notice, the employer is liable to pay the employee for each week of the period of notice a sum not less than a week's pay.

(2) The employer's liability under this section is conditional on the employee being ready and willing to do work of a reasonable nature and amount to earn a week's pay.

(3) Subsection (2) does not apply—

(a) in respect of any period during which the employee is incapable of work because of sickness or injury,

(b) in respect of any period during which the employee is absent from work wholly or partly because of pregnancy or childbirth [or on]⁴ [adoption leave, parental leave or paternity leave]⁵, or

(c) in respect of any period during which the employee is absent from work in accordance with the terms of his employment relating to holidays.

---

¹ Words inserted by Employment Relations Act 1999 c.26 Sch 4 (III) para 10
² Words substituted by Employment Act 2002 c.22 Sch 7 para 29 (2)
³ Words inserted by Employment Act 2002 c.22 Sch 7 para 29 (3)
⁴ Words inserted by Employment Relations Act 1999 c.26 Sch 4 (III) para 11
⁵ Words substituted by Employment Act 2002 c.22 Sch 7 para 30 (2)

(4) Any payment made to an employee by his employer in respect of a period within subsection (3) (whether by way of sick pay, statutory sick pay, maternity pay, statutory maternity pay, [paternity pay, statutory paternity pay, adoption pay, statutory adoption pay,][1] holiday pay or otherwise) shall be taken into account for the purposes of this section as if it were remuneration paid by the employer in respect of that period.

(5) Where notice was given by the employee, the employer's liability under this section does not arise unless and until the employee leaves the service of the employer in pursuance of the notice.

Short-term incapacity benefit and industrial injury benefit

90.—(1) This section has effect where the arrangements in force relating to **11-107** the employment are such that—
    (a) payments by way of sick pay are made by the employer to employees to whom the arrangements apply, in cases where any such employees are incapable of work because of sickness or injury, and
    (b) in calculating any payment so made to any such employee an amount representing, or treated as representing, short-term incapacity benefit or industrial injury benefit is taken into account, whether by way of deduction or by way of calculating the payment as a supplement to that amount.

(2) If—
    (a) during any part of the period of notice the employee is incapable of work because of sickness or injury,
    (b) one or more payments by way of sick pay are made to him by the employer in respect of that part of the period of notice, and
    (c) in calculating any such payment such an amount as is referred to in paragraph (b) of subsection (1) is taken into account as mentioned in that paragraph,
for the purposes of section 88 or 89 the amount so taken into account shall be treated as having been paid by the employer to the employee by way of sick pay in respect of that part of that period, and shall go towards meeting the liability of the employer under that section accordingly.

Supplementary

91.—(1) An employer is not liable under section 88 or 89 to make any **11-108** payment in respect of a period during which an employee is absent from work with the leave of the employer granted at the request of the employee, including any period of time off taken in accordance with—
    (a) Part VI of this Act, or
    (b) section 168 or 170 of the Trade Union and Labour Relations (Consolidation) Act 1992 (trade union duties and activities).

(2) No payment is due under section 88 or 89 in consequence of a notice to terminate a contract given by an employee if, after the notice is given and on or before the termination of the contract, the employee takes part in a strike of employees of the employer.

(3) If, during the period of notice, the employer breaks the contract of employment, payments received under section 88 or 89 in respect of the part of the period after the breach go towards mitigating the damages recoverable by the employee for loss of earnings in that part of the period of notice.

---

[1] Words inserted by Employment Act 2002 c.22 Sch 7 para 30 (3)

(4) If, during the period of notice, the employee breaks the contract and the employer rightfully treats the breach as terminating the contract, no payment is due to the employee under section 88 or 89 in respect of the part of the period falling after the termination of the contract.

(5) If an employer fails to give the notice required by section 86, the rights conferred by sections 87 to 90 and this section shall be taken into account in assessing his liability for breach of the contract.

(6) Sections 86 to 90 and this section apply in relation to a contract all or any of the terms of which are terms which take effect by virtue of any provision contained in or having effect under an Act (whether public or local) as in relation to any other contract; and the reference in this subsection to an Act includes, subject to any express provision to the contrary, an Act passed after this Act.

Written statement of reasons for dismissal

Right to written statement of reasons for dismissal

11-109   **92.**—(1) An employee is entitled to be provided by his employer with a written statement giving particulars of the reasons for the employee's dismissal—

(a) if the employee is given by the employer notice of termination of his contract of employment,

(b) if the employee's contract of employment is terminated by the employer without notice, or

[(c) if the employee is employed under a limited-term contract and the contract terminates by virtue of the limiting event without being renewed under the same contract.][1]

(2) Subject to [subsections (4) and (4A)][2], an employee is entitled to a written statement under this section only if he makes a request for one; and a statement shall be provided within fourteen days of such a request.

(3) Subject to [subsections (4) and (4A)][3], an employee is not entitled to a written statement under this section unless on the effective date of termination he has been, or will have been, continuously employed for a period of not less than [one year][4] ending with that date.

(4) An employee is entitled to a written statement under this section without having to request it and irrespective of whether she has been continuously employed for any period if she is dismissed—

(a) at any time while she is pregnant, or

(b) after childbirth in circumstances in which her [ordinary or additional maternity leave period][5] ends by reason of the dismissal.

[(4A) An employee who is dismissed while absent from work during an ordinary or additional adoption leave period is entitled to a written statement under this section without having to request it and irrespective of whether he has been continuously employed for any period if he is dismissed in circumstances in which that period ends by reason of the dismissal.][6]

(5) A written statement under this section is admissible in evidence in any proceedings.

---

[1] Substituted by SI 2002/2034 Sch 2 (1) para 3 (5)
[2] Words substituted by Employment Act 2002 c.22 Sch 7 para 31
[3] Words substituted by Employment Act 2002 c.22 Sch 7 para 31
[4] Words substituted by SI 1999/1436 art 2
[5] Words substituted by Employment Relations Act 1999 c.26 Sch 4 (III) para 12
[6] Inserted by Employment Act 2002 c.22 Sch 7 para 31

(6) Subject to subsection (7), in this section "the effective date of termination"—

    (a) in relation to an employee whose contract of employment is terminated by notice, means the date on which the notice expires,

    (b) in relation to an employee whose contract of employment is terminated without notice, means the date on which the termination takes effect, and

    [(c) in relation to an employee who is employed under a limited-term contract which terminates by virtue of the limiting event without being renewed under the same contract, means the date on which the termination takes effect.][1]

(7) Where—

    (a) the contract of employment is terminated by the employer, and

    (b) the notice required by section 86 to be given by an employer would, if duly given on the material date, expire on a date later than the effective date of termination (as defined by subsection (6)),

the later date is the effective date of termination.

(8) In subsection (7)(b) "the material date" means—

    (a) the date when notice of termination was given by the employer, or

    (b) where no notice was given, the date when the contract of employment was terminated by the employer.

Complaints to [employment tribunal][2]

93.—(1) A complaint may be presented to an [employment tribunal][3] by an **11-110** employee on the ground that—

    (a) the employer unreasonably failed to provide a written statement under section 92, or

    (b) the particulars of reasons given in purported compliance with that section are inadequate or untrue.

(2) Where an [employment tribunal][4] finds a complaint under this section well-founded, the tribunal—

    (a) may make a declaration as to what it finds the employer's reasons were for dismissing the employee, and

    (b) shall make an award that the employer pay to the employee a sum equal to the amount of two weeks' pay.

(3) An [employment tribunal][5] shall not consider a complaint under this section relating to the reasons for a dismissal unless it is presented to the tribunal at such a time that the tribunal would, in accordance with section 111, consider a complaint of unfair dismissal in respect of that dismissal presented at the same time.

---

[1] Substituted by SI 2002/2034 Sch 2 (1) para 3 (6)
[2] Words substituted by Employment Rights (Dispute Resolution) Act 1998 c.8 Pt I s 1 (2)
[3] Words substituted by Employment Rights (Dispute Resolution) Act 1998 c.8 Pt I s 1 (2)
[4] Words substituted by Employment Rights (Dispute Resolution) Act 1998 c.8 Pt I s 1 (2)
[5] Words substituted by Employment Rights (Dispute Resolution) Act 1998 c.8 Pt I s 1 (2)

PART X

UNFAIR DISMISSAL

CHAPTER I

RIGHT NOT TO BE UNFAIRLY DISMISSED

The right

The right

11-111   **94.**—(1) An employee has the right not to be unfairly dismissed by his employer.

(2) Subsection (1) has effect subject to the following provisions of this Part (in particular sections 108 to 110) and to the provisions of the Trade Union and Labour Relations (Consolidation) Act 1992 (in particular sections 237 to 239).

Dismissal

Circumstances in which an employee is dismissed

11-112   **95.**—(1) For the purposes of this Part an employee is dismissed by his employer if (and, subject to subsection (2) and section 96, only if)—

    (a) the contract under which he is employed is terminated by the employer (whether with or without notice),

    [(b) he is employed under a limited-term contract and that contract terminates by virtue of the limiting event without being renewed under the same contract, or]¹

    (c) the employee terminates the contract under which he is employed (with or without notice) in circumstances in which he is entitled to terminate it without notice by reason of the employer's conduct.

(2) An employee shall be taken to be dismissed by his employer for the purposes of this Part if—

    (a) the employer gives notice to the employee to terminate his contract of employment, and

    (b) at a time within the period of that notice the employee gives notice to the employer to terminate the contract of employment on a date earlier than the date on which the employer's notice is due to expire;

and the reason for the dismissal is to be taken to be the reason for which the employer's notice is given.

11-113   **96.** [...]²

Effective date of termination

11-114   **97.**—(1) Subject to the following provisions of this section, in this Part "the effective date of termination"—

    (a) in relation to an employee whose contract of employment is terminated by notice, whether given by his employer or by the employee, means the date on which the notice expires,

---

¹ Substituted by SI 2002/2034 Sch 2 (1) para 3 (7)
² Repealed by Employment Relations Act 1999 c.26 Sch 9 para 1

(b) in relation to an employee whose contract of employment is terminated without notice, means the date on which the termination takes effect, and

[(c) in relation to an employee who is employed under a limited-term contract which terminates by virtue of the limiting event without being renewed under the same contract, means the date on which the termination takes effect.]¹

(2) Where—

(a) the contract of employment is terminated by the employer, and

(b) the notice required by section 86 to be given by an employer would, if duly given on the material date, expire on a date later than the effective date of termination (as defined by subsection (1)),

for the purposes of sections 108(1), 119(1) and 227(3) the later date is the effective date of termination.

(3) In subsection (2)(b) "the material date" means—

(a) the date when notice of termination was given by the employer, or

(b) where no notice was given, the date when the contract of employment was terminated by the employer.

(4) Where—

(a) the contract of employment is terminated by the employee,

(b) the material date does not fall during a period of notice given by the employer to terminate that contract, and

(c) had the contract been terminated not by the employee but by notice given on the material date by the employer, that notice would have been required by section 86 to expire on a date later than the effective date of termination (as defined by subsection (1)),

for the purposes of sections 108(1), 119(1) and 227(3) the later date is the effective date of termination.

(5) In subsection (4) "the material date" means—

(a) the date when notice of termination was given by the employee, or

(b) where no notice was given, the date when the contract of employment was terminated by the employee.

(6) [...]²

Fairness

General

98.—(1) In determining for the purposes of this Part whether the dismissal **11-115** of an employee is fair or unfair, it is for the employer to show—

(a) the reason (or, if more than one, the principal reason) for the dismissal, and

(b) that it is either a reason falling within subsection (2) or some other substantial reason of a kind such as to justify the dismissal of an employee holding the position which the employee held.

(2) A reason falls within this subsection if it—

(a) relates to the capability or qualifications of the employee for performing work of the kind which he was employed by the employer to do,

(b) relates to the conduct of the employee,

---

¹ Substituted by SI 2002/2034 Sch 2 (1) para 3 (8)
² Repealed by Employment Relations Act 1999 c.26 Sch 9 para 1

(c) is that the employee was redundant, or

(d) is that the employee could not continue to work in the position which he held without contravention (either on his part or on that of his employer) of a duty or restriction imposed by or under an enactment.

(3) In subsection (2)(a)—

(a) "capability", in relation to an employee, means his capability assessed by reference to skill, aptitude, health or any other physical or mental quality, and

(b) "qualifications", in relation to an employee, means any degree, diploma or other academic, technical or professional qualification relevant to the position which he held.

(4) Where the employer has fulfilled the requirements of subsection (1), the determination of the question whether the dismissal is fair or unfair (having regard to the reason shown by the employer)—

(a) depends on whether in the circumstances (including the size and administrative resources of the employer's undertaking) the employer acted reasonably or unreasonably in treating it as a sufficient reason for dismissing the employee, and

(b) shall be determined in accordance with equity and the substantial merits of the case.

(5) [...]^1

(6) [Subsection (4)]^2 is subject to—

(a) sections [98A]^3 to 107 of this Act, and

(b) sections 152, 153 and 238 of the Trade Union and Labour Relations (Consolidation) Act 1992 (dismissal on ground of trade union membership or activities or in connection with industrial action).

[Procedural fairness

11-116   **98A.**—(1) An employee who is dismissed shall be regarded for the purposes of this Part as unfairly dismissed if—

(a) one of the procedures set out in Part 1 of Schedule 2 to the Employment Act 2002 (dismissal and disciplinary procedures) applies in relation to the dismissal,

(b) the procedure has not been completed, and

(c) the non-completion of the procedure is wholly or mainly attributable to failure by the employer to comply with its requirements.

(2) Subject to subsection (1), failure by an employer to follow a procedure in relation to the dismissal of an employee shall not be regarded for the purposes of section 98(4)(a) as by itself making the employer's action unreasonable if he shows that he would have decided to dismiss the employee if he had followed the procedure.

(3) For the purposes of this section, any question as to the application of a procedure set out in Part 1 of Schedule 2 to the Employment Act 2002, completion of such a procedure or failure to comply with the requirements of such a procedure shall be determined by reference to regulations under section 31 of that Act.]^4

---

^{1} Repealed by Employment Relations Act 1999 c.26 Sch 9 para 1
^{2} Words substituted by Employment Relations Act 1999 c.26 Sch 4 (III) para 15 (b)
^{3} Words inserted by Employment Act 2002 c.22 Sch 7 para 32
^{4} Inserted by Employment Act 2002 c.22 s 34 (2)

[Leave for family reasons

99.—(1) An employee who is dismissed shall be regarded for the purposes of **11-117** this Part as unfairly dismissed if—

(a) the reason or principal reason for the dismissal is of a prescribed kind, or

(b) the dismissal takes place in prescribed circumstances.

(2) In this section "prescribed" means prescribed by regulations made by the Secretary of State.

(3) A reason or set of circumstances prescribed under this section must relate to—

(a) pregnancy, childbirth or maternity,

(b) ordinary, compulsory or additional maternity leave,

[(ba) ordinary or additional adoption leave,][1]

(c) parental leave,

[(ca) paternity leave, or][2]

(d) time off under section 57A;

and it may also relate to redundancy or other factors.

(4) A reason or set of circumstances prescribed under subsection (1) satisfies subsection (3)(c) or (d) if it relates to action which an employee—

(a) takes,

(b) agrees to take, or

(c) refuses to take,

under or in respect of a collective or workforce agreement which deals with parental leave.

(5) Regulations under this section may—

(a) make different provision for different cases or circumstances;

(b) apply any enactment, in such circumstances as may be specified and subject to any conditions specified, in relation to persons regarded as unfairly dismissed by reason of this section.][3]

Health and safety cases

100.—(1) An employee who is dismissed shall be regarded for the purposes **11-118** of this Part as unfairly dismissed if the reason (or, if more than one, the principal reason) for the dismissal is that—

(a) having been designated by the employer to carry out activities in connection with preventing or reducing risks to health and safety at work, the employee carried out (or proposed to carry out) any such activities,

(b) being a representative of workers on matters of health and safety at work or member of a safety committee—

(i) in accordance with arrangements established under or by virtue of any enactment, or

(ii) by reason of being acknowledged as such by the employer,

the employee performed (or proposed to perform) any functions as such a representative or a member of such a committee,

[(ba) the employee took part (or proposed to take part) in consultation with the employer pursuant to the Health and Safety (Consultation with Employees) Regulations 1996 or in an election of representatives

---

[1] Inserted by Employment Act 2002 c.22 Sch 7 para 33 (2)
[2] Inserted by Employment Act 2002 c.22 Sch 7 para 33 (3)
[3] Substituted by Employment Relations Act 1999 c.26 Sch 4 (III) para 16

of employee safety within the meaning of those Regulations (whether as a candidate or otherwise),][1]

(c) being an employee at a place where—
   (i) there was no such representative or safety committee, or
   (ii) there was such a representative or safety committee but it was not reasonably practicable for the employee to raise the matter by those means,

he brought to his employer's attention, by reasonable means, circumstances connected with his work which he reasonably believed were harmful or potentially harmful to health or safety,

(d) in circumstances of danger which the employee reasonably believed to be serious and imminent and which he could not reasonably have been expected to avert, he left (or proposed to leave) or (while the danger persisted) refused to return to his place of work or any dangerous part of his place of work, or

(e) in circumstances of danger which the employee reasonably believed to be serious and imminent, he took (or proposed to take) appropriate steps to protect himself or other persons from the danger.

(2) For the purposes of subsection (1)(e) whether steps which an employee took (or proposed to take) were appropriate is to be judged by reference to all the circumstances including, in particular, his knowledge and the facilities and advice available to him at the time.

(3) Where the reason (or, if more than one, the principal reason) for the dismissal of an employee is that specified in subsection (1)(e), he shall not be regarded as unfairly dismissed if the employer shows that it was (or would have been) so negligent for the employee to take the steps which he took (or proposed to take) that a reasonable employer might have dismissed him for taking (or proposing to take) them.

Shop workers and betting workers who refuse Sunday work

11-119   **101.**—(1) Where an employee who is—
   (a) a protected shop worker or an opted-out shop worker, or
   (b) a protected betting worker or an opted-out betting worker,

is dismissed, he shall be regarded for the purposes of this Part as unfairly dismissed if the reason (or, if more than one, the principal reason) for the dismissal is that he refused (or proposed to refuse) to do shop work, or betting work, on Sunday or on a particular Sunday.

(2) Subsection (1) does not apply in relation to an opted-out shop worker or an opted-out betting worker where the reason (or principal reason) for the dismissal is that he refused (or proposed to refuse) to do shop work, or betting work, on any Sunday or Sundays falling before the end of the notice period.

(3) A shop worker or betting worker who is dismissed shall be regarded for the purposes of this Part as unfairly dismissed if the reason (or, if more than one, the principal reason) for the dismissal is that the shop worker or betting worker gave (or proposed to give) an opting-out notice to the employer.

(4) For the purposes of section 36(2)(b) or 41(1)(b), the appropriate date in relation to this section is the effective date of termination.

---
[1] Inserted by SI 1996/1513 reg 8

[Working time cases

101A.—(1) An employee who is dismissed shall be regarded for the purposes **11-120** of this Part as unfairly dismissed if the reason (or, if more than one, the principal reason) for the dismissal is that the employee –

(a) refused (or proposed to refuse) to comply with a requirement which the employer imposed (or proposed to impose) in contravention of the Working Time Regulations 1998,

(b) refused (or proposed to refuse) to forgo a right conferred on him by those Regulations,

(c) failed to sign a workforce agreement for the purposes of those Regulations, or to enter into, or agree to vary or extend, any other agreement with his employer which is provided for in those Regulations, or

(d) being –

    (i) a representative of members of the workforce for the purposes of Schedule 1 to those Regulations, or

    (ii) a candidate in an election in which any person elected will, on being elected, be such a representative,

performed (or proposed to perform) any functions or activities as such a representative or candidate.]¹

[(2) A reference in this section to the Working Time Regulations 1998 includes a reference to the Merchant Shipping (Working Time: Inland Waterways) Regulations 2003.]²

Trustees of occupational pension schemes

102.—(1) An employee who is dismissed shall be regarded for the purposes **11-121** of this Part as unfairly dismissed if the reason (or, if more than one, the principal reason) for the dismissal is that, being a trustee of a relevant occupational pension scheme which relates to his employment, the employee performed (or proposed to perform) any functions as such a trustee.

[(1A) This section applies to an employee who is a director of a company which is a trustee of a relevant occupational pension scheme as it applies to an employee who is a trustee of such a scheme (references to such a trustee being read for this purpose as references to such a director).]³

(2) In this section "relevant occupational pension scheme" means an occupational pension scheme (as defined in section 1 of the Pension Schemes Act 1993 established under a trust.

Employee representatives

103.—[(1) An employee who is dismissed shall be regarded for the purposes **11-122** of this Part as unfairly dismissed if the reason (or, if more than one, the principal reason) for the dismissal is that the employee, being—

(a) an employee representative for the purposes of Chapter II of Part IV of the Trade Union and Labour Relations (Consolidation) Act 1992 (redundancies) or Regulations 10 and 11 of the Transfer of Undertakings (Protection of Employment) Regulations 1981, or

(b) a candidate in an election in which any person elected will, on being elected, be such an employee representative,

---

¹ Inserted by SI 1998/1833 reg 32 (1)
² Inserted by SI 2003/3049 Sch 2 para 3
³ Inserted by Welfare Reform and Pensions Act 1999 c.30 Sch 2 para 19 (4)

performed (or proposed to perform) any functions or activities as such an employee representative or candidate.][1]

[(2) An employee who is dismissed shall be regarded for the purposes of this Part as unfairly dismissed if the reason (or, if more than one, the principal reason) for the dismissal is that the employee took part in an election of employee representatives for the purposes of Chapter II of Part IV of the Trade Union and Labour Relations (Consolidation) Act 1992 (redundancies) or Regulations 10 and 11 of the Transfer of Undertakings (Protection of Employment) Regulations 1981.][2]

[Protected disclosure

11-123   **103A.** An employee who is dismissed shall be regarded for the purposes of this Part as unfairly dismissed if the reason (or, if more than one, the principal reason) for the dismissal is that the employee made a protected disclosure.][3]

Assertion of statutory right

11-124   **104.**—(1) An employee who is dismissed shall be regarded for the purposes of this Part as unfairly dismissed if the reason (or, if more than one, the principal reason) for the dismissal is that the employee—

(a) brought proceedings against the employer to enforce a right of his which is a relevant statutory right, or

(b) alleged that the employer had infringed a right of his which is a relevant statutory right.

(2) It is immaterial for the purposes of subsection (1)—

(a) whether or not the employee has the right, or

(b) whether or not the right has been infringed;

but, for that subsection to apply, the claim to the right and that it has been infringed must be made in good faith.

(3) It is sufficient for subsection (1) to apply that the employee, without specifying the right, made it reasonably clear to the employer what the right claimed to have been infringed was.

(4) The following are relevant statutory rights for the purposes of this section—

(a) any right conferred by this Act for which the remedy for its infringement is by way of a complaint or reference to an [employment tribunal][4],

(b) the right conferred by section 86 of this Act, [...][5]

(c) the rights conferred by sections 68, 86, 146, 168, [168A,][6] 169 and 170 of the Trade Union and Labour Relations (Consolidation) Act 1992 (deductions from pay, union activities and time off)[, and][7]

[(d) the rights conferred by the Working Time Regulations 1998 [or the Merchant Shipping (Working Time: Inland Waterways) Regulations 2003][8].][9]

[(5) In this section any reference to an employer includes, where the right in question is conferred by section 63A, the principal (within the meaning of section

---

[1] Existing s 103 renumbered as s 103 (1) by SI 1999/1925 reg 13
[2] Words inserted by SI 1999/1925 reg 13
[3] Words inserted by Public Interest Disclosure Act 1998 c.23 s 5
[4] Words substituted by Employment Rights (Dispute Resolution) Act 1998 c.8 Pt I s 1 (2)
[5] Word repealed by SI 1998/1833 Pt IV reg 32 (2) (a)
[6] Words inserted by Employment Act 2002 c.22 Sch 7 para 34
[7] Word and para (d) inserted by SI 1998/1833 Pt IV reg 32 (2) (b)
[8] Words inserted by SI 1998/1833 reg 32 (2)
[9] Words and para (d) inserted by SI 1998/1833 Pt IV reg 32 (2) (b)

63A(3)) [or the Merchant Shipping (Working Time: Inland Waterways) Regulations 2003][1].][2]

[The national minimum wage

104A.—(1) An employee who is dismissed shall be regarded for the purposes **11-125** of this Part as unfairly dismissed if the reason (or, if more than one, the principal reason) for the dismissal is that—

(a) any action was taken, or was proposed to be taken, by or on behalf of the employee with a view to enforcing, or otherwise securing the benefit of, a right of the employee's to which this section applies; or

(b) the employer was prosecuted for an offence under section 31 of the National Minimum Wage Act 1998 as a result of action taken by or on behalf of the employee for the purpose of enforcing, or otherwise securing the benefit of, a right of the employee's to which this section applies; or

(c) the employee qualifies, or will or might qualify, for the national minimum wage or for a particular rate of national minimum wage.

(2) It is immaterial for the purposes of paragraph (a) or (b) of subsection (1) above—

(a) whether or not the employee has the right, or

(b) whether or not the right has been infringed,

but, for that subsection to apply, the claim to the right and, if applicable, the claim that it has been infringed must be made in good faith.

(3) The following are the rights to which this section applies—

(a) any right conferred by, or by virtue of, any provision of the National Minimum Wage Act 1998 for which the remedy for its infringement is by way of a complaint to an employment tribunal; and

(b) any right conferred by section 17 of the National Minimum Wage Act 1998 (worker receiving less than national minimum wage entitled to additional remuneration).][3]

[Tax credits

104B—(1) An employee who is dismissed shall be regarded for the purposes **11-126** of this Part as unfairly dismissed if the reason (or, if more than one, the principal reason) for the dismissal is that—

(a) any action was taken, or was proposed to be taken, by or on behalf of the employee with a view to enforcing, or otherwise securing the benefit of, a right conferred on the employee by regulations under section 25 of the Tax Credits Act 2002,

(b) a penalty was imposed on the employer, or proceedings for a penalty were brought against him, under that Act, as a result of action taken by or on behalf of the employee for the purpose of enforcing, or otherwise securing the benefit of, such a right, or

(c) the employee is entitled, or will or may be entitled, to working tax credit.

(2) It is immaterial for the purposes of subsection (1)(a) or (b)—

(a) whether or not the employee has the right, or

(b) whether or not the right has been infringed,

---

[1] Words inserted by SI 2003/3049 Sch 2 para 3 (4)
[2] Inserted by Teaching and Higher Education Act 1998 c.30 Sch 3 para 13
[3] Inserted by National Minimum Wage Act 1998 c.39 s 25 (1)

but, for those provisions to apply, the claim to the right and (if applicable) the claim that it has been infringed must be made in good faith.]¹

[Flexible working

11-127 **104C** An employee who is dismissed shall be regarded for the purposes of this Part as unfairly dismissed if the reason (or, if more than one, the principal reason) for the dismissal is that the employee—

    (a) made (or proposed to make) an application under section 80F,

    (b) exercised (or proposed to exercise) a right conferred on him under section 80G,

    (c) brought proceedings against the employer under section 80H, or

    (d) alleged the existence of any circumstance which would constitute a ground for bringing such proceedings.]²

Redundancy

11-128 **105.**—(1) An employee who is dismissed shall be regarded for the purposes of this Part as unfairly dismissed if—

    (a) the reason (or, if more than one, the principal reason) for the dismissal is that the employee was redundant,

    (b) it is shown that the circumstances constituting the redundancy applied equally to one or more other employees in the same undertaking who held positions similar to that held by the employee and who have not been dismissed by the employer, and

    (c) it is shown that any of [[subsections (2) to (7C)]³]⁴ [, (7E) and (7F)]⁵ applies.

    (2) [...]⁶

(3) This subsection applies if the reason (or, if more than one, the principal reason) for which the employee was selected for dismissal was one of those specified in subsection (1) of section 100 (read with subsections (2) and (3) of that section).

Replacements

11-129 **106.**—(1) Where this section applies to an employee he shall be regarded for the purposes of section 98(1)(b) as having been dismissed for a substantial reason of a kind such as to justify the dismissal of an employee holding the position which the employee held.

    (2) This section applies to an employee where—

    (a) on engaging him the employer informs him in writing that his employment will be terminated on the resumption of work by another employee who is, or will be, absent wholly or partly because of pregnancy or childbirth, [or on adoption leave]⁷ and

    (b) the employer dismisses him in order to make it possible to give work to the other employee.

    (3) This section also applies to an employee where—

    (a) on engaging him the employer informs him in writing that his employment will be terminated on the end of a suspension of another

---

¹ Substituted by Tax Credits Act 2002 c.21 Sch 1 para 3 (2)
² Inserted by Employment Act 2002 c.22 Pt IV s 47 (4)
³ Words substituted by Employment Relations Act 1999 c.26 Sch 5 para 5 (2)
⁴ Words inserted by SI 1999/3323 Pt VII reg 29 (1)
⁵ Words substituted by SI 2002/2034 Sch 2 (1) para 3 (9)
⁶ Repealed by Employment Relations Act 1999 c.26 Sch 9 para 1
⁷ Words inserted by Employment Act 2002 c.22 Sch 7 para 35

employee from work on medical grounds or maternity grounds (within the meaning of Part VII, and

(b) the employer dismisses him in order to make it possible to allow the resumption of work by the other employee.

(4) Subsection (1) does not affect the operation of section 98(4) in a case to which this section applies.

Pressure on employer to dismiss unfairly

107.—(1) This section applies where there falls to be determined for the **11-130** purposes of this Part a question—

(a) as to the reason, or principal reason, for which an employee was dismissed,

(b) whether the reason or principal reason for which an employee was dismissed was a reason fulfilling the requirement of section 98(1)(b), or

(c) whether an employer acted reasonably in treating the reason or principal reason for which an employee was dismissed as a sufficient reason for dismissing him.

(2) In determining the question no account shall be taken of any pressure which by calling, organising, procuring or financing a strike or other industrial action, or threatening to do so, was exercised on the employer to dismiss the employee; and the question shall be determined as if no such pressure had been exercised.

Exclusion of right

Qualifying period of employment

108.—(1) Section 94 does not apply to the dismissal of an employee unless **11-131** he has been continuously employed for a period of not less than [one year]¹ ending with the effective date of termination.

(2) If an employee is dismissed by reason of any such requirement or recommendation as is referred to in section 64(2), subsection (1) has effect in relation to that dismissal as if for the words "[one year]²" there were substituted the words "one month".

(3) Subsection (1) does not apply if—

(a) [...]³

(b) subsection (1) of section 99 (read with subsection (2) of that section) or subsection (3) of that section applies,

(c) subsection (1) of section 100 (read with subsections (2) and (3) of that section applies,

(d) subsection (1) of section 101 (read with subsection (2) of that section) or subsection (3) of that section applies,

[(dd) section 101A applies,]⁴

(e) section 102 applies,

(f) section 103 applies,

[(ff) section 103A applies,]⁵

---

¹ Words substituted by SI 1999/1436 art 3
² Words substituted by SI 1999/1436 art 4
³ Repealed by Employment Relations Act 1999 c.26 Sch 9 para 1
⁴ Inserted by SI 1998/1833 Pt IV reg 32 (4)
⁵ Inserted by Public Interest Disclosure Act 1998 c.23 s 7 (1)

(g) subsection (1) of section 104 (read with subsections (2) and (3) of that section) applies, [...][1]

[(gg) subsection (1) of section 104A (read with subsection (2) of that section) applies, [...][2]][3]

[(gh) subsection (1) of section 104B (read with subsection (2) of that section) applies.][4]

(h) section 105 applies [, [...][5]][6] [...][7]

[(hh) paragraph (3) or (6) of regulation 28 of the Transnational Information and Consultation of Employees Regulations 1999 (read with paragraphs (4) and (7) of that regulation) applies, [...][8]][9]

[(i) paragraph (1) of regulation 7 of the Part-time Workers (Prevention of Less Favourable Treatment) Regulations 2000 applies [, or][10]][11]

[(j) paragraph (1) of regulation 6 of the Fixed-term Employees (Prevention of Less Favourable Treatment) Regulations 2002 applies.][12]

Upper age limit

11-132   **109.**—(1) Section 94 does not apply to the dismissal of an employee if on or before the effective date of termination he has attained—

(a) in a case where—

(i) in the undertaking in which the employee was employed there was a normal retiring age for an employee holding the position held by the employee, and

(ii) the age was the same whether the employee holding that position was a man or a woman,

that normal retiring age, and

(b) in any other case, the age of sixty-five.

(2) Subsection (1) does not apply if—

(a) [...][13]

(b) subsection (1) of section 99 (read with subsection (2) of that section) or subsection (3) of that section applies,

(c) subsection (1) of section 100 (read with subsections (2) and (3) of that section) applies,

(d) subsection (1) of section 101 (read with subsection (2) of that section) or subsection (3) of that section applies,

[(dd) section 101A applies,][14]

(e) section 102 applies,

(f) section 103 applies,

[(ff) section 103A applies,][15]

---

1 Word repealed by National Minimum Wage Act 1998 c.39 Sch 3 para 1
2 Word repealed by Tax Credits Act 1999 c.10 Sch 6 para 1
3 Inserted by National Minimum Wage Act 1998 c.39 s 25 (3)
4 Substituted by Tax Credits Act 2002 c.21 Sch 1 para 3 (4)
5 Word repealed by SI 2000/1551 Sch 1 para 2 (2)
6 Inserted by SI 1999/3323 Pt VII reg 29 (2)
7 Word repealed by SI 2000/1551 Sch 1 para 2 (2)
8 Words repealed by SI 2002/2034 Sch 2 (1) para 3 (11)
9 Inserted by SI 1999/3323 Pt VII reg 29 (2)
10 Words nserted by SI 2002/2034 Sch 2 (1) para 3 (11)
11 Inserted by SI 2000/1551 Sch 1 para 2 (2)
12 Inserted by SI 2002/2034 Sch 2 (1) para 3 (11)
13 Repealed by Employment Relations Act 1999 c.26 Sch 9 para 1
14 Inserted by SI 1998/1833 Pt IV reg 32 (4)
15 Inserted by Public Interest Disclosure Act 1998 c.23 s 7 (2)

(g) subsection (1) of section 104 (read with subsections (2) and (3) of that section) applies, [...]¹

[(gg) subsection (1) of section 104A (read with subsection (2) of that section) applies, [...]²]³

[(gh) subsection (1) of section 104B (read with subsection (2) of that section) applies, [...]⁴]⁵

(h) section 105 applies [, [...]⁶]⁷[...]⁸

[(hh) paragraph (3) or (6) of regulation 28 of the Transnational Information and Consultation of Employees Regulations 1999 (read with paragraphs (4) and (7) of that regulation) applies [,]⁹]¹⁰

[(i) paragraph (1) of regulation 7 of the Part-time Workers (Prevention of Less Favourable Treatment) Regulations 2000 applies [, or]¹¹]¹²

[(j) paragraph (1) of regulation 6 of the Fixed-term Employees (Prevention of Less Favourable Treatment) Regulations 2002 applies.]¹³

Dismissal procedures agreements

110.—(1) Where a dismissal procedures agreement is designated by an order **11-133** under subsection (3) which is for the time being in force—

(a) the provisions of that agreement relating to dismissal shall have effect in substitution for any rights under section 94, and

(b) accordingly, section 94 does not apply to the dismissal of an employee from any employment if it is employment to which, and he is an employee to whom, those provisions of the agreement apply.

[(2) But if the agreement includes provision that it does not apply to dismissals of particular descriptions, subsection (1) does not apply in relation to a dismissal of any such description.]¹⁴

(3) An order designating a dismissal procedures agreement may be made by the Secretary of State, on an application being made to him jointly by all the parties to the agreement, if he is satisfied that—

(a) every trade union which is a party to the agreement is an independent trade union,

(b) the agreement provides for procedures to be followed in cases where an employee claims that he has been, or is in the course of being, unfairly dismissed,

(c) those procedures are available without discrimination to all employees falling within any description to which the agreement applies,

(d) the remedies provided by the agreement in respect of unfair dismissal are on the whole as beneficial as (but not necessarily identical with) those provided in respect of unfair dismissal by this Part,

---

¹ Words repealed by National Minimum Wage Act 1998 c.39 Sch 3 para 1
² Word repealed by Tax Credits Act 1999 c.10 Sch 6 para 1
³ Inserted by National Minimum Wage Act 1998 c.39 s 25 (4)
⁴ Word repealed by SI 1999/3323 Pt VII reg 29 (3)
⁵ Inserted by Tax Credits Act 1999 c.10 Sch 3 para 3 (4)
⁶ Word repealed by SI 2000/1551 Sch 1 para 2 (3)
⁷ Inserted by SI 1999/3323 Pt VII reg 29 (3)
⁸ Word repealed by SI 2000/1551 Sch 1 para 2 (3)
⁹ Inserted by SI 2000/1551 Sch 1 para 2 (3)
¹⁰ Inserted by SI 1999/3323 Pt VII reg 29 (3)
¹¹ Inserted by SI 2002/2034 Sch 2 (1) para 3 (12)
¹² Inserted by SI 2000/1551 Sch 1 para 2 (3)
¹³ Inserted by SI 2002/2034 Sch 2 (1) para 3 (12)
¹⁴ Substituted by Employment Rights (Dispute Resolution) Act 1998 c.8 Pt II s 12 (1)

[(e) the agreement includes provision either for arbitration in every case or for—
　　(i) arbitration where (by reason of equality of votes or for any other reason) a decision under the agreement cannot otherwise be reached, and
　　(ii) a right to submit to arbitration any question of law arising out of such a decision, and][1]
(f) the provisions of the agreement are such that it can be determined with reasonable certainty whether or not a particular employee is one to whom the agreement applies.

[(3A) The Secretary of State may by order amend subsection (3) so as to add to the conditions specified in that subsection such conditions as he may specify in the order.][2]

(4) If at any time when an order under subsection (3) is in force in relation to a dismissal procedures agreement the Secretary of State is satisfied, whether on an application made to him by any of the parties to the agreement or otherwise, either—
(a) that it is the desire of all the parties to the agreement that the order should be revoked, or
(b) that the agreement no longer satisfied all the conditions specified in subsection (3),
the Secretary of State shall revoke the order by an order under this subsection.

(5) The transitional provisions which may be made in an order under subsection (4) include, in particular, provisions directing—
(a) that an employee—
　　(i) shall not be excluded from his right under section 94 where the effective date of termination falls within a transitional period which ends with the date on which the order takes effect and which is specified in the order, and
　　(ii) shall have an extended time for presenting a complaint under section 111 in respect of a dismissal where the effective date of termination falls within that period, and
(b) that, where the effective date of termination falls within such a transitional period, an [employment tribunal][3] shall, in determining any complaint of unfair dismissal presented by an employee to whom the dismissal procedures agreement applies, have regard to such considerations as are specified in the order (in addition to those specified in this Part and [section 10(4) and (5) of the Employment Tribunals Act 1996][4]).

[(6) Where an award is made under a designated dismissal procedures agreement—
(a) in England and Wales it may be enforced, by leave of a county court, in the same manner as a judgment of the court to the same effect and, where leave is given, judgment may be entered in terms of the award, and
(b) in Scotland it may be recorded for execution in the Books of Council and Session and shall be enforceable accordingly.][5]

---

[1] Substituted by Employment Rights (Dispute Resolution) Act 1998 c.8 Pt II s 12 (2)
[2] Inserted by Employment Act 2002 c.22 s 44
[3] Words substituted by Employment Rights (Dispute Resolution) Act 1998 c.8 Pt I s 1 (2)
[4] Words substituted by Employment Rights (Dispute Resolution) Act 1998 c.8 Pt I s 1 (2)
[5] Inserted by Employment Rights (Dispute Resolution) Act 1998 c.8 Pt II s 12 (3)

Chapter II

Remedies for Unfair Dismissal

Introductory

Complaints to [employment tribunal][1]

111.—(1) A complaint may be presented to an [employment tribunal][2] **11-134** against an employer by any person that he was unfairly dismissed by the employer.

(2) Subject to subsection (3), an [employment tribunal][3] shall not consider a complaint under this section unless it is presented to the tribunal—

(a) before the end of the period of three months beginning with the effective date of termination, or

(b) within such further period as the tribunal considers reasonable in a case where it is satisfied that it was not reasonably practicable for the complaint to be presented before the end of that period of three months.

(3) Where a dismissal is with notice, an [employment tribunal][4] shall consider a complaint under this section if it is presented after the notice is given but before the effective date of termination.

(4) In relation to a complaint which is presented as mentioned in subsection (3), the provisions of this Act, so far as they relate to unfair dismissal, have effect as if—

(a) references to a complaint by a person that he was unfairly dismissed by his employer included references to a complaint by a person that his employer has given him notice in such circumstances that he will be unfairly dismissed when the notice expires,

(b) references to reinstatement included references to the withdrawal of the notice by the employer,

(c) references to the effective date of termination included references to the date which would be the effective date of termination on the expiry of the notice, and

(d) references to an employee ceasing to be employed included references to an employee having been given notice of dismissal.

The remedies: orders and compensation

112.—(1) This section applies where, on a complaint under section 111, an **11-135** [employment tribunal][5] finds that the grounds of the complaint are well-founded.

(2) The tribunal shall—

(a) explain to the complainant what orders may be made under section 113 and in what circumstances they may be made, and

(b) ask him whether he wishes the tribunal to make such an order.

(3) If the complainant expresses such a wish, the tribunal may make an order under section 113.

[1] Words substituted by Employment Rights (Dispute Resolution) Act 1998 c.8 Pt I s 1 (2)
[2] Words substituted by Employment Rights (Dispute Resolution) Act 1998 c.8 Pt I s 1 (2)
[3] Words substituted by Employment Rights (Dispute Resolution) Act 1998 c.8 Pt I s 1 (2)
[4] Words substituted by Employment Rights (Dispute Resolution) Act 1998 c.8 Pt I s 1 (2)
[5] Words substituted by Employment Rights (Dispute Resolution) Act 1998 c.8 Pt I s 1 (2)

(4) If no order is made under section 113, the tribunal shall make an award of compensation for unfair dismissal (calculated in accordance with [sections 118 to 127A][1] [...][2] [...][3]) to be paid by the employer to the employee.

Orders for reinstatement or re-engagement

The orders

11-136   **113.** An order under this section may be—
   (a) an order for reinstatement (in accordance with section 114), or
   (b) an order for re-engagement (in accordance with section 115), as the tribunal may decide.

Order for reinstatement

11-137   **114.**—(1) An order for reinstatement is an order that the employer shall treat the complainant in all respects as if he had not been dismissed.
   (2) On making an order for reinstatement the tribunal shall specify—
   (a) any amount payable by the employer in respect of any benefit which the complainant might reasonably be expected to have had but for the dismissal (including arrears of pay) for the period between the date of termination of employment and the date of reinstatement,
   (b) any rights and privileges (including seniority and pension rights) which must be restored to the employee, and
   (c) the date by which the order must be complied with.
   (3) If the complainant would have benefited from an improvement in his terms and conditions of employment had he not been dismissed, an order for reinstatement shall require him to be treated as if he had benefited from that improvement from the date on which he would have done so but for being dismissed.
   (4) In calculating for the purposes of subsection (2)(a) any amount payable by the employer, the tribunal shall take into account, so as to reduce the employer's liability, any sums received by the complainant in respect of the period between the date of termination of employment and the date of reinstatement by way of—
   (a) wages in lieu of notice or ex gratia payments paid by the employer, or
   (b) remuneration paid in respect of employment with another employer,
and such other benefits as the tribunal thinks appropriate in the circumstances.
   (5) [...][4]

Order for re-engagement

11-138   **115.**—(1) An order for re-engagement is an order, on such terms as the tribunal may decide, that the complainant be engaged by the employer, or by a successor of the employer or by an associated employer, in employment comparable to that from which he was dismissed or other suitable employment.
   (2) On making an order for re-engagement the tribunal shall specify the terms on which re-engagement is to take place, including—
   (a) the identity of the employer,
   (b) the nature of the employment,
   (c) the remuneration for the employment,

---

[1] Words substituted by Employment Rights (Dispute Resolution) Act 1998 c.8 Sch 1 para 19
[2] Words repealed by Employment Relations Act 1999 c.26 Sch 9 para 1
[3] Words repealed by Employment Relations Act 1999 c.26 Sch 9 para 1
[4] Repealed by Employment Relations Act 1999 c.26 Sch 9 para 1

(d) any amount payable by the employer in respect of any benefit which the complainant might reasonably be expected to have had but for the dismissal (including arrears of pay) for the period between the date of termination of employment and the date of re-engagement,

(e) any rights and privileges (including seniority and pension rights) which must be restored to the employee, and

(f) the date by which the order must be complied with.

(3) In calculating for the purposes of subsection (2)(d) any amount payable by the employer, the tribunal shall take into account, so as to reduce the employer's liability, any sums received by the complainant in respect of the period between the date of termination of employment and the date of re-engagement by way of—

(a) wages in lieu of notice or ex gratia payments paid by the employer, or

(b) remuneration paid in respect of employment with another employer,

and such other benefits as the tribunal thinks appropriate in the circumstances.

(4) [...]¹

Choice of order and its terms

116.—(1) In exercising its discretion under section 113 the tribunal shall first **11-139** consider whether to make an order for reinstatement and in so doing shall take into account—

(a) whether the complainant wishes to be reinstated,

(b) whether it is practicable for the employer to comply with an order for reinstatement, and

(c) where the complainant caused or contributed to some extent to the dismissal, whether it would be just to order his reinstatement.

(2) If the tribunal decides not to make an order for reinstatement it shall then consider whether to make an order for re-engagement and, if so, on what terms.

(3) In so doing the tribunal shall take into account—

(a) any wish expressed by the complainant as to the nature of the order to be made,

(b) whether it is practicable for the employer (or a successor or an associated employer) to comply with an order for re-engagement, and

(c) where the complainant caused or contributed to some extent to the dismissal, whether it would be just to order his re-engagement and (if so) on what terms.

(4) Except in a case where the tribunal takes into account contributory fault under subsection (3)(c) it shall, if it orders re-engagement, do so on terms which are, so far as is reasonably practicable, as favourable as an order for reinstatement.

(5) Where in any case an employer has engaged a permanent replacement for a dismissed employee, the tribunal shall not take that fact into account in determining, for the purposes of subsection (1)(b) or (3)(b), whether it is practicable to comply with an order for reinstatement or re-engagement.

(6) Subsection (5) does not apply where the employer shows—

(a) that it was not practicable for him to arrange for the dismissed employee's work to be done without engaging a permanent replacement, or

(b) that—

¹ Repealed by Employment Relations Act 1999 c.26 Sch 9 para 1

(i) he engaged the replacement after the lapse of a reasonable period, without having heard from the dismissed employee that he wished to be reinstated or re-engaged, and

(ii) when the employer engaged the replacement it was no longer reasonable for him to arrange for the dismissed employee's work to be done except by a permanent replacement.

Enforcement of order and compensation

11-140   **117.**—(1) An [employment tribunal][1] shall make an award of compensation, to be paid by the employer to the employee, if—

(a) an order under section 113 is made and the complainant is reinstated or re-engaged, but

(b) the terms of the order are not fully complied with.

(2) Subject to section 124 [...][2], the amount of the compensation shall be such as the tribunal thinks fit having regard to the loss sustained by the complainant in consequence of the failure to comply fully with the terms of the order.

(3) Subject to subsections (1) and (2) [...][3], if an order under section 113 is made but the complainant is not reinstated or re-engaged in accordance with the order, the tribunal shall make—

(a) an award of compensation for unfair dismissal (calculated in accordance with [sections 118 to 127A][4]), and

(b) except where this paragraph does not apply, an additional award of compensation of [an amount not less than twenty-six nor more than fifty-two weeks' pay][5],

to be paid by the employer to the employee.

(4) Subsection (3)(b) does not apply where—

(a) the employer satisfies the tribunal that it was not practicable to comply with the order, [...][6]

(b) [...][7]

(5) [...][8]

(6) [...][9]

(7) Where in any case an employer has engaged a permanent replacement for a dismissed employee, the tribunal shall not take that fact into account in determining for the purposes of subsection (4)(a) whether it was practicable to comply with the order for reinstatement or re-engagement unless the employer shows that it was not practicable for him to arrange for the dismissed employee's work to be done without engaging a permanent replacement.

(8) Where in any case an [employment tribunal][10] finds that the complainant has unreasonably prevented an order under section 113 from being complied with, in making an award of compensation for unfair dismissal [...][11] it shall take that conduct into account as a failure on the part of the complainant to mitigate his loss.

---

[1] Words substituted by Employment Rights (Dispute Resolution) Act 1998 c.8 Pt I s 1 (2)
[2] Words repealed by Employment Relations Act 1999 c.26 Sch 9 para 1
[3] Words repealed by Employment Relations Act 1999 c.26 Sch 9 para 1
[4] Words substituted by Employment Rights (Dispute Resolution) Act 1998 c.8 Sch 1 para 20
[5] Words substituted by Employment Relations Act 1999 c.26 s 33 (2)
[6] Repealed by Employment Relations Act 1999 c.26 Sch 9 para 1
[7] Repealed by Employment Relations Act 1999 c.26 Sch 9 para 1
[8] Repealed by Employment Relations Act 1999 c.26 Sch 9 para 1
[9] Repealed by Employment Relations Act 1999 c.26 Sch 9 para 1
[10] Words substituted by Employment Rights (Dispute Resolution) Act 1998 c.8 Pt I s 1 (2)
[11] Words repealed by Employment Rights (Dispute Resolution) Act 1998 c.8 Sch 2 para 1

Compensation

General

118.—(1) [...]^1 Where a tribunal makes an award of compensation for unfair **11-141** dismissal under section 112(4) or 117(3)(a) the award shall consist of—

    (a) a basic award (calculated in accordance with sections 119 to 122 and 126, and

    (b) a compensatory award (calculated in accordance with [...]^2 [sections 123, 124, 126 and 127A(1), (3) and (4)]^3).

(2)

(3) [...]^4

[(4) Where section 127A(2) applies, the award shall also include a supplementary award.]^5

Basic award

119.—(1) Subject to the provisions of this section, sections 120 to 122 and **11-142** section 126, the amount of the basic award shall be calculated by—

    (a) determining the period, ending with the effective date of termination, during which the employee has been continuously employed,

    (b) reckoning backwards from the end of that period the number of years of employment falling within that period, and

    (c) allowing the appropriate amount for each of those years of employment.

(2) In subsection (1)(c) "the appropriate amount" means—

    (a) one and a half weeks' pay for a year of employment in which the employee was not below the age of forty-one,

    (b) one week's pay for a year of employment (not within paragraph (a)) in which he was not below the age of twenty-two, and

    (c) half a week's pay for a year of employment not within paragraph (a) or (b).

(3) Where twenty years of employment have been reckoned under subsection (1), no account shall be taken under that subsection of any year of employment earlier than those twenty years.

(4) Where the effective date of termination is after the sixty-fourth anniversary of the day of the employee's birth, the amount arrived at under subsections (1) to (3) shall be reduced by the appropriate fraction.

(5) In subsection (4) "the appropriate fraction" means the fraction of which—

    (a) the numerator is the number of whole months reckoned from the sixty-fourth anniversary of the day of the employee's birth in the period beginning with that anniversary and ending with the effective date of termination, and

    (b) the denominator is twelve.

(6) [...]^6

---

^{1} Words repealed by Employment Relations Act 1999 c.26 Sch 9 para 1
^{2} Word repealed by Employment Relations Act 1999 c.26 Sch 9 para 1
^{3} Words inserted by Employment Relations Act 1999 c.26 Sch 9 para 1
^{4} Repealed by Employment Relations Act 1999 c.26 Sch 9 para 1
^{5} Inserted by Employment Rights (Dispute Resolution) Act 1998 c.8 Sch 1 para 21 (3)
^{6} Repealed by Employment Relations Act 1999 c.26 Sch 9 para 1

Basic award: minimum in certain cases

11-143 **120.**—(1) The amount of the basic award (before any reduction under section 122) shall not be less than [£3,600][1] where the reason (or, if more than one, the principal reason)—

  (a) in a redundancy case, for selecting the employee for dismissal, or

  (b) otherwise, for the dismissal,

is one of those specified in [section 100(1)(a) and (b), 101A(d), 102(1) or 103][2].

  (2) [...][3]

Basic award of two weeks' pay in certain cases

11-144 **121.** The amount of the basic award shall be two weeks' pay where the tribunal finds that the reason (or, where there is more than one, the principal reason) for the dismissal of the employee is that he was redundant and the employee—

  (a) by virtue of section 138 is not regarded as dismissed for the purposes of Part XI, or

  (b) by virtue of section 141 is not, or (if he were otherwise entitled) would not be, entitled to a redundancy payment.

Basic award: reductions

11-145 **122.**—(1) Where the tribunal finds that the complainant has unreasonably refused an offer by the employer which (if accepted) would have the effect of reinstating the complainant in his employment in all respects as if he had not been dismissed, the tribunal shall reduce or further reduce the amount of the basic award to such extent as it considers just and equitable having regard to that finding.

  (2) Where the tribunal considers that any conduct of the complainant before the dismissal (or, where the dismissal was with notice, before the notice was given) was such that it would be just and equitable to reduce or further reduce the amount of the basic award to any extent, the tribunal shall reduce or further reduce that amount accordingly.

  (3) Subsection (2) does not apply in a redundancy case unless the reason for selecting the employee for dismissal was one of those specified in [section 100(1)(a) and (b), 101A(d), 102(1) or 103][4]; and in such a case subsection (2) applies only to so much of the basic award as is payable because of section 120.

  [(3A) Where the complainant has been awarded any amount in respect of the dismissal under a designated dismissal procedures agreement, the tribunal shall reduce or further reduce the amount of the basic award to such extent as it considers just and equitable having regard to that award.][5]

  (4) The amount of the basic award shall be reduced or further reduced by the amount of—

  (a) any redundancy payment awarded by the tribunal under Part XI in respect of the same dismissal, or

  (b) any payment made by the employer to the employee on the ground that the dismissal was by reason of redundancy (whether in pursuance of Part XI or otherwise).

---

[1] Figure substituted by SI 2003/3038 Sch 1 para 1
[2] Words inserted by SI 1998/1833 Pt IV reg 32 (5)
[3] Repealed by Employment Relations Act 1999 c.26 Sch 9 para 1
[4] Words inserted by SI 1998/1833 Pt IV reg 32 (5)
[5] Inserted by Employment Rights (Dispute Resolution) Act 1998 c.8 Sch 1 para 22

Compensatory award

123.—(1) Subject to the provisions of this section and [sections 124, 126, 127 **11-146**
and 127A(1), (3) and (4)][1], the amount of the compensatory award shall be such
amount as the tribunal considers just and equitable in all the circumstances
having regard to the loss sustained by the complainant in consequence of the
dismissal in so far as that loss is attributable to action taken by the employer.

(2) The loss referred to in subsection (1) shall be taken to include—

(a) any expenses reasonably incurred by the complainant in consequence
of the dismissal, and

(b) subject to subsection (3), loss of any benefit which he might reasonably
be expected to have had but for the dismissal.

(3) The loss referred to in subsection (1) shall be taken to include in respect
of any loss of—

(a) any entitlement or potential entitlement to a payment on account of
dismissal by reason of redundancy (whether in pursuance of Part XI or
otherwise), or

(b) any expectation of such a payment,

only the loss referable to the amount (if any) by which the amount of that
payment would have exceeded the amount of a basic award (apart from any
reduction under section 122 in respect of the same dismissal.

(4) In ascertaining the loss referred to in subsection (1) the tribunal shall
apply the same rule concerning the duty of a person to mitigate his loss as applies
to damages recoverable under the common law of England and Wales or (as the
case may be) Scotland.

(5) In determining, for the purposes of subsection (1), how far any loss
sustained by the complainant was attributable to action taken by the employer,
no account shall be taken of any pressure which by—

(a) calling, organising, procuring or financing a strike or other industrial
action, or

(b) threatening to do so,

was exercised on the employer to dismiss the employee; and that question shall
be determined as if no such pressure had been exercised.

(6) Where the tribunal finds that the dismissal was to any extent caused or
contributed to by any action of the complainant, it shall reduce the amount of the
compensatory award by such proportion as it considers just and equitable
having regard to that finding.

(7) If the amount of any payment made by the employer to the employee on
the ground that the dismissal was by reason of redundancy (whether in pursuance
of Part XI or otherwise) exceeds the amount of the basic award which would be
payable but for section 122(4), that excess goes to reduce the amount of the compensatory award.

Limit of compensatory award etc

124.—(1) The amount of—   **11-147**

(a) any compensation awarded to a person under section 117(1) and (2), or

(b) a compensatory award to a person calculated in accordance with
section 123,

shall not exceed [£55,000][2].

---

[1] Words substituted by Employment Rights (Dispute Resolution) Act 1998 c.8 Sch 1 para 23
[2] Figure substituted by SI 2003/3038 Sch 1 para 1

[(1A) Subsection (1) shall not apply to compensation awarded, or a compensatory award made, to a person in a case where he is regarded as unfairly dismissed by virtue of section 100, 103A, 105(3) or 105(6A).][1]

(2) [...][2]

(3) In the case of compensation awarded to a person under section 117(1) and (2), the limit imposed by this section may be exceeded to the extent necessary to enable the award fully to reflect the amount specified as payable under section 114(2)(a) or section 115(2)(d).

(4) Where—

(a) a compensatory award is an award under paragraph (a) of subsection (3) of section 117, and

(b) an additional award falls to be made under paragraph (b) of that subsection,

the limit imposed by this section on the compensatory award may be exceeded to the extent necessary to enable the aggregate of the compensatory and additional awards fully to reflect the amount specified as payable under section 114(2)(a) or section 115(2)(d).

(5) The limit imposed by this section applies to the amount which the [employment tribunal][3] would, apart from this section, award in respect of the subject matter of the complaint after taking into account—

(a) any payment made by the respondent to the complainant in respect of that matter, and

(b) any reduction in the amount of the award required by any enactment or rule of law.

11-148   125.—[...][4]

Acts which are both unfair dismissal and discrimination

11-149   126.—(1) This section applies where compensation falls to be awarded in respect of any act both under—

(a) the provisions of this Act relating to unfair dismissal, and

[(b) any one or more of the Sex Discrimination Act 1975, the Race Relations Act 1976 [...][5], the Disability Discrimination Act 1995 [and the Employment Equality (Sexual Orientation) Regulations 2003.][6]][7]

(2) An [employment tribunal][8] shall not award compensation under any one of those Acts [or Regulations][9] in respect of any loss or other matter which is or has been taken into account under [any other of them][10] by the tribunal (or another [employment tribunal][11]) in awarding compensation on the same or another complaint in respect of that act.

11-150   127. [...][12]

---

[1] Inserted by Employment Relations Act 1999 c.26 s 37 (1)
[2] Repealed by Employment Relations Act 1999 c.26 Sch 9 para 1
[3] Words substituted by Employment Rights (Dispute Resolution) Act 1998 c.8 Pt I s 1 (2)
[4] Repealed by Employment Relations Act 1999 c.26 Sch 9
[5] Word repealed by SI 2003/1661 Sch 5 para 2
[6] Word inserted by SI 2003/1661 Sch 5 para 2
[7] Substituted by Employment Rights (Dispute Resolution) Act 1998 c.8 Pt III s 14 (3)
[8] Words substituted by Employment Rights (Dispute Resolution) Act 1998 c.8 Pt I s 1 (2)
[9] Word inserted by SI 2003/1661 Sch 5 para 2
[10] Words substituted by Employment Rights (Dispute Resolution) Act 1998 c.8 Pt III s 14 (4) (b)
[11] Words substituted by Employment Rights (Dispute Resolution) Act 1998 c.8 Pt I s 1 (2)
[12] Repealed by Employment Relations Act 1999 c.26 Sch 9 para 1

[Internal appeal procedures

127A.—(1) Where in a case in which an award of compensation for unfair **11-151** dismissal falls to be made under section 112(4) or 117(3)(a) the tribunal finds that—

(a) the employer provided a procedure for appealing against dismissal, and

(b) the complainant was, at the time of the dismissal or within a reasonable period afterwards, given written notice stating that the employer provided the procedure and including details of it, but

(c) the complainant did not appeal against the dismissal under the procedure (otherwise than because the employer prevented him from doing so),

the tribunal shall reduce the compensatory award included in the award of compensation for unfair dismissal by such amount (if any) as it considers just and equitable.

(2) Where in a case in which an award of compensation for unfair dismissal falls to be made under section 112(4) or 117(3)(a) the tribunal finds that—

(a) the employer provided a procedure for appealing against dismissal, but

(b) the employer prevented the complainant from appealing against the dismissal under the procedure,

the award of compensation for unfair dismissal shall include a supplementary award of such amount (if any) as the tribunal considers just and equitable.

(3) In determining the amount of a reduction under subsection (1) or a supplementary award under subsection (2) the tribunal shall have regard to all the circumstances of the case, including in particular the chances that an appeal under the procedure provided by the employer would have been successful.

(4) The amount of such a reduction or supplementary award shall not exceed the amount of two weeks' pay.][1]

Interim relief

Interim relief pending determination of complaint

128.—(1) An employee who presents a complaint to an [employment **11-152** tribunal][2]—

(a) that he has been unfairly dismissed by his employer, and

(b) that the reason (or, if more than one, the principal reason) for the dismissal is one of those specified in [section 100(1)(a) and (b), 101A(d), 102(1), 103 or 103A][3][or in paragraph 161(2) of Schedule A1 to the Trade Union and Labour Relations (Consolidation) Act 1992][4],

may apply to the tribunal for interim relief.

(2) The tribunal shall not entertain an application for interim relief unless it is presented to the tribunal before the end of the period of seven days immediately following the effective date of termination (whether before, on or after that date).

(3) The tribunal shall determine the application for interim relief as soon as practicable after receiving the application.

[1] Inserted by Employment Rights (Dispute Resolution) Act 1998 c.8 Pt III s 13
[2] Words substituted by Employment Rights (Dispute Resolution) Act 1998 c.8 Pt I s 1 (2)
[3] Words substituted by Public Interest Disclosure Act 1998 c.23 s 9
[4] Words inserted by Employment Relations Act 1999 c.26 s 6

(4) The tribunal shall give to the employer not later than seven days before the date of the hearing a copy of the application together with notice of the date, time and place of the hearing.

(5) The tribunal shall not exercise any power it has of postponing the hearing of an application for interim relief except where it is satisfied that special circumstances exist which justify it in doing so.

Procedure on hearing of application and making of order

11-153 **129.**—(1) This section applies where, on hearing an employee's application for interim relief, it appears to the tribunal that it is likely that on determining the complaint to which the application relates the tribunal will find that the reason (or, if more than one, the principal reason) for his dismissal is one of those specified in [section 100(1)(a) and (b), 101A(d), 102(1), 103 or 103A][1] [or in paragraph 161(2) of Schedule A1 to the Trade Union and Labour Relations (Consolidation) Act 1992][2].

(2) The tribunal shall announce its findings and explain to both parties (if present)—

(a) what powers the tribunal may exercise on the application, and

(b) in what circumstances it will exercise them.

(3) The tribunal shall ask the employer (if present) whether he is willing, pending the determination or settlement of the complaint—

(a) to reinstate the employee (that is, to treat him in all respects as if he had not been dismissed), or

(b) if not, to re-engage him in another job on terms and conditions not less favourable than those which would have been applicable to him if he had not been dismissed.

(4) For the purposes of subsection (3)(b) "terms and conditions not less favourable than those which would have been applicable to him if he had not been dismissed" means, as regards seniority, pension rights and other similar rights, that the period prior to the dismissal should be regarded as continuous with his employment following the dismissal.

(5) If the employer states that he is willing to reinstate the employee, the tribunal shall make an order to that effect.

(6) If the employer—

(a) states that he is willing to re-engage the employee in another job, and

(b) specifies the terms and conditions on which he is willing to do so,

the tribunal shall ask the employee whether he is willing to accept the job on those terms and conditions.

(7) If the employee is willing to accept the job on those terms and conditions, the tribunal shall make an order to that effect.

(8) If the employee is not willing to accept the job on those terms and conditions—

(a) where the tribunal is of the opinion that the refusal is reasonable, the tribunal shall make an order for the continuation of his contract of employment, and

(b) otherwise, the tribunal shall make no order.

(9) If on the hearing of an application for interim relief the employer—

(a) fails to attend before the tribunal, or

(b) states that he is unwilling either to reinstate or re-engage the employee as mentioned in subsection (3),

---

[1] Words substituted by Public Interest Disclosure Act 1998 c.23 s 9

[2] Words inserted by Employment Relations Act 1999 c.26 s 6

the tribunal shall make an order for the continuation of the employee's contract of employment.

Order for continuation of contract of employment

130.—(1) An order under section 129 for the continuation of a contract of **11-154** employment is an order that the contract of employment continue in force—

(a) for the purposes of pay or any other benefit derived from the employment, seniority, pension rights and other similar matters, and

(b) for the purposes of determining for any purpose the period for which the employee has been continuously employed,

from the date of its termination (whether before or after the making of the order) until the determination or settlement of the complaint.

(2) Where the tribunal makes such an order it shall specify in the order the amount which is to be paid by the employer to the employee by way of pay in respect of each normal pay period, or part of any such period, falling between the date of dismissal and the determination or settlement of the complaint.

(3) Subject to the following provisions, the amount so specified shall be that which the employee could reasonably have been expected to earn during that period, or part, and shall be paid—

(a) in the case of a payment for any such period falling wholly or partly after the making of the order, on the normal pay day for that period, and

(b) in the case of a payment for any past period, within such time as may be specified in the order.

(4) If an amount is payable in respect only of part of a normal pay period, the amount shall be calculated by reference to the whole period and reduced proportionately.

(5) Any payment made to an employee by an employer under his contract of employment, or by way of damages for breach of that contract, in respect of a normal pay period, or part of any such period, goes towards discharging the employer's liability in respect of that period under subsection (2); and, conversely, any payment under that subsection in respect of a period goes towards discharging any liability of the employer under, or in respect of breach of, the contract of employment in respect of that period.

(6) If an employee, on or after being dismissed by his employer, receives a lump sum which, or part of which, is in lieu of wages but is not referable to any normal pay period, the tribunal shall take the payment into account in determining the amount of pay to be payable in pursuance of any such order.

(7) For the purposes of this section, the amount which an employee could reasonably have been expected to earn, his normal pay period and the normal pay day for each such period shall be determined as if he had not been dismissed.

Application for variation or revocation of order

131.—(1) At any time between— **11-155**

(a) the making of an order under section 129, and

(b) the determination or settlement of the complaint,

the employer or the employee may apply to an [employment tribunal][1] for the revocation or variation of the order on the ground of a relevant change of circumstances since the making of the order.

---

[1] Words substituted by Employment Rights (Dispute Resolution) Act 1998 c.8 Pt I s 1 (2)

(2) Section 128 and 129 apply in relation to such an application as in relation to an original application for interim relief except that, in the case of an application by the employer, section 128(4) has effect with the substitution of a reference to the employee for the reference to the employer.

Consequence of failure to comply with order

11-156   **132.**—(1) If, on the application of an employee, an [employment tribunal][1] is satisfied that the employer has not complied with the terms of an order for the reinstatement or re-engagement of the employee under section 129(5) or (7), the tribunal shall—

(a) make an order for the continuation of the employee's contract of employment, and

(b) order the employer to pay compensation to the employee.

(2) Compensation under subsection (1)(b) shall be of such amount as the tribunal considers just and equitable in all the circumstances having regard—

(a) to the infringement of the employee's right to be reinstated or reengaged in pursuance of the order, and

(b) to any loss suffered by the employee in consequence of the non-compliance.

(3) Section 130 applies to an order under subsection (1)(a) as in relation to an order under section 129.

(4) If on the application of an employee an [employment tribunal][2] is satisfied that the employer has not complied with the terms of an order for the continuation of a contract of employment subsection (5) or (6) applies.

(5) Where the non-compliance consists of a failure to pay an amount by way of pay specified in the order—

(a) the tribunal shall determine the amount owed by the employer on the date of the determination, and

(b) if on that date the tribunal also determines the employee's complaint that he has been unfairly dismissed, it shall specify that amount separately from any other sum awarded to the employee.

(6) In any other case, the tribunal shall order the employer to pay the employee such compensation as the tribunal considers just and equitable in all the circumstances having regard to any loss suffered by the employee in consequence of the non-compliance.

Death of employer or employee

11-157   **133.**—(1) Where—

(a) an employer has given notice to an employee to terminate his contract of employment, and

(b) before that termination the employee or the employer dies,

this Part applies as if the contract had been duly terminated by the employer by notice expiring on the date of the death.

(2) Where—

(a) an employee's contract of employment has been terminated,

(b) by virtue of subsection (2) or (4) of section 97 a date later than the effective date of termination as defined in subsection (1) of that section is to be treated for certain purposes as the effective date of termination, and

(c) the employer or the employee dies before that date,

---

[1] Words substituted by Employment Rights (Dispute Resolution) Act 1998 c.8 Pt I s 1 (2)

[2] Words substituted by Employment Rights (Dispute Resolution) Act 1998 c.8 Pt I s 1 (2)

subsection (2) or (4) of section 97 applies as if the notice referred to in that subsection as required by section 86 expired on the date of the death.

(3) Where an employee has died, sections 113 to 116 do not apply; and, accordingly, if the [employment tribunal][1] finds that the grounds of the complaint are well-founded, the case shall be treated as falling within section 112(4) as a case in which no order is made under section 113.

(4) Subsection (3) does not prejudice an order for reinstatement or re-engagement made before the employee's death.

(5) Where an order for reinstatement or re-engagement has been made and the employee dies before the order is complied with—

   (a) if the employer has before the death refused to reinstate or re-engage the employee in accordance with the order, subsections (3) to (6) of section 117 apply, and an award shall be made under subsection (3)(b) of that section, unless the employer satisfies the tribunal that it was not practicable at the time of the refusal to comply with the order, and

   (b) if there has been no such refusal, subsections (1) and (2) of that section apply if the employer fails to comply with any ancillary terms of the order which remain capable of fulfilment after the employee's death as they would apply to such a failure to comply fully with the terms of an order where the employee had been reinstated or re-engaged.

PART XI

REDUNDANCY PAYMENTS ETC

CHAPTER I

RIGHT TO REDUNDANCY PAYMENT

The right

135.—(1) An employer shall pay a redundancy payment to any employee of **11-158** his if the employee—

   (a) is dismissed by the employer by reason of redundancy, or

   (b) is eligible for a redundancy payment by reason of being laid off or kept on short-time.

(2) Subsection (1) has effect subject to the following provisions of this Part (including, in particular, sections 140 to 144, 149 to 152, 155 to 161 and 164).

CHAPTER II

RIGHT ON DISMISSAL BY REASON OF REDUNDANCY

Dismissal by reason of redundancy

Circumstances in which an employee is dismissed

136.—(1) Subject to the provisions of this section and sections 137 and 138, **11-159** for the purposes of this Part an employee is dismissed by his employer if (and only if)—

---

[1] Words substituted by Employment Rights (Dispute Resolution) Act 1998 c.8 Pt I s 1 (2)

(a) the contract under which he is employed by the employer is terminated by the employer (whether with or without notice),

[(b) he is employed under a limited term contract and that contract terminates by virtue of the limiting event without being renewed under the same contract, or][1]

(c) the employee terminates the contract under which he is employed (with or without notice) in circumstances in which he is entitled to terminate it without notice by reason of the employer's conduct.

(2) Subsection (1)(c) does not apply if the employee terminates the contract without notice in circumstances in which he is entitled to do so by reason of a lock-out by the employer.

(3) An employee shall be taken to be dismissed by his employer for the purposes of this Part if—

(a) the employer gives notice to the employee to terminate his contract of employment, and

(b) at a time within the obligatory period of notice the employee gives notice in writing to the employer to terminate the contract of employment on a date earlier than the date on which the employer's notice is due to expire.

(4) In this Part the "obligatory period of notice", in relation to notice given by an employer to terminate an employee's contract of employment, means—

(a) the actual period of the notice in a case where the period beginning at the time when the notice is given and ending at the time when it expires is equal to the minimum period which (by virtue of any enactment or otherwise) is required to be given by the employer to terminate the contract of employment, and

(b) the period which—

(i) is equal to the minimum period referred to in paragraph (a), and

(ii) ends at the time when the notice expires,

in any other case.

(5) Where in accordance with any enactment or rule of law—

(a) an act on the part of an employer, or

(b) an event affecting an employer (including, in the case of an individual, his death),

operates to terminate a contract under which an employee is employed by him, the act or event shall be taken for the purposes of this Part to be a termination of the contract by the employer.

11-160   137. [...][2]

No dismissal in cases of renewal of contract or re-engagement

11-161   138.—(1) Where—

(a) an employee's contract of employment is renewed, or he is re-engaged under a new contract of employment in pursuance of an offer (whether in writing or not) made before the end of his employment under the previous contract, and

(b) the renewal or re-engagement takes effect either immediately on, or after an interval of not more than four weeks after, the end of that employment,

---

[1] Substituted by SI 2002/2034 Sch 2 (1) para 3 (13)

[2] Repealed by Employment Relations Act 1999 c.26 Sch 9 para 1

the employee shall not be regarded for the purposes of this Part as dismissed by his employer by reason of the ending of his employment under the previous contract.

(2) Subsection (1) does not apply if—

    (a) the provisions of the contract as renewed, or of the new contract, as to—

        (i) the capacity and place in which the employee is employed, and

        (ii) the other terms and conditions of his employment,

    differ (wholly or in part) from the corresponding provisions of the previous contract, and

    (b) during the period specified in subsection (3)—

        (i) the employee (for whatever reason) terminates the renewed or new contract, or gives notice to terminate it and it is in consequence terminated, or

        (ii) the employer, for a reason connected with or arising out of any difference between the renewed or new contract and the previous contract, terminates the renewed or new contract, or gives notice to terminate it and it is in consequence terminated.

(3) The period referred to in subsection (2)(b) is the period—

    (a) beginning at the end of the employee's employment under the previous contract, and

    (b) ending with—

        (i) the period of four weeks beginning with the date on which the employee starts work under the renewed or new contract, or

        (ii) such longer period as may be agreed in accordance with subsection (6) for the purpose of retraining the employee for employment under that contract;

and is in this Part referred to as the "trial period".

(4) Where subsection (2) applies, for the purposes of this Part—

    (a) the employee shall be regarded as dismissed on the date on which his employment under the previous contract (or, if there has been more than one trial period, the original contract) ended, and

    (b) the reason for the dismissal shall be taken to be the reason for which the employee was then dismissed, or would have been dismissed had the offer (or original offer) of renewed or new employment not been made, or the reason which resulted in that offer being made.

(5) Subsection (2) does not apply if the employee's contract of employment is again renewed, or he is again re-engaged under a new contract of employment, in circumstances such that subsection (1) again applies.

(6) For the purposes of subsection (3)(b)(ii) a period of retraining is agreed in accordance with this subsection only if the agreement—

    (a) is made between the employer and the employee or his representative before the employee starts work under the contract as renewed, or the new contract,

    (b) is in writing,

    (c) specifies the date on which the period of retraining ends, and

    (d) specifies the terms and conditions of employment which will apply in the employee's case after the end of that period.

Redundancy

11-162   **139.**—(1) For the purposes of this Act an employee who is dismissed shall be taken to be dismissed by reason of redundancy if the dismissal is wholly or mainly attributable to—

(a) the fact that his employer has ceased or intends to cease—

    (i) to carry on the business for the purposes of which the employee was employed by him, or

    (ii) to carry on that business in the place where the employee was so employed, or

(b) the fact that the requirements of that business—

    (i) for employees to carry out work of a particular kind, or

    (ii) for employees to carry out work of a particular kind in the place where the employee was employed by the employer,

have ceased or diminished or are expected to cease or diminish.

(2) For the purposes of subsection (1) the business of the employer together with the business or businesses of his associated employers shall be treated as one (unless either of the conditions specified in paragraphs (a) and (b) of that subsection would be satisfied without so treating them).

(3) For the purposes of subsection (1) the activities carried on by a local education authority with respect to the schools maintained by it, and the activities carried on by the [governing bodies][1] of those schools, shall be treated as one business (unless either of the conditions specified in paragraphs (a) and (b) of that subsection would be satisfied without so treating them).

(4) Where—

(a) the contract under which a person is employed is treated by section 136(5) as terminated by his employer by reason of an act or event, and

(b) the employee's contract is not renewed and he is not re-engaged under a new contract of employment,

he shall be taken for the purposes of this Act to be dismissed by reason of redundancy if the circumstances in which his contract is not renewed, and he is not re-engaged, are wholly or mainly attributable to either of the facts stated in paragraphs (a) and (b) of subsection (1).

(5) In its application to a case within subsection (4), paragraph (a)(i) of subsection (1) has effect as if the reference in that subsection to the employer included a reference to any person to whom, in consequence of the act or event, power to dispose of the business has passed.

(6) In subsection (1) "cease" and "diminish" mean cease and diminish either permanently or temporarily and for whatever reason.

Exclusions

Summary dismissal

11-163   **140.**—(1) Subject to subsections (2) and (3), an employee is not entitled to a redundancy payment by reason of dismissal where his employer, being entitled to terminate his contract of employment without notice by reason of the employee's conduct, terminates it either—

(a) without notice,

(b) by giving shorter notice than that which, in the absence of conduct entitling the employer to terminate the contract without notice, the employer would be required to give to terminate the contract, or

---

[1] Words substituted by Education Act 2002 c.32 Sch 21 para 31

(c) by giving notice which includes, or is accompanied by, a statement in writing that the employer would, by reason of the employee's conduct, be entitled to terminate the contract without notice.

(2) Where an employee who—

(a) has been given notice by his employer to terminate his contract of employment, or

(b) has given notice to his employer under section 148(1) indicating his intention to claim a redundancy payment in respect of lay-off or short-time,

takes part in a strike at any relevant time in circumstances which entitle the employer to treat the contract of employment as terminable without notice, subsection (1) does not apply if the employer terminates the contract by reason of his taking part in the strike.

(3) Where the contract of employment of an employee who—

(a) has been given notice by his employer to terminate his contract of employment, or

(b) has given notice to his employer under section 148(1) indicating his intention to claim a redundancy payment in respect of lay-off or short-time,

is terminated as mentioned in subsection (1) at any relevant time otherwise than by reason of his taking part in a strike, an [employment tribunal][1] may determine that the employer is liable to make an appropriate payment to the employee if on a reference to the tribunal it appears to the tribunal, in the circumstances of the case, to be just and equitable that the employee should receive it.

(4) In subsection (3) "appropriate payment" means—

(a) the whole of the redundancy payment to which the employee would have been entitled apart from subsection (1), or

(b) such part of that redundancy payment as the tribunal thinks fit.

(5) In this section "relevant time"—

(a) in the case of an employee who has been given notice by his employer to terminate his contract of employment, means any time within the obligatory period of notice, and

(b) in the case of an employee who has given notice to his employer under section 148(1), means any time after the service of the notice.

Renewal of contract or re-engagement

141.—(1) This section applies where an offer (whether in writing or not) is **11-164** made to an employee before the end of his employment—

(a) to renew his contract of employment, or

(b) to re-engage him under a new contract of employment,

with renewal or re-engagement to take effect either immediately on, or after an interval of not more than four weeks after, the end of his employment.

(2) Where subsection (3) is satisfied, the employee is not entitled to a redundancy payment if he unreasonably refuses the offer.

(3) This subsection is satisfied where—

(a) the provisions of the contract as renewed, or of the new contract, as to—

(i) the capacity and place in which the employee would be employed, and

(ii) the other terms and conditions of his employment,

---

[1] Words substituted by Employment Rights (Dispute Resolution) Act 1998 c.8 Pt I s 1 (2)

would not differ from the corresponding provisions of the previous contract, or

(b) those provisions of the contract as renewed, or of the new contract, would differ from the corresponding provisions of the previous contract but the offer constitutes an offer of suitable employment in relation to the employee.

(4) The employee is not entitled to a redundancy payment if—

(a) his contract of employment is renewed, or he is re-engaged under a new contract of employment, in pursuance of the offer,

(b) the provisions of the contract as renewed or new contract as to the capacity or place in which he is employed or the other terms and conditions of his employment differ (wholly or in part) from the corresponding provisions of the previous contract,

(c) the employment is suitable in relation to him, and

(d) during the trial period he unreasonably terminates the contract, or unreasonably gives notice to terminate it and it is in consequence terminated.

Employee anticipating expiry of employer's notice

11-165   **142.**—(1) Subject to subsection (3), an employee is not entitled to a redundancy payment where—

(a) he is taken to be dismissed by virtue of section 136(3) by reason of giving to his employer notice terminating his contract of employment on a date earlier than the date on which notice by the employer terminating the contract is due to expire,

(b) before the employee's notice is due to expire, the employer gives him a notice such as is specified in subsection (2), and

(c) the employee does not comply with the requirements of that notice.

(2) The employer's notice referred to in subsection (1)(b) is a notice in writing—

(a) requiring the employee to withdraw his notice terminating the contract of employment and to continue in employment until the date on which the employer's notice terminating the contract expires, and

(b) stating that, unless he does so, the employer will contest any liability to pay to him a redundancy payment in respect of the termination of his contract of employment.

(3) An [employment tribunal][1] may determine that the employer is liable to make an appropriate payment to the employee if on a reference to the tribunal it appears to the tribunal, having regard to—

(a) the reasons for which the employee seeks to leave the employment, and

(b) the reasons for which the employer requires him to continue in it,

to be just and equitable that the employee should receive the payment.

(4) In subsection (3) "appropriate payment"means—

(a) the whole of the redundancy payment to which the employee would have been entitled apart from subsection (1), or

(b) such part of that redundancy payment as the tribunal thinks fit.

Strike during currency of employer's notice

11-166   **143.**—(1) This section applies where—

---

[1] Words substituted by Employment Rights (Dispute Resolution) Act 1998 c.8 Pt I s 1 (2)

(a) an employer has given notice to an employee to terminate his contract of employment ("notice of termination"),

(b) after the notice is given the employee begins to take part in a strike of employees of the employer, and

(c) the employer serves on the employee a notice of extension.

(2) A notice of extension is a notice in writing which—

(a) requests the employee to agree to extend the contract of employment beyond the time of expiry by a period comprising as many available days as the number of working days lost by striking ("the proposed period of extension"),

(b) indicates the reasons for which the employer makes that request, and

(c) states that the employer will contest any liability to pay the employee a redundancy payment in respect of the dismissal effected by the notice of termination unless either—

   (i) the employee complies with the request, or

   (ii) the employer is satisfied that, in consequence of sickness or injury or otherwise, the employee is unable to comply with it or that (even though he is able to comply with it) it is reasonable in the circumstances for him not to do so.

(3) Subject to subsections (4) and (5), if the employee does not comply with the request contained in the notice of extension, he is not entitled to a redundancy payment by reason of the dismissal effected by the notice of termination.

(4) Subsection (3) does not apply if the employer agrees to pay a redundancy payment to the employee in respect of the dismissal effected by the notice of termination even though he has not complied with the request contained in the notice of extension.

(5) An [employment tribunal][1] may determine that the employer is liable to make an appropriate payment to the employee if on a reference to the tribunal it appears to the tribunal that—

(a) the employee has not complied with the request contained in the notice of extension and the employer has not agreed to pay a redundancy payment in respect of the dismissal effected by the notice of termination, but

(b) either the employee was unable to comply with the request or it was reasonable in the circumstances for him not to comply with it.

(6) In subsection (5) "appropriate payment" means—

(a) the whole of the redundancy payment to which the employee would have been entitled apart from subsection (3), or

(b) such part of that redundancy payment as the tribunal thinks fit.

(7) If the employee—

(a) complies with the request contained in the notice of extension, or

(b) does not comply with it but attends at his proper or usual place of work and is ready and willing to work on one or more (but not all) of the available days within the proposed period of extension,

the notice of termination has effect, and shall be deemed at all material times to have had effect, as if the period specified in it had been appropriately extended; and section 87 to 91 accordingly apply as if the period of notice required by section 86 were extended to a corresponding extent.

(8) In subsection (7) "appropriately extended" means—

---

[1] Words substituted by Employment Rights (Dispute Resolution) Act 1998 c.8 Pt I s 1 (2)

(a) in a case within paragraph (a) of that subsection, extended beyond the time of expiry by an additional period equal to the proposed period of extension, and

(b) in a case within paragraph (b) of that subsection, extended beyond the time of expiry up to the end of the day (or last of the days) on which he attends at his proper or usual place of work and is ready and willing to work.

Provisions supplementary to section 143

11-167   **144.**—(1) For the purposes of section 143 an employee complies with the request contained in a notice of extension if, but only if, on each available day within the proposed period of extension, he—

(a) attends at his proper or usual place of work, and

(b) is ready and willing to work,

whether or not he has signified his agreement to the request in any other way.

(2) The reference in section 143(2) to the number of working days lost by striking is a reference to the number of working days in the period—

(a) beginning with the date of service of the notice of termination, and

(b) ending with the time of expiry,

which are days on which the employee in question takes part in a strike of employees of his employer.

(3) In section 143 and this section—

"available day", in relation to an employee, means a working day beginning at or after the time of expiry which is a day on which he is not taking part in a strike of employees of the employer,

"available day within the proposed period of extension" means an available day which begins before the end of the proposed period of extension,

"time of expiry", in relation to a notice of termination, means the time at which the notice would expire apart from section 143, and

"working day", in relation to an employee, means a day on which, in accordance with his contract of employment, he is normally required to work.

(4) Neither the service of a notice of extension nor any extension by virtue of section 143(7) of the period specified in a notice of termination affects—

(a) any right either of the employer or of the employee to terminate the contract of employment (whether before, at or after the time of expiry) by a further notice or without notice, or

(b) the operation of this Part in relation to any such termination of the contract of employment.

Supplementary

The relevant date

11-168   **145.**—(1) For the purposes of the provisions of this Act relating to redundancy payments "the relevant date" in relation to the dismissal of an employee has the meaning given by this section.

(2) Subject to the following provisions of this section, "the relevant date"—

(a) in relation to an employee whose contract of employment is terminated by notice, whether given by his employer or by the employee, means the date on which the notice expires,

(b) in relation to an employee whose contract of employment is terminated without notice, means the date on which the termination takes effect, and

[(c) in relation to an employee who is employed under a limited-term contract which terminates by virtue of the limiting event without being renewed under the same contract, means the date on which the termination takes effect.]¹

(3) Where the employee is taken to be dismissed by virtue of section 136(3) the "relevant date" means the date on which the employee's notice to terminate his contract of employment expires.

(4) Where the employee is regarded by virtue of section 138(4) as having been dismissed on the date on which his employment under an earlier contract ended, "the relevant date" means—

(a) for the purposes of section 164(1), the date which is the relevant date as defined by subsection (2) in relation to the renewed or new contract or, where there has been more than one trial period, the last such contract, and

(b) for the purposes of any other provision, the date which is the relevant date as defined by subsection (2) in relation to the previous contract or, where there has been more than one such trial period, the original contract.

(5) Where—

(a) the contract of employment is terminated by the employer, and

(b) the notice required by section 86 to be given by an employer would, if duly given on the material date, expire on a date later than the relevant date (as defined by the previous provisions of this section),

for the purposes of sections 155, 162(1) and 227(3) the later date is the relevant date.

(6) In subsection (5)(b) "the material date" means—

(a) the date when notice of termination was given by the employer, or

(b) where no notice was given, the date when the contract of employment was terminated by the employer.

(7) [...]²

Provisions supplementing sections 138 and 141

146.—(1) In section 138 and 141—   **11-169**

(a) references to re-engagement are to re-engagement by the employer or an associated employer, and

(b) references to an offer are to an offer made by the employer or an associated employer.

(2) For the purposes of the application of section 138(1) or 141(1) to a contract under which the employment ends on a Friday, Saturday or Sunday—

(a) the renewal or re-engagement shall be treated as taking effect immediately on the ending of the employment under the previous contract if it takes effect on or before the next Monday after that Friday, Saturday or Sunday, and

(b) the interval of four weeks to which those provisions refer shall be calculated as if the employment had ended on that next Monday.

(3) [...]³

---

¹ Substituted by SI 2002/2034 Sch 2 (1) para 3 (14)
² Repealed by Employment Relations Act 1999 c.26 Sch 9 para 1
³ Repealed by Employment Relations Act 1999 c.26 Sch 9 para 1

CHAPTER III

RIGHT BY REASON OF LAY-OFF OR SHORT-TIME

Lay-off and short-time

Meaning of "lay-off" and "short-time"

11-170   **147.**—(1) For the purposes of this Part an employee shall be taken to be laid off for a week if—

(a) he is employed under a contract on terms and conditions such that his remuneration under the contract depends on his being provided by the employer with work of the kind which he is employed to do, but

(b) he is not entitled to any remuneration under the contract in respect of the week because the employer does not provide such work for him.

(2) For the purposes of this Part an employee shall be taken to be kept on short-time for a week if by reason of a diminution in the work provided for the employee by his employer (being work of a kind which under his contract the employee is employed to do) the employee's remuneration for the week is less than half a week's pay.

Eligibility by reason of lay-off or short-time

11-171   **148.**—(1) Subject to the following provisions of this Part, for the purposes of this Part an employee is eligible for a redundancy payment by reason of being laid off or kept on short-time if—

(a) he gives notice in writing to his employer indicating (in whatever terms) his intention to claim a redundancy payment in respect of lay-off or short-time (referred to in this Part as "notice of intention to claim"), and

(b) before the service of the notice he has been laid off or kept on short-time in circumstances in which subsection (2) applies.

(2) This subsection applies if the employee has been laid off or kept on short-time—

(a) for four or more consecutive weeks of which the last before the service of the notice ended on, or not more than four weeks before, the date of service of the notice, or

(b) for a series of six or more weeks (of which not more than three were consecutive) within a period of thirteen weeks, where the last week of the series before the service of the notice ended on, or not more than four weeks before, the date of service of the notice.

Exclusions

Counter-notices

11-172   **149.** Where an employee gives to his employer notice of intention to claim but—

(a) the employer gives to the employee, within seven days after the service of that notice, notice in writing (referred to in this Part as a "counter-notice") that he will contest any liability to pay to the employee a redundancy payment in pursuance of the employee's notice, and

(b) the employer does not withdraw the counter-notice by a subsequent notice in writing, the employee is not entitled to a redundancy payment in pursuance of his notice of intention to claim except in accordance with a decision of an [employment tribunal][1].

Resignation

150.—(1) An employee is not entitled to a redundancy payment by reason of **11-173** being laid off or kept on short-time unless he terminates his contract of employment by giving such period of notice as is required for the purposes of this section before the end of the relevant period.

(2) The period of notice required for the purposes of this section—
  (a) where the employee is required by his contract of employment to give more than one week's notice to terminate the contract, is the minimum period which he is required to give, and
  (b) otherwise, is one week.

(3) In subsection (1) "the relevant period"—
  (a) if the employer does not give a counter-notice within seven days after the service of the notice of intention to claim, is three weeks after the end of those seven days,
  (b) if the employer gives a counter-notice within that period of seven days but withdraws it by a subsequent notice in writing, is three weeks after the service of the notice of withdrawal, and
  (c) if—
    (i) the employer gives a counter-notice within that period of seven days, and does not so withdraw it, and
    (ii) a question as to the right of the employee to a redundancy payment in pursuance of the notice of intention to claim is referred to an [employment tribunal][2],
is three weeks after the tribunal has notified to the employee its decision on that reference.

(4) For the purposes of subsection (3)(c) no account shall be taken of—
  (a) any appeal against the decision of the tribunal, or
  (b) any proceedings or decision in consequence of any such appeal.

Dismissal

151.—(1) An employee is not entitled to a redundancy payment by reason of **11-174** being laid off or kept on short-time if he is dismissed by his employer.

(2) Subsection (1) does not prejudice any right of the employee to a redundancy payment in respect of the dismissal.

Likelihood of full employment

152.—(1) An employee is not entitled to a redundancy payment in pursuance **11-175** of a notice of intention to claim if—
  (a) on the date of service of the notice it was reasonably to be expected that the employee (if he continued to be employed by the same employer) would, not later than four weeks after that date, enter on a period of employment of not less than thirteen weeks during which he would not be laid off or kept on short-time for any week, and
  (b) the employer gives a counter-notice to the employee within seven days after the service of the notice of intention to claim.

(2) Subsection (1) does not apply where the employee—

---

[1] Words substituted by Employment Rights (Dispute Resolution) Act 1998 c.8 Pt I s 1 (2)
[2] Words substituted by Employment Rights (Dispute Resolution) Act 1998 c.8 Pt I s 1 (2)

(a) continues or has continued, during the next four weeks after the date of service of the notice of intention to claim, to be employed by the same employer, and

(b) is or has been laid off or kept on short-time for each of those weeks.

Supplementary

The relevant date

11-176   **153.** For the purposes of the provisions of this Act relating to redundancy payments "the relevant date" in relation to a notice of intention to claim or a right to a redundancy payment in pursuance of such a notice—

(a) in a case falling within paragraph (a) of subsection (2) of section 148, means the date on which the last of the four or more consecutive weeks before the service of the notice came to an end, and

(b) in a case falling within paragraph (b) of that subsection, means the date on which the last of the series of six or more weeks before the service of the notice came to an end.

Provisions supplementing sections 148 and 152

11-177   **154.** For the purposes of sections 148(2) and 152(2)—

(a) it is immaterial whether a series of weeks consists wholly of weeks for which the employee is laid off or wholly of weeks for which he is kept on short-time or partly of the one and partly of the other, and

(b) no account shall be taken of any week for which an employee is laid off or kept on short-time where the lay-off or short-time is wholly or mainly attributable to a strike or a lock-out (whether or not in the trade or industry in which the employee is employed and whether in Great Britain or elsewhere).

CHAPTER IV

GENERAL EXCLUSIONS FROM RIGHT

Qualifying period of employment

11-178   **155.** An employee does not have any right to a redundancy payment unless he has been continuously employed for a period of not less than two years ending with the relevant date.

Upper age limit

11-179   **156.**—(1) An employee does not have any right to a redundancy payment if before the relevant date he has attained—

(a) in a case where—

(i) in the business for the purposes of which the employee was employed there was a normal retiring age of less than sixty-five for an employee holding the position held by the employee, and

(ii) the age was the same whether the employee holding that position was a man or woman,

that normal retiring age, and

(b) in any other case, the age of sixty-five.

(2) [...]¹

---

¹ Repealed by Employment Relations Act 1999 c.26 Sch 9 para 1

Exemption orders

157.—(1) Where an order under this section is in force in respect of an **11-180** agreement covered by this section, an employee who, immediately before the relevant date, is an employee to whom the agreement applies does not have any right to a redundancy payment.

(2) An agreement is covered by this section if it is an agreement between—

(a) one or more employers or organisations of employers, and

(b) one or more trade unions representing employees,

under which employees to whom the agreement applies have a right in certain circumstances to payments on the termination of their contracts of employment.

(3) Where, on the application of all the parties to an agreement covered by this section, the Secretary of State is satisfied, having regard to the provisions of the agreement, that the employees to whom the agreement applies should not have any right to a redundancy payment, he may make an order under this section in respect of the agreement.

(4) The Secretary of State shall not make an order under this section in respect of an agreement unless the agreement indicates (in whatever terms) the willingness of the parties to it to submit to an [employment tribunal][1] any question arising under the agreement as to—

(a) the right of an employee to a payment on the termination of his employment, or

(b) the amount of such a payment.

(5) An order revoking an earlier order under this section may be made in pursuance of an application by all or any of the parties to the agreement in question or in the absence of such an application.

(6) [...][2]

Chapter V

Other Provisions about Redundancy Payments

Amount of a redundancy payment

162.—(1) The amount of a redundancy payment shall be calculated by— **11-181**

(a) determining the period, ending with the relevant date, during which the employee has been continuously employed,

(b) reckoning backwards from the end of that period the number of years of employment falling within that period, and

(c) allowing the appropriate amount for each of those years of employment.

(2) In subsection (1)(c) "the appropriate amount" means—

(a) one and a half weeks' pay for a year of employment in which the employee was not below the age of forty-one,

(b) one week's pay for a year of employment (not within paragraph (a)) in which he was not below the age of twenty-two, and

(c) half a week's pay for each year of employment not within paragraph (a) or (b).

(3) Where twenty years of employment have been reckoned under subsection (1), no account shall be taken under that subsection of any year of employment earlier than those twenty years.

---

[1] Words substituted by Employment Rights (Dispute Resolution) Act 1998 c.8 Pt I s 1 (2)

[2] Repealed by Employment Relations Act 1999 c.26 Sch 9 para 1

(4) Where the relevant date is after the sixty-fourth anniversary of the day of the employee's birth, the amount arrived at under subsections (1) to (3) shall be reduced by the appropriate fraction.

(5) In subsection (4) "the appropriate fraction" means the fraction of which—

    (a) the numerator is the number of whole months reckoned from the sixty-fourth anniversary of the day of the employee's birth in the period beginning with that anniversary and ending with the relevant date, and

    (b) the denominator is twelve.

(6) Subsections (1) to (5) apply for the purposes of any provision of this Part by virtue of which an [employment tribunal][1] may determine that an employer is liable to pay to an employee—

    (a) the whole of the redundancy payment to which the employee would have had a right apart from some other provision, or

    (b) such part of the redundancy payment to which the employee would have had a right apart from some other provision as the tribunal thinks fit,

as if any reference to the amount of a redundancy payment were to the amount of the redundancy payment to which the employee would have been entitled apart from that other provision.

(7) [...][2]

(8) This section has effect subject to any regulations under section 158 by virtue of which the amount of a redundancy payment, or part of a redundancy payment, may be reduced.

References to [employment tribunals][3]

11-182   **163.**—(1) Any question arising under this Part as to—

    (a) the right of an employee to a redundancy payment, or

    (b) the amount of a redundancy payment,

shall be referred to and determined by an [employment tribunal][4].

(2) For the purposes of any such reference, an employee who has been dismissed by his employer shall, unless the contrary is proved, be presumed to have been so dismissed by reason of redundancy.

(3) Any question whether an employee will become entitled to a redundancy payment if he is not dismissed by his employer and he terminates his contract of employment as mentioned in section 150(1) shall for the purposes of this Part be taken to be a question as to the right of the employee to a redundancy payment.

(4) Where an order under section 157 is in force in respect of an agreement, this section has effect in relation to any question arising under the agreement as to the right of an employee to a payment on the termination of his employment, or as to the amount of such a payment, as if the payment were a redundancy payment and the question arose under this Part.

Claims for redundancy payment

11-183   **164.**—(1) An employee does not have any right to a redundancy payment unless, before the end of the period of six months beginning with the relevant date—

    (a) the payment has been agreed and paid,

---

[1] Words substituted by Employment Rights (Dispute Resolution) Act 1998 c.8 Pt I s 1 (2)
[2] Repealed by Employment Relations Act 1999 c.26 Sch 9 para 1
[3] Words substituted by Employment Rights (Dispute Resolution) Act 1998 c.8 Pt I s 1 (2)
[4] Words substituted by Employment Rights (Dispute Resolution) Act 1998 c.8 Pt I s 1 (2)

(b) the employee has made a claim for the payment by notice in writing given to the employer,

(c) a question as to the employee's right to, or the amount of, the payment has been referred to an [employment tribunal][1], or

(d) a complaint relating to his dismissal has been presented by the employee under section 111.

(2) An employee is not deprived of his right to a redundancy payment by subsection (1) if, during the period of six months immediately following the period mentioned in that subsection, the employee—

(a) makes a claim for the payment by notice in writing given to the employer,

(b) refers to an [employment tribunal][2] a question as to his right to, or the amount of, the payment, or

(c) presents a complaint relating to his dismissal under section 111,

and it appears to the tribunal to be just and equitable that the employee should receive a redundancy payment.

(3) In determining under subsection (2) whether it is just and equitable that an employee should receive a redundancy payment an [employment tribunal][3] shall have regard to—

(a) the reason shown by the employee for his failure to take any such step as is referred to in subsection (2) within the period mentioned in subsection (1), and

(b) all the other relevant circumstances.

Written particulars of redundancy payment

165.—(1) On making any redundancy payment, otherwise than in pursuance **11-184** of a decision of a tribunal which specifies the amount of the payment to be made, the employer shall give to the employee a written statement indicating how the amount of the payment has been calculated.

(2) An employer who without reasonable excuse fails to comply with subsection (1) is guilty of an offence and liable on summary conviction to a fine not exceeding level 1 on the standard scale.

(3) If an employer fails to comply with the requirements of subsection (1), the employee may by notice in writing to the employer require him to give to the employee a written statement complying with those requirements within such period (not being less than one week beginning with the day on which the notice is given) as may be specified in the notice.

(4) An employer who without reasonable excuse fails to comply with a notice under subsection (3) is guilty of an offence and liable on summary conviction to a fine not exceeding level 3 on the standard scale.

Applications for payments

166.—(1) Where an employee claims that his employer is liable to pay to him **11-185** an employer's payment and either—

(a) that the employee has taken all reasonable steps, other than legal proceedings, to recover the payment from the employer and the employer has refused or failed to pay it, or has paid part of it and has refused or failed to pay the balance,

---

[1] Words substituted by Employment Rights (Dispute Resolution) Act 1998 c.8 Pt I s 1 (2)
[2] Words substituted by Employment Rights (Dispute Resolution) Act 1998 c.8 Pt I s 1 (2)
[3] Words substituted by Employment Rights (Dispute Resolution) Act 1998 c.8 Pt I s 1 (2)

[(aa) a payment which his employer is liable to make to him under an agreement to refrain from instituting or continuing proceedings for a contravention or alleged contravention of section 135 which has effect by virtue of section 203(2)(e) or (f), or][1]

(b) that the employer is insolvent and the whole or part of the payment remains unpaid,

the employee may apply to the Secretary of State for a payment under this section.

(2) In this Part "employer's payment", in relation to an employee, means—

(a) a redundancy payment which his employer is liable to pay to him under this Part, or

(b) a payment which his employer is, under an agreement in respect of which an order is in force under section 157, liable to make to him on the termination of his contract of employment.

(3) In relation to any case where (in accordance with any provision of this Part) an employment tribunal determines that an employer is liable to pay part (but not the whole) of a redundancy payment the reference in subsection (2)(a) to a redundancy payment is to the part of the redundancy payment.

(4) In subsection (1)(a) "legal proceedings"—

(a) does not include any proceedings before an employment tribunal, but

(b) includes any proceedings to enforce a decision or award of an employment tribunal.

(5) An employer is insolvent for the purposes of subsection (1)(b)—

(a) where the employer is an individual, if (but only if) subsection (6) is satisfied,

(b) where the employer is a company, if (but only if) subsection (7) is satisfied, and

(c) where the employer is a limited liability partnership, if (but only if) subsection (8) is satisfied.

(6) This subsection is satisfied in the case of an employer who is an individual—

(a) in England and Wales if—

(i) he has been adjudged bankrupt or has made a composition or arrangement with his creditors, or

(ii) he has died and his estate falls to be administered in accordance with an order under section 421 of the Insolvency Act 1986, and

(b) in Scotland if—

(i) sequestration of his estate has been awarded or he has executed a trust deed for his creditors or has entered into a composition contract, or

(ii) he has died and a judicial factor appointed under section 11A of the Judicial Factors (Scotland) Act 1889 is required by that section to divide his insolvent estate among his creditors.

(7) This subsection is satisfied in the case of an employer which is a company—

(a) if a winding up [...][2] order has been made, or a resolution for voluntary winding up has been passed, with respect to the company,

[(aa) if the company is in administration for the purposes of the Insolvency Act 1986,][3]

---

[1] Inserted by Employment Rights (Dispute Resolution) Act 1998 c.8 s 11 (2)

[2] Words repealed by Enterprise Act 2002 c.40 Sch 26

[3] Words inserted by Enterprise Act 2002 c.40 Sch 17 para 49 (2) (b)

(b) if a receiver or (in England and Wales only) a manager of the company's undertaking has been duly appointed, or (in England and Wales only) possession has been taken, by or on behalf of the holders of any debentures secured by a floating charge, of any property of the company comprised in or subject to the charge, or

(c) if a voluntary arrangement proposed in the case of the company for the purposes of Part I of the Insolvency Act 1986 has been approved under that Part of that Act.

(8) This subsection is satisfied in the case of an employer which is a limited liability partnership—

(a) if a winding-up order, an administration order or a determination for a voluntary winding-up has been made with respect to the limited liability partnership,

(b) if a receiver or (in England and Wales only) a manager of the undertaking of the limited liability partnership has been duly appointed, or (in England and Wales only) possession has been taken, by or on behalf of the holders of any debentures secured by a floating charge, of any property of the limited liability partnership comprised in or subject to the charge, or

(c) if a voluntary arrangement proposed in the case of the limited liability partnership for the purpose of Part I of the Insolvency Act 1986 has been approved under that Part of that Act.

Making of payments

167.—(1) Where, on an application under section 166 by an employee in relation to an employer's payment, the Secretary of State is satisfied that the requirements specified in subsection (2) are met, he shall pay to the employee out of the National Insurance Fund a sum calculated in accordance with section 168 but reduced by so much (if any) of the employer's payment as has already been paid. **11-186**

(2) The requirements referred to in subsection (1) are—

(a) that the employee is entitled to the employer's payment, and

(b) that one of the conditions specified in paragraphs (a) and (b) of subsection (1) of section 166 is fulfilled,

and, in a case where the employer's payment is a payment such as is mentioned in subsection (2)(b) of that section, that the employee's right to the payment arises by virtue of a period of continuous employment (computed in accordance with the provisions of the agreement in question) which is not less than two years.

(3) Where under this section the Secretary of State pays a sum to an employee in respect of an employer's payment—

(a) all rights and remedies of the employee with respect to the employer's payment, or (if the Secretary of State has paid only part of it) all the rights and remedies of the employee with respect to that part of the employer's payment, are transferred to and vest in the Secretary of State, and

(b) any decision of an [employment tribunal][1] requiring the employer's payment to be paid to the employee has effect as if it required that payment, or that part of it which the Secretary of State has paid, to be paid to the Secretary of State.

(4) Any money recovered by the Secretary of State by virtue of subsection (3) shall be paid into the National Insurance Fund.

[1] Words substituted by Employment Rights (Dispute Resolution) Act 1998 c.8 Pt I s 1 (2)

Amount of payments

11-187   **168.**—(1) The sum payable to an employee by the Secretary of State under section 167—

(a) where the employer's payment to which the employee's application under section 166 relates is a redundancy payment or a part of a redundancy payment, is a sum equal to the amount of the redundancy payment or part,

[(aa) where the employer's payment to which the employee's application under section 166 relates is a payment which his employer is liable to make to him under an agreement having effect by virtue of section 203(2)(e) or (f), is a sum equal to the amount of the employer's payment or of any redundancy payment which the employer would have been liable to pay to the employee but for the agreement, whichever is less, and][1]

(b) where the employer's payment to which the employee's application under section 166 relates is a payment which the employer is liable to make under an agreement in respect of which an order is in force under section 157, is a sum equal to the amount of the employer's payment or of the relevant redundancy payment, whichever is less.

(2) The reference in subsection (1)(b) to the amount of the relevant redundancy payment is to the amount of the redundancy payment which the employer would have been liable to pay to the employee on the assumptions specified in subsection (3).

(3) The assumptions referred to in subsection (2) are that—

(a) the order in force in respect of the agreement had not been made,

(b) the circumstances in which the employer's payment is payable had been such that the employer was liable to pay a redundancy payment to the employee in those circumstances,

(c) the relevant date, in relation to any such redundancy payment, had been the date on which the termination of the employee's contract of employment is treated as having taken effect for the purposes of the agreement, and

(d) in so far as the provisions of the agreement relating to the circumstances in which the continuity of an employee's period of employment is to be treated as broken, and the weeks which are to count in computing a period of employment, are inconsistent with the provisions of Chapter I of Part XIV, the provisions of the agreement were substituted for those provisions.

Information relating to applications for payments

11-188   **169.**—(1) Where an employee makes an application to the Secretary of State under section 166, the Secretary of State may, by notice in writing given to the employer, require the employer—

(a) to provide the Secretary of State with such information, and

(b) to produce for examination on behalf of the Secretary of State documents in his custody or under his control of such description,

as the Secretary of State may reasonably require for the purpose of determining whether the application is well-founded.

(2) Where a person on whom a notice is served under subsection (1) fails without reasonable excuse to comply with a requirement imposed by the notice,

---

[1] Inserted by Employment Rights (Dispute Resolution) Act 1998 c.8 Pt II s 11 (3)

he is guilty of an offence and liable on summary conviction to a fine not exceeding level 3 on the standard scale.

(3) A person is guilty of an offence if—

    (a) in providing any information required by a notice under subsection (1), he makes a statement which he knows to be false in a material particular or recklessly makes a statement which is false in a material particular, or

    (b) he produces for examination in accordance with a notice under subsection (1) a document which to his knowledge has been willfully falsified.

(4) A person guilty of an offence under subsection (3) is liable—

    (a) on summary conviction, to a fine not exceeding the statutory maximum or to imprisonment for a term not exceeding three months, or to both, or

    (b) on conviction on indictment, to a fine or to imprisonment for a term not exceeding two years, or to both.

References to [employment tribunals][1]

170.—(1) Where on an application made to the Secretary of State for a **11-189** payment under section 166 it is claimed that an employer is liable to pay an employer's payment, there shall be referred to an [employment tribunal][2]—

    (a) any question as to the liability of the employer to pay the employer's payment, and

    (b) any question as to the amount of the sum payable in accordance with section 168.

(2) For the purposes of any reference under this section an employee who has been dismissed by his employer shall, unless the contrary is proved, be presumed to have been so dismissed by reason of redundancy.

PART XII

INSOLVENCY OF EMPLOYERS

Employee's rights on insolvency of employer

182. If, on an application made to him in writing by an employee, the **11-190** Secretary of State is satisfied that—

    (a) the employee's employer has become insolvent,

    (b) the employee's employment has been terminated, and

    (c) on the appropriate date the employee was entitled to be paid the whole or part of any debt to which this Part applies,

the Secretary of State shall, subject to section 186, to pay the employee out of the National Insurance Fund the amount to which, in the opinion of the Secretary of State, the employee is entitled in respect of the debt.

Insolvency

183.—(1) An employer has become insolvent for the purposes of this Part—   **11-191**

---

[1] Words substituted by Employment Rights (Dispute Resolution) Act 1998 c.8 Pt I s 1 (2)
[2] Words substituted by Employment Rights (Dispute Resolution) Act 1998 c.8 Pt I s 1 (2)

(a) where the employer is an individual, if (but only if) subsection (2) is satisfied, [...][1]

(b) where the employer is a company, if (but only if) subsection (3) is satisfied[, and][2]

[(c) where the employer is a limited liability partnership, if (but only if) subsection (4) is satisfied.][3]

(2) This subsection is satisfied in the case of an employer who is an individual—

    (a) in England and Wales if—

        (i) he has been adjudged bankrupt or has made a composition or arrangement with his creditors, or

        (ii) he has died and his estate falls to be administered in accordance with an order under section 421 of the Insolvency Act 1986, and

    (b) in Scotland if—

        (i) sequestration of his estate has been awarded or he has executed a trust deed for his creditors or has entered into a composition contract, or

        (ii) he has died and a judicial factor appointed under section 11A of the Judicial Factors (Scotland) Act 1889 is required by that section to divide his insolvent estate among his creditors.

(3) This subsection is satisfied in the case of an employer which is a company—

    (a) if a winding up order [...][4] has been made, or a resolution for voluntary winding up has been passed, with respect to the company,

    [(aa) if the company is in administration for the purposes of the Insolvency Act 1986,][5]

    (b) if a receiver or (in England and Wales only) a manager of the company's undertaking has been duly appointed, or (in England and Wales only) possession has been taken, by or on behalf of the holders of any debentures secured by a floating charge, of any property of the company comprised in or subject to the charge, or

    (c) if a voluntary arrangement proposed in the case of the company for the purposes of Part I of the Insolvency Act 1986 has been approved under that Part of that Act.

[(4) This subsection is satisfied in the case of an employer which is a limited liability partnership—

    (a) if a winding-up order, an administration order or a determination for a voluntary winding-up has been made with respect to the limited liability partnership,

    (b) if a receiver or (in England and Wales only) a manager of the undertaking of the limited liability partnership has been duly appointed, or (in England and Wales only) possession has been taken, by or on behalf of the holders of any debentures secured by a floating charge, of any property of the limited liability partnership comprised in or subject to the charge, or

---

[1] Word repealed by SI 2001/1090 Sch 5 para 19 (2)

[2] Word inserted by SI 2001/1090 Sch 5 para 19 (2)

[3] Inserted by SI 2001/1090 Sch 5 para 19 (2)

[4] Words repealed by Enterprise Act 2002 c.40 Sch 17 para 49

[5] Inserted by Enterprise Act 2002 c.40 Sch 17 para 49

(c) if a voluntary arrangement proposed in the case of the limited liability partnership for the purposes of Part I of the Insolvency Act 1986 has been approved under that Part of that Act.]¹

Debts to which Part applies

184.—(1) This part applies to the following debts— **11-192**
  (a) any arrears of pay in respect of one or more (but not more than eight) weeks,
  (b) any amount which the employer is liable to pay the employee for the period of notice required by section 86(1) or (2) or for any failure of the employer to give the period of notice required by section 86(1),
  (c) any holiday pay—
    (i) in respect of a period or periods of holiday not exceeding six weeks in all, and
    (ii) to which the employee became entitled during the twelve months ending with the appropriate date,
  (d) any basic award of compensation for unfair dismissal, [or so much of an award under a designated dismissal procedures agreement as does not exceed any basic award of compensation for unfair dismissal to which the employee would be entitled but for the agreement,]² and
  (e) any reasonable sum by way of reimbursement of the whole or part of any fee or premium paid by an apprentice or articled clerk.

(2) For the purposes of subsection (1)(a) the following amounts shall be treated as arrears of pay—
  (a) a guarantee payment,
  (b) any payment for time off under Part VI of this Act or section 169 of the Trade Union and Labour Relations (Consolidation) Act 1992 (payment for time off for carrying out trade union duties etc.),
  (c) remuneration on suspension on medical grounds under section 64 of this Act and remuneration on suspension on maternity grounds under section 68 of this Act, and
  (d) remuneration under a protective award under section 189 of the Trade Union and Labour Relations (Consolidation) Act 1992.

(3) In subsection (1)(c) "holiday pay", in relation to an employee, means —
  (a) pay in respect of a holiday actually taken by the employee, or
  (b) any accrued holiday pay which, under the employee's contract of employment, would in the ordinary course have become payable to him in respect of the period of a holiday if his employment with the employer had continued until he became entitled to a holiday.

(4) A sum shall be taken to be reasonable for the purposes of subsection (1)(e) in a case where a trustee in bankruptcy, or (in Scotland) a permanent or interim trustee (within the meaning of the Bankruptcy (Scotland) Act 1985), or liquidator has been or is required to be appointed—
  (a) as respects England and Wales, if it is admitted to be reasonable by the trustee in bankruptcy or liquidator under section 348 of the Insolvency Act 1986 (effect of bankruptcy on apprenticeships etc.), whether as originally enacted or as applied to the winding up of a company by rules under section 411 of that Act, and

---

¹ Inserted by SI 2001/1090 Sch 5 para 19 (3)
² Words inserted by Employment Rights (Dispute Resolution) Act 1998 c.8 Pt II s 12 (4)

(b) as respects Scotland, if it is accepted by the permanent or interim
trustee or liquidator for the purposes of the sequestration or winding
up.

The appropriate date

11-193   **185.** In this Part "the appropriate date"—

(a) in relation to arrears of pay (not being remuneration under a protective
award made under section 189 of the Trade Union and Labour Relations
(Consolidation) Act 1992) and to holiday pay, means the date on which
the employer became insolvent,

(b) in relation to a basic award of compensation for unfair dismissal and
to remuneration under a protective award so made, means whichever is
the latest of—

  (i) the date on which the employer became insolvent,
  (ii) the date of the termination of the employee's employment, and
  (iii) the date on which the award was made, and

(c) in relation to any other debt to which this Part applies, means
whichever is the later of—

  (i) the date on which the employer became insolvent, and
  (ii) the date of the termination of the employee's employment.

Limit on amount payable under section 182

11-194   **186.**—(1) The total amount payable to an employee in respect of any debt to
which this Part applies, where the amount of the debt is referable to a period of
time, shall not exceed—

(a) [£270][1] in respect of any one week, or

(b) in respect of a shorter period, an amount bearing the same proportion
to [£270][2] as that shorter period bears to a week.

(2) [...][3]

Role of relevant officer

11-195   **187.**—(1) Where a relevant officer has been, or is required to be, appointed in
connection with an employer's insolvency, the Secretary of State shall not make a
payment under section 182 in respect of a debt until he has received a statement
from the relevant officer of the amount of that debt which appears to have been
owed to the employee on the appropriate date and to remain unpaid.

(2) If the Secretary of State is satisfied that he does not require a statement
under subsection (1) in order to determine the amount of a debt which was owed
to the employee on the appropriate date and remains unpaid, he may make a
payment under section 182 in respect of the debt without having received such a
statement.

(3) A relevant officer shall, on request by the Secretary of State, provide him
with a statement for the purposes of subsection (1) as soon as is reasonably practicable.

(4) The following are relevant officers for the purposes of this section—

(a) a trustee in bankruptcy or a permanent or interim trustee (within the
meaning of the Bankruptcy (Scotland) Act 1985),

(b) a liquidator,

(c) an administrator,

---

[1] Figure substituted by SI 2003/3038 Sch 1
[2] Figure substituted by SI 2003/3038 Sch 1
[3] Repealed by Employment Relations Act 1999 c.26 Sch 9 para 1

(d) a receiver or manager,

(e) a trustee under a composition or arrangement between the employer and his creditors, and

(f) a trustee under a trust deed for his creditors executed by the employer.

(5) In subsection (4)(e) "trustee"includes the supervisor of a voluntary arrangement proposed for the purposes of, and approved under, Part I or VIII of the Insolvency Act 1986.

Complaints to [employment tribunals][1]

188.—(1) A person who has applied for a payment under section 182 may **11-196** present a complaint to an [employment tribunal][2]—

(a) that the Secretary of State has failed to make any such payment, or

(b) that any such payment made by him is less than the amount which should have been paid.

(2) An [employment tribunal][3] shall not consider a complaint under subsection (1) unless it is presented—

(a) before the end of the period of three months beginning with the date on which the decision of the Secretary of State on the application was communicated to the applicant, or

(b) within such further period as the tribunal considers reasonable in a case where it is not reasonably practicable for the complaint to be presented before the end of that period of three months.

(3) Where an [employment tribunal][4] finds that the Secretary of State ought to make a payment under section 182, the tribunal shall—

(a) make a declaration to that effect, and

(b) declare the amount of any such payment which it finds the Secretary of State ought to make.

Transfer to Secretary of State of rights and remedies

189.—(1) Where, in pursuance of section 182, the Secretary of State makes a **11-197** payment to an employee in respect of a debt to which this Part applies—

(a) on the making of the payment any rights and remedies of the employee in respect of the debt (or, if the Secretary of State has paid only part of it, in respect of that part) become rights and remedies of the Secretary of State, and

(b) any decision of an [employment tribunal][5] requiring an employer to pay that debt to the employee has the effect that the debt (or the part of it which the Secretary of State has paid) is to be paid to the Secretary of State.

(2) Where a debt (or any part of a debt) in respect of which the Secretary of State has made a payment in pursuance of section 182 constitutes—

(a) a preferential debt within the meaning of the Insolvency Act 1986 for the purposes of any provision of that Act (including any such provision as applied by any order made under that Act) or any provision of the Companies Act 1985, or

(b) a preferred debt within the meaning of the Bankruptcy (Scotland) Act 1985 for the purposes of any provision of that Act (including any such

---

[1] Words substituted by Employment Rights (Dispute Resolution) Act 1998 c.8 Pt I s 1 (2)

[2] Words substituted by Employment Rights (Dispute Resolution) Act 1998 c.8 Pt I s 1 (2)

[3] Words substituted by Employment Rights (Dispute Resolution) Act 1998 c.8 Pt I s 1 (2)

[4] Words substituted by Employment Rights (Dispute Resolution) Act 1998 c.8 Pt I s 1 (2)

[5] Words substituted by Employment Rights (Dispute Resolution) Act 1998 c.8 Pt I s 1 (2)

provision as applied by section 11A of the Judicial Factors (Scotland) Act 1889),

the rights which become rights of the Secretary of State in accordance with subsection (1) include any right arising under any such provision by reason of the status of the debt (or that part of it) as a preferential or preferred debt.

(3) In computing for the purposes of any provision mentioned in subsection (2)(a) or (b) the aggregate amount payable in priority to other creditors of the employer in respect of—

    (a) any claim of the Secretary of State to be paid in priority to other creditors of the employer by virtue of subsection (2), and

    (b) any claim by the employee to be so paid made in his own right,

any claim of the Secretary of State to be so paid by virtue of subsection (2) shall be treated as if it were a claim of the employee.

(4) [...][1]

(5) Any sum recovered by the Secretary of State in exercising any right, or pursuing any remedy, which is his by virtue of this section shall be paid into the National Insurance Fund.

Power to obtain information

11-198   **190.**—(1) Where an application is made to the Secretary of State under section 182 in respect of a debt owed by an employer, the Secretary of State may require—

    (a) the employer to provide him with such information as he may reasonably require for the purpose of determining whether the application is well-founded, and

    (b) any person having the custody or control of any relevant records or other documents to produce for examination on behalf of the Secretary of State any such document in that person's custody or under his control which is of such a description as the Secretary of State may require.

(2) Any such requirement—

    (a) shall be made by notice in writing given to the person on whom the requirement is imposed, and

    (b) may be varied or revoked by a subsequent notice so given.

(3) If a person refuses or wilfully neglects to furnish any information or produce any document which he has been required to furnish or produce by a notice under this section he is guilty of an offence and liable on summary conviction to a fine not exceeding level 3 on the standard scale.

(4) If a person, in purporting to comply with a requirement of a notice under this section, knowingly or recklessly makes any false statement he is guilty of an offence and liable on summary conviction to a fine not exceeding level 5 on the standard scale.

(5) Where an offence under this section committed by a body corporate is proved—

    (a) to have been committed with the consent or connivance of, or

    (b) to be attributable to any neglect on the part of,

any director, manager, secretary or other similar officer of the body corporate, or any person who was purporting to act in any such capacity, he (as well as the body corporate) is guilty of the offence and liable to be proceeded against and punished accordingly.

---

[1] Words repealed by Enterprise Act 2002 c.40 Sch 17 para 49

(6) Where the affairs of a body corporate are managed by its members, subsection (5) applies in relation to the acts and defaults of a member in connection with his functions of management as if he were a director of the body corporate.

PART XIII

MISCELLANEOUS

Chapter II

Other Miscellaneous Matters

Restrictions on disclosure of information

National security

202.—(1) Where in the opinion of any Minister of the Crown the disclosure **11-199** of any information would be contrary to the interests of national security—
  (a) nothing in any of the provisions to which this section applies requires any person to disclose the information, and
  (b) no person shall disclose the information in any proceedings in any court or tribunal relating to any of those provisions.
(2) This section applies to—
  (a) Part I, so far as it relates to employment particulars,
  (b) in Part V, sections 44, 45A, 47 and 47C, and sections 48 and 49 so far as relating to those sections,
  (c) in Part VI, sections 55 to 57B and 61 to 63,
  (d) in Part VII, sections 66 to 68, and sections 69 and 70 so far as relating to those sections,
  (e) Part VIII,
  (f) in Part IX, sections 92 and 93 where they apply by virtue of section 92(4),
  (g) Part X so far as relating to a dismissal which is treated as unfair—
    [(i) by section 99, 100, 101A(d) or 103, or by section 104 in its application in relation to time off under section 57A,][1]
    (ii) by subsection (1) of section 105 by reason of the application of subsection (2), (3) or (6) of that section, or by reason of the application of subsection (4A) in so far as it applies where the reason (or, if more than one, the principal reason) for which an employee was selected for dismissal was that specified in section 101A(d) and
  (h) this Part and Parts XIV and XV (so far as relating to any of the provisions in paragraphs (a) to (g)).

Contracting out etc. and remedies

Restrictions on contracting out

203.—(1) Any provision in an agreement (whether a contract of employment **11-200** or not) is void in so far as it purports—

---

[1] Substituted by Employment Relations Act 1999 c.26 Sch 4 Pt III para 36 (c)

    (a) to exclude or limit the operation of any provision of this Act, or

    (b) to preclude a person from bringing any proceedings under this Act before an [employment tribunal][1].

(2) Subsection (1)—

    (a) does not apply to any provision in a collective agreement excluding rights under section 28 if an order under section 35 is for the time being in force in respect of it,

    (b) does not apply to any provision in a dismissal procedures agreement excluding the right under section 94 if that provision is not to have effect unless an order under section 110 is for the time being in force in respect of it,

    (c) does not apply to any provision in an agreement if an order under section 157 is for the time being in force in respect of it,

    (d) [...][2]

    (e) does not apply to any agreement to refrain from instituting or continuing proceedings where a conciliation officer has taken action under [section 18 of the Employment Tribunals Act 1996][3], and

    (f) does not apply to any agreement to refrain from instituting or continuing [...][4] any proceedings within [the following provisions of section 18(1) of the Employment Tribunals Act 1996 (cases where conciliation available)—

        [(i) paragraph (d) (proceedings under this Act),

        (ii) paragraph (h) (proceedings arising out of the Part-time Workers (Prevention of Less Favourable Treatment) Regulations 2000),][5]

        [(iii) paragraph (i) (proceedings arising out of the Fixed-term Employees (Prevention of Less Favourable Treatment) Regulations 2002),

        (iv) paragraph (j) (proceedings under those Regulations),][6]

if the conditions regulating compromise agreements under this Act are satisfied in relation to the agreement.

(3) For the purposes of subsection (2)(f) the conditions regulating compromise agreements under this Act are that—

    (a) the agreement must be in writing,

    (b) the agreement must relate to the particular [proceedings][7],

    (c) the employee or worker must have received [advice from a relevant independent adviser][8] as to the terms and effect of the proposed agreement and, in particular, its effect on his ability to pursue his rights before an [employment tribunal][9],

    (d) there must be in force, when the adviser gives the advice, a [contract of insurance, or an indemnity provided for members of a profession or professional body,][10] covering the risk of a claim by the employee or worker in respect of loss arising in consequence of the advice,

    (e) the agreement must identify the adviser, and

---

[1] Words substituted by Employment Rights (Dispute Resolution) Act 1998 c.8 Pt I s 1 (2)
[2] Repealed by SI 2002/2034 Sch 2 (1) para 3 (17) (a)
[3] Words substituted by Employment Rights (Dispute Resolution) Act 1998 c.8 Pt I s 1 (2)
[4] Words repealed by Employment Rights (Dispute Resolution) Act 1998 c.8 Sch 2 para 1
[5] Inserted by SI 2001/1107 reg 3
[6] Inserted by SI 2002/2034 Sch 2 (1) para 3 (17) (b)
[7] Words substituted by Employment Rights (Dispute Resolution) Act 1998 c.8 Sch 1 para 24 (2)
[8] Words substituted by Employment Rights (Dispute Resolution) Act 1998 c.8 Pt II s 9 (2) (e)
[9] Words substituted by Employment Rights (Dispute Resolution) Act 1998 c.8 Pt I s 1 (2)
[10] Words substituted by Employment Rights (Dispute Resolution) Act 1998 c.8 Pt II s 10 (2) (e)

(f) the agreement must state that the conditions regulating compromise agreements under this Act are satisfied.

[(3A) A person is a relevant independent adviser for the purposes of subsection (3)(c)—

    (a) if he is a qualified lawyer,

    (b) if he is an officer, official, employee or member of an independent trade union who has been certified in writing by the trade union as competent to give advice and as authorised to do so on behalf of the trade union,

    (c) if he works at an advice centre (whether as an employee or a volunteer) and has been certified in writing by the centre as competent to give advice and as authorised to do so on behalf of the centre, or

    (d) if he is a person of a description specified in an order made by the Secretary of State.

(3B) But a person is not a relevant independent adviser for the purposes of subsection (3)(c) in relation to the employee or worker—

    (a) if he is, is employed by or is acting in the matter for the employer or an associated employer,

    (b) in the case of a person within subsection (3A)(b) or (c), if the trade union or advice centre is the employer or an associated employer,

    (c) in the case of a person within subsection (3A)(c), if the employee or worker makes a payment for the advice received from him, or

    (d) in the case of a person of a description specified in an order under subsection (3A)(d), if any condition specified in the order in relation to the giving of advice by persons of that description is not satisfied.

(4) In subsection (3A)(a) "qualified lawyer" means—

    (a) as respects England and Wales, a barrister (whether in practice as such or employed to give legal advice), a solicitor who holds a practising certificate, or a person other than a barrister or solicitor who is an authorised advocate or authorised litigator (within the meaning of the Courts and Legal Services Act 1990), and

    (b) as respects Scotland, an advocate (whether in practice as such or employed to give legal advice), or a solicitor who holds a practising certificate.][1]

[(5) An agreement under which the parties agree to submit a dispute to arbitration—

    (a) shall be regarded for the purposes of subsection (2)(e) and (f) as being an agreement to refrain from instituting or continuing proceedings if—

        (i) the dispute is covered by a scheme having effect by virtue of an order under section 212A of the Trade Union and Labour Relations (Consolidation) Act 1992, and

        (ii) the agreement is to submit it to arbitration in accordance with the scheme, but

    (b) shall be regarded as neither being nor including such an agreement in any other case.][2]

---

[1] S 203 (3A), (3B) and (4) substituted for s 203 (4) by Employment Rights (Dispute Resolution) Act 1998 c.8 Sch 1 para 24 (3)

[2] Inserted by Employment Rights (Dispute Resolution) Act 1998 c.8 Pt II s 8 (5)

Law governing employment

11-201   **204.**—(1) For the purposes of this Act it is immaterial whether the law which (apart from this Act) governs any person's employment is the law of the United Kingdom, or of a part of the United Kingdom, or not.

   (2) [...]¹

PART XIV

INTERPRETATION

CHAPTER I

CONTINUOUS EMPLOYMENT

Introductory

11-202   **210.**—(1) References in any provision of this Act to a period of continuous employment are (unless provision is expressly made to the contrary) to a period computed in accordance with this Chapter.

   (2) In any provision of this Act which refers to a period of continuous employment expressed in months or years—

      (a) a month means a calendar month, and

      (b) a year means a year of twelve calendar months.

   (3) In computing an employee's period of continuous employment for the purposes of any provision of this Act, any question—

      (a) whether the employee's employment is of a kind counting towards a period of continuous employment, or

      (b) whether periods (consecutive or otherwise) are to be treated as forming a single period of continuous employment,

shall be determined week by week; but where it is necessary to compute the length of an employee's period of employment it shall be computed in months and years of twelve months in accordance with section 211.

   (4) Subject to sections 215 to 217, a week which does not count in computing the length of a period of continuous employment breaks continuity of employment.

   (5) A person's employment during any period shall, unless the contrary is shown, be presumed to have been continuous.

Period of continuous employment

11-203   **211.**—(1) An employee's period of continuous employment for the purposes of any provision of this Act—

      (a) (subject to subsections (2) and (3)) begins with the day on which the employee starts work, and

      (b) ends with the day by reference to which the length of the employee's period of continuous employment is to be ascertained for the purposes of the provision.

   (2) For the purposes of sections 155 and 162(1), and employee's period of continuous employment shall be treated as beginning on the employee's eighteenth birthday if that is later than the day on which the employee starts work.

---

¹ Repealed by Employment Relations Act 1999 c.26 Sch 9 para 1

(3) If an employee's period of continuous employment includes one or more periods which (by virtue of section 215, 216 or 217) while not counting in computing the length of the period do not break continuity of employment, the beginning of the period shall be treated as postponed by the number of days falling within that intervening period, or the aggregate number of days falling within those periods, calculated in accordance with the section in question.

Weeks counting in computing period

212.—(1) Any week during the whole or part of which an employee's **11-204** relations with his employer are governed by a contract of employment counts in computing the employee's period of employment.

(2) [...]¹

(3) Subject to subsection (4), any week (not within subsection (1)) during the whole or part of which an employee is—

    (a) incapable of work in consequence of sickness or injury,

    (b) absent from work on account of a temporary cessation of work, [or]²

    (c) absent from work in circumstances such that, by arrangement or custom, he is regarded as continuing in the employment of his employer for any purpose, [...]³

    (d) [...]⁴

counts in computing the employee's period of employment.

(4) Not more than twenty-six weeks count under subsection (3)(a) [...]⁵ between any periods falling under subsection (1).

Intervals in employment

213.—(1) Where in the case of an employee a date later than the date which **11-205** would be the effective date of termination by virtue of subsection (1) of section 97 is treated for certain purposes as the effective date of termination by virtue of subsection (2) or (4) of that section, the period of the interval between the two dates counts as a period of employment in ascertaining for the purposes of section 108(1) or 119(1) the period for which the employee has been continuously employed.

(2) Where an employee is by virtue of section 138(1) regarded for the purposes of Part XI as not having been dismissed by reason of a renewal or re-engagement taking effect after an interval, the period of the interval counts as a period of employment in ascertaining for the purposes of section 155 or 162(1) the period for which the employee has been continuously employed (except so far as it is to be disregarded under section 214 or 215).

(3) Where in the case of an employee a date later than the date which would be the relevant date by virtue of subsections (2) to (4) of section 145 is treated for certain purposes as the relevant date by virtue of subsection (5) of that section, the period of the interval between the two dates counts as a period of employment in ascertaining for the purposes of section 155 or 162(1) the period for which the employee has been continuously employed (except so far as it is to be disregarded under section 214 or 215).

¹ Repealed by Employment Relations Act 1999 c.26 Sch 9 para 1
² Word inserted by Employment Relations Act 1999 c.26 Sch 4 (III) para 38 (3) (a)
³ Word repealed by Employment Relations Act 1999 c.26 Sch 9 para 1
⁴ Repealed by Employment Relations Act 1999 c.26 Sch 9 para 1
⁵ Words repealed by Employment Relations Act 1999 c.26 Sch 9 para 1

Special provisions for redundancy payments

11-206 **214.**—(1) This section applies where a period of continuous employment has to be determined in relation to an employee for the purposes of the application of section 155 or 162(1).

(2) The continuity of a period of employment is broken where—

(a) a redundancy payment has previously been paid to the employee (whether in respect of dismissal or in respect of lay-off or short-time), and

(b) the contract of employment under which the employee was employed was renewed (whether by the same or another employer) or the employee was re-engaged under a new contract of employment (whether by the same or another employer).

(3) The continuity of a period of employment is also broken where—

(a) a payment has been made to the employee (whether in respect of the termination of his employment or lay-off or short-time) in accordance with a scheme under section 1 of the Superannuation Act 1972 or arrangements falling within section 177(3), and

(b) he commenced new, or renewed, employment.

(4) The date on which the person's continuity of employment is broken by virtue of this section—

(a) if the employment was under a contract of employment, is the date which was the relevant date in relation to the payment mentioned in subsection (2)(a) or (3)(a), and

(b) if the employment was otherwise than under a contract of employment, is the date which would have been the relevant date in relation to the payment mentioned in subsection (2)(a) or (3)(a) had the employment been under a contract of employment.

(5) For the purposes of this section a redundancy payment shall be treated as having been paid if—

(a) the whole of the payment has been paid to the employee by the employer,

(b) a tribunal has determined liability and found that the employer must pay part (but not all) of the redundancy payment and the employer has paid that part, or

(c) the Secretary of State has paid a sum to the employee in respect of the redundancy payment under section 167.

Employment abroad etc.

11-207 **215.**—(1) This Chapter applies to a period of employment—

(a) (subject to the following provisions of this section) even where during the period the employee was engaged in work wholly or mainly outside Great Britain, and

(b) even where the employee was excluded by or under this Act from any right conferred by this Act.

(2) For the purposes of sections 155 and 162(1) a week of employment does not count in computing a period of employment if the employee—

(a) was employed outside Great Britain during the whole or part of the week, and

(b) was not during that week an employed earner for the purposes of the Social Security Contributions and Benefits Act 1992 in respect of whom a secondary Class 1 contribution was payable under that Act (whether or not the contribution was in fact paid).

(3) Where by virtue of subsection (2) a week of employment does not count in computing a period of employment, the continuity of the period is not broken by reason only that the week does not count in computing the period; and the number of days which, for the purposes of section 211(3), fall within the intervening period is seven for each week within this subsection.

(4) Any question arising under subsection (2) whether—

(a) a person was an employed earner for the purposes of the Social Security Contributions and Benefits Act 1992, or

(b) if so, whether a secondary Class 1 contribution was payable in respect of him under that Act,

shall be determined by an officer of the Commissioners of Inland Revenue.

[(5) Part II of the Social Security Contributions (Transfer of Functions, etc.) Act 1999 (decisions and appeals) shall apply in relation to the determination of any issue by the Inland Revenue under subsection (4) as if it were a decision falling within section 8(1) of that Act.

(6) Subsection (2) does not apply in relation to a person who is—

(a) employed as a master or seaman in a British ship, and

(b) ordinarily resident in Great Britain.][1]

Industrial disputes

216.—(1) A week does not count under section 212 if during the week, or any part of the week, the employee takes part in a strike.   **11-208**

(2) The continuity of an employee's period of employment is not broken by a week which does not count under this Chapter (whether or not by virtue only of subsection (1)) if during the week, or any part of the week, the employee takes part in a strike; and the number of days which, for the purposes of section 211(3), fall within the intervening period is the number of days between the last working day before the strike and the day on which work was resumed.

(3) The continuity of an employee's period of employment is not broken by a week if during the week, or any part of the week, the employee is absent from work because of a lock-out by the employer; and the number of days which, for the purposes of section 211(3), fall within the intervening period is the number of days between the last working day before the lock-out and the day on which work was resumed.

Change of employer

218.—(1) Subject to the provisions of this section, this Chapter relates only   **11-209**
to employment by the one employer.

(2) If a trade or business, or an undertaking (whether or not established by or under an Act), is transferred from one person to another—

(a) the period of employment of an employee in the trade or business or undertaking at the time of the transfer counts as a period of employment with the transferee, and

(b) the transfer does not break the continuity of the period of employment.

(3) If by or under an Act (whether public or local and whether passed before or after this Act) a contract of employment between any body corporate and an employee is modified and some other body corporate is substituted as the employer—

---

[1] Substituted by Social Security Contributions (Transfer of Functions, etc.) Act 1999 c.2 Sch 7 para 21 (3)

    (a) the employee's period of employment at the time when the modification takes effect counts as a period of employment with the second body corporate, and

    (b) the change of employer does not break the continuity of the period of employment.

(4) If on the death of an employer the employee is taken into the employment of the personal representatives or trustees of the deceased—

    (a) the employee's period of employment at the time of the death counts as a period of employment with the employer's personal representatives or trustees, and

    (b) the death does not break the continuity of the period of employment.

(5) If there is a change in the partners, personal representatives or trustees who employ any person—

    (a) the employee's period of employment at the time of the change counts as a period of employment with the partners, personal representatives or trustees after the change, and

    (b) the change does not break the continuity of the period of employment.

(6) If an employee of an employer is taken into the employment of another employer who, at the time when the employee enters the second employer's employment, is an associated employer of the first employer—

    (a) the employee's period of employment at that time counts as a period of employment with the second employer, and

    (b) the change of employer does not break the continuity of the period of employment.

(7) If an employee of the [governing body][1] of a school maintained by a local education authority is taken into the employment of the authority or an employee of a local education authority is taken into the employment of the [governing body][2] of a school maintained by the authority—

    (a) his period of employment at the time of the change of employer counts as a period of employment with the second employer, and

    (b) the change does not break the continuity of the period of employment.

(8) If a person employed in relevant employment by a health service employer is taken into relevant employment by another such employer, his period of employment at the time of the change of employer counts as a period of employment with the second employer and the change does not break the continuity of the period of employment.

(9) For the purposes of subsection (8) employment is relevant employment if it is employment of a description—

    (a) in which persons are engaged while undergoing professional training which involves their being employed successively by a number of different health service employers, and

    (b) which is specified in an order made by the Secretary of State.

(10) The following are health service employers for the purposes of subsections (8) and (9)—

    (a) Health Authorities established under section 8 of the National Health Service Act 1977,

    (b) Special Health Authorities established under section 11 of that Act,

    [(bb) Primary Care Trusts established under section 16A of that Act,][3]

---

[1] Words substituted in relation to Wales by Education Act 2002 c.32 Sch 21 para 32
[2] Words substituted in relation to Wales by Education Act 2002 c.32 Sch 21 para 32
[3] Inserted by SI 2000/90 Sch 1 para 30 (3)

(c) National Health Service trusts established under Part I of the National Health Service and Community Care Act 1990,

[(ca) NHS foundation trusts,][1]

(d) [...][2]

(e) the Public Health Laboratory Service Board.

Reinstatement or re-engagement of dismissed employee

219.—(1) Regulations made by the Secretary of State may make provision— **11-210**

(a) for preserving the continuity of a person's period of employment for the purposes of this Chapter or for the purposes of this Chapter as applied by or under any other enactment specified in the regulations, or

(b) for modifying or excluding the operation of section 214 subject to the recovery of any such payment as is mentioned in that section,

in cases where [...][3] a dismissed employee is reinstated[, re-engaged or otherwise re-employed][4] by his employer or by a successor or associated employer of that employer [in any circumstances prescribed by the regulations][5].

(2) [...][6]

(3) [...][7]

(4) [...][8]

CHAPTER II

A WEEK'S PAY

Introductory

Introductory

220. The amount of a week's pay of an employee shall be calculated for the **11-211**
purposes of this Act in accordance with this Chapter.

Employments with normal working hours

General

221.—(1) This section and sections 222 and 223 apply where there are **11-212**
normal working hours for the employee when employed under the contract of employment in force on the calculation date.

(2) Subject to section 222, if the employee's remuneration for employment in normal working hours (whether by the hour or week or other period) does not vary with the amount of work done in the period, the amount of a week's pay is the amount which is payable by the employer under the contract of employment

---

[1] Inserted by Health and Social Care (Community Health and Standards) Act 2003 c.43 Sch 4 para 101

[2] Repealed by Health and Social Care (Community Health and Standards) Act 2003 c.43 Sch 14

[3] Words repealed by Employment Rights (Dispute Resolution) Act 1998 c.8 Sch 2 para 1

[4] Words substituted by Employment Rights (Dispute Resolution) Act 1998 c.8 Sch 1 para 25 (2) (b)

[5] Words inserted by Employment Rights (Dispute Resolution) Act 1998 c.8 Sch 1 para 25 (2) (c)

[6] Repealed by Employment Rights (Dispute Resolution) Act 1998 c.8 Sch 2 para 1

[7] Repealed by Employment Rights (Dispute Resolution) Act 1998 c.8 Sch 2 para 1

[8] Repealed by Employment Rights (Dispute Resolution) Act 1998 c.8 Sch 2 para 1

in force on the calculation date if the employee works throughout his normal working hours in a week.

(3) Subject to section 222, if the employee's remuneration for employment in normal working hours (whether by the hour or week or other period) does vary with the amount of work done in the period, the amount of a week's pay is the amount of remuneration for the number of normal working hours in a week calculated at the average hourly rate of remuneration payable by the employer to the employee in respect of the period of twelve weeks ending—

    (a) where the calculation date is the last day of a week, with that week, and

    (b) otherwise, with the last complete week before the calculation date.

(4) In this section references to remuneration varying with the amount of work done includes remuneration which may include any commission or similar payment which varies in amount.

(5) This section is subject to sections 227 and 228.

Remuneration varying according to time of work

11-213   **222.**—(1) This section applies if the employee is required under the contract of employment in force on the calculation date to work during normal working hours on days of the week, or at times of the day, which differ from week to week or over a longer period so that the remuneration payable for, or apportionable to, any week varies according to the incidence of those days or times.

(2) The amount of a week's pay is the amount of remuneration for the average number of weekly normal working hours at the average hourly rate of remuneration.

(3) For the purposes of subsection (2)—

    (a) the average number of weekly hours is calculated by dividing by twelve the total number of the employee's normal working hours during the relevant period of twelve weeks, and

    (b) the average hourly rate of remuneration is the average hourly rate of remuneration payable by the employer to the employee in respect of the relevant period of twelve weeks.

(4) In subsection (3) "the relevant period of twelve weeks" means the period of twelve weeks ending—

    (a) where the calculation date is the last day of a week, with that week, and

    (b) otherwise, with the last complete week before the calculation date.

(5) This section is subject to sections 227 and 228.

Supplementary

11-214   **223.**—(1) For the purposes of sections 221 and 222, in arriving at the average hourly rate of remuneration, only—

    (a) the hours when the employee was working, and

    (b) the remuneration payable for, or apportionable to, those hours,

shall be brought in.

(2) If for any of the twelve weeks mentioned in sections 221 and 222 no remuneration within subsection (1)(b) was payable by the employer to the employee, account shall be taken of remuneration in earlier weeks so as to bring up to twelve the number of weeks of which account is taken.

(3) Where—

    (a) in arriving at the average hourly rate of remuneration, account has to be taken of remuneration payable for, or apportionable to, work done in hours other than normal working hours, and

(b) the amount of that remuneration was greater than it would have been if the work had been done in normal working hours (or, in a case within section 234(3), in normal working hours falling within the number of hours without overtime),

account shall be taken of that remuneration as if the work had been done in such hours and the amount of that remuneration had been reduced accordingly.

Employments with no normal working hours

Employments with no normal working hours

224.—(1) This section applies where there are no normal working hours for **11-215** the employee when employed under the contract of employment in force on the calculation date.

(2) The amount of a week's pay is the amount of the employee's average weekly remuneration in the period of twelve weeks ending—

(a) where the calculation date is the last day of a week, with that week, and

(b) otherwise, with the last complete week before the calculation date.

(3) In arriving at the average weekly remuneration no account shall be taken of a week in which no remuneration was payable by the employer to the employee and remuneration in earlier weeks shall be brought in so as to bring up to twelve the number of weeks of which account is taken.

(4) This section is subject to sections 227 and 228.

The calculation date

Rights during employment

225.—(1) Where the calculation is for the purposes of section 30, the calcula- **11-216** tion date is—

(a) where the employee's contract has been varied, or a new contract entered into, in connection with a period of short-time working, the last day on which the original contract was in force, and

(b) otherwise, the day in respect of which the guarantee payment is payable.

(2) Where the calculation is for the purposes of section 53 or 54, the calculation date is the day on which the employer's notice was given.

(3) Where the calculation is for the purposes of section 56, the calculation date is the day of the appointment.

(4) Where the calculation is for the purposes of section 62, the calculation date is the day on which the time off was taken or on which it is alleged the time off should have been permitted.

[(4A) Where the calculation is for the purposes of section 63B, the calculation date is the day on which the time off was taken or on which it is alleged the time off should have been permitted.][1]

(5) Where the calculation is for the purposes of section 69—

(a) in the case of an employee suspended on medical grounds, the calculation date is the day before that on which the suspension begins, and

(b) in the case of an employee suspended on maternity grounds, the calculation date is—

---

[1] Inserted by Teaching and Higher Education Act 1998 c.30 Sch 3 para 14

[(i) where the day before that on which the suspension begins falls during a period of ordinary or additional maternity leave, the day before the beginning of that period,]¹

(ii) otherwise, the day before that on which the suspension begins.

[(6) Where the calculation is for the purposes of section 80I, the calculation date is the day on which the application under section 80F was made.]²

Rights on termination

11-217   **226.**—(1) Where the calculation is for the purposes of section 88 or 89, the calculation date is the day immediately preceding the first day of the period of notice required by section 86(1) or (2).

(2) Where the calculation is for the purposes of section 93, 117 or 125, the calculation date is—

(a) if the dismissal was with notice, the date on which the employer's notice was given, and

(b) otherwise, the effective date of termination.

(3) Where the calculation is for the purposes of [section 119, 121 or 127A]³, the calculation date is—

(a) [...]⁴

(b) if by virtue of subsection (2) or (4) of section 97 a date later than the effective date of termination as defined in subsection (1) of that section is to be treated for certain purposes as the effective date of termination, the effective date of termination as so defined, and

(c) otherwise, the date specified in subsection (6).

(4) Where the calculation is for the purposes of section 147(2), the calculation date is the day immediately preceding the first of the four, or six, weeks referred to in section 148(2).

(5) Where the calculation is for the purposes of section 162, the calculation date is—

(a) [...]⁵

(b) if by virtue of subsection (5) of section 145 a date is to be treated for certain purposes as the relevant date which is later than the relevant date as defined by the previous provisions of that section, the relevant date as so defined, and

(c) otherwise, the date specified in subsection (6).

(6) The date referred to in subsections (3)(c) and (5)(c) is the date on which notice would have been given had—

(a) the contract been terminable by notice and been terminated by the employer giving such notice as is required by section 86 to terminate the contract, and

(b) the notice expired on the effective date of termination, or the relevant date,

(whether or not those conditions were in fact fulfilled).

---

¹ Substituted by Employment Relations Act 1999 c.26 Sch 4 (III) para 39
² Inserted by Employment Act 2002 c.22 Sch 7 para 45
³ Words substituted by Employment Rights (Dispute Resolution) Act 1998 c.8 Sch 1 para 26
⁴ Repealed by Employment Relations Act 1999 c.26 Sch 9 para 1
⁵ Words repealed by Employment Relations Act 1999 c.26 Sch 9 para 1

Maximum amount of week's pay

Maximum amount

227.—(1) For the purpose of calculating—   **11-218**
[(za) an award of compensation under section 80I(1)(b).][1]
(a) a basic award of compensation for unfair dismissal,
(b) an additional award of compensation for unfair dismissal,
[(ba) an award under section 112(5), or][2]
(c) a redundancy payment,
the amount of a week's pay shall not exceed [£270][3].
(2) [...][4]
(3) [...][5]
(4) [...][6]

Miscellaneous

New employments and other special cases

228.—(1) In any case in which the employee has not been employed for a   **11-219**
sufficient period to enable a calculation to be made under the preceding
provisions of this Chapter, the amount of a week's pay is the amount which fairly
represents a week's pay.
(2) In determining that amount the [employment tribunal][7]—
(a) shall apply as nearly as may be such of the preceding provisions of this
Chapter as it considers appropriate, and
(b) may have regard to such of the considerations specified in subsection
(3) as it thinks fit.
(3) The considerations referred to in subsection (2)(b) are—
(a) any remuneration received by the employee in respect of the
employment in question,
(b) the amount offered to the employee as remuneration in respect of the
employment in question,
(c) the remuneration received by other persons engaged in relevant
comparable employment with the same employer, and
(d) the remuneration received by other persons engaged in relevant
comparable employment with other employers.
(4) The Secretary of State may by regulations provide that in cases
prescribed by the regulations the amount of a week's pay shall be calculated in
such manner as may be so prescribed.

Supplementary

229.—(1) In arriving at—   **11-220**
(a) an average hourly rate of remuneration, or
(b) average weekly remuneration,
under this Chapter, account shall be taken of work for a former employer
within the period for which the average is to be taken if, by virtue of Chapter I of

---

[1] Inserted by Employment Act 2002 c.22 Sch 7 para 47 (2)
[2] Inserted by Employment Act 2002 c.22 Sch 7 para 47 (2)
[3] Figure substituted by SI 2003/3038 Sch 1 para 1
[4] Repealed by Employment Relations Act 1999 c.26 Sch 9 para 1
[5] Repealed by Employment Relations Act 1999 c.26 Sch 9 para 1
[6] Repealed by Employment Relations Act 1999 c.26 Sch 9 para 1
[7] Words substituted by Employment Rights (Dispute Resolution) Act 1998 c.8 Pt I s 1 (2)

this Part, a period of employment with the former employer counts as part of the employee's continuous period of employment.

(2) Where under this Chapter account is to be taken of remuneration or other payments for a period which does not coincide with the periods for which the remuneration or other payments are calculated, the remuneration or other payments shall be apportioned in such manner as may be just.

CHAPTER III

OTHER INTERPRETATION PROVISIONS

Employees, workers etc

11-221   **230.**—(1) In this Act "employee" means an individual who has entered into or works under (or, where the employment has ceased, worked under) a contract of employment.

(2) In this Act "contract of employment" means a contract of service or apprenticeship, whether express or implied, and (if it is express) whether oral or in writing.

(3) In this Act "worker" (except in the phrases "shop worker" and "betting worker") means an individual who has entered into or works under (or, where the employment has ceased, worked under)—

(a) a contract of employment, or

(b) any other contract, whether express or implied and (if it is express) whether oral or in writing, whereby the individual undertakes to do or perform personally any work or services for another party to the contract whose status is not by virtue of the contract that of a client or customer of any profession or business undertaking carried on by the individual;

and any reference to a worker's contract shall be construed accordingly.

(4) In this Act "employer", in relation to an employee or a worker, means the person by whom the employee or worker is (or, where the employment has ceased, was) employed.

(5) In this Act "employment"—

(a) in relation to an employee, means (except for the purposes of section 171) employment under a contract of employment, and

(b) in relation to a worker, means employment under his contract;

and "employed" shall be construed accordingly.

[(6) This section has effect subject to sections 43K and 47B(3); and for the purposes of Part XIII so far as relating to Part IVA or section 47B, "worker" "worker's contract" and, in relation to a worker, "employer", "employment" and "employed" have the extended meaning given by section 43K.][1]

Associated employers

11-222   **231.** For the purposes of this Act any two employers shall be treated as associated if—

(a) one is a company of which the other (directly or indirectly) has control, or

(b) both are companies of which a third person (directly or indirectly) has control;

and "associated employer" shall be construed accordingly.

---

[1] Inserted by Public Interest Disclosure Act 1998 c.23 s 15 (1)

Other definitions

235.—(1) In this Act, except in so far as the context otherwise requires— **11-223**

"act" and "action" each includes omission and references to doing an act or taking action shall be construed accordingly,

"basic award of compensation for unfair dismissal" shall be construed in accordance with section 118,

"business" includes a trade or profession and includes any activity carried on by a body of persons (whether corporate or unincorporated),

"childbirth" means the birth of a living child or the birth of a child whether living or dead after twenty-four weeks of pregnancy,

"collective agreement" has the meaning given by section 178(1) and (2) of the Trade Union and Labour Relations (Consolidation) Act 1992,

"conciliation officer" means an officer designated by the Advisory, Conciliation and Arbitration Service under section 211 of that Act,

"dismissal procedures agreement" means an agreement in writing with respect to procedures relating to dismissal made by or on behalf of one or more independent trade unions and one or more employers or employers' associations,

"employers' association" has the same meaning as in the Trade Union and Labour Relations (Consolidation) Act 1992,

"expected week of childbirth" means the week, beginning with midnight between Saturday and Sunday, in which it is expected that childbirth will occur,

"guarantee payment" has the meaning given by section 28,

"independent trade union" means a trade union which—

   (a) is not under the domination or control of an employer or a group of employers or of one or more employers' associations, and

   (b) is not liable to interference by an employer or any such group or association (arising out of the provision of financial or material support or by any other means whatever) tending towards such control,

"job", in relation to an employee, means the nature of the work which he is employed to do in accordance with his contract and the capacity and place in which he is so employed,

["paternity leave" means leave under section 80A or 80B,][1]

[...][2]

"position", in relation to an employee, means the following matters taken as a whole—

   (a) his status as an employee,

   (b) the nature of his work, and

   (c) his terms and conditions of employment,

["protected disclosure" has the meaning given by section 43A.][3]

"redundancy payment" has the meaning given by Part XI,

"relevant date" has the meaning given by sections 145 and 153,

"renewal" includes extension, and any reference to renewing a contract or a fixed term shall be construed accordingly,

---

[1] Definition inserted by Employment Act 2002 c.22 Sch 7 para 48 (2)
[2] Definitions repealed by Employment Relations Act 1999 c.26 Sch 9 para 1
[3] Definition inserted by Public Interest Disclosure Act 1998 c.23 s 15 (2)

"statutory provision" means a provision, whether of a general or a special nature, contained in, or in any document made or issued under, any Act, whether of a general or special nature,

"successor", in relation to the employer of an employee, means (subject to subsection (2)) a person who in consequence of a change occurring (whether by virtue of a sale or other disposition or by operation of law) in the ownership of the undertaking, or of the part of the undertaking, for the purposes of which the employee was employed, has become the owner of the undertaking or part,

"trade union" has the meaning given by section 1 of the Trade Union and Labour Relations (Consolidation) Act 1992,

"week" —

    (a) in Chapter I of this Part means a week ending with Saturday, and

    (b) otherwise, except in [sections 80A, 80B and 86][1], means, in relation to an employee whose remuneration is calculated weekly by a week ending with a day other than Saturday, a week ending with that other day and, in relation to any other employee, a week ending with Saturday.

(2) The definition of "successor" in subsection (1) has effect (subject to the necessary modifications) in relation to a case where—

    (a) the person by whom an undertaking or part of an undertaking is owned immediately before a change is one of the persons by whom (whether as partners, trustees or otherwise) it is owned immediately after the change, or

    (b) the persons by whom an undertaking or part of an undertaking is owned immediately before a change (whether as partners, trustees or otherwise) include the persons by whom, or include one or more of the persons by whom, it is owned immediately after the change,

as it has effect where the previous owner and the new owner are wholly different persons.

[(2A) For the purposes of this Act a contract of employment is a "limited-term contract" if—

    (a) the employment under the contract is not intended to be permanent, and

    (b) provision is accordingly made in the contract for it to terminate by virtue of a limiting event.

(2B) In this Act, "limiting event", in relation to a contract of employment means—

    (a) in the case of a contract for a fixed-term, the expiry of the term,

    (b) in the case of a contract made in contemplation of the performance of a specific task, the performance of the task, and

    (c) in the case of a contract which provides for its termination on the occurrence of an event (or the failure of an event to occur), the occurrence of the event (or the failure of the event to occur).][2]

(3) References in this Act to redundancy, dismissal by reason of redundancy and similar expressions shall be construed in accordance with section 139.

(4) In sections 136(2), 154 and 216(3) and paragraph 14 of Schedule 2 "lock-out" means —

    (a) the closing of a place of employment,

---

[1] Words substituted by Employment Act 2002 c.22 Sch 7 para 48 (3)
[2] Inserted by SI 2002/2034 Sch 2 (1) para 3 (18)

(b) the suspension of work, or

(c) the refusal by an employer to continue to employ any number of persons employed by him in consequence of a dispute,

done with a view to compelling persons employed by the employer, or to aid another employer in compelling persons employed by him, to accept terms or conditions of or affecting employment.

(5) In sections 91(2), 140(2) and (3), 143(1), 144(2) and (3), 154 and 216(1) and (2) and paragraph 14 of Schedule 2 "strike" means—

(a) the cessation of work by a body of employed persons acting in combination, or

(b) a concerted refusal, or a refusal under a common understanding, of any number of employed persons to continue to work for an employer in consequence of a dispute,

done as a means of compelling their employer or any employed person or body of employed persons, or to aid other employees in compelling their employer or any employed person or body of employed persons, to accept or not to accept terms or conditions of or affecting employment.

Asylum and Immigration Act 1996

CHAPTER 49

Persons subject to immigration control

Restrictions on employment

8.—(1) Subject to subsection (2) below, if any person ("the employer") **12-001** employs a person subject to immigration control ("the employee") who has attained the age of 16, the employer shall be guilty of an offence if—

(a) the employee has not been granted leave to enter or remain in the United Kingdom; or

(b) the employee's leave is not valid and subsisting, or is subject to a condition precluding him from taking up the employment,

and (in either case) the employee does not satisfy such conditions as may be specified in an order made by the Secretary of State.

[(2) It is a defence for a person charged with an offence under this section to prove that before the employment began any relevant requirement of an order of the Secretary of State under subsection (2A) was complied with.

(2A) An order under this subsection may—

(a) require the production to an employer of a document of a specified description;

(b) require the production to an employer of one document of each of a number of specified descriptions;

(c) require an employer to take specified steps to retain, copy or record the content of a document produced to him in accordance with the order;

(d) make provision which applies generally or only in specified circumstances;

(e) make different provision for different circumstances.][1]

---

[1] Substituted by Nationality, Immigration and Asylum Act 2002 c.41 Pt VII s 147 (2)

(3) The defence afforded by subsection (2) above shall not be available in any case where the employer knew that his employment of the employee would constitute an offence under this section.

(4) A person guilty of an offence under this section shall be liable on summary conviction to a fine not exceeding level 5 on the standard scale.

(5) Where an offence under this section committed by a body corporate is proved to have been committed with the consent or connivance of, or to be attributable to any neglect on the part of—

> (a) any director, manager, secretary or other similar officer of the body corporate, or
>
> (b) any person who was purporting to act in any such capacity,

he as well as the body corporate shall be guilty of the offence and shall be liable to be proceeded against and punished accordingly.

(6) Where the affairs of a body corporate are managed by its members, subsection (5) above shall apply in relation to the acts and defaults of a member in connection with his functions of management as if he were a director of the body corporate.

[(6A) Where an offence under this section is committed by a partnership (other than a limited partnership) each partner shall be guilty of the offence and shall be liable to be proceeded against and punished accordingly.

(6B) Subsection (5) shall have effect in relation to a limited partnership as if—

> (a) a reference to a body corporate were a reference to a limited partnership, and
>
> (b) a reference to an officer of the body were a reference to a partner.][1]

(7) An order under this section shall be made by statutory instrument which shall be subject to annulment in pursuance of a resolution of either House of Parliament.

(8) In this section—

> "contract of employment" means a contract of service or apprenticeship, whether express or implied, and (if it is express) whether it is oral or in writing;
>
> "employ" means employ under a contract of employment and "employment"shall be construed accordingly.

[(9) Section 28(1) of the Immigration Act 1971 (c. 77) (extended time limit for prosecution) shall apply in relation to an offence under this section.

(10) An offence under this section shall be treated as—

> (a) a relevant offence for the purpose of sections 28B and 28D of that Act (search, entry and arrest), and
>
> (b) an offence under Part III of that Act (criminal proceedings) for the purposes of sections 28E, 28G and 28H (search after arrest).][2]

[Code of practice

12-002   8A.—(1) The Secretary of State must issue a code of practice as to the measures which an employer is to be expected to take, or not to take, with a view to securing that, while avoiding the commission of an offence under section 8, he also avoids unlawful discrimination.

(2) "Unlawful discrimination" means—

> (a) discrimination in contravention of section 4(1) of the Race Relations Act 1976 ("the 1976 Act"); or

---

[1] Inserted by Nationality, Immigration and Asylum Act 2002 c.41 Pt VII s 147 (3)
[2] Inserted by Nationality, Immigration and Asylum Act 2002 c.41 Pt VII s 147 (4)

(b) in relation to Northern Ireland, discrimination in contravention of Article 6(1) of the Race Relations (Northern Ireland) Order 1997 ("the 1997 Order").

(3) Before issuing the code, the Secretary of State must—

(a) prepare and publish a draft of the proposed code; and

(b) consider any representations about it which are made to him.

(4) In preparing the draft, the Secretary of State must consult—

(a) the Commission for Racial Equality;

(b) the Equality Commission for Northern Ireland; and

(c) such organisations and bodies (including organisations or associations of organisations representative of employers or of workers) as he considers appropriate.

(5) If the Secretary of State decides to proceed with the code, he must lay a draft of the code before both Houses of Parliament.

(6) The draft code may contain modifications to the original proposals made in the light of representations to the Secretary of State.

(7) After laying the draft code before Parliament, the Secretary of State may bring the code into operation by an order made by statutory instrument.

(8) An order under subsection (7)—

(a) shall be subject to annulment in pursuance of a resolution of either House of Parliament;

(b) may contain such transitional provisions or savings as appear to the Secretary of State to be necessary or expedient in connection with the code.

(9) A failure on the part of any person to observe a provision of the code does not of itself make him liable to any proceedings.

(10) But the code is admissible in evidence—

(a) in proceedings under the 1976 Act before an employment tribunal;

(b) in proceedings under the 1997 Order before an industrial tribunal.

(11) If any provision of the code appears to the tribunal to be relevant to any question arising in such proceedings, that provision is to be taken into account in determining the question.

(12) The Secretary of State may from time to time revise the whole or any part of the code and issue the code as revised.

(13) The provisions of this section also apply (with appropriate modifications) to any revision, or proposed revision, of the code.][1]

Data Protection Act 1998

CHAPTER 29

PART I

PRELIMINARY

Basic interpretative provisions

1.—(1) In this Act, unless the context otherwise requires— **13-001**

---

[1] Inserted by Immigration and Asylum Act 1999 c.33 Pt I s 22

"data" means information which—
   (a) is being processed by means of equipment operating automatically in response to instructions given for that purpose,
   (b) is recorded with the intention that it should be processed by means of such equipment,
   (c) is recorded as part of a relevant filing system or with the intention that it should form part of a relevant filing system, or
   (d) does not fall within paragraph (a), (b) or (c) but forms part of an accessible record as defined by section 68;

"data controller" means , subject to subsection (4), a person who (either alone or jointly or in common with other persons) determines the purposes for which and the manner in which any personal data are, or are to be, processed;
"data processor" , in relation to personal data, means any person (other than an employee of the data controller) who processes the data on behalf of the data controller;
"data subject" means an individual who is the subject of personal data;
"personal data" means data which relate to a living individual who can be identified—
   (a) from those data, or
   (b) from those data and other information which is in the possession of, or is likely to come into the possession of, the data controller,
   and includes any expression of opinion about the individual and any indication of the intentions of the data controller or any other person in respect of the individual;
"processing", in relation to information or data, means obtaining, recording or holding the information or data or carrying out any operation or set of operations on the information or data, including—
   (a) organisation, adaptation or alteration of the information or data,
   (b) retrieval, consultation or use of the information or data,
   (c) disclosure of the information or data by transmission, dissemination or otherwise making available, or
   (d) alignment, combination, blocking, erasure or destruction of the information or data;

"relevant filing system" means any set of information relating to individuals to the extent that, although the information is not processed by means of equipment operating automatically in response to instructions given for that purpose, the set is structured, either by reference to individuals or by reference to criteria relating to individuals, in such a way that specific information relating to a particular individual is readily accessible.
   (2) In this Act, unless the context otherwise requires—
   (a) "obtaining" or "recording", in relation to personal data, includes obtaining or recording the information to be contained in the data, and
   (b) "using" or "disclosing", in relation to personal data, includes using or disclosing the information contained in the data.
   (3) In determining for the purposes of this Act whether any information is recorded with the intention—
   (a) that it should be processed by means of equipment operating automatically in response to instructions given for that purpose, or

    (b) that it should form part of a relevant filing system,

it is immaterial that it is intended to be so processed or to form part of such a system only after being transferred to a country or territory outside the European Economic Area.

(4) Where personal data are processed only for purposes for which they are required by or under any enactment to be processed, the person on whom the obligation to process the data is imposed by or under that enactment is for the purposes of this Act the data controller.

Sensitive personal data

2. In this Act "sensitive personal data" means personal data consisting of information as to— **13-002**

    (a) the racial or ethnic origin of the data subject,

    (b) his political opinions,

    (c) his religious beliefs or other beliefs of a similar nature,

    (d) whether he is a member of a trade union (within the meaning of the Trade Union and Labour Relations (Consolidation) Act 1992),

    (e) his physical or mental health or condition,

    (f) his sexual life,

    (g) the commission or alleged commission by him of any offence, or

    (h) any proceedings for any offence committed or alleged to have been committed by him, the disposal of such proceedings or the sentence of any court in such proceedings.

The special purposes

3. In this Act "the special purposes" means any one or more of the following— **13-003**

    (a) the purposes of journalism,

    (b) artistic purposes, and

    (c) literary purposes.

The data protection principles

4.—(1) References in this Act to the data protection principles are to the principles set out in Part I of Schedule 1. **13-004**

(2) Those principles are to be interpreted in accordance with Part II of Schedule 1.

(3) Schedule 2 (which applies to all personal data) and Schedule 3 (which applies only to sensitive personal data) set out conditions applying for the purposes of the first principle; and Schedule 4 sets out cases in which the eighth principle does not apply.

(4) Subject to section 27(1), it shall be the duty of a data controller to comply with the data protection principles in relation to all personal data with respect to which he is the data controller.

PART II

RIGHTS OF DATA SUBJECTS AND OTHERS

Right of access to personal data

13-005   7.—(1) Subject to the following provisions of this section and to [sections 8, 9 and 9A][1], an individual is entitled—

(a) to be informed by any data controller whether personal data of which that individual is the data subject are being processed by or on behalf of that data controller,

(b) if that is the case, to be given by the data controller a description of—
    (i) the personal data of which that individual is the data subject,
    (ii) the purposes for which they are being or are to be processed, and
    (iii) the recipients or classes of recipients to whom they are or may be disclosed,

(c) to have communicated to him in an intelligible form—
    (i) the information constituting any personal data of which that individual is the data subject, and
    (ii) any information available to the data controller as to the source of those data, and

(d) where the processing by automatic means of personal data of which that individual is the data subject for the purpose of evaluating matters relating to him such as, for example, his performance at work, his credit worthiness, his reliability or his conduct, has constituted or is likely to constitute the sole basis for any decision significantly affecting him, to be informed by the data controller of the logic involved in that decision-taking.

(2) A data controller is not obliged to supply any information under subsection (1) unless he has received—

(a) a request in writing, and

(b) except in prescribed cases, such fee (not exceeding the prescribed maximum) as he may require.

[(3) Where a data controller—

(a) reasonably requires further information in order to satisfy himself as to the identity of the person making a request under this section and to locate the information which that person seeks, and

(b) has informed him of that requirement,

the data controller is not obliged to comply with the request unless he is supplied with that further information.][2]

(4) Where a data controller cannot comply with the request without disclosing information relating to another individual who can be identified from that information, he is not obliged to comply with the request unless—

(a) the other individual has consented to the disclosure of the information to the person making the request, or

(b) it is reasonable in all the circumstances to comply with the request without the consent of the other individual.

(5) In subsection (4) the reference to information relating to another individual includes a reference to information identifying that individual as the source of the information sought by the request; and that subsection is not to be

---

[1] Words substituted by Freedom of Information Act 2000 c.36 Pt VII s 69
[2] Substituted by Freedom of Information Act 2000 c.36 Sch 6 para 1

construed as excusing a data controller from communicating so much of the information sought by the request as can be communicated without disclosing the identity of the other individual concerned, whether by the omission of names or other identifying particulars or otherwise.

(6) In determining for the purposes of subsection (4)(b) whether it is reasonable in all the circumstances to comply with the request without the consent of the other individual concerned, regard shall be had, in particular, to—

    (a) any duty of confidentiality owed to the other individual,

    (b) any steps taken by the data controller with a view to seeking the consent of the other individual,

    (c) whether the other individual is capable of giving consent, and

    (d) any express refusal of consent by the other individual.

(7) An individual making a request under this section may, in such cases as may be prescribed, specify that his request is limited to personal data of any prescribed description.

(8) Subject to subsection (4), a data controller shall comply with a request under this section promptly and in any event before the end of the prescribed period beginning with the relevant day.

(9) If a court is satisfied on the application of any person who has made a request under the foregoing provisions of this section that the data controller in question has failed to comply with the request in contravention of those provisions, the court may order him to comply with the request.

(10) In this section—

    "prescribed" means prescribed by the [Secretary of State][1] by regulations:

    "the prescribed maximum" means such amount as may be prescribed:

    "the prescribed period" means forty days or such other period as may be prescribed:

    "the relevant day", in relation to a request under this section, means the day on which the data controller receives the request or, if later, the first day on which the data controller has both the required fee and the information referred to in subsection (3).

(11) Different amounts or periods may be prescribed under this section in relation to different cases.

Provisions supplementary to section 7

8.—(1) The [Secretary of State][2] may by regulations provide that, in such cases as may be prescribed, a request for information under any provision of subsection (1) of section 7 is to be treated as extending also to information under other provisions of that subsection. **13-006**

(2) The obligation imposed by section 7(1)(c)(i) must be complied with by supplying the data subject with a copy of the information in permanent form unless—

    (a) the supply of such a copy is not possible or would involve disproportionate effort, or

    (b) the data subject agrees otherwise;

and where any of the information referred to in section 7(1)(c)(i) is expressed in terms which are not intelligible without explanation the copy must be accompanied by an explanation of those terms.

---

[1] Words substituted by SI 2003/1887 Sch 2 para 9
[2] Words substituted by SI 2003/1887 Sch 2 para 9

(3) Where a data controller has previously complied with a request made under section 7 by an individual, the data controller is not obliged to comply with a subsequent identical or similar request under that section by that individual unless a reasonable interval has elapsed between compliance with the previous request and the making of the current request.

(4) In determining for the purposes of subsection (3) whether requests under section 7 are made at reasonable intervals, regard shall be had to the nature of the data, the purposes for which the data are processed and the frequency with which the data are altered.

(5) Section 7(1)(d) is not to be regarded as requiring the provision of information as to the logic involved in any decision-taking if, and to the extent that, the information constitutes a trade secret.

(6) The information to be supplied pursuant to a request under section 7 must be supplied by reference to the data in question at the time when the request is received, except that it may take account of any amendment or deletion made between that time and the time when the information is supplied, being an amendment or deletion that would have been made regardless of the receipt of the request.

(7) For the purposes of section 7(4) and (5) another individual can be identified from the information being disclosed if he can be identified from that information, or from that and any other information which, in the reasonable belief of the data controller, is likely to be in, or to come into, the possession of the data subject making the request.

Application of section 7 where data controller is credit reference agency

13-007   **9.**—(1) Where the data controller is a credit reference agency, section 7 has effect subject to the provisions of this section.

(2) An individual making a request under section 7 may limit his request to personal data relevant to his financial standing, and shall be taken to have so limited his request unless the request shows a contrary intention.

(3) Where the data controller receives a request under section 7 in a case where personal data of which the individual making the request is the data subject are being processed by or on behalf of the data controller, the obligation to supply information under that section includes an obligation to give the individual making the request a statement, in such form as may be prescribed by the [Secretary of State][1] by regulations, of the individual's rights—

(a) under section 159 of the Consumer Credit Act 1974, and

(b) to the extent required by the prescribed form, under this Act.

[Unstructured personal data held by public authorities

13-008   **9A.**—(1) In this section "unstructured personal data" means any personal data falling within paragraph (e) of the definition of "data" in section 1(1), other than information which is recorded as part of, or with the intention that it should form part of, any set of information relating to individuals to the extent that the set is structured by reference to individuals or by reference to criteria relating to individuals.

(2) A public authority is not obliged to comply with subsection (1) of section 7 in relation to any unstructured personal data unless the request under that section contains a description of the data.

[1] Words substituted by SI 2003/1887 Sch 2 para 9 (1) (a)

(3) Even if the data are described by the data subject in his request, a public authority is not obliged to comply with subsection (1) of section 7 in relation to unstructured personal data if the authority estimates that the cost of complying with the request so far as relating to those data would exceed the appropriate limit.

(4) Subsection (3) does not exempt the public authority from its obligation to comply with paragraph (a) of section 7(1) in relation to the unstructured personal data unless the estimated cost of complying with that paragraph alone in relation to those data would exceed the appropriate limit.

(5) In subsections (3) and (4) "the appropriate limit" means such amount as may be prescribed by the [Secretary of State][1] by regulations, and different amounts may be prescribed in relation to different cases.

(6) Any estimate for the purposes of this section must be made in accordance with regulations under section 12(5) of the Freedom of Information Act 2000.][2]

Right to prevent processing likely to cause damage or distress

10.—(1) Subject to subsection (2), an individual is entitled at any time by **13-009** notice in writing to a data controller to require the data controller at the end of such period as is reasonable in the circumstances to cease, or not to begin, processing, or processing for a specified purpose or in a specified manner, any personal data in respect of which he is the data subject, on the ground that, for specified reasons—

    (a) the processing of those data or their processing for that purpose or in that manner is causing or is likely to cause substantial damage or substantial distress to him or to another, and

    (b) that damage or distress is or would be unwarranted.

(2) Subsection (1) does not apply—

    (a) in a case where any of the conditions in paragraphs 1 to 4 of Schedule 2 is met, or

    (b) in such other cases as may be prescribed by the [Secretary of State][3] by order.

(3) The data controller must within twenty-one days of receiving a notice under subsection (1) ("the data subject notice") give the individual who gave it a written notice—

    (a) stating that he has complied or intends to comply with the data subject notice, or

    (b) stating his reasons for regarding the data subject notice as to any extent unjustified and the extent (if any) to which he has complied or intends to comply with it.

(4) If a court is satisfied, on the application of any person who has given a notice under subsection (1) which appears to the court to be justified (or to be justified to any extent), that the data controller in question has failed to comply with the notice, the court may order him to take such steps for complying with the notice (or for complying with it to that extent) as the court thinks fit.

(5) The failure by a data subject to exercise the right conferred by subsection (1) or section 11(1) does not affect any other right conferred on him by this Part.

---

[1] Words substituted by SI 2003/1887 Sch 2 Para 12 (1) (b)
[2] Inserted by Freedom of Information Act 2000 c.36 Pt VII s 69
[3] Words substituted by SI 2003/1887 Sch 2 para 9

SCHEDULES

THE DATA PROTECTION PRINCIPLES

THE PRINCIPLES

13-010   1. Personal data shall be processed fairly and lawfully and, in particular, shall not be processed unless—

    (a) at least one of the conditions in Schedule 2 is met, and

    (b) in the case of sensitive personal data, at least one of the conditions in Schedule 3 is also met.

13-011   2. Personal data shall be obtained only for one or more specified and lawful purposes, and shall not be further processed in any manner incompatible with that purpose or those purposes.

13-012   3. Personal data shall be adequate, relevant and not excessive in relation to the purpose or purposes for which they are processed.

13-013   4. Personal data shall be accurate and, where necessary, kept up to date.

13-014   5. Personal data processed for any purpose or purposes shall not be kept for longer than is necessary for that purpose or those purposes.

13-015   6. Personal data shall be processed in accordance with the rights of data subjects under this Act.

13-016   7. Appropriate technical and organisational measures shall be taken against unauthorised or unlawful processing of personal data and against accidental loss or destruction of, or damage to, personal data.

13-017   8. Personal data shall not be transferred to a country or territory outside the European Economic Area unless that country or territory ensures an adequate level of protection for the rights and freedoms of data subjects in relation to the processing of personal data.

INTERPRETATION OF THE PRINCIPLES IN PART I

The first principle

13-018   1.— (1) In determining for the purposes of the first principle whether personal data are processed fairly, regard is to be had to the method by which they are obtained, including in particular whether any person from whom they are obtained is deceived or misled as to the purpose or purposes for which they are to be processed.

    (2) Subject to paragraph 2, for the purposes of the first principle data are to be treated as obtained fairly if they consist of information obtained from a person who—

    (a) is authorised by or under any enactment to supply it, or

    (b) is required to supply it by or under any enactment or by any convention or other instrument imposing an international obligation on the United Kingdom.

13-019   2.— (1) Subject to paragraph 3, for the purposes of the first principle personal data are not to be treated as processed fairly unless—

    (a) in the case of data obtained from the data subject, the data controller ensures so far as practicable that the data subject has, is provided with, or has made readily available to him, the information specified in sub-paragraph (3), and

    (b) in any other case, the data controller ensures so far as practicable that, before the relevant time or as soon as practicable after that time, the data subject has, is provided with, or has made readily available to him, the information specified in sub-paragraph (3).

    (2) In sub-paragraph (1)(b) "the relevant time" means—

    (a) the time when the data controller first processes the data, or

    (b) in a case where at that time disclosure to a third party within a reasonable period is envisaged—

        (i) if the data are in fact disclosed to such a person within that period, the time when the data are first disclosed,

(ii) if within that period the data controller becomes, or ought to become, aware that the data are unlikely to be disclosed to such a person within that period, the time when the data controller does become, or ought to become, so aware, or

(iii) in any other case, the end of that period.

(3) The information referred to in sub-paragraph (1) is as follows, namely—

(a) the identity of the data controller,

(b) if he has nominated a representative for the purposes of this Act, the identity of that representative,

(c) the purpose or purposes for which the data are intended to be processed, and

(d) any further information which is necessary, having regard to the specific circumstances in which the data are or are to be processed, to enable processing in respect of the data subject to be fair.

3.— (1) Paragraph 2(1)(b) does not apply where either of the primary conditions in sub-paragraph (2), together with such further conditions as may be prescribed by the [Secretary of State][1] by order, are met. **13-020**

(2) The primary conditions referred to in sub-paragraph (1) are—

(a) that the provision of that information would involve a disproportionate effort, or

(b) that the recording of the information to be contained in the data by, or the disclosure of the data by, the data controller is necessary for compliance with any legal obligation to which the data controller is subject, other than an obligation imposed by contract.

4.— (1) Personal data which contain a general identifier falling within a description prescribed by the [Secretary of State][2] by order are not to be treated as processed fairly and lawfully unless they are processed in compliance with any conditions so prescribed in relation to general identifiers of that description. **13-021**

(2) In sub-paragraph (1) "a general identifier" means any identifier (such as, for example, a number or code used for identification purposes) which—

(a) relates to an individual, and

(b) forms part of a set of similar identifiers which is of general application.

The second principle

5. The purpose or purposes for which personal data are obtained may in particular be specified— **13-022**

(a) in a notice given for the purposes of paragraph 2 by the data controller to the data subject, or

(b) in a notification given to the Commissioner under Part III of this Act.

6. In determining whether any disclosure of personal data is compatible with the purpose or purposes for which the data were obtained, regard is to be had to the purpose or purposes for which the personal data are intended to be processed by any person to whom they are disclosed. **13-023**

The fourth principle

7. The fourth principle is not to be regarded as being contravened by reason of any inaccuracy in personal data which accurately record information obtained by the data controller from the data subject or a third party in a case where— **13-024**

(a) having regard to the purpose or purposes for which the data were obtained and further processed, the data controller has taken reasonable steps to ensure the accuracy of the data, and

(b) if the data subject has notified the data controller of the data subject's view that the data are inaccurate, the data indicate that fact.

The sixth principle

8. A person is to be regarded as contravening the sixth principle if, but only if— **13-025**

(a) he contravenes section 7 by failing to supply information in accordance with that section,

(b) he contravenes section 10 by failing to comply with a notice given under subsection (1) of that section to the extent that the notice is justified or by failing to give a notice under subsection (3) of that section,

(c) he contravenes section 11 by failing to comply with a notice given under subsection (1) of that section, [...][3]

---

[1] Words substituted by SI 2003/1887 Sch 2 para 9

[2] Words substituted by SI 2003/1887 Sch 2 para 9

[3] Word repealed by Data Protection Act 1998 c.29 Sch 13 para 5

(d) he contravenes section 12 by failing to comply with a notice given under subsection (1) or (2)(b) of that section or by failing to give a notification under subsection (2)(a) of that section or a notice under subsection (3) of that section, [or

(e) he contravenes section 12A by failing to comply with a notice given under subsection (1) of that section to the extent that the notice is justified.]¹

The seventh principle

13-026   **9.** Having regard to the state of technological development and the cost of implementing any measures, the measures must ensure a level of security appropriate to—

(a) the harm that might result from such unauthorised or unlawful processing or accidental loss, destruction or damage as are mentioned in the seventh principle, and

(b) the nature of the data to be protected.

13-027   **10.** The data controller must take reasonable steps to ensure the reliability of any employees of his who have access to the personal data.

13-028   **11.** Where processing of personal data is carried out by a data processor on behalf of a data controller, the data controller must in order to comply with the seventh principle—

(a) choose a data processor providing sufficient guarantees in respect of the technical and organisational security measures governing the processing to be carried out, and

(b) take reasonable steps to ensure compliance with those measures.

13-029   **12.** Where processing of personal data is carried out by a data processor on behalf of a data controller; the data controller is not to be regarded as complying with the seventh principle unless—

(a) the processing is carried out under a contract—

(i) which is made or evidenced in writing, and

(ii) under which the data processor is to act only on instructions from the data controller, and

(b) the contract requires the data processor to comply with obligations equivalent to those imposed on a data controller by the seventh principle.

The eighth principle

13-030   **13.** An adequate level of protection is one which is adequate in all the circumstances of the case, having regard in particular to—

(a) the nature of the personal data,

(b) the country or territory of origin of the information contained in the data,

(c) the country or territory of final destination of that information,

(d) the purposes for which and period during which the data are intended to be processed,

(e) the law in force in the country or territory in question,

(f) the international obligations of that country or territory,

(g) any relevant codes of conduct or other rules which are enforceable in that country or territory (whether generally or by arrangement in particular cases), and

(h) any security measures taken in respect of the data in that country or territory.

13-031   **14.** The eighth principle does not apply to a transfer falling within any paragraph of Schedule 4, except in such circumstances and to such extent as the [Secretary of State]² may by order provide.

13-032   **15.**— (1) Where—

(a) in any proceedings under this Act any question arises as to whether the requirement of the eighth principle as to an adequate level of protection is met in relation to the transfer of any personal data to a country or territory outside the European Economic Area, and

(b) a Community finding has been made in relation to transfers of the kind in question,

that question is to be determined in accordance with that finding.

(2) In sub-paragraph (1) "Community finding" means a finding of the European Commission, under the procedure provided for in Article 31(2) of the Data Protection Directive, that a country or territory outside the European Economic Area does, or does not, ensure an adequate level of protection within the meaning of Article 25(2) of the Directive.

---

¹ Paragraph (e) and the word 'or' immediatley preceeding it inserted by Data Protection Act 1998 c.29 Sch 13 para 5

² Words substituted by SI 2003/1887 Sch 2 para 9

CONDITIONS RELEVANT FOR PURPOSES OF THE FIRST PRINCIPLE: PROCESSING
OF ANY PERSONAL DATA

1. The data subject has given his consent to the processing.   **13-033**

2. The processing is necessary—   **13-034**
   - (a) for the performance of a contract to which the data subject is a party, or
   - (b) for the taking of steps at the request of the data subject with a view to entering into a contract.

3. The processing is necessary for compliance with any legal obligation to which the data **13-035** controller is subject, other than an obligation imposed by contract.

4. The processing is necessary in order to protect the vital interests of the data subject.   **13-036**

5. The processing is necessary—   **13-037**
   - (a) for the administration of justice,
   - (b) for the exercise of any functions conferred on any person by or under any enactment,
   - (c) for the exercise of any functions of the Crown, a Minister of the Crown or a government department, or
   - (d) for the exercise of any other functions of a public nature exercised in the public interest by any person.

6.— (1) The processing is necessary for the purposes of legitimate interests pursued by the data **13-038** controller or by the third party or parties to whom the data are disclosed, except where the processing is unwarranted in any particular case by reason of prejudice to the rights and freedoms or legitimate interests of the data subject.
   (2) The [Secretary of State][1] may by order specify particular circumstances in which this condition is, or is not, to be taken to be satisfied.

CONDITIONS RELEVANT FOR PURPOSES OF THE FIRST PRINCIPLE: PROCESSING
OF SENSITIVE PERSONAL DATA

1. The data subject has given his explicit consent to the processing of the personal data.   **13-039**

2.— (1) The processing is necessary for the purposes of exercising or performing any right or **13-040** obligation which is conferred or imposed by law on the data controller in connection with employment.
   (2) The [Secretary of State][2] may by order—
   - (a) exclude the application of sub-paragraph (1) in such cases as may be specified, or
   - (b) provide that, in such cases as may be specified, the condition in sub-paragraph (1) is not to be regarded as satisfied unless such further conditions as may be specified in the order are also satisfied.

3. The processing is necessary—   **13-041**
   - (a) in order to protect the vital interests of the data subject or another person, in a case where—
     - (i) consent cannot be given by or on behalf of the data subject, or
     - (ii) the data controller cannot reasonably be expected to obtain the consent of the data subject, or
   - (b) in order to protect the vital interests of another person, in a case where consent by or on behalf of the data subject has been unreasonably withheld.

4. The processing—   **13-042**
   - (a) is carried out in the course of its legitimate activities by any body or association which—
     - (i) is not established or conducted for profit, and
     - (ii) exists for political, philosophical, religious or trade-union purposes,
   - (b) is carried out with appropriate safeguards for the rights and freedoms of data subjects,

---

[1] Words substituted by SI 2003/1887 Sch 2 para 9
[2] Words substituted by SI 2003/1887 Sch 2 para 9

(c) relates only to individuals who either are members of the body or association or have regular contact with it in connection with its purposes, and

(d) does not involve disclosure of the personal data to a third party without the consent of the data subject.

13-043 **5.** The information contained in the personal data has been made public as a result of steps deliberately taken by the data subject.

13-044 **6.** The processing—

(a) is necessary for the purpose of, or in connection with, any legal proceedings (including prospective legal proceedings),

(b) is necessary for the purpose of obtaining legal advice, or

(c) is otherwise necessary for the purposes of establishing, exercising or defending legal rights.

13-045 **7.**— (1) The processing is necessary—

(a) for the administration of justice,

(b) for the exercise of any functions conferred on any person by or under an enactment, or

(c) for the exercise of any functions of the Crown, a Minister of the Crown or a government department.

(2) The [Secretary of State][1] may by order—

(a) exclude the application of sub-paragraph (1) in such cases as may be specified, or

(b) provide that, in such cases as may be specified, the condition in sub-paragraph (1) is not to be regarded as satisfied unless such further conditions as may be specified in the order are also satisfied.

13-046 **8.**— (1) The processing is necessary for medical purposes and is undertaken by—

(a) a health professional, or

(b) a person who in the circumstances owes a duty of confidentiality which is equivalent to that which would arise if that person were a health professional.

(2) In this paragraph "medical purposes" includes the purposes of preventative medicine, medical diagnosis, medical research, the provision of care and treatment and the management of health care services.

13-047 **9.**— (1) The processing—

(a) is of sensitive personal data consisting of information as to racial or ethnic origin,

(b) is necessary for the purpose of identifying or keeping under review the existence or absence of equality of opportunity or treatment between persons of different racial or ethnic origins, with a view to enabling such equality to be promoted or maintained, and

(c) is carried out with appropriate safeguards for the rights and freedoms of data subjects.

(2) The [Secretary of State][2] may by order specify circumstances in which processing falling within sub-paragraph (1)(a) and (b) is, or is not, to be taken for the purposes of sub-paragraph (1)(c) to be carried out with appropriate safeguards for the rights and freedoms of data subjects.

10. The personal data are processed in circumstances specified in an order made by the [Secretary of State][3] for the purposes of this paragraph.

---

[1] Words substituted by SI 2003/1887 Sch 2 para 9
[2] Words substituted by SI 2003/1887 Sch 2 para 9
[3] Words substituted by SI 2003/1887 Sch 2 para 9

National Minimum Wage Act 1998

CHAPTER 39

Entitlement to the national minimum wage

Workers to be paid at least the national minimum wage

1.—(1) A person who qualifies for the national minimum wage shall be **14-001**
remunerated by his employer in respect of his work in any pay reference period at
a rate which is not less than the national minimum wage.

(2) A person qualifies for the national minimum wage if he is an individual
who—

    (a) is a worker;

    (b) is working, or ordinarily works, in the United Kingdom under his
contract; and

    (c) has ceased to be of compulsory school age.

(3) The national minimum wage shall be such single hourly rate as the
Secretary of State may from time to time prescribe.

(4) For the purposes of this Act a "pay reference period" is such period as
the Secretary of State may prescribe for the purpose.

(5) Subsections (1) to (4) above are subject to the following provisions of this
Act.

Records

Duty of employers to keep records

9. For the purposes of this Act, the Secretary of State may by regulations **14-002**
make provision requiring employers—

    (a) to keep, in such form and manner as may be prescribed, such records
as may be prescribed; and

    (b) to preserve those records for such period as may be prescribed.

Worker's right of access to records

10.—(1) A worker may, in accordance with the following provisions of this **14-003**
section,—

    (a) require his employer to produce any relevant records; and

    (b) inspect and examine those records and copy any part of them.

(2) The rights conferred by subsection (1) above are exercisable only if the
worker believes on reasonable grounds that he is or may be being, or has or may
have been, remunerated for any pay reference period by his employer at a rate
which is less than the national minimum wage.

(3) The rights conferred by subsection (1) above are exercisable only for the
purpose of establishing whether or not the worker is being, or has been, remunerated for any pay reference period by his employer at a rate which is less than the
national minimum wage.

(4) The rights conferred by subsection (1) above are exercisable—

    (a) by the worker alone; or

    (b) by the worker accompanied by such other person as the worker may
think fit.

(5) The rights conferred by subsection (1) above are exercisable only if the worker gives notice (a "production notice") to his employer requesting the production of any relevant records relating to such period as may be described in the notice.

(6) If the worker intends to exercise the right conferred by subsection (4)(b) above, the production notice must contain a statement of that intention.

(7) Where a production notice is given, the employer shall give the worker reasonable notice of the place and time at which the relevant records will be produced.

(8) The place at which the relevant records are produced must be—
   (a) the worker's place of work; or
   (b) any other place at which it is reasonable, in all the circumstances, for the worker to attend to inspect the relevant records; or
   (c) such other place as may be agreed between the worker and the employer.

(9) The relevant records must be produced—
   (a) before the end of the period of fourteen days following the date or receipt of the production notice; or
   (b) at such later time as may be agreed during that period between the worker and the employer.

(10) In this section—
   "records" means records which the worker's employer is required to keep and, at the time of receipt of the production notice, preserve in accordance with section 9 above;
   "relevant records" means such parts of, or such extracts from, any records as are relevant to establishing whether or not the worker has, for any pay reference period to which the records relate, been remunerated by the employer at a rate which is at least equal to the national minimum wage.

Failure of employer to allow access to records

14-004   **11.**—(1) A complaint may be presented to an employment tribunal by a worker on the ground that the employer—
   (a) failed to produce some or all of the relevant records in accordance with subsections (8) and (9) of section 10 above; or
   (b) failed to allow the worker to exercise some or all of the rights conferred by subsection (1)(b) or (4)(b) of that section.

(2) Where an employment tribunal finds a complaint under this section well-founded, the tribunal shall—
   (a) make a declaration to that effect; and
   (b) make an award that the employer pay to the worker a sum equal to 80 times the hourly amount of the national minimum wage (as in force when the award is made).

(3) An employment tribunal shall not consider a complaint under this section unless it is presented to the tribunal before the expiry of the period of three months following—
   (a) the end of the period of fourteen days mentioned in paragraph (a) of subsection (9) of section 10 above; or
   (b) in a case where a later day was agreed under paragraph (b) of that subsection, that later day.

(4) Where the employment tribunal is satisfied that it was not reasonably practicable for a complaint under this section to be presented before the expiry of

the period of three months mentioned in subsection (3) above, the tribunal may consider the complaint if it is presented within such further period as the tribunal considers reasonable.

(5) Expressions used in this section and in section 10 above have the same meaning in this section as they have in that section.

Employer to provide worker with national minimum wage statement

12.—(1) Regulations may make provision for the purpose of conferring on a **14-005** worker the right to be given by his employer, at or before the time at which any payment of remuneration is made to the worker, a written statement.

(2) The regulations may make provision with respect to the contents of any such statement and may, in particular, require it to contain—

(a) prescribed information relating to this Act or any regulations under it; or

(b) prescribed information for the purpose of assisting the worker to determine whether he has been remunerated at a rate at least equal to the national minimum wage during the period to which the payment of remuneration relates.

(3) Any statement required to be given under this section to a worker by his employer may, if the worker is an employee, be included in the written itemised pay statement required to be given to him by his employer under section 8 of the Employment Rights Act 1996 or Article 40 of the Employment Rights (Northern Ireland) Order 1996, as the case may be.

(4) The regulations may make provision for the purpose of applying—

(a) sections 11 and 12 of the Employment Rights Act 1996 (references to employment tribunals and determination of references), or

(b) in relation to Northern Ireland, Articles 43 and 44of the Employment Rights (Northern Ireland) Order 1996 (references to industrial tribunals and determination of references),

in relation to a worker and any such statement as is mentioned in subsection (1) above as they apply in relation to an employee and a statement required to be given to him by his employer under section 8 of that Act or Article 40 of that Order, as the case may be.

Enforcement

Non-compliance: worker entitled to additional remuneration

17.—(1) If a worker who qualifies for the national minimum wage is remuner- **14-006** ated for any pay reference period by his employer at a rate which is less than the national minimum wage, the worker shall be taken to be entitled under this contract to be paid, as additional remuneration in respect of that period, the amount described in subsection (2) below.

[(2) That amount is the difference between–

(a) the remuneration received by the worker as a worker employed in agriculture for the pay reference period from his employer; and

(b) the amount which he would have received as a worker employed in agriculture for that period had he been remunerated by the employer at the minimum rate applicable under this Act][1]

---

[1] Para 17 (2) substituted for paras 17 (2) and (3) by Agricultural Wages Act 1948 (11&12Geo6) c.47 s 3A

Rights not to suffer unfair dismissal or other detriment

The right not to suffer detriment

14-007   **23.**—(1) A worker has the right not to be subjected to any detriment by any act, or any deliberate failure to act, by his employer, done on the ground that—

    (a) any action was taken, or was proposed to be taken, by or on behalf of the worker with a view to enforcing, or otherwise securing the benefit of, a right of the worker's to which this section applies; or

    (b) the employer was prosecuted for an offence under section 31 below as a result of action taken by or on behalf of the worker for the purpose of enforcing, or otherwise securing the benefit of, a right of the worker's to which this section applies; or

    (c) the worker qualifies, or will or might qualify, for the national minimum wage or for a particular rate of national minimum wage.

    (2) It is immaterial for the purposes of paragraph (a) or (b) of subsection (1) above—

    (a) whether or not the worker has the right, or

    (b) whether or not the right has been infringed,

but, for that subsection to apply, the claim to the right and, if applicable, the claim that it has been infringed must be made in good faith.

    (3) The following are the rights to which this section applies—

    (a) any right conferred by, or by virtue of, any provision of this Act for which the remedy for its infringement is by way of a complaint to an employment tribunal; and

    (b) any right conferred by section 17 above.

    [(4) This section does not apply where the detriment in question amounts to dismissal within the meaning of—

    (a) Part X of the Employment Rights Act 1996 (unfair dismissal), or

    (b) Part XI of the Employment Rights (Northern Ireland) Order 1996 (corresponding provision for Northern Ireland),

except where in relation to Northern Ireland the person in question is dismissed in circumstances in which, by virtue of Article 240 of that Order (fixed term contracts), Part XI does not apply to the dismissal.][1]

Enforcement of the right

14-008   **24.**—(1) A worker may present a complaint to an employment tribunal that he has been subjected to a detriment in contravention of section 23 above.

    (2) Subject to the following provisions of this section, the provisions of—

    (a) sections 48(2) to (4) and 49 of the Employment Rights Act 1996 (complaints to employment tribunals and remedies), or

    (b) in relation to Northern Ireland, Articles 71(2) to (4) and 72 of the Employment Rights (Northern Ireland) Order 1996 (complaints to industrial tribunals and remedies),

shall apply in relation to a complaint under this section as they apply in relation to a complaint under section 48 of that Act or Article 71 of that Order (as the case may be), but taking references in those provisions to the employer as references to the employer within the meaning of section 23(1) above.

    (3) Where—

    (a) the detriment to which the worker is subjected is the termination of his worker's contract, but

---
[1] Substituted by Employment Relations Act 1999 c.26 s 18 (4)

    (b) that contract is not a contract of employment,

any compensation awarded under section 49 of the Employment Rights Act 1996 or Article 72 of the Employment Rights (Northern Ireland) Order 1996 by virtue of subsection (2) above must not exceed the limit specified in subsection (4) below.

    (4) The limit mentioned in subsection (3) above is the total of—

    (a) the sum which would be the basic award for unfair dismissal, calculated in accordance with section 119 of the Employment Rights Act 1996 or Article 153 of the Employment Rights (Northern Ireland) Order 1996 (as the case may be), if the worker had been an employee and the contract terminated had been a contract of employment; and

    (b) the sum for the time being specified in section 124(1) of that Act or Article 158(1) of that Order (as the case may be) which is the limit for a compensatory award to a person calculated in accordance with section 123 of that Act or Article 157 of that Order (as the case may be).

    (5) Where the worker has been working under arrangements which do not fall to be regarded as a worker's contract for the purposes of—

    (a) the Employment Rights Act 1996, or

    (b) in relation to Northern Ireland, the Employment Rights (Northern Ireland) Order 1996,

he shall be treated for the purposes of subsections (3) and (4) above as if any arrangements under which he has been working constituted a worker's contract falling within section 230(3)(b) of that Act or Article 3(3)(b) of that Order (as the case may be).

Civil procedure, evidence and appeals

Reversal of burden of proof

    28.—(1) Where in any civil proceedings any question arises as to whether an individual qualifies or qualified at any time for the national minimum wage, it shall be presumed that the individual qualifies or, as the case may be, qualified at that time for the national minimum wage unless the contrary is established. **14-009**

Special classes of person

Agency workers who are not otherwise "workers"

    34.—(1) This section applies in any case where an individual ("the agency workers")— **14-010**

    (a) is supplied by a person ("the agent") to do work for another ("the principal") under a contract or other arrangements made between the agent and the principal; but

    (b) is not, as respects that work, a worker, because of the absence of a worker's contract between the individual and the agent or the principal; and

    (c) is not a party to a contract under which he undertakes to do the work for another party to the contract whose status is, by virtue of the contract, that of a client or customer of any profession or business undertaking carried on by the individual.

    (2) In a case where this section applies, the other provisions of this Act shall have effect as if there were a worker's contract for the doing of the work by the agency worker made between the agency worker and—

(a) whichever of the agent and the principal is responsible for paying the agency worker in respect of the work; or

(b) if neither the agent nor the principal is so responsible, whichever of them pays the agency worker in respect of the work.

Home workers who are not otherwise "workers"

14-011   **35.**—(1) In determining for the purposes of this Act whether a home worker is or is not a worker, section 54(3)(b) below shall have effect as if for the word "personally" there were substituted "(whether personally or otherwise)".

(2) In this section "home worker" means an individual who contracts with a person, for the purposes of that person's business, for the execution of work to be done in a place not under the control or management of that person.

Miscellaneous

Application of Act to superior employers

14-012   **48.** Where—

(a) the immediate employer of a worker is himself in the employment of some other person, and

(b) the worker is employed on the premises of that other person,

that other person shall be deemed for the purposes of this Act to be the employer of the worker jointly with the immediate employer.

Restrictions on contracting out

14-013   **49.**—(1) Any provision in any agreement (whether a worker's contract or not) is void in so far as it purports—

(a) to exclude or limit the operation of any provision of this Act; or

(b) to preclude a person from bringing proceedings under this Act before an employment tribunal.

(2) Subsection (1) above does not apply to any agreement to refrain from instituting or continuing proceedings where a conciliation officer has taken action under—

(a) section 18 of the Employment Tribunals Act 1996 (conciliation), or

(b) in relation to Northern Ireland, Article 20 of the Industrial Tribunals (Northern Ireland) Order 1996.

(3) Subsection (1) above does not apply to any agreement to refrain from instituting or continuing before an employment tribunal any proceedings within—

(a) section 18(1)(dd) of the Employment Tribunals Act 1996 (proceedings under or by virtue of this Act where conciliation is available), or

(b) in relation to Northern Ireland, Article 20(1)(cc) of the Industrial Tribunals (Northern Ireland) Order 1996,

if the conditions regulating compromise agreements under this Act are satisfied in relation to the agreement.

(4) For the purposes of subsection (3) above the conditions regulating compromise agreements under this Act are that—

(a) the agreement must be in writing,

(b) the agreement must relate to the particular proceedings,

(c) the employee or worker must have received advice from a relevant independent adviser as to the terms and effect of the proposed agreement and, in particular, its effect on his ability to pursue his rights before an employment tribunal,

    (d) there must be in force, when the adviser gives the advice, a contract of insurance, or an indemnity provided for members of a profession or a professional body, covering the risk of a claim by the employee or worker in respect of loss arising in consequence of the advice,

    (e) the agreement must identify the adviser, and

    (f) the agreement must state that the conditions regulating compromise agreements under this Act are satisfied.

(5) A person is a relevant independent adviser for the purposes of subsection (4)(c) above—

    (a) if he is a qualified lawyer,

    (b) if he is an officer, official, employee or member of an independent trade union who has been certified in writing by the trade union as competent to give advice and as authorised to do so on behalf of the trade union,

    (c) if he works at an advice centre (whether as an employee or a volunteer) and has been certified in writing by the centre as competent to give advice and as authorised to do so on behalf of the centre, or

    (d) if he is a person of a description specified in an order made by the Secretary of State.

(6) But a person is not a relevant independent adviser for the purposes of subsection (4)(c) above in relation to the employee or worker—

    (a) if he is employed by, or is acting in the matter for, the employer or an associated employer,

    (b) in the case of a person within subsection (5)(b) or (c) above, if the trade union or advice centre is the employer or an associated employer,

    (c) in the case of a person within subsection (5)(c) above, if the employee or worker makes a payment for the advice received from him, or

    (d) in the case of a person of a description specified in an order under subsection (5)(d) above, if any condition specified in the order in relation to the giving of advice by persons of that description is not satisfied.

(7) In this section "qualified lawyer" means —

    (a) as respects England and Wales—

        (i) a barrister (whether in practice as such or employed to give legal advice);

        (ii) a solicitor who holds a practising certificate; or

        (iii) a person other than a barrister or solicitor who is an authorised advocate or authorised litigator (within the meaning of the Courts and Legal Services Act 1990);

    (b) as respects Scotland—

        (i) an advocate (whether in practice as such or employed to give legal advice); or

        (ii) a solicitor who holds a practising certificate; and

    (c) as respects Northern Ireland—

        (i) a barrister (whether in practice as such or employed to give legal advice); or

        (ii) a solicitor who holds a practising certificate.

(8) For the purposes of this section any two employers shall be treated as associated if—

    (a) one is a company of which the other (directly or indirectly) has control; or

(b) both are companies of which a third person (directly or indirectly) has control;

and "associated employer" shall be construed accordingly.

(9) In the application of this section in relation to Northern Ireland—

(a) subsection (4)(c) above shall have effect as if for "advice from a relevant independent adviser" there were substituted "independent legal advice from a qualified lawyer"; and

(b) subsection (4)(d) above shall have effect as if for "contract of insurance, or an indemnity provided for members of a profession or a professional body," there were substituted "policy of insurance".

(10) In subsection (4) above, as it has effect by virtue of subsection (9) above, "independent", in relation to legal advice received by an employee or worker, means that the advice is given by a lawyer who is not acting in the matter for the employer or an associated employer.

(11) The Secretary of State may by order repeal subsections (9) and (10) above and this subsection.

Supplementary

Meaning of "worker", "employee" etc

14-014   **54.**—(1) In this Act "employee" means an individual who has entered into or works under (or, where the employment has ceased, worked under) a contract of employment.

(2) In this Act "contract of employment" means a contract of service or apprenticeship, whether express or implied, and (if it is express) whether oral or in writing.

(3) In this Act "worker" (except in the phrases "agency worker" and "home worker") means an individual who has entered into or works under (or, where the employment has ceased, worked under)—

(a) a contract of employment; or

(b) any other contract, whether express or implied and (if it is express) whether oral or in writing, whereby the individual undertakes to do or perform personally any work or services for another party to the contract whose status is not by virtue of the contract that of a client or customer of any profession or business undertaking carried on by the individual;

and any reference to a worker's contract shall be construed accordingly.

(4) In this Act "employer", in relation to an employee or a worker, means the person by whom the employee or worker is (or, where the employment has ceased, was) employed.

(5) In this Act "employment" —

(a) in relation to an employee, means employment under a contract of employment; and

(b) in relation to a worker, means employment under his contract;

and "employed" shall be construed accordingly.

Human Rights Act 1998

CHAPTER 42

Introduction

The Convention Rights

1.—(1) In this Act "the Convention rights" means the rights and fundamental **15-001** freedoms set out in—
  (a) Articles 2 to 12 and 14 of the Convention,
  (b) Articles 1 to 3 of the First Protocol, and
  (c) Articles 1 and 2 of the Sixth Protocol,
as read with Articles 16 to 18 of the Convention.

(2) Those Articles are to have effect for the purposes of this Act subject to any designated derogation or reservation (as to which see sections 14 and 15).

(3) The Articles are set out in Schedule 1.

(4) The [Secretary of State][1] may by order make such amendments to this Act as he considers appropriate to reflect the effect, in relation to the United Kingdom, of a protocol.

(5) In subsection (4) "protocol" means a protocol to the Convention—
  (a) which the United Kingdom has ratified; or
  (b) which the United Kingdom has signed with a view to ratification.

(6) No amendment may be made by an order under subsection (4) so as to come into force before the protocol concerned is in force in relation to the United Kingdom.

Interpretation of Convention rights

2.—(1) A court or tribunal determining a question which has arisen in **15-002** connection with a Convention right must take into account any—
  (a) judgment, decision, declaration or advisory opinion of the European Court of Human Rights,
  (b) opinion of the Commission given in a report adopted under Article 31 of the Convention,
  (c) decision of the Commission in connection with Article 26 or 27(2) of the Convention, or
  (d) decision of the Committee of Ministers taken under Article 46 of the Convention,
whenever made or given, so far as, in the opinion of the court or tribunal, it is relevant to the proceedings in which that question has arisen.

(2) Evidence of any judgment, decision, declaration or opinion of which account may have to be taken under this section is to be given in proceedings before any court or tribunal in such manner as may be provided by rules.

(3) In this section "rules" means rules of court or, in the case of proceedings before a tribunal, rules made for the purposes of this section—
  (a) by [...][2] the Secretary of State, in relation to any proceedings outside Scotland;
  (b) by the Secretary of State, in relation to proceedings in Scotland; or

---

[1] Words substituted by SI 2003/1887 Sch 2 para 10
[2] Words repealed by SI 2003/1887 Sch 2 para 10

    (c) by a Northern Ireland department, in relation to proceedings before a tribunal in Northern Ireland—
        (i) which deals with transferred matters; and
        (ii) for which no rules made under paragraph (a) are in force.

Legislation

Interpretation of legislation

15-003   **3.**—(1) So far as it is possible to do so, primary legislation and subordinate legislation must be read and given effect in a way which is compatible with the Convention rights.

    (2) This section—
    (a) applies to primary legislation and subordinate legislation whenever enacted;
    (b) does not affect the validity, continuing operation or enforcement of any incompatible primary legislation; and
    (c) does not affect the validity, continuing operation or enforcement of any incompatible subordinate legislation if (disregarding any possibility of revocation) primary legislation prevents removal of the incompatibility.

Declaration of incompatibility

15-004   **4.**—(1) Subsection (2) applies in any proceedings in which a court determines whether a provision of primary legislation is compatible with a Convention right.

    (2) If the court is satisfied that the provision is incompatible with a Convention right, it may make a declaration of that incompatibility.

    (3) Subsection (4) applies in any proceedings in which a court determines whether a provision of subordinate legislation, made in the exercise of a power conferred by primary legislation, is compatible with a Convention right.

    (4) If the court is satisfied—
    (a) that the provision is incompatible with a Convention right, and
    (b) that (disregarding any possibility of revocation) the primary legislation concerned prevents removal of the incompatibility,
it may make a declaration of that incompatibility.

    (5) In this section "court" means —
    (a) the House of Lords;
    (b) the Judicial Committee of the Privy Council;
    (c) the Courts-Martial Appeal Court;
    (d) in Scotland, the High Court of Justiciary sitting otherwise than as a trial court or the Court of Session;
    (e) in England and Wales or Northern Ireland, the High Court or the Court of Appeal.

    (6) A declaration under this section ("a declaration of incompatibility")—
    (a) does not affect the validity, continuing operation or enforcement of the provision in respect of which it is given; and
    (b) is not binding on the parties to the proceedings in which it is made.

Public authorities

Acts of public authorities

6.—(1) It is unlawful for a public authority to act in a way which is incompati- **15-005**
ble with a Convention right.

(2) Subsection (1) does not apply to an act if—
  (a) as the result of one or more provisions of primary legislation, the
      authority could not have acted differently; or
  (b) in the case of one or more provisions of, or made under, primary legisla-
      tion which cannot be read or given effect in a way which is compatible
      with the Convention rights, the authority was acting so as to give effect
      to or enforce those provisions.

(3) In this section "public authority" includes—
  (a) a court or tribunal, and
  (b) any person certain of whose functions are functions of a public nature,
but does not include either House of Parliament or a person exercising
functions in connection with proceedings in Parliament.

(4) In subsection (3) "Parliament" does not include the House of Lords in its
judicial capacity.

(5) In relation to a particular act, a person is not a public authority by virtue
only of subsection (3)(b) if the nature of the act is private.

(6) "An act" includes a failure to act but does not include a failure to—
  (a) introduce in, or lay before, Parliament a proposal for legislation; or
  (b) make any primary legislation or remedial order.

SCHEDULES

Section 1(3)　　　　　　　　　Schedule 1

THE ARTICLES

THE CONVENTION

RIGHTS AND FREEDOMS

Right to life

Article 2—1. Everyone's right to life shall be protected by law. No one shall be deprived of his life **15-006**
intentionally save in the execution of a sentence of a court following his conviction of a crime for which
this penalty is provided by law.

2. Deprivation of life shall not be regarded as inflicted in contravention of this Article when it
results from the use of force which is no more than absolutely necessary:
  (a) in defence of any person from unlawful violence;
  (b) in order to effect a lawful arrest or to prevent the escape of a person lawfully detained;
  (c) in action lawfully taken for the purpose of quelling a riot or insurrection.

Prohibition of torture

Article 3 No one shall be subjected to torture or to inhuman or degrading treatment or **15-007**
punishment.

Prohibition of slavery and forced labour

15-008   **Article 4**—1. No one shall be held in slavery or servitude.

2. No one shall be required to perform forced or compulsory labour.

3. For the purpose of this Article the term "forced or compulsory labour" shall not include:

  (a) any work required to be done in the ordinary course of detention imposed according to the provisions of Article 5 of this Convention or during conditional release from such detention;

  (b) any service of a military character or, in case of conscientious objectors in countries where they are recognised, service exacted instead of compulsory military service;

  (c) any service exacted in case of an emergency or calamity threatening the life or well-being of the community;

  (d) any work or service which forms part of normal civic obligations.

Right to liberty and security

15-009   **Article 5**—1. Everyone has the right to liberty and security of a person. No one shall be deprived of his liberty save in the following cases and in accordance with a procedure prescribed by law:

  (a) the lawful detention of a person after conviction by a competent court;

  (b) the lawful arrest or detention of a person for non-compliance with the lawful order of a court or in order to secure the fulfilment of any obligation prescribed by law;

  (c) the lawful arrest or detention of a person effected for the purpose of bringing him before the competent legal authority on reasonable suspicion of having committed an offence or when it is reasonably considered necessary to prevent his committing an offence or fleeing after having done so;

  (d) the detention of a minor by lawful order for the purpose of educational supervision or his lawful detention for the purpose of bringing him before the competent legal authority;

  (e) the lawful detention of persons for the prevention of the spreading of infectious diseases, of persons of unsound mind, alcoholics or drug addicts or vagrants;

  (f) the lawful arrest or detention of a person to prevent his effecting an unauthorised entry into the country or of a person against whom action is being taken with a view to deportation or extradition.

2. Everyone who is arrested shall be informed promptly, in a language which he understands, of the reasons for his arrest and of any charge against him.

3. Everyone arrested or detained in accordance with the provisions of paragraph 1(c) of this Article shall be brought promptly before a judge or other officer authorised by law to exercise judicial power and shall be entitled to trial within a reasonable time or to release pending trial. Release may be conditioned by guarantees to appear for trial.

4. Everyone who is deprived of his liberty by arrest or detention shall be entitled to take proceedings by which the lawfulness of his detention shall be decided speedily by a court and his release ordered if the detention is not lawful.

5. Everyone who has been the victim of arrest or detention in contravention of the provisions of this Article shall have an enforceable right to compensation.

Right to a fair trial

15-010   **Article 6**—1. In the determination of his civil rights and obligations or of any criminal charge against him, everyone is entitled to a fair and public hearing within a reasonable time by an independent and impartial tribunal established by law. Judgment shall be pronounced publicly but the press and public may be excluded from all or part of the trial in the interest of morals, public order or national security in a democratic society, where the interests of juveniles or the protection of the private life of the parties so require, or to the extent strictly necessary in the opinion of the court in special circumstances where publicity would prejudice the interests of justice.

2. Everyone charged with a criminal offence shall be presumed innocent until proved guilty according to law.

3. Everyone charged with a criminal offence has the following minimum rights:

  (a) to be informed promptly, in a language which he understands and in detail, of the nature and cause of the accusation against him;

  (b) to have adequate time and facilities for the preparation of his defence;

  (c) to defend himself in person or through legal assistance of his own choosing or, if he has not sufficient means to pay for legal assistance, to be given it free when the interests of justice so require;

(d) to examine or have examined witnesses against him and to obtain the attendance and examination of witnesses on his behalf under the same conditions as witnesses against him;

(e) to have the free assistance of an interpreter if he cannot understand or speak the language used in court.

No punishment without law

Article 7—1. No one shall be held guilty of any criminal offence on account of any act or **15-011** omission which did not constitute a criminal offence under national or international law at the time when it was committed. Nor shall a heavier penalty be imposed than the one that was applicable at the time the criminal offence was committed.

2. This Article shall not prejudice the trial and punishment of any person for any act or omission which, at the time when it was committed, was criminal according to the general principles of law recognised by civilised nations.

Right to respect for private and family life

Article 8—1. Everyone has the right to respect for his private and family life, his home and his cor- **15-012** respondence.

2. There shall be no interference by a public authority with the exercise of this right except such as is in accordance with the law and is necessary in a democratic society in the interests of national security, public safety or the economic well-being of the country, for the prevention of disorder or crime, for the protection of health or morals, or for the protection of the rights and freedoms of others.

Freedom of thought, conscience and religion

Article 9—1. Everyone has the right to freedom of thought, conscience and religion, this right **15-013** includes freedom to change his religion or belief and freedom, either alone or in community with others and in public or private, to manifest his religion or belief, in worship, teaching, practice and observance.

2. Freedom to manifest one's religion or beliefs shall be subject only to such limitation as are prescribed by law and are necessary in a democratic society in the interests of public safety, for the protection of public order, health or morals, or for the protection of the rights and freedoms of others.

Freedom of expression

Article 10—1. Everyone has the right to freedom of expression. This right shall include freedom **15-014** to hold opinions and to receive and impart information and ideas without interference by public authority and regardless of frontiers. This Article shall not prevent States from requiring the licensing of broadcasting, television or cinema enterprises.

2. The exercise of these freedoms, since it carries with it duties and responsibilities, may be subject to such formalities, conditions, restrictions or penalties as are prescribed by law and are necessary in a democratic society, in the interests of national security, territorial integrity or public safety, for the prevention of disorder or crime, for the protection of health or morals, for the protection of the reputation or rights of others, for preventing the disclosure of information received in confidence, or for maintaining the authority and impartiality of the judiciary.

Freedom of assembly and association

Article 11—1. Everyone has the right to freedom of peaceful assembly and to freedom of associa- **15-015** tion with others, including the right to form and to join trade unions for the protection of his interests.

2. No restrictions shall be placed on the exercise of these rights other than such as are prescribed by law and are necessary in a democratic society in the interests of national security or public safety, for the prevention of disorder or crime, for the protection of health or morals or for the protection of the rights and freedoms of others. This Article shall not prevent the imposition of lawful restrictions on the exercise of these rights by members of the armed forces, of the police or of the administration of the State.

Right to marry

Article 12 Men and women of marriageable age have the right to marry and to found a family, **15-016** according to the national laws governing the exercise of this right.

Prohibition of discrimination

15-017   **Article 14** The enjoyment of the rights and freedoms set forth in this Convention shall be secured without discrimination on any ground such as sex, race, colour, language, religion, political or other opinion, national or social origin, association with a national minority, property, birth or other status.

Restrictions on political activity of aliens

15-018   **Article 16** Nothing in Articles 10, 11 and 14 shall be regarded as preventing the High Contracting Parties from imposing restrictions on the political activity of aliens.

Prohibition of abuse of rights

15-019   **Article 17** Nothing in this Convention may be interpreted as implying for any State, group or person any right to engage in any activity or perform any act aimed at the destruction of any of the rights and freedoms set forth herein or at their limitation to a greater extent than is provided for in the Convention.

Limitation on use of restrictions on rights

15-020   **Article 18** The restrictions permitted under this Convention to the said rights and freedoms shall not be applied for any purpose other than those for which they have been prescribed.

Employment Relations Act 1999

CHAPTER 26

Trade unions

Blacklists

16-001   **3.**—(1) The Secretary of State may make regulations prohibiting the compilation of lists which—

    (a) contain details of members of trade unions or persons who have taken part in the activities of trade unions, and

    (b) are compiled with a view to being used by employers or employment agencies for the purposes of discrimination in relation to recruitment or in relation to the treatment of workers.

(2) The Secretary of State may make regulations prohibiting—

    (a) the use of lists to which subsection (1) applies;

    (b) the sale or supply of lists to which subsection (1) applies.

(3) Regulations under this section may, in particular—

    (a) confer jurisdiction (including exclusive jurisdiction) on employment tribunals and on the Employment Appeal Tribunal;

    (b) include provision for or about the grant and enforcement of specified remedies by courts and tribunals;

    (c) include provision for the making of awards of compensation calculated in accordance with the regulations;

    (d) include provision permitting proceedings to be brought by trade unions on behalf of members in specified circumstances;

(e) include provision about cases where an employee is dismissed by his employer and the reason or principal reason for the dismissal, or why the employee was selected for dismissal, relates to a list to which subsection (1) applies;

(f) create criminal offences;

(g) in specified cases or circumstances, extend liability for a criminal offence created under paragraph (f) to a person who aids the commission of the offence or to a person who is an agent, principal, employee, employer or officer of a person who commits the offence;

(h) provide for specified obligations or offences not to apply in specified circumstances;

(i) include supplemental, incidental, consequential and transitional provision, including provision amending an enactment;

(j) make different provision for different cases or circumstances.

(4) Regulations under this section creating an offence may not provide for it to be punishable—

(a) by imprisonment,

(b) by a fine in excess of level 5 on the standard scale in the case of an offence triable only summarily, or

(c) by a fine in excess of the statutory maximum in the case of summary conviction for an offence triable either way.

(5) In this section—

"list" includes any index or other set of items whether recorded electronically or by any other means, and

"worker" has the meaning given by section 13.

(6) Subject to subsection (5), expressions used in this section and in the Trade Union and Labour Relations (Consolidation) Act 1992 have the same meaning in this section as in that Act.

Disciplinary and grievance hearings

Right to be accompanied

10.—(1) This section applies where a worker— **16-002**

(a) is required or invited by his employer to attend a disciplinary or grievance hearing, and

(b) reasonably requests to be accompanied at the hearing.

(2) Where this section applies the employer must permit the worker to be accompanied at the hearing by a single companion who—

(a) is chosen by the worker and is within subsection (3),

(b) is to be permitted to address the hearing (but not to answer questions on behalf of the worker), and

(c) is to be permitted to confer with the worker during the hearing.

(3) A person is within this subsection if he is—

(a) employed by a trade union of which he is an official within the meaning of sections 1 and 119 of the Trade Union and Labour Relations (Consolidation) Act 1992,

(b) an official of a trade union (within that meaning) whom the union has reasonably certified in writing as having experience of, or as having received training in, acting as a worker's companion at disciplinary or grievance hearings, or

(c) another of the employer's workers.

(4) If—

(a) a worker has a right under this section to be accompanied at a hearing,

(b) his chosen companion will not be available at the time proposed for the hearing by the employer, and

(c) the worker proposes an alternative time which satisfies subsection (5),

the employer must postpone the hearing to the time proposed by the worker.

(5) An alternative time must—

(a) be reasonable, and

(b) fall before the end of the period of five working days beginning with the first working day after the day proposed by the employer.

(6) An employer shall permit a worker to take time off during working hours for the purpose of accompanying another of the employer's workers in accordance with a request under subsection (1)(b).

(7) Sections 168(3) and (4), 169 and 171 to 173 of the Trade Union and Labour Relations (Consolidation) Act 1992 (time off for carrying out trade union duties) shall apply in relation to subsection (6) above as they apply in relation to section 168(1) of that Act.

Employment Act 2002

CHAPTER 22

PART 3

DISPUTE RESOLUTION ETC

Statutory procedures

Statutory dispute resolution procedures

17-001 **29.**—(1) Schedule 2 (which sets out the statutory dispute resolution procedures) shall have effect.

(2) The Secretary of State may by order—

(a) amend Schedule 2;

(b) make provision for the Schedule to apply, with or without modifications, as if—

(i) any individual of a description specified in the order who would not otherwise be an employee for the purposes of the Schedule were an employee for those purposes; and

(ii) a person of a description specified in the order were, in the case of any such individual, the individual's employer for those purposes.

(3) Before making an order under this section, the Secretary of State must consult the Advisory, Conciliation and Arbitration Service.

Contracts of employment

17-002 **30.**—(1) Every contract of employment shall have effect to require the employer and employee to comply, in relation to any matter to which a statutory procedure applies, with the requirements of the procedure.

(2) Subsection (1) shall have effect notwithstanding any agreement to the contrary, but does not affect so much of an agreement to follow a particular procedure as requires the employer or employee to comply with a requirement which is additional to, and not inconsistent with, the requirements of the statutory procedure.

(3) The Secretary of State may for the purpose of this section by regulations make provision about the application of the statutory procedures.

(4) In this section, "contract of employment" has the same meaning as in the Employment Rights Act 1996 (c. 18).

Non-completion of statutory procedure: adjustment of awards

31.—(1) This section applies to proceedings before an employment tribunal **17-003** relating to a claim under any of the jurisdictions listed in Schedule 3 by an employee.

(2) If, in the case of proceedings to which this section applies, it appears to the employment tribunal that—

    (a) the claim to which the proceedings relate concerns a matter to which one of the statutory procedures applies,

    (b) the statutory procedure was not completed before the proceedings were begun, and

    (c) the non-completion of the statutory procedure was wholly or mainly attributable to failure by the employee—

        (i) to comply with a requirement of the procedure, or

        (ii) to exercise a right of appeal under it,

it must, subject to subsection (4), reduce any award which it makes to the employee by 10 per cent, and may, if it considers it just and equitable in all the circumstances to do so, reduce it by a further amount, but not so as to make a total reduction of more than 50 per cent.

(3) If, in the case of proceedings to which this section applies, it appears to the employment tribunal that—

    (a) the claim to which the proceedings relate concerns a matter to which one of the statutory procedures applies,

    (b) the statutory procedure was not completed before the proceedings were begun, and

    (c) the non-completion of the statutory procedure was wholly or mainly attributable to failure by the employer to comply with a requirement of the procedure,

it must, subject to subsection (4), increase any award which it makes to the employee by 10 per cent and may, if it considers it just and equitable in all the circumstances to do so, increase it by a further amount, but not so as to make a total increase of more than 50 per cent.

(4) The duty under subsection (2) or (3) to make a reduction or increase of 10 per cent does not apply if there are exceptional circumstances which would make a reduction or increase of that percentage unjust or inequitable, in which case the tribunal may make no reduction or increase or a reduction or increase of such lesser percentage as it considers just and equitable in all the circumstances.

(5) Where an award falls to be adjusted under this section and under section 38, the adjustment under this section shall be made before the adjustment under that section.

(6) The Secretary of State may for the purposes of this section by regulations—

    (a) make provision about the application of the statutory procedures;

    (b) make provision about when a statutory procedure is to be taken to be completed;

    (c) make provision about what constitutes compliance with a requirement of a statutory procedure;

    (d) make provision about circumstances in which a person is to be treated as not subject to, or as having complied with, such a requirement;

    (e) make provision for a statutory procedure to have effect in such circumstances as may be specified by the regulations with such modifications as may be so specified;

    (f) make provision about when an employee is required to exercise a right of appeal under a statutory procedure.

  (7) The Secretary of State may by order—

    (a) amend Schedule 3 for the purpose of—

      (i) adding a jurisdiction to the list in that Schedule, or

      (ii) removing a jurisdiction from that list;

    (b) make provision, in relation to a jurisdiction listed in Schedule 3, for this section not to apply to proceedings relating to claims of a description specified in the order;

    (c) make provision for this section to apply, with or without modifications, as if—

      (i) any individual of a description specified in the order who would not otherwise be an employee for the purposes of this section were an employee for those purposes, and

      (ii) a person of a description specified in the order were, in the case of any such individual, the individual's employer for those purposes.

Complaints about grievances

17-004   **32.**—(1) This section applies to the jurisdictions listed in Schedule 4.

  (2) An employee shall not present a complaint to an employment tribunal under a jurisdiction to which this section applies if—

    (a) it concerns a matter in relation to which the requirement in paragraph 6 or 9 of Schedule 2 applies, and

    (b) the requirement has not been complied with.

  (3) An employee shall not present a complaint to an employment tribunal under a jurisdiction to which this section applies if—

    (a) it concerns a matter in relation to which the requirement in paragraph 6 or 9 of Schedule 2 has been complied with, and

    (b) less than 28 days have passed since the day on which the requirement was complied with.

  (4) An employee shall not present a complaint to an employment tribunal under a jurisdiction to which this section applies if—

    (a) it concerns a matter in relation to which the requirement in paragraph 6 or 9 of Schedule 2 has been complied with, and

    (b) the day on which the requirement was complied with was more than one month after the end of the original time limit for making the complaint.

  (5) In such circumstances as the Secretary of State may specify by regulations, an employment tribunal may direct that subsection (4) shall not apply in relation to a particular matter.

  (6) An employment tribunal shall be prevented from considering a complaint presented in breach of subsections (2) to (4), but only if—

    (a) the breach is apparent to the tribunal from the information supplied to it by the employee in connection with the bringing of the proceedings, or

    (b) the tribunal is satisfied of the breach as a result of his employer raising the issue of compliance with those provisions in accordance with regulations under section 7 of the Employment Tribunals Act 1996 (c. 17) (employment tribunal procedure regulations).

(7) The Secretary of State may for the purposes of this section by regulations—

    (a) make provision about the application of the procedures set out in Part 2 of Schedule 2;

    (b) make provision about what constitutes compliance with paragraph 6 or 9 of that Schedule;

    (c) make provision about circumstances in which a person is to be treated as having complied with paragraph 6 or 9 of that Schedule;

    (d) make provision for paragraph 6 or 9 of that Schedule to have effect in such circumstances as may be specified by the regulations with such modifications as may be so specified.

(8) The Secretary of State may by order—

    (a) amend, repeal or replace any of subsections (2) to (4);

    (b) amend Schedule 4;

    (c) make provision for this section to apply, with or without modifications, as if—

        (i) any individual of a description specified in the order who would not otherwise be an employee for the purposes of this section were an employee for those purposes, and

        (ii) a person of a description specified in the order were, in the case of any such individual, the individual's employer for those purposes.

(9) Before making an order under subsection (8)(a), the Secretary of State must consult the Advisory, Conciliation and Arbitration Service.

(10) In its application to orders under subsection (8)(a), section 51(1)(b) includes power to amend this section.

Consequential adjustment of time limits

33.—(1) The Secretary of State may, in relation to a jurisdiction listed in **17-005** Schedule 3 or 4, by regulations make provision about the time limit for beginning proceedings in respect of a claim concerning a matter to which a statutory procedure applies.

(2) Regulations under this section may, in particular—

    (a) make provision extending, or authorising the extension of, the time for beginning proceedings,

    (b) make provision about the exercise of a discretion to extend the time for beginning proceedings, or

    (c) make provision treating proceedings begun out of time as begun within time.

Employment particulars

Failure to give statement of employment particulars etc

17-006   **38.**—(1) This section applies to proceedings before an employment tribunal relating to a claim by an employee under any of the jurisdictions listed in Schedule 5.

(2) If in the case of proceedings to which this section applies—

    (a) the employment tribunal finds in favour of the employee, but makes no award to him in respect of the claim to which the proceedings relate, and

    (b) when the proceedings were begun the employer was in breach of his duty to the employee under section 1(1) or 4(1) of the Employment Rights Act 1996 (c. 18) (duty to give a written statement of initial employment particulars or of particulars of change),

the tribunal must, subject to subsection (5), make an award of the minimum amount to be paid by the employer to the employee and may, if it considers it just and equitable in all the circumstances, award the higher amount instead.

(3) If in the case of proceedings to which this section applies—

    (a) the employment tribunal makes an award to the employee in respect of the claim to which the proceedings relate, and

    (b) when the proceedings were begun the employer was in breach of his duty to the employee under section 1(1) or 4(1) of the Employment Rights Act 1996,

the tribunal must, subject to subsection (5), increase the award by the minimum amount and may, if it considers it just and equitable in all the circumstances, increase the award by the higher amount instead.

(4) In subsections (2) and (3)—

    (a) references to the minimum amount are to an amount equal to two weeks' pay, and

    (b) references to the higher amount are to an amount equal to four weeks' pay.

(5) The duty under subsection (2) or (3) does not apply if there are exceptional circumstances which would make an award or increase under that subsection unjust or inequitable.

(6) The amount of a week's pay of an employee shall—

    (a) be calculated for the purposes of this section in accordance with Chapter 2 of Part 14 of the Employment Rights Act 1996 (c. 18), and

    (b) not exceed the amount for the time being specified in section 227 of that Act (maximum amount of week's pay).

(7) For the purposes of Chapter 2 of Part 14 of the Employment Rights Act 1996 as applied by subsection (6), the calculation date shall be taken to be—

    (a) if the employee was employed by the employer on the date the proceedings were begun, that date, and

    (b) if he was not, the effective date of termination as defined by section 97 of that Act.

(8) The Secretary of State may by order—

    (a) amend Schedule 5 for the purpose of—

        (i) adding a jurisdiction to the list in that Schedule, or

        (ii) removing a jurisdiction from that list;

(b) make provision, in relation to a jurisdiction listed in Schedule 5, for this section not to apply to proceedings relating to claims of a description specified in the order;

(c) make provision for this section to apply, with or without modifications, as if—

(i) any individual of a description specified in the order who would not otherwise be an employee for the purposes of this section were an employee for those purposes, and

(ii) a person of a description specified in the order were, in the case of any such individual, the individual's employer for those purposes.

SCHEDULES

Section 29   Schedule 2

STATUTORY DISPUTE RESOLUTION PROCEDURES

DISMISSAL AND DISCIPLINARY PROCEDURES

STANDARD PROCEDURE

Step 1: statement of grounds for action and invitation to meeting

1.—(1) The employer must set out in writing the employee's alleged conduct or characteristics, or other circumstances, which lead him to contemplate dismissing or taking disciplinary action against the employee.   **17-007**

(2) The employer must send the statement or a copy of it to the employee and invite the employee to attend a meeting to discuss the matter.

Step 2: meeting

2.—(1) The meeting must take place before action is taken, except in the case where the disciplinary action consists of suspension.   **17-008**

(2) The meeting must not take place unless—

(a) the employer has informed the employee what the basis was for including in the statement under paragraph 1(1) the ground or grounds given in it, and

(b) the employee has had a reasonable opportunity to consider his response to that information.

(3) The employee must take all reasonable steps to attend the meeting.

(4) After the meeting, the employer must inform the employee of his decision and notify him of the right to appeal against the decision if he is not satisfied with it.

Step 3: appeal

3.—(1) If the employee does wish to appeal, he must inform the employer.   **17-009**

(2) If the employee informs the employer of his wish to appeal, the employer must invite him to attend a further meeting.

(3) The employee must take all reasonable steps to attend the meeting.

(4) The appeal meeting need not take place before the dismissal or disciplinary action takes effect.

(5) After the appeal meeting, the employer must inform the employee of his final decision.

MODIFIED PROCEDURE

Step 1: statement of grounds for action

17-010   **4.** The employer must—
    (a) set out in writing—
        (i) the employee's alleged misconduct which has led to the dismissal,
        (ii) what the basis was for thinking at the time of the dismissal that the employee was guilty of the alleged misconduct, and
        (iii) the employee's right to appeal against dismissal, and
    (b) send the statement or a copy of it to the employee.

Step 2: appeal

17-011   **5.**—(1) If the employee does wish to appeal, he must inform the employer.
(2) If the employee informs the employer of his wish to appeal, the employer must invite him to attend a meeting.
(3) The employee must take all reasonable steps to attend the meeting.
(4) After the appeal meeting, the employer must inform the employee of his final decision.

GRIEVANCE PROCEDURES

STANDARD PROCEDURE

Step 1: statement of grievance

17-012   **6.** The employee must set out the grievance in writing and send the statement or a copy of it to the employer.

Step 2: meeting

17-013   **7.**—(1) The employer must invite the employee to attend a meeting to discuss the grievance.
(2) The meeting must not take place unless—
    (a) the employee has informed the employer what the basis for the grievance was when he made the statement under paragraph 6, and
    (b) the employer has had a reasonable opportunity to consider his response to that information.
(3) The employee must take all reasonable steps to attend the meeting.
(4) After the meeting, the employer must inform the employee of his decision as to his response to the grievance and notify him of the right to appeal against the decision if he is not satisfied with it.

Step 3: appeal

17-014   **8.**—(1) If the employee does wish to appeal, he must inform the employer.
(2) If the employee informs the employer of his wish to appeal, the employer must invite him to attend a further meeting.
(3) The employee must take all reasonable steps to attend the meeting.
(4) After the appeal meeting, the employer must inform the employee of his final decision.

MODIFIED PROCEDURE

Step 1: statement of grievance

17-015   **9.** The employee must—
    (a) set out in writing—
        (i) the grievance, and
        (ii) the basis for it, and
    (b) send the statement or a copy of it to the employer.

Step 2: response

10. The employer must set out his response in writing and send the statement or a copy of it to the **17-016** employee.

GENERAL REQUIREMENTS

Introductory

11. The following requirements apply to each of the procedures set out above (so far as **17-017** applicable).

Timetable

12. Each step and action under the procedure must be taken without unreasonable delay.   **17-018**

Meetings

13.—(1) Timing and location of meetings must be reasonable.   **17-019**

(2) Meetings must be conducted in a manner that enables both employer and employee to explain their cases.

(3) In the case of appeal meetings which are not the first meeting, the employer should, as far as is reasonably practicable, be represented by a more senior manager than attended the first meeting (unless the most senior manager attended that meeting).

SUPPLEMENTARY

Status of meetings

14. A meeting held for the purposes of this Schedule is a hearing for the purposes of section **17-020** 13(4) and (5) of the Employment Relations Act 1999 (c. 26) (definition of "disciplinary hearing" and "grievance hearing" in relation to the right to be accompanied under section 10 of that Act).

Scope of grievance procedures

15.—(1) The procedures set out in Part 2 are only applicable to matters raised by an employee **17-021** with his employer as a grievance.

(2) Accordingly, those procedures are only applicable to the kind of disclosure dealt with in Part 4A of the Employment Rights Act 1996 (c. 18) (protected disclosures of information) if information is disclosed by an employee to his employer in circumstances where—

  (a) the information relates to a matter which the employee could raise as a grievance with his employer, and
  (b) it is the intention of the employee that the disclosure should constitute the raising of the matter with his employer as a grievance.

Section 31   Schedule 3

TRIBUNAL JURISDICTIONS TO WHICH SECTION 31 APPLIES

Section 2 of the Equal Pay Act 1970 (c. 41) (equality clauses)
Section 63 of the Sex Discrimination Act 1975 (c. 65) (discrimination in the employment field)
Section 54 of the Race Relations Act 1976 (c. 74) (discrimination in the employment field)
Section 146 of the Trade Union and Labour Relations (Consolidation) Act 1992 (c. 52) (detriment in relation to trade union membership and activities)
Paragraph 156 of Schedule A1 to that Act (detriment in relation to union recognition rights)
Section 8 of the Disability Discrimination Act 1995 (c. 50) (discrimination in the employment field)
Section 23 of the Employment Rights Act 1996 (c. 18) (unauthorised deductions and payments)
Section 48 of that Act (detriment in employment)
Section 111 of that Act (unfair dismissal)
Section 163 of that Act (redundancy payments)
Section 24 of the National Minimum Wage Act 1998 (c. 39) (detriment in relation to national minimum wage)
Schedule 3 to the Tax Credits Act 1999 (c. 10) (detriment in relation to tax credits)

The Employment Tribunal Extension of Jurisdiction (England and Wales) Order 1994 (SI 1994/1623) (breach of employment contract and termination)
The Employment Tribunal Extension of Jurisdiction (Scotland) Order 1994 (SI 1994/1624) (corresponding provision for Scotland)
Regulation 30 of the Working Time Regulations 1998 (SI 1998/1833) (breach of regulations)
Regulation 32 of the Transnational Information and Consultation of Employees Regulations 1999 (SI 1999/3323) (detriment relating to European Works Councils)

Section 32 Schedule 4

TRIBUNAL JURISDICTIONS TO WHICH SECTION 32 APPLIES

Section 2 of the Equal Pay Act 1970 (c. 41) (equality clauses)
Section 63 of the Sex Discrimination Act 1975 (c. 65) (discrimination in the employment field)
Section 54 of the Race Relations Act 1976 (c. 74) (discrimination in the employment field)
Section 146 of the Trade Union and Labour Relations (Consolidation) Act 1992 (c. 52) (detriment in relation to trade union membership and activities)
Paragraph 156 of Schedule A1 to that Act (detriment in relation to union recognition rights)
Section 8 of the Disability Discrimination Act 1995 (c. 50) (discrimination in the employment field)
Section 23 of the Employment Rights Act 1996 (c. 18) (unauthorised deductions and payments)
Section 48 of that Act (detriment in employment)
Section 111 of that Act (unfair dismissal)
Section 163 of that Act (redundancy payments)
Section 24 of the National Minimum Wage Act 1998 (c. 39) (detriment in relation to national minimum wage)
Schedule 3 to the Tax Credits Act 1999 (c. 10) (detriment in relation to tax credits)
Regulation 30 of the Working Time Regulations 1998 (SI 1998/1833) (breach of regulations)
Regulation 32 of the Transnational Information and Consultation of Employees Regulations 1999 (SI 1999/3323) (detriment relating to European Works Councils)

Section 38 Schedule 5

TRIBUNAL JURISDICTIONS TO WHICH SECTION 38 APPLIES

Section 2 of the Equal Pay Act 1970 (equality clauses)
Section 63 of the Sex Discrimination Act 1975 (c. 65) (discrimination in the employment field)
Section 54 of the Race Relations Act 1976 (c. 74) (discrimination in the employment field)
Section 146 of the Trade Union and Labour Relations (Consolidation) Act 1992 (c. 52) (detriment in relation to trade union membership and activities)
Paragraph 156 of Schedule A1 to that Act (detriment in relation to union recognition rights)
Section 8 of the Disability Discrimination Act 1995 (c. 50) (discrimination in the employment field)
Section 23 of the Employment Rights Act 1996 (c. 18) (unauthorised deductions and payments)
Section 48 of that Act (detriment in employment)
Section 111 of that Act (unfair dismissal)
Section 163 of that Act (redundancy payments)
Section 24 of the National Minimum Wage Act 1998 (c. 39) (detriment in relation to national minimum wage)
Schedule 3 to the Tax Credits Act 1999 (c. 10) (detriment in relation to tax credits)
The Employment Tribunal Extension of Jurisdiction (England and Wales) Order 1994 (SI 1994/1623) (breach of employment contract and termination)
The Employment Tribunal Extension of Jurisdiction (Scotland) Order 1994 (SI 1994/1624) (corresponding provision for Scotland)
Regulation 30 of the Working Time Regulations 1998 (SI 1998/1833) (breach of regulations)
Regulation 32 of the Transnational Information and Consultation of Employees Regulations 1999 (SI 1999/3323) (detriment relating to European Works Councils)

Employment Relations Bill 2004

PART 3

RIGHTS OF TRADE UNION MEMBERS, WORKERS AND EMPLOYEES

Inducements and detriments in respect of membership etc. of independent trade union

Inducements relating to union membership or activities

28.—(1) After section 145 of the 1992 Act insert—   **18-001**

"Inducements
145A Inducements relating to union membership or activities
A worker has the right not to have an offer made to him by his employer for the sole or main purpose of inducing the worker—
- (a) not to be or seek to become a member of an independent trade union,
- (b) not to take part, at an appropriate time, in the activities of an independent trade union,
- (c) not to make use, at an appropriate time, of trade union services, or
- (d) to be or become a member of any trade union or of a particular trade union or of one of a number of particular trade unions.

(2) In subsection (1) "an appropriate time" means—
- (a) a time outside the worker's working hours, or
- (b) a time within his working hours at which, in accordance with arrangements agreed with or consent given by his employer, it is permissible for him to take part in the activities of a trade union or (as the case may be) make use of trade union services.

(3) In subsection (2) "working hours", in relation to a worker, means any time when, in accordance with his contract of employment (or other contract personally to do work or perform services), he is required to be at work.

(4) In subsections (1) and (2)—
- (a) "trade union services" means services made available to the worker by an independent trade union by virtue of his membership of the union, and
- (b) references to a worker's "making use" of trade union services include his consenting to the raising of a matter on his behalf by an independent trade union of which he is a member.(5) A worker may present a complaint to an employment tribunal on the ground that his employer has made him an offer in contravention of this section.

145B Inducements relating to collective bargaining
(1) A worker who is a member of an independent trade union which is recognised by his employer has the right not to have an offer made to him by his employer if—

(a) acceptance of the offer, together with other workers' acceptance of offers which the employer also makes to them, would have the prohibited result, and

(b) the employer's sole or main purpose in making the offers is to achieve that result.

(2) The prohibited result is that the workers' terms of employment, or any of those terms, will no longer be determined by collective agreement negotiated by or on behalf of the union.

(3) It is immaterial for the purposes of subsection (1) whether the offers are made to the workers simultaneously.

(4) Having terms of employment determined by collective agreement shall not be regarded for the purposes of section 145A (or section 146 or 152) as making use of a trade union service.

(5) A worker may present a complaint to an employment tribunal on the ground that his employer has made him an offer in contravention of this section.

145C Time limit for proceedings

An employment tribunal shall not consider a complaint under section 145A or 145B unless it is presented—

(a) before the end of the period of three months beginning with the date when the offer was made or, where the offer is part of a series of similar offers to the worker, the date when the last of them was made, or

(b) where the tribunal is satisfied that it was not reasonably practicable for the complaint to be presented before the end of that period, within such further period as it considers reasonable.

145D Consideration of complaint

(1) On a complaint under section 145A it shall be for the employer to show what was his sole or main purpose in making the offer.

(2) On a complaint under section 145B it shall be for the employer to show what was his sole or main purpose in making the offers.

(3) On a complaint under section 145A or 145B, in determining any question whether the employer made the offer (or offers) or the purpose for which he did so, no account shall be taken of any pressure which was exercised on him by calling, organising, procuring or financing a strike or other industrial action, or by threatening to do so; and that question shall be determined as if no such pressure had been exercised.

(4) In determining whether an employer's sole or main purpose in making offers was the purpose mentioned in section 145B(1), the matters taken into account must include any evidence—

(a) that when the offers were made the employer had recently changed or sought to change, or did not wish to use, arrangements agreed with the union for collective bargaining, or

(b) that the offers were made only to particular workers, and were made with the sole or main purpose of rewarding those particular workers for their high level of performance or of retaining them because of their special value to the employer.

145E Remedies

(1) Subsections (2) and (3) apply where the employment tribunal finds that a complaint under section 145A or 145B is well-founded

(2) The tribunal—

(a) shall make a declaration to that effect, and

(b) shall make an award to be paid by the employer to the complainant in respect of the offer complained of.

(3) The amount of the award shall be fl2,500 (subject to any adjustment of the award that may fall to be made under Part 3 of the Employment Act 2002).

(4) Where an offer made in contravention of section 145A or 145B is accepted—

(a) if the acceptance results in the worker's agreeing to vary his terms of employment, the employer cannot enforce the agreement to vary, or recover any sum paid or other asset transferred by him under the agreement to vary;

(b) if as a result of the acceptance the worker's terms of employment are varied, nothing in section 145A or 145B makes the variation unenforce-able by either party.

(5) Nothing in this section or sections 145A and 145B prejudices any right conferred by section 146 or 149.

(6) In ascertaining any amount of compensation under section 149, no reduction shall be made on the ground—

(a) that the complainant caused or contributed to his loss, or to the act or failure complained of, by accepting or not accepting an offer made in contravention of section 145A or 145B, or

(b) that the complainant has received or is entitled to an award under this section.

145F Interpretation and other supplementary provisions

(1) References in sections 145A to 145E to being or becoming a member of a trade union include references—

(a) to being or becoming a member of a particular branch or section of that union, and

(b) to being or becoming a member of one of a number of particular branches or sections of that union.

(2) References in those sections—

(a) to taking part in the activities of a trade union, and

(b) to services made available by a trade union by virtue of membership of the union,

shall be construed in accordance with subsection (1).

(3) The remedy of a worker for infringement of the right conferred on him by section 145A or 145B is by way of a complaint to an employment tribunal in accordance with this Part, and not otherwise.

Extension of protection against detriment for union membership etc.

29.—(1) Section 146 of the 1992 Act (action short of dismissal on grounds **18-002** related to union membership or activities) is amended in accordance with subsections (2) to (5).

(2) For "An employee" in each of subsections (1), (3) and (5), and "an employee" in each of subsections (2) and (4), substitute "A worker" and "a worker" respectively.

(3) In subsection (2)—

(a) for "employee's" substitute "worker's"; and

(b) after "contract of employment" insert "(or other contract personally to do work or perform services)".

(4) In subsection (3), for "his contract of employment" substitute "a contract of employment".

(5) For subsection (6) substitute—

"(5A) This section does not apply where—

(a) the worker is an employee; and

(b) the detriment in question amounts to dismissal."

(6) In the sidenote to section 146 of the 1992 Act, and in the cross-heading immediately preceding it, for "Action short of dismissal" substitute "Detriment".

(7) In section 151(2) of the 1992 Act (supplementary provision), for "an employee" substitute "a worker".

(8) In the sidenote to section 152 of the 1992 Act, and in the cross-heading immediately preceding it, after "Dismissal" insert "of employee".

Detriment for use of union services or refusal of inducement

18-003 **30.**—(1) Section 146 of the 1992 Act (action short of dismissal on grounds related to union membership or activities) is also amended in accordance with subsections (2) to (4).

(2) In subsection (1), omit "or" at the end of paragraph (b) and after that paragraph insert—

(ba) preventing or deterring him from making use of trade union services at an appropriate time, or penalising him for doing so, or

(3) In subsection (2)—

(a) for "(1)(b)" substitute "(1)"; and

(b) in paragraph (b), after "the activities of a trade union" insert "or (as the case may be) make use of trade union services".

(4) After subsection (2) insert—

"(2A) In this section—

(a) "trade union services" means services made available to the worker by an independent trade union by virtue of his membership of the union, and

(b) references to a worker's "making use" of trade union services include his consenting to the raising of a matter on his behalf by an independent trade union of which he is a member.

(2B) If an independent trade union of which a worker is a member raises a matter on his behalf (with or without his consent), penalising the worker for that is to be treated as penalising him as mentioned in subsection (1)(ba).

(2C) A worker also has the right not to be subjected to any detriment as an individual by any act, or any deliberate failure to act, by his employer if the act or failure takes place because of the worker's failure to accept an offer made in contravention of section 145A or 145B.

(2D) For the purposes of subsection (2C), not conferring a benefit that, if the offer had been accepted by the worker, would have been conferred on him under the resulting agreement shall be taken to be subjecting him to a detriment as an individual (and to be a deliberate failure to act)."

(5) In section 148 of the 1992 Act (consideration of complaint under section 146), omit subsections (3) to (5).

(6) In section 151 of the 1992 Act, in subsection (1) (references in sections 146 to 150 to being etc. a member of a union to include being etc. a member of a branch or section) omit "; and references to taking part in the activities of a trade union shall be similarly construed".

(7) After that subsection insert—

"(1A) References in those sections—
    (a) to taking part in the activities of a trade union, and
    (b) to services made available by a trade union by virtue of membership of the union,
shall be construed in accordance with subsection (1)."

(8) Omit section 17 of the Employment Relations Act 1999 (c. 26) (which is superseded by this section and section 31).

Dismissal for use of union services or refusal of inducement

31.—(1) Section 152 of the 1992 Act (dismissal on grounds related to union membership or activities) is amended as follows.   **18-004**

(2) In subsection (1), omit "or" at the end of each of paragraphs (a) and (b) and after paragraph (b) insert—
    (ba) had made use, or proposed to make use, of trade union services at an appropriate time,
    (bb) had failed to accept an offer made in contravention of section 145A or 145B, or

(3) In subsection (2)—
    (a) for "(1)(b)" substitute "(1)"; and
    (b) in paragraph (b), after "the activities of a trade union" insert "or (as the case may be) make use of trade union services".

(4) After subsection (2) insert—
"(2A) In this section—
    (a) "trade union services" means services made available to the employee by an independent trade union by virtue of his membership of the union, and
    (b) references to an employee's "making use" of trade union services include his consenting to the raising of a matter on his behalf by an independent trade union of which he is a member.
Where the reason or one of the reasons for the dismissal was that an independent trade union (with or without the employee's consent) raised a matter on behalf of the employee as one of its members, the reason shall be treated as falling within subsection (1)(ba)."

(5) In subsection (4) (references to being etc. a member of a union to include being etc. a member of a branch or section) omit "; and references to taking part in the activities of a trade union shall be similarly construed".

(6) After that subsection add—
"(5) References in this section—
    (a) to taking part in the activities of a trade union, and
    (b) to services made available by a trade union by virtue of membership of the union,
shall be construed in accordance with subsection (4)."

Exclusion and expulsion from trade unions

Exclusion or expulsion from trade union attributable to conduct

32.—(1) Section 174 of the 1992 Act (right not to be excluded or expelled from trade union) is amended as follows.   **18-005**

(2) In subsection (2)(d) for "his conduct" substitute "conduct of his (other than excluded conduct) and the conduct to which it is wholly or mainly attributable is not protected conduct".

(3) For subsection (4) substitute—

"(4) For the purposes of subsection (2)(d) "excluded conduct", in relation to an individual, means—

(a) conduct which consists in his being or ceasing to be, or having been or ceased to be, a member of another trade union,

(b) conduct which consists in his being or ceasing to be, or having been or ceased to be, employed by a particular employer or at a particular place, or

(c) conduct to which section 65 (conduct for which an individual may not be disciplined by a union) applies or would apply if the references in that section to the trade union which is relevant for the purposes of that section were references to any trade union.

(4A) For the purposes of subsection (2)(d) "protected conduct" is conduct which consists in the individual's being or ceasing to be, or having been or ceased to be, a member of a political party.

(4B) Conduct which consists of activities undertaken by an individual as a member of a political party is not conduct falling within subsection (4A)."

(4) In section 176 of that Act (remedies for infringement of right not to be excluded or expelled), after subsection (1) insert—

"(1A) If a tribunal makes a declaration under subsection (1) and it appears to the tribunal that the exclusion or expulsion was mainly attributable to conduct falling within section 174(4A) it shall make a declaration to that effect.

(1B) If a tribunal makes a declaration under subsection (1A) and it appears to the tribunal that the other conduct to which the exclusion or expulsion was attributable consisted wholly or mainly of acting in a way which was contrary to the rules of the union (whether or not the complainant was a member of the union at the time at which he acted in that way) it shall make a declaration to that effect."

(5) In subsection (3)(a) of that section, after "declaration" insert "under subsection (1)".

(6) After subsection (6) of that section insert—

"(6A) If on the date on which the application was made the applicant had not been admitted or re-admitted to the union, the award shall not be less than £5,900.

(6B) Subsection (6A) does not apply in a case where the tribunal which made the declaration under subsection (1) also made declarations under subsections (1A) and (1B)."

(7) In sections 174 and 176 of the 1992 Act references to the conduct of an individual include references to conduct which took place before the coming into force of this section.

Other rights of workers and employees

Disapplication of qualifying period and upper age limit for unfair dismissal

18-006   34.—For section 154 of the 1992 Act substitute—

"154 Disapplication of qualifying period and upper age limit for unfair dismissal

Sections 108(1) and 109(1) of the Employment Rights Act 1996 (qualifying period and upper age limit for unfair dismissal protection) do not apply to a dismissal which by virtue of section 152 or 153 is regarded as unfair for the purposes of Part 10 of that Act."

Role of companion at disciplinary or grievance hearing

35.—(1) For subsection (2) of section 10 of the Employment Relations Act **18-007** 1999 (c. 26) (duty of employers to permit workers to be accompanied at disciplinary and grievance hearings) substitute—

"(2A) Where this section applies, the employer must permit the worker to be accompanied at the hearing by one companion who—
(a) is chosen by the worker; and
(b) is within subsection (3).

(2B) The employer must permit the worker's companion to—
(a) address the hearing in order to do any or all of the following—
(i) put the worker's case;
(ii) sum up that case;
(iii) respond on the worker's behalf to any view expressed at the hearing;
(b) confer with the worker during the hearing.

(2C) Subsection (2B) does not require the employer to permit the worker's companion to—
(a) answer questions on behalf of the worker;
(b) address the hearing if the worker indicates at it that he does not wish his companion to do so; or
(c) use the powers conferred by that subsection in a way that prevents the employer from explaining his case or prevents any other person at the hearing from making his contribution to it."

(2) In section 11(1) of that Act (complaint to employment tribunal), for "10(2)" insert "10(2A), (2B)".

(3) In section 12 of that Act (right not to be subjected to a detriment or dismissal)—
(a) in subsections (1)(a) and (3)(a) for "10(2)" substitute "10(2A), (2B)"; and
(b) after subsection (6) add—
"(7) References in this section to a worker having accompanied or sought to accompany another worker include references to his having exercised or sought to exercise any of the powers conferred by section 10(2A) or (2B)."

Flexible working

38.—(1) In section 237(1A)(a) of the 1992 Act (cases where employee may **18-008** complain of unfair dismissal despite participation in unofficial industrial action)—
(a) for "or 103A" substitute ", 103A or 104C"; and
(b) for "and protected disclosure" substitute ", protected disclosure and flexible working".

(2) In subsection (2A)(a) of section 238 of that Act (cases where employment tribunal to determine whether dismissal of an employee is unfair despite limitation in subsection (2) of that section—
(a) for "or 103" substitute ", 103 or 104C"; and

(b) for "and employee representative" substitute ", employee representative and flexible working".

(3) After subsection (7B) of section 105 of the Employment Rights Act 1996 (c. 18) insert—

"(7BA) This subsection applies if the reason (or, if more than one, the principal reason) for which the employee was selected for dismissal was one of those specified in section 104C."

(4) In section 108(3) of that Act (exceptions to one year qualifying period of continuous employment for claims for unfair dismissal), after paragraph (gh) insert—

"(gi) section 104C applies,".

(5) In section 109(2) of that Act (exceptions to upper age limit for claims for unfair dismissal), after paragraph (gh) insert—

"(gi) section 104C applies,".

Information and consultation: Great Britain

18-009   **39.**—(1) The Secretary of State may make regulations for the purpose of conferring on employees of an employer to whom the regulations apply, or on representatives of those employees, rights—

(a) to be informed by the employer about prescribed matters;

(b) to be consulted by the employer about prescribed matters.

(2) Regulations made under subsection (1) must make provision as to the employers to whom the regulations apply which may include provision—

(a) applying the regulations by reference to factors including the number of employees in the United Kingdom in the employer's undertaking;

(b) as to the method by which the number of employees in an employer's undertaking is to be calculated; and

(c) applying the regulations to different descriptions of employer with effect from different dates.

(3) Regulations made under subsection (1) may make provision—

(a) as to the circumstances in which the rights mentioned in subsection (1) arise and the extent of those rights;

(b) for and about the initiation and conduct of negotiations between employers to whom the regulations apply and their employees for the purposes of reaching an agreement satisfying prescribed conditions about the provision of information to the employees, and consultation of them (whether that provision or consultation is to be direct or through representatives);

(c) about the representatives the employees may have for the purposes of the regulations and the method by which those representatives are to be selected;

(d) as to the resolution of disputes and the enforcement of obligations imposed by the regulations or by an agreement of the kind mentioned in paragraph (b).

(4) Regulations made under subsection (1) may—

(a) confer jurisdiction (including exclusive jurisdiction) on employment tribunals and on the Employment Appeal Tribunal;

(b) confer functions on the Central Arbitration Committee;

(c) require or authorise the holding of ballots;

(d) amend, apply with or without modifications, or make provision similar to any provision of the Employment Rights Act 1996 (c. 18) (including, in particular, Parts 5, 10 and 13), the Employment Tribunals Act 1996 (c. 17) or the 1992 Act;

(e) include supplemental, incidental, consequential and transitional provision, including provision amending any enactment;

(f) make different provision for different cases or circumstances.

(5) Regulations made under subsection (1) may make any provision which appears to the Secretary of State to be necessary or expedient—

(a) for the purpose of implementing Directive 2002/14/EC of the European Parliament and of the Council of 11 March 2002 establishing a general framework for informing and consulting employees in the European Community;

(b) for the purpose of dealing with any matter arising out of or related to the United Kingdom's obligations under that Directive.

(6) Nothing in subsections (2) to (5) prejudices the generality of this section.

(7) Regulations under this section shall be made by statutory instrument.

(8) No such regulations may be made unless a draft of the regulations has been laid before Parliament and approved by a resolution of each House of Parliament.

(9) In this section "prescribed" means prescribed by regulations under this section.

Information and consultation: Northern Ireland

40.—(1) The Department for Employment and Learning may make regula- **18-010** tions for the purpose of conferring on employees of an employer to whom the regulations apply, or on representatives of those employees, rights—

(a) to be informed by the employer about prescribed matters;

(b) to be consulted by the employer about prescribed matters.

(2) Regulations made under subsection (1) must make provision as to the employers to whom the regulations apply which may include provision—

(a) applying the regulations by reference to factors including the number of employees in the United Kingdom in the employer's undertaking;

(b) as to the method by which the number of employees in an employer's undertaking is to be calculated; and

(c) applying the regulations to different descriptions of employer with effect from different dates.

(3) Regulations made under subsection (1) may make provision—

(a) as to the circumstances in which the rights mentioned in subsection (1) arise and the extent of those rights;

(b) for and about the initiation and conduct of negotiations between employers to whom the regulations apply and their employees for the purposes of reaching an agreement satisfying prescribed conditions about the provision of information to the employees, and consultation of them (whether that provision or consultation is to be direct or through representatives);

(c) about the representatives the employees may have for the purposes of the regulations and the method by which those representatives are to be selected;

(d) as to the resolution of disputes and the enforcement of obligations imposed by the regulations or by an agreement of the kind mentioned in paragraph (b).

(4) Regulations made under subsection (1) may—

(a) confer jurisdiction (including exclusive jurisdiction) on industrial tribunals and on the High Court;

(b) confer functions on the Industrial Court;

(c) require or authorise the holding of ballots;

(d) amend, apply with or without modifications, or make provision similar to any provision of—

    (i) the Industrial Relations (Northern Ireland) Order 1992 (S.I. 1992/807 (N.I. 5));

    (ii) the Trade Union and Labour Relations (Northern Ireland) Order 1995 (S.I. 1995/1980 (N.I. 12));

    (iii) the Employment Rights (Northern Ireland) Order 1996 (S.I. 1996/1919 (N.I. 16)) (including, in particular, Parts 6, 11 and 15); or

    (iv) the Industrial Tribunals (Northern Ireland) Order 1996 (S.I. 1996/1921 (N.I. 18));

(e) include supplemental, incidental, consequential and transitional provision, including provision amending any enactment;

(f) make different provision for different cases or circumstances.

(5) Regulations made under subsection (1) may make any provision which appears to the Department for Employment and Learning to be necessary or expedient—

(a) for the purpose of implementing Directive 2002/14/EC of the European Parliament and of the Council of 11 March 2002 establishing a general framework for informing and consulting employees in the European Community;

(b) for the purpose of dealing with any matter arising out of or related to the United Kingdom's obligations under that Directive.

(6) Nothing in subsections (2) to (5) prejudices the generality of this section.

(7) Power to make regulations under this section is exercisable by statutory rule for the purposes of the Statutory Rules (Northern Ireland) Order 1979 (S.I. 1979/1573 (N.I. 12)).

(8) No regulations under this section may be made unless a draft of the regulations has been laid before and approved by a resolution of the Northern Ireland Assembly.

(9) In this section—

"enactment" includes—

(a) a provision of an Act;

(b) a provision of, or of any instrument made under, Northern Ireland legislation; and

(c) a provision of subordinate legislation;

"the Industrial Court" means the Industrial Court constituted under Article 91 of the Industrial Relations (Northern Ireland) Order 1992 (S.I. 1992/807 (N.I. 5));

"industrial tribunals" has the meaning given by section 42(5) of the Interpretation Act (Northern Ireland) 1954 (c. 33 (N.I.)); and

"prescribed" means prescribed by regulations under this section.

The Transfer of Undertakings (Protection of Employment) Regulations 1981

(S.I. 1794)

Citation, commencement and extent

1.—(1) These Regulations may be cited as the Transfer of Undertakings **19-001** (Protection of Employment) Regulations 1981.

(2) These Regulations, except Regulations 4 to 9 and 14 shall come into operation on 1st February 1982 and Regulations 4 to 9 and 14 shall come into operation on 1st May 1982.

(3) These Regulations, except Regulations 11(10) and 13(3) and (4), extend to Northern Ireland.

Interpretation

2.—(1) In these Regulations— **19-002**
   "collective agreement", "employers' association", and "trade union" have
      the same meanings respectively as in the 1974 Act or, in Northern
      Ireland, the 1976 Order;
   "collective bargaining" has the same meaning as it has in the 1975 Act or,
      in Northern Ireland, the 1976 Order;
   "contract of employment" means any agreement between an employee and
      his employer determining the terms and conditions of his
      employment;
   "employee" means any individual who works for another person whether
      under a contract of service or apprenticeship or otherwise but does not
      include anyone who provides services under a contract for services
      and references to a person's employer shall be construed accordingly;
   "the 1974 Act", "the 1975 Act", "the 1978 Act" and "the 1976 Order" mean,
      respectively, the Trade Union and Labour Relations Act 1974, the
      Employment Protection Act 1975, the Employment Protection (Con-
      solidation) Act 1978 and the Industrial Relations (Northern Ireland)
      Order 1976;
   "recognised", in relation to a trade union, means recognised to any extent
      by an employer, or two or more associated employers, (within the
      meaning of the 1978 Act, or, in Northern Ireland, the 1976 Order, for
      the purpose of collective bargaining;
   "relevant transfer" means a transfer to which these Regulations apply and
      "transferor" and "transferee" shall be construed accordingly; and
   "undertaking" includes any trade or business [...][1].

(2) References in these Regulations to the transfer of part of an undertaking are references to a transfer of a part which is being transferred as a business and, accordingly, do not include references to a transfer of a ship without more.

(3) For the purposes of these Regulations the representative of a trade union recognised by an employer is an official or other person authorised to carry on collective bargaining with that employer by that union.

---

[1] Words repealed by Trade Union Reform and Employment Rights Act 1993 c.19 Pt II s 33 (2)

A relevant transfer

19-003   **3.**—(1) Subject to the provisions of these Regulations, these Regulations apply to a transfer from one person to another of an undertaking situated immediately before the transfer in the United Kingdom or a part of one which is so situated.

(2) Subject as aforesaid, these Regulations so apply whether the transfer is effected by sale or by some other disposition or by operation of law.

(3) Subject as aforesaid, these Regulations so apply notwithstanding—

(a) that the transfer is governed or effected by the law of a country or territory outside the United Kingdom;

(b) that persons employed in the undertaking or part transferred ordinarily work outside the United Kingdom;

(c) that the employment of any of those persons is governed by any such law.

(4) It is hereby declared that a transfer of an undertaking or part of [one—][1]

[(a) may be effected by a series of two or more transactions; and

(b) may take place whether or not any property is transferred to the transferee by the transferor.][2]

(5) Where, in consequence (whether directly or indirectly) of the transfer of an undertaking or part of one which was situated immediately before the transfer in the United Kingdom, a ship within the meaning of the Merchant Shipping Act 1894 registered in the United Kingdom ceases to be so registered, these Regulations shall not affect the right conferred by section 5 of the Merchant Shipping Act 1970 (right of seamen to be discharged when ship ceases to be registered in the United Kingdom) on a seaman employed in the ship.

Transfers by receivers and liquidators

19-004   **4.**—(1) Where the receiver of the property or part of the property of a company or, in the case of a creditors' voluntary winding up, the liquidator of a company [or the administrator of a company appointed under Part II of the Insolvency Act 1986][3] transfers the company's undertaking, or part of the company's undertaking (the "relevant undertaking") to a wholly owned subsidiary of the company, the transfer shall for the purposes of these Regulations be deemed not to have been effected until immediately before—

(a) the transferee company ceases (otherwise than by reason of its being wound up) to be a wholly owned subsidiary of the transferor company; or

(b) the relevant undertaking is transferred by the transferee company to another person;

whichever first occurs, and, for the purposes of these Regulations, the transfer of the relevant undertaking shall be taken to have been effected immediately before that date by one transaction only.

(2) In this Regulation—

"creditors' voluntary winding up" has the same meaning as in the Companies Act 1948 or, in Northern Ireland, the Companies Act (Northern Ireland) 1960; and

---

[1] Words substituted by Trade Union Reform and Employment Rights Act 1993 c.19 Pt II s 33 (3)

[2] Substituted by Trade Union Reform and Employment Rights Act 1993 c.19 Pt II s 33 (3)

[3] Words inserted by SI 1987/442 reg 2

"wholly owned subsidiary" has the same meaning as it has for the purposes of section 150 of the Companies Act 1948 andsection 144 of the Companies Act (Northern Ireland) 1960.

Effect of relevant transfer on contracts of employment, etc

5.—(1) [Except where objection is made under paragraph (4A) below, a][1] **19-005** relevant transfer shall not operate so as to terminate the contract of employment of any person employed by the transferor in the undertaking or part transferred but any such contract which would otherwise have been terminated by the transfer shall have effect after the transfer as if originally made between the person so employed and the transferee.

(2) Without prejudice to paragraph (1) above, [but subject to paragraph (4A) below,][2] on the completion of a relevant transfer—

   (a) all the transferor's rights, powers, duties and liabilities under or in connection with any such contract, shall be transferred by virtue of this Regulation to the transferee; and

   (b) anything done before the transfer is completed by or in relation to the transferor in respect of that contract or a person employed in that undertaking or part shall be deemed to have been done by or in relation to the transferee.

(3) Any reference in paragraph (1) or (2) above to a person employed in an undertaking or part of one transferred by a relevant transfer is a reference to a person so employed immediately before the transfer, including, where the transfer is effected by a series of two or more transactions, a person so employed immediately before any of those transactions.

(4) Paragraph (2) above shall not transfer or otherwise affect the liability of any person to be prosecuted for, convicted of and sentenced for any offence.

[(4A) Paragraphs (1) and (2) above shall not operate to transfer his contract of employment and the rights, powers, duties and liabilities under or in connection with it if the employee informs the transferor or the transferee that he objects to becoming employed by the transferee.

(4B) Where an employee so objects the transfer of the undertaking or part in which he is employed shall operate so as to terminate his contract of employment with the transferor but he shall not be treated, for any purpose, as having been dismissed by the transferor.][3]

(5) [Paragraphs (1) and (4A) above are][4] without prejudice to any right of an employee arising apart from these Regulations to terminate his contract of employment without notice if a substantial change is made in his working conditions to his detriment; but no such right shall arise by reason only that, under that paragraph, the identity of his employer changes unless the employee shows that, in all the circumstances, the change is a significant change and is to his detriment.

Effect of relevant transfer on collective agreements

6. Where at the time of a relevant transfer there exists a collective agreement **19-006** made by or on behalf of the transferor with a trade union recognised by the

---

[1] Words inserted by Trade Union Reform and Employment Rights Act 1993 c.19 Pt II s 33 (4) (a)

[2] Words inserted by Trade Union Reform and Employment Rights Act 1993 c.19 Pt II s 33 (4) (b)

[3] Inserted by Trade Union Reform and Employment Rights Act 1993 c.19 Pt II s 33 (4) (c)

[4] Words substituted by Trade Union Reform and Employment Rights Act 1993 c.19 Pt II s 33 (4) (d)

transferor in respect of any employee whose contract of employment is preserved by Regulation 5(1) above, then,—

   (a) without prejudice to section 18 of the 1974 Act or Article 63 of the 1976 Order (collective agreements presumed to be unenforceable in specified circumstances) that agreement, in its application in relation to the employee, shall, after the transfer, have effect as if made by or on behalf of the transferee with that trade union, and accordingly anything done under or in connection with it, in its application as aforesaid, by or in relation to the transferor before the transfer, shall, after the transfer, be deemed to have been done by or in relation to the transferee; and

   (b) any order made in respect of that agreement, in its application in relation to the employee, shall, after the transfer, have effect as if the transferee were a party to the agreement.

[Exclusion of occupational pensions schemes

19-007   **7.**—(1) Regulations 5 and 6 above shall not apply—

   (a) to so much of a contract of employment or collective agreement as relates to an occupational pension scheme within the meaning of the Social Security Pensions Act 1975 or the Social Security Pensions (Northern Ireland) Order 1975; or

   (b) to any rights, powers, duties or liabilities under or in connection with any such contract or subsisting by virtue of any such agreement and relating to such a scheme or otherwise arising in connection with that person's employment and relating to such a scheme.

   (2) For the purposes of paragraph (1) above any provisions of an occupational pension scheme which do not relate to benefits for old age, invalidity or survivors shall be treated as not being part of the scheme.][1]

Dismissal of employee because of relevant transfer

19-008   **8.**—(1) Where either before or after a relevant transfer, any employee of the transferor or transferee is dismissed, that employee shall be treated for the purposes of Part V of the 1978 Act and Articles 20 to 41 of the 1976 Order (unfair dismissal) as unfairly dismissed if the transfer or a reason connected with it is the reason or principal reason for his dismissal.

   (2) Where an economic, technical or organisational reason entailing changes in the workforce of either the transferor or the transferee before or after a relevant transfer is the reason or principal reason for dismissing an employee—

   (a) paragraph (1) above shall not apply to his dismissal; but

   (b) without prejudice to the application of section 57(3) of the 1978 Act or Article 22(10) of the 1976 Order (test of fair dismissal), the dismissal shall for the purposes of section 57(1)(b) of that Act and Article 22(1)(b) of that Order (substantial reason for dismissal) be regarded as having been for a substantial reason of a kind such as to justify the dismissal of an employee holding the position which that employee held.

   (3) The provisions of this Regulation apply whether or not the employee in question is employed in the undertaking or part of the undertaking transferred or to be transferred.

   (4) Paragraph (1) above shall not apply in relation to the dismissal of any employee which was required by reason of the application of section 5 of the Aliens Restriction (Amendment) Act 1919 to his employment.

---

[1] Reg 7 renumbered as reg 7 (1) and reg 7 (2) inserted by Trade Union Reform and Employment Rights Act 1993 c.19 Pt II s 33 (5)

[(5) Paragraph (1) above shall not apply in relation to a dismissal of an employee if—
    (a) the application of section 54 of the 1978 Act to the dismissal of the employee is excluded by or under any provision of Part V or sections 141 to 149 of the 1978 Act or of section 237 or 238 of the Trade Union and Labour Relations (Consolidation) Act 1992; or
    (b) the application of Article 20 of the 1976 Order to the dismissal of the employee is excluded by or under any provision of Part III or Article 76 of that Order.][1]

Effect of relevant transfer on trade union recognition

9.—(1) This Regulation applies where after a relevant transfer the undertaking **19-009** or part of the undertaking transferred maintains an identity distinct from the remainder of the transferee's undertaking.

(2) Where before such a transfer an independent trade union is recognised to any extent by the transferor in respect of employees of any description who in consequence of the transfer become employees of the transferee, then, after the transfer—
    (a) the union shall be deemed to have been recognised by the transferee to the same extent in respect of employees of that description so employed; and
    (b) any agreement for recognition may be varied or rescinded accordingly.

Duty to inform and consult [...][2] representatives

10.—(1) In this Regulation and Regulation 11 below [references to affected **19-010** employees, in relation to a relevant transfer, are to any employees of the transferor or the transferee (whether or not employed in the undertaking or the part of the undertaking to be transferred) who may be affected by the transfer or may be affected by measures taken in connection with it; and references to the employer shall be construed accordingly][3].

(2) Long enough before a relevant transfer to enable [the employer of any affected employees to consult all the persons who are appropriate representatives of any of those affected employees,][4] the employer shall inform those representatives of—
    (a) the fact that the relevant transfer is to take place, when, approximately, it is to take place and the reasons for it; and
    (b) the legal, economic and social implications of the transfer for the affected employees; and
    (c) the measures which he envisages he will, in connection with the transfer, take in relation to those employees or, if he envisages that no measures will be so taken, that fact; and
    (d) if the employer is the transferor, the measures which the transferee envisages he will, in connection with the transfer, take in relation to such of those employees as, by virtue of Regulation 5 above, become employees of the transferee after the transfer or, if he envisages that no measures will be so taken, that fact.

[(2A) For the purposes of this Regulation the appropriate representatives of any employees are-

---

[1] Inserted by SI 1995/2587 reg 8
[2] Words repealed by SI 1995/2587 reg 9 (11)
[3] Words substituted by SI 1995/2587 reg 9 (2)
[4] Words substituted by SI 1995/2587 reg 9 (3)

    (a) if the employees are of a description in respect of which an independent trade union is recognised by their employer, representatives of the trade union, or

    (b) in any other case, whichever of the following employee representatives the employer chooses:-

        (i) employee representatives appointed or elected by the affected employees otherwise than for the purposes of this Regulation, who (having regard to the purposes for and the method by which they were appointed or elected) have authority from those employees to receive information and to be consulted about [the transfer][1] on their behalf;

        (ii) employee representatives elected by them, for the purposes of this Regulation, in an election satisfying the requirements of Regulation 10A(1).][2]

(3) The transferee shall give the transferor such information at such a time as will enable the transferor to perform the duty imposed on him by virtue of paragraph (2)(d) above.

(4) The information which is to be given to the [appropriate representatives shall be given to each of them by being delivered to them, or sent by post to an address notified by them to the employer, or (in the case of representatives of a trade union)][3] sent by post to the union at the address of its head or main office.

(5) Where an employer of any affected employees envisages that he will, in connection with the transfer, be taking measures in relation to any such employees [[he shall consult all the persons who are appropriate representatives of any of the affected employees in relation to whom he envisages taking measures][4] with a view to seeking their agreement to measures to be taken][5].

(6) In the course of those consultations the employer shall—

    (a) consider any representations made by the [appropriate][6] representatives; and

    (b) reply to those representations and, if he rejects any of those representations, state his reasons.

[(6A) The employer shall allow the appropriate representatives access to the affected employees and shall afford to those representatives such accommodation and other facilities as may be appropriate.][7]

(7) If in any case there are special circumstances which render it not reasonably practicable for an employer to perform a duty imposed on him by any of [paragraphs (2) to (6)][8], he shall take all such steps towards performing that duty as are reasonably practicable in the circumstances.

[(8) Where—

    (a) the employer has invited any of the affected employees to elect employee representatives, and

    (b) the invitation was issued long enough before the time when the employer is required to give information under paragraph (2) above to allow them to elect representatives by that time,

[1] Words substituted by SI 1999/2402 reg 3
[2] Substituted by SI 1999/1925 reg 8 (2)
[3] Words substituted by SI 1995/2587 reg 9 (5)
[4] Words substituted by SI 1995/2587 reg 9 (6)
[5] Words inserted by Trade Union Reform and Employment Rights Act 1993 c.19 Pt II s 33 (6)
[6] Word substituted by SI 1995/2587 reg 9 (7)
[7] Inserted by SI 1995/2587 reg 9 (8)
[8] Words substituted by SI 1995/2587 reg 9 (9)

the employer shall be treated as complying with the requirements of this Regulation in relation to those employees if he complies with those requirements as soon as is reasonably practicable after the election of the representatives.][1]

[(8A) If, after the employer has invited affected employees to elect representatives, they fail to do so within a reasonable time, he shall give to each affected employee the information set out in paragraph (2).][2]

[**10A.**—(1) The requirements for the election of employee representatives under **19-011** Regulation 10(2A) are that—

   (a) the employer shall make such arrangements as are reasonably practical to ensure that the election is fair;

   (b) the employer shall determine the number of representatives to be elected so that there are sufficient representatives to represent the interests of all the affected employees having regard to the number and classes of those employees;

   (c) the employer shall determine whether the affected employees should be represented either by representatives of all the affected employees or by representatives of particular classes of those employees;

   (d) before the election the employer shall determine the term of office as employee representatives so that it is of sufficient length to enable information to be given and consultations under Regulation 10 to be completed;

   (e) the candidates for election as employee representatives are affected employees on the date of the election;

   (f) no affected employee is unreasonably excluded from standing for election;

   (g) all affected employees on the date of the election are entitled to vote for employee representatives;

   (h) the employees entitled to vote may vote for as many candidates as there are representatives to be elected to represent them or, if there are to be representatives for particular classes of employees, may vote for as many candidates as there are representatives to be elected to represent their particular class of employee;

   (i) the election is conducted so as to secure that—

      (i) so far as is reasonably practicable, those voting do so in secret, and

      (ii) the votes given at the election are accurately counted.

(2) Where, after an election of employee representatives satisfying the requirements of paragraph (1) has been held, one of those elected ceases to act as an employee representative and any of those employees are no longer represented, those employees shall elect another representative by an election satisfying the requirements of paragraph (1)(a), (e), (f) and (i).][3]

Failure to inform or consult

11.—[(1) Where an employer has failed to comply with a requirement of **19-012** Regulation 10 or Regulation 10A, a complaint may be presented to an employment tribunal on that ground–

   (a) in the case of a failure relating to the election of employee representatives, by any of his employees who are affected employees;

---

[1] Inserted by SI 1995/2587 reg 9 (10)
[2] Inserted by SI 1999/1925 reg 8 (3)
[3] Inserted by SI 1999/1925 reg 9

 (b) in the case of any other failure relating to employee representatives, by any of the employee representatives to whom the failure related,

 (c) in the case of failure relating to representatives of a trade union, by the trade union, and

 (d) in any other case, by any of his employees who are affected employees.][1]

(2) If on a complaint under paragraph (1) above a question arises whether or not it was reasonably practicable for an employer to perform a particular duty or what steps he took towards performing it, it shall be for him to show—

 (a) that there were special circumstances which rendered it not reasonably practicable for him to perform the duty; and

 (b) that he took all such steps towards its performance as were reasonably practicable in those circumstances.

[(2A) If on a complaint under paragraph (1) a question arises as to whether or not any employee representative was an appropriate representative for the purposes of Regulation 10, it shall be for the employer to show that the employee representative had the necessary authority to represent the affected employees.

(2B) On a complaint under sub-paragraph (1)(a) it shall be for the employer to show that the requirements in Regulation 10A have been satisfied.][2]

(3) On any such complaint against a transferor that he had failed to perform the duty imposed upon him by virtue of paragraph (2)(d) or, so far as relating thereto, paragraph (7) of Regulation 10 above, he may not show that it was not reasonably practicable for him to perform the duty in question for the reason that the transferee had failed to give him the requisite information at the requisite time in accordance with Regulation 10(3) above unless he gives the transferee notice of his intention to show that fact; and the giving of the notice shall make the transferee a party to the proceedings.

(4) Where the tribunal finds a complaint under paragraph (1) above well-founded it shall make a declaration to that effect and may—

 (a) order the employer to pay appropriate compensation to such descriptions of affected employees as may be specified in the award; or

 (b) if the complaint is that the transferor did not perform the duty mentioned in paragraph (3) above and the transferor (after giving due notice) shows the facts so mentioned, order the transferee to pay appropriate compensation to such descriptions of affected employees as may be specified in the award.

(5) An employee may present a complaint to an [employment tribunal][3] on the ground that he is an employee of a description to which an order under paragraph (4) above relates and that the transferor or the transferee has failed, wholly or in part, to pay him compensation in pursuance of the order.

(6) Where the tribunal finds a complaint under paragraph (5) above well-founded it shall order the employer to pay the complainant the amount of compensation which it finds is due to him.

(7) [...][4]

(8) An [employment tribunal][5] shall not consider a complaint under paragraph (1) or (5) above unless it is presented to the tribunal before the end of the period of three months beginning with—

---

[1] Substituted by SI 1999/1925 reg 10 (2)

[2] Inserted by SI 1999/1925 reg 10 (3)

[3] Words substituted by Employment Rights (Dispute Resolution) Act 1998 c.8 Pt I s 1 (2)

[4] Repealed by Trade Union Reform and Employment Rights Act 1993 c.19 Sch 10 para 1

[5] Words substituted by Employment Rights (Dispute Resolution) Act 1998 c.8 Pt I s 1 (2)

(a) the date on which the relevant transfer is completed, in the case of a complaint under paragraph (1);

(b) the date of the tribunal's order under paragraph (4) above, in the case of a complaint under paragraph (5);

or within such further period as the tribunal considers reasonable in a case where it is satisfied that it was not reasonably practicable for the complaint to be presented before the end of the period of three months.

(9) Section 129 of the 1978 Act (complaint to be sole remedy for breach of relevant rights) and section 133 of that Act (functions of conciliation officer) and Articles 58(2) and 62 of the 1976 Order (which make corresponding provision for Northern Ireland) shall apply to the rights conferred by this Regulation and to proceedings under this Regulation as they apply to the rights conferred by that Act or that Order and the industrial tribunal proceedings mentioned therein.

(10) An appeal shall lie and shall lie only to the Employment Appeal Tribunal on a question of law arising from any decision of, or arising in any proceedings before, an industrial tribunal under or by virtue of these Regulations; and section 13(1) of the Tribunals and Inquiries Act 1971 (appeal from certain tribunals to the High Court) shall not apply in relation to any such proceedings.

(11) In this Regulation "appropriate compensation" means such sum not exceeding [thirteen weeks' pay]¹ for the employee in question as the tribunal considers just and equitable having regard to the seriousness of the failure of the employer to comply with his duty.

(12) Schedule 14 to the 1978 Act or, in Northern Ireland, Schedule 2 to the 1976 Order shall apply for calculating the amount of a week's pay for any employee for the purposes of paragraph (11) above; and, for the purposes of that calculation, the calculation date shall be—

(a) in the case of an employee who is dismissed by reason of redundancy (within the meaning of section 81 of the 1978 Act or, in Northern Ireland, section 11 of the Contracts of Employment and Redundancy Payments Act (Northern Ireland) 1965 the date which is the calculation date for the purposes of any entitlement of his to a redundancy payment (within the meaning of that section or which would be that calculation date if he were so entitled;

(b) in the case of an employee who is dismissed for any other reason, the effective date of termination (within the meaning of section 55 of the 1978 Act or, in Northern Ireland, Article 21 of the 1976 Order) of his contract of employment;

(c) in any other case, the date of the transfer in question.

[Construction of references to employee representatives

11A. For the purposes of Regulations 10 and 11 above persons are employee representatives if— **19-013**

(a) they have been elected by employees for the specific purpose of being given information and consulted by their employer under Regulation 10 above; or

(b) having been elected [or appointed]² by employees otherwise than for that specific purpose, it is appropriate (having regard to the purposes for which they were elected) for their employer to inform and consult them under that Regulation,

---

¹ Words substituted by SI 1999/1925 reg 10 (4)
² Words Inserted by SI 1999/1925 reg 11 (2)

and (in either case) they are employed by the employer at the time when they are elected [or appointed][1].][2]

Restriction on contracting out

19-014   **12.** Any provision of any agreement (whether a contract of employment or not) shall be void in so far as it purports to exclude or limit the operation of Regulation 5, 8 or 10 above or to preclude any person from presenting a complaint to an [employment tribunal][3] under Regulation 11 above.

Exclusion of employment abroad or as dock worker

19-015   **13.**—(1) Regulations 8, 10 and 11 of these Regulations do not apply to employment where under his contract of employment the employee ordinarily works outside the United Kingdom.

(2) For the purposes of this Regulation a person employed to work on board a ship registered in the United Kingdom shall, unless—

   (a) the employment is wholly outside the United Kingdom, or

   (b) he is not ordinarily resident in the United Kingdom,

be regarded as a person who under his contract ordinarily works in the United Kingdom.

(3) Nothing in these Regulations applies in relation to any person employed as a registered dock worker unless he is wholly or mainly engaged in work which is not dock work.

(4) Paragraph (3) above shall be construed as if it were contained in section 145 of the 1978 Act.

Consequential amendments

19-016   **14.**—(1) In section 4(4) of the 1978 Act (written statement to be given to employee on change of his employer), in paragraph (b), the reference to paragraph 17 of Schedule 13 to that Act (continuity of employment where change of employer) shall include a reference to these Regulations.

(2) In section 4(6A) of the Contracts of Employment and Redundancy Payments Act (Northern Ireland) 1965, in paragraph (b), the reference to paragraph 10 of Schedule 1 to that Act shall include a reference to these Regulations.

The Disability Discrimination (Meaning of Disability) Regulations 1996

(S.I. 1455)

Citation and commencement

20-001   **1.** These Regulations may be cited as the Disability Discrimination (Meaning of Disability) Regulations 1996 and shall come into force on 30th July 1996.

---
[1] Words inserted by SI 1999/1925 reg 11 (3)
[2] Inserted by SI 1995/2587 reg 11
[3] Words substituted by Employment Rights (Dispute Resolution) Act 1998 c.8 Pt I s 1 (2)

Interpretation

2. In these Regulations-   **20-002**
"the Act" means the Disability Discrimination Act 1995; and
"addition" includes a dependency.

Addictions

3.—(1) Subject to paragraph (2) below, addiction to alcohol, nicotine or any **20-003** other substance is to be treated as not amounting to an impairment for the purposes of the Act.

(2) Paragraph (1) above does not apply to addiction which was originally the result of administration of medically prescribed drugs or other medical treatment.

Other conditions not to be treated as impairments

4.—(1) For the purposes of the Act the following conditions are to be treated **20-004** as not amounting to impairments:-
  (a) a tendency to set fires,
  (b) a tendency to steal,
  (c) a tendency to physical or sexual abuse of other persons,
  (d) exhibitionism, and
  (e) voyeurism.

(2) Subject to paragraph (3) below for the purposes of the Act the condition known as seasonal allergic rhinitis shall be treated as not amounting to an impairment.

(3) Paragraph (2) above shall not prevent that condition from being taken into account for the purposes of the Act where it aggravates the effect of another condition.

Tattoos and piercings

5. For the purposes of paragraph 3 of Schedule 1 to the Act a severe disfigure- **20-005** ment is not to be treated as having a substantial adverse effect on the ability of the person concerned to carry out normal day-to-day activities if it consists of –
  (a) a tattoo (which has not been removed), or
  (b) a piercing of the body for decorative or other non-medical purposes, including any object attached through the piercing for such purposes.

Babies and Young Children

6. For the purposes of the Act where a child under six years of age has an **20-006** impairment which does not have an effect falling within paragraph 4(1) of Schedule 1 to the Act that impairment is to be taken to have a substantial and long-term adverse effect on the ability of that child to carry out normal day-to-day activities where it would normally have a substantial and long-term adverse effect on the ability of a person aged 6 years or over to carry out normal day-to-day activities.

The Working Time Regulations 1998

(S.I. 1833)

PART I

GENERAL

Citation, commencement and extent

21-001   **1.**—(1) These Regulations may be cited as the Working Time Regulations 1998 and shall come into force on 1st October 1998.

(2) These Regulations extend to Great Britain only.

Interpretation

21-002   **2.**—(1) In these Regulations—

"the 1996 Act" means the Employment Rights Act 1996;

"adult worker" means a worker who has attained the age of 18;

"the armed forces" means any of the naval, military and air forces of the Crown;

"calendar year" means the period of twelve months beginning with 1st January in any year;

"the civil protection services" includes the police, fire brigades and ambulance services, the security and intelligence services, customs and immigration officers, the prison service, the coastguard, and lifeboat crew and other voluntary rescue services;

"collective agreement" means a collective agreement within the meaning of section 178 of the Trade Union and Labour Relations (Consolidation) Act 1992, the trade union parties to which are independent trade unions within the meaning of section 5 of that Act;

"day" means a period of 24 hours beginning at midnight;

"employer", in relation to a worker, means the person by whom the worker is (or, where the employment has ceased, was) employed;

"employment", in relation to a worker, means employment under his contract, and

"employed", shall be construed accordingly;

["fishing vessel" has the same meaning as in section 313 of the Merchant Shipping Act 1995;

"mobile worker" means any worker employed as a member of travelling or flying personnel by an undertaking which operates transport services for passengers or goods by road or air;][1]

"night time", in relation to a worker, means a period—

    (a) the duration of which is not less than seven hours, and

    (b) which includes the period between midnight and 5 a.m.,

which is determined for the purposes of these Regulations by a relevant agreement, or, in default of such a determination, the period between 11 p.m. and 6 a.m.;

"night work" means work during night time;

"night worker" means a worker—

---

[1] Definitions inserted by SI 2003/1684 reg 3

(a) who, as a normal course, works at least three hours of his daily working time during night time, or

(b) who is likely, during night time, to work at least such proportion of his annual working time as may be specified for the purposes of these Regulations in a collective agreement or a workforce agreement;

and, for the purpose of paragraph (a) of this definition, a person works hours as a normal course (without prejudice to the generality of that expression) if he works such hours on the majority of days on which he works;

["offshore work" means work performed mainly on or from offshore installations (including drilling rigs), directly or indirectly in connection with the exploration, extraction or exploitation of mineral resources, including hydrocarbons, and diving in connection with such activities, whether performed from an offshore installation or a vessel;][1]

"relevant agreement", in relation to a worker, means a workforce agreement which applies to him, any provision of a collective agreement which forms part of a contract between him and his employer, or any other agreement in writing which is legally enforceable as between the worker and his employer;

"relevant training" means work experience provided pursuant to a training course or programme, training for employment, or both, other than work experience or training–

(a) the immediate provider of which is an educational institution or a person whose main business is the provision of training, and

(b) which is provided on a course run by that institution or person;

"rest period", in relation to a worker, means a period which is not working time, other than a rest break or leave to which the worker is entitled under these Regulations;

["the restricted period", in relation to a worker, means the period between 10 p.m. and 6 a.m.or, where the worker's contract provides for him to work after 10 p.m., the period between 11 p.m. and 7 a.m.][2]

["ship" has the same meaning as in section 313 of the Merchant Shipping Act 1995;][3]

"worker" means an individual who has entered into or works under (or, where the employment has ceased, worked under)–

(a) a contract of employment; or

(b) any other contract, whether express or implied and (if it is express) whether oral or in writing, whereby the individual undertakes to do or perform personally any work or services for another party to the contract whose status is not by virtue of the contract that of a client or customer of any profession or business taking carried on by the individual;

and any reference to a worker's contract shall be construed accordingly;

"worker employed in agriculture" has the same meaning as in the Agricultural Wages Act 1948 or the Agricultural Wages (Scotland) Act 1949, and a reference to a worker partly employed in agriculture is to a worker employed

---

[1] Definition inserted by SI 2003/1684 reg 3
[2] Definition inserted by SI 2002/3128 reg 3
[3] Definition inserted by SI 2003/1684 reg 3

in agriculture whose employer also employs him for non-agricultural purposes;

"workforce agreement" means an agreement between an employer and workers employed by him or their representatives in respect of which the conditions set out in Schedule 1 to these Regulations are satisfied;

"working time", in relation to a worker, means –

    (a) any period during which he is working, at his employer's disposal and carrying out his activity or duties,

    (b) any period during which he is receiving relevant training, and

    (c) any additional period which is to be treated as working time for the purpose of these Regulations under a relevant agreement;

and "work" shall be construed accordingly;

"Working Time Directive" means Council Directive 93/104/EC of 23rd November 1993 concerning certain aspects of the organization of working time;

"young worker" means a worker who has attained the age of 15 but not the age of 18 and who, as respects England and Wales, is over compulsory school age (construed in accordance with section 8 of the Education Act 1996) and, as respects Scotland, is over school age (construed in accordance with section 31 of the Education (Scotland) Act 1980), and

"Young Workers Directive" means Council Directive 94/33/EC of 22nd June 1994 on the protection of young people at work.

(2) In the absence of a definition in these Regulations, words and expressions used in particular provisions which are also used in corresponding provisions of the Working Time Directive or the Young Workers Directive have the same meaning as they have in those corresponding provisions.

(3) In these Regulations –

    (a) a reference to a numbered regulation is to the regulation in these Regulations bearing that number;

    (b) a reference in a regulation to a numbered paragraph is to the paragraph in that regulation bearing that number; and

    (c) a reference in a paragraph to a lettered sub-paragraph is to the sub-paragraph in that paragraph bearing that letter.

PART II

RIGHTS AND OBLIGATIONS CONCERNING WORKING TIME

General

21-003   **3.**—(1) The provisions of this Part have effect subject to the exceptions provided for in Part III of these Regulations.

[(2) Where, in this Part, separate provision is made as respects the same matter in relation to young workers, the provision relating to workers generally applies only to adult workers and those young workers to whom, by virtue of any exception in Part 3, the provision relating to young workers does not apply.][1]

---

[1] Inserted by SI 2002/3128 reg 4

Maximum weekly working time

4.—(1) [Unless his employer has first obtained the worker's agreement in **21-004** writing to perform such work][1], a worker's working time, including overtime, in any reference period which is applicable in his case shall not exceed an average of 48 hours for each seven days.

(2) An employer shall take all reasonable steps, in keeping with the need to protect the health and safety of workers, to ensure that the limit specified in paragraph (1) is complied with in the case of each worker employed by him in relation to whom it applies [and shall keep up-to-date records of all workers who carry out work to which it does not apply by reason of the fact that the employer has obtained the worker's agreement as mentioned in paragraph (1)][2].

(3) Subject to paragraphs (4) and (5) and any agreement under regulation 23(b), the reference periods which apply in the case of a worker are–

- (a) where a relevant agreement provides for the application of this regulation in relation to successive periods of 17 weeks, each such period, or
- (b) in any other case, any period of 17 weeks in the course of his employment.

(4) Where a worker has worked for his employer for less than 17 weeks, the reference period applicable in his case is the period that has elapsed since he started work for his employer.

(5) Paragraphs (3) and (4) shall apply to a worker who is excluded from the scope of certain provisions of these Regulations by regulation 21 as if for each reference to 17 weeks there were substituted a reference to 26 weeks.

(6) For the purposes of this regulation, a worker's average working time for each seven days during a reference period shall be determined according to the formula– $(A + B)/C$ where–

A is the aggregate number of hours comprised in the worker's working time during the course of the reference period;

B is the aggregate number of hours comprised in his working time during the course of the period beginning immediately after the end of the reference period and ending when the number of days in that subsequent period on which he has worked equals the number of excluded days during the reference period; and

C is the number of weeks in the reference period.

(7) In paragraph (6), "excluded days" means days comprised in–

- (a) any period of annual leave taken by the worker in exercise of his entitlement under regulation 13;
- (b) any period of sick leave taken by the worker;
- (c) any period of maternity, [paternity, adoption or parental][3] leave taken by the worker; and
- (d) any period in respect of which the limit specified in paragraph (1) did not apply in relation to the worker [by reason of the fact that the employer has obtained the worker's agreement as mentioned in paragraph (1)][4].

Agreement to exclude the maximum

5.—(1) [...][5] **21-005**

---

[1] Words substituted by SI 1999/3372 reg 3 (1) (a)
[2] Words inserted by SI 1999/3372 reg 3 (1) (b)
[3] Words inserted by SI 2002/3128 reg 5
[4] Words substituted by SI 1999/3372 reg 3 (1) (c)
[5] Repealed by SI 1999/3372 reg 3 (2) (a)

(2) An agreement for the purposes of [regulation 4][1]–

(a) may either relate to a specified period or apply indefinitely; and

(b) subject to any provision in the agreement for a different period of notice, shall be terminable by the worker by giving not less than seven days' notice to his employer in writing.

(3) Where an agreement for the purposes of [regulation 4][2] makes provision for the termination of the agreement after a period of notice, the notice period provided for shall not exceed three months.

(4) [...][3]

[Maximum working time for young workers

21-006   **5A.**—(1) A young worker's working time shall not exceed -

(a) eight hours a day, or

(b) 40 hours per week

(2) If, on any day, or, as the case may be, during any week, a young worker is employed by more than one employer, his working time shall be determined for the purpose of paragraph (1) by aggregating the number of hours worked by him for each employer.

(3) For the purposes of paragraphs (1) and (2), a week starts at midnight between Sunday and Monday.

(4) An employer shall take all reasonable steps, in keeping with the need to protect the health and safety of workers, to ensure that the limits specified in paragraph (1) are complied with in the case of each worker employed by him in relation to whom they apply.][4]

Length of night work

21-007   **6.**—(1) A night worker's normal hours of work in any reference period which is applicable in his case shall not exceed an average of eight hours for each 24 hours.

(2) An employer shall take all reasonable steps, in keeping with the need to protect the health and safety or workers, to ensure that the limit specified in paragraph (1) is complied with in the case of each night worker employed by him.

(3) The reference periods which apply in the case of a night worker are–

(a) where a relevant agreement provides for the application of this regulation in relation to successive periods of 17 weeks, each such period, or

(b) in any other case, any period of 17 weeks in the course of his employment.

(4) Where a worker has worked for his employer for less than 17 weeks, the reference period applicable in his case is the period that has elapsed since he started work for his employer.

(5) For the purposes of this regulation, a night worker's average normal hours of work for each 24 hours during a reference period shall be determined according to the formula – $^A/_{(B - C)}$ where –

A is the number of hours during the reference period which are normal working hours for that worker;

B is the number of days during the reference period, and

---

[1] Words substituted by SI 1999/3372 reg 3 (2) (b)

[2] Words substituted by SI 1999/3372 reg 3 (2) (b)

[3] Repealed by SI 1999/3372 reg 3 (2) (a)

[4] Inserted by SI 2002/3128 reg 6

C is the total number of hours during the reference period comprised in rest periods spent by the worker in pursuance of his entitlement under regulation 11, divided by 24.

(7) An employer shall ensure that no night worker employed by him whose work involves special hazards or heavy physical or mental strain works for more than eight hours in any 24-hour period during which the night worker performs night work.

(8) For the purposes of paragraph (7), the work of a night worker shall be regarded as involving special hazards or heavy physical or mental strain if –

    (a) it is identified as such in –

        (i) a collective agreement, or

        (ii) a workforce agreement,

    which takes account of the specific effects and hazards of night work, or

    (b) it is recognised in a risk assessment made by the employer under [regulation 3 of the Management of Health and Safety at Work Regulations 1999][1] as involving a significant risk to the health or safety of workers employed by him.

[Night work by young workers

6A. An employer shall ensure that no young worker employed by him works **21-008** during the restricted period.][2]

Health assessment and transfer of night workers to day work

7.—(1) An employer –   **21-009**

    (a) shall not assign an adult worker to work which is to be undertaken during periods such that the worker will become a night worker unless –

        (i) the employer has ensured that the worker will have the opportunity of a free health assessment before he takes up the assignment; or

        (ii) the worker had a health assessment before being assigned to work to be undertaken during such periods on an earlier occasion, and the employer has no reason to believe that that assessment is no longer valid, and

    (b) shall ensure that each night worker employed by him has the opportunity of a free health assessment at regular intervals of whatever duration may be appropriate in his case.

(2) Subject to paragraph (4), an employer –

    (a) shall not assign a young worker to work during [the restricted period][3] unless –

        (i) the employer has ensured that the young worker will have the opportunity of a free assessment of his health and capacities before he takes up the assignment; or

        (ii) the young worker had an assessment of his health and capacities before being assigned to work during the restricted period on an earlier occasion, and the employer has no reason to believe that that assessment is no longer valid; and

    (b) shall ensure that each young worker employed by him and assigned to work during the restricted period has the opportunity of a free

---

[1] Words substituted by SI 1999/3242 Sch 2 para 1

[2] Inserted by SI 2002/3128 reg 8

[3] Words inserted by SI 2002/3128 reg 9

assessment of his health and capacities at regular intervals of whatever duration may be appropriate in his case.

(3) For the purposes of paragraphs (1) and (2), an assessment is free if it is at no cost to the worker to whom it relates.

(4) The requirements in paragraph (2) do not apply in a case where the work a young worker is assigned to do is of an exceptional nature.

(5) No person shall disclose an assessment made for the purposes of this regulation to any person other than the worker to whom it relates, unless –

    (a) the worker has given his consent in writing to the disclosure, or

    (b) the disclosure is confined to a statement that the assessment shows the worker to be fit –

        (i) in a case where paragraph (1)(a)(i) or (2)(a)(i) applies, to take up an assignment, or

        (ii) in a case where paragraph (1)(b) or (2)(b) applies, to continue to undertake an assignment.

(6) Where –

    (a) a registered medical practitioner has advised an employer that a worker employed by the employer is suffering from health problems which the practitioner considers to be connected with the fact that the worker performs night work, and

    (b) it is possible for the employer to transfer the worker to work –

        (i) to which the worker is suited, and

        (ii) which is to be undertaken during periods such that the worker will cease to be a night worker,

the employer shall transfer the worker accordingly.

Pattern of work

21-010   **8.** Where the pattern according to which an employer organizes work is such as to put the health and safety of a worker employed by him at risk, in particular because the work is monotonous or the work-rate is predetermined, the employer shall ensure that the worker is given adequate rest breaks.

Records

21-011   **9.** An employer shall –

    (a) keep records which are adequate to show whether the limits specified in regulations 4(1), [5A(1)][1] and 6(1) and (7) and the requirements in regulations [6A and][2] 7(1) and (2) are being complied with in the case of each worker employed by him in relation to whom they apply; and

    (b) retain such records for two years from the date on which they were made.

Daily rest

21-012   **10.**—(1) [A worker][3] is entitled to a rest period of not less than eleven consecutive hours in each 24-hour period during which he works for his employer.

(2) Subject to paragraph (3), a young worker is entitled to a rest period of not less than twelve consecutive hours in each 24-hour period during which he works for his employer.

---

[1] Words inserted by SI 2002/3128 reg 10 (a)
[2] Words inserted by SI 2002/3128 reg 10 (b)
[3] Words inserted by SI 2002/3128 reg 11

(3) The minimum rest period provided for in paragraph (2) may be interrupted in the case of activities involving periods of work that are split up over the day or of short duration.

Weekly rest period

11.—(1) Subject to paragraph (2), [a worker][1] is entitled to an uninterrupted **21-013** rest period of not less than 24 hours in each seven-day period during which he works for his employer.

(2) If his employer so determines, [a worker][2] shall be entitled to either –
- (a) two uninterrupted rest periods each of not less than 24 hours in each 14-day period during which he works for his employer; or
- (b) one uninterrupted rest period of not less than 48 hours in each such 14-day period,

in place of the entitlement provided for in paragraph (1).

(3) Subject to paragraph (8), a young worker is entitled to a rest period of not less than 48 hours in each seven-day period during which he works for his employer.

(4) For the purpose of paragraphs (1) to (3), a seven-day period or (as the case may be) 14-day period shall be taken to begin –
- (a) at such times on such days as may be provided for for the purposes of this regulation in a relevant agreement; or
- (b) where there are no provisions of a relevant agreement which apply, at the start of each week or (as the case may be) every other week.

(5) In a case where, in accordance with paragraph (4), 14-day periods are to be taken to begin at the start of every other week, the first such period applicable in the case of a particular worker shall be taken to begin –
- (a) if the worker's employment began on or before the date on which these Regulations come into force, on 5th October 1998; or
- (b) if the worker's employment begins after the date on which these Regulations come into force, at the start of the week in which that employment begins.

(6) For the purposes of paragraphs (4) and (5), a week starts at midnight between Sunday and Monday.

(7) The minimum rest period to which [a worker][3] is entitled under paragraph (1) or (2) shall not include any part of a rest period to which the worker is entitled under regulation 10(1), except where this is justified by objective or technical reasons or reasons concerning the organization of work.

(8) The minimum rest period to which a young worker is entitled under paragraph (3)–
- (a) may be interrupted in the case of activities involving periods of work that are split up over the day or are of short duration; and
- (b) may be reduced where this is justified by technical or organization reasons, but not to less than 36 consecutive hours.

Rest breaks

12.—(1) Where [a worker's][4] daily working time is more than six hours, he is **21-014** entitled to a rest break.

---

[1] Words inserted by SI 2002/3128 reg 11
[2] Words inserted by SI 2002/3128 reg 11
[3] Words inserted by SI 2002/3128 reg 11
[4] Words inserted by SI 2002/3128 reg 13 (a)

(2) The details of the rest break to which [a worker]¹ is entitled under paragraph (1), including its duration and the terms on which it is granted, shall be in accordance with any provisions for the purposes of this regulation which are contained in a collective agreement or a workforce agreement.

(3) Subject to the provisions of any applicable collective agreement or workforce agreement, the rest break provided for in paragraph (1) is an uninterrupted period of not less than 20 minutes, and the worker is entitled to spend it away from his workstation if he has one.

(4) Where a young worker's daily working time is more than four and a half hours, he is entitled to a rest break of at least 30 minutes, which shall be consecutive if possible, and he is entitled to spend it away from his workstation if he has one.

(5) If, on any day, a young worker is employed by more than one employer, his daily working time shall be determined for the purpose of paragraph (4) by aggregating the number of hours worked by him for each employer.

Entitlement to annual leave

21-015   **13.**—[(1) Subject to paragraph (5), a worker is entitled to four weeks' annual leave in each leave year.]²

(2) [...]³

(3) A worker's leave year, for the purposes of this regulation, begins–
    (a) on such date during the calendar year as may be provided for in a relevant agreement; or
    (b) where there are no provisions of a relevant agreement which apply–
        (i) if the worker's employment began on or before 1st October 1998, on that date and each subsequent anniversary of that date; or
        (ii) if the worker's employment begins after 1st October 1998, on the date on which that employment begins and each subsequent anniversary of that date.

(4) Paragraph (3) does not apply to a worker to whom Schedule 2 applies (workers employed in agriculture) except where, in the case of a worker partly employed in agriculture, a relevant agreement so provides.

(5) Where the date on which a worker's employment begins is later than the date on which (by virtue of a relevant agreement) his first leave year begins, the leave to which he is entitled in that leave year is a proportion of the period applicable under [paragraph (1)]⁴ equal to the proportion of that leave year remaining on the date on which his employment begins.

(6) Where by virtue of paragraph [...]⁵ (5) the period of leave to which a worker is entitled is or includes a proportion of a week, the proportion shall be determined in days and any fraction of a day shall be treated as a whole day.

(7) [...]⁶

(8) [...]⁷

(9) Leave to which a worker is entitled under this regulation may be taken in instalments, but–
    (a) it may only be taken in the leave year in respect of which it is due, and

¹ Words inserted by SI 2002/3128 reg 13 (b)
² Substituted by SI 2001/3256 reg 2 (2)
³ Repealed by SI 2001/3256 reg 2 (3)
⁴ Words substituted by SI 2001/3256 reg 2 (4)
⁵ Words repealed by SI 2001/3256 reg 2 (5)
⁶ Repealed by SI 2001/3256 reg 2 (6)
⁷ Repealed by SI 2001/3256 reg 2 (6)

(b) it may not be replaced by a payment in lieu except where the worker's employment is terminated.

Compensation related to entitlement to leave

14.—(1) This regulation applies where—

21-016

(a) a worker's employment is terminated during the course of his leave year, and

(b) on the date on which the termination takes effect ("the termination date"), the proportion he has taken of the leave to which he is entitled in the leave year under [regulation 13][1] differs from the proportion of the leave year which has expired.

(2) Where the proportion of leave taken by the worker is less than the proportion of the leave year which has expired, his employer shall make him a payment in lieu of leave in accordance with paragraph (3).

(3) The payment due under paragraph (2) shall be—

(a) such sum as may be provided for for the purposes of this regulation in a relevant agreement, or

(b) where there are no provisions of a relevant agreement which apply, a sum equal to the amount that would be due to the worker under regulation 16 in respect of a period of leave determined according to the formula— $(A \times B) - C$

where—

A is the period of leave to which the worker is entitled under [regulation 13][2];

B is the proportion of the worker's leave year which expired before the termination date, and

C is the period of leave taken by the worker between the start of the leave year and the termination date.

(4) A relevant agreement may provide that, where the proportion of leave taken by the worker exceeds the proportion of the leave year which has expired, he shall compensate his employer, whether by a payment, by undertaking additional work or otherwise.

Dates on which leave is taken

15.—(1) A worker may take leave to which he is entitled under [regulation **21-017** 13][3] on such days as he may elect by giving notice to his employer in accordance with paragraph (3), subject to any requirement imposed on him by his employer under paragraph (2).

(2) A worker's employer may require the worker—

(a) to take leave to which the worker is entitled under [regulation 13][4]; or

(b) not to take such leave,

on particular days, by giving notice to the worker in accordance with paragraph (3).

(3) A notice under paragraph (1) or (2)—

(a) may relate to all or part of the leave to which a worker is entitled in a leave year;

---

[1] Words substituted by SI 2001/3256 reg 3
[2] Words substituted by SI 2001/3256 reg 3
[3] Words substituted by SI 2001/3256 reg 3
[4] Words substituted by SI 2001/3256 reg 3

(b) shall specify the days on which leave is or (as the case may be) is not to be taken and, where the leave on a particular day is to be in respect of only part of the day, its duration; and

(c) shall be given to the employer or, as the case may be, the worker before the relevant date.

(4) The relevant date, for the purposes of paragraph (3), is the date—

(a) in the case of a notice under paragraph (1) or (2)(a), twice as many days in advance of the earliest day specified in the notice as the number of days or part-days to which the notice relates, and

(b) in the case of a notice under paragraph (2)(b), as many days in advance of the earliest day so specified as the number of days or part-days to which the notice relates.

(5) Any right or obligation under paragraphs (1) to (4) may be varied or excluded by a relevant agreement.

(6) This regulation does not apply to a worker to whom Schedule 2 applies (workers employed in agriculture) except where, in the case of a worker partly employed in agriculture, a relevant agreement so provides.

[Leave during the first year of employment

21-018   **15A.**—(1) During the first year of his employment, the amount of leave a worker may take at any time in exercise of his entitlement under regulation 13 is limited to the amount which is deemed to have accrued in his case at that time under paragraph (2), as modified under paragraph (3) in a case where that paragraph applies, less the amount of leave (if any) that he has already taken during that year.

(2) For the purposes of paragraph (1), leave is deemed to accrue over the course of the worker's first year of employment, at the rate of one-twelfth of the amount specified in regulation 13(1) on the first day of each month of that year.

(3) Where the amount of leave that has accrued in a particular case includes a fraction of a day other than a half-day, the fraction shall be treated as a half-day if it is less than a half-day and as a whole day if it is more than a half-day.

(4) This regulation does not apply to a worker whose employment began on or before 25th October 2001.][1]

Payment in respect of periods of leave

21-019   **16.**—(1) A worker is entitled to be paid in respect of any period of annual leave to which he is entitled under regulation 13, at the rate of a week's pay in respect of each week of leave.

(2) Sections 221 to 224 of the 1996 Act shall apply for the purpose of determining the amount of a week's pay for the purposes of this regulation, subject to the modifications set out in paragraph (3).

(3) The provisions referred to in paragraph (2) shall apply—

(a) as if references to the employee were references to the worker;

(b) as if references to the employee's contract of employment were references to the worker's contract;

(c) as if the calculation date were the first day of the period of leave in question; and

(d) as if the references to sections 227 and 228 did not apply.

(4) A right to payment under paragraph (1) does not affect any right of a worker to remuneration under his contract ("contractual remuneration").

---

[1] Inserted by SI 2001/3256 reg 4

(5) Any contractual remuneration paid to a worker in respect of a period of leave goes towards discharging any liability of the employer to make payments under this regulation in respect of that period; and, conversely, any payment of remuneration under this regulation in respect of a period goes towards discharging any liability of the employer to pay contractual remuneration in respect of that period.

Entitlements under other provisions

17. Where during any period a worker is entitled to a rest period, rest break **21-020** or annual leave both under a provisions of these Regulations and under a separate provision (including a provision of his contract), he may not exercise the two rights separately, but may, in taking a rest period, break or leave during that period, take advantage of whichever right is, in any particular respect, the more favourable.

PART III

EXCEPTIONS

[Excluded sectors

18.—(1) These Regulations do not apply –   **21-021**
  (a) to workers to whom the European Agreement on the organisation of working time of seafarers dated 30th September 1998 and put into effect by Council Directive 1999/63/EC of 21st June 1999 applies;
  (b) to workers on board a sea-going fishing vessel; or
  [(c) to workers to whom the Merchant Shipping (Working Time: Inland Waterways) Regulations 2003 apply.]¹
  (2) Regulations 4(1) and (2), 6(1), (2) and (7), 7(1) and (6), 8, 10(1), 11(1) and (2), 12(1), 13 and 16 do not apply –
  (a) where characteristics peculiar to certain specific services such as the armed forces or the police, or to certain specific activities in the civil protection services, inevitably conflict with the provisions of these Regulations;
  (b) to workers to whom the European Agreement on the organisation of working time of mobile staff in civil aviation concluded on 22nd March 2000 and implemented by Council Directive 2000/79/EC of 27th November 2000 applies; or
  (c) to the activities of workers who are doctors in training.
  (3) Paragraph (2)(c) has effect only until 31st July 2004.
  (4) Regulations 4(1) and (2), 6(1), (2) and (7), 8, 10(1), 11(1) and (2) and 12(1) do not apply to workers to whom Directive 2002/15/EC of the European Parliament and of the Council on the organisation of the working time of persons performing mobile road transport activities, dated 11th March 2002 applies.]²

Domestic service

19. Regulations 4(1) and (2), [5A(1) and (4),]³ 6(1), (2) and (7), [6A,]⁴ 7(1), (2) **21-022** and (6) and 8 do not apply in relation to a worker employed as a domestic servant in a private household.

¹ Substituted by SI 2003/3049 Sch 2 para 6
² Substituted by SI 2003/1684 reg 4
³ Words inserted by SI 2002/3128 reg 14
⁴ Words inserted by SI 2002/3128 reg 14

Unmeasured working time

21-023   **20.**—[(1) Regulations 4(1) and (2), 6(1), (2) and (7), 10(1), 11(1) and (2) and 12(1) do not apply in relation to a worker where, on account of the specific characteristics of the activity in which he is engaged, the duration of his working time is not measured or predetermined or can be determined by the worker himself, as may be the case for–

(a) managing executives or other persons with autonomous decision-taking powers;

(b) family workers; or

(c) workers officiating at religious ceremonies in churches and religious communities.

(2) Where part of the working time of a worker is measured or predetermined or cannot be determined by the worker himself but the specific characteristics of the activity are such that, without being required to do so by the employer, the worker may also do work the duration of which is not measured or predetermined or can be determined by the worker himself, regulations 4(1) and (2) and 6(1), (2) and (7) apply only to so much of his work as is measured or predetermined or cannot be determined by the worker himself.]¹

Other special case

21-024   **21.** Subject to regulation 24, regulations 6(1), (2) and (7), 10(1), 11(1) and (2) and 12(1) do not apply in relation to a worker–

(a) where the worker's activities are such that his place of work and place of residence are distant from one another, [including cases where the worker is employed in offshore work,]² or his different places of work are distant from one another;

(b) where the worker is engaged in security and surveillance activities requiring a permanent presence in order to protect property and persons, as may be the case for security guards and caretakers or security firms;

(c) where the worker's activities involve the need for continuity of service or production, as may be the case in relation to–

(i) services relating to the reception, treatment or care provided by hospitals or similar establishments [(including the activities of doctors in training)]³, residential institutions and prisons;

(ii) work at docks or airports;

(iii) press, radio, television, cinematographic production, postal and telecommunications services and civil protection services;

(iv) gas, water and electricity production, transmission and distribution, household refuse collection and incineration;

(v) industries in which work cannot be interrupted on technical grounds;

(vi) research and development activities;

(vii) agriculture;

[(viii) the carriage of passengers on regular urban transport services;]⁴

(d) where there is a foreseeable surge of activity, as may be the case in relation to–

---

¹ Inserted by SI 1999/3372 reg 4
² Words inserted by SI 2003/1684 reg 5
³ Words inserted by SI 2003/1684 reg 5
⁴ Inserted by SI 2003/1684 reg 5

      (i) agriculture;
      (ii) tourism; and
      (iii) postal services;
  (e) where the worker's activities are affected by–
      (i) an occurrence due to unusual and unforeseeable circumstances, beyond the control of the worker's employer;
      (ii) exceptional events, the consequences of which could not have been avoided despite the exercise of all due care by the employer; or
      (iii) an accident or the imminent risk of an accident.
  [(f) where the worker works in railway transport and–
      (i) his activities are intermittent;
      (ii) he spends his working time on board trains; or
      (iii) his activities are linked to transport timetables and to ensuring the continuity and regularity of traffic.][1]

Shift workers

22.—(1) Subject to regulation 24–   **21-025**
  (a) regulation 10(1) does not apply in relation to a shift worker when he changes shift and cannot take a daily rest period between the end of one shift and the start of the next one;
  (b) paragraphs (1) and (2) of regulation 11 do not apply in relation to a shift worker when he changes shift and cannot take a weekly rest period between the end of one shift and the start of the next one; and
  (c) neither regulation 10(1) nor paragraphs (1) and (2) of regulation 11 apply to workers engaged in activities involving periods of work split up over the day, as may be the case for cleaning staff.
 (2) For the purposes of this regulation–
    "shift worker" means any worker whose work schedule is part of shift work; and
    "shift work" means any method of organizing work in shifts whereby workers succeed each other at the same workstations according to a certain pattern, including a rotating pattern, and which may be continuous or discontinuous, entailing the need for workers to work at different times over a given period of days or weeks.

Collective and workforce agreements

23. A collective agreement or a workforce agreement may–   **21-026**
  (a) modify or exclude the application of regulations 6(1) to (3) and (7), 10(1), 11(1) and (2) and 12(1), and
  (b) for objective or technical reasons or reasons concerning the organization of work, modify the application of regulation 4(3) and (4) by the substitution, for each reference to 17 weeks, of a different period, being a period not exceeding 52 weeks,
in relation to particular workers or groups of workers.

Compensatory rest

24. Where the application of any provision of these Regulations is excluded **21-027** by regulation 21 or 22, or is modified or excluded by means of a collective agreement or a workforce agreement under regulation 23(a), and a worker is

---

[1] Inserted by SI 2003/1684 reg 5

accordingly required by his employer to work during a period which would otherwise be a rest period or rest break –

    (a) his employer shall wherever possible allow him to take an equivalent period of compensatory rest, and

    (b) in exceptional cases in which it is not possible, for objective reasons, to grant such a period of rest, his employer shall afford him such protection as may be appropriate in order to safeguard the worker's health and safety.

[Mobile workers

21-028   **24A.**—(1) Regulations 6(1), (2) and (7), 10(1), 11(1) and (2) and 12(1) do not apply to a mobile worker in relation to whom the application of those regulations is not excluded by any provision of regulation 18.

(2) A mobile worker, to whom paragraph (1) applies, is entitled to adequate rest, except where the worker's activities are affected by any of the matters referred to in regulation 21(e).

(3) For the purposes of this regulation, "adequate rest" means that a worker has regular rest periods, the duration of which are expressed in units of time and which are sufficiently long and continuous to ensure that, as a result of fatigue or other irregular working patterns, he does not cause injury to himself, to fellow workers or to others and that he does not damage his health, either in the short term or in the longer term.][1]

Workers in the armed forces

21-029   **25.**—(1) Regulation 9 does not apply in relation to a worker serving as a member of the armed forces.

(2) Regulations [5A, 6A,][2] 10(2) and 11(3) do not apply in relation to a young worker serving as a member of the armed forces.

(3) In a case where a young worker is accordingly required to work during [the restricted period, or is not permitted the minimum rest period provided for in regulation 10(2) or 11(3)][3], he shall be allowed an appropriate period of compensatory rest.

[Doctors in training

21-030   **25A.**—(1) Paragraph (1) of regulation 4 is modified in its application to workers who are doctors in training as follows –

    (a) for the reference to 48 hours there is substituted a reference to 58 hours with effect from 1st August 2004 until 31st July 2007;

    (b) for the reference to 48 hours there is substituted a reference to 56 hours with effect from 1st August 2007 until 31st July 2009.

(2) In the case of workers who are doctors in training, paragraphs (3)(5) of regulation 4 shall not apply and paragraphs (3) and (4) of this regulation shall apply in their place.

(3) Subject to paragraph (4), the reference period which applies in the case of a worker who is a doctor in training is, with effect from 1st August 2004–

    (a) where a relevant agreement provides for the application of this regulation in relation to successive periods of 26 weeks, each such period; and

---

[1] Inserted by SI 2003/1684 reg 6
[2] Words inserted by SI 2002/3128 reg 15
[3] Words substituted by SI 2002/3128 reg 15 (b)

(b) in any other case, any period of 26 weeks in the course of his employment.

(4) Where a doctor in training has worked for his employer for less than 26 weeks, the reference period applicable in his case is the period that has elapsed since he started work for his employer.][1]

[Workers employed in offshore work

25B.—(1) In the case of workers employed in offshore work, paragraphs **21-031** (3)(5) of regulation 4 shall not apply and paragraphs (2) and (3) of this regulation shall apply in their place.

(2) Subject to paragraph (3), the reference period which applies in the case of workers employed in offshore work is—

(a) where a relevant agreement provides for the application of this regulation in relation to successive periods of 52 weeks, each such period; and

(b) in any other case, any period of 52 weeks in the course of his employment.

(3) Where a worker employed in offshore work has worked for his employer for less than 52 weeks, the reference period applicable in his case is the period that has elapsed since he started work for his employer.][2]

26.—[...][3]   **21-032**

Young workers: force majeure

27.—(1) Regulations [5A, 6A,][4] 10(2) and 12(4) do not apply in relation to a **21-033** young worker where his employer requires him to undertake work which no adult worker is available to perform and which—

(a) is occasioned by either—
  (i) an occurrence due to unusual and unforseeable circumstances, beyond the employer's control, or
  (ii) exceptional events, the consequences of which could not have been avoided despite the exercise of all due care by the employer;

(b) is of a temporary nature; and

(c) must be performed immediately.

(2) Where the application of regulation [5A, 6A,][5] 10(2) or 12(4) is excluded by paragraph (1), and a young worker is accordingly required to work during a period which would otherwise be a rest period or rest break, his employer shall allow him to take an equivalent period of compensatory rest within the following three weeks.

[Other exceptions relating to young workers

27A.—(1) Regulation 5A does not apply in relation to a young worker **21-034** where—

(a) the young worker's employer requires him to undertake work which is necessary either to maintain continuity of service or production or to respond to a surge in demand for a service or product;

(b) no adult worker is available to perform the work, and

---

[1] Inserted by SI 2003/1684 reg 7
[2] Inserted by SI 2003/1684 reg 8
[3] Repealed by SI 2003/1684 reg 9
[4] Words inserted by SI 2002/3128 reg 18
[5] Words inserted by SI 2002/3128 reg 18

    (c) performing the work would not adversely affect the young worker's education or training

    (2) Regulation 6A does not apply to a young worker employed –

        (a) in a hospital or cleaning establishment

        (b) in connection with cultural, artistic, sporting or advertising activities in the circumstances referred to in paragraph (1)

    (3) Regulation 6A does not apply, except in so far as it prohibits work between midnight and 4 a.m, in relation to a young worker employed in –

        (a) agriculture

        (b) retail trading

        (c) postal or newspaper deliveries

        (d) a catering business

        (e) a hotel, public house, restaurant, bar or similar establishment, or

        (f) a bakery

in the circumstances referred to in paragraph (1).

    (4) Where the application of regulation 6A is excluded by paragraph (2) or (3), and a young worker is accordingly required to work during a period which would otherwise be a rest period or rest break—

        (a) he shall be supervised by an adult worker where such supervision is necessary for the young worker's protection, and

        (b) he shall be allowed an equivalent period of compensatory rest.][1]

[Enforcement

21-035   **28.**—(1) In this regulation, regulations 29–29E and Schedule 3–

    "the 1974 Act" means the Health and Safety at Work etc. Act 1974;

    "the Civil Aviation Authority" means the authority referred to in section 2(1) of the Civil Aviation Act 1982;

    "code of practice" includes a standard, a specification and any other documentary form of practical guidance;

    "the Commission" means the Health and Safety Commission referred to in section 10(2) of the 1974 Act;

    "enforcement authority" means the Executive, a local authority, the Civil Aviation Authority or VOSA;

    "the Executive" means the Health and Safety Executive referred to in section 10(5) of the 1974 Act;

    "local authority" means –

        (a) in relation to England, a county council so far as they are the council for an area for which there are no district councils, a district council, a London borough council, the Common Council of the City of London, the Sub-Treasurer of the Inner Temple or the Under-Treasurer of the Middle Temple;

        (b) in relation to Wales, a county council or a county borough council;

        (c) in relation to Scotland, a council constituted under section 2 of the Local Government etc. (Scotland) Act 1994;

    "premises" includes any place and, in particular, includes –

        (a) any vehicle, vessel, aircraft or hovercraft;

        (b) any installation on land (including the foreshore and other land intermittently covered by water), any offshore installation, and any other installation (whether floating, or resting on the seabed or

---

[1] Inserted by SI 2002/3128 reg 17

the subsoil thereof, or resting on other land covered with water or the subsoil thereof) and

(c) any tent or movable structure;

"relevant civil aviation worker" means a mobile worker who works mainly on board civil aircraft, excluding any worker to whom regulation 18(2)(b) applies;

"the relevant requirements" means the following provisions –

(a) regulations 4(2), 5A(4), 6(2) and (7), 6A, 7(1), (2) and (6), 8, 9 and 27A(4)(a);

(b) regulation 24, in so far as it applies where regulation 6(1), (2) or (7) is modified or excluded, and

(c) regulation 24A(2), in so far as it applies where regulations 6(1), (2) or (7) is excluded;

"relevant road transport worker" means a mobile worker to whom one or more of the following applies –

(a) Council Regulation (EEC) 3820/85,

(b) the European Agreement concerning the Work of Crews of Vehicles engaged in International Road Transport (AETR) of 1st July 1970, and

(c) the United Kingdom domestic driver's hours code, which is set out in Part VI of the Transport Act 1968;

"the relevant statutory provisions" means –

(a) the provisions of the 1974 Act and of any regulations made under powers contained in that Act; and

(b) while and to the extent that they remain in force, the provisions of the Acts mentioned in Schedule 1 to the 1974 Act and which are specified in the third column of that Schedule and the regulations, orders or other instruments of a legislative character made or having effect under a provision so specified; and

"VOSA" means the Vehicle and Operator Services Agency.

(2) It shall be the duty of the Executive to make adequate arrangements for the enforcement of the relevant requirements except to the extent that –

(a) a local authority is made responsible for their enforcement by paragraph (3);

(b) the Civil Aviation Authority is made responsible for their enforcement by paragraph (5); or

(c) VOSA is made responsible for their enforcement by paragraph (6).

(3) Where the relevant requirements apply in relation to workers employed in premises in respect of which a local authority is responsible, under the Health and Safety (Enforcing Authority) Regulations 1998, for enforcing any of the relevant statutory provisions, it shall be the duty of that authority to enforce those requirements.

(4) The duty imposed on local authorities by paragraph (3) shall be performed in accordance with such guidance as may be given to them by the Commission.

(5) It shall be the duty of the Civil Aviation Authority to enforce the relevant requirements in relation to relevant civil aviation workers.

(6) It shall be the duty of VOSA to enforce the relevant requirements in relation to relevant road transport workers.

(7) The provisions of Schedule 3 shall apply in relation to the enforcement of the relevant requirements.

(8) Any function of the Commission under the 1974 Act which is exercisable in relation to the enforcement by the Executive of the relevant statutory provisions shall be exercisable in relation to the enforcement by the Executive of the relevant requirements.

Offences

21-036   **29.**—(1) An employer who fails to comply with any of the relevant requirements shall be guilty of an offence.

(2) The provisions of paragraph (3) shall apply where an inspector is exercising or has exercised any power conferred by Schedule 3.

(3) It is an offence for a person—

    (a) to contravene any requirement imposed by the inspector under paragraph 2 of Schedule 3;

    (b) to prevent or attempt to prevent any other person from appearing before the inspector or from answering any question to which the inspector may by virtue of paragraph 2(2)(e) of Schedule 3 require an answer;

    (c) to contravene any requirement or prohibition imposed by an improvement notice or a prohibition notice (including any such notice as is modified on appeal);

    (d) intentionally to obstruct the inspector in the exercise or performance of his powers or duties;

    (e) to use or disclose any information in contravention of paragraph 8 of Schedule 3;

    (f) to make a statement which he knows to be false or recklessly to make a statement which is false, where the statement is made in purported compliance with a requirement to furnish any information imposed by or under these Regulations.

(4) An employer guilty of an offence under paragraph (1) shall be liable—

    (a) on summary conviction, to a fine not exceeding the statutory maximum;

    (b) on conviction on indictment, to a fine.

(5) A person guilty of an offence under paragraph (3) shall be liable to the penalty prescribed in relation to that provision by paragraphs (6), (7) or (8) as the case may be.

(6) A person guilty of an offence under sub-paragraph (3)(a), (b) or (d) shall be liable on summary conviction to a fine not exceeding level 5 on the standard scale.

(7) A person guilty of an offence under sub-paragraph (3)(c) shall be liable—

    (a) on summary conviction, to imprisonment for a term not exceeding three months, or a fine not exceeding the statutory maximum;

    (b) on conviction on indictment, to imprisonment for a term not exceeding two years, or a fine, or both.

(8) A person guilty of an offence under any of the sub-paragraphs of paragraph (3) not falling within paragraphs (6) or (7) above, shall be liable—

    (a) on summary conviction, to a fine not exceeding the statutory maximum;

(b) on conviction on indictment –

    (i) if the offence is under sub-paragraph (3)(e), to imprisonment for a term not exceeding two years or a fine or both;

    (ii) if the offence is not one to which the preceding sub-paragraph applies, to a fine.

(9) The provisions set out in regulations 29A–29E below shall apply in relation to the offences provided for in paragraphs (1) and (3).

Offences due to fault of other person

29A. Where the commission by any person of an offence is due to the act or **21-037** default of some other person, that other person shall be guilty of the offence, and a person may be charged with and convicted of the offence by virtue of this paragraph whether or not proceedings are taken against the first-mentioned person.

Offences by bodies corporate

29B.—(1) Where an offence committed by a body corporate is proved to **21-038** have been committed with the consent or connivance of, or to have been attributable to any neglect on the part of, any director, manager, secretary or other similar officer of the body corporate or a person who was purporting to act in any such capacity, he as well as the body corporate shall be guilty of that offence and shall be liable to be proceeded against and punished accordingly.

(2) Where the affairs of a body corporate are managed by its members, the preceding paragraph shall apply in relation to the acts and defaults of a member in connection with his functions of management as if he were a director of the body corporate.

Restriction on institution of proceedings in England and Wales

29C. Proceedings for an offence shall not, in England and Wales, be **21-039** instituted except by an inspector or by or with the consent of the Director of Public Prosecutions.

Prosecutions by inspectors

29D.—(1) An inspector, if authorised in that behalf by an enforcement **21-040** authority, may, although not of counsel or a solicitor, prosecute before a magistrate's court proceedings for an offence under these Regulations.

(2) This regulation shall not apply to Scotland.

Power of court to order cause of offence to be remedied

29E.—(1) Where a person is convicted of an offence in respect of any **21-041** matters which appear to the court to be matters which it is in his power to remedy, the court may, in addition to or instead of imposing any punishment, order him, within such time as may be fixed by the order, to take such steps as may be specified in the order for remedying the said matters.

(2) The time fixed by an order under paragraph (1) may be extended or further extended by order of the court on an application made before the end of that time as originally fixed or as extended under this paragraph, as the case may be.

(3) Where a person is ordered under paragraph (1) to remedy any matters, that person shall not be liable under these Regulations in respect of those matters

in so far as they continue during the time fixed by the order or any further time allowed under paragraph (2).][1]

Remedies

21-042 **30.**—(1) A worker may present a complaint to an employment tribunal that his employer –
  (a) has refused to permit him to exercise any right he has under –
    (i) regulation 10(1) or (2), 11(1), (2) or (3), 12(1) or (4) or 13;
    (ii) regulation 24, in so far as it applies where regulation 10(1), 11(1) or (2) or 12(1) is modified or excluded; [...][2]
    [(iii) regulation 24A, in so far as it applies where regulation 10(1), 11(1) or (2) or 12(1) is excluded; or
    (iv) regulation 25(3), 27A(4)(b) or 27(2); or][3]
  (b) has failed to pay him the whole or any part of any amount due to him under regulation 14(2) or 16(1).
  (2) An employment tribunal shall not consider a complaint under this regulation unless it is presented –
  (a) before the end of the period of three months (or, in a case to which regulation 38(2) applies, six months) beginning with the date on which it is alleged that the exercise of the right should have been permitted (or in the case of a rest period or leave extending over more than one day, the date on which it should have been permitted to begin) or, as the case may be, the payment should have been made;
  (b) within such further period as the tribunal considers reasonable in a case where it is satisfied that it was not reasonably practicable for the complaint to be presented before the end of that period of three or, as the case may be, six months.
  (3) Where an employment tribunal finds a complaint under paragraph (1)(a) well-founded, the tribunal –
  (a) shall make a declaration to that effect, and
  (b) may make an award of compensation to be paid by the employer to the worker.
  (4) The amount of the compensation shall be such as the tribunal considers just and equitable in all the circumstances having regard to –
  (a) the employer's default in refusing to permit the worker to exercise his right, and
  (b) any loss sustained by the worker which is attributable to the matters complained of.
  (5) Where on a complaint under paragraph (1)(b) an employment tribunal finds that an employer has failed to pay a worker in accordance with regulation 14(2) or 16(1), it shall order the employer to pay to the worker the amount which it finds to be due to him.

Regulation 2   Schedule 1

WORKFORCE AGREEMENTS

21-043 **1.** An agreement is a workforce agreement for the purposes of these Regulations if the following conditions are satisfied –
  (a) the agreement is in writing;

---

[1] Section 28, 29, 29A–29E substituted for section 8 and 9 by SI 2003/1684 Pt IV reg 10
[2] Words repealed by SI 2003/1684 reg 11
[3] Substituted by SI 2003/1684 reg 11

(b) it has effect for a specified period not exceeding five years;

(c) it applies either –

    (i) to all of the relevant members of the workforce, or

    (ii) to all of the relevant members of the workforce who belong to a particular group;

(d) the agreement is signed –

    (i) in the case of an agreement of the kind referred to in sub-paragraph (c)(i), by the representatives of the workforce, and in the case of an agreement of the kind referred to in sub-paragraph (c)(ii) by the representatives of the group to which the agreement applies (excluding, in either case, any representative not a relevant member of the workforce on the date on which the agreement was first made available for signature), or

    (ii) if the employer employed 20 or fewer workers on the date referred to in sub-paragraph (d)(i), either by the appropriate representatives in accordance with that sub-paragraph or by the majority of the workers employed by him;

(e) before the agreement was made available for signature, the employer provided all the workers to whom it was intended to apply on the date on which it came into effect with copies of the text of the agreement and such guidance as those workers might reasonably require in order to understand it fully.

2. For the purposes of this Schedule –   **21-044**

"a particular group" is a group of the relevant members of a workforce who undertake a particular function, work at a particular workplace or belong to a particular department or unit within their employer's business;

"relevant members of the workforce" are all of the workers employed by a particular employer, excluding any worker whose terms and conditions of employment are provided for, wholly or in part, in a collective agreement;

"representatives of the workforce" are workers duly elected to represent the relevant members of the workforce, "representatives of the group" are workers duly elected to represent the members of a particular group, and representatives are "duly elected" if the election at which they were elected satisfied the requirements of paragraph 3 of this Schedule.

3. The requirements concerning elections referred to in paragraph 2 are that –   **21-045**

(a) the number of representatives to be elected is determined by the employer;

(b) the candidates for election as representatives of the workforce are relevant members of the workforce, and the candidates for election as representatives of a group are members of the group;

(c) no worker who is eligible to be a candidate is unreasonably excluded from standing for election;

(d) all the relevant members of the workforce are entitled to vote for representatives of the workforce, and all the members of a particular group are entitled to vote for representatives of the group;

(e) the workers entitled to vote may vote for as many candidates as there are representatives to be elected;

(f) the election is conducted so as to secure that –

    (i) so far as is reasonably practicable, those voting do so in secret, and

    (ii) the votes given at the election are fairly and accurately counted.

The National Minimum Wage Regulations 1999

(S.I. 584)

PART I

GENERAL AND INTERPRETATION

Citation and commencement

22-001   **1.** These Regulations may be cited as the National Minimum Wage Regulations 1999 and shall come into force on 1st April 1999.

Interpretation

General interpretative provisions

22-002   **2.**—(1) In these Regulations –
  "the Act" means the National Minimum Wage Act 1998;
  "allowance", other than in regulation 8(b), means any payment paid by the employer to a worker attributable to a particular aspect of his working arrangements or to his working or personal circumstances that is not consolidated into his standard pay, but does not include an allowance designed to refund a worker in respect of expenses incurred by him in connection with his employment;
  "arrangements made by the Government" means –
  (a) in England and Wales, arrangements made by the Secretary of State under section 2 of the Employment and Training Act 1973,
  (b) in Scotland, arrangements made by the Secretary of State under section 2 of the Employment and Training Act 1973 or by Scottish Enterprise or Highlands and Islands Enterprise under section 2 of the Enterprise and New Towns (Scotland) Act 1990,
  (c) in Northern Ireland, arrangements made by the Department of Economic Development under section 1 of the Employment and Training Act (Northern Ireland) 1950;

  "employer" has the meaning given to it by section 54(4) of the Act but, in relation to a worker (as defined in section 54(3) of the Act), includes in addition, except in paragraph (6) of regulation 12–
  (a) an agent or principal in relation to whom, by virtue of section 34(2) of the Act, the provisions of the Act have effect as if there were a worker's contract between him and an agency worker for the doing of work by the agency worker, and
  (b) an employer of a home worker who is a worker by virtue of section 35 of the Act;
  "performance bonus" means a performance bonus or other merit payment attributable to the quality or amount of work done in the course of more than one pay reference period, and not therefore payable directly in respect of work done in specific hours;
  "the total of reductions" means the total of reductions determined in accordance with regulations 31 to 37;

"the total of remuneration" means the total of money payments determined in accordance with regulation 30;

"pay reference period" has the meaning assigned to it by regulation 10;

"worker" has the same meaning as in section 54(3) of the Act but, except in [paragraph (3), (5) and (6) of regulation 12][1], includes in addition –

    (a) an agency worker in relation to whom, by virtue of section 34(2) of the Act, the provisions of the Act have effect as if there were a worker's contract for the doing of his work between him and an agent or principal; and

    (b) a home worker who is a worker by virtue of section 35 of the Act.

(2) In these Regulations "work" does not include work (of whatever description) relating to the employer's family household done by a worker where the conditions in sub-paragraphs (a) or (b) are satisfied.

    (a) The conditions to be satisfied under this sub-paragraph are –

        (i) that the worker resides in the family home of the employer for whom he works,

        (ii) that the worker is not a member of that family, but is treated as such, in particular as regards to the provision of accommodation and meals and the sharing of tasks and leisure activities;

        (iii) that the worker is neither liable to any deduction, nor to make any payment to the employer, or any other person, in respect of the provision of the living accommodation or meals; and

        (iv) that, had the work been done by a member of the employer's family, it would not be treated as being performed under a worker's contract or as being work because the conditions in sub-paragraph (b) would be satisfied.

    (b) The conditions to be satisfied under this sub-paragraph are –

        (i) that the worker is a member of the employer's family,

        (ii) that the worker resides in the family home of the employer,

        (iii) that the worker shares in the tasks and activities of the family,

and that the work is done in that context.

(3) In these Regulations "work" does not include work (of whatever description) relating to an employer's family business, done by a worker who satisfies the conditions in paragraph (4).

    (4) The conditions to be satisfied under this paragraph are –

        (i) that the worker is a member of the employer's family,

        (ii) that the worker resides in the family home of the employer,

        (iii) that the worker participates in the running of the family business,

and that the work is done in that context.

The meaning of time work

3. In these Regulations "time work" means –   **22-003**

    (a) work that is paid for under a worker's contract by reference to the time for which a worker works and is not salaried hours work;

    (b) work that is paid for under a worker's contract by reference to a measure of the output of the worker per hour or other period of time during the whole of which the worker is required to work, and is not salaried hours work; and

---

[1] Words inserted by SI 2001/1108 reg 2

(c) work that would fall within paragraph (b) but for the fact that the worker is paid by reference to the length of the period of time alone when his output does not exceed a particular level.

The meaning of salaried hours work

22-004   **4.**—(1) In these Regulations "salaried hours work" means work–
  (a) that is done under a contract to do salaried hours work; and
  (b) that falls within paragraph (6) below.
  (2) A contract to do salaried hours work is a contract under which a worker–
  (a) is entitled to be paid for an ascertainable basic number of hours in a year (referred to in this regulation as "the basic hours"); and
  (b) is entitled, in respect of hours that consist of or include the basic hours, to be paid an annual salary–
    (i) by equal weekly or monthly instalments of wages, or
    (ii) by monthly instalments of wages that vary but have the result that the worker is entitled to be paid an equal amount in each quarter,
regardless of the number of hours in respect of which the worker is entitled to the annual salary that are actually worked by him (if any) in any particular week or month; and
  (c) has, in respect of those hours, no entitlement to any payment other than his annual salary or no such entitlement other than an entitlement to a performance bonus.
  (3) A contract that satisfies the conditions in paragraph (2) does so–
  (a) whether or not all the basic hours are working hours;
  (b) whether or not the worker can be required under his contract to work, or does in fact work, any hours in addition to the total of hours in respect of which he is entitled to his annual salary, and regardless of any payments made in respect of those additional hours.
  (4) Circumstances having the result that in practice a worker may not be or is not paid by equal instalments of wages, or by an equal amount in each quarter, for hours in respect of which he is entitled under his contract only to his annual salary do not prevent the contract from being a contract for salaried hours work, for example–
  (a) that a worker may be awarded a performance bonus,
  (b) that the amount of a worker's annual salary may be varied,
  (c) that by virtue of regulation 22 or 23 the worker is entitled to the national minimum wage in respect of hours in addition to his basic hours when, under his contract, there is no entitlement to any payment in addition to his annual salary for those additional hours (or to no payment in addition other than a performance bonus), and
  (d) that the worker's employment may start or terminate during a week or month with the result that the worker is paid a proportionate amount of his annual salary for the week or month in question.
  (5) The fact that, by reason of an absence from work for hours in respect of which his annual salary is normally payable, a worker is entitled under his contract, in respect of those hours, to be paid less than he would be but for the absence or to no payment does not prevent the worker's contract from being a contract for salaried hours work.
  (6) The work done under a contract to do salaried hours work that falls within this paragraph, and is therefore salaried hours work, is work in respect of which the worker is entitled to no payment in addition to his annual salary, or to no payment in addition to his annual salary other than a performance bonus.

(7) References in regulation 22 to work or hours of work in respect of which a worker is entitled to no payment other than his annual salary refer also to work or hours of work in respect of which the only payment to which the worker is entitled other than his annual salary is payment of a performance bonus.

The meaning of output work

5. In these Regulations "output work" means work that is paid for under a **22-005** worker's contract that is not time work and, but for the effect of the Act and these Regulations or anything done pursuant to these Regulations, would be paid for under that contract wholly by reference to the number of pieces made or processed by the worker, or wholly by reference to some other measure of output such as the number or value of sales made or transactions completed by the worker or as a result of his work.

The meaning of unmeasured work

6. In these Regulations "unmeasured work" means any other work that is not **22-006** time work, salaried hours work or output work including, in particular, work in respect of which there are no specified hours and the worker is required to work when needed or when work is available.

Travelling

7. A worker is to be treated as travelling for the purposes of regulations 15(2), **22-007** 16(2) and (5)(b), 17(1), 18(1) and 19(1)(b) if –
    (a) he is in the course of a journey by a mode of transport or is making a journey on foot;
    (b) he is waiting at a place of departure to begin his journey by a mode of transport;
    (c) where his journey is broken, he is waiting at a place of departure for his journey to re-commence either by the same or another mode of transport, except for any time during such a period he spends in taking a rest break; or
    (d) he is waiting at the end of a journey, in the case of regulations 15(2), 16(2), 17(1) and 18(1), for the purpose of carrying out his duties, or, in the case of regulations 16(5)(b) and 19(1)(b), to receive training, except for any time before he is due to carry out his duties or receive training which he spends in taking a rest break.

The meaning of payments

8. References in these Regulations to payments paid by the employer to the **22-008** worker are references to payments paid by the employer to the worker in his capacity as a worker before any deductions are made, excluding–
    (a) any payment by way of an advance under an agreement for a loan or by way of an advance of wages;
    (b) any payment by way of a pension, by way of an allowance or gratuity in connection with the worker's retirement or as compensation for loss of office;
    (c) any payment of an award made by a court or tribunal or to settle proceedings which have been or might be brought before a court or tribunal, other than the payment of an amount due under the worker's contract;
    (d) any payment referable to the worker's redundancy;
    (e) any payment by way of an award under a suggestions scheme.

Benefits in kind not to count as payments

22-009   **9.** For the purposes of these Regulations the following shall not be treated as payments by the employer to the worker –

    (a) any benefit in kind provided to the worker, whether or not a monetary value is attached to the benefit, other than living accommodation;

    (b) any voucher, stamp or similar document capable of being exchanged for money, goods or services (or for any combination of those things) provided by the employer to the worker.

The pay reference period

22-010   **10.**—(1) The pay reference period is a month or, in the case of a worker who is paid wages by reference to a period shorter than a month, that period.

(2) When a worker's contract terminates regulations 14 and 30 to 37 shall be applied in relation to payments made in the period of a month beginning with the day immediately following the last day on which the worker worked under the contract as if such payments had been made in the worker's final pay reference period.

PART II

THE RATE OF THE NATIONAL MINIMUM WAGE

The rate and exclusions

The rate of the national minimum wage

22-011   **11.** The single hourly rate of the national minimum wage is [£4.50][1].

Workers who do not qualify for the national minimum wage

22-012   **12.**—(1) Workers who have not attained the age of 18 do not qualify for the national minimum wage.

(2) A worker who –

    (a) has not attained the age of 26,

    (b) is employed under a contract of apprenticeship or, in accordance with paragraph (3), is to be treated as employed under a contract of apprenticeship, and

    (c) is within the first 12 months after the commencement of that employment or has not attained the age of 19,

does not qualify for the national minimum wage in respect of work done for his employer under that contract.

[(3) A person is to be treated for the purposes of paragraph (2)(b) as a worker who is employed under a contract of apprenticeship if, and only if, he is –

    (a) a worker within the meaning given by section 54(3) of the Act; and

    (b) engaged –

        (i) in England or Wales, under the Government arrangements known, at 1st October 2000, as National Traineeships, Modern Apprenticeships, Foundation Modern Apprenticeships or Advanced Modern Apprenticeships;

        (ii) in Scotland, under the Government arrangements known, at 1st October 2000, as Skillseekers or Modern Apprenticeships and the

---

[1] Figure substituted by SI 2003/1923 reg 2

arrangements are for the purpose of gaining a Scottish Vocational Qualification at Level 2 or 3 or a National Vocational Qualification at Level 2 or 3; or

    (iii) in Northern Ireland, under the Government arrangements known, at 1st October 2000, as Jobskills Traineeships or Modern Apprenticeships.][1]

(4) For the purposes of paragraph (2)(c) a worker does not commence employment with an employer where he has previously been employed by another employer and continuity of employment is preserved between the two employments by or under any enactment.

(5) A [person][2] who is participating in a scheme, designed to provide him with training, work experience or temporary work, or to assist him in seeking or obtaining work, which is [...][3]–

    [(a) a scheme provided to him under Government arrangements that are not specified in paragraph (3)(b),

    (b) a scheme provided to him under Government arrangements that are specified in paragraph (3)(b), unless the person is a worker within the meaning given by section 54(3) of the Act by virtue of his participation in the scheme, or

    (c) a scheme, not being one provided to him under Government arrangements, funded in whole or in part under the European Social Fund,][4]

does not qualify for the national minimum wage in respect of work done for his employer as part of that scheme except to the extent that paragraph (6) or (7) otherwise provides.

(6) Paragraph (5) does not apply to a [person who is a worker within the meaning given by section 54(3) of the Act and][5] is participating in a scheme falling within sub-paragraph (a) of paragraph (5) if he is employed by the employer for whom he works under the scheme, unless the worker is engaged, for a period not exceeding three weeks, in a trial period of work with a prospective employer under [Government arrangements][6].

(7) Paragraph (5) does not apply to an employee who is participating in a scheme falling within sub-paragraph [(c)][7] of paragraph (5) if he is employed by the employer for whom he works under the scheme, unless the employee is engaged, for a period not exceeding three weeks, in a trial period of work with a prospective employer under [Government arrangements][8].

[(8) A worker who is attending a higher education course, and before the course ends is required, as part of that course, to attend a period of work experience not exceeding one year, does not qualify for the national minimum wage in respect of work done for his employer as part of that course.][9]

(9) For the purposes of paragraph (8) a "higher education course" means –

    (a) in England and Wales, a course of a description referred to in Schedule 6 to the Education Reform Act 1988;

    (b) in Scotland, a course of a description falling within section 38 of the Further and Higher Education (Scotland) Act 1992;

---

[1] Substituted by SI 2000/1989 reg 4 (1)
[2] Word substituted by SI 2001/1108 reg 3
[3] Word repealed by SI 2001/1108 reg 3
[4] Substituted by SI 2001/1108 reg 4
[5] Words substituted by SI 2000/1989 reg 4 (2)
[6] Words substituted by SI 2001/1108 reg 5
[7] Word substituted by SI 2001/1108 reg 6
[8] Words substituted by SI 2001/1108 reg 6
[9] Substituted by SI 2000/1989 reg 4 (3)

(c) in Northern Ireland, a course of a description referred to in Schedule 1 to the Further Education (Northern Ireland) Order 1997.

(10) A worker who satisfies the condition set out in paragraph (11) and is participating in a scheme which satisfies the conditions set out in paragraph (12), under which he is provided with shelter and other benefits (which may include money benefits) in return for performing work, does not qualify for the national minimum wage in respect of work performed for his employer under that scheme.

(11) A worker satisfies the condition referred to in paragraph (10) if, immediately before his entry into the scheme –

(a) he was either homeless or residing in a hostel for homeless persons; and

(b) he –

   (i) was in receipt of, or entitled to, income support or income-based job seekers' allowance, or

   (ii) was not entitled to receive either of those benefits only because he was not habitually resident in the United Kingdom.

(12) A scheme satisfies this paragraph if –

(a) the arrangements under which the scheme operates prevent the person operating the scheme or any other person from making a profit out of the provision of the scheme, other than one which may only be applied in running the scheme or other schemes satisfying the requirements of this paragraph or, where the person operating the scheme is a charity, for a purpose, being a purpose of the charity, relating to the alleviation of poverty;

(b) every person participating in the scheme satisfies the condition set out in paragraph (11), or would satisfy it if he were a worker;

(c) the accommodation available under the scheme is provided by the person operating the scheme or under arrangements made between that person and another person; and

(d) the work done under the scheme is both provided by, and performed for, the person operating the scheme.

Workers who qualify for the national minimum wage at a different rate

22-013   **13.**—(1) The hourly rate of the national minimum wage is [£3.80][1] for a worker who has attained the age of 18 but not the age of 22.

(2) The hourly rate of the national minimum wage is [£3.80][2] for a worker who –

(a) has attained the age of 22;

(b) is within the first six months after the commencement of his employment with an employer;

(c) has not previously been employed either by that employer or by an associated employer of that employer; and

(d) has entered into an agreement with the employer requiring the worker to take part in accredited training on at least 26 days between the commencement of his employment or, if later, the day upon which he entered into the agreement, and the end of the six month period referred to in sub-paragraph (b).

(3) In this regulation "accredited training" means –

---

[1] Figure substituted by SI 2003/1923 reg 3
[2] Figure substituted by SI 2003/1923 reg 3

(b) training by means of a course leading to a qualification accredited or awarded by the Scottish Qualifications Authority, other than qualifications known as Standard Grade, Higher Grade and Certificate of Sixth Year Studies;

(c) a course which prepares students in Northern Ireland to obtain a vocational qualification which corresponds to, or falls within a class corresponding to, any qualification or class of qualification [which—][1]

[(i) was, immediately before 1 April 2001, approved for the purposes of sub-paragraph (a) of Schedule 2 to the Further and Higher Education Act 1992, or

(ii) is approved under section 98 or 99 of the Learning and Skills Act 2000 for the purposes of section 97 of that Act;][2]

(d) training provided by the worker's employer where—

(i) the training is recognised in England and Wales, both as being directed towards the achievement of a National Vocational Qualification at any level, and as including at least 50% of the requirements of the relevant level, by an awarding body accredited for this purpose by virtue of an accreditation agreement with the Qualifications and Curriculum Authority to which it is a party,

(ii) the training is recognised in Scotland, both as being directed towards the achievement of a Scottish Vocational Qualification at any level, and as including at least 50% of the requirements of the relevant level, by an awarding body accredited for this purpose by virtue of an accreditation agreement with the Scottish Qualifications Authority to which it is a party,

(iii) the training is recognised in Northern Ireland, both as being directed towards the achievement of a National Vocational Qualification at any level, and as including at least 50% of the requirements of the relevant level, by an awarding body accredited for this purpose by virtue of an accreditation agreement with the Qualifications and Curriculum Authority to which it is a party;

(e) where the worker is engaged as part of his work in a training scheme falling within the provision made for persons of 18 or over who (at the time of commencing their engagement in the scheme) have not attained the age of 25, under the arrangements made by the Government known as the "New Deal" (or under any other title by which those arrangements may subsequently become known)–

[(i) in England and Wales, training by means of a course which—

(a) prepares students to obtain a vocational qualification which, immediately before 1 April 2001, was, or fell within a class, approved for the purposes of sub-paragraph (a) of Schedule 2 to the Further and Higher Education Act 1992, or

(b) leads to an external qualification approved under section 98 or 99 of the Learning and Skills Act 2000 for the purposes of section 97 of that Act,][3]

(ii) in Scotland, training by means of a course or programme of a description mentioned in section 6(1) of the Further and Higher Education (Scotland) Act 1992,

(iii) in Northern Ireland, training by means of a relevant course.

---

[1] Word substituted by SI 2001/2673 reg 5 (1) (b)
[2] Substituted by SI 2001/2673 reg 5 (1) (b)
[3] Substituted by SI 2001/2673 reg 5 (1) (c)

(4) For the purposes of paragraph (2)(b) a worker does not commence employment with an employer where he has previously been employed by another employer and continuity of employment is preserved between the two employments by or under any enactment.

(5) For the purposes of paragraph (2)(c) two employers shall be treated as associated if–

    (a) one is a company of which the other (directly or indirectly) has control; or

    (b) both are companies of which a third person (directly or indirectly) has control.

(6) For the purposes of paragraph (3)(e)(iii) "relevant course" means –

    (a) a course which prepares students in Northern Ireland to obtain a vocational qualification which corresponds to, or falls within a class corresponding to, any qualification or class of [qualification which—][1]

        [(i) was, immediately before 1st April 2001, approved for the purposes of sub-paragraph (a) of Schedule 2 to the Further and Higher Education Act 1992, or

       (ii) is approved under section 98 or 99 of the Learning and Skills Act 2000 for the purposes of section 97 of that Act;][2]

    (b) a course which prepares students to qualify for–

        (i) the General Certificate of Secondary Education, or

       (ii) the General Certificate of Education at Advanced Level or Advanced Supplementary Level (including special papers);

    (c) a course which corresponds to any course [which was, immediately before 1st April 2001][3] approved by the Secretary of State under, and for the purposes of, paragraph (c) of Schedule 2 to the Further and Higher Education Act 1992, which prepares students for entry to a course of higher education;

    (d) a course which prepares students for entry to another course falling within paragraphs (a) to (c);

    (e) a course of basic literacy in English;

    (f) a course to improve the knowledge of English of those for whom English is not the language spoken at home;

    (g) a course to teach the basics of mathematics;

    (h) a course to teach independent living and communication skills to persons having learning difficulties which prepares them for entry to another course falling within paragraphs (d) to (g) above.

(7) Paragraphs (1) and (2) do not apply in relation to a worker who, by virtue of regulation 12, does not qualify for the national minimum wage.

Method of determining whether the national minimum wage has been paid

22-014   **14.**—(1) The hourly rate paid to a worker in a pay reference period shall be determined by dividing the total calculated in accordance with paragraph (2) by the number of hours specified in paragraph (3).

(2) The total referred to in paragraph (1) shall be calculated by subtracting from the total of remuneration in the pay reference period determined under regulation 30, the total of reductions determined under regulations 31 to 37.

(3) The hours referred to in paragraph (1) are the total number of hours of time work, salaried hours work, output work and unmeasured work worked by

---

[1] Words substituted by SI 2001/2673 reg 5 (2) (a)
[2] Substituted by SI 2001/2673 reg 5 (2) (a)
[3] Words substituted by SI 2001/2673 reg 5 (2) (b)

the worker in the pay reference period that have been ascertained in accordance with [regulations 20 to 29A][1].

[Determining the applicable national minimum rate

14A.—(1) The hourly rate at which a worker is entitled to be remunerated in **22-015** respect of his work in any pay reference period is the rate, prescribed by regulations, that is in force on the first day of that period.][2]

The Maternity and Parental Leave etc. Regulations 1999

(S.I. 3312)

PART 1

GENERAL

Citation and commencement

1. These Regulations may be cited as the Maternity and Parental Leave etc. **23-001** Regulations 1999 and shall come into force on 15th December 1999.

Interpretation

2.—(1) In these Regulations– **23-002**
"the 1996 Act" means the Employment Rights Act 1996;
["additional adoption leave" means leave under section 75B of the 1996
     Act;][3]
"additional maternity leave" means leave under section 73 of the 1996 Act;
"business" includes a trade or profession and includes any activity carried
     on by a body of persons (whether corporate or unincorporated);
"child" means a person under the age of eighteen;
"childbirth" means the birth of a living child or the birth of a child whether
     living or dead after 24 weeks of pregnancy;
"collective agreement" means a collective agreement within the meaning of
     section 178 of the Trade Union and Labour Relations (Consolidation)
     Act 1992, the trade union parties to which are independent trade
     unions within the meaning of section 5 of that Act;
"contract of employment" means a contract of service or apprenticeship,
     whether express or implied, and (if it is express) whether oral or in
     writing;
"disability living allowance" means the disability living allowance provided
     for in Part III of the Social Security Contributions and Benefits Act
     1992;
"employee" means an individual who has entered into or works under (or,
     where the employment has ceased, worked under) a contract of
     employment;

---

[1] Words substituted by SI 2000/1989 reg 5
[2] Inserted by SI 2002/1999 reg 4
[3] Definition inserted by SI 2002/2789 reg 4 (a)

"employer" means the person by whom an employee is (or, where the employment has ceased, was) employed;

"expected week of childbirth" means the week, beginning with midnight between Saturday and Sunday, in which it is expected that childbirth will occur, and "week of childbirth" means the week, beginning with midnight between Saturday and Sunday, in which childbirth occurs;

"job", in relation to an employee returning after [...][1] maternity leave or parental leave, means the nature of the work which she is employed to do in accordance with her contract and the capacity and place in which she is so employed;

"ordinary maternity leave" means leave under section 71 of the 1996 Act;

"parental leave" means leave under regulation 13(1);

"parental responsibility" has the meaning given by section 3 of the Children Act 1989, and "parental responsibilities" has the meaning given by section 1(3) of the Children (Scotland) Act 1995;

["statutory leave" means leave provided for in Part 8 of the 1996 Act;][2]

"workforce agreement" means an agreement between an employer and his employees or their representatives in respect of which the conditions set out in Schedule 1 to these Regulations are satisfied.

(2) A reference in any provision of these Regulations to a period of continuous employment is to a period computed in accordance with Chapter I of Part XIV of the 1996 Act, as if that provision were a provision of that Act.

(3) For the purposes of these Regulations any two employers shall be treated as associated if –

(a) one is a company of which the other (directly or indirectly) has control; or

(b) both are companies of which a third person (directly or indirectly) has control;

and "associated employer" shall be construed accordingly.

(4) In these Regulations, unless the context otherwise requires,–

(a) a reference to a numbered regulation or schedule is to the regulation or schedule in these Regulations bearing that number;

(b) a reference in a regulation or schedule to a numbered paragraph is to the paragraph in that regulation or schedule bearing that number, and

(c) a reference in a paragraph to a lettered sub-paragraph is to the sub-paragraph in that paragraph bearing that letter.

Application

23-003   **3.**—(1) The provisions of Part II of these Regulations have effect only in relation to employees whose expected week of childbirth begins on or after 30th April 2000.

(2) Regulation 19 (protection from detriment) has effect only in relation to an act or failure to act which takes place on or after 15th December 1999.

(3) For the purposes of paragraph (2)–

(a) where an act extends over a period, the reference to the date of the act is a reference to the last day of that period, and

(b) a failure to act is to be treated as done when it was decided on.

(4) For the purposes of paragraph (3), in the absence of evidence establishing the contrary an employer shall be taken to decide on a failure to act –

(a) when he does an act inconsistent with doing the failed act, or

---

[1] Word repealed by SI 2002/2789 reg 4 (b)

[2] Definition inserted by SI 2002/2789 reg 4 (c)

(b) if he has done no such inconsistent act, when the period expires within which he might reasonably have been expected to do the failed act if it was to be done.

(5) Regulation 20 (unfair dismissal) has effect only in relation to dismissals where the effective date of termination (within the meaning of section 97 of the 1996 Act) falls on or after 15th December 1999.

PART II

MATERNITY LEAVE

Entitlement to ordinary maternity leave

4.—(1) An employee is entitled to ordinary maternity leave provided that she **23-004** satisfies the following conditions –

(a) [no later than the end of the fifteenth week before her expected week of childbirth][1], or, if that is not reasonably practicable, as soon as is reasonably practicable, she notifies her employer of –
  (i) her pregnancy;
  (ii) the expected week of childbirth, and
  (iii) the date on which she intends her ordinary maternity leave period to start,

and

(b) if requested to do so by her employer, she produces for his inspection a certificate from –
  (i) a registered medical practitioner, or
  (ii) a registered midwife,

stating the expected week of childbirth [and of the date on which her absence on that account began][2].

[(1A) An employee who has notified her employer under paragraph (1)(a)(iii) of the date on which she intends her ordinary maternity leave period to start may subsequently vary that date, provided that she notifies her employer of the variation at least—

(a) 28 days before the date varied, or
(b) 28 days before the new date,

whichever is the earlier, or, if that is not reasonably practicable, as soon as is reasonably practicable.][3]

(2) [Notification under paragraph (1)(a)(iii) or (1A)][4]–

(a) shall be given in writing, if the employer so requests, and
(b) shall not specify a date earlier than the beginning of the eleventh week before the expected week of childbirth.

(3) Where, by virtue of regulation 6(1)(b), an employee's ordinary maternity leave period commences with [the day which follows][5] the first day after the beginning of [the fourth week][6] before the expected week of childbirth on which she is absent from work wholly or partly because of pregnancy –

(a) paragraph (1) does not require her to notify her employer of the date specified in that paragraph, but

---

[1] Words substituted by SI 2002/2789 reg 5 (a)
[2] Words inserted by SI 2002/2789 reg 5 (d) (iii)
[3] Inserted by SI 2002/2789 reg 5 (b)
[4] Words substituted by SI 2002/2789 reg 5 (c)
[5] Words inserted by SI 2002/2789 reg 5 (d) (i)
[6] Words substituted by SI 2002/2789 reg 5 (d) (ii)

(b) (whether or not she has notified him of that date) she is not entitled to ordinary maternity leave unless she notifies him as soon as is reasonably practicable that she is absent from work wholly or partly because of pregnancy.

(4) Where, by virtue of regulation 6(2), an employee's ordinary maternity leave period commences [on the day which follows][1] the day on which childbirth occurs –

(a) paragraph (1) does not require her to notify her employer of the date specified in that paragraph, but

(b) (whether or not she has notified him of that date) she is not entitled to ordinary maternity leave unless she notifies him as soon as is reasonably practicable after the birth that she has given birth [and of the date on which the birth occurred][2].

(5) The notification provided for in paragraphs (3)(b) and (4)(b) shall be given in writing, if the employer so requests.

Entitlement to additional maternity leave

23-005   **5.** An employee who satisfies the following conditions is entitled to additional maternity leave –

(a) she is entitled to ordinary maternity leave, and

(b) she has, at the beginning of [the fourteenth week][3] before the expected week of childbirth, been continuously employed for a period of not less than [26 weeks][4].

Commencement of maternity leave periods

23-006   **6.**—(1) Subject to paragraph (2), an employee's ordinary maternity leave period commences with the earlier of –

(a) the date which [...][5] she notifies to her employer[, in accordance with regulation 4,][6] as the date on which she intends her ordinary maternity leave period to start, [or, if by virtue of the provision for variation in that regulation she has notified more than one such date, the last date she notifies,][7] and

(b) [the day which follows][8] the first day after the beginning of [the fourth week][9] before the expected week of childbirth on which she is absent from work wholly or partly because of pregnancy.

(2) Where the employee's ordinary maternity leave period has not commenced by virtue of paragraph (1) when childbirth occurs, her ordinary maternity leave period commences [on the day which follows][10] the day on which childbirth occurs.

(3) An employee's additional maternity leave period commences on the day after the last day of her ordinary maternity leave period.

---

[1] Words substituted by SI 2002/2789 reg 5 (e) (i)
[2] Words inserted by SI 2002/2789 reg 5 (e) (ii)
[3] Words substituted by SI 2002/2789 reg 6 (a)
[4] Words substituted by SI 2002/2789 reg 6 (b)
[5] Words repealed by SI 2002/2789 reg 7 (a) (i)
[6] Words inserted by SI 2002/2789 reg 7 (a) (ii)
[7] Words inserted by SI 2002/2789 reg 7 (a) (iii)
[8] Words inserted by SI 2002/2789 reg 7 (b) (i)
[9] Words substituted by SI 2002/2789 reg 7 (b) (ii)
[10] Words substituted by SI 2002/2789 reg 7 (c)

Duration of maternity leave periods

7.—(1) Subject to paragraphs (2) and (5), an employee's ordinary maternity **23-007** leave period continues for the period of [26 weeks][1] from its commencement, or until the end of the compulsory maternity leave period provided for in regulation 8 if later.

(2) Subject to paragraph (5), where any requirement imposed by or under any relevant statutory provision prohibits the employee from working for any period after the end of the period determined under paragraph (1) by reason of her having recently given birth, her ordinary maternity leave period continues until the end of that later period.

(3) In paragraph (2), "relevant statutory provision" means a provision of–
  (a) an enactment, or
  (b) an instrument under an enactment,
other than a provision for the time being specified in an order under section 66(2) of the 1996 Act.

(4) Subject to paragraph (5), where an employee is entitled to additional maternity leave her additional maternity leave period continues until the end of the period of [26 weeks from the day on which it commenced][2].

(5) Where the employee is dismissed after the commencement of an ordinary or additional maternity leave period but before the time when (apart from this paragraph) that period would end, the period ends at the time of the dismissal.

[(6) An employer who is notified under any provision of regulation 4 of the date on which, by virtue of any provision of regulation 6, an employee's ordinary maternity leave period will commence or has commenced shall notify the employee of the date on which—
  (a) if the employee is entitled only to ordinary maternity leave, her ordinary maternity leave period will end, or
  (b) if the employee is entitled to both ordinary and additional maternity leave, her additional maternity leave period will end.

(7) The notification provided for in paragraph (6) shall be given to the employee—
  (a) where the employer is notified under regulation 4(1)(a)(iii), (3)(b) or (4)(b), within 28 days of the date on which he received the notification;
  (b) where the employer is notified under regulation 4(1A), within 28 days of the date on which the employee's ordinary maternity leave period commenced.][3]

Compulsory maternity leave

8. The prohibition in section 72 of the 1996 Act, against permitting an **23-008** employee who satisfies prescribed conditions to work during a particular period (referred to as a "compulsory maternity leave period"), applies–
  (a) in relation to an employee who is entitled to ordinary maternity leave, and
  (b) in respect of the period of two weeks which commences with the day on which childbirth occurs.

[Application of terms and conditions during ordinary maternity leave

9.—(1) An employee who takes ordinary maternity leave—   **23-009**

---

[1] Words substituted by SI 2002/2789 reg 8 (a)
[2] Words substituted by SI 2002/2789 reg 8 (b)
[3] Inserted by SI 2002/2789 reg 8 (c)

(a) is entitled, during the period of leave, to the benefit of all of the terms and conditions of employment which would have applied if she had not been absent, and

(b) is bound, during that period, by any obligations arising under those terms and conditions, subject only to the exception in section 71(4)(b) of the 1996 Act.

(2) In paragraph (1)(a), "terms and conditions" has the meaning given by section 71(5) of the 1996 Act, and accordingly does not include terms and conditions about remuneration.

(3) For the purposes of section 71 of the 1996 Act, only sums payable to an employee by way of wages or salary are to be treated as remuneration.][1]

Redundancy during maternity leave

23-010   **10.**—(1) This regulation applies where, during an employee's ordinary or additional maternity leave period, it is not practicable by reason of redundancy for her employer to continue to employ her under her existing contract of employment.

(2) Where there is a suitable available vacancy, the employee is entitled to be offered (before the end of her employment under her existing contract) alternative employment with her employer or his successor, or an associated employer, under a new contract of employment which complies with paragraph (3) (and takes effect immediately on the ending of her employment under the previous contract).

(3) The new contract of employment must be such that—

(a) the work to be done under it is of a kind which is both suitable in relation to the employee and appropriate for her to do in the circumstances, and

(b) its provisions as to the capacity and place in which she is to be employed, and as to the other terms and conditions of her employment, are not substantially less favourable to her than if she had continued to be employed under the previous contract.

Requirement to notify intention to return during a maternity leave period

23-011   **11.**—(1) An employee who intends to return to work earlier than the end of her ordinary maternity leave period or, where she is entitled to [both ordinary and][2] additional maternity leave, the end of her additional maternity leave period, shall give to her employer not less than [28 days'][3] notice of the date on which she intends to return.

(2) If an employee attempts to return to work earlier than the end of a maternity leave period without complying with paragraph (1), her employer is entitled to postpone her return to a date such as will secure, subject to paragraph (3), that he has [28 days'][4] notice of her return.

(3) An employer is not entitled under paragraph (2) to postpone an employee's return to work to a date after the end of the relevant maternity leave period.

(4) If an employee whose return to work has been postponed under paragraph (2) has been notified that she is not to return to work before the date to which her return was postponed, the employer is under no contractual

[1] Substituted by SI 2002/2789 reg 9
[2] Words inserted by SI 2002/2789 reg 10 (a) (i)
[3] Words substituted by SI 2002/2789 reg 10 (a) (ii)
[4] Words substituted by SI 2002/2789 reg 10 (b)

obligation to pay her remuneration until the date to which her return was postponed if she returns to work before that date.

[(5) This regulation does not apply in a case where the employer did not notify the employee in accordance with regulation 7(6) and (7) of the date on which the relevant maternity leave period would end.][1]

12. [...][2]

23-012

PART III

PARENTAL LEAVE

Entitlement to parental leave

13.—(1) An employee who—

23-013

    (a) has been continuously employed for a period of not less than a year [or is to be treated as having been so employed by virtue of paragraph (1A)][3]; and

    (b) has, or expects to have, responsibility for a child,

is entitled, in accordance with these Regulations, to be absent from work on parental leave for the purpose of caring for that child.

[(1A) If, in a case where regulation 15(2) or (3) applies—

    (a) the employee was employed, during the period between 15th December 1998 and 9th January 2002, by a person other than the person who was his employer on 9th January 2002, and

    (b) the period of his employment by that person (or, if he was employed by more than one person during that period, any such person) was not less than a year,

then, for the purposes of paragraph (1), he shall be treated as having been continuously employed for a period of not less than a year.;][4]

(2) An employee has responsibility for a child, for the purpose of paragraph (1), if—

    (a) he has parental responsibility or, in Scotland, parental responsibilities for the child; or

    (b) he has been registered as the child's father under any provision of section 10(1) or 10A(1) of the Births and Deaths Registration Act 1953 or of section 18(1) or (2) of the Registration of Births, Deaths and Marriages (Scotland) Act 1965.

(3) [...][5]

Extent of entitlement

14.—(1) [Except in the case referred to in paragraph (1A), an employee is entitled][6] to thirteen weeks' leave in respect of any individual child.

23-014

[(1A) An employee is entitled to eighteen weeks' leave in respect of a child who is entitled to a disability living allowance.][7]

---

[1] Inserted by SI 2002/2789 reg 10 (c)
[2] Repealed by SI 2002/2789 reg 11
[3] Words inserted by SI 2001/4010 reg 3 (a)
[4] Inserted by SI 2001/4010 reg 3 (b)
[5] Repealed by SI 2001/4010 reg 3 (c)
[6] Words substituted by SI 2001/4010 reg 4 (a)
[7] Inserted by SI 2001/4010 reg 4 (b)

(2) Where the period for which an employee is normally required, under his contract of employment, to work in the course of a week does not vary, a week's leave for the employee is a period of absence from work which is equal in duration to the period for which he is normally required to work.

(3) Where the period for which an employee is normally required, under his contract of employment, to work in the course of a week varies from week to week or over a longer period, or where he is normally required under his contract to work in some weeks but not in others, a week's leave for the employee is a period of absence from work which is equal in duration to the period calculated by dividing the total of the periods for which he is normally required to work in a year by 52.

(4) Where an employee takes leave in periods shorter than the period which constitutes, for him, a week's leave under whichever of paragraphs (2) and (3) is applicable in his case, he completes a week's leave when the aggregate of the periods of leave he has taken equals the period constituting a week's leave for him under the applicable paragraph.

23-015   [15.—(1) Except in the cases referred to in paragraphs (2)-(4), an employee may not exercise any entitlement to parental leave in respect of a child after the date of the child's fifth birthday or, in the case of a child placed with the employee for adoption by him, on or after—

    (a) the fifth anniversary of the date on which the placement began, or
    (b) the date of the child's eighteenth birthday,
whichever is the earlier.

    (2) In the case of child—
    (a) born before 15th December 1999, whose fifth birthday was or is on or after that date, or
    (b) placed with the employee for adoption by him before 15th December 1999, the fifth anniversary of whose placement was or is on or after that date,
not being a case to which paragraph (3) or (4) applies, any entitlement to parental leave may not be exercised after 31st March 2005.

    (3) In the case of a child who is entitled to a disability living allowance, any entitlement to parental leave may not be exercised on or after the date of the child's eighteenth birthday.

    (4) In a case where—
    (a) the provisions set out in Schedule 2 apply, and
    (b) the employee was unable to take leave in respect of a child within the time permitted in the case of that child under paragraphs (1) or (2) because the employer postponed the period of leave under paragraph 6 of that Schedule,
the entitlement to leave is exercisable until the end of the period to which the leave was postponed.][1]

Default provisions in respect of parental leave

23-016   16. The provisions set out in Schedule 2 apply in relation to parental leave in the case of an employee whose contract of employment does not include a provision which—

    (a) confers an entitlement to absence from work for the purpose of caring for a child, and

---

[1] Substituted by SI 2001/4010 reg 5

(b) incorporates or operates by reference to all or part of a collective agreement or workforce agreement.

PART IV

PROVISIONS APPLICABLE IN RELATION TO MORE THAN ONE KIND OF ABSENCE

Application of terms and conditions during periods of leave

17. An employee who takes additional maternity leave or parental leave– **23-017**
   (a) is entitled, during the period of leave, to the benefit of her employer's implied obligation to her of trust and confidence and any terms and conditions of her employment relating to–
      (i) notice of the termination of the employment contract by her employer;
      (ii) compensation in the event of redundancy, or
      (iii) disciplinary or grievance procedures;
   (b) is bound, during that period, by her implied obligation to her employer of good faith and any terms and conditions of her employment relating to–
      (i) notice of the termination of the employment contract by her;
      (ii) the disclosure of confidential information;
      (iii) the acceptance of gifts or other benefits, or
      (iv) the employee's participation in any other business.

[Right to return after maternity or parental leave

18.—(1) An employee who returns to work after a period of ordinary **23-018**
maternity leave, or a period of parental leave of four weeks or less, which was—
   (a) an isolated period of leave, or
   (b) the last of two or more consecutive periods of statutory leave which did not include any period of additional maternity leave or additional adoption leave, or a period of parental leave of more than four weeks,
is entitled to return to the job in which she was employed before her absence.
   (2) An employee who returns to work after—
   (a) a period of additional maternity leave, or a period of parental leave of more than four weeks, whether or not preceded by another period of statutory leave, or
   (b) a period of ordinary maternity leave, or a period of parental leave of four weeks or less, not falling within the description in paragraph (1)(a) or (b) above,
is entitled to return from leave to the job in which she was employed before her absence or, if it is not reasonably practicable for the employer to permit her to return to that job, to another job which is both suitable for her and appropriate for her to do in the circumstances.
   (3) The reference in paragraphs (1) and (2) to the job in which an employee was employed before her absence is a reference to the job in which she was employed—
   (a) if her return is from an isolated period of statutory leave, immediately before that period began;

(b) if her return is from consecutive periods of statutory leave, immediately before the first such period.

(4) This regulation does not apply where regulation 10 applies.][1]

[Incidents of the right to return

23-019   **18A.**—(1) An employee's right to return under regulation 18(1) or (2) is a right to return—

    (a) with her seniority, pension rights and similar rights—

        (i) in a case where the employee is returning from additional maternity leave, or consecutive periods of statutory leave which included a period of additional maternity leave or additional adoption leave, as they would have been if the period or periods of her employment prior to her additional maternity leave or (as the case may be) additional adoption leave were continuous with the period of employment following it;

        (ii) in any other case, as they would have been if she had not been absent, and

    (b) on terms and conditions not less favourable than those which would have applied if she had not been absent.

(2) The provision in paragraph (1)(a)(i) concerning the treatment of periods of additional maternity leave or additional adoption leave is subject to the requirements of paragraphs 5 and 6 of Schedule 5 to the Social Security Act 1989 (equal treatment under pension schemes: maternity absence and family leave).

(3) The provisions in paragraph (1)(a)(ii) and (b) for an employee to be treated as if she had not been absent refer to her absence—

    (a) if her return is from an isolated period of statutory leave, since the beginning of that period;

    (b) if her return is from consecutive periods of statutory leave, since the beginning of the first such period.][2]

Protection from detriment

23-020   **19.**—(1) An employee is entitled under section 47C of the 1996 Act not to be subjected to any detriment by any act, or any deliberate failure to act, by her employer done for any of the reasons specified in paragraph (2).

(2) The reasons referred to in paragraph (1) are that the employee –

    (a) is pregnant;

    (b) has given birth to a child;

    (c) is the subject of a relevant requirement, or a relevant recommendation, as defined by section 66(2) of the 1996 Act;

    (d) took, sought to take or availed herself of the benefits of, ordinary maternity leave;

    (e) took or sought to take –

        (i) additional maternity leave;

        (ii) parental leave, or

        (iii) time off under section 57A of the 1996 Act;

    [(ee) failed to return after a period of ordinary or additional maternity leave in a case where—

        (i) the employer did not notify her, in accordance with regulation 7(6) and (7) or otherwise, of the date on which the period in

---

[1] Substituted by SI 2002/2789 reg 12
[2] Substituted by SI 2002/2789 reg 12

question would end, and she reasonably believed that that period had not ended, or

    (ii) the employer gave her less than 28 days' notice of the date on which the period in question would end, and it was not reasonably practicable for her to return on that date;][1]

(f) declined to sign a workforce agreement for the purpose of these Regulations, or

(g) being–

    (i) a representative of members of the workforce for the purpose of Schedule 1, or

    (ii) a candidate in an election in which any person elected will, on being elected, become such a representative,

performed (or proposed to perform) any functions or activities as such a representative or candidate.

(3) For the purpose of paragraph (2)(d), a woman avails herself of the benefits of ordinary maternity leave if, during her ordinary maternity leave period, she avails herself of the benefit of any of the terms and conditions of her employment preserved by section 71 of the 1996 Act [and regulation 9][2] during that period.

(4) Paragraph (1) does not apply in a case where the detriment in question amounts to dismissal within the meaning of Part X of the 1996 Act.

(5) Paragraph (2)(b) only applies where the act or failure to act takes place during the employee's ordinary or additional maternity leave period.

(6) For the purpose of paragraph(5)–

(a) where an act extends over a period, the reference to the date of the act is a reference to the last day of that period, and

(b) a failure to act is to be treated as done when it was decided on.

(7) For the purposes of paragraph (6), in the absence of evidence establishing the contrary an employer shall be taken to decide on a failure act–

(a) when he does an act inconsistent with doing the failed act, or

(b) if he has done no such inconsistent act, when the period expires within which he might reasonably have been expected to do the failed act if it were to be done.

Unfair dismissal

20.—(1) An employee who is dismissed is entitled under section 99 of the **23-021** 1996 Act to be regarded for the purposes of Part X of that Act as unfairly dismissed if–

(a) the reason or principal reason for the dismissal is of a kind specified in paragraph (3), or

(b) the reason or principal reason for the dismissal is that the employee is redundant, and regulation 10 has not been complied with.

(2) An employee who is dismissed shall also be regarded for the purposes of Part X of the 1996 Act as unfairly dismissed if–

(a) the reason (or, if more than one, the principal reason) for the dismissal is that the employee was redundant;

(b) it is shown that the circumstances constituting the redundancy applied equally to one or more employees in the same undertaking who held positions similar to that held by the employee and who have not been dismissed by the employer, and

---

[1] Inserted by SI 2002/2789 reg 13 (a)
[2] Words inserted by SI 2002/2789 reg 13 (b)

(c) it is shown that the reason (or, if more than one, the principal reason) for which the employee was selected for dismissal was a reason of a kind specified in paragraph (3).

(3) The kinds of reason referred to in paragraph (1) and (2) are reasons connected with –

(a) the pregnancy of the employee;

(b) the fact that the employee has given birth to a child;

(c) the application of a relevant requirement, or a relevant recommendation, as defined by section 66(2) of the 1996 Act;

(d) the fact that she took, sought to take or availed herself of the benefits of, ordinary maternity leave;

(e) the fact that she took or sought to take –

 (i) additional maternity leave;

 (ii) parental leave, or

 (iii) time off under section 57A of the 1996 Act;

[(ee) the fact that she failed to return after a period of ordinary or additional maternity leave in a case where—

 (i) the employer did not notify her, in accordance with regulation 7(6) and (7) or otherwise, of the date on which the period in question would end, and she reasonably believed that that period had not ended, or

 (ii) the employer gave her less than 28 days' notice of the date on which the period in question would end, and it was not reasonably practicable for her to return on that date;][1]

(f) the fact that she declined to sign a workforce agreement for the purposes of these Regulations, or

(g) the fact that the employee, being –

 (i) a representative of members of the workforce for the purposes of Schedule 1, or

 (ii) a candidate in an election in which any person elected will, on being elected, become such a representative,

performed (or proposed to perform) any functions or activities as such a representative or candidate.

(4) Paragraphs (1)(b) and (3)(b) only apply where the dismissal ends the employee's ordinary or additional maternity leave period.

(5) Paragraphs (3) of regulation 19 applies for the purposes of paragraph (3)(d) as it applies for the purpose of paragraph (2)(d) of that regulation.

(6) Paragraph (1) does not apply in relation to an employee if –

(a) immediately before the end of her additional maternity leave period (or, if it ends by reason of dismissal, immediately before the dismissal) the number of employees employed by her employer, added to the number employed by any associated employer of his, did not exceed five, and

(b) it is not reasonably practicable for the employer (who may be the same employer or a successor of his) to permit her to return to a job which is both suitable for her and appropriate for her to do in the circumstances or for an associated employer to offer her a job of that kind.

(7) Paragraph (1) does not apply in relation to an employee if –

(a) it is not reasonably practicable for a reason other than redundancy for the employer (who may be the same employer or a successor of his) to

---

[1] Inserted by SI 2002/2789 reg 14

permit her to a job which is both suitable for her and appropriate for her to do in the circumstances;

(b) an associated employer offers her a job of that kind, and

(c) she accepts or unreasonably refuses that offer.

(8) Where on a complaint of unfair dismissal any question arises as to whether the operation of paragraph (1) is excluded by the provisions of paragraph (6) or (7), it is for the employer to show that the provisions in question were satisfied in relation to the complainant.

Contractual rights to maternity or parental leave

21.—(1) This regulation applies where an employee is entitled to –   **23-022**

(a) ordinary maternity leave;

(b) additional maternity leave, or

(c) parental leave,

(referred to in paragraph (2) as a "statutory right") and also to a right which corresponds to that right and which arises under the employee's contract of employment or otherwise.

(2) In a case where this regulation applies –

(a) the employee may not exercise the statutory right and the corresponding right separately but may, in taking the leave for which the two rights provide, take advantage of whichever right is, in any particular respect, the more favourable, and

(b) the provisions of the 1996 Act and of these Regulations relating to the statutory right apply, subject to any modifications necessary to give effect to any more favourable contractual terms, to the exercise of the composite right described in sub-paragraph (a) as they apply to the exercise of the statutory right.

Calculation of a week's pay

22. Where –   **23-023**

(a) under Chapter II of part XIV of the 1996 Act, the amount of a week's pay of an employee falls to be calculated by reference to the average rate of remuneration, or the average amount of remuneration, payable to the employee in respect of a period of twelve weeks ending on a particular date (referred to as "the calculation date");

(b) during a week in that period, the employee was absent from work on ordinary or additional maternity leave or parental leave, and

(c) remuneration is payable to the employee in respect of that week under her contract of employment, but the amount payable is less than the amount that would be payable if she were working,

that week shall be disregarded for the purpose of the calculation and account shall be taken of remuneration in earlier weeks so as to bring up to twelve the number of weeks of which account is taken.

Regulation 2(1)   Schedule 1

WORKFORCE AGREEMENTS

1. An agreement is a workforce agreement for the purposes of these Regulations if the following   **23-024**
conditions are satisfied –

(a) the agreement is in writing;

(b) it has effect for a specified period not exceeding five years;

(c) it applies either –

(i) to all of the relevant members of the workforce, or

(ii) to all of the relevant members of the workforce who belong to a particular group;

(d) the agreement is signed –

(i) in the case of an agreement of the kind referred to in sub-paragraph (c)(i), by the representatives of the workforce, and in the case of an agreement of the kind referred to in sub-paragraph (c)(ii), by the representatives of the group to which the agreement applies (excluding, in either case, any representative not a relevant member of the workforce on the date on which the agreement was first made available for signature), or

(ii) if the employer employed 20 or fewer employees on the date referred to in sub-paragraph (d)(i), either by the appropriate representatives in accordance with that sub-paragraph or by the majority of the employees employed by him;

and

(e) before the agreement was made available for signature, the employer provided all the employees to whom it was intended to apply on the date on which it came into effect with copies of the text of the agreement and such guidance as those employees might reasonably require in order to understand it in full.

23-025 **2.** For the purposes of this Schedule –

"a particular group" is a group of the relevant members of a workforce who undertake a particular function, work at a particular workplace or belong to a particular department or unit within their employer's business;

"relevant members of the workforce" are all of the employees employed by a particular employer, excluding any employee whose terms and conditions of employment are provided for, wholly or in part, in a collective agreement;

"representatives of the workforce" are employees duly elected to represent the relevant members of the workforce, "representatives of the group" are employees duly elected to represent the members of a particular group, and representatives are "duly elected" if the election at which they were elected satisfied the requirements of paragraph 3 of this Schedule.

23-026 **3.** The requirements concerning elections referred to in paragraph 2 are that –

(a) the number of representatives to be elected is determined by the employer;

(b) the candidates for election as representatives of the workforce are relevant members of the workforce, and the candidates for election as representatives of a group are members of the group;

(c) no employee who is eligible to be a candidate is unreasonably excluded from standing for election;

(d) all the relevant members of the workforce are entitled to vote for representatives of the workforce, and all the members of a particular group are entitled to vote for representatives of the group;

(e) the employees entitled to vote may vote for as many candidates as there are representatives to be elected, and

(f) the election is conducted so as to secure that –

(i) so far as is reasonably practicable, those voting do so in secret, and

(ii) the votes given at the election are fairly and accurately counted.

Regulation 16   Schedule 2

DEFAULT PROVISIONS IN RESPECT OF PARENTAL LEAVE

Conditions of entitlement

23-027 **1.** An employee may not exercise any entitlement to parental leave unless –

(a) he has complied with any request made by his employer to produce for the employer's inspection evidence of his entitlement, of the kind described in paragraph 2;

(b) he has given his employer notice, in accordance with whichever of paragraphs 3 to 5 is applicable, of the period of leave he proposes to take, and

(c) in a case where paragraph 6 applies, his employer has not postponed the period of leave in accordance with that paragraph.

23-028 **2.** The evidence to be produced for the purpose of paragraph 1(a) is such evidence as may reasonably be required of –

(a) the employee's responsibility or expected responsibility for the child in respect of whom the employee proposes to take parental leave;

(b) the child's date of birth or, in the case of a child who was placed with the employee for adoption, the date on which the placement began, and

(c) in a case where the employee's right to exercise an entitlement to parental leave under regulation 15, or to take a particular period of leave under paragraph 7, depends upon whether the child is entitled to a disability living allowance, the child's entitlement to that allowance.

[**2A.** Where regulation 13(1A) applies, and the employee's entitlement to parental leave arises out of a period of employment by a person other than the person who was his employer on 9th January 2002, the employee may not exercise the entitlement unless he has given his employer notice of that period of employment, and provided him with such evidence of it as the employer may reasonably require.][1]   **23-029**

Notice to be given to employer

3. Except in a case where paragraph 4 or 5 applies, the notice required for the purpose of paragraph 1(b) is notice which –   **23-030**
(a) specifies the dates on which the period of leave is to begin and end, and
(b) is given to the employer at least 21 days before the date on which that period is to begin.

4. Where the employee is the father of the child in respect of whom the leave is to be taken, and the period of leave is to begin on the date on which the child is born, the notice required for the purpose of paragraph 1(b) is notice which–   **23-031**
(a) specifies the expected week of childbirth and the duration of the period of leave, and
(b) is given to the employer at least 21 days before the beginning of the expected week of childbirth.

5. Where the child in respect of whom the leave is to be taken is to be placed with the employee for adoption by him and the leave is to begin on the date of the placement, the notice required for the purpose of paragraph 1(b) is notice which–   **23-032**
(a) specifies the week in which the placement is expected to occur and the duration of the period of leave, and
(b) is given to the employer at least 21 days before the beginning of that week, or, if that is not reasonably practicable, as soon as is reasonably practicable.

Postponement of leave

6. An employer may postpone a period of parental leave where–   **23-033**
(a) neither paragraph 4 nor paragraph 5 applies, and the employee has accordingly given the employer notice in accordance with paragraph 3;
(b) the employer considers that the operation of his business would be unduly disrupted if the employee took leave during the period identified in his notice;
(c) the employer agrees to permit the employee to take a period of leave–
    (i) of the same duration as the period identified in the employee's notice, [...][2]
    (ii) beginning on a date determined by the employer after consulting the employee, which is no later than six months after the commencement of that period; [and][3]
    [(iii) ending before the date of the child's eighteenth birthday.][4]
(d) the employer gives the employee notice in writing of the postponement which–
    (i) states the reason for it, and
    (ii) specifies the dates on which the period of leave the employer agrees to permit the employee to take will begin and end,
and
(e) that notice is given to the employee not more than seven days after the employee's notice was given to the employer.

Minimum periods of leave

7. An employee may not take parental leave in a period other than the period which constitutes a week's leave for him under regulation 14 or a multiple of that period, except in a case where the child in respect of whom leave is taken is entitled to a disability living allowance.   **23-034**

---

[1] Inserted by SI 2001/4010 reg 6 (a)
[2] Word repealed by SI 2001/4010 reg 6 (b) (i)
[3] Word inserted by SI 2001/4010 reg 6 (b) (ii)
[4] Inserted by SI 2001/4010 reg 6 (b) (iii)

Maximum annual leave allowance

23-035   **8.** An employee may not take more than four weeks' leave in respect of any individual child during a particular year.

23-036   **9.** For the purposes of paragraph 8, a year is the period of twelve months beginning –
    (a) except where sub-paragraph (b) applies, on the date on which the employee first became entitled to take parental leave in respect of the child in question, or
    (b) in a case where the employee's entitlement has been interrupted at the end of period of continuous employment, on the date on which the employee most recently became entitled to take parental leave in respect of that child,
and each successive period of twelve months beginning on the anniversary of that date.

The Part-time Workers (Prevention of Less Favourable Treatment) Regulations 2000

(S.I. 1551)

PART I

GENERAL AND INTERPRETATION

Citation commencement and interpretation

24-001   **1.**—(1) These Regulations may be cited as the Part-time Workers (Prevention of Less Favourable Treatment) Regulations 2000 and shall come into force on 1st July 2000.

    (2) In these Regulations –
    "the 1996 Act" means the Employment Rights Act 1996;
    "contract of employment" means a contract of service or of apprenticeship, whether express or implied, and (if it is express) whether oral or in writing;
    "employee" means an individual who has entered into or works under or (except where a provision of these Regulations otherwise requires) where the employment has ceased, worked under a contract of employment;
    "employer", in relation to any employee or worker, means the person by whom the employee or worker is or (except where a provision of these Regulations otherwise requires) where the employment has ceased, was employed;
    "pro rata principle" means that where a comparable full-time worker receives or is entitled to receive pay or any other benefit, a part-time worker is to receive or be entitled to receive not less than the proportion of that pay or other benefit that the number of his weekly hours bears to the number of weekly hours of the comparable full-time worker;
    "worker" means an individual who has entered into or works under or (except where a provision of these Regulations otherwise requires) where the employment has ceased, worked under –
    (a) a contract of employment; or
    (b) any other contract, whether express or implied and (if it is express) whether oral or in writing, whereby the individual

undertakes to do or perform personally any work or services for another party to the contract whose status is not by virtue of the contract that of a client or customer of any profession or business undertaking carried on by the individual.

(3) In the definition of the pro rata principle and in regulations 3 and 4 "weekly hours" means the number of hours a worker is required to work under his contract of employment in a week in which he has no absences from work and does not work any overtime or, where the number of such hours varies according to a cycle, the average number of such hours.

Meaning of full-time worker, part-time worker and comparable full-time worker

2.—(1) A worker is a full-time worker for the purpose of these Regulations if **24-002** he is paid wholly or in part by reference to the time he works and, having regard to the custom and practice of the employer in relation to workers employed by the worker's employer under the same type of contract, is identifiable as a full-time worker.

(2) A worker is a part-time worker for the purpose of these Regulations if he is paid wholly or in part by reference to the time he works and, having regard to the custom and practice of the employer in relation to workers employed by the worker's employer under the same type of contract, is not identifiable as a full-time worker.

[(3) For the purposes of paragraphs (1), (2) and (4), the following shall be regarded as being employed under different types of contract—

(a) employees employed under a contract that is not a contract of apprenticeship;
(b) employees employed under a contract of apprenticeship;
(c) workers who are not employees;
(d) any other description of worker that it is reasonable for the employer to treat differently from other workers on the ground that workers of that description have a different type of contract.][1]

(4) A full-time worker is a comparable full-time worker in relation to a part-time worker if, at the time when the treatment that is alleged to be less favourable to the part-time worker takes place–

(a) both workers are–
    (i) employed by the same employer under the same type of contract, and
    (ii) engaged in the same or broadly similar work having regard, where relevant, to whether they have a similar level of qualification, skills and experience; and
(b) the full-time worker works or is based at the same establishment as the part-time worker or, where there is no full-time worker working or based at that establishment who satisfies the requirements of sub-paragraph (a), works or is based at a different establishment and satisfies those requirements.

Workers becoming part-time

3.—(1) This regulation applies to a worker who– **24-003**

---
[1] Substituted by SI 2002/2035 reg 2 (a)

     (a) was identifiable as a full-time worker in accordance with regulation 2(1); and

     (b) following a termination or variation of his contract, continues to work under a new or varied contract, whether of the same type or not, that requires him to work for a number of weekly hours that is lower than the number he was required to work immediately before the termination or variation.

(2) Notwithstanding regulation 2(4), regulation 5 shall apply to a worker to whom this regulation applies as if he were a part-time worker and as if there were a comparable full-time worker employed under the terms that applied to him immediately before the variation or termination.

(3) The fact that this regulation applies to a worker does not affect any right he may have under these Regulations by virtue of regulation 2(4).

Workers returning part-time after absence

24-004   **4.**—(1) This regulation applies to a worker who—

     (a) was identifiable as a full-time worker in accordance with regulation 2(1) immediately before a period of absence (whether the absence followed a termination of the worker's contract or not);

     (b) returns to work for the same employer within a period of less than twelve months beginning with the day on which the period of absence started;

     (c) returns to the same job or to a job at the same level under a contract, whether it is a different contract or a varied contract and regardless of whether it is of the same type, under which he is required to work for a number of weekly hours that is lower than the number he was required to work immediately before the period of absence.

(2) Notwithstanding regulation 2(4), regulation 5 shall apply to a worker to whom this regulation applies ("the returning worker") as if he were a part-time worker and as if there were a comparable full-time worker employed under—

     (a) the contract under which the returning worker was employed immediately before the period of absence; or

     (b) where it is shown that, had the returning worker continued to work under the contract mentioned in sub-paragraph (a) a variation would have been made to its term during the period of absence, the contract mentioned in that sub-paragraph including that variation.

(3) The fact that this regulation applies to a worker does not affect any right he may have under these Regulations by virtue of regulation 2(4).

PART II

RIGHTS AND REMEDIES

Less favourable treatment of part-time workers

24-005   **5.**—(1) A part-time worker has the right not to be treated by his employer less favourably than the employer treats a comparable full-time worker—

     (a) as regards the terms of his contract; or

     (b) by being subjected to any other detriment by any act, or deliberate failure to act, of his employer.

(2) The right conferred by paragraph (1) applies only if—

     (a) the treatment is on the ground that the worker is a part-time worker, and

(b) the treatment is not justified on objective grounds.

(3) In determining whether a part-time worker has been treated less favourably than a comparable full-time worker the pro rata principle shall be applied unless it is inappropriate.

(4) A part-time worker paid at a lower rate for overtime worked by him in a period than a comparable full-time worker is or would be paid for overtime worked by him in the same period shall not, for that reason, be regarded as treated less favourably than the comparable full-time worker where, or to the extent that, the total number of hours worked by the part-time worker in the period, including overtime, does not exceed the number of hours the comparable full-time worker is required to work in the period, disregarding absences from work and overtime.

Right to receive a written statement of reasons for less favourable treatment

6.—(1) If a worker who considers that his employer may have treated him in **24-006** a manner which infringes a right conferred on him by regulation 5 requests in writing from his employer a written statement giving particulars of the reasons for the treatment, the worker is entitled to be provided with such a statement within twenty-one days of his request.

(2) A written statement under this regulation is admissible as evidence in any proceedings under these Regulations.

(3) If it appears to the tribunal in any proceedings under these Regulations—
　　(a) that the employer deliberately, and without reasonable excuse, omitted to provide a written statement, or
　　(b) that the written statement is evasive or equivocal,
it may draw any inference which it considers it just and equitable to draw, including an inference that the employer has infringed the right in question.

(4) This regulation does not apply where the treatment in question consists of the dismissal of an employee, and the employee is entitled to a written statement of reasons for his dismissal under section 92 of the 1996 Act.

Unfair dismissal and the right not to be subjected to detriment

7.—(1) An employee who is dismissed shall be regarded as unfairly dismissed **24-007** for the purposes of Part X of the 1996 Act if the reason (or, if more than one, the principal reason) for the dismissal is a reason specified in paragraph (3).

(2) A worker has the right not to be subjected to any detriment by any act, or any deliberate failure to act, by his employer done on a ground specified in paragraph (3).

(3) The reasons or, as the case may be, grounds are—
　　(a) that the worker has—
　　　　(i) brought proceedings against the employer under these Regulations;
　　　　(ii) requested from his employer a written statement of reasons under regulation 6;
　　　　(iii) given evidence or information in connection with such proceedings brought by any worker;
　　　　(iv) otherwise done anything under these Regulations in relation to the employer or any other person;
　　　　(v) alleged that the employer had infringed these Regulations; or
　　　　(vi) refused (or proposed to refuse) to forgo a right conferred on him by these Regulations, or

(b) that the employer believes or suspects that the worker has done or intends to do any of the things mentioned in sub-paragraph (a).

(4) Where the reason or principal reason for dismissal or, as the case may be, ground for subjection to any act or deliberate failure to act, is that mentioned in paragraph (3)(a)(v), or (b) so far as it relates thereto, neither paragraph (1) nor paragraph (2) applies if the allegation made by the worker is false and not made in good faith.

(5) Paragraph (2) does not apply where the determent in question amounts to the dismissal of an employee within the meaning of Part X of the 1996 Act.

Complaints to employment tribunals etc

24-008   **8.**—(1) Subject to regulation 7(5), a worker may present a complaint to an employment tribunal that his employer has infringed a right conferred on him by regulation 5 or 7(2).

(2) Subject to paragraph (3), an employment tribunal shall not consider a complaint under this regulation unless it is presented before the end of the period of three months (or, in a case to which regulation 13 applies, six months) beginning with the date of the less favourable treatment or detriment to which the complaint relates or, where an act or failure to act is part of a series of similar acts or failures comprising the less favourable treatment or detriment, the last of them.

(3) A tribunal may consider any such complaint which is out of time if, in all the circumstances of the case, it considers that it is just and equitable to do so.

(4) For the purposes of calculating the date of the less favourable treatment or detriment under paragraph (2)–

(a) where a term in a contract is less favourable, that treatment shall be treated, subject to paragraph (b), as taking place on each day of the period during which the term is less favourable;

(b) where an application relies on regulation 3 or 4 the less favourable treatment shall be treated as occurring on, and only on, in the case of regulation 3, the first day on which the applicant worked under the new or varied contract and, in the case of regulation 4, the day on which the applicant returned; and

(c) a deliberate failure to act contrary to regulation 5 or 7(2) shall be treated as done when it was decided on.

(5) In the absence of evidence establishing the contrary, a person shall be taken for the purposes of paragraph (4)(c) to decide not to act –

(a) when he does an act inconsistent with doing the failed act; or

(b) if he has done no such inconsistent act, when the period expires within which he might reasonably have been expected to have done the failed act if it was to be done.

(6) Where a worker presents a complaint under this regulation it is for the employer to identify the ground for the less favourable treatment or detriment.

(7) Where an employment tribunal finds that a complaint presented to it under this regulation is well founded, it shall take such of the following steps as it considers just and equitable –

(a) making a declaration as to the rights of the complainant and the employer in relation to the matters to which the complaint relates;

(b) ordering the employer to pay compensation to the complainant;

(c) recommending that the employer take, within a specified period, action appearing to the tribunal to be reasonable, in all the circumstances of the case, for the purpose of obviating or reducing the adverse effect on the complainant of any matter to which the complaint relates.

(9) [...][1]

(10) The loss shall be taken to include –

(a) any expenses reasonably incurred by the complainant in consequence of the infringement, and

(b) loss of any benefit which he might reasonably be expected to have had but for the infringement.

(11) Compensation in respect of treating a worker in a manner which infringes the right conferred on him by regulation 5 shall not include compensation for injury to feelings.

(12) In ascertaining the loss the tribunal shall apply the same rule concerning the duty of a person to mitigate his loss as applies to damages recoverable under the common law of England and Wales or (as the case may be) Scotland.

(13) Where the tribunal finds that the act, or failure to act, to which the complaint relates was to any extent caused or contributed to by action of the complaint relates was to any extent caused or contributed to by action of the complainant, it shall reduce the amount of the compensation by such proportion as it considers just and equitable having regard to that finding.

(14) If the employer fails, without reasonable justification, to comply with a recommendation made by an employment tribunal under paragraph (7)(c) the tribunal may, if it thinks it just and equitable to do so –

(a) increase the amount of compensation required to be paid to the complainant in respect of the complaint, where an order was made under paragraph (7)(b); or

(b) make an order under paragraph (7)(b).

Restrictions on contracting out

9. Section 203 of the 1996 Act (restrictions on contracting out) shall apply in **24-009** relation to these Regulations as if they were contained in that Act.

Amendments to primary legislation

10. The amendments in the Schedule to these Regulations shall have effect.   **24-010**

PART III

MISCELLANEOUS

Liability of employers and principals

11.—(1) Anything done by a person in the course of his employment shall be **24-011** treated for the purposes of these Regulations as also done by his employer, whether or not it was done with the employer's knowledge or approval.

(2) Anything done by a person as agent for the employer with the authority of the employer shall be treated for the purposes of these Regulations as also done by the employer.

(3) In proceedings under these Regulations against any person in respect of an act alleged to have been done by a worker of his, it shall be a defence for that person to prove that he took such steps as were reasonably practicable to prevent the worker from –

---

[1] Repealed by SI 2002/2035 reg 2 (b) (ii)

(a) doing that act; or

(b) doing, in the course of his employment, acts of that discription.

The Fixed-term Employees (Prevention of Less Favourable Treatment) Regulations 2002

(S.I. 2034)

PART 1

GENERAL AND INTERPRETATION

Citation, commencement and interpretation

25-001   **1.**—(1) These Regulations may be cited as the Fixed-term Employees (Prevention of Less Favourable Treatment) Regulations 2002 and shall come into force on 1st October 2002.

(2) In these Regulations—

"the 1996 Act" means the Employment Rights Act 1996;

"collective agreement" means a collective agreement within the meaning of section 178 of the Trade Union and Labour Relations (Consolidation) Act 1992; the trade union parties to which are independent trade unions within the meaning of section 5 of that Act;

"employer", in relation to any employee, means the person by whom the employee is (or, where the employment has ceased, was) employed;

"fixed-term contract" means a contract of employment that, under its provisions determining how it will terminate in the normal course, will terminate—

(a) on the expiry of a specific term,

(b) on the completion of a particular task, or

(c) on the occurrence or non-occurrence of any other specific event other than the attainment by the employee of any normal and bona fide retiring age in the establishment for an employee holding the position held by him,

and any reference to "fixed-term" shall be construed accordingly;

"fixed-term employee" means an employee who is employed under a fixed-term contract;

"permanent employee" means an employee who is not employed under a fixed-term contract, and any reference to "permanent employment" shall be construed accordingly;

"pro rata principle" means that where a comparable permanent employee receives or is entitled to pay or any other benefit, a fixed-term employee is to receive or be entitled to such proportion of that pay or other benefit as is reasonable in the circumstances having regard to the length of his contract of employment and to the terms on which the pay or other benefit is offered;

"renewal" includes extension and references to renewing a contract shall be construed accordingly;

"workforce agreement" means an agreement between an employer and his employees or their representatives in respect of which the conditions set out in Schedule 1 to these Regulations are satisfied.

Comparable employees

2.—(1) For the purposes of these Regulations, an employee is a comparable **25-002** permanent employee in relation to a fixed-term employee if, at the time when the treatment that is alleged to be less favourable to the fixed-term employee takes place,

    (a) both employees are—
        (i) employed by the same employer, and
        (ii) engaged in the same or broadly similar work having regard, where relevant, to whether they have a similar level of qualification and skills; and
    (b) the permanent employee works or is based at the same establishment as the fixed-term employee or, where there is no comparable permanent employee working or based at that establishment who satisfies the requirements of sub-paragraph (a), works or is based at a different establishment and satisfies those requirements.

(2) For the purposes of paragraph (1), an employee is not a comparable permanent employee if his employment has ceased.

PART 2

RIGHTS AND REMEDIES

Less favourable treatment of fixed-term employees

3.—(1) A fixed-term employee has the right not to be treated by his employer **25-003** less favourably than the employer treats a comparable permanent employee—

    (a) as regards the terms of his contract; or
    (b) by being subjected to any other detriment by any act, or deliberate failure to act, of his employer.

(2) Subject to paragraphs (3) and (4), the right conferred by paragraph (1) includes in particular the right of the fixed-term employee in question not to be treated less favourably than the employer treats a comparable permanent employee in relation to—

    (a) any period of service qualification relating to any particular condition of service,
    (b) the opportunity to receive training, or
    (c) the opportunity to secure any permanent position in the establishment.

(3) The right conferred by paragraph (1) applies only if—

    (a) the treatment is on the ground that the employee is a fixed-term employee, and
    (b) the treatment is not justified on objective grounds.

(4) Paragraph (3)(b) is subject to regulation 4.

(5) In determining whether a fixed-term employee has been treated less favourably than a comparable permanent employee, the pro rata principle shall be applied unless it is inappropriate.

(6) In order to ensure that an employee is able to exercise the right conferred by paragraph (1) as described in paragraph (2)(c) the employee has the right to be informed by his employer of available vacancies in the establishment.

(7) For the purposes of paragraph (6) an employee is "informed by his employer" only if the vacancy is contained in an advertisement which the employee has a reasonable opportunity of reading in the course of his employment or the employee is given reasonable notification of the vacancy in some other way.

Objective justification

25-004 **4.**—(1) Where a fixed-term employee is treated by his employer less favourably than the employer treats a comparable permanent employee as regards any term of his contract, the treatment in question shall be regarded for the purposes of regulation 3(3)(b) as justified on objective grounds if the terms of the fixed-term employee's contract of employment, taken as a whole, are at least as favourable as the terms of the comparable permanent employee's contract of employment.

(2) Paragraph (1) is without prejudice to the generality of regulation 3(3)(b).

Right to receive a written statement of reasons for less favourable treatment

25-005 **5.**—(1) If an employee who considers that his employer may have treated him in a manner which infringes a right conferred on him by regulation 3 requests in writing from his employer a written statement giving particulars of the reasons for the treatment, the employee is entitled to be provided with such a statement within twenty-one days of his request.

(2) A written statement under this regulation is admissible as evidence in any proceedings under these Regulations.

(3) If it appears to the tribunal in any proceedings under these Regulations—
  (a) that the employer deliberately, and without reasonable excuse, omitted to provide a written statement, or
  (b) that the written statement is evasive or equivocal,
it may draw any inference which it considers it just and equitable to draw, including an inference that the employer has infringed the right in question.

(4) This regulation does not apply where the treatment in question consists of the dismissal of an employee, and the employee is entitled to a written statement of reasons for his dismissal under section 92 of the 1996 Act.

Unfair dismissal and the right not to be subjected to detriment

25-006 **6.**—(1) An employee who is dismissed shall be regarded as unfairly dismissed for the purposes of Part 10 of the 1996 Act if the reason (or, if more than one, the principal reason) for the dismissal is a reason specified in paragraph (3).

(2) An employee has the right not to be subjected to any detriment by any act, or any deliberate failure to act, of his employer done on a ground specified in paragraph (3).

(3) The reasons or, as the case may be, grounds are—
  (a) that the employee—
     (i) brought proceedings against the employer under these Regulations;
     (ii) requested from his employer a written statement under regulation 5 or regulation 9;
     (iii) gave evidence or information in connection with such proceedings brought by any employee;
     (iv) otherwise did anything under these Regulations in relation to the employer or any other person;

    (v) alleged that the employer had infringed these Regulations;

    (vi) refused (or proposed to refuse) to forgo a right conferred on him by these Regulations;

    (vii) declined to sign a workforce agreement for the purposes of these Regulations, or

    (viii) being—

        (aa) a representative of members of the workforce for the purposes of Schedule 1, or

        (bb) a candidate in an election in which any person elected will, on being elected,

        become such a representative,

        performed (or proposed to perform) any functions or activities as such a representative or candidate, or

  (b) that the employer believes or suspects that the employee has done or intends to do any of the things mentioned in sub-paragraph (a).

(4) Where the reason or principal reason for dismissal or, as the case may be, ground for subjection to any act or deliberate failure to act, is that mentioned in paragraph (3)(a)(v), or (b) so far as it relates thereto, neither paragraph (1) nor paragraph (2) applies if the allegation made by the employee is false and not made in good faith.

(5) Paragraph (2) does not apply where the detriment in question amounts to dismissal within the meaning of Part 10 of the 1996 Act.

Complaints to employment tribunals etc

7.—(1) An employee may present a complaint to an employment tribunal **25-007** that his employer has infringed a right conferred on him by regulation 3, or (subject to regulation 6(5)), regulation 6(2).

(2) Subject to paragraph (3), an employment tribunal shall not consider a complaint under this regulation unless it is presented before the end of the period of three months beginning—

  (a) in the case of an alleged infringement of a right conferred by regulation 3(1) or 6(2), with the date of the less favourable treatment or detriment to which the complaint relates or, where an act or failure to act is part of a series of similar acts or failures comprising the less favourable treatment or detriment, the last of them;

  (b) in the case of an alleged infringement of the right conferred by regulation 3(6), with the date, or if more than one the last date, on which other individuals, whether or not employees of the employer, were informed of the vacancy.

(3) A tribunal may consider any such complaint which is out of time if, in all the circumstances of the case, it considers that it is just and equitable to do so.

(4) For the purposes of calculating the date of the less favourable treatment or detriment under paragraph (2)(a)—

  (a) where a term in a contract is less favourable, that treatment shall be treated, subject to paragraph (b), as taking place on each day of the period during which the term is less favourable;

  (b) a deliberate failure to act contrary to regulation 3 or 6(2) shall be treated as done when it was decided on.

(5) In the absence of evidence establishing the contrary, a person shall be taken for the purposes of paragraph (4)(b) to decide not to act—

  (a) when he does an act inconsistent with doing the failed act; or

(b) if he has done no such inconsistent act, when the period expires within which he might reasonably have been expected to have done the failed act if it was to be done.

(6) Where an employee presents a complaint under this regulation in relation to a right conferred on him by regulation 3 or 6(2) it is for the employer to identify the ground for the less favourable treatment or detriment.

(7) Where an employment tribunal finds that a complaint presented to it under this regulation is well founded, it shall take such of the following steps as it considers just and equitable—

(a) making a declaration as to the rights of the complainant and the employer in relation to the matters to which the complaint relates;

(b) ordering the employer to pay compensation to the complainant;

(c) recommending that the employer take, within a specified period, action appearing to the tribunal to be reasonable, in all the circumstances of the case, for the purpose of obviating or reducing the adverse effect on the complainant of any matter to which the complaint relates.

(8) Where a tribunal orders compensation under paragraph (7)(b), the amount of the compensation awarded shall be such as the tribunal considers just and equitable in all the circumstances having regard to—

(a) the infringement to which the complaint relates, and

(b) any loss which is attributable to the infringement.

(9) The loss shall be taken to include—

(a) any expenses reasonably incurred by the complainant in consequence of the infringement, and

(b) loss of any benefit which he might reasonably be expected to have had but for the infringement.

(10) Compensation in respect of treating an employee in a manner which infringes the right conferred on him by regulation 3 shall not include compensation for injury to feelings.

(11) In ascertaining the loss the tribunal shall apply the same rule concerning the duty of a person to mitigate his loss as applies to damages recoverable under the common law of England and Wales or (as the case may be) the law of Scotland.

(12) Where the tribunal finds that the act, or failure to act, to which the complaint relates was to any extent caused or contributed to by action of the complainant, it shall reduce the amount of the compensation by such proportion as it considers just and equitable having regard to that finding.

(13) If the employer fails, without reasonable justification, to comply with a recommendation made by an employment tribunal under paragraph (7)(c) the tribunal may, if it thinks it just and equitable to do so—

(a) increase the amount of compensation required to be paid to the complainant in respect of the complaint, where an order was made under paragraph (7)(b); or

(b) make an order under paragraph (7)(b).

Successive fixed-term contracts

25-008　　**8.**—(1) This regulation applies where—

(a) an employee is employed under a contract purporting to be a fixed-term contract, and

(b) the contract mentioned in sub-paragraph (a) has previously been renewed, or the employee has previously been employed on a fixed-term contract before the start of the contract mentioned in sub-paragraph (a).

(2) Where this regulation applies then, with effect from the date specified in paragraph (3), the provision of the contract mentioned in paragraph (1)(a) that restricts the duration of the contract shall be of no effect, and the employee shall be a permanent employee, if—

 (a) the employee has been continuously employed under the contract mentioned in paragraph 1(a), or under that contract taken with a previous fixed-term contract, for a period of four years or more, and

 (b) the employment of the employee under a fixed-term contract was not justified on objective grounds—

  (i) where the contract mentioned in paragraph (1)(a) has been renewed, at the time when it was last renewed;

  (ii) where that contract has not been renewed, at the time when it was entered into.

(3) The date referred to in paragraph (2) is whichever is the later of—

 (a) the date on which the contract mentioned in paragraph (1)(a) was entered into or last renewed, and

 (b) the date on which the employee acquired four years' continuous employment.

(4) For the purposes of this regulation Chapter 1 of Part 14 of the 1996 Act shall apply in determining whether an employee has been continuously employed, and any period of continuous employment falling before the 10th July 2002 shall be disregarded.

(5) A collective agreement or a workforce agreement may modify the application of paragraphs (1) to (3) of this regulation in relation to any employee or specified description of employees, by substituting for the provisions of paragraph (2) or paragraph (3), or for the provisions of both of those paragraphs, one or more different provisions which, in order to prevent abuse arising from the use of successive fixed-term contracts, specify one or more of the following—

 (a) the maximum total period for which the employee or employees of that description may be continuously employed on a fixed-term contract or on successive fixed-term contracts;

 (b) the maximum number of successive fixed-term contracts and renewals of such contracts under which the employee or employees of that description may be employed; or

 (c) objective grounds justifying the renewal of fixed-term contracts, or the engagement of the employee or employees of that description under successive fixed-term contracts,

and those provisions shall have effect in relation to that employee or an employee of that description as if they were contained in paragraphs (2) and (3).

Right to receive written statement of variation

9.—(1) If an employee who considers that, by virtue of regulation 8, he is a **25-009** permanent employee requests in writing from his employer a written statement confirming that his contract is no longer fixed-term or that he is now a permanent employee, he is entitled to be provided, within twenty-one days of his request, with either—

 (a) such a statement, or

 (b) a statement giving reasons why his contract remains fixed-term.

(2) If the reasons stated under paragraph (1)(b) include an assertion that there were objective grounds for the engagement of the employee under a fixed-term contract, or the renewal of such a contract, the statement shall include a statement of those grounds.

(3) A written statement under this regulation is admissible as evidence in any proceedings before a court, an employment tribunal and the Commissioners of the Inland Revenue.

(4) If it appears to the court or tribunal in any proceedings—

    (a) that the employer deliberately, and without reasonable excuse, omitted to provide a written statement, or

    (b) that the written statement is evasive or equivocal,

it may draw any inference which it considers it just and equitable to draw.

(5) An employee who considers that, by virtue of regulation 8, he is a permanent employee may present an application to an employment tribunal for a declaration to that effect.

(6) No application may be made under paragraph (5) unless—

    (a) the employee in question has previously requested a statement under paragraph (1) and the employer has either failed to provide a statement or given a statement of reasons under paragraph (1)(b), and

    (b) the employee is at the time the application is made employed by the employer.

PART 3

MISCELLANEOUS

Restrictions on contracting out

25-010   **10.** Section 203 of the 1996 Act (restrictions on contracting out) shall apply in relation to these Regulations as if they were contained in that Act.

Amendments to primary legislation

25-011   **11.** The amendments in Part 1 of Schedule 2 to these Regulations shall have effect subject to the transitional provisions in Part 2 of the Schedule.

Liability of employers and principals

25-012   **12.**—(1) Anything done by a person in the course of his employment shall be treated for the purposes of these Regulations as also done by his employer, whether or not it was done with the employer's knowledge or approval.

(2) Anything done by a person as agent for the employer with the authority of the employer shall be treated for the purposes of these Regulations as also done by the employer.

(3) In proceedings under these Regulations against any person in respect of an act alleged to have been done by an employee of his, it shall be a defence for that person to prove that he took such steps as were reasonably practicable to prevent the employee from—

    (a) doing that act, or

    (b) doing, in the course of his employment, acts of that description.

The Paternity and Adoption Leave Regulations 2002

(S.I. 2788)

PART 1

GENERAL

Citation and commencement

1. These Regulations may be cited as the Paternity and Adoption Leave Regulations 2002 and shall come into force on 8th December 2002.   **26-001**

Interpretation

2.—(1) In these Regulations—   **26-002**
    "the 1996 Act" means the Employment Rights Act 1996;
    "additional adoption leave" means leave under section 75B of the 1996 Act;
    "additional maternity leave" means leave under section 73 of the 1996 Act;
    "adopter", in relation to a child, means a person who has been matched
        with the child for adoption, or, in a case where two people have been
        matched jointly, whichever of them has elected to be the child's
        adopter for the purposes of these Regulations;
    "adoption agency" has the meaning given, in relation to England and
        Wales, by section 1(4) of the Adoption Act 1976 and, in relation to
        Scotland, by section 1(4) of the Adoption (Scotland) Act 1978;
    "adoption leave" means ordinary or additional adoption leave;
    "child" means a person who is, or when placed with an adopter for
        adoption was, under the age of 18;
    "contract of employment" means a contract of service or apprenticeship,
        whether express or implied, and (if it is express) whether oral or in
        writing;
    "employee" means an individual who has entered into or works under (or,
        where the employment has ceased, worked under) a contract of
        employment;
    "employer" means the person by whom an employee is (or, where the
        employment has ceased, was) employed;
    "expected week", in relation to the birth of a child, means the week,
        beginning with midnight between Saturday and Sunday, in which it is
        expected that the child will be born;
    "ordinary adoption leave" means leave under section 75A of the 1996 Act;
    "parental leave" means leave under regulation 13(1) of the Maternity and
        Parental Leave etc. Regulations 1999;
    "partner", in relation to a child's mother or adopter, means a person
        (whether of a different sex or the same sex) who lives with the mother
        or adopter and the child in an enduring family relationship but is not a
        relative of the mother or adopter of a kind specified in paragraph (2);
    "paternity leave" means leave under regulation 4 or regulation 8 of these
        Regulations;
    "statutory leave" means leave provided for in Part 8 of the 1996 Act.

(2) The relatives of a child's mother or adopter referred to in the definition of "partner" in paragraph (1) are the mother's or adopter's parent, grandparent, sister, brother, aunt or uncle.

(3) References to relationships in paragraph (2)—

(a) are to relationships of the full blood or half blood or, in the case of an adopted person, such of those relationships as would exist but for the adoption, and

(b) include the relationship of a child with his adoptive, or former adoptive, parents,

but do not include any other adoptive relationships.

(4) For the purposes of these Regulations—

(a) a person is matched with a child for adoption when an adoption agency decides that that person would be a suitable adoptive parent for the child, either individually or jointly with another person, and

(b) a person is notified of having been matched with a child on the date on which he receives notification of the agency's decision, under regulation 11(2) of the Adoption Agencies Regulations 1983 or regulation 12(3) of the Adoption Agencies (Scotland) Regulations 1996;

(c) a person elects to be a child's adopter, in a case where the child is matched with him and another person jointly, if he and that person agree, at the time at which they are matched, that he and not the other person will be the adopter.

(5) A reference in any provision of these Regulations to a period of continuous employment is to a period computed in accordance with Chapter 1 of Part 14 of the 1996 Act, as if that provision were a provision of that Act.

(6) For the purposes of these Regulations, any two employers shall be treated as associated if—

(a) one is a company of which the other (directly or indirectly) has control; or

(b) both are companies of which a third person (directly or indirectly) has control;

and "associated employer" shall be construed accordingly.

Application

26-003   **3.**—(1) The provisions relating to paternity leave under regulation 4 below have effect only in relation to children—

(a) born on or after 6th April 2003, or

(b) whose expected week of birth begins on or after that date.

(2) The provisions relating to paternity leave under regulation 8 and adoption leave under regulation 15 below have effect only in relation to children—

(a) matched with a person who is notified of having been matched on or after 6th April 2003, or

(b) placed for adoption on or after that date.

(3) Regulation 28 (protection from detriment) has effect only in relation to an act or failure to act which takes place on or after 8th December 2002.

(4) For the purposes of paragraph (3)—

(a) where an act extends over a period, the reference to the date of the act is a reference to the last day of that period, and

(b) a failure to act is to be treated as done when it was decided on.

(5) For the purposes of paragraph (4), in the absence of evidence establishing the contrary an employer shall be taken to decide on a failure to act—

    (a) when he does an act inconsistent with doing the failed act, or

    (b) if he has done no such inconsistent act, when the period expires within which he might reasonably have been expected to do the failed act if it was to be done.

(6) Regulation 29 (unfair dismissal) has effect only in relation to dismissals where the effective date of termination (within the meaning of section 97 of the 1996 Act) falls on or after 8th December 2002.

PART 2

PATERNITY LEAVE

Entitlement to paternity leave: birth

4.—(1) An employee is entitled to be absent from work for the purpose of **26-004** caring for a child or supporting the child's mother if he—

    (a) satisfies the conditions specified in paragraph (2), and

    (b) has complied with the notice requirements in regulation 6 and, where applicable, the evidential requirements in that regulation.

(2) The conditions referred to in paragraph (1) are that the employee—

    (a) has been continuously employed for a period of not less than 26 weeks ending with the week immediately preceding the 14th week before the expected week of the child's birth;

    (b) is either—

        (i) the father of the child or;

        (ii) married to or the partner of the child's mother, but not the child's father;

    (c) has, or expects to have—

        (i) if he is the child's father, responsibility for the upbringing of the child;

        (ii) if he is the mother's husband or partner but not the child's father, the main responsibility (apart from any responsibility of the mother) for the upbringing of the child.

(3) An employee shall be treated as having satisfied the condition in paragraph (2)(a) on the date of the child's birth notwithstanding the fact that he has not then been continuously employed for a period of not less than 26 weeks, where—

    (a) the date on which the child is born is earlier than the 14th week before the week in which its birth is expected, and

    (b) the employee would have been continuously employed for such a period if his employment had continued until that 14th week.

(4) An employee shall be treated as having satisfied the condition in paragraph (2)(b)(ii) if he would have satisfied it but for the fact that the child's mother has died.

(5) An employee shall be treated as having satisfied the condition in paragraph (2)(c) if he would have satisfied it but for the fact that the child was stillborn after 24 weeks of pregnancy or has died.

(6) An employee's entitlement to leave under this regulation shall not be affected by the birth, or expected birth, of more than one child as a result of the same pregnancy.

Options in respect of leave under regulation 4

26-005   **5.**—(1) An employee may choose to take either one week's leave or two consecutive weeks' leave in respect of a child under regulation 4.

(2) The leave may only be taken during the period which begins with the date on which the child is born and ends—

> (a) except in the case referred to in sub-paragraph (b), 56 days after that date;

> (b) in a case where the child is born before the first day of the expected week of its birth, 56 days after that day.

(3) Subject to paragraph (2) and, where applicable, paragraph (4), an employee may choose to begin his period of leave on—

> (a) the date on which the child is born;

> (b) the date falling such number of days after the date on which the child is born as the employee may specify in a notice under regulation 6, or

> (c) a predetermined date, specified in a notice under that regulation, which is later than the first day of the expected week of the child's birth.

(4) In a case where the leave is in respect of a child whose expected week of birth begins before 6th April 2003, an employee may choose to begin a period of leave only on a predetermined date, specified in a notice under regulation 6, which is at least 28 days after the date on which that notice is given.

Notice and evidential requirements for leave under regulation 4

26-006   **6.**—(1) An employee must give his employer notice of his intention to take leave in respect of a child under regulation 4, specifying—

> (a) the expected week of the child's birth;

> (b) the length of the period of leave that, in accordance with regulation 5(1), the employee has chosen to take, and

> (c) the date on which, in accordance with regulation 5(3) or (4), the employee has chosen that his period of leave should begin.

(2) The notice provided for in paragraph (1) must be given to the employer—

> (a) in or before the 15th week before the expected week of the child's birth, or

> (b) in a case where it was not reasonably practicable for the employee to give the notice in accordance with sub-paragraph (a), as soon as is reasonably practicable.

(3) Where the employer requests it, an employee must also give his employer a declaration, signed by the employee, to the effect that the purpose of his absence from work will be that specified in regulation 4(1) and that he satisfies the conditions of entitlement in regulation 4(2)(b) and (c)

(4) An employee who has given notice under paragraph (1) may vary the date he has chosen as the date on which his period of leave will begin, subject to paragraph (5) and provided that he gives his employer notice of the variation—

> (a) where the variation is to provide for the employee's period of leave to begin on the date on which the child is born, at least 28 days before the first day of the expected week of the child's birth;

> (b) where the variation is to provide for the employee's period of leave to begin on a date that is a specified number of days (or a different specified number of days) after the date on which the child is born, at least 28 days before the date falling that number of days after the first day of the expected week of the child's birth;

(c) where the variation is to provide for the employee's period of leave to begin on a predetermined date (or a different predetermined date), at least 28 days before that date,

or, if it is not reasonably practicable to give the notice at least 28 days before whichever day or date is relevant, as soon as is reasonably practicable.

(5) In a case where regulation 5(4) applies, an employee may only vary the date which he has chosen as the date on which his period of leave will begin by substituting a different predetermined date.

(6) In a case where—

(a) the employee has chosen to begin his period of leave on a particular pre-determined date, and

(b) the child is not born on or before that date,

the employee must vary his choice of date, by substituting a later predetermined date or (except in a case where regulation 5(4) applies) exercising an alternative option under regulation 5(3), and give his employer notice of the variation as soon as is reasonably practicable.

(7) An employee must give his employer a further notice, as soon as is reasonably practicable after the child's birth, of the date on which the child was born.

(8) Notice under paragraph (1), (4), (6) or (7) shall be given in writing, if the employer so requests.

Commencement of leave under regulation 4

7.—(1) Except in the case referred to in paragraph (2), an employee's period **26-007** of paternity leave under regulation 4 begins on the date specified in his notice under regulation 6(1), or, where he has varied his choice of date under regulation 6(4) or (6), on the date specified in his notice under that provision (or the last such notice if he has varied his choice more than once).

(2) In a case where—

(a) the employee has chosen to begin his period of leave on the date on which the child is born, and

(b) he is at work on that date,

the employee's period of leave begins on the day after that date.

Entitlement to paternity leave: adoption

8.—(1) An employee is entitled to be absent from work for the purpose of **26-008** caring for a child or supporting the child's adopter if he—

(a) satisfies the conditions specified in paragraph (2), and

(b) has complied with the notice requirements in regulation 10 and, where applicable, the evidential requirements in that regulation.

(2) The conditions referred to in paragraph (1) are that the employee—

(a) has been continuously employed for a period of not less than 26 weeks ending with the week in which the child's adopter is notified of having been matched with the child;

(b) is either married to or the partner of the child's adopter, and

(c) has, or expects to have, the main responsibility (apart from the responsi-bility of the adopter) for the upbringing of the child.

(3) In paragraph (2)(a), "week" means the period of seven days beginning with Sunday.

(4) An employee shall be treated as having satisfied the condition in paragraph (2)(b) if he would have satisfied it but for the fact that the child's adopter died during the child's placement.

(5) An employee shall be treated as having satisfied the condition in paragraph (2)(c) if he would have satisfied it but for the fact that the child's placement with the adopter has ended.

(6) An employee's entitlement to leave under this regulation shall not be affected by the placement for adoption of more than one child as part of the same arrangement.

Options in respect of leave under regulation 8

26-009   **9.**—(1) An employee may choose to take either one week's leave or two consecutive weeks' leave in respect of a child under regulation 8.

(2) The leave may only be taken during the period of 56 days beginning with the date on which the child is placed with the adopter.

(3) Subject to paragraph (2) and, where applicable, paragraph (4), an employee may choose to begin a period of leave under regulation 8 on—
   (a) the date on which the child is placed with the adopter;
   (b) the date falling such number of days after the date on which the child is placed with the adopter as the employee may specify in a notice under regulation 10, or
   (c) a predetermined date, specified in a notice under that regulation, which is later than the date on which the child is expected to be placed with the adopter.

(4) In a case where the adopter was notified of having been matched with the child before 6th April 2003, the employee may choose to begin a period of leave only on a predetermined date, specified in a notice under regulation 10, which is at least 28 days after the date on which that notice is given.

Notice and evidential requirements for leave under regulation 8

26-010   **10.**—(1) An employee must give his employer notice of his intention to take leave in respect of a child under regulation 8, specifying—
   (a) the date on which the adopter was notified of having been matched with the child;
   (b) the date on which the child is expected to be placed with the adopter;
   (c) the length of the period of leave that, in accordance with regulation 9(1), the employee has chosen to take, and
   (d) the date on which, in accordance with regulation 9(3) or (4), the employee has chosen that his period of leave should begin.

(2) The notice provided for in paragraph (1) must be given to the employer—
   (a) no more than seven days after the date on which the adopter is notified of having been matched with the child, or
   (b) in a case where it was not reasonably practicable for the employee to give notice in accordance with sub-paragraph (a), as soon as is reasonably practicable.

(3) Where the employer requests it, an employee must also give his employer a declaration, signed by the employee, to the effect that the purpose of his absence from work will be that specified in regulation 8(1) and that he satisfies the conditions of entitlement in regulation 8(2)(b) and (c).

(4) An employee who has given notice under paragraph (1) may vary the date he has chosen as the date on which his period of leave will begin, subject to paragraph (5) and provided that he gives his employer notice of the variation—
   (a) where the variation is to provide for the employee's period of leave to begin on the date on which the child is placed with the adopter, at least 28 days before the date specified in the employee's notice under

paragraph (1) as the date on which the child is expected to be placed with the adopter;

(b) where the variation is to provide for the employee's period of leave to begin on a date that is a specified number of days (or a different specified number of days) after the date on which the child is placed with the adopter, at least 28 days before the date falling that number of days after the date specified in the employee's notice under paragraph (1) as the date on which the child is expected to be placed with the adopter;

(c) where the variation is to provide for the employee's period of leave to begin on a predetermined date, at least 28 days before that date, or, if it is not reasonably practicable to give the notice at least 28 days before whichever date is relevant, as soon as is reasonably practicable.

(5) In a case where regulation 9(4) applies, an employee may only vary the date which he has chosen as the date on which his period of leave will begin by substituting a different predetermined date.

(6) In a case where—

(a) the employee has chosen to begin his period of leave on a particular pre-determined date, and

(b) the child is not placed with the adopter on or before that date,

the employee must vary his choice of date, by substituting a later predetermined date or (except in a case where regulation 9(4) applies) exercising an alternative option under regulation 9(3), and give his employer notice of the variation as soon as is reasonably practicable.

(7) An employee must give his employer a further notice, as soon as is reasonably practicable after the child's placement, of the date on which the child was placed.

(8) Notice under paragraph (1), (4), (6) or (7) shall be given in writing, if the employer so requests.

Commencement of leave under regulation 8

11.—(1) Except in the case referred to in paragraph (2), an employee's period **26-011** of paternity leave under regulation 8 begins on the date specified in his notice under regulation 10(1), or, where he has varied his choice of date under regulation 10(4) or (6), on the date specified in his notice under that provision (or the last such date if he has varied his choice more than once).

(2) In a case where—

(a) the employee has chosen to begin his period of leave on the date on which the child is placed with the adopter, and

(b) he is at work on that date,

the employee's period of leave begins on the day after that date.

Application of terms and conditions during paternity leave

12.—(1) An employee who takes paternity leave—   **26-012**

(a) is entitled, during the period of leave, to the benefit of all of the terms and conditions of employment which would have applied if he had not been absent, and

(b) is bound, during that period, by any obligations arising under those terms and conditions, subject only to the exception in section 80C(1)(b) of the 1996 Act.

(2) In paragraph (1)(a), "terms and conditions of employment" has the meaning given by section 80C(5) of the 1996 Act, and accordingly does not include terms and conditions about remuneration.

(3) For the purposes of section 80C of the 1996 Act, only sums payable to an employee by way of wages or salary are to be treated as remuneration.

Right to return after paternity leave

26-013   **13.**—(1) An employee who returns to work after a period of paternity leave which was—

(a) an isolated period of leave, or

(b) the last of two or more consecutive periods of statutory leave, which did not include any period of additional maternity leave or additional adoption leave or a period of parental leave of more than four weeks,

is entitled to return from leave to the job in which he was employed before his absence.

(2) An employee who returns to work after a period of paternity leave not falling within the description in paragraph (1)(a) or (b) above is entitled to return from leave to the job in which he was employed before his absence, or, if it is not reasonably practicable for the employer to permit him to return to that job, to another job which is both suitable for him and appropriate for him to do in the circumstances.

(3) The reference in paragraphs (1) and (2) to the job in which an employee was employed before his absence is a reference to the job in which he was employed—

(a) if his return is from an isolated period of paternity leave, immediately before that period began;

(b) if his return is from consecutive periods of statutory leave, immediately before the first such period.

Incidents of the right to return after paternity leave

26-014   **14.**—(1) An employee's right to return under regulation 13 is a right to return—

(a) with his seniority, pension rights and similar rights—

(i) in a case where the employee is returning from consecutive periods of statutory leave which included a period of additional adoption leave or additional maternity leave, as they would have been if the period or periods of his employment prior to the additional adoption leave or (as the case may be) additional maternity leave were continuous with the period of employment following it;

(ii) in any other case, as they would have been if he had not been absent, and

(b) on terms and conditions not less favourable than those which would have applied if he had not been absent.

(2) The provision in paragraph (1)(a)(i) concerning the treatment of periods of additional maternity leave or additional adoption leave is subject to the requirements of paragraphs 5 and 6 of Schedule 5 to the Social Security Act 1989 (equal treatment under pension schemes: maternity absence and family leave).

(3) The provisions in paragraph (1)(a)(ii) and (b) for an employee to be treated as if he had not been absent refer to his absence—

(a) if his return is from an isolated period of paternity leave, since the beginning of that period;

(b) if his return is from consecutive periods of statutory leave, since the beginning of the first such period.

[Determining the applicable national minimum rate

14A. The hourly rate at which a worker is entitled to be remunerated in **26-015** respect of his work in any pay reference period is the rate, prescribed by regulations, that is in force on the first day of that period.][1]

PART 3

ADOPTION LEAVE

Entitlement to ordinary adoption leave

15.—(1) An employee is entitled to ordinary adoption leave in respect of a **26-016** child if he—
 (a) satisfies the conditions specified in paragraph (2), and
 (b) has complied with the notice requirements in regulation 17 and, where applicable, the evidential requirements in that regulation.
 (2) The conditions referred to in paragraph (1) are that the employee—
 (a) is the child's adopter;
 (b) has been continuously employed for a period of not less than 26 weeks ending with the week in which he was notified of having been matched with the child, and
 (c) has notified the agency that he agrees that the child should be placed with him and on the date of placement.
 (3) In paragraph (2)(b), "week" means the period of seven days beginning with Sunday.
 (4) An employee's entitlement to leave under this regulation shall not be affected by the placement for adoption of more than one child as part of the same arrangement.

Options in respect of ordinary adoption leave

16.—(1) Except in the case referred to in paragraph (2), an employee may **26-017** choose to begin a period of ordinary adoption leave on—
 (a) the date on which the child is placed with him for adoption, or
 (b) a predetermined date, specified in a notice under regulation 17, which is no more than 14 days before the date on which the child is expected to be placed with the employee and no later than that date.
 (2) In a case where the employee was notified of having been matched with the child before 6th April 2003, the employee may choose to begin a period of leave only on a predetermined date, specified in a notice under regulation 17, which is after 6th April 2003 and at least 28 days after the date on which that notice is given.

Notice and evidential requirements for ordinary adoption leave

17.—(1) An employee must give his employer notice of his intention to take **26-018** ordinary adoption leave in respect of a child, specifying—
 (a) the date on which the child is expected to be placed with him for adoption, and

[1] Inserted by SI 2002/1999 reg 4

(b) the date on which, in accordance with regulation 16(1) or (2), the employee has chosen that his period of leave should begin.

(2) The notice provided for in paragraph (1) must be given to the employer—

(a) no more than seven days after the date on which the employee is notified of having been matched with the child for the purposes of adoption, or

(b) in a case where it was not reasonably practicable for the employee to give notice in accordance with sub-paragraph (a), as soon as is reasonably practicable.

(3) Where the employer requests it, an employee must also provide his employer with evidence, in the form of one or more documents issued by the adoption agency that matched the employee with the child, of—

(a) the name and address of the agency;

(b) [...]¹

(c) the date on which the employee was notified that he had been matched with the child, and

(d) the date on which the agency expects to place the child with the employee.

(4) An employee who has given notice under paragraph (1) may vary the date he has chosen as the date on which his period of leave will begin, subject to paragraph (5) and provided that he gives his employer notice of the variation—

(a) where the variation is to provide for the employee's period of leave to begin on the date on which the child is placed with him for adoption, at least 28 days before the date specified in his notice under paragraph (1) as the date on which the child is expected to be placed with him;

(b) where the variation is to provide for the employee's period of leave to begin on a predetermined date (or a different predetermined date), at least 28 days before that date,

or, if it is not reasonably practicable to give the notice 28 days before whichever date is relevant, as soon as is reasonably practicable.

(5) In a case where regulation 16(2) applies, an employee may only vary the date which he has chosen as the date on which his period of leave will begin by substituting a different predetermined date.

(6) Notice under paragraph (1) or (4) shall be given in writing, if the employer so requests.

(7) An employer who is given notice under paragraph (1) or (4) of the date on which an employee has chosen that his period of ordinary adoption leave should begin shall notify the employee, within 28 days of his receipt of the notice, of the date on which the period of additional adoption leave to which the employee will be entitled (if he satisfies the conditions in regulation 20(1)) after his period of ordinary adoption leave ends.

(8) The notification provided for in paragraph (7) shall be given to the employee—

(a) where the employer is given notice under paragraph (1), within 28 days of the date on which he received that notice;

(b) where the employer is given notice under paragraph (4), within 28 days of the date on which the employee's ordinary adoption leave period began.

¹ Repealed by SI 2004/923 reg 3

Duration and commencement of ordinary adoption leave

18.—(1) Subject to regulations 22 and 24, an employee's ordinary adoption **26-019** leave period is a period of 26 weeks.

(2) Except in the case referred to in paragraph (3), an employee's ordinary adoption leave period begins on the date specified in his notice under regulation 17(1), or, where he has varied his choice of date under regulation 17(4), on the date specified in his notice under that provision (or the last such date if he has varied his choice more than once).

(3) In a case where—

(a) the employee has chosen to begin his period of leave on the date on which the child is placed with him, and

(b) he is at work on that date,

the employee's period of leave begins on the day after that date.

Application of terms and conditions during ordinary adoption leave

19.—(1) An employee who takes ordinary adoption leave— **26-020**

(a) is entitled, during the period of leave, to the benefit of all of the terms and conditions of employment which would have applied if he had not been absent, and

(b) is bound, during that period, by any obligations arising under those terms and conditions, subject only to the exception in section 75A(3)(b) of the 1996 Act.

(2) In paragraph (1)(a), "terms and conditions of employment" has the meaning given by section 75A(4) of the 1996 Act, and accordingly does not include terms and conditions about remuneration.

(3) For the purposes of section 75A of the 1996 Act, only sums payable to an employee by way of wages or salary are to be treated as remuneration.

Additional adoption leave: entitlement, duration and commencement

20.—(1) An employee is entitled to additional adoption leave in respect of a **26-021** child if—

(a) the child was placed with him for adoption,

(b) he took ordinary adoption leave in respect of the child, and

(c) his ordinary adoption leave period did not end prematurely under regulation 22(2)(a) or 24.

(2) Subject to regulations 22 and 24, an employee's additional adoption leave period is a period of 26 weeks beginning on the day after the last day of his ordinary adoption leave period.

Application of terms and conditions during additional adoption leave

21. An employee who takes additional adoption leave— **26-022**

(a) is entitled, during the period of leave, to the benefit of his employer's implied obligation to him of trust and confidence and of any terms and conditions of his employment relating to—

(i) notice of the termination of the employment contract by his employer;

(ii) compensation in the event of redundancy, or

(iii) disciplinary or grievance procedures; and

(b) is bound, during that period, by his implied obligation to his employer of good faith and of any terms and conditions of his employment relating to—

(i) notice of the termination of the employment contract by him,

(ii) the disclosure of confidential information;

(iii) the acceptance of gifts or other benefits, or

(iv) the employee's participation in any other business.

Disrupted placement in the course of adoption leave

26-023   **22.**—(1) This regulation applies where—

(a) an employee has begun a period of adoption leave in respect of a child before the placement of the child with him, and the employee is subsequently notified that the placement will not be made, or

(b) during an employee's period of adoption leave in respect of a child placed with him—

(i) the child dies, or

(ii) the child is returned to the adoption agency under section 30(3) of the Adoption Act 1976 or section 30(3) of the Adoption (Scotland) Act 1978.

(2) Subject to regulation 24, in a case where this regulation applies—

(a) except in the circumstances referred to in sub-paragraphs (b) and (c), the employee's adoption leave period ends eight weeks after the end of the relevant week specified in paragraph (3);

(b) where the employee is taking ordinary adoption leave and the period of 26 weeks provided for in regulation 18 ends within eight weeks of the end of the relevant week—

(i) the employee's ordinary adoption leave period ends on the expiry of the 26-week period;

(ii) the employee is entitled to additional adoption leave, and

(iii) the employee's additional adoption leave period ends eight weeks after the end of the relevant week;

(c) where the employee is taking additional adoption leave and the period of 26 weeks provided for in regulation 20 ends within eight weeks of the end of the relevant week, the employee's additional adoption leave period ends on the expiry of the 26-week period.

(3) The relevant week referred to in paragraph (2) is—

(a) in a case falling within paragraph (1)(a), the week during which the person with whom the child was to be placed for adoption is notified that the placement will not be made;

(b) in a case falling within paragraph (1)(b)(i), the week during which the child dies;

(c) in a case falling within paragraph (1)(b)(ii), the week during which the child is returned.

(4) In paragraph (3), "week" means the period of seven days beginning with Sunday.

Redundancy during adoption leave

26-024   **23.**—(1) This regulation applies where, during an employee's ordinary or additional adoption leave period, it is not practicable by reason of redundancy for his employer to continue to employ him under his existing contract of employment.

(2) Where there is a suitable available vacancy, the employee is entitled to be offered (before the end of his employment under his existing contract) alternative employment with his employer or his employer's successor, or an associated employer, under a new contract of employment which complies with paragraph

(3) and takes effect immediately on the ending of his employment under the previous contract.

(3) The new contract of employment must be such that—

    (a) the work to be done under it is of a kind which is both suitable in relation to the employee and appropriate for him to do in the circumstances, and

    (b) its provisions as to the capacity and place in which he is to be employed, and as to the other terms and conditions of his employment, are not substantially less favourable to him than if he had continued to be employed under the previous contract.

Dismissal during adoption leave

24. Where an employee is dismissed after an ordinary or additional adoption **26-025** leave period has begun but before the time when (apart from this regulation) that period would end, the period ends at the time of the dismissal.

Requirement to notify intention to return during adoption leave period

25.—(1) An employee who intends to return to work earlier than the end of **26-026** his additional adoption leave period must give his employer at least 28 days' notice of the date on which he intends to return.

(2) If an employee attempts to return to work earlier than the end of his additional adoption leave period without complying with paragraph (1), his employer is entitled to postpone his return to a date such as will secure, subject to paragraph (3), that he has at least 28 days' notice of the employee's return.

(3) An employer is not entitled under paragraph (2) to postpone an employee's return to work to a date after the end of the employee's additional adoption leave period.

(4) If an employee whose return has been postponed under paragraph (2) has been notified that he is not to return to work before the date to which his return was postponed, the employer is under no contractual obligation to pay him remuneration until the date to which his return was postponed if he returns to work before that date.

(5) This regulation does not apply in a case where the employer did not notify the employee in accordance with regulation 17(7) and (8) of the date on which the employee's additional adoption leave period would end.

(6) In a case where an employee's adoption leave is curtailed because regulation 22 applies, the references in this regulation to the end of an employee's additional adoption leave period are references to the date on which that period would have ended had that regulation not applied, irrespective of whether it was the employee's ordinary adoption leave period or his additional adoption leave period that was curtailed.

Right to return after adoption leave

26.—(1) An employee who returns to work after a period of ordinary **26-027** adoption leave which was—

    (a) an isolated period of leave, or

    (b) the last of two or more consecutive periods of statutory leave, which did not include any period of additional maternity leave or additional adoption leave or a period of parental leave of more than four weeks,

is entitled to return from leave to the job in which he was employed before his absence.

(2) An employee who returns to work after—

(a) a period of additional adoption leave, whether or not preceded by another period of statutory leave, or

(b) a period of ordinary adoption leave not falling within the description in paragraph (1)(a) or (b) above,

is entitled to return from leave to the job in which he was employed before his absence, or, if it is not reasonably practicable for the employer to permit him to return to that job, to another job which is both suitable for him and appropriate for him to do in the circumstances.

(3) The reference in paragraphs (1) and (2) to the job in which an employee was employed before his absence is a reference to the job in which he was employed—

(a) if his return is from an isolated period of adoption leave, immediately before that period began;

(b) if his return is from consecutive periods of statutory leave, immediately before the first such period.

(4) This regulation does not apply where regulation 23 applies.

Incidents of the right to return from adoption leave

26-028   **27.**—(1) An employee's right to return under regulation 26 is to return—

(a) with his seniority, pension rights and similar rights—

(i) in a case where the employee is returning from additional adoption leave, or consecutive periods of statutory leave which included a period of additional adoption leave or additional maternity leave, as they would have been if the period or periods of his employment prior to his additional adoption leave or (as the case may be) additional maternity leave were continuous with the period of employment following it;

(ii) in any other case, as they would have been if he had not been absent, and

(b) on terms and conditions [...]¹ not less favourable than those which would have been applied to him if he had not been absent.

(2) The provision in paragraph (1)(a)(i) concerning the treatment of periods of additional adoption leave or additional maternity leave is subject to the requirements of paragraphs 5 and 6 of Schedule 5 to the Social Security Act 1989 (equal treatment under pension schemes: maternity absence and family leave).

(3) The provisions in paragraph (1)(a)(ii) and (b) for an employee to be treated as if he had not been absent refer to his absence—

(a) if his return is from an isolated period of ordinary adoption leave, since the beginning of that period;

(b) if his return is from consecutive periods of statutory leave, since the beginning of the first such period.

---

¹ Words repealed by SI 2004/923 reg 4

PART 4

PROVISIONS APPLICABLE IN RELATION TO BOTH PATERNITY AND ADOPTION LEAVE

Protection from detriment

28.—(1) An employee is entitled under section 47C of the 1996 Act not to be **26-029** subjected to any detriment by any act, or any deliberate failure to act, by his employer because—
   (a) the employee took or sought to take paternity leave or ordinary or additional adoption leave;
   (b) the employer believed that the employee was likely to take ordinary or additional adoption leave, or
   (c) the employee failed to return after a period of additional adoption leave in a case where—
       (i) the employer did not notify him, in accordance with regulation 17(7) and (8) or otherwise, of the date on which that period ended, and he reasonably believed that the period had not ended, or
       (ii) the employer gave him less than 28 days' notice of the date on which the period would end, and it was not reasonably practicable for him to return on that date.
   (2) Paragraph (1) does not apply where the detriment in question amounts to dismissal within the meaning of Part 10 of the 1996 Act.

Unfair dismissal

29.—(1) An employee who is dismissed is entitled under section 99 of the **26-030** 1996 Act to be regarded for the purpose of Part 10 of that Act as unfairly dismissed if—
   (a) the reason or principal reason for the dismissal is of a kind specified in paragraph (3), or
   (b) the reason or principal reason for the dismissal is that the employee is redundant, and regulation 23 has not been complied with.
   (2) An employee who is dismissed shall also be regarded for the purposes of Part 10 of the 1996 Act as unfairly dismissed if—
   (a) the reason (or, if more than one, the principal reason) for the dismissal is that the employee was redundant;
   (b) it is shown that the circumstances constituting the redundancy applied equally to one or more employees in the same undertaking who had positions similar to that held by the employee and who have not been dismissed by the employer, and
   (c) it is shown that the reason (or, if more than one, the principal reason) for which the employee was selected for dismissal was a reason of a kind specified in paragraph (3).
   (3) The kinds of reason referred to in paragraph (1) and (2) are reasons connected with the fact that—
   (a) the employee took, or sought to take, paternity or adoption leave;
   (b) the employer believed that the employee was likely to take ordinary or additional adoption leave, or
   (c) the employee failed to return after a period of additional adoption leave in a case where—

(i) the employer did not notify him, in accordance with regulation 17(7) and (8) or otherwise, of the date on which that period would end, and he reasonably believed that the period had not ended, or

(ii) the employer gave him less than 28 days' notice of the date on which the period would end, and it was not reasonably practicable for him to return on that date.

(4) Paragraph (1) does not apply in relation to an employee who took adoption leave if—

(a) immediately before the end of his additional adoption leave period (or, if it ends by reason of dismissal, immediately before the dismissal) the number of employees employed by his employer, added to the number employed by any associated employer of his employer, did not exceed five, and

(b) it is not reasonably practicable for the employer (who may be the same employer or a successor of his) to permit the employee to return to a job which is both suitable for the employee and appropriate for him to do in the circumstances or for an associated employer to offer the employee a job of that kind.

(5) Paragraph (1) does not apply in relation to an employee if—

(a) it is not reasonably practicable for a reason other than redundancy for the employer (who may be the same employer or a successor of his) to permit the employee to return to a job which is both suitable for the employee and appropriate for him to do in the circumstances;

(b) an associated employer offers the employee a job of that kind, and

(c) the employee accepts or unreasonably refuses that offer.

(6) Where, on a complaint of unfair dismissal, any question arises as to whether the operation of paragraph (1) is excluded by the provisions of paragraph (4) or (5), it is for the employer to show that the provisions in question were satisfied in relation to the complainant.

Contractual rights to paternity or adoption leave

26-031   **30.**—(1) This regulation applies where an employee is entitled to—

(a) paternity leave,

(b) ordinary adoption leave, or

(c) additional adoption leave,

(referred to in paragraph (2) as a "statutory right") and also to a right which corresponds to that right and which arises under the employee's contract of employment or otherwise.

(2) In a case where this regulation applies—

(a) the employee may not exercise the statutory right and the corresponding right separately but may, in taking the leave for which the two rights provide, take advantage of whichever right is, in any particular respect, the more favourable, and

(b) the provisions of the 1996 Act and of these Regulations relating to the statutory right apply, subject to any modifications necessary to give effect to any more favourable contractual terms, to the exercise of the composite right described in sub-paragraph (a) as they apply to the exercise of the statutory right.

Calculation of a week's pay

26-032   **31.** Where—

(a) under Chapter 2 of Part 14 of the 1996 Act, the amount of a week's pay of an employee falls to be calculated by reference to the average rate of remuneration, or the average amount of remuneration, payable to the employee in respect of a period of twelve weeks ending on a particular date (referred to as "the calculation date");

(b) during a week in that period, the employee was absent from work on paternity leave or ordinary or additional adoption leave, and

(c) remuneration is payable to the employee in respect of that week under his contract of employment, but the amount payable is less than the amount that would be payable if he were working,

that week shall be disregarded for the purpose of the calculation and account shall be taken of remuneration in earlier weeks so as to bring up to twelve the number of weeks of which account is taken.

The Flexible Working (Procedural Requirements) Regulations 2002

(S.I. 3207)

Citation and commencement

1. These Regulations may be cited as the Flexible Working (Procedural **27-001** Requirements) Regulations 2002 and shall come into force on 6th April 2003.

Interpretation

2.—(1) In these Regulations— **27-002**

"the 1996 Act" means the Employment Rights Act 1996;

"application" means an application under section 80F of the 1996 Act (statutory right to request a contract variation);

"contract of employment" means a contract of service or apprenticeship, whether express or implied, and (if it is express) whether oral or in writing;

"contract variation" means a change in the terms and conditions of a contract of employment of a kind specified in section 80F(1)(a) of the 1996 Act;

"electronic communication" means an electronic communication within the meaning of section 15(1) of the Electronic Communications Act 2000;

"employee" means an individual who has entered into or works under (or, where the employment has ceased, worked under) a contract of employment;

"employer" means the person by whom an employee is (or, where the employment has ceased, was) employed;

"worker" means an individual who has entered into or works under (or, where the employment has ceased, worked under)—

(a) a contract of employment, or

(b) any other contract, whether express or implied and (if it is express) whether oral or in writing, whereby the individual undertakes to do or perform personally any work or services for another party to the contract whose status is not by virtue of the contract that of a client or customer of any profession or business undertaking carried on by the individual.

"writing" includes writing delivered by means of electronic communication.

(2) For the purposes of these Regulations, unless the contrary is proved, an application is taken as having been made on the day the application is received.

(3) The reference in paragraph (2) to the day on which an application is received is a reference—

(a) in relation to an application transmitted by electronic communication, to the day on which it is transmitted,

(b) in relation to an application sent by post, to the day on which the application would be delivered in the ordinary course of post.

(4) For the purpose of these Regulations, unless the contrary is proved, a notice is taken as being given—

(a) in relation to a notice transmitted by electronic communication, on the day on which it is transmitted,

(b) in relation to a notice sent by post, the day on which the notice would be delivered in the ordinary course of post.

The meeting to discuss an application with an employee

27-003   **3.**—(1) Subject to paragraph (2) and regulation 13, an employer to whom an application for a contract variation is made shall hold a meeting to discuss the application with the employee within 28 days after the date on which the application is made.

(2) Paragraph (1) does not apply where the employer agrees to the application and notifies the employee accordingly in writing within the period referred to in that paragraph.

(3) A notice under paragraph (2) shall specify—

(a) the contract variation agreed to, and

(b) the date from which the variation is to take effect.

27-004   **4.** Where a meeting is held to discuss an application the employer shall give the employee notice of his decision on the application within 14 days after the date of the meeting.

27-005   **5.** A notice under regulation 4 shall—

(a) be in writing,

(b)

(i) where the employer's decision is to agree to the application, specify the contract variation agreed to and state the date on which the variation is to take effect,

(ii) where the decision is to refuse the application, state which of the grounds for refusal specified in section 80G(1)(b) of the 1996 Act are considered by the employer to apply, contain a sufficient explanation as to why those grounds apply in relation to the application, and set out the appeal procedure, and

(c) be dated.

Appeals

27-006   **6.** An employee is entitled to appeal against his employer's decision to refuse an application by giving notice in accordance with regulation 7 within 14 days after the date on which notice of the decision is given.

7. A notice of appeal under regulation 6 shall—   **27-007**
  (a) be in writing,
  (b) set out the grounds of appeal, and
  (c) be dated.

8.—(1) Subject to paragraph (2), the employer shall hold a meeting with the **27-008**
employee to discuss the appeal within 14 days after the employee's notice under
regulation 6 is given.
  (2) Paragraph (1) does not apply where, within 14 days after the date on
which notice under regulation 6 is given, the employer—
  (a) upholds the appeal, and
  (b) notifies the employee in writing of his decision, specifying the contract
       variation agreed to and stating the date from which the contract
       variation is to take effect.

9. Where a meeting is held to discuss the appeal, the employer shall notify the **27-009**
employee of his decision on the appeal within 14 days after the date of the
meeting.

10. Notice under regulation 9 shall—   **27-010**
  (a) be in writing,
  (b)
       (i) where the employer upholds the appeal, specify the contract
            variation agreed to and state the date from which the variation is to
            take effect, or
       (ii) where the employer dismisses the appeal, state the grounds for the
            decision and contain a sufficient explanation as to why those
            grounds apply, and
  (c) be dated.

11. The time and place of a meeting under regulation 3(1) or 8(1) shall be **27-011**
convenient to the employer and the employee.

Extension of periods

12.—(1) An employer and an employee may agree to an extension of any of **27-012**
the periods referred to in regulations 3, 4, 6, 8, 9 and 13.
  (2) An agreement under paragraph (1) must be recorded in writing by the
employer.
  (3) The employer's record referred to in paragraph (2) must—
  (a) specify what period the extension relates to,
  (b) specify the date on which the extension is to end,
  (c) be dated, and
  (d) be sent to the employee.

13. Where the individual who would ordinarily consider an application is **27-013**
absent from work on annual leave or on sick leave on the day on which the application is made, the period referred to in regulation 3(1) commences on the day the
individual returns to work or 28 days after the application is made, whichever is
the sooner.

Right to be accompanied

14.—(1) This regulation applies where—   **27-014**
  (a) a meeting is held under regulation 3(1) or 8(1), and

(b) the employee reasonably requests to be accompanied at the meeting.

(2) Where this regulation applies the employer must permit the employee to be accompanied at the meeting by a single companion who—

(a) is chosen by the employee and is within paragraph (3),

(b) is to be permitted to address the meeting (but not to answer questions on behalf of the employee), and

(c) is to be permitted to confer with the employee during the meeting.

(3) A person comes within this paragraph if he is a worker employed by the same employer as the employee.

(4) If—

(a) an employee has a right under this regulation to be accompanied at a meeting,

(b) his chosen companion will not be available at the time proposed for the meeting by the employer, and

(c) the employee proposes an alternative time which satisfies paragraph (5),

the employer must postpone the meeting to the time proposed by the employee.

(5) An alternative time must—

(a) be convenient for employer, employee and companion, and

(b) fall before the end of the period of seven days beginning with the first day after the day proposed by the employer.

(6) An employer shall permit a worker to take time off during working hours for the purpose of accompanying an employee in accordance with a request under paragraph (1)(b).

(7) Sections 168(3) and (4), 169 and 171 to 173 of the Trade Union and Labour Relations (Consolidation) Act 1992 (time off for carrying out trade union duties) shall apply in relation to paragraph (6) above as they apply in relation to section 168(1) of that Act.

Complaint to employment tribunal

27-015   **15.**—(1) An employee may present a complaint to an employment tribunal that his employer has failed, or threatened to fail, to comply with regulation 14(2) or (4).

(2) A tribunal shall not consider a complaint under this regulation in relation to a failure or threat unless the complaint is presented—

(a) before the end of the period of three months beginning with the date of the failure or threat, or

(b) within such further period as the tribunal considers reasonable in a case where it is satisfied that it was not reasonably practicable for the complaint to be presented before the end of that period of three months.

(3) Where a tribunal finds that a complaint under this regulation is well-founded it shall order the employer to pay compensation to the worker of an amount not exceeding two weeks' pay.

(4) Chapter 2 of Part 14 of the 1996 Act (calculation of a week's pay) shall apply for the purposes of paragraph (3); and in applying that Chapter the calculation date shall be taken to be the date on which the relevant meeting took place (or was to have taken place).

(5) The limit in section 227(1) of the Employment Rights Act 1996 (maximum amount of a week's pay) shall apply for the purposes of paragraph (3) above.

Detriment and dismissal

16.—(1) A person has the right not to be subjected to any detriment by any **27-016**
act, or any deliberate failure to act, by his employer done on the ground that
he—

    (a) exercised or sought to exercise the right under regulation 14(2) or (4),
       or

    (b) accompanied or sought to accompany an employee pursuant to a
       request under that regulation.

(2) Section 48 of the 1996 Act shall apply in relation to contraventions of
paragraph (1) above as it applies in relation to contraventions of certain sections
of that Act.

(3) A person who is dismissed shall be regarded for the purposes of Part 10
of the 1996 Act as unfairly dismissed if the reason (or, if more than one, the
principle reason) for the dismissal is that he—

    (a) exercised or sought to exercise his right under regulation 14(2) or (4),
       or

    (b) accompanied or sought to accompany an employee pursuant to a
       request under that regulation.

(4) Sections 108 and 109 of the 1996 Act (qualifying period of employment
and upper age limit) shall not apply in relation to paragraph (3) above.

(5) Sections 128 to 132 of the 1996 Act (interim relief) shall apply in relation
to dismissal for the reason specified in paragraph 3(a) or (b) above as they apply
in relation to dismissal for a reason specified in section 128(1)(b) of that Act.

(6) In the application of Chapter 2 of Part 10 of the 1996 Act in relation to
paragraph (3) above, a reference to an employee shall be taken as a reference to a
worker.

Withdrawal of application by the employee

17.—(1) An employer shall treat an application as withdrawn where the **27-017**
employee has—

    (a) notified to him whether orally or in writing that he is withdrawing the
       application,

    (b) without reasonable cause, failed to attend a meeting under regulation
       3(1) or 8(1) more than once, or

    (c) without reasonable cause, refused to provide the employer with informa-
       tion the employer requires in order to assess whether the contract
       variation should be agreed to.

(2) An employer shall confirm the withdrawal of the application to the
employee in writing unless the employee has provided him with written notice of
the withdrawal under paragraph 1(a).

Flexible Working (Eligibility, Complaints and Remedies) Regulations 2002

(S.I. 3236)

Citation and commencement

28-001 **1.**—These Regulations may be cited as the Flexible Working (Eligibility, Complaints and Remedies) Regulations 2002 and shall come into force on 6th April 2003.

Interpretation

28-002 **2.**—(1) In these Regulations—

"the 1996 Act" means the Employment Rights Act 1996;

"the Procedure Regulations" means the Flexible Working (Procedural Requirements) Regulations 2002;

"adopter", in relation to a child, means a person who has been matched with the child for adoption;

"application" means an application under section 80F of the 1996 Act (statutory right to request contract variation);

"contract of employment" means a contract of service or apprenticeship, whether express or implied, and (if it is express) whether oral or in writing;

"contract variation", means a change in the terms and conditions of a contract of employment of a kind specified in section 80F(1)(a) of the 1996 Act;

"electronic communication" means an electronic communication within the meaning of section 15(1) of the Electronic Communications Act 2000;

"employee" means an individual who has entered into or works under (or, where the employment has ceased, worked under) a contract of employment;

"employer" means the person by whom an employee is (or, where the employment has ceased, was) employed;

"foster parent" means a foster parent within the meaning of regulation 2(1) of the Fostering Services Regulations 2002 or a foster carer within the meaning of regulation 2(1) of the Fostering of Children (Scotland) Regulations 1996;

"guardian" means a person appointed as a guardian under section 5 of the Children Act 1989 or section 7 or 11 of the Children (Scotland) Act 1995;

"partner", in relation to a child's mother, father, adopter, guardian or foster parent, means a person (whether of a different sex or the same sex) who lives with the child and the mother, father, adopter, guardian or foster parent in an enduring family relationship but is not a relative of the mother, father, adopter, guardian or foster parent of a kind specified in paragraph (2);

"writing includes writing delivered by means of electronic communication.

(2) The relatives of a child's mother, father, adopter, guardian or foster parent referred to in the definition of "partner" in paragraph (1) are the mother's,

father's adopter's, guardian's or foster parent's parent, grandparent, sister, brother, aunt or uncle.

(3) References to relationships in paragraph (2)—

    (a) are to relationships of the full blood or half blood or, in the case of an adopted person, such as those relationships as would exist but for the adoption, and

    (b) include the relationship of a child with his adoptive, or former adoptive, parents,

but do not include any other adoptive relationships.

Entitlement to request a contract variation

3.—(1) An employee is entitled to make an application to his employer for a **28-003** contract variation if he—

    (a) has been continuously employed for a period of not less than 26 weeks;

    (b) is either—

        (i) the mother, father, adopter, guardian or foster parent of the child or;

        (ii) married to or the partner of the child's mother, father, adopter, guardian or foster parent;

    (c) has, or expects to have responsibility for the upbringing of the child.

(2) The reference in paragraph (1) to a period of continuous employment is to a period computed in accordance with Chapter 1 of Part 14 of the 1996 Act, as if that paragraph were a provision of that Act.

Form of the application

4. An application shall— **28-004**

    (a) be made in writing,

    (b) state whether a previous application has been made by the employee to the employer and, if so, when, and

    (c) be dated.

Date when an application is taken as made

5.—(1) Unless the contrary is proved, an application is taken as having been **28-005** made on the day the application is received.

(2) The reference in paragraph (1) to the day on which an application is received is a reference—

    (a) in relation to an application transmitted by electronic communication, to the day on which it is transmitted,

    (b) in relation to an application sent by post, to the day on which the application would be delivered in the ordinary course of post.

Breaches of the Procedure Regulations by the employer entitling an employee to make a complaint to an employment tribunal

6. The breaches of the Procedure Regulations which entitle an employee to **28-006** make a complaint to an employment tribunal under section 80H of the 1996 Act notwithstanding the fact that his application has not been disposed of by agreement or withdrawn are—

    (a) failure to hold a meeting in accordance with regulation 3(1) or 8(1),

    (b) failure to notify a decision in accordance with regulation 4 or 9.

Compensation

28-007   7. The maximum amount of compensation that an employment tribunal may award under section 80I of the 1996 Act where it finds a complaint by an employee under section 80H of the Act well-founded is 8 weeks' pay.

The Employment Equality (Religion or Belief) Regulations 2003

Whereas a draft of these Regulations was laid before Parliament in accordance with paragraph 2 of Schedule 2 to the European Communities Act 1972, and was approved by resolution of each House of Parliament; Now, therefore, the Secretary of State, being a Minister designated for the purposes of section 2(2) of the European Communities Act 1972 in relation to discrimination, in exercise of the powers conferred by that section, hereby makes the following Regulations:–

(S.I. 1660)

PART 1

GENERAL

Citation, commencement and extent

29-001   1.—(1) These Regulations may be cited as the Employment Equality (Religion or Belief) Regulations 2003, and shall come into force on 2nd December 2003.

(2) These Regulations do not extend to Northern Ireland.

Interpretation

29-002   2.—(1) In these Regulations, "religion or belief" means any religion, religious belief, or similar philosophical belief.

(2) In these Regulations, references to discrimination are to any discrimination falling within regulation 3 (discrimination on grounds of religion or belief) or 4 (discrimination by way of victimisation) and related expressions shall be construed accordingly, and references to harassment shall be construed in accordance with regulation 5 (harassment on grounds of religion or belief).

(3) In these Regulations–

  "act" includes a deliberate omission;

  ["benefits", except in regulation 9A (trustees and managers of occupational pension schemes), includes facilities and services;][1]

  "detriment" does not include harassment within the meaning of regulation 5;

  references to "employer", in their application to a person at any time seeking to employ another, include a person who has no employees at that time;

---

[1] Substituted by SI 2003/2828 reg 3 (2)

"employment" means employment under a contract of service or of apprenticeship or a contract personally to do any work, and related expressions shall be construed accordingly;

"Great Britain", except where the context otherwise requires in regulation 26 (protection of Sikhs from discrimination in connection with requirements as to wearing of safety helmets), includes such of the territorial waters of the United Kingdom as are adjacent to Great Britain;

"Minister of the Crown" includes the Treasury and the Defence Council; and

"school", in England and Wales, has the meaning given by section 4 of the Education Act 1996, and, in Scotland, has the meaning given by section 135(1) of the Education (Scotland) Act 1980, and references to a school are to an institution in so far as it is engaged in the provision of education under those sections.

Discrimination on grounds of religion or belief

3.—(1) For the purposes of these Regulations, a person ("A") discriminates **29-003** against another person ("B") if—

(a) on grounds of religion or belief, A treats B less favourably than he treats or would treat other persons; or

(b) A applies to B a provision, criterion or practice which he applies or would apply equally to persons not of the same religion or belief as B, but—

(i) which puts or would put persons of the same religion or belief as B at a particular disadvantage when compared with other persons,

(ii) which puts B at that disadvantage, and

(iii) which A cannot show to be a proportionate means of achieving a legitimate aim.

(2) The reference in paragraph (1)(a) to religion or belief does not include A's religion or belief.

(3) A comparison of B's case with that of another person under paragraph (1) must be such that the relevant circumstances in the one case are the same, or not materially different, in the other.

Discrimination by way of victimisation

4.—(1) For the purposes of these Regulations, a person ("A") discriminates **29-004** against another person ("B") if he treats B less favourably than he treats or would treat other persons in the same circumstances, and does so by reason that B has—

(a) brought proceedings against A or any other person under these Regulations;

(b) given evidence or information in connection with proceedings brought by any person against A or any other person under these Regulations;

(c) otherwise done anything under or by reference to these Regulations in relation to A or any other person; or

(d) alleged that A or any other person has committed an act which (whether or not the allegation so states) would amount to a contravention of these Regulations,

or by reason that A knows that B intends to do any of those things, or suspects that B has done or intends to do any of them.

(2) Paragraph (1) does not apply to treatment of B by reason of any allegation made by him, or evidence or information given by him, if the allegation, evidence or information was false and not made (or, as the case may be, given) in good faith.

Harassment on grounds of religion or belief

29-005   **5.**—(1) For the purposes of these Regulations, a person ("A") subjects another person ("B") to harassment where, on grounds of religion or belief, A engages in unwanted conduct which has the purpose or effect of–

(a) violating B's dignity; or

(b) creating an intimidating, hostile, degrading, humiliating or offensive environment for B.

(2) Conduct shall be regarded as having the effect specified in paragraph (1)(a) or (b) only if, having regard to all the circumstances, including in particular the perception of B, it should reasonably be considered as having that effect.

PART II

DISCRIMINATION IN EMPLOYMENT AND VOCATIONAL TRAINING

Applicants and employees

29-006   **6.**—(1) It is unlawful for an employer, in relation to employment by him at an establishment in Great Britain, to discriminate against a person–

(a) in the arrangements he makes for the purpose of determining to whom he should offer employment;

(b) in the terms on which he offers that person employment; or

(c) by refusing to offer, or deliberately not offering, him employment.

(2) It is unlawful for an employer, in relation to a person whom he employs at an establishment in Great Britain, to discriminate against that person–

(a) in the terms of employment which he affords him;

(b) in the opportunities which he affords him for promotion, a transfer, training, or receiving any other benefit;

(c) by refusing to afford him, or deliberately not affording him, any such opportunity; or

(d) by dismissing him, or subjecting him to any other detriment.

(3) It is unlawful for an employer, in relation to employment by him at an establishment in Great Britain, to subject to harassment a person whom he employs or who has applied to him for employment.

(4) Paragraph (2) does not apply to benefits of any description if the employer is concerned with the provision (for payment or not) of benefits of that description to the public, or to a section of the public which includes the employee in question, unless–

(a) that provision differs in a material respect from the provision of the benefits by the employer to his employees; or

(b) the provision of the benefits to the employee in question is regulated by his contract of employment; or

(c) the benefits relate to training.

(5) In paragraph (2)(d) reference to the dismissal of a person from employment includes reference–

(a) to the termination of that person's employment by the expiration of any period (including a period expiring by reference to an event or circumstance), not being a termination immediately after which the employment is renewed on the same terms; and

(b) to the termination of that person's employment by any act of his (including the giving of notice) in circumstances such that he is entitled to terminate it without notice by reason of the conduct of the employer.

Exception for genuine occupational requirement

7.—(1) In relation to discrimination falling within regulation 3 (discrimination on grounds of religion or belief)– **29-007**

(a) regulation 6(1)(a) or (c) does not apply to any employment;

(b) regulation 6(2)(b) or (c) does not apply to promotion or transfer to, or training for, any employment; and

(c) regulation 6(2)(d) does not apply to dismissal from any employment, where paragraph (2) or (3) applies.

(2) This paragraph applies where, having regard to the nature of the employment or the context in which it is carried out–

(a) being of a particular religion or belief is a genuine and determining occupational requirement;

(b) it is proportionate to apply that requirement in the particular case; and

(c) either–

(i) the person to whom that requirement is applied does not meet it, or

(ii) the employer is not satisfied, and in all the circumstances it is reasonable for him not to be satisfied, that that person meets it,

and this paragraph applies whether or not the employer has an ethos based on religion or belief.

(3) This paragraph applies where an employer has an ethos based on religion or belief and, having regard to that ethos and to the nature of the employment or the context in which it is carried out–

(a) being of a particular religion or belief is a genuine occupational requirement for the job;

(b) it is proportionate to apply that requirement in the particular case; and

(c) either–

(i) the person to whom that requirement is applied does not meet it, or

(ii) the employer is not satisfied, and in all the circumstances it is reasonable for him not to be satisfied, that that person meets it.

Contract workers

8.—(1) It is unlawful for a principal, in relation to contract work at an establishment in Great Britain, to discriminate against a contract worker– **29-008**

(a) in the terms on which he allows him to do that work;

(b) by not allowing him to do it or continue to do it;

(c) in the way he affords him access to any benefits or by refusing or deliberately not affording him access to them; or

(d) by subjecting him to any other detriment.

(2) It is unlawful for a principal, in relation to contract work at an establishment in Great Britain, to subject a contract worker to harassment.

(3) A principal does not contravene paragraph (1)(b) by doing any act in relation to a contract worker where, if the work were to be done by a person taken

into the principal's employment, that act would be lawful by virtue of regulation 7 (exception for genuine occupational requirement).

(4) Paragraph (1) does not apply to benefits of any description if the principal is concerned with the provision (for payment or not) of benefits of that description to the public, or to a section of the public to which the contract worker in question belongs, unless that provision differs in a material respect from the provision of the benefits by the principal to his contract workers.

(5) In this regulation–

"principal" means a person ("A") who makes work available for doing by individuals who are employed by another person who supplies them under a contract made with A;

"contract work" means work so made available; and

"contract worker" means any individual who is supplied to the principal under such a contract.

Meaning of employment and contract work at establishment in Great Britain

29-009   **9.**—(1) For the purposes of this Part ("the relevant purposes"), employment is to be regarded as being at an establishment in Great Britain if the employee–

(a) does his work wholly or partly in Great Britain; or

(b) does his work wholly outside Great Britain and paragraph (2) applies.

(2) This paragraph applies if–

(a) the employer has a place of business at an establishment in Great Britain;

(b) the work is for the purposes of the business carried on at that establishment; and

(c) the employee is ordinarily resident in Great Britain–

(i) at the time when he applies for or is offered the employment, or

(ii) at any time during the course of the employment.

(3) The reference to "employment" in paragraph (1) includes–

(a) employment on board a ship only if the ship is registered at a port of registry in Great Britain, and

(b) employment on an aircraft or hovercraft only if the aircraft or hovercraft is registered in the United Kingdom and operated by a person who has his principal place of business, or is ordinarily resident, in Great Britain.

(4) Subject to paragraph (5), for the purposes of determining if employment concerned with the exploration of the sea bed or sub-soil or the exploitation of their natural resources is outside Great Britain, this regulation has effect as if references to Great Britain included–

(a) any area designated under section 1(7) of the Continental Shelf Act 1964 except an area or part of an area in which the law of Northern Ireland applies; and

(b) in relation to employment concerned with the exploration or exploitation of the Frigg Gas Field, the part of the Norwegian sector of the Continental Shelf described in Schedule 1.

(5) Paragraph (4) shall not apply to employment which is concerned with the exploration or exploitation of the Frigg Gas Field unless the employer is–

(a) a company registered under the Companies Act 1985;

(b) an oversea company which has established a place of business within Great Britain from which it directs the exploration or exploitation in question; or

(c) any other person who has a place of business within Great Britain from which he directs the exploration or exploitation in question.

(6) In this regulation–

"the Frigg Gas Field" means the naturally occurring gas-bearing sand formations of the lower Eocene age located in the vicinity of the intersection of the line of latitude 59 degrees 53 minutes North and of the dividing line between the sectors of the Continental Shelf of the United Kingdom and the Kingdom of Norway and includes all other gas-bearing strata from which gas at the start of production is capable of flowing into the above-mentioned gas-bearing sand formations;

"oversea company" has the same meaning as in section 744 of the Companies Act 1985.

(7) This regulation applies in relation to contract work within the meaning of regulation 8 as it applies in relation to employment; and, in its application to contract work, references to "employee", "employer" and "employment" are references to (respectively) "contract worker", "principal" and "contract work" within the meaning of regulation 8.

[Trustees and managers of occupational pension schemes

9A.—(1) It is unlawful, except in relation to rights accrued or benefits **29-010** payable in respect of periods of service prior to the coming into force of these Regulations, for the trustees or managers of an occupational pension scheme to discriminate against a member or prospective member of the scheme in carrying out any of their functions in relation to it (including in particular their functions relating to the admission of members to the scheme and the treatment of members of it).

(2) It is unlawful for the trustees or managers of an occupational pension scheme, in relation to the scheme, to subject to harassment a member or prospective member of it.

(3) Schedule 1A (occupational pension schemes) shall have effect for the purposes of–

(a) defining terms used in this regulation and in that Schedule;
(b) treating every occupational pension scheme as including a non-discrimination rule;
(c) giving trustees or managers of an occupational pension scheme power to alter the scheme so as to secure conformity with the non-discrimination rule;
(d) making provision in relation to the procedures, and remedies which may be granted, on certain complaints relating to occupational pension schemes presented to an employment tribunal under regulation 28 (jurisdiction of employment tribunals).][1]

Office-holders etc

10.—(1) It is unlawful for a relevant person, in relation to an appointment to **29-011** an office or post to which this regulation applies, to discriminate against a person–

(a) in the arrangements which he makes for the purpose of determining to whom the appointment should be offered;
(b) in the terms on which he offers him the appointment; or
(c) by refusing to offer him the appointment.

---

[1] Inserted by SI 2003/2828 reg 3 (3)

(2) It is unlawful, in relation to an appointment to an office or post to which this regulation applies and which is an office or post referred to in paragraph (8)(b), for a relevant person on whose recommendation (or subject to whose approval) appointments to the office or post are made, to discriminate against a person—

    (a) in the arrangements which he makes for the purpose of determining who should be recommended or approved in relation to the appointment; or

    (b) in making or refusing to make a recommendation, or giving or refusing to give an approval, in relation to the appointment.

(3) It is unlawful for a relevant person, in relation to a person who has been appointed to an office or post to which this regulation applies, to discriminate against him—

    (a) in the terms of the appointment;

    (b) in the opportunities which he affords him for promotion, a transfer, training or receiving any other benefit, or by refusing to afford him any such opportunity;

    (c) by terminating the appointment; or

    (d) by subjecting him to any other detriment in relation to the appointment.

(4) It is unlawful for a relevant person, in relation to an office or post to which this regulation applies, to subject to harassment a person—

    (a) who has been appointed to the office or post;

    (b) who is seeking or being considered for appointment to the office or post; or

    (c) who is seeking or being considered for a recommendation or approval in relation to an appointment to an office or post referred to in paragraph (8)(b).

(5) Paragraphs (1) and (3) do not apply to any act in relation to an office or post where, if the office or post constituted employment, that act would be lawful by virtue of regulation 7 (exception for genuine occupational requirement); and paragraph (2) does not apply to any act in relation to an office or post where, if the office or post constituted employment, it would be lawful by virtue of regulation 7 to refuse to offer the person such employment.

(6) Paragraph (3) does not apply to benefits of any description if the relevant person is concerned with the provision (for payment or not) of benefits of that description to the public, or a section of the public to which the person appointed belongs, unless—

    (a) that provision differs in a material respect from the provision of the benefits by the relevant person to persons appointed to offices or posts which are the same as, or not materially different from, that which the person appointed holds; or

    (b) the provision of the benefits to the person appointed is regulated by the terms and conditions of his appointment; or

    (c) the benefits relate to training.

(7) In paragraph (3)(c) the reference to the termination of the appointment includes a reference—

    (a) to the termination of the appointment by the expiration of any period (including a period expiring by reference to an event or circumstance), not being a termination immediately after which the appointment is renewed on the same terms and conditions; and

(b) to the termination of the appointment by any act of the person appointed (including the giving of notice) in circumstances such that he is entitled to terminate the appointment without notice by reason of the conduct of the relevant person.

(8) This regulation applies to –

(a) any office or post to which persons are appointed to discharge functions personally under the direction of another person, and in respect of which they are entitled to remuneration; and

(b) any office or post to which appointments are made by (or on the recommendation of or subject to the approval of) a Minister of the Crown, a government department, the National Assembly for Wales or any part of the Scottish Administration,

but not to a political office or a case where regulation 6 (applicants and employees), 8 (contract workers), 12 (barristers), 13 (advocates) or 14 (partnerships) applies, or would apply but for the operation of any other provision of these Regulations.

(9) For the purposes of paragraph (8)(a) the holder of an office or post –

(a) is to be regarded as discharging his functions under the direction of another person if that other person is entitled to direct him as to when and where he discharges those functions;

(b) is not to be regarded as entitled to remuneration merely because he is entitled to payments –

    (i) in respect of expenses incurred by him in carrying out the functions of the office or post, or

    (ii) by way of compensation for the loss of income or benefits he would or might have received from any person had he not been carrying out the functions of the office or post.

(10) In this regulation –

(a) appointment to an office or post does not include election to an office or post;

(b) "political office" means –

    (i) any office of the House of Commons held by a member of it,

    (ii) a life peerage within the meaning of the Life Peerages Act 1958, or any office of the House of Lords held by a member of it,

    (iii) any office mentioned in Schedule 2 (Ministerial offices) to the House of Commons Disqualification Act 1975,

    (iv) the offices of Leader of the Opposition, Chief Opposition Whip or Assistant Opposition Whip within the meaning of the Ministerial and other Salaries Act 1975,

    (v) any office of the Scottish Parliament held by a member of it,

    (vi) a member of the Scottish Executive within the meaning of section 44 of the Scotland Act 1998, or a junior Scottish Minister within the meaning of section 49 of that Act,

    (vii) any office of the National Assembly for Wales held by a member of it,

    (viii) in England, any office of a county council, a London borough council, a district council, or a parish council held by a member of it,

    (ix) in Wales, any office of a county council, a county borough council, or a community council held by a member of it,

    (x) in relation to a council constituted under section 2 of the Local Government etc (Scotland) Act 1994 or a community council established under section 51 of the Local Government (Scotland) Act 1973, any office of such a council held by a member of it,

(xi) any office of the Greater London Authority held by a member of it,

(xii) any office of the Common Council of the City of London held by a member of it,

(xiii) any office of the Council of the Isles of Scilly held by a member of it,

(xiv) any office of a political party;

(c) "relevant person", in relation to an office or post, means –

(i) any person with power to make or terminate appointments to the office or post, or to determine the terms of appointment,

(ii) any person with power to determine the working conditions of a person appointed to the office or post in relation to opportunities for promotion, a transfer, training or for receiving any other benefit, and

(iii) any person or body referred to in paragraph (8)(b) on whose recommendation or subject to whose approval appointments are made to the office or post;

(d) references to making a recommendation include references to making a negative recommendation; and

(e) references to refusal include references to deliberate omission.

Police

29-012   **11.**—(1) For the purposes of this Part, the holding of the office of constable shall be treated as employment –

(a) by the chief officer of police as respects any act done by him in relation to a constable or that office;

(b) by the police authority as respects any act done by it in relation to a constable or that office.

(2) For the purposes of regulation 22 (liability of employers and principals)–

(a) the holding of the office of constable shall be treated as employment by the chief officer of police (and as not being employment by any other person); and

(b) anything done by a person holding such an office in the performance, or purported performance, of his functions shall be treated as done in the course of that employment.

(3) There shall be paid out of the police fund –

(a) any compensation, costs or expenses awarded against a chief officer of police in any proceedings brought against him under these Regulations, and any costs or expenses incurred by him in any such proceedings so far as not recovered by him in the proceedings; and

(b) any sum required by a chief officer of police for the settlement of any claim made against him under these Regulations if the settlement is approved by the police authority.

(4) Any proceedings under these Regulations which, by virtue of paragraph (1), would lie against a chief officer of police shall be brought against the chief officer of police for the time being or, in the case of a vacancy in that office, against the person for the time being performing the functions of that office; and references in paragraph (3) to the chief officer of police shall be construed accordingly.

(5) A police authority may, in such cases and to such extent as appear to it to be appropriate, pay out of the police fund –

(a) any compensation, costs or expenses awarded in proceedings under these Regulations against a person under the direction and control of the chief officer of police;

(b) any costs or expenses incurred and not recovered by such a person in such proceedings; and

(c) any sum required in connection with the settlement of a claim that has or might have given rise to such proceedings.

(6) Paragraphs (1) and (2) apply to a police cadet and appointment as a police cadet as they apply to a constable and the office of constable.

(7) Subject to paragraph (8), in this regulation –

"chief officer of police" –

(a) in relation to a person appointed, or an appointment falling to be made, under a specified Act, has the same meaning as in the Police Act 1996,

(b) in relation to a person appointed, or an appointment falling to be made, under section 9(1)(b) or 55(1)(b) of the Police Act 1997 (police members of the National Criminal Intelligence Service and the National Crime Squad) means the Director General of the National Criminal Intelligence Service or, as the case may be, the Director General of the National Crime Squad,

(c) in relation to a person appointed, or an appointment falling to be made, under the Police (Scotland) Act 1967, means the chief constable of the relevant police force,

(d) in relation to any other person or appointment means the officer or other person who has the direction and control of the body of constables or cadets in question;

"police authority" –

(a) in relation to a person appointed, or an appointment falling to be made, under a specified Act, has the same meaning as in the Police Act 1996,

(b) in relation to a person appointed, or an appointment falling to be made, under section 9(1)(b) or 55(1)(b) of the Police Act 1997, means the Service Authority for the National Criminal Intelligence Service or, as the case may be, the Service Authority for the National Crime Squad,

(c) in relation to a person appointed, or an appointment falling to be made, under the Police (Scotland) Act 1967, has the meaning given in that Act,

(d) in relation to any other person or appointment, means the authority by whom the person in question is or on appointment would be paid;

"police cadet" means any person appointed to undergo training with a view to becoming a constable;

"police fund" –

(a) in relation to a chief officer of police within sub-paragraph (a) of the above definition of that term, has the same meaning as in the Police Act 1996,

(b) in relation to a chief officer of police within sub-paragraph (b) of that definition, means the service fund established under section 16 or (as the case may be) section 61 of the Police Act 1997,

(c) in any other case means money provided by the police authority; and

"specified Act" means the Metropolitan Police Act 1829, the City of London Police Act 1839 or the Police Act 1996.

(8) In relation to a constable of a force who is not under the direction and control of the chief officer of police for that force, references in this regulation to the chief officer of police are references to the chief officer of the force under whose direction and control he is, and references in this regulation to the police authority are references to the relevant police authority for that force.

Barristers

29-013   **12.**—(1) It is unlawful for a barrister or barrister's clerk, in relation to any offer of a pupillage or tenancy, to discriminate against a person—

(a) in the arrangements which are made for the purpose of determining to whom the pupillage or tenancy should be offered;

(b) in respect of any terms on which it is offered; or

(c) by refusing, or deliberately not offering, it to him.

(2) It is unlawful for a barrister or barrister's clerk, in relation to a pupil or tenant in the set of chambers in question, to discriminate against him—

(a) in respect of any terms applicable to him as a pupil or tenant;

(b) in the opportunities for training, or gaining experience, which are afforded or denied to him;

(c) in the benefits which are afforded or denied to him; or

(d) by terminating his pupillage, or by subjecting him to any pressure to leave the chambers or other detriment.

(3) It is unlawful for a barrister or barrister's clerk, in relation to a pupillage or tenancy in the set of chambers in question, to subject to harassment a person who is, or has applied to be, a pupil or tenant.

(4) It is unlawful for any person, in relation to the giving, withholding or acceptance of instructions to a barrister, to discriminate against any person by subjecting him to a detriment, or to subject him to harassment.

(5) In this regulation—

"barrister's clerk" includes any person carrying out any of the functions of a barrister's clerk;

"pupil", "pupillage" and "set of chambers" have the meanings commonly associated with their use in the context of barristers practising in independent practice; and

"tenancy" and "tenant" have the meanings commonly associated with their use in the context of barristers practising in independent practice, but also include reference to any barrister permitted to work in a set of chambers who is not a tenant.

(6) This regulation extends to England and Wales only.

Advocates

29-014   **13.**—(1) It is unlawful for an advocate, in relation to taking any person as his pupil, to discriminate against a person—

(a) in the arrangements which he makes for the purpose of determining whom he will take as his pupil;

(b) in respect of any terms on which he offers to take any person as his pupil; or

(c) by refusing to take, or deliberately not taking, a person as his pupil.

(2) It is unlawful for an advocate, in relation to a person who is his pupil, to discriminate against him—

(a) in respect of any terms applicable to him as a pupil;

(b) in the opportunities for training, or gaining experience, which are afforded or denied to him;

(c) in the benefits which are afforded or denied to him; or

(d) by terminating the relationship, or by subjecting him to any pressure to terminate the relationship or other detriment.

(3) It is unlawful for an advocate, in relation to a person who is his pupil or taking any person as his pupil, to subject such a person to harassment.

(4) It is unlawful for any person, in relation to the giving, withholding or acceptance of instructions to an advocate, to discriminate against any person by subjecting him to a detriment, or to subject him to harassment.

(5) In this regulation—

"advocate" means a member of the Faculty of Advocates practising as such; and

"pupil" has the meaning commonly associated with its use in the context of a person training to be an advocate.

(6) This regulation extends to Scotland only.

Partnerships

14.—(1) It is unlawful for a firm, in relation to a position as partner in the **29-015** firm, to discriminate against a person—

(a) in the arrangements they make for the purpose of determining to whom they should offer that position;

(b) in the terms on which they offer him that position;

(c) by refusing to offer, or deliberately not offering, him that position; or

(d) in a case where the person already holds that position—

(i) in the way they afford him access to any benefits or by refusing to afford, or deliberately not affording, him access to them, or

(ii) by expelling him from that position, or subjecting him to any other detriment.

(2) It is unlawful for a firm, in relation to a position as partner in the firm, to subject to harassment a person who holds or has applied for that position.

(3) Paragraphs (1)(a) to (c) and (2) apply in relation to persons proposing to form themselves into a partnership as they apply in relation to a firm.

(4) Paragraph (1) does not apply to any act in relation to a position as partner where, if the position were employment, that act would be lawful by virtue of regulation 7 (exception for genuine occupational requirement).

(5) In the case of a limited partnership references in this regulation to a partner shall be construed as references to a general partner as defined in section 3 of the Limited Partnerships Act 1907.

(6) This regulation applies to a limited liability partnership as it applies to a firm; and, in its application to a limited liability partnership, references to a partner in a firm are references to a member of the limited liability partnership.

(7) In this regulation, "firm" has the meaning given by section 4 of the Partnership Act 1890.

(8) In paragraph (1)(d) reference to the expulsion of a person from a position as partner includes reference –

    (a) to the termination of that person's partnership by the expiration of any period (including a period expiring by reference to an event or circumstance), not being a termination immediately after which the partnership is renewed on the same terms; and

    (b) to the termination of that person's partnership by any act of his (including the giving of notice) in circumstances such that he is entitled to terminate it without notice by reason of the conduct of the other partners.

Trade organisations

29-016   **15.**—(1) It is unlawful for a trade organisation to discriminate against a person –

    (a) in the terms on which it is prepared to admit him to membership of the organisation; or

    (b) by refusing to accept, or deliberately not accepting, his application for membership.

(2) It is unlawful for a trade organisation, in relation to a member of the organisation, to discriminate against him –

    (a) in the way it affords him access to any benefits or by refusing or deliberately omitting to afford him access to them;

    (b) by depriving him of membership, or varying the terms on which he is a member; or

    (c) by subjecting him to any other detriment.

(3) It is unlawful for a trade organisation, in relation to a person's membership or application for membership of that organisation, to subject that person to harassment.

(4) In this regulation –

    "trade organisation" means an organisation of workers, an organisation of employers, or any other organisation whose members carry on a particular profession or trade for the purposes of which the organisation exists;

    "profession" includes any vocation or occupation; and

    "trade" includes any business.

Qualifications bodies

29-017   **16.**—(1) It is unlawful for a qualifications body to discriminate against a person –

    (a) in the terms on which it is prepared to confer a professional or trade qualification on him;

    (b) by refusing or deliberately not granting any application by him for such a qualification; or

    (c) by withdrawing such a qualification from him or varying the terms on which he holds it.

(2) It is unlawful for a qualifications body, in relation to a professional or trade qualification conferred by it, to subject to harassment a person who holds or applies for such a qualification.

(3) In this regulation –

    "qualifications body" means any authority or body which can confer a professional or trade qualification, but it does not include –

    (a) an educational establishment to which regulation 20 (institutions of further and higher education) applies, or would apply but for the operation of any other provision of these Regulations, or

    (b) a school;

"confer" includes renew or extend;

"professional or trade qualification" means any authorisation, qualification, recognition, registration, enrolment, approval or certification which is needed for, or facilitates engagement in, a particular profession or trade;

"profession" and "trade" have the same meaning as in regulation 15.

Providers of vocational training

17.—(1) It is unlawful, in relation to a person seeking or undergoing training **29-018** which would help fit him for any employment, for any training provider to discriminate against him—

    (a) in the terms on which the training provider affords him access to any training;

    (b) by refusing or deliberately not affording him such access;

    (c) by terminating his training; or

    (d) by subjecting him to any other detriment during his training.

(2) It is unlawful for a training provider, in relation to a person seeking or undergoing training which would help fit him for any employment, to subject him to harassment.

(3) Paragraph (1) does not apply if the discrimination only concerns training for employment which, by virtue of regulation 7 (exception for genuine occupational requirement), the employer could lawfully refuse to offer the person seeking training.

(4) In this regulation—

"training" includes—

    (a) facilities for training; and

    (b) practical work experience provided by an employer to a person whom he does not employ;

"training provider" means any person who provides, or makes arrangements for the provision of, training which would help fit another person for any employment, but it does not include—

    (a) an employer in relation to training for persons employed by him;

    (b) an educational establishment to which regulation 20 (institutions of further and higher education) applies, or would apply but for the operation of any other provision of these Regulations; or

    (c) a school.

Employment agencies, careers guidance etc

18.—(1) It is unlawful for an employment agency to discriminate against a **29-019** person—

    (a) in the terms on which the agency offers to provide any of its services;

    (b) by refusing or deliberately not providing any of its services; or

    (c) in the way it provides any of its services.

(2) It is unlawful for an employment agency, in relation to a person to whom it provides its services, or who has requested it to provide its services, to subject that person to harassment.

(3) Paragraph (1) does not apply to discrimination if it only concerns employment which, by virtue of regulation 7 (exception for genuine occupational requirement), the employer could lawfully refuse to offer the person in question.

(4) An employment agency shall not be subject to any liability under this regulation if it proves that–

    (a) it acted in reliance on a statement made to it by the employer to the effect that, by reason of the operation of paragraph (3), its action would not be unlawful, and

    (b) it was reasonable for it to rely on the statement.

(5) A person who knowingly or recklessly makes a statement such as is referred to in paragraph (4)(a) which in a material respect is false or misleading commits an offence, and shall be liable on summary conviction to a fine not exceeding level 5 on the standard scale.

(6) For the purposes of this regulation–

    (a) "employment agency" means a person who, for profit or not, provides services for the purpose of finding employment for workers or supplying employers with workers, but it does not include–

        (i) an educational establishment to which regulation 20 (institutions of further and higher education) applies, or would apply but for the operation of any other provision of these Regulations, or

        (ii) a school; and

    (b) references to the services of an employment agency include guidance on careers and any other services related to employment.

Assisting persons to obtain employment etc

29-020   **19.**—(1) It is unlawful for the Secretary of State to discriminate against any person by subjecting him to a detriment, or to subject a person to harassment, in the provision of facilities or services under section 2 of the Employment and Training Act 1973 (arrangements for assisting persons to obtain employment).

(2) It is unlawful for Scottish Enterprise or Highlands and Islands Enterprise to discriminate against any person by subjecting him to a detriment, or to subject a person to harassment, in the provision of facilities or services under such arrangements as are mentioned in section 2(3) of the Enterprise and New Towns (Scotland) Act 1990 (arrangements analogous to arrangements in pursuance of the said Act of 1973).

(3) This regulation does not apply in a case where–

    (a) regulation 17 (providers of vocational training) applies, or would apply but for the operation of any other provision of these Regulations, or

    (b) the Secretary of State is acting as an employment agency within the meaning of regulation 18.

Institutions of further and higher education

29-021   **20.**—(1) [Subject to paragraph (4A), it][1] is unlawful, in relation to an educational establishment to which this regulation applies, for the governing body of that establishment to discriminate against a person–

    (a) in the terms on which it offers to admit him to the establishment as a student;

    (b) by refusing or deliberately not accepting an application for his admission to the establishment as a student; or

    (c) where he is a student of the establishment–

[1] Words inserted by SI 2004/437 reg 3 (1)

(i) in the way it affords him access to any benefits,

(ii) by refusing or deliberately not affording him access to them, or

(iii) by excluding him from the establishment or subjecting him to any other detriment.

(2) It is unlawful, in relation to an educational establishment to which this regulation applies, for the governing body of that establishment to subject to harassment a person who is a student at the establishment, or who has applied for admission to the establishment as a student.

(3) Paragraph (1) does not apply if the discrimination only concerns training which would help fit a person for employment which, by virtue of regulation 7 (exception for genuine occupational requirement), the employer could lawfully refuse to offer the person in question.

(4) [Subject to paragraph (4A),][1] this regulation applies to the following educational establishments in England and Wales, namely–

(a) an institution within the further education sector (within the meaning of section 91(3) of the Further and Higher Education Act 1992);

(b) a university;

(c) an institution, other than a university, within the higher education sector (within the meaning of section 91(5) of the Further and Higher Education Act 1992).

[(4A) In relation to an institution specified in Schedule 1B, this regulation applies with the modification set out in that Schedule.][2]

(5) This regulation applies to the following educational establishments in Scotland, namely–

(a) a college of further education within the meaning of section 36(1) of the Further and Higher Education (Scotland) Act 1992 under the management of a board of management within the meaning of Part I of that Act;

(b) a college of further education maintained by an education authority in the exercise of its further education functions in providing courses of further education within the meaning of section 1(5)(b)(ii) of the Education (Scotland) Act 1980;

(c) any other educational establishment (not being a school) which provides further education within the meaning of section 1 of the Further and Higher Education (Scotland) Act 1992;

(d) an institution within the higher education sector (within the meaning of Part II of the Further and Higher Education (Scotland) Act 1992);

(e) a central institution (within the meaning of section 135 of the Education (Scotland) Act 1980).

(6) In this regulation–

"education authority" has the meaning given by section 135(1) of the Education (Scotland) Act 1980;

"governing body" includes–

(a) the board of management of a college referred to in paragraph (5)(a), and

(b) the managers of a college or institution referred to in paragraph (5)(b) or (e);

"student" means any person who receives education at an educational establishment to which this regulation applies; and

---

[1] Words inserted by SI 2004/437 reg 3 (1)

[2] Inserted by SI 2004/437 reg 3 (2)

"university" includes a university college and the college, school or hall of a university.

Relationships which have come to an end

29-022   **21.**—(1) In this regulation a "relevant relationship" is a relationship during the course of which an act of discrimination against, or harassment of, one party to the relationship ("B") by the other party to it ("A") is unlawful by virtue of any preceding provision of this Part.

(2) Where a relevant relationship has come to an end, it is unlawful for A—

(a) to discriminate against B by subjecting him to a detriment; or

(b) to subject B to harassment,

where the discrimination or harassment arises out of and is closely connected to that relationship.

(3) In paragraph (1), reference to an act of discrimination or harassment which is unlawful includes, in the case of a relationship which has come to an end before the coming into force of these Regulations, reference to an act of discrimination or harassment which would, after the coming into force of these Regulations, be unlawful.

PART III

OTHER UNLAWFUL ACTS

Liability of employers and principals

29-023   **22.**—(1) Anything done by a person in the course of his employment shall be treated for the purposes of these Regulations as done by his employer as well as by him, whether or not it was done with the employer's knowledge or approval.

(2) Anything done by a person as agent for another person with the authority (whether express or implied, and whether precedent or subsequent) of that other person shall be treated for the purposes of these Regulations as done by that other person as well as by him.

(3) In proceedings brought under these Regulations against any person in respect of an act alleged to have been done by an employee of his it shall be a defence for that person to prove that he took such steps as were reasonably practicable to prevent the employee from doing that act, or from doing in the course of his employment acts of that description.

Aiding unlawful acts

29-024   **23.**—(1) A person who knowingly aids another person to do an act made unlawful by these Regulations shall be treated for the purpose of these Regulations as himself doing an unlawful act of the like description.

(2) For the purposes of paragraph (1) an employee or agent for whose act the employer or principal is liable under regulation 22 (or would be so liable but for regulation 22(3)) shall be deemed to aid the doing of the act by the employer or principal.

(3) A person does not under this regulation knowingly aid another to do an unlawful act if—

(a) he acts in reliance on a statement made to him by that other person that, by reason of any provision of these Regulations, the act which he aids would not be unlawful; and

(b) it is reasonable for him to rely on the statement.

(4) A person who knowingly or recklessly makes a statement such as is referred to in paragraph (3)(a) which in a material respect is false or misleading commits an offence, and shall be liable on summary conviction to a fine not exceeding level 5 on the standard scale.

PART IV

GENERAL EXCEPTIONS FROM PARTS II AND III

Exception for national security

24. Nothing in Part II or III shall render unlawful an act done for the **29-025** purpose of safeguarding national security, if the doing of the act was justified by that purpose.

Exceptions for positive action

25.—(1) Nothing in Part II or III shall render unlawful any act done in or in **29-026** connection with–
> (a) affording persons of a particular religion or belief access to facilities for training which would help fit them for particular work; or
> (b) encouraging persons of a particular religion or belief to take advantage of opportunities for doing particular work,

where it reasonably appears to the person doing the act that it prevents or compensates for disadvantages linked to religion or belief suffered by persons of that religion or belief doing that work or likely to take up that work.

(2) Nothing in Part II or III shall render unlawful any act done by a trade organisation within the meaning of regulation 15 in or in connection with–
> (a) affording only members of the organisation who are of a particular religion or belief access to facilities for training which would help fit them for holding a post of any kind in the organisation; or
> (b) encouraging only members of the organisation who are of a particular religion or belief to take advantage of opportunities for holding such posts in the organisation,

where it reasonably appears to the organisation that the act prevents or compensates for disadvantages linked to religion or belief suffered by those of that religion or belief holding such posts or likely to hold such posts.

(3) Nothing in Part II or III shall render unlawful any act done by a trade organisation within the meaning of regulation 15 in or in connection with encouraging only persons of a particular religion or belief to become members of the organisation where it reasonably appears to the organisation that the act prevents or compensates for disadvantages linked to religion or belief suffered by persons of that religion or belief who are, or are eligible to become, members.

Protection of Sikhs from discrimination in connection with requirements as to wearing of safety helmets

26.—(1) Where–   **29-027**
> (a) any person applies to a Sikh any provision, criterion or practice relating to the wearing by him of a safety helmet while he is on a construction site; and
> (b) at the time when he so applies the provision, criterion or practice that person has no reasonable grounds for believing that the Sikh would not wear a turban at all times when on such a site,

then, for the purposes of regulation 3(1)(b)(iii), the provision, criterion or practice shall be taken to be one which cannot be shown to be a proportionate means of achieving a legitimate aim.

(2) Any special treatment afforded to a Sikh in consequence of section 11(1) or (2) of the Employment Act 1989 (exemption of Sikhs from requirements as to wearing of safety helmets on construction sites) shall not be regarded as giving rise, in relation to any other person, to any discrimination falling within regulation 3.

(3) In this regulation–

"construction site" means any place in Great Britain where any building operations or works of engineering construction are being undertaken, but does not include any site within the territorial sea adjacent to Great Britain unless there are being undertaken on that site such operations or works as are activities falling within Article 8(a) of the Health and Safety at Work etc Act 1974 (Application outside Great Britain) Order 2001; and

"safety helmet" means any form of protective headgear.

(4) In this regulation–

(a) any reference to a Sikh is a reference to a follower of the Sikh religion; and

(b) any reference to a Sikh being on a construction site is a reference to his being there whether while at work or otherwise.

PART V

ENFORCEMENT

Restriction of proceedings for breach of Regulations

29-028   **27.**—(1) Except as provided by these Regulations no proceedings, whether civil or criminal, shall lie against any person in respect of an act by reason that the act is unlawful by virtue of a provision of these Regulations.

(2) Paragraph (1) does not prevent the making of an application for judicial review [or the investigation or determination of any matter in accordance with Part X (investigations: the Pensions Ombudsman) of the Pension Schemes Act 1993 by the Pensions Ombudsman][1].

Jurisdiction of employment tribunals

29-029   **28.**—(1) A complaint by any person ("the complainant") that another person ("the respondent")–

(a) has committed against the complainant an act to which this regulation applies; or

(b) is by virtue of regulation 22 (liability of employers and principals) or 23 (aiding unlawful acts) to be treated as having committed against the complainant such an act,

may be presented to an employment tribunal.

(2) This regulation applies to any act of discrimination or harassment which is unlawful by virtue of any provision of Part II other than–

(a) where the act is one in respect of which an appeal or proceedings in the nature of an appeal may be brought under any enactment, regulation 16 (qualifications bodies);

---

[1] Words inserted by SI 2003/2828 reg 3 (4)

   (b) regulation 20 (institutions of further and higher education); or

   (c) where the act arises out of and is closely connected to a relationship between the complainant and the respondent which has come to an end but during the course of which an act of discrimination against, or harassment of, the complainant by the respondent would have been unlawful by virtue of regulation 20, regulation 21 (relationships which have come to an end).

(3) In paragraph (2)(c), reference to an act of discrimination or harassment which would have been unlawful includes, in the case of a relationship which has come to an end before the coming into force of these Regulations, reference to an act of discrimination or harassment which would, after the coming into force of these Regulations, have been unlawful.

(4) In this regulation, "enactment" includes an enactment comprised in, or in an instrument made under, an Act of the Scottish Parliament.

Burden of proof: employment tribunals

29.—(1) This regulation applies to any complaint presented under regulation **29-030** 28 to an employment tribunal.

(2) Where, on the hearing of the complaint, the complainant proves facts from which the tribunal could, apart from this regulation, conclude in the absence of an adequate explanation that the respondent—

   (a) has committed against the complainant an act to which regulation 28 applies; or

   (b) is by virtue of regulation 22 (liability of employers and principals) or 23 (aiding unlawful acts) to be treated as having committed against the complainant such an act,

the tribunal shall uphold the complaint unless the respondent proves that he did not commit, or as the case may be, is not to be treated as having committed, that act.

Remedies on complaints in employment tribunals

30.—(1) Where an employment tribunal finds that a complaint presented to **29-031** it under regulation 28 is well-founded, the tribunal shall make such of the following as it considers just and equitable—

   (a) an order declaring the rights of the complainant and the respondent in relation to the act to which the complaint relates;

   (b) an order requiring the respondent to pay to the complainant compensation of an amount corresponding to any damages he could have been ordered by a county court or by a sheriff court to pay to the complainant if the complaint had fallen to be dealt with under regulation 31 (jurisdiction of county and sheriff courts);

   (c) a recommendation that the respondent take within a specified period action appearing to the tribunal to be practicable for the purpose of obviating or reducing the adverse effect on the complainant of any act of discrimination or harassment to which the complaint relates.

(2) As respects an unlawful act of discrimination falling within regulation 3(1)(b), if the respondent proves that the provision, criterion or practice was not applied with the intention of treating the complainant unfavourably on grounds of religion or belief, an order may be made under paragraph (1)(b) only if the employment tribunal—

(a) makes such order under paragraph (1)(a) (if any) and such recommendation under paragraph (1)(c) (if any) as it would have made if it had no power to make an order under paragraph (1)(b); and

(b) (where it makes an order under paragraph (1)(a) or a recommendation under paragraph (1)(c) or both) considers that it is just and equitable to make an order under paragraph (1)(b) as well.

(3) If without reasonable justification the respondent to a complaint fails to comply with a recommendation made by an employment tribunal under paragraph (1)(c), then, if it thinks it just and equitable to do so–

(a) the tribunal may increase the amount of compensation required to be paid to the complainant in respect of the complaint by an order made under paragraph (1)(b); or

(b) if an order under paragraph (1)(b) was not made, the tribunal may make such an order.

(4) Where an amount of compensation falls to be awarded under paragraph (1)(b), the tribunal may include in the award interest on that amount subject to, and in accordance with, the provisions of the Employment Tribunals (Interest on Awards in Discrimination Cases) Regulations 1996.

[(5) This regulation has effect subject to paragraph 7 of Schedule 1A (occupational pension schemes).][1]

The Employment Equality (Sexual Orientation) Regulations 2003

Whereas a draft of these Regulations was laid before Parliament in accordance with paragraph 2 of Schedule 2 to the European Communities Act 1972, and was approved by resolution of each House of Parliament; Now, therefore, the Secretary of State, being a Minister designated for the purposes of section 2(2) of the European Communities Act 1972 in relation to discrimination, in exercise of the powers conferred by that section, hereby makes the following Regulations:–

(S.I. 1661)

PART I

GENERAL

Citation, commencement and extent

30-001   **1.**—(1) These Regulations may be cited as the Employment Equality (Sexual Orientation) Regulations 2003, and shall come into force on 1st December 2003.

(2) These Regulations do not extend to Northern Ireland.

Interpretation

30-002   **2.**—(1) In these Regulations, "sexual orientation" means a sexual orientation towards–

(a) persons of the same sex;

(b) persons of the opposite sex; or

---
[1] Inserted by SI 2003/2828 reg 3 (5)

(c) persons of the same sex and of the opposite sex.

(2) In these Regulations, references to discrimination are to any discrimination falling within regulation 3 (discrimination on grounds of sexual orientation) or 4 (discrimination by way of victimisation) and related expressions shall be construed accordingly, and references to harassment shall be construed in accordance with regulation 5 (harassment on grounds of sexual orientation).

(3) In these Regulations –

"act" includes a deliberate omission;

["benefits", except in regulation 9A (trustees and managers of occupational pension schemes), includes facilities and services;][1]

"detriment" does not include harassment within the meaning of regulation 5;

references to "employer", in their application to a person at any time seeking to employ another, include a person who has no employees at that time;

"employment" means employment under a contract of service or of apprenticeship or a contract personally to do any work, and related expressions shall be construed accordingly;

"Great Britain" includes such of the territorial waters of the United Kingdom as are adjacent to Great Britain;

"Minister of the Crown" includes the Treasury and the Defence Council; and

"school", in England and Wales, has the meaning given by section 4 of the Education Act 1996, and, in Scotland, has the meaning given by section 135(1) of the Education (Scotland) Act 1980, and references to a school are to an institution in so far as it is engaged in the provision of education under those sections.

Discrimination on grounds of sexual orientation

3.—(1) For the purposes of these Regulations, a person ("A") discriminates **30-003** against another person ("B") if –

(a) on grounds of sexual orientation, A treats B less favourably than he treats or would treat other persons; or

(b) A applies to B a provision, criterion or practice which he applies or would apply equally to persons not of the same sexual orientation as B, but –

(i) which puts or would put persons of the same sexual orientation as B at a particular disadvantage when compared with other persons,

(ii) which puts B at that disadvantage, and

(iii) which A cannot show to be a proportionate means of achieving a legitimate aim.

(2) A comparison of B's case with that of another person under paragraph (1) must be such that the relevant circumstances in the one case are the same, or not materially different, in the other.

Discrimination by way of victimisation

4.—(1) For the purposes of these Regulations, a person ("A") discriminates **30-004** against another person ("B") if he treats B less favourably than he treats or would

---

[1] Definition substituted by SI 2003/2827 reg 3 (2)

treat other persons in the same circumstances, and does so by reason that B has—

    (a) brought proceedings against A or any other person under these Regulations;

    (b) given evidence or information in connection with proceedings brought by any person against A or any other person under these Regulations;

    (c) otherwise done anything under or by reference to these Regulations in relation to A or any other person; or

    (d) alleged that A or any other person has committed an act which (whether or not the allegation so states) would amount to a contravention of these Regulations,

or by reason that A knows that B intends to do any of those things, or suspects that B has done or intends to do any of them.

(2) Paragraph (1) does not apply to treatment of B by reason of any allegation made by him, or evidence or information given by him, if the allegation, evidence or information was false and not made (or, as the case may be, given) in good faith.

Harassment on grounds of sexual orientation

30-005   **5.**—(1) For the purposes of these Regulations, a person ("A") subjects another person ("B") to harassment where, on grounds of sexual orientation, A engages in unwanted conduct which has the purpose or effect of—

    (a) violating B's dignity; or

    (b) creating an intimidating, hostile, degrading, humiliating or offensive environment for B.

(2) Conduct shall be regarded as having the effect specified in paragraph (1)(a) or (b) only if, having regard to all the circumstances, including in particular the perception of B, it should reasonably be considered as having that effect.

PART II

DISCRIMINATION IN EMPLOYMENT AND VOCATIONAL TRAINING

Applicants and employees

30-006   **6.**—(1) It is unlawful for an employer, in relation to employment by him at an establishment in Great Britain, to discriminate against a person—

    (a) in the arrangements he makes for the purpose of determining to whom he should offer employment;

    (b) in the terms on which he offers that person employment; or

    (c) by refusing to offer, or deliberately not offering, him employment.

(2) It is unlawful for an employer, in relation to a person whom he employs at an establishment in Great Britain, to discriminate against that person—

    (a) in the terms of employment which he affords him;

    (b) in the opportunities which he affords him for promotion, a transfer, training, or receiving any other benefit;

    (c) by refusing to afford him, or deliberately not affording him, any such opportunity; or

    (d) by dismissing him, or subjecting him to any other detriment.

(3) It is unlawful for an employer, in relation to employment by him at an establishment in Great Britain, to subject to harassment a person whom he employs or who has applied to him for employment.

(4) Paragraph (2) does not apply to benefits of any description if the employer is concerned with the provision (for payment or not) of benefits of that description to the public, or to a section of the public which includes the employee in question, unless –

    (a) that provision differs in a material respect from the provision of the benefits by the employer to his employees; or

    (b) the provision of the benefits to the employee in question is regulated by his contract of employment; or

    (c) the benefits relate to training.

(5) In paragraph (2)(d) reference to the dismissal of a person from employment includes reference –

    (a) to the termination of that person's employment by the expiration of any period (including a period expiring by reference to an event or circumstance), not being a termination immediately after which the employment is renewed on the same terms; and

    (b) to the termination of that person's employment by any act of his (including the giving of notice) in circumstances such that he is entitled to terminate it without notice by reason of the conduct of the employer.

Exception for genuine occupational requirement etc

7.—(1) In relation to discrimination falling within regulation 3 (discrimina- **30-007** tion on grounds of sexual orientation)–

    (a) regulation 6(1)(a) or (c) does not apply to any employment;

    (b) regulation 6(2)(b) or (c) does not apply to promotion or transfer to, or training for, any employment; and

    (c) regulation 6(2)(d) does not apply to dismissal from any employment,

where paragraph (2) or (3) applies.

(2) This paragraph applies where, having regard to the nature of the employment or the context in which it is carried out –

    (a) being of a particular sexual orientation is a genuine and determining occupational requirement;

    (b) it is proportionate to apply that requirement in the particular case; and

    (c) either –

        (i) the person to whom that requirement is applied does not meet it, or

        (ii) the employer is not satisfied, and in all the circumstances it is reasonable for him not to be satisfied, that that person meets it,

and this paragraph applies whether or not the employment is for purposes of an organised religion.

(3) This paragraph applies where –

    (a) the employment is for purposes of an organised religion;

    (b) the employer applies a requirement related to sexual orientation –

        (i) so as to comply with the doctrines of the religion, or

        (ii) because of the nature of the employment and the context in which it is carried out, so as to avoid conflicting with the strongly held religious convictions of a significant number of the religion's followers; and

    (c) either –

        (i) the person to whom that requirement is applied does not meet it, or

(ii) the employer is not satisfied, and in all the circumstances it is reasonable for him not to be satisfied, that that person meets it.

Contract workers

30-008   **8.**—(1) It is unlawful for a principal, in relation to contract work at an establishment in Great Britain, to discriminate against a contract worker—

(a) in the terms on which he allows him to do that work;

(b) by not allowing him to do it or continue to do it;

(c) in the way he affords him access to any benefits or by refusing or deliberately not affording him access to them; or

(d) by subjecting him to any other detriment.

(2) It is unlawful for a principal, in relation to contract work at an establishment in Great Britain, to subject a contract worker to harassment.

(3) A principal does not contravene paragraph (1)(b) by doing any act in relation to a contract worker where, if the work were to be done by a person taken into the principal's employment, that act would be lawful by virtue of regulation 7 (exception for genuine occupational requirement etc).

(4) Paragraph (1) does not apply to benefits of any description if the principal is concerned with the provision (for payment or not) of benefits of that description to the public, or to a section of the public to which the contract worker in question belongs, unless that provision differs in a material respect from the provision of the benefits by the principal to his contract workers.

(5) In this regulation—

"principal" means a person ("A") who makes work available for doing by individuals who are employed by another person who supplies them under a contract made with A;

"contract work" means work so made available; and

"contract worker" means any individual who is supplied to the principal under such a contract.

Meaning of employment and contract work at establishment in Great Britain

30-009   **9.**—(1) For the purposes of this Part ("the relevant purposes"), employment is to be regarded as being at an establishment in Great Britain if the employee—

(a) does his work wholly or partly in Great Britain; or

(b) does his work wholly outside Great Britain and paragraph (2) applies.

(2) This paragraph applies if—

(a) the employer has a place of business at an establishment in Great Britain;

(b) the work is for the purposes of the business carried on at that establishment; and

(c) the employee is ordinarily resident in Great Britain—

(i) at the time when he applies for or is offered the employment, or

(ii) at any time during the course of the employment.

(3) The reference to "employment" in paragraph (1) includes—

(a) employment on board a ship only if the ship is registered at a port of registry in Great Britain, and

(b) employment on an aircraft or hovercraft only if the aircraft or hovercraft is registered in the United Kingdom and operated by a person who has his principal place of business, or is ordinarily resident, in Great Britain.

(4) Subject to paragraph (5), for the purposes of determining if employment concerned with the exploration of the sea bed or sub-soil or the exploitation of

their natural resources is outside Great Britain, this regulation has effect as if references to Great Britain included –

 (a) any area designated under section 1(7) of the Continental Shelf Act 1964 except an area or part of an area in which the law of Northern Ireland applies; and

 (b) in relation to employment concerned with the exploration or exploitation of the Frigg Gas Field, the part of the Norwegian sector of the Continental Shelf described in Schedule 1.

(5) Paragraph (4) shall not apply to employment which is concerned with the exploration or exploitation of the Frigg Gas Field unless the employer is –

 (a) a company registered under the Companies Act 1985;

 (b) an oversea company which has established a place of business within Great Britain from which it directs the exploration or exploitation in question; or

 (c) any other person who has a place of business within Great Britain from which he directs the exploration or exploitation in question.

(6) In this regulation –

 "the Frigg Gas Field" means the naturally occurring gas-bearing sand formations of the lower Eocene age located in the vicinity of the intersection of the line of latitude 59 degrees 53 minutes North and of the dividing line between the sectors of the Continental Shelf of the United Kingdom and the Kingdom of Norway and includes all other gas-bearing strata from which gas at the start of production is capable of flowing into the above-mentioned gas-bearing sand formations;

 "oversea company" has the same meaning as in section 744 of the Companies Act 1985.

(7) This regulation applies in relation to contract work within the meaning of regulation 8 as it applies in relation to employment; and, in its application to contract work, references to "employee", "employer" and "employment" are references to (respectively) "contract worker", "principal" and "contract work" within the meaning of regulation 8.

[Trustees and managers of occupational pension schemes

9A.—(1) It is unlawful, except in relation to rights accrued or benefits **30-010** payable in respect of periods of service prior to the coming into force of these Regulations, for the trustees or managers of an occupational pension scheme to discriminate against a member or prospective member of the scheme in carrying out any of their functions in relation to it (including in particular their functions relating to the admission of members to the scheme and the treatment of members of it).

(2) It is unlawful for the trustees or managers of an occupational pension scheme, in relation to the scheme, to subject to harassment a member or prospective member of it.

(3) Schedule 1A (occupational pension schemes) shall have effect for the purposes of –

 (a) defining terms used in this regulation and in that Schedule;

 (b) treating every occupational pension scheme as including a non-discrimination rule;

 (c) giving trustees or managers of an occupational pension scheme power to alter the scheme so as to secure conformity with the non-discrimination rule;

(d) making provision in relation to the procedures, and remedies which may be granted, on certain complaints relating to occupational pension schemes presented to an employment tribunal under regulation 28 (jurisdiction of employment tribunals).][1]

Office-holders etc

30-011　　**10.**—(1) It is unlawful for a relevant person, in relation to an appointment to an office or post to which this regulation applies, to discriminate against a person—

(a) in the arrangements which he makes for the purpose of determining to whom the appointment should be offered;

(b) in the terms on which he offers him the appointment; or

(c) by refusing to offer him the appointment.

(2) It is unlawful, in relation to an appointment to an office or post to which this regulation applies and which is an office or post referred to in paragraph (8)(b), for a relevant person on whose recommendation (or subject to whose approval) appointments to the office or post are made, to discriminate against a person—

(a) in the arrangements which he makes for the purpose of determining who should be recommended or approved in relation to the appointment; or

(b) in making or refusing to make a recommendation, or giving or refusing to give an approval, in relation to the appointment.

(3) It is unlawful for a relevant person, in relation to a person who has been appointed to an office or post to which this regulation applies, to discriminate against him—

(a) in the terms of the appointment;

(b) in the opportunities which he affords him for promotion, a transfer, training or receiving any other benefit, or by refusing to afford him any such opportunity;

(c) by terminating the appointment; or

(d) by subjecting him to any other detriment in relation to the appointment.

(4) It is unlawful for a relevant person, in relation to an office or post to which this regulation applies, to subject to harassment a person—

(a) who has been appointed to the office or post;

(b) who is seeking or being considered for appointment to the office or post; or

(c) who is seeking or being considered for a recommendation or approval in relation to an appointment to an office or post referred to in paragraph (8)(b).

(5) Paragraphs (1) and (3) do not apply to any act in relation to an office or post where, if the office or post constituted employment, that act would be lawful by virtue of regulation 7 (exception for genuine occupational requirement etc); and paragraph (2) does not apply to any act in relation to an office or post where, if the office or post constituted employment, it would be lawful by virtue of regulation 7 to refuse to offer the person such employment.

(6) Paragraph (3) does not apply to benefits of any description if the relevant person is concerned with the provision (for payment or not) of benefits of that description to the public, or a section of the public to which the person appointed belongs, unless—

---

[1] Inserted by SI 2003/2827 reg 3 (3)

(a) that provision differs in a material respect from the provision of the benefits by the relevant person to persons appointed to offices or posts which are the same as, or not materially different from, that which the person appointed holds; or

(b) the provision of the benefits to the person appointed is regulated by the terms and conditions of his appointment; or

(c) the benefits relate to training.

(7) In paragraph (3)(c) the reference to the termination of the appointment includes a reference—

(a) to the termination of the appointment by the expiration of any period (including a period expiring by reference to an event or circumstance), not being a termination immediately after which the appointment is renewed on the same terms and conditions; and

(b) to the termination of the appointment by any act of the person appointed (including the giving of notice) in circumstances such that he is entitled to terminate the appointment without notice by reason of the conduct of the relevant person.

(8) This regulation applies to—

(a) any office or post to which persons are appointed to discharge functions personally under the direction of another person, and in respect of which they are entitled to remuneration; and

(b) any office or post to which appointments are made by (or on the recommendation of or subject to the approval of) a Minister of the Crown, a government department, the National Assembly for Wales or any part of the Scottish Administration,

but not to a political office or a case where regulation 6 (applicants and employees), 8 (contract workers), 12 (barristers), 13 (advocates) or 14 (partnerships) applies, or would apply but for the operation of any other provision of these Regulations.

(9) For the purposes of paragraph (8)(a) the holder of an office or post—

(a) is to be regarded as discharging his functions under the direction of another person if that other person is entitled to direct him as to when and where he discharges those functions;

(b) is not to be regarded as entitled to remuneration merely because he is entitled to payments—

(i) in respect of expenses incurred by him in carrying out the functions of the office or post, or

(ii) by way of compensation for the loss of income or benefits he would or might have received from any person had he not been carrying out the functions of the office or post.

(10) In this regulation—

(a) appointment to an office or post does not include election to an office or post;

(b) "political office" means—

(i) any office of the House of Commons held by a member of it,

(ii) a life peerage within the meaning of the Life Peerages Act 1958, or any office of the House of Lords held by a member of it,

(iii) any office mentioned in Schedule 2 (Ministerial offices) to the House of Commons Disqualification Act 1975,

(iv) the offices of Leader of the Opposition, Chief Opposition Whip or Assistant Opposition Whip within the meaning of the Ministerial and other Salaries Act 1975,

    (v) any office of the Scottish Parliament held by a member of it,

    (vi) a member of the Scottish Executive within the meaning of section 44 of the Scotland Act 1998, or a junior Scottish Minister within the meaning of section 49 of that Act,

    (vii) any office of the National Assembly for Wales held by a member of it,

    (viii) in England, any office of a county council, a London borough council, a district council, or a parish council held by a member of it,

    (ix) in Wales, any office of a county council, a county borough council, or a community council held by a member of it,

    (x) in relation to a council constituted under section 2 of the Local Government etc (Scotland) Act 1994 or a community council established under section 51 of the Local Government (Scotland) Act 1973, any office of such a council held by a member of it,

    (xi) any office of the Greater London Authority held by a member of it,

    (xii) any office of the Common Council of the City of London held by a member of it,

    (xiii) any office of the Council of the Isles of Scilly held by a member of it,

    (xiv) any office of a political party;

(c) "relevant person", in relation to an office or post, means–

    (i) any person with power to make or terminate appointments to the office or post, or to determine the terms of appointment,

    (ii) any person with power to determine the working conditions of a person appointed to the office or post in relation to opportunities for promotion, a transfer, training or for receiving any other benefit, and

    (iii) any person or body referred to in paragraph (8)(b) on whose recommendation or subject to whose approval appointments are made to the office or post;

(d) references to making a recommendation include references to making a negative recommendation; and

(e) references to refusal include references to deliberate omission.

Police

30-012   **11.**—(1) For the purposes of this Part, the holding of the office of constable shall be treated as employment–

(a) by the chief officer of police as respects any act done by him in relation to a constable or that office;

(b) by the police authority as respects any act done by it in relation to a constable or that office.

(2) For the purposes of regulation 22 (liability of employers and principals)–

(a) the holding of the office of constable shall be treated as employment by the chief officer of police (and as not being employment by any other person); and

(b) anything done by a person holding such an office in the performance, or purported performance, of his functions shall be treated as done in the course of that employment.

(3) There shall be paid out of the police fund–

    (a) any compensation, costs or expenses awarded against a chief officer of police in any proceedings brought against him under these Regulations, and any costs or expenses incurred by him in any such proceedings so far as not recovered by him in the proceedings; and

    (b) any sum required by a chief officer of police for the settlement of any claim made against him under these Regulations if the settlement is approved by the police authority.

(4) Any proceedings under these Regulations which, by virtue of paragraph (1), would lie against a chief officer of police shall be brought against the chief officer of police for the time being or, in the case of a vacancy in that office, against the person for the time being performing the functions of that office; and references in paragraph (3) to the chief officer of police shall be construed accordingly.

(5) A police authority may, in such cases and to such extent as appear to it to be appropriate, pay out of the police fund –

    (a) any compensation, costs or expenses awarded in proceedings under these Regulations against a person under the direction and control of the chief officer of police;

    (b) any costs or expenses incurred and not recovered by such a person in such proceedings; and

    (c) any sum required in connection with the settlement of a claim that has or might have given rise to such proceedings.

(6) Paragraphs (1) and (2) apply to a police cadet and appointment as a police cadet as they apply to a constable and the office of constable.

(7) Subject to paragraph (8), in this regulation –

"chief officer of police" –

    (a) in relation to a person appointed, or an appointment falling to be made, under a specified Act, has the same meaning as in the Police Act 1996,

    (b) in relation to a person appointed, or an appointment falling to be made, under section 9(1)(b) or 55(1)(b) of the Police Act 1997 (police members of the National Criminal Intelligence Service and the National Crime Squad) means the Director General of the National Criminal Intelligence Service or, as the case may be, the Director General of the National Crime Squad,

    (c) in relation to a person appointed, or an appointment falling to be made, under the Police (Scotland) Act 1967, means the chief constable of the relevant police force,

    (d) in relation to any other person or appointment means the officer or other person who has the direction and control of the body of constables or cadets in question;

"police authority" –

    (a) in relation to a person appointed, or an appointment falling to be made, under a specified Act, has the same meaning as in the Police Act 1996,

    (b) in relation to a person appointed, or an appointment falling to be made, under section 9(1)(b) or 55(1)(b) of the Police Act 1997, means the Service Authority for the National Criminal Intelligence Service or, as the case may be, the Service Authority for the National Crime Squad,

(c) in relation to a person appointed, or an appointment falling to be made, under the Police (Scotland) Act 1967, has the meaning given in that Act,

(d) in relation to any other person or appointment, means the authority by whom the person in question is or on appointment would be paid;

"police cadet" means any person appointed to undergo training with a view to becoming a constable;

"police fund"–

(a) in relation to a chief officer of police within sub-paragraph (a) of the above definition of that term, has the same meaning as in the Police Act 1996,

(b) in relation to a chief officer of police within sub-paragraph (b) of that definition, means the service fund established under section 16 or (as the case may be) section 61 of the Police Act 1997,

(c) in any other case means money provided by the police authority; and

"specified Act" means the Metropolitan Police Act 1829, the City of London Police Act 1839 or the Police Act 1996.

(8) In relation to a constable of a force who is not under the direction and control of the chief officer of police for that force, references in this regulation to the chief officer of police are references to the chief officer of the force under whose direction and control he is, and references in this regulation to the police authority are references to the relevant police authority for that force.

Barristers

30-013   **12.**—(1) It is unlawful for a barrister or barrister's clerk, in relation to any offer of a pupillage or tenancy, to discriminate against a person–

(a) in the arrangements which are made for the purpose of determining to whom the pupillage or tenancy should be offered;

(b) in respect of any terms on which it is offered; or

(c) by refusing, or deliberately not offering, it to him.

(2) It is unlawful for a barrister or barrister's clerk, in relation to a pupil or tenant in the set of chambers in question, to discriminate against him–

(a) in respect of any terms applicable to him as a pupil or tenant;

(b) in the opportunities for training, or gaining experience, which are afforded or denied to him;

(c) in the benefits which are afforded or denied to him; or

(d) by terminating his pupillage, or by subjecting him to any pressure to leave the chambers or other detriment.

(3) It is unlawful for a barrister or barrister's clerk, in relation to a pupillage or tenancy in the set of chambers in question, to subject to harassment a person who is, or has applied to be, a pupil or tenant.

(4) It is unlawful for any person, in relation to the giving, withholding or acceptance of instructions to a barrister, to discriminate against any person by subjecting him to a detriment, or to subject him to harassment.

(5) In this regulation–

"barrister's clerk" includes any person carrying out any of the functions of a barrister's clerk;

"pupil", "pupillage" and "set of chambers" have the meanings commonly associated with their use in the context of barristers practising in independent practice; and "tenancy" and "tenant" have the meanings commonly associated with their use in the context of barristers practising in independent practice, but also include reference to any barrister permitted to work in a set of chambers who is not a tenant.

(6) This regulation extends to England and Wales only.

Advocates

13.—(1) It is unlawful for an advocate, in relation to taking any person as his **30-014** pupil, to discriminate against a person –

(a) in the arrangements which he makes for the purpose of determining whom he will take as his pupil;

(b) in respect of any terms on which he offers to take any person as his pupil; or

(c) by refusing to take, or deliberately not taking, a person as his pupil.

(2) It is unlawful for an advocate, in relation to a person who is his pupil, to discriminate against him –

(a) in respect of any terms applicable to him as a pupil;

(b) in the opportunities for training, or gaining experience, which are afforded or denied to him;

(c) in the benefits which are afforded or denied to him; or

(d) by terminating the relationship, or by subjecting him to any pressure to terminate the relationship or other detriment.

(3) It is unlawful for an advocate, in relation to a person who is his pupil or taking any person as his pupil, to subject such a person to harassment.

(4) It is unlawful for any person, in relation to the giving, withholding or acceptance of instructions to an advocate, to discriminate against any person by subjecting him to a detriment, or to subject him to harassment.

(5) In this regulation –

"advocate" means a member of the Faculty of Advocates practising as such; and

"pupil" has the meaning commonly associated with its use in the context of a person training to be an advocate.

(6) This regulation extends to Scotland only.

Partnerships

14.—(1) It is unlawful for a firm, in relation to a position as partner in the **30-015** firm, to discriminate against a person –

(a) in the arrangements they make for the purpose of determining to whom they should offer that position;

(b) in the terms on which they offer him that position;

(c) by refusing to offer, or deliberately not offering, him that position; or

(d) in a case where the person already holds that position –

(i) in the way they afford him access to any benefits or by refusing to afford, or deliberately not affording, him access to them, or

(ii) by expelling him from that position, or subjecting him to any other detriment.

(2) It is unlawful for a firm, in relation to a position as partner in the firm, to subject to harassment a person who holds or has applied for that position.

(3) Paragraphs (1)(a) to (c) and (2) apply in relation to persons proposing to form themselves into a partnership as they apply in relation to a firm.

(4) Paragraph (1) does not apply to any act in relation to a position as partner where, if the position were employment, that act would be lawful by virtue of regulation 7 (exception for genuine occupational requirement etc).

(5) In the case of a limited partnership references in this regulation to a partner shall be construed as references to a general partner as defined in section 3 of the Limited Partnerships Act 1907.

(6) This regulation applies to a limited liability partnership as it applies to a firm; and, in its application to a limited liability partnership, references to a partner in a firm are references to a member of the limited liability partnership.

(7) In this regulation, "firm" has the meaning given by section 4 of the Partnership Act 1890.

(8) In paragraph (1)(d) reference to the expulsion of a person from a position as partner includes reference–

  (a) to the termination of that person's partnership by the expiration of any period (including a period expiring by reference to an event or circumstance), not being a termination immediately after which the partnership is renewed on the same terms; and

  (b) to the termination of that person's partnership by any act of his (including the giving of notice) in circumstances such that he is entitled to terminate it without notice by reason of the conduct of the other partners.

Trade organisations

30-016   **15.**—(1) It is unlawful for a trade organisation to discriminate against a person–

  (a) in the terms on which it is prepared to admit him to membership of the organisation; or

  (b) by refusing to accept, or deliberately not accepting, his application for membership.

(2) It is unlawful for a trade organisation, in relation to a member of the organisation, to discriminate against him–

  (a) in the way it affords him access to any benefits or by refusing or deliberately omitting to afford him access to them;

  (b) by depriving him of membership, or varying the terms on which he is a member; or

  (c) by subjecting him to any other detriment.

(3) It is unlawful for a trade organisation, in relation to a person's membership or application for membership of that organisation, to subject that person to harassment.

(4) In this regulation–

  "trade organisation" means an organisation of workers, an organisation of employers, or any other organisation whose members carry on a particular profession or trade for the purposes of which the organisation exists;

  "profession" includes any vocation or occupation; and

  "trade" includes any business.

Qualifications bodies

30-017   **16.**—(1) It is unlawful for a qualifications body to discriminate against a person–

  (a) in the terms on which it is prepared to confer a professional or trade qualification on him;

    (b) by refusing or deliberately not granting any application by him for such a qualification; or

    (c) by withdrawing such a qualification from him or varying the terms on which he holds it.

(2) It is unlawful for a qualifications body, in relation to a professional or trade qualification conferred by it, to subject to harassment a person who holds or applies for such a qualification.

(3) Paragraph (1) does not apply to a professional or trade qualification for purposes of an organised religion where a requirement related to sexual orientation is applied to the qualification so as to comply with the doctrines of the religion or avoid conflicting with the strongly held religious convictions of a significant number of the religion's followers.

(4) In this regulation—

    "qualifications body" means any authority or body which can confer a professional or trade qualification, but it does not include—

        (a) an educational establishment to which regulation 20 (institutions of further and higher education) applies, or would apply but for the operation of any other provision of these Regulations, or

        (b) a school;

    "confer" includes renew or extend;

    "professional or trade qualification" means any authorisation, qualification, recognition, registration, enrolment, approval or certification which is needed for, or facilitates engagement in, a particular profession or trade;

    "profession" and "trade" have the same meaning as in regulation 15.

Providers of vocational training

17.—(1) It is unlawful, in relation to a person seeking or undergoing training **30-018** which would help fit him for any employment, for any training provider to discriminate against him—

    (a) in the terms on which the training provider affords him access to any training;

    (b) by refusing or deliberately not affording him such access;

    (c) by terminating his training; or

    (d) by subjecting him to any other detriment during his training.

(2) It is unlawful for a training provider, in relation to a person seeking or undergoing training which would help fit him for any employment, to subject him to harassment.

(3) Paragraph (1) does not apply if the discrimination only concerns training for employment which, by virtue of regulation 7 (exception for genuine occupational requirement etc), the employer could lawfully refuse to offer the person seeking training.

(4) In this regulation—

    "training" includes—

        (a) facilities for training; and

        (b) practical work experience provided by an employer to a person whom he does not employ;

    "training provider" means any person who provides, or makes arrangements for the provision of, training which would help fit another person for any employment, but it does not include—

        (a) an employer in relation to training for persons employed by him;

(b) an educational establishment to which regulation 20 (institutions of further and higher education) applies, or would apply but for the operation of any other provision of these Regulations; or

(c) a school.

Employment agencies, careers guidance etc

30-019   **18.**—(1) It is unlawful for an employment agency to discriminate against a person—

(a) in the terms on which the agency offers to provide any of its services;

(b) by refusing or deliberately not providing any of its services; or

(c) in the way it provides any of its services.

(2) It is unlawful for an employment agency, in relation to a person to whom it provides its services, or who has requested it to provide its services, to subject that person to harassment.

(3) Paragraph (1) does not apply to discrimination if it only concerns employment which, by virtue of regulation 7 (exception for genuine occupational requirement etc), the employer could lawfully refuse to offer the person in question.

(4) An employment agency shall not be subject to any liability under this regulation if it proves that—

(a) it acted in reliance on a statement made to it by the employer to the effect that, by reason of the operation of paragraph (3), its action would not be unlawful, and

(b) it was reasonable for it to rely on the statement.

(5) A person who knowingly or recklessly makes a statement such as is referred to in paragraph (4)(a) which in a material respect is false or misleading commits an offence, and shall be liable on summary conviction to a fine not exceeding level 5 on the standard scale.

(6) For the purposes of this regulation—

(a) "employment agency" means a person who, for profit or not, provides services for the purpose of finding employment for workers or supplying employers with workers, but it does not include—

(i) an educational establishment to which regulation 20 (institutions of further and higher education) applies, or would apply but for the operation of any other provision of these Regulations, or

(ii) a school; and

(b) references to the services of an employment agency include guidance on careers and any other services related to employment.

Assisting persons to obtain employment etc

30-020   **19.**—(1) It is unlawful for the Secretary of State to discriminate against any person by subjecting him to a detriment, or to subject a person to harassment, in the provision of facilities or services under section 2 of the Employment and Training Act 1973 (arrangements for assisting persons to obtain employment).

(2) It is unlawful for Scottish Enterprise or Highlands and Islands Enterprise to discriminate against any person by subjecting him to a detriment, or to subject a person to harassment, in the provision of facilities or services under such arrangements as are mentioned in section 2(3) of the Enterprise and New Towns (Scotland) Act 1990 (arrangements analogous to arrangements in pursuance of the said Act of 1973).

(3) This regulation does not apply in a case where—

(a) regulation 17 (providers of vocational training) applies, or would apply but for the operation of any other provision of these Regulations, or

(b) the Secretary of State is acting as an employment agency within the meaning of regulation 18.

Institutions of further and higher education

20.—(1) It is unlawful, in relation to an educational establishment to which **30-021** this regulation applies, for the governing body of that establishment to discriminate against a person—

(a) in the terms on which it offers to admit him to the establishment as a student;

(b) by refusing or deliberately not accepting an application for his admission to the establishment as a student; or

(c) where he is a student of the establishment—

  (i) in the way it affords him access to any benefits,

  (ii) by refusing or deliberately not affording him access to them, or

  (iii) by excluding him from the establishment or subjecting him to any other detriment.

(2) It is unlawful, in relation to an educational establishment to which this regulation applies, for the governing body of that establishment to subject to harassment a person who is a student at the establishment, or who has applied for admission to the establishment as a student.

(3) Paragraph (1) does not apply if the discrimination only concerns training which would help fit a person for employment which, by virtue of regulation 7 (exception for genuine occupational requirement etc), the employer could lawfully refuse to offer the person in question.

(4) This regulation applies to the following educational establishments in England and Wales, namely—

(a) an institution within the further education sector (within the meaning of section 91(3) of the Further and Higher Education Act 1992);

(b) a university;

(c) an institution, other than a university, within the higher education sector (within the meaning of section 91(5) of the Further and Higher Education Act 1992).

(5) This regulation applies to the following educational establishments in Scotland, namely—

(a) a college of further education within the meaning of section 36(1) of the Further and Higher Education (Scotland) Act 1992 under the management of a board of management within the meaning of Part I of that Act;

(b) a college of further education maintained by an education authority in the exercise of its further education functions in providing courses of further education within the meaning of section 1(5)(b)(ii) of the Education (Scotland) Act 1980;

(c) any other educational establishment (not being a school) which provides further education within the meaning of section 1 of the Further and Higher Education (Scotland) Act 1992;

(d) an institution within the higher education sector (within the meaning of Part II of the Further and Higher Education (Scotland) Act 1992);

(e) a central institution (within the meaning of section 135 of the Education (Scotland) Act 1980).

(6) In this regulation—

"education authority" has the meaning given by section 135(1) of the Education (Scotland) Act 1980;

"governing body" includes –

(a) the board of management of a college referred to in paragraph (5)(a), and

(b) the managers of a college or institution referred to in paragraph (5)(b) or (e);

"student" means any person who receives education at an educational establishment to which this regulation applies; and

"university" includes a university college and the college, school or hall of a university.

Relationships which have come to an end

30-022   **21.**—(1) In this regulation a "relevant relationship" is a relationship during the course of which an act of discrimination against, or harassment of, one party to the relationship ("B") by the other party to it ("A") is unlawful by virtue of any preceding provision of this Part.

(2) Where a relevant relationship has come to an end, it is unlawful for A –

(a) to discriminate against B by subjecting him to a detriment; or

(b) to subject B to harassment,

where the discrimination or harassment arises out of and is closely connected to that relationship.

(3) In paragraph (1), reference to an act of discrimination or harassment which is unlawful includes, in the case of a relationship which has come to an end before the coming into force of these Regulations, reference to an act of discrimination or harassment which would, after the coming into force of these Regulations, be unlawful.

PART III

OTHER UNLAWFUL ACTS

Liability of employers and principals

30-023   **22.**—(1) Anything done by a person in the course of his employment shall be treated for the purposes of these Regulations as done by his employer as well as by him, whether or not it was done with the employer's knowledge or approval.

(2) Anything done by a person as agent for another person with the authority (whether express or implied, and whether precedent or subsequent) of that other person shall be treated for the purposes of these Regulations as done by that other person as well as by him.

(3) In proceedings brought under these Regulations against any person in respect of an act alleged to have been done by an employee of his it shall be a defence for that person to prove that he took such steps as were reasonably practicable to prevent the employee from doing that act, or from doing in the course of his employment acts of that description.

Aiding unlawful acts

30-024   **23.**—(1) A person who knowingly aids another person to do an act made unlawful by these Regulations shall be treated for the purpose of these Regulations as himself doing an unlawful act of the like description.

(2) For the purposes of paragraph (1) an employee or agent for whose act the employer or principal is liable under regulation 22 (or would be so liable but for regulation 22(3)) shall be deemed to aid the doing of the act by the employer or principal.

(3) A person does not under this regulation knowingly aid another to do an unlawful act if –

    (a) he acts in reliance on a statement made to him by that other person that, by reason of any provision of these Regulations, the act which he aids would not be unlawful; and

    (b) it is reasonable for him to rely on the statement.

(4) A person who knowingly or recklessly makes a statement such as is referred to in paragraph (3)(a) which in a material respect is false or misleading commits an offence, and shall be liable on summary conviction to a fine not exceeding level 5 on the standard scale.

PART IV

GENERAL EXCEPTIONS FROM PARTS II AND III

Exception for national security

24. Nothing in Part II or III shall render unlawful an act done for the **30-025** purpose of safeguarding national security, if the doing of the act was justified by that purpose.

Exception for benefits dependent on marital status

25. Nothing in Part II or III shall render unlawful anything which prevents **30-026** or restricts access to a benefit by reference to marital status.

Exceptions for positive action

26.—(1) Nothing in Part II or III shall render unlawful any act done in or in **30-027** connection with –

    (a) affording persons of a particular sexual orientation access to facilities for training which would help fit them for particular work; or

    (b) encouraging persons of a particular sexual orientation to take advantage of opportunities for doing particular work,

where it reasonably appears to the person doing the act that it prevents or compensates for disadvantages linked to sexual orientation suffered by persons of that sexual orientation doing that work or likely to take up that work.

(2) Nothing in Part II or III shall render unlawful any act done by a trade organisation within the meaning of regulation 15 in or in connection with –

    (a) affording only members of the organisation who are of a particular sexual orientation access to facilities for training which would help fit them for holding a post of any kind in the organisation; or

    (b) encouraging only members of the organisation who are of a particular sexual orientation to take advantage of opportunities for holding such posts in the organisation,

where it reasonably appears to the organisation that the act prevents or compensates for disadvantages linked to sexual orientation suffered by those of that sexual orientation holding such posts or likely to hold such posts.

(3) Nothing in Part II or III shall render unlawful any act done by a trade organisation within the meaning of regulation 15 in or in connection with

encouraging only persons of a particular sexual orientation to become members of the organisation where it reasonably appears to the organisation that the act prevents or compensates for disadvantages linked to sexual orientation suffered by persons of that sexual orientation who are, or are eligible to become, members.

PART V

ENFORCEMENT

Restriction of proceedings for breach of Regulations

30-028   **27.**—(1) Except as provided by these Regulations no proceedings, whether civil or criminal, shall lie against any person in respect of an act by reason that the act is unlawful by virtue of a provision of these Regulations.

(2) Paragraph (1) does not prevent the making of an application for judicial review [or the investigation or determination of any matter in accordance with Part X (investigations: the Pensions Ombudsman) of the Pension Schemes Act 1993 by the Pensions Ombudsman][1].

Jurisdiction of employment tribunals

30-029   **28.**—(1) A complaint by any person ("the complainant") that another person ("the respondent")–

(a) has committed against the complainant an act to which this regulation applies; or

(b) is by virtue of regulation 22 (liability of employers and principals) or 23 (aiding unlawful acts) to be treated as having committed against the complainant such an act,

may be presented to an employment tribunal.

(2) This regulation applies to any act of discrimination or harassment which is unlawful by virtue of any provision of Part II other than–

(a) where the act is one in respect of which an appeal or proceedings in the nature of an appeal may be brought under any enactment, regulation 16 (qualifications bodies);

(b) regulation 20 (institutions of further and higher education); or

(c) where the act arises out of and is closely connected to a relationship between the complainant and the respondent which has come to an end but during the course of which an act of discrimination against, or harassment of, the complainant by the respondent would have been unlawful by virtue of regulation 20, regulation 21 (relationships which have come to an end).

(3) In paragraph (2)(c), reference to an act of discrimination or harassment which would have been unlawful includes, in the case of a relationship which has come to an end before the coming into force of these Regulations, reference to an act of discrimination or harassment which would, after the coming into force of these Regulations, have been unlawful.

(4) In this regulation, "enactment" includes an enactment comprised in, or in an instrument made under, an Act of the Scottish Parliament.

---

[1] Words inserted by SI 2003/2827 reg 3 (4)

Burden of proof: employment tribunals

29.—(1) This regulation applies to any complaint presented under regulation **30-030** 28 to an employment tribunal.

(2) Where, on the hearing of the complaint, the complainant proves facts from which the tribunal could, apart from this regulation, conclude in the absence of an adequate explanation that the respondent—

   (a) has committed against the complainant an act to which regulation 28 applies; or

   (b) is by virtue of regulation 22 (liability of employers and principals) or 23 (aiding unlawful acts) to be treated as having committed against the complainant such an act,

the tribunal shall uphold the complaint unless the respondent proves that he did not commit, or as the case may be, is not to be treated as having committed, that act.

Remedies on complaints in employment tribunals

30.—(1) Where an employment tribunal finds that a complaint presented to **30-031** it under regulation 28 is well-founded, the tribunal shall make such of the following as it considers just and equitable—

   (a) an order declaring the rights of the complainant and the respondent in relation to the act to which the complaint relates;

   (b) an order requiring the respondent to pay to the complainant compensation of an amount corresponding to any damages he could have been ordered by a county court or by a sheriff court to pay to the complainant if the complaint had fallen to be dealt with under regulation 31 (jurisdiction of county and sheriff courts);

   (c) a recommendation that the respondent take within a specified period action appearing to the tribunal to be practicable for the purpose of obviating or reducing the adverse effect on the complainant of any act of discrimination or harassment to which the complaint relates.

(2) As respects an unlawful act of discrimination falling within regulation 3(1)(b), if the respondent proves that the provision, criterion or practice was not applied with the intention of treating the complainant unfavourably on grounds of sexual orientation, an order may be made under paragraph (1)(b) only if the employment tribunal—

   (a) makes such order under paragraph (1)(a) (if any) and such recommendation under paragraph (1)(c) (if any) as it would have made if it had no power to make an order under paragraph (1)(b); and

   (b) (where it makes an order under paragraph (1)(a) or a recommendation under paragraph (1)(c) or both) considers that it is just and equitable to make an order under paragraph (1)(b) as well.

(3) If without reasonable justification the respondent to a complaint fails to comply with a recommendation made by an employment tribunal under paragraph (1)(c), then, if it thinks it just and equitable to do so—

   (a) the tribunal may increase the amount of compensation required to be paid to the complainant in respect of the complaint by an order made under paragraph (1)(b); or

   (b) if an order under paragraph (1)(b) was not made, the tribunal may make such an order.

(4) Where an amount of compensation falls to be awarded under paragraph (1)(b), the tribunal may include in the award interest on that amount subject to,

and in accordance with, the provisions of the Employment Tribunals (Interest on Awards in Discrimination Cases) Regulations 1996.

[(5) This regulation has effect subject to paragraph 7 of Schedule 1A (occupational pension schemes).][1]

The Employment Act 2002 (Dispute Resolution) Regulations 2004

Whereas a draft of these Regulations was laid before Parliament in accordance with section 51 (4) of the Employment Act 2002 and approved by a resolution of each House of Parliament: Now, therefore, the Secretary of State, in exercise of the powers conferred on her by sections 31 (6), 32 (7), 33 and 51 (1) (a) and (b) of that Act, hereby makes the following Regulations:

(S.I. 752)

Citation and Commencement

31-001   1. These Regulations may be cited as the Employment Act 2002 (Dispute Resolution) Regulations 2004 and shall come into force on 1st October 2004.

Interpretation

31-002   2.—(1) In these Regulations–
"the 1992 Act" means the Trade Union and Labour Relations (Consolidation) Act 1992;
"the 1996 Act" means the Employment Rights Act 1996;
"the 1999 Act" means the Employment Relations Act 1999;
"the 2002 Act" means the Employment Act 2002;
"action" means any act or omission;
"applicable statutory procedure" means the statutory procedure that applies in relation to a particular case by virtue of these Regulations;
"collective agreement" has the meaning given to it by section 178(1) of the 1992 Act;
"dismissal and disciplinary procedures" means the statutory procedures set out in Part 1 of Schedule 2;
"dismissed" has the meaning given to it in section 95(1)(a) and (b) of the 1996 Act;
"employers association" has the meaning given to it by section 122 of the 1992 Act;
"grievance" means a complaint by an employee about action which his employer has taken or is contemplating taking in relation to him;
"grievance procedures" means the statutory procedures set out in Part 2 of Schedule 2;
"independent trade union" has the meaning given to it by section 5 of the 1992 Act;

---

[1] Inserted by SI 2003/2827 reg 3 (5)

"modified dismissal procedure" means the procedure set out in Chapter 2 of Part 1 of Schedule 2;

"modified grievance procedure" means the procedure set out in Chapter 2 of Part 2 of Schedule 2;

"non-completion" of a statutory procedure includes non-commencement of such a procedure except where the term is used in relation to the non-completion of an identified requirement of a procedure or to circumstances where a procedure has already been commenced;

"party" means the employer or the employee;

"relevant disciplinary action" means action, short of dismissal, which the employer asserts to be based wholly or mainly on the employees conduct or capability, other than suspension on full pay or the issuing of warnings (whether oral or written);

"standard dismissal and disciplinary procedure" means the procedure set out in Chapter 1 of Part 1 of Schedule 2;

"standard grievance procedure" means the procedure set out in Chapter 1 of Part 2 of Schedule 2;

and a reference to a Schedule is a reference to a Schedule to the 2002 Act.

(2) In determining whether a meeting or written communication fulfils a requirement of Schedule 2, it is irrelevant whether the meeting or communication deals with any other matter (including a different matter required to be dealt with in a meeting or communication intended to fulfil a requirement of Schedule 2).

Application of dismissal and disciplinary procedures

3.—(1) Subject to paragraph (2) and regulation 4, the standard dismissal and **31-003** disciplinary procedure applies when an employer contemplates dismissing or taking relevant disciplinary action against an employee.

(2) Subject to regulation 4, the modified dismissal procedure applies in relation to a dismissal where—

(a) the employer dismissed the employee by reason of his conduct without notice,

(b) the dismissal occurred at the time the employer became aware of the conduct or immediately thereafter,

(c) the employer was entitled, in the circumstances, to dismiss the employee by reason of his conduct without notice or any payment in lieu of notice, and

(d) it was reasonable for the employer, in the circumstances, to dismiss the employee before enquiring into the circumstances in which the conduct took place,

but neither of the dismissal and disciplinary procedures applies in relation to such a dismissal where the employee presents a complaint relating to the dismissal to an employment tribunal at a time when the employer has not complied with paragraph 4 of Schedule 2.

Dismissals to which the dismissal and disciplinary procedures do not apply

4.—(1) Neither of the dismissal and disciplinary procedures applies in **31-004** relation to the dismissal of an employee where—

(a) all the employees of a description or in a category to which the employee belongs are dismissed, provided that the employer offers to re-engage all the employees so dismissed either before or upon the termination of their contracts;

(b) the dismissal is one of a number of dismissals in respect of which the duty in section 188 of the 1992 Act (duty of employer to consult representatives when proposing to dismiss as redundant a certain number of employees) applies;

(c) at the time of the employees dismissal he is taking part in –

    (i) an unofficial strike or other unofficial industrial action, or

    (ii) a strike or other industrial action (being neither unofficial industrial action nor protected industrial action), unless the circumstances of the dismissal are such that, by virtue of section 238(2) of the 1992 Act, an employment tribunal is entitled to determine whether the dismissal was fair or unfair;

(d) the reason (or, if more than one, the principal reason) for the dismissal is that the employee took protected industrial action and the dismissal would be regarded, by virtue of section 238A(2) of the 1992 Act, as unfair for the purposes of Part 10 of the 1996 Act;

(e) the employers business suddenly ceases to function, because of an event unforeseen by the employer, with the result that it is impractical for him to employ any employees;

(f) the reason (or, if more than one principal reason) for the dismissal is that the employee could not continue to work in the position which he held without contravention (either on his part or on that of his employer) of a duty or restriction imposed by or under any enactment; or

(g) the employee is one to whom a dismissal procedures agreement designated by an order under section 110 of the 1996 Act applies at the date of dismissal.

(2) For the purposes of paragraph (1)–

"unofficial" shall be construed in accordance with subsections (2) to (4) of section 237 of the 1992 Act;

"strike" has the meaning given to it by section 246 of the 1992 Act;

"protected industrial action" shall be construed in accordance with section 238A(1) of the 1992 Act;

and an employer shall be regarded as offering to re-engage an employee if that employer, a successor of that employer or an associated employer of that employer offers to re-engage the employee, either in the job which he held immediately before the date of dismissal or in a different job which would be suitable in his case.

Circumstances in which parties are treated as complying with the dismissal and disciplinary procedures

31-005   **5.**—(1) Where–

(a) either of the dismissal and disciplinary procedures is the applicable statutory procedure in relation to a dismissal,

(b) the employee presents an application for interim relief to an employment tribunal pursuant to section 128 of the 1996 Act (interim relief pending determination of complaint) in relation to his dismissal, and

(c) at the time the application is presented, the requirements of paragraphs 1 and 2 or, as the case may be, paragraph 4 of Schedule 2 have been complied with but the requirements of paragraph 3 or 5 of Schedule 2 have not,

the parties shall be treated as having complied with the requirements of paragraph 3 or 5 of Schedule 2.

(2) Where either of the dismissal and disciplinary procedures is the applicable statutory procedure in relation to the dismissal of an employee or to relevant disciplinary action taken against an employee but –
  (a) at the time of the dismissal or the taking of the action an appropriate procedure exists,
  (b) the employee is entitled to appeal under that procedure against his dismissal or the relevant disciplinary action taken against him instead of appealing to his employer, and
  (c) the employee has appealed under that procedure,
the parties shall be treated as having complied with the requirements of paragraph 3 or 5 of Schedule 2.

(3) For the purposes of paragraph (2) a procedure is appropriate if it –
  (a) gives the employee an effective right of appeal against dismissal or disciplinary action taken against him, and
  (b) operates by virtue of a collective agreement made between two or more employers or an employers association and one or more independent trade unions.

Application of the grievance procedures

6.—(1) The grievance procedures apply, in accordance with the paragraphs **31-006** (2) to (7) of this regulation, in relation to any grievance about action by the employer that could form the basis of a complaint by an employee to an employment tribunal under a jurisdiction listed in Schedule 3 or 4, or could do so if the action took place.

(2) Subject to paragraphs (3) to (7), the standard grievance procedure applies in relation to any such grievance.

(3) Subject to paragraphs (4) to (7), the modified grievance procedure applies in relation to a grievance where –
  (a) the employee has ceased to be employed by the employer;
  (b) the employer –
    (i) was unaware of the grievance before the employment ceased, or
    (ii) was so aware but the standard grievance procedure was not commenced or was not completed before the last day of the employees employment; and
  (c) the parties have agreed in writing in relation to the grievance, whether before, on or after that day, but after the employer became aware of the grievance, that the modified procedure should apply.

(4) Neither of the grievance procedures applies where –
  (a) the employee has ceased to be employed by the employer;
  (b) neither procedure has been commenced; and
  (c) since the employee ceased to be employed it has ceased to be reasonably practicable for him to comply with paragraph 6 or 9 of Schedule 2.

(5) Neither of the grievance procedures applies where the grievance is that the employer has dismissed or is contemplating dismissing the employee.

(6) Neither of the grievance procedures applies where the grievance is that the employer has taken or is contemplating taking relevant disciplinary action against the employee unless one of the reasons for the grievance is a reason mentioned in regulation 7(1).

(7) Neither of the grievance procedures applies where regulation 11(1) applies.

Circumstances in which parties are treated as complying with the grievance procedures

31-007   **7.**—(1) Where the grievance is that the employer has taken or is contemplating taking relevant disciplinary action against the employee and one of the reasons for the grievance is—

(a) that the relevant disciplinary action amounted to or, if it took place, would amount to unlawful discrimination, or

(b) that the grounds on which the employer took the action or is contemplating taking it were or are unrelated to the grounds on which he asserted that he took the action or is asserting that he is contemplating taking it,

the standard grievance procedure or, as the case may be, modified grievance procedure shall apply but the parties shall be treated as having complied with the applicable procedure if the employee complies with the requirement in paragraph (2).

(2) The requirement is that the employee must set out the grievance in a written statement and send the statement or a copy of it to the employer—

(a) where either of the dismissal and disciplinary procedures is being followed, before the meeting referred to in paragraph 3 or 5 (appeals under the dismissal and disciplinary procedures) of Schedule 2, or

(b) where neither of those procedures is being followed, before presenting any complaint arising out of the grievance to an employment tribunal.

(3) In paragraph (1)(a) "unlawful discrimination" means an act or omission in respect of which a right of complaint lies to an employment tribunal under any of the following tribunal jurisdictions (specified in Schedules 3 and 4)—

section 2 of the Equal Pay Act 1970;

section 63 of the Sex Discrimination Act 1975;

section 54 of the Race Relations Act 1976;

section 17A of the Disability Discrimination Act 1995;

regulation 28 of the Employment Equality (Religion or Belief) Regulations 2003;

regulation 28 of the Employment Equality (Sexual Orientation) Regulations 2003.

31-008   **8.**—(1) Where—

(a) the standard grievance procedure is the applicable statutory procedure,

(b) the employee has ceased to be employed by the employer,

(c) paragraph 6 of Schedule 2 has been complied with (whether before or after the end of his employment); and

(d) since the end of his employment it has ceased to be reasonably practicable for the employee, or his employer, to comply with the requirements of paragraph 7 or 8 of Schedule 2,

the parties shall be treated, subject to paragraph (2), as having complied with such of those paragraphs of Schedule 2 as have not been complied with.

(2) In a case where paragraph (1) applies and the requirements of paragraphs 7(1) to (3) of Schedule 2 have been complied with but the requirement in paragraph 7(4) of Schedule 2 has not, the employer shall be treated as having failed to comply with paragraph 7(4) unless he informs the employee in writing of his decision as to his response to the grievance.

9.—(1) Where either of the grievance procedures is the applicable statutory **31-009** procedure, the parties shall be treated as having complied with the requirements of the procedure if a person who is an appropriate representative of the employee having the grievance has –
  (a) written to the employer setting out the grievance; and
  (b) specified in writing to the employer (whether in setting out the grievance or otherwise) the names of at least two employees, of whom one is the employee having the grievance, as being the employees on behalf of whom he is raising the grievance.

(2) For the purposes of paragraph (1), a person is an appropriate representative if, at the time he writes to the employer setting out the grievance, he is –
  (a) an official of an independent trade union recognised by the employer for the purposes of collective bargaining in respect of a description of employees that includes the employee having the grievance, or
  (b) an employee of the employer who is an employee representative elected or appointed by employees consisting of or including employees of the same description as the employee having the grievance and who, having regard to the purposes for which and method by which he was elected or appointed, has the authority to represent employees of that description under an established procedure for resolving grievances agreed between employee representatives and the employer.

(3) For the purposes of paragraph (2)(a) the terms "official", "recognised" and "collective bargaining" have the meanings given to them by, respectively, sections 119, 178(3) and 178(1) of the 1992 Act.

Where either of the grievance procedures is the applicable statutory procedure but –
  10. (a) at the time the employee raises his grievance there is a procedure in **31-010** operation, under a collective agreement made between two or more employers or an employers association and one or more independent trade unions, that provides for employees of the employer to raise grievances about the behaviour of the employer and have them considered, and
  (b) the employee is entitled to raise his grievance under that procedure and does so,
the parties shall be treated as having complied with the applicable statutory procedure.

General circumstances in which the statutory procedures do not apply or are treated as being complied with

11.—(1) Where the circumstances specified in paragraph (3) apply and in con- **31-011** sequence the employer or employee does not commence the procedure that would otherwise be the applicable statutory procedure (by complying with paragraph 1, 4, 6 or 9 of Schedule 2), the procedure does not apply.

(2) Where the applicable statutory procedure has been commenced, but the circumstances specified in paragraph (3) apply and in consequence a party does not comply with a subsequent requirement of the procedure, the parties shall be treated as having complied with the procedure.

(3) The circumstances referred to in paragraphs (1) and (2) are that –
  (a) the party has reasonable grounds to believe that commencing the procedure or complying with the subsequent requirement would result

in a significant threat to himself, his property, any other person or the property of any other person;

(b) the party has been subjected to harassment and has reasonable grounds to believe that commencing the procedure or complying with the subsequent requirement would result in his being subjected to further harassment; or

(c) it is not practicable for the party to commence the procedure or comply with the subsequent requirement within a reasonable period.

(4) In paragraph (3)(b), "harassment" means conduct which has the purpose or effect of –

(a) violating the persons dignity, or

(b) creating an intimidating, hostile, degrading, humiliating or offensive environment for him,

but conduct shall only be regarded as having that purpose or effect if, having regard to all the circumstances, including in particular the perception of the person who was the subject of the conduct, it should reasonably be considered as having that purpose or effect.

Failure to comply with the statutory procedures

31-012　　**12.**—(1) If either party fails to comply with a requirement of an applicable statutory procedure, including a general requirement contained in Part 3 of Schedule 2, then, subject to paragraph (2), the non-completion of the procedure shall be attributable to that party and neither party shall be under any obligation to comply with any further requirement of the procedure.

(2) Except as mentioned in paragraph (4), where the parties are to be treated as complying with the applicable statutory procedure, or any requirement of it, there is no failure to comply with the procedure or requirement.

(3) Notwithstanding that if regulation 11(1) applies the procedure that would otherwise be the applicable statutory procedure does not apply, where that regulation applies because the circumstances in sub-paragraph (a) or (b) of regulation 11(3) apply and it was the behaviour of one of the parties that resulted in those circumstances applying, that party shall be treated as if –

(a) the procedure had applied, and

(b) there had been a failure to comply with a requirement of the procedure that was attributable to him.

(4) In a case where regulation 11(2) applies in relation to a requirement of the applicable statutory procedure because the circumstances in sub-paragraph (a) or (b) of regulation 11(3) apply, and it was the behaviour of one of the parties that resulted in those circumstances applying, the fact that the requirement was not complied with shall be treated as being a failure, attributable to that party, to comply with a requirement of the procedure.

Failure to attend a meeting

31-013　　**13.**—(1) Without prejudice to regulation 11(2) and (3)(c), if it is not reasonably practicable for –

(a) the employee, or, if he is exercising his right under section 10 of the 1999 Act (right to be accompanied), his companion; or

(b) the employer,

to attend a meeting organised in accordance with the applicable statutory procedure for a reason which was not foreseeable when the meeting was arranged, the employee or, as the case may be, employer shall not be treated as having failed to comply with that requirement of the procedure.

(2) In the circumstances set out in paragraph (1), the employer shall continue to be under the duty in the applicable statutory procedure to invite the employee to attend a meeting and, where the employee is exercising his rights under section 10 of the 1999 Act and the employee proposes an alternative time under subsection (4) of that section, the employer shall be under a duty to invite the employee to attend a meeting at that time.

(3) The duty to invite the employee to attend a meeting referred to in paragraph (2) shall cease if the employer has invited the employee to attend two meetings and paragraph (1) applied in relation to each of them.

(4) Where the duty in paragraph (2) has ceased as a result of paragraph (3), the parties shall be treated as having complied with the applicable statutory procedure.

Questions to obtain information not to constitute statement of grievance

14.—(1) Where a person aggrieved questions a respondent under any of the **31-014** provisions set out in paragraph (2), those questions shall not constitute a statement of grievance under paragraph 6 or 9 of Schedule 2.

(2) The provisions referred to in paragraph (1) are –
> section 7B of the Equal Pay Act 1970;
> section 74 of the Sex Discrimination Act 1975;
> section 65 of the Race Relations Act 1976;
> section 56 of the Disability Discrimination Act 1995;
> regulation 33 of the Employment Equality (Religion or Belief) Regulations 2003;
> regulation 33 of the Employment Equality (Sexual Orientation) Regulations 2003.

Extension of time limits

15.—(1) Where a complaint is presented to an employment tribunal under a **31-015** jurisdiction listed in Schedule 3 or 4 and –
> (a) either of the dismissal and disciplinary procedures is the applicable statutory procedure and the circumstances specified in paragraph (2) apply; or
> (b) either of the grievance procedures is the applicable statutory procedure and the circumstances specified in paragraph (3) apply;

the normal time limit for presenting the complaint is extended for a period of three months beginning with the day after the day on which it would otherwise have expired.

(2) The circumstances referred to in paragraph (1)(a) are that the employee presents a complaint to the tribunal after the expiry of the normal time limit for presenting the complaint but had reasonable grounds for believing, when that time limit expired, that a dismissal or disciplinary procedure, whether statutory or otherwise (including an appropriate procedure for the purposes of regulation 5(2)), was being followed in respect of matters that consisted of or included the substance of the tribunal complaint.

(3) The circumstances referred to in paragraph (1)(b) are that the employee presents a complaint to the tribunal –
> (a) within the normal time limit for presenting the complaint but in circumstances in which section 32(2) or (3) of the 2002 Act does not permit him to do so; or

(b) after the expiry of the normal time limit for presenting the complaint, having complied with paragraph 6 or 9 of Schedule 2 in relation to his grievance within that normal time limit.

(4) For the purposes of paragraph (3) and section 32 of the 2002 Act the following acts shall be treated, in a case to which the specified regulation applies, as constituting compliance with paragraph 6 or 9 of Schedule 2–

(a) in a case to which regulation 7(1) applies, compliance by the employee with the requirement in regulation 7(2);

(b) in a case to which regulation 9(1) applies, compliance by the appropriate representative with the requirement in sub-paragraph (a) or (b) of that regulation, whichever is the later; and

(c) in a case to which regulation 10 applies, the raising of his grievance by the employee in accordance with the procedure referred to in that regulation.

(5) In this regulation "the normal time limit" means–

(a) subject to sub-paragraph (b), the period within which a complaint under the relevant jurisdiction must be presented if there is to be no need for the tribunal, in order to be entitled to consider it to–

(i) exercise any discretion, or

(ii) make any determination as to whether it is required to consider the complaint, that the tribunal would have to exercise or make in order to consider a complaint presented outside that period; and

(b) in relation to claims brought under the Equal Pay Act 1970, the period ending on the date on or before which proceedings must be instituted in accordance with section 2(4) of that Act.

National security

31-016   Where it would not be possible to comply with an applicable statutory procedure without disclosing information the disclosure of which would be contrary to the interests of national security, nothing in these Regulations requires either party to comply with that procedure.

Amendments to secondary legislation

31-017   **16.** The statutory instruments referred to in this regulation shall be amended as follows–

17. (a) in the Sex Discrimination (Questions and Replies) Order 1975, for paragraph (a) of article 5 there shall be substituted–

(a) where it was served before a complaint had been presented to a tribunal, if it was so served–

(i) within the period of three months beginning when the act complained of was done; or

(ii) where the period under section 76 of the Act within which proceedings must be brought is extended by regulation 15 of the Employment Act 2002 (Dispute Resolution) Regulations 2004, within that extended period;

(b) in the Race Relations (Questions and Replies) Order 1977, for paragraph (a) of article 5 there shall be substituted–

(a) where it was served before a complaint had been presented to a tribunal, if it was so served–

(i) within the period of three months beginning when the act complained of was done; or

(ii) where the period under section 68 of the Act within which proceedings must be brought is extended by regulation 15 of the Employment Act 2002 (Dispute Resolution) Regulations 2004, within that extended period;

(c) in article 7 of the Employment Tribunals Extension of Jurisdiction (England and Wales) Order 1994, after paragraph (b) there shall be inserted –

    (ba) where the period within which a complaint must be presented in accordance with paragraph (a) or (b) is extended by regulation 15 of the Employment Act 2002 (Dispute Resolution)Regulations 2004, the period within which the complaint must be presented shall be the extended period rather than the period in paragraph (a) or (b).

(d) in article 7 of the Employment Tribunals Extension of Jurisdiction (Scotland) Order 1994, after paragraph (b) there shall be inserted –

    (ba) where the period within which a complaint must be presented in accordance with paragraph (a) or (b) is extended by regulation 15 of the Employment Act 2002 (Dispute Resolution) Regulations 2004, the period within which the complaint must be presented shall be the extended period rather than the period in paragraph (a) or (b).

(e) in regulation (2) of the Employment Protection (Continuity of Employment) Regulations 1996, the word "or" at the end of paragraph (d) shall be omitted and after paragraph (e) there shall be inserted –

or

    (f) a decision taken arising out of the use of a statutory dispute resolution procedure contained in Schedule 2 to the Employment Act 2002 in a case where, in accordance with the Employment Act 2002 (Dispute Resolution) Regulations 2004, such a procedure applies.

(f) in regulation 30(2)(b) of the Working Time Regulations 1998, after paragraph (2) there shall be inserted –

(2A) Where the period within which a complaint must be presented in accordance with paragraph (2) is extended by regulation 15 of the Employment Act 2002 (Dispute Resolution) Regulations 2004, the period within which the complaint must be presented shall be the extended period rather than the period in paragraph (2).

(g) in the Employment Equality (Religion or Belief) Regulations 2003 –

    (i) for regulation 33(4)(a) there shall be substituted –

where it was served before a complaint had been presented to a tribunal, if it was so served –

        (i) within the period of three months beginning when the act complained of was done; or

        (ii) where paragraph (1A) of regulation 34 applies, within the extended period;

and

    (ii) in regulation 34, after paragraph (1) there shall be inserted –

(1A) Where the period within which a complaint must be presented in accordance with paragraph (1) is extended by regulation 15 of the Employment Act 2002 (Dispute Resolution) Regulations 2004, the period within which the complaint must be presented shall be the extended period rather than the period in paragraph (1).

and
(h) in the Employment Equality (Sexual Orientation) Regulations 2003–
   (i) for regulation 33(4)(a) there shall be substituted–
where it was served before a complaint had been presented to a tribunal, if it was so served–
     (i) within the period of three months beginning when the act complained of was done; or
     (ii) where paragraph (1A) of regulation 34 applies, within the extended period;
and
   (ii) in regulation 34, after paragraph (1) there shall be inserted–
(1A) Where the period within which a complaint must be presented in accordance with paragraph (1) is extended by regulation 15 of the Employment Act 2002 (Dispute Resolution) Regulations 2004, the period within which the complaint must be presented shall be the extended period rather than the period in paragraph (1).

Transitional Provisions

31-018   These Regulations shall apply–
18. (a) in relation to dismissal and relevant disciplinary action, where the employer first contemplates dismissing or taking such action against the employee after these Regulations come into force; and
(b) in relation to grievances, where the action about which the employee complains occurs or continues after these Regulations come into force,
but shall not apply in relation to a grievance where the action continues after these Regulations come into force if the employee has raised a grievance about the action with the employer before they come into force.

CONSOLIDATED VERSION OF THE TREATY ESTABLISHING THE EUROPEAN COMMUNITY

Part One

Principles

Article 13

A-001

1. Without prejudice to the other provisions of this Treaty and within the limits of the powers conferred by it upon the Community, the Council, acting unanimously on a proposal from the Commission and after consulting the European Parliament, may take appropriate action to combat discrimination based on sex, racial or ethnic origin, religion or belief, disability, age or sexual orientation.

2. By way of derogation from paragraph 1, when the Council adopts Community incentive measures, excluding any harmonisation of the laws and regulations of the Member States, to support action taken by the Member States in order to contribute to the achievement of the objectives referred to in paragraph 1, it shall act in accordance with the procedure referred to in Article 251.

TITLE III

FREE MOVEMENT OF PERSONS, SERVICES AND CAPITAL

Chapter 1

Workers

Article 39

1. Freedom of movement for workers shall be secured within the A-002 Community.

2. Such freedom of movement shall entail the abolition of any discrimination based on nationality between workers of the Member States as regards employment, remuneration and other conditions of work and employment.

3. It shall entail the right, subject to limitations justified on grounds of public policy, public security or public health:

    (a) to accept offers of employment actually made;

    (b) to move freely within the territory of Member States for this purpose;

    (c) to stay in a Member State for the purpose of employment in accordance with the provisions governing the employment of nationals of that State laid down by law, regulation or administrative action;

    (d) to remain in the territory of a Member State after having been employed in that State, subject to conditions which shall be embodied in implementing regulations to be drawn up by the Commission.

4. The provisions of this article shall not apply to employment in the public service.

Chapter 2

Right of establishment

Article 43

A-003   Within the framework of the provisions set out below, restrictions on the freedom of establishment of nationals of a Member State in the territory of another Member State shall be prohibited. Such prohibition shall also apply to restrictions on the setting-up of agencies, branches or subsidiaries by nationals of any Member State established in the territory of any Member State.

Freedom of establishment shall include the right to take up and pursue activities as self-employed persons and to set up and manage undertakings, in particular companies or firms within the meaning of the second paragraph of Article 48, under the conditions laid down for its own nationals by the law of the country where such establishment is effected, subject to the provisions of the chapter relating to capital.

TITLE XI

SOCIAL POLICY, EDUCATION, VOCATIONAL TRAINING AND YOUTH

Chapter 1

Social provisions

Article 136

A-004   The Community and the Member States, having in mind fundamental social rights such as those set out in the European Social Charter signed at Turin on 18 October 1961 and in the 1989 Community Charter of the Fundamental Social Rights of Workers, shall have as their objectives the promotion of employment, improved living and working conditions, so as to make possible their harmonisation while the improvement is being maintained, proper social protection, dialogue between management and labour, the development of human resources with a view to lasting high employment and the combating of exclusion.

To this end the Community and the Member States shall implement measures which take account of the diverse forms of national practices, in particular in the field of contractual relations, and the need to maintain the competitiveness of the Community economy.

They believe that such a development will ensue not only from the functioning of the common market, which will favour the harmonisation of social systems, but also from the procedures provided for in this Treaty and from the approximation of provisions laid down by law, regulation or administrative action.

Article 137

A-005   (1) With a view to achieving the objectives of Article 136, the Community shall support and complement the activities of the Member States in the following fields:

(a) improvement in particular of the working environment to protect workers' health and safety;

(b) working conditions;

(c) social security and social protection of workers;

(d) protection of workers where their employment contract is terminated;

(e) the information and consultation of workers;

(f) representation and collective defence of the interests of workers and employers, including co-determination, subject to paragraph 5;

(g) conditions of employment for third-country nationals legally residing in Community territory;

(h) the integration of persons excluded from the labour market, without prejudice to Article 150;

(i) equality between men and women with regard to labour market opportunities and treatment at work;

(j) the combating of social exclusion;

(k) the modernisation of social protection systems without prejudice to point (c).

(2) To this end, the Council:

(a) may adopt measures designed to encourage cooperation between Member States through initiatives aimed at improving knowledge, developing exchanges of information and best practices, promoting innovative approaches and evaluating experiences, excluding any harmonisation of the laws and regulations of the Member States;

(b) may adopt, in the fields referred to in paragraph 1(a) to (i), by means of directives, minimum requirements for gradual implementation, having regard to the conditions and technical rules obtaining in each of the Member States. Such directives shall avoid imposing administrative, financial and legal constraints in a way which would hold back the creation and development of small and medium-sized undertakings.

The Council shall act in accordance with the procedure referred to in Article 251 after consulting the Economic and Social Committee and the Committee of the Regions, except in the fields referred to in paragraph 1(c), (d), (f) and (g) of this article, where the Council shall act unanimously on a proposal from the Commission, after consulting the European Parliament and the said Committees. The Council, acting unanimously on a proposal from the Commission, after consulting the European Parliament, may decide to render the procedure referred to in Article 251 applicable to paragraph 1(d), (f) and (g) of this article.

(3) A Member State may entrust management and labour, at their joint request, with the implementation of directives adopted pursuant to paragraph 2.

In this case, it shall ensure that, no later than the date on which a directive must be transposed in accordance with Article 249, management and labour have introduced the necessary measures by agreement, the Member State concerned being required to take any necessary measure enabling it at any time to be in a position to guarantee the results imposed by that directive.

(4) The provisions adopted pursuant to this article:

—shall not affect the right of Member States to define the fundamental principles of their social security systems and must not significantly affect the financial equilibrium thereof,

—shall not prevent any Member State from maintaining or introducing more stringent protective measures compatible with this Treaty.

(5) The provisions of this article shall not apply to pay, the right of association, the right to strike or the right to impose lock-outs.

Article 138

A-006   (1) The Commission shall have the task of promoting the consultation of management and labour at Community level and shall take any relevant measure to facilitate their dialogue by ensuring balanced support for the parties.

(2) To this end, before submitting proposals in the social policy field, the Commission shall consult management and labour on the possible direction of Community action.

(3) If, after such consultation, the Commission considers Community action advisable, it shall consult management and labour on the content of the envisaged proposal. Management and labour shall forward to the Commission an opinion or, where appropriate, a recommendation.

(4) On the occasion of such consultation, management and labour may inform the Commission of their wish to initiate the process provided for in Article 139. The duration of the procedure shall not exceed nine months, unless the management and labour concerned and the Commission decide jointly to extend it.

Article 139

A-007   (1) Should management and labour so desire, the dialogue between them at Community level may lead to contractual relations, including agreements.

(2) Agreements concluded at Community level shall be implemented either in accordance with the procedures and practices specific to management and labour and the Member States or, in matters covered by Article 137, at the joint request of the signatory parties, by a Council decision on a proposal from the Commission.

The Council shall act by qualified majority, except where the agreement in question contains one or more provisions relating to one of the areas for which unanimity is required pursuant to Article 137(2). In that case, it shall act unanimously.

Article 140

A-008   (1) With a view to achieving the objectives of Article 136 and without prejudice to the other provisions of this Treaty, the Commission shall encourage cooperation between the Member States and facilitate the coordination of their action in all social policy fields under this chapter, particularly in matters relating to:

—employment,
—labour law and working conditions,
—basic and advanced vocational training,
—social security,
—prevention of occupational accidents and diseases,
—occupational hygiene,
—the right of association and collective bargaining between employers and workers.

To this end, the Commission shall act in close contact with Member States by making studies, delivering opinions and arranging consultations both on problems arising at national level and on those of concern to international organisations.

Before delivering the opinions provided for in this article, the Commission shall consult the Economic and Social Committee.

Article 141

(1) Each Member State shall ensure that the principle of equal pay for male **A-009** and female workers for equal work or work of equal value is applied.

(2) For the purpose of this article, "pay" means the ordinary basic or minimum wage or salary and any other consideration, whether in cash or in kind, which the worker receives directly or indirectly, in respect of his employment, from his employer.

Equal pay without discrimination based on sex means:
  (a) that pay for the same work at piece rates shall be calculated on the basis of the same unit of measurement;
  (b) that pay for work at time rates shall be the same for the same job.

(3) The Council, acting in accordance with the procedure referred to in Article 251, and after consulting the Economic and Social Committee, shall adopt measures to ensure the application of the principle of equal opportunities and equal treatment of men and women in matters of employment and occupation, including the principle of equal pay for equal work or work of equal value.

(4) With a view to ensuring full equality in practice between men and women in working life, the principle of equal treatment shall not prevent any Member State from maintaining or adopting measures providing for specific advantages in order to make it easier for the underrepresented sex to pursue a vocational activity or to prevent or compensate for disadvantages in professional careers.

Council Directive of 10 February 1975 on the approximation of the laws of the Member States relating to the application of the principle of equal pay for men and women (75/117/EEC)

Article 1

The principle of equal pay for men and women outlined in Article 119 of the **A-010** Treaty, hereinafter called ɪprinciple of equal payɪ, means, for the same work or for work to which equal value is attributed, the elimination of all discrimination on grounds of sex with regard to all aspects and conditions of remuneration. In particular, where a job classification system is used for determining pay, it must be based on the same criteria for both men and women and so drawn up as to exclude any discrimination on grounds of sex.

Article 2

Member States shall introduce into their national legal systems such **A-011** measures as are necessary to enable all employees who consider themselves wronged by failure to apply the principle of equal pay to pursue their claims by judicial process after possible recourse to other competent authorities.

Article 3

Member States shall abolish all discrimination between men and women **A-012** arising from laws, regulations or administrative provisions which is contrary to the principle of equal pay.

Article 4

A-013 Member States shall take the necessary measures to ensure that provisions appearing in collective agreements, wage scales, wage agreements or individual contracts of employment which are contrary to the principle of equal pay shall be, or may be declared, null and void or may be amended.

Article 5

A-014 Member States shall take the necessary measures to protect employees against dismissal by the employer as a reaction to a complaint within the under-taking or to any legal proceedings aimed at enforcing compliance with the principle of equal pay.

Article 6

A-015 Member States shall, in accordance with their national circumstances and legal systems, take the measures necessary to ensure that the priciple of equal pay is applied. They shall see that effective means are available to take care that this principle is observed.

Council Directive 76/207/EEC of 9 February 1976 on the implementation of the principle of equal treatment for men and women as regards access to employment, vocational training and promotion, and working conditions (76/207/EEC)

Article 1

A-016 1. The purpose of this Directive is to put into effect in the Member States the principle of equal treatment for men and women as regards access to employment, including promotion, and to vocational training and as regards working conditions and, on the conditions referred to in paragraph 2, social security. This principle is herinafter referred to as "the principle of equal treatment."

1a. Member States shall actively take into account the objective of equality between men and women when formulating and implementing laws, regulations, administrative provisions, policies and activities in the areas referred to in paragraph 1.

2. With a view to ensuring the progressive implementation of the principle of equal treatment in matters of social security, the Council, acting on a proposal from the Commission, will adopt provisions defining its substance, its scope and the arrangements for its application.

Article 2

A-017 1. For the purposes of the following provisions, the principle of equal treatment shall mean that there shall be no discrimination whatsoever on grounds of sex either directly or indirectly by reference in particular to marital or family status.

2. For the purposes of this Directive, the following definitions shall apply:

—direct discrimination: where one person is treated less favourably on grounds of sex than another is, has been or would be treated in a comparable situation,

—indirect discrimination: where an apparently neutral provision, criterion or practice would put persons of one sex at a particular disadvantage compared with persons of the other sex, unless that provision, criterion or practice is objectively justified by a legitimate aim, and the means of achieving that aim are appropriate and necessary,

—harassment: where an unwanted conduct related to the sex of a person occurs with the purpose or effect of violating the dignity of a person, and of creating an intimidating, hostile, degrading, humiliating or offensive environment,

—sexual harassment: where any form of unwanted verbal, non-verbal or physical conduct of a sexual nature occurs, with the purpose or effect of violating the dignity of a person, in particular when creating an intimidating, hostile, degrading, humiliating or offensive environment.

3. Harassment and sexual harassment within the meaning of this Directive shall be deemed to be discrimination on the grounds of sex and therefore prohibited.

A person's rejection of, or submission to, suchconduct may not be used as a basis for a decision affecting that person.

4. An instruction to discriminate against persons on grounds of sex shall be deemed to be discrimination within the meaning of this Directive.

5. Member States shall encourage, in accordance with national law, collective agreements or practice, employers and those responsible for access to vocational training to take measures to prevent all forms of discrimination on grounds of sex, in particular harassment and sexual harassment at the workplace.

6. Member States may provide, as regards access to employment including the training leading thereto, that a difference of treatment which is based on a characteristic related to sex shall not constitute discrimination where, by reason of the nature of the particular occupational activities concerned or of the context in which they are carried out, sucha characteristic constitutes a genuine and determining occupational requirement, provided that the objective is legitimate and the requirement is proportionate.

7. This Directive shall be without prejudice to provisions concerning the protection of women, particularly as regards pregnancy and maternity.

A woman on maternity leave shall be entitled, after the end of her period of maternity leave, to return to her job or to an equivalent post on terms and conditions which are no less favourable to her and to benefit from any improvement in working conditions to which she would be entitled during her absence.

Less favourable treatment of a woman related to pregnancy or maternity leave within the meaning of Directive 92/85/EEC shall constitute discrimination within the meaning of this Directive.

This Directive shall also be without prejudice to the provisions of Council Directive 96/34/EC of 3 June 1996 on the framework agreement on parental leave concluded by UNICE, CEEP and the ETUC (1) and of Council Directive 92/85/EEC of 19 October 1992 on the introduction of measures to encourage improvements in the safety and health at work of pregnant workers and workers who have recently given birth or are breastfeeding (tenth individual Directive within the meaning of Article 16(1) of Directive 89/391/EEC) (2). It is also without prejudice to the right of Member States to recognise distinct rights to paternity and/or adoption leave. Those Member States which recognise such rights shall take the necessary measures to protect working men and women against dismissal due to exercising those rights and ensure that, at the end of such leave, they shall be entitled to return to their jobs or to equivalent posts on terms and conditions which are no less favourable to them, and to benefit from any improvement in working conditions to which they would have been entitled during their absence.

8. Member States may maintain or adopt measures within the meaning of Article 141(4) of the Treaty with a view to ensuring full equality in practice between men and women.

Article 3

A-018   1. Application of the principle of equal treatment means that there shall be no direct or indirect discrimination on the grounds of sex in the public or private sectors, including public bodies, in relation to:

> (a) conditions for access to employment, to self-employment or to occupation, including selection criteria and recruitment conditions, whatever the branch of activity and at all levels of the professional hierarchy, including promotion;
>
> (b) access to all types and to all levels of vocational guidance, vocational training, advanced vocational training and retraining, including practical work experience;
>
> (c) employment and working conditions, including dismissals, as well as pay as provided for in Directive 75/117/EEC;
>
> (d) membership of, and involvement in, an organisation of workers or employers, or any organisation whose members carry on a particular profession, including the benefits provided for by such organisations.

2. To that end, Member States shall take the necessary measures to ensure that:

> (a) any laws, regulations and administrative provisions contrary to the principle of equal treatment are abolished;
>
> (b) any provisions contrary to the principle of equal treatment which are included in contracts or collective agreements, internal rules of undertakings or rules governing the independent occupations and professions and workers' and employers' organisations shall be, or may be declared, null and void or are amended.

Article 6

A-019   1. Member States shall ensure that judicial and/or administrative procedures, including where they deem it appropriate conciliation procedures, for the enforcement of obligations under this Directive are available to all persons who consider themselves wronged by failure to apply the principle of equal treatment to them, even after the relationship in which the discrimination is alleged to have occurred has ended.

2. Member States shall introduce into their national legal systems suchmeasures as are necessary to ensure real and effective compensation or reparation as the Member States so determine for the loss and damage sustained by a person injured as a result of discrimination contrary to Article 3, in a way which is dissuasive and proportionate to the damage suffered; such compensation or reparation may not be restricted by the fixing of a prior upper limit, except in cases where the employer can prove that the only damage suffered by an applicant as a result of discrimination within the meaning of this Directive is the refusal to take his/her job application into consideration.

3. Member States shall ensure that associations, organisations or other legal entities which have, in accordance with the criteria laid down by their national law, a legitimate interest in ensuring that the provisions of this Directive are complied with, may engage, either on behalf or in support of the complainants, with his or her approval, in any judicial and/or administrative procedure provided for the enforcement of obligations under this Directive.

4. Paragraphs 1 and 3 are without prejudice to national rules relating to time limits for bringing actions as regards the principle of equal treatment.

Article 7

Member States shall introduce into their national legal systems such **A-020** measures as are necessary to protect employees, including those who are employees' representatives provided for by national laws and/or practices, against dismissal or other adverse treatment by the employer as a reaction to a complaint within the undertaking or to any legal proceedings aimed at enforcing compliance withth e principle of equal treatment.

Council Directive of 14 October 1991 on an employer's obligation to inform employees of the conditions applicable to the contract or employment relationship (91/533/EEC)

Article 1   Scope

1. This Directive shall apply to every paid employee having a contract or **A-021** employment relationship defined by the law in force in a Member State and/or governed by the law in force in a Member State.

2. Member States may provide that this Directive shall not apply to employees having a contract or employment relationship:
   (a) –with a total duration not exceeding one month, and/or
   –with a working week not exceeding eight hours; or
   (b) of a casual and/or specific nature provided, in these cases, that its non-application is justified by objective considerations.

Article 2   Obligation to provide information

1. An employer shall be obliged to notify an employee to whom this Directive **A-022** applies, hereinafter referred to as 'the employee', of the essential aspects of the contract or employment relationship.

2. The information referred to in paragraph 1 shall cover at least the following:
   (a) the identities of the parties;
   (b) the place of work; where there is no fixed or main place of work, the principle that the employee is employed at various places and the registered place of business or, where appropriate, the domicile of the employer;
   (c)
      (i) the title, grade, nature or category of the work for which the employee is employed; or
      (ii) a brief specification or description of the work;
   (d) the date of commencement of the contract or employment relationship;

    (e) in the case of a temporary contract or employment relationship, the expected duration thereof;

    (f) the amount of paid leave to which the employee is entitled or, where this cannot be indicated when the information is given, the procedures for allocating and determining such leave;

    (g) the length of the periods of notice to be observed by the employer and the employee should their contract or employment relationship be terminated or, where this cannot be indicated when the information is given, the method for determining such periods of notice;

    (h) the initial basic amount, the other component elements and the frequency of payment of the remuneration to which the employee is entitled;

    (i) the length of the employee's normal working day or week;

    (j) where appropriate;

        (i) the collective agreements governing the employee's conditions of work; or

        (ii) in the case of collective agreements concluded outside the business by special joint bodies or institutions, the name of the competent body or joint institution within which the agreements were concluded.

3. The information referred to in paragraph 2 (f), (g), (h) and (i) may, where appropriate, be given in the form of a reference to the laws, regulations and administrative or statutory provisions or collective agreements governing those particular points.

Article 3   Means of information

A-023   1. The information referred to in Article 2 (2) may be given to the employee, not later than two months after the commencement of employment, in the form of:

    (a) a written contract of employment; and/or

    (b) a letter of engagement; and/or

    (c) one or more other written documents, where one of these documents contains at least all the information referred to in Article 2 (2) (a), (b), (c), (d), (h) and (i).

2. Where none of the documents referred to in paragraph 1 is handed over to the employee within the prescribed period, the employer shall be obliged to give the employee, not later than two months after the commencement of employment, a written declaration signed by the employer and containing at least the information referred to in Article 2 (2).

Where the document(s) referred to in paragraph 1 contain only part of the information required, the written declaration provided for in the first subparagraph of this paragraph shall cover the remaining information.

3. Where the contract or employment relationship comes to an end before expiry of a period of two months as from the date of the start of work, the information provided for in Article 2 and in this Article must be made available to the employee by the end of this period at the latest.

Article 4   Expatriate employees

A-024   1. Where an employee is required to work in a country or countries other than the Member State whose law and/or practice governs the contract or employment relationship, the document(s) referred to in Article 3 must be in his/

her possession before his/her departure and must include at least the following additional information:

    (a) the duration of the employment abroad;

    (b) the currency to be used for the payment of remuneration;

    (c) where appropriate, the benefits in cash or kind attendant on the employment abroad;

    (d) where appropriate, the conditions governing the employee's repatriation.

2. The information referred to in paragraph 1 (b) and (c) may, where appropriate, be given in the form of a reference to the laws, regulations and administrative or statutory provisions or collective agreements governing those particular points.

3. Paragraphs 1 and 2 shall not apply if the duration of the employment outside the country whose law and/or practice governs the contract or employment relationship is one month or less.

Article 5   Modification of aspects of the contract or employment relationship and procedural rules

1. Any change in the details referred to in Articles 2 (2) and 4 (1) must be the **A-025** subject of a written document to be given by the employer to the employee at the earliest opportunity and not later than one month after the date of entry into effect of the change in question.

2. The written document referred to in paragraph 1 shall not be compulsory in the event of a change in the laws, regulations and administrative or statutory provisions or collective agreements cited in the documents referred to in Article 3, supplemented, where appropriate, pursuant to Article 4 (1).

Article 6   Form and proof of the existence of a contract or employment relationship and procedural rules

This Directive shall be without prejudice to national law and practice **A-026** concerning:

    –the form of the contract or employment relationship,

    –proof as regards the existence and content of a contract or employment relationship,

    –the relevant procedural rules.

Council Directive 92/85/EEC of 19 October 1992 on the introduction of measures to encourage improvements in the safety and health at work of pregnant workers and workers who have recently given birth or are breastfeeding (tenth individual Directive within the meaning of Article 16 (1) of Directive 89/391/EEC)

SECTION I PURPOSE AND DEFINITIONS

Article 1   Purpose

1. The purpose of this Directive, which is the tenth individual Directive **A-027** within the meaning of Article 16 (1) of Directive 89/391/EEC, is to implement measures to encourage improvements in the safety and health at work of pregnant workers and workers who have recently given birth or who are breastfeeding.

2. The provisions of Directive 89/391/EEC, except for Article 2 (2) thereof, shall apply in full to the whole area covered by paragraph 1, without prejudice to any more stringent and/or specific provisions contained in this Directive.

3. This Directive may not have the effect of reducing the level of protection afforded to pregnant workers, workers who have recently given birth or who are breastfeeding as compared with the situation which exists in each Member State on the date on which this Directive is adopted.

Article 2   Definitions

A-028   For the purposes of this Directive:

(a) pregnant worker shall mean a pregnant worker who informs her employer of her condition, in accordance with national legislation and/ or national practice;

(b) worker who has recently given birth shall mean a worker who has recently given birth within the meaning of national legislation and/or national practice and who informs her employer of her condition, in accordance with that legislation and/or practice;

(c) worker who is breastfeeding shall mean a worker who is breastfeeding within the meaning of national legislation and/or national practice and who informs her employer of her condition, in accordance with that legislation and/or practice.

SECTION II GENERAL PROVISIONS

Article 3   Guidelines

A-029   1. In consultation with the Member States and assisted by the Advisory Committee on Safety, Hygiene and Health Protection at Work, the Commission shall draw up guidelines on the assessment of the chemical, physical and biological agents and industrial processes considered hazardous for the safety or health of workers within the meaning of Article 2.

The guidelines referred to in the first subparagraph shall also cover movements and postures, mental and physical fatigue and other types of physical and mental stress connected with the work done by workers within the meaning of Article 2.

2. The purpose of the guidelines referred to in paragraph 1 is to serve as a basis for the assessment referred to in Article 4 (1).

To this end, Member States shall bring these guidelines to the attention of all employers and all female workers and/or their representatives in the respective Member State.

Article 4   Assessment and information

A-030   1. For all activities liable to involve a specific risk of exposure to the agents, processes or working conditions of which a non-exhaustive list is given in Annex I, the employer shall assess the nature, degree and duration of exposure, in the undertaking and/or establishment concerned, of workers within the meaning of Article 2, either directly or by way of the protective and preventive services referred to in Article 7 of Directive 89/391/EEC, in order to:

–assess any risks to the safety or health and any possible effect on the pregnancys or breastfeeding of workers within the meaning of Article 2,

–decide what measures should be taken.

2. Without prejudice to Article 10 of Directive 89/391/EEC, workers within the meaning of Article 2 and workers likely to be in one of the situations referred

to in Article 2 in the undertaking and/or establishment concerned and/or their representatives shall be informed of the results of the assessment referred to in paragraph 1 and of all measures to be taken concerning health and safety at work.

Article 5 Action further to the results of the assessment

1. Without prejudice to Article 6 of Directive 89/391/EEC, if the results of **A-031** the assessment referred to in Article 4 (1) reveal a risk to the safety or health or an effect on the pregnancy or breastfeeding of a worker within the meaning of Article 2, the employer shall take the necessary measures to ensure that, by temporarily adjusting the working conditions and/or the working hours of the worker concerned, the exposure of that worker to such risks is avoided.

2. If the adjustment of her working conditions and/or working hours is not technically and/or objectively feasible, or cannot reasonably be required on duly substantiated grounds, the employer shall take the necessary measures to move the worker concerned to another job.

3. If moving her to another job is not technically and/or objectively feasible or cannot reasonably be required on duly substantiated grounds, the worker concerned shall be granted leave in accordance with national legislation and/or national practice for the whole of the period necessary to protect her safety or health.

4. The provisions of this Article shall apply mutatis mutandis to the case where a worker pursuing an activity which is forbidden pursuant to Article 6 becomes pregnant or starts breastfeeding and informs her employer thereof.

Article 6 Cases in which exposure is prohibited

In addition to the general provisions concerning the protection of workers, in **A-032** particular those relating to the limit values for occupational exposure:

1. pregnant workers within the meaning of Article 2 (a) may under no circumstances be obliged to perform duties for which the assessment has revealed a risk of exposure, which would jeopardize safety or health, to the agents and working conditions listed in Annex II, Section A;

2. workers who are breastfeeding, within the meaning of Article 2 (c), may under no circumstances be obliged to perform duties for which the assessment has revealed a risk of exposure, which would jeopardize safety or health, to the agents and working conditions listed in Annex II, Section B.

Article 7 Night Work

1. Member States shall take the necessary measures to ensure that workers **A-033** referred to in Article 2 are not obliged to perform night work during their pregnancy and for a period following childbirth which shall be determined by the national authority competent for safety and health, subject to submission, in accordance with the procedures laid down by the Member States, of a medical certificate stating that this is necessary for the safety or health of the worker concerned.

2. The measures referred to in paragraph 1 must entail the possibility, in accordance with national legislation and/or national practice, of:

   (a) transfer to daytime work; or
   (b) leave from work or extension of maternity leave where such a transfer is not technically and/or objectively feasible or cannot reasonably by required on duly substantiated grounds.

Article 8   Maternity Leave

A-034   1. Member States shall take the necessary measures to ensure that workers within the meaning of Article 2 are entitled to a continuous period of maternity leave of a least 14 weeks allocated before and/or after confinement in accordance with national legislation and/or practice.

2. The maternity leave stipulated in paragraph 1 must include compulsory maternity leave of at least two weeks allocated before and/or after confinement in accordance with national legislation and/or practice.

Article 9   Time off for ante-natal examinations

A-035   Member States shall take the necessary measures to ensure that pregnant workers within the meaning of Article 2 (a) are entitled to, in accordance with national legislation and/or practice, time off, without loss of pay, in order to attend ante-natal examinations, if such examinations have to take place during working hours.

Article 10   Prohibition of dismissal

A-036   In order to guarantee workers, within the meaning of Article 2, the exercise of their health and safety protection rights as recognized under this Article, it shall be provided that:

1. Member States shall take the necessary measures to prohibit the dismissal of workers, within the meaning of Article 2, during the period from the beginning of their pregnancy to the end of the maternity leave referred to in Article 8 (1), save in exceptional cases not connected with their condition which are permitted under national legislation and/or practice and, where applicable, provided that the competent authority has given its consent;

2. if a worker, within the meaning of Article 2, is dismissed during the period referred to in point 1, the employer must cite duly substantiated grounds for her dismissal in writing;

3. Member States shall take the necessary measures to protect workers, within the meaning of Article 2, from consequences of dismissal which is unlawful by virtue of point 1.

Article 11   Employment rights

A-037   In order to guarantee workers within the meaning of Article 2 the exercise of their health and safety protection rights as recognized in this Article, it shall be provided that:

1. in the cases referred to in Articles 5, 6 and 7, the employment rights relating to the employment contract, including the maintenance of a payment to, and/or entitlement to an adequate allowance for, workers within the meaning of Article 2, must be ensured in accordance with national legislation and/or national practice;

2. in the case referred to in Article 8, the following must be ensured:
   (a) the rights connected with the employment contract of workers within the meaning of Article 2, other than those referred to in point (b) below;
   (b) maintenance of a payment to, and/or entitlement to an adequate allowance for, workers within the meaning of Article 2;

3. the allowance referred to in point 2 (b) shall be deemed adequate if it guarantees income at least equivalent to that which the worker

concerned would receive in the event of a break in her activities on grounds connected with her state of health, subject to any ceiling laid down under national legislation;

4. Member States may make entitlement to pay or the allowance referred to in points 1 and 2 (b) conditional upon the worker concerned fulfilling the conditions of eligibilty for such benefits laid down under national legislation.

These conditions may under no circumstances provide for periods of previous employment in excess of 12 months immediately prior to the presumed date of confinement.

Article 12   Defence of rights

Member States shall introduce into their national legal systems such **A-038** measures as are necessary to enable all workers who should themselves wronged by failure to comply with the obligations arising from this Directive to pursue their claims by judicial process (and/or, in accordance with national laws and/or practices) by recourse to other competent authorities.

Council Directive 93/104/EC of 23 November 1993 concerning certain aspects of the organization of working time

SECTION I SCOPE AND DEFINITIONS

Article 1   Purpose and scope

1. This Directive lays down minimum safety and health requirements for the **A-039** organization of working time.
2. This Directive applies to:
   (a) minimum periods of daily rest, weekly rest and annual leave, to breaks and maximum weekly working time; and
   (b) certain aspects of night work, shift work and patterns of work.
3. This Directive shall apply to all sectors of activity, both public and private, within the meaning of Article 2 of Directive 89/391/EEC, without prejudice to Article 17 of this Directive, with the exception of air, rail, road, sea, inland waterway and lake transport, sea fishing, other work at sea and the activities of doctors in training;
4. The provisions of Directive 89/391/EEC are fully applicable to the matters referred to in paragraph 2, without prejudice to more stringent and/or specific provisions contained in this Directive.

Article 2   Definitions

For the purposes of this Directive, the following definitions shall apply: **A-040**
   1. working time shall mean any period during which the worker is working, at the employer's disposal and carrying out his activity or duties, in accordance with national laws and/or practice;
   2. rest period shall mean any period which is not working time;
   3. night time shall mean any period of not less than seven hours, as defined by national law, and which must include in any case the period between midnight and 5 a. m.;
   4. night worker shall mean:
      (a) on the one hand, any worker, who, during night time, works at least three hours of his daily working time as a normal course; and

(b) on the other hand, any worker who is likely during night time to work a certain proportion of his annual working time, as defined at the choice of the Member State concerned:

(i) by national legislation, following consultation with the two sides of industry; or

(ii) by collective agreements or agreements concluded between the two sides of industry at national or regional level;

5. shift work shall mean any method of organizing work in shifts whereby workers succeed each other at the same work stations according to a certain pattern, including a rotating pattern, and which may be continuous or discontinuous, entailing the need for workers to work at different times over a given period of days or weeks;

6. shift worker shall mean any worker whose work schedule is part of shift work.

SECTION II MINIMUM REST PERIODS - OTHER ASPECTS OF THE ORGANIZATION OF WORKING TIME

Article 3   Daily Rest

A-041   Member States shall take the measures necessary to ensure that every worker is entitled to a minimum daily rest period of 11 consecutive hours per 24-hour period.

Article 4   Breaks

A-042   Member States shall take the measures necessary to ensure that, where the working day is longer than six hours, every worker is entitled to a rest break, the details of which, including duration and the terms on which it is granted, shall be laid down in collective agreements or agreements between the two sides of industry or, failing that, by national legislation.

Article 5   Weekly rest period

A-043   Member States shall take the measures necessary to ensure that, per each seven-day period, every worker is entitled to a minimum uninterrupted rest period of 24 hours plus the 11 hours' daily rest referred to in Article 3.

The minimum rest period referred to in the first subparagraph shall in principle include Sunday.

If objective, technical or work organization conditions so justify, a minimum rest period of 24 hours may be applied.

Article 6   Maximum weekly working time

A-044   Member States shall take the measures necessary to ensure that, in keeping with the need to protect the safety and health of workers:

1. the period of weekly working time is limited by means of laws, regulations or administrative provisions or by collective agreements or agreements between the two sides of industry;

2. the average working time for each seven-day period, including overtime, does not exceed 48 hours.

Article 7   Annual leave

A-045   1. Member States shall take the measures necessary to ensure that every worker is entitled to paid annual leave of at least four weeks in accordance with the conditions for entitlement to, and granting of, such leave laid down by national legislation and/or practice.

2. The minimum period of paid annual leave may not be replaced by an allowance in lieu, except where the employment relationship is terminated.

SECTION III NIGHT WORK - SHIFT WORK - PATTERNS OF WORK

Article 8   Length of night work

Member States shall take the measures necessary to ensure that: A-046
1. normal hours of work for night workers do not exceed an average of eight hours in any 24-hour period;
2. night workers whose work involves special hazards or heavy physical or mental strain do not work more than eight hours in any period of 24 hours during which they perform night work.

For the purposes of the aforementioned, work involving special hazards or heavy physical or mental strain shall be defined by national legislation and/or practice or by collective agreements or agreements concluded between the two sides of industry, taking account of the specific effects and hazards of night work.

Article 9   Health assessment and transfer of night workers to day work

1. Member States shall take the measures necessary to ensure that: A-047
   (a) night workers are entitled to a free health assessment before their assignment and thereafter at regular intervals;
   (b) night workers suffering from health problems recognized as being connected with the fact that they perform night work are transferred whenever possible to day work to which they are suited.

2. The free health assessment referred to in paragraph 1 (a) must comply with medical confidentiality.

3. The free health assessment referred to in paragraph 1 (a) may be conducted within the national health system.

Article 10   Guarantees for night-time working

Member States may make the work of certain categories of night workers A-048 subject to certain guarantees, under conditions laid down by national legislation and/or practice, in the case of workers who incur risks to their safety or health linked to night-time working.

Article 11   Notification of regular use of night workers

Member States shall take the measures necessary to ensure that an employer A-049 who regularly uses night workers brings this information to the attention of the competent authorities if they so request.

Article 12   Safety and health protection

Member States shall take the measures necessary to ensure that: A-050
1. night workers and shift workers have safety and health protection appropriate to the nature of their work;
2. appropriate protection and prevention services or facilities with regard to the safety and health of night workers and shift workers are equivalent to those applicable to other workers and are available at all times.

Article 13   Pattern of work

A-051   Member States shall take the measures necessary to ensure that an employer who intends to organize work according to a certain pattern takes account of the general principle of adapting work to the worker, with a view, in particular, to alleviating monotonous work and work at a predetermined work-rate, depending on the type of activity, and of safety and health requirements, especially as regards breaks during working time.

SECTION IV MISCELLANEOUS PROVISIONS

Article 14   More specific Community provisions

A-052   The provisions of this Directive shall not apply where other Community instruments contain more specific requirements concerning certain occupations or occupational activities.

Article 15   More favourable provisions

A-053   This Directive shall not affect Member States' right to apply or introduce laws, regulations or administrative provisions more favourable to the protection of the safety and health of workers or to facilitate or permit the application of collective agreements or agreements concluded between the two sides of industry which are more favourable to the protection of the safety and health of workers.

Article 16   Reference periods

A-054   Member States may lay down:
1. for the application of Article 5 (weekly rest period), a reference period not exceeding 14 days;
2. for the application of Article 6 (maximum weekly working time), a reference period not exceeding four months.
   The periods of paid annual leave, granted in accordance with Article 7, and the periods of sick leave shall not be included or shall be neutral in the calculation of the average;
3. for the application of Article 8 (length of night work), a reference period defined after consultation of the two sides of industry or by collective agreements or agreements concluded between the two sides of industry at national or regional level.
   If the minimum weekly rest period of 24 hours required by Article 5 falls within that reference period, it shall not be included in the calculation of the average.

Council Directive 94/33/EC of 22 June 1994 on the protection of young people at work

SECTION I

Article 1   Purpose

A-055   1. Member States shall take the necessary measures to prohibit work by children. They shall ensure, under the conditions laid down by this Directive, that the minimum working or employment age is not lower than the minimum age at which compulsory full-time schooling as imposed by national law ends or 15 years in any event.

2. Member States ensure that work by adolescents is strictly regulated and protected under the conditions laid down in this Directive.

3. Member States shall ensure in general that employers guarantee that young people have working conditions which suit their age.

They shall ensure that young people are protected against economic exploitation and against any work likely to harm their safety, health or physical, mental, moral or social development or to jeopardize their education.

Article 2   Scope

1. This Directive shall apply to any person under 18 years of age having an **A-056** employment contract or an employment relationship defined by the law in force in a Member State and/or governed by the law in force in a Member State.

2. Member States may make legislative or regulatory provision for this Directive not to apply, within the limits and under the conditions which they set by legislative or regulatory provision, to occasional work or short-term work involving:
- (a) domestic service in a privat household, or
- (b) work regarded as not being harmful, damaging or dangerous to young people in a family undertaking.

Article 3   Definitions

For the purposes of this Directive: **A-057**
- (a) 'young person' shall mean any person under 18 years of age referred to in Article 2 (1);
- (b) 'child' shall mean any young person of less than 15 years of age or who is still subject to compulsory full-time schooling under national law;
- (c) 'adolescent' shall mean any young person of at least 15 years of age but less than 18 years of age who is no longer subject to compulsory full-time schooling under national law;
- (d) 'light work' shall mean all work which, on account of the inherent nature of the tasks which it involves and the particular conditions under which they are performed:
  - (i) is not likely to be harmful to the safety, health or development of children, and
  - (ii) is not such as to be harmful to their attendance at school, their participation in vocational guidance or training programmes approved by the competent authority or their capacity to benefit from the instruction received;
- (e) 'working time' shall mean any period during which the young person is at work, at the employer's disposal and carrying out his activity or duties in accordance with national legislation and/or practice;
- (f) 'rest period' shall mean any period which is not working time.

Article 4   Prohibition of work by children

1. Member States shall adopt the measures necessary to prohibit work by **A-058** children.

2. Taking into account the objectives set out in Article 1, Member States may make legislative or regulatory provision for the prohibition of work by children not to apply to:
- (a) children pursuing the activities set out in Article 5;

(b) children of at least 14 years of age working under a combined work/ training scheme or an in-plant work-experience scheme, provided that such work is done in accordance with the conditions laid down by the competent authority;

(c) children of at least 14 years of age performing light work other than that covered by Article 5; light work other than that covered by Article 5 may, however, be performed by children of 13 years of age for a limited number of hours per week in the case of categories of work determined by national legislation.

3. Member States that make use of the opinion referred to in paragraph 2 (c) shall determine, subject to the provisions of this Directive, the working conditions relating to the light work in question.

Article 5   Cultural or similar activities

A-059   1. The employment of children for the purposes of performance in cultural, artistic, sports or advertising activities shall be subject to prior authorization to be given by the competent authority in individual cases.

2. Member States shall by legislative or regulatory provision lay down the working conditions for children in the cases referred to in paragraph 1 and the details of the prior authorization procedure, on condition that the activities:

(i) are not likely to be harmful to the safety, health or development of children, and

(ii) are not such as to be harmful to their attendance at school, their participation in vocational guidance or training programmes approved by the competent authority or their capacity to benefit from the instruction received.

3. By way of derogation from the procedure laid down in paragraph 1, in the case of children of at least 13 years of age, Member States may authorize, by legislative or regulatory provision, in accordance with conditions which they shall determine, the employment of children for the purposes of performance in cultural, artistic, sports or advertising activities.

4. The Member States which have a specific authorization system for modelling agencies with regard to the activities of children may retain that system.

SECTION II

Article 6   General obligations on employers

A-060   1. Without prejudice to Article 4 (1), the employer shall adopt the measures necessary to protect the safety and health of young people, taking particular account of the specific risks referred to in Article 7 (1).

2. The employer shall implement the measures provided for in paragraph 1 on the basis of an assessment of the hazards to young people in connection with their work. The assessment must be made before young people begin work and when there is any major change in working conditions and must pay particular attention to the following points:

(a) the fitting-out and layout of the workplace and the workstation;

(b) the nature, degree and duration of exposure to physical, biological and chemical agents;

(c) the form, range and use of work equipment, in particular agents, machines, apparatus and devices, and the way in which they are handled;

(d) the arrangement of work processes and operations and the way in which these are combined (organization of work);

(e) the level of training and instruction given to young people.

Where this assessment shows that there is a risk to the safety, the physical or mental health or development of young people, an appropriate free assessment and monitoring of their health shall be provided at regular intervals without prejudice to Directive 89/391/EEC.

The free health assessment and monitoring may form part of a national health system.

3. The employer shall inform young people of possible risks and of all measures adopted concerning their safety and health.

Furthermore, he shall inform the legal representatives of children of possible risks and of all measures adopted concerning children's safety and health.

4. The employer shall involve the protective and preventive services referred to in Article 7 of Directive 89/391/EEC in the planning, implementation and monitoring of the safety and health conditions applicable to young people.

Article 7   Vulnerability of young people - Prohibition of work

1. Member States shall ensure that young people are protected from any **A-061** specific risks to their safety, health and development which are a consequence of their lack of experience, of absence of awareness of existing or potential risks or of the fact that young people have not yet fully matured.

2. Without prejudice to Article 4 (1), Member States shall to this end prohibit the employment of young people for:

(a) work which is objectively beyond their phyiscal or psychological capacity;

(b) work involving harmful exposure to agents which are toxic, carcinogenic, cause heritable genetic damage, or harm to the unborn child or which in any other way chronically affect human health;

(c) work involving harmful exposure to radiation;

(d) work involving the risk of accidents which it may be assumed cannot be recognized or avoided by young persons owing to their insufficient attention to safety or lack of experience or training; or

(e) work in which there is a risk to health from extreme cold or heat, or from noise or vibration.

Work which is likely to entail specific risks for young people within the meaning of paragraph 1 includes:

– work involving harmful exposure to the physical, biological and chemical agents referred to in point I of the Annex, and

– processes and work referred to in point II of the Annex.

3. Member States may, by legislative or regulatory provision, authorize derogations from paragraph 2 in the case of adolescents where such derogations are indispensable for their vocational training, provided that protection of their safety and health is ensured by the fact that the work is performed under the supervision of a competent person within the meaning of Article 7 of Directive 89/391/EEC and provided that the protection afforded by that Directive is guaranteed.

Article 8   Working time

1. Member States which make use of the option in Article 4 (2) (b) or (c) **A-062** shall adopt the measures necessary to limit the working time of children to:

(a) eight hours a day and 40 hours a week for work performed under a combined work/training scheme or an in-plant work-experience scheme;

(b) two hours on a school day and 12 hours a week for work performed in term-time outside the hours fixed for school attendance, provided that this is not prohibited by national legislation and/or practice;

in no circumstances may the daily working time exceed seven hours; this limit may be raised to eight hours in the case of children who have reached the age of 15;

(c) seven hours a day and 35 hours a week for work performed during a period of at least a week when school is not operating; these limits may be raised to eight hours a day and 40 hours a week in the case of chidren who have reached the age of 15;

(d) seven hours a day and 35 hours a week for light work performed by children no longer subject to compulsory full-time schooling under national law.

2. Member States shall adopt the measures necessary to limit the working time of adolescents to eight hours a day and 40 hours a week.

3. The time spent on training by a young person working under a theoretical and/or practical combined work/training scheme or an in-plant work-experience scheme shall be counted as working time.

4. Where a young person is employed by more than one employer, working days and working time shall be cumulative.

5. Member States may, by legislative or regulatory provision, authorize derogations from paragraph 1 (a) and paragraph 2 either by way of exception or where there are objective grounds for so doing.

Member States shall, by legislative or regulatory provision, determine the conditions, limits and procedure for implementing such derogations.

Article 9   Night work

A-063   1. (a) Member States which make use of the option in Article 4 (2) (b) or (c) shall adopt the measures necessary to prohibit work by children between 8 p.m. and 6 a.m.

(b) Member States shall adopt the measures necessary to prohibit work by adolescents either between 10 p.m. and 6 a.m. or between 11 p.m. and 7 a.m.

2. (a) Member States may, by legislative or regulatory provision, authorize work by adolescents in specific areas of activity during the period in which night work is prohibited as referred to in paragraph 1 (b).

In that event, Member States shall take appropriate measures to ensure that the adolescent is supervised by an adult where such supervision is necessary for the adolescent's protection.

(b) If point (a) is applied, work shall continue to be prohibited between midnight and 4 a.m.

However, Member States may, by legislative or regulatory provision, authorize work by adolescents during the period in which night work is prohibited in the following cases, where there are objective grounds for so doing and provided that adolescents are allowed suitable compensatory rest time and that the objectives set out in Article 1 are not called into question:

– work performed in the shipping or fisheries sectors;
– work performed in the context of the armed forces or the police;
– work performed in hospitals or similar establishments;
– cultural, artistic, sports or advertising activities.

3. Prior to any assignment to night work and at regular intervals thereafter, adolescents shall be entitled to a free assessment of their health and capacities, unless the work they do during the period during which work is prohibited is of an exceptional nature.

Article 10   Rest period

1. (a) Member States which make use of the option in Article 4 (2) (b) or (c) **A-064** shall adopt the measures necessary to ensure that, for each 24-hour period, children are entitled to a minimum rest period of 14 consecutive hours.

(b) Member States shall adopt the measures necessary to ensure that, for each 24-hour period, adolescents are entitled to a minimum rest period of 12 consecutive hours.

2. Member States shall adopt the measures necessary to ensure that, for each seven-day period:

–children in respect of whom they have made use of the option in Article 4
   (2) (b) or (c), and
–adolescents

are entitled to a minimum rest period of two days, which shall be consecutive if possible.Where justified by technical or organization reasons, the minimum rest period may be reduced, but may in no circumstances be less than 36 consecutive hours. The minimum rest period referred to in the first and second subparagraphs shall in principle include Sunday.

3. Member States may, by legislative or regulatory provision, provide for the minimum rest periods referred to in pargraphs 1 and 2 to be interrupted in the case of activities involving periods of work that are split up over the day or are of short duration.

4. Member States may make legislative or regulatory provision for derogations from paragraph 1 (b) and paragraph 2 in respect of adolescents in the following cases, where there are objective grounds for so doing and provided that they are granted appropriate compensatory rest time and that the objetives set out in Article 1 are not called into question:

(a)   work performed in the shipping or fisheries sectors;
(b)   work performed in the context of the armed forces or the police;
(c)   work performed in hospitals or similar establishments;
(d)   work performed in agriculture;
(e)   work performed in the tourism industry or in the hotel, restaurant and
     café sector;
(f)   activities involving periods of work split up over the day.

Article 11   Annual rest

Member States which make use of the option referred to in Article 4 (2) (b) **A-065** or (c) shall see to it that a period free of any work is included, as far as possible, in the school holidays of children subject to compulsory full-time schooling under national law.

Article 12   Breaks

Member States shall adopt the measures necessary to ensure that, where **A-066** daily working time is more than four and a half hours, young people are entitled to a break of at least 30 minutes, which shall be consecutive if possible.

Article 13   Work by adolescents in the event of force majeure

A-067   Member States may, by legislative or regulatory provision, authorize derogations from Article 8 (2), Article 9 (1) (b), Article 10 (1) (b) and, in the case of
adolescents, Article 12, for work in the circumstances referred to in Article 5 (4)
of Directive 89/391/EEC, provided that such work is of a temporary nature and
must be performed immediately, that adult workers are not available and that the
adolescents are allowed equivalent compensatory rest time within the following
three weeks.

Council Directive 97/80/EC of 15 December 1997 on the burden of proof in cases of discrimination based on sex

Article 1   Aim

A-068   The aim of this Directive shall be to ensure that the measures taken by the
Member States to implement the principle of equal treatment are made more
effective, in order to enable all persons who consider themselves wronged because
the principle of equal treatment has not been applied to them to have their
rights asserted by judicial process after possible recourse to other competent
bodies.

Article 2   Definitions

A-069   1. For the purposes of this Directive, the principle of equal treatment shall
mean that there shall be no discrimination whatsoever based on sex, either
directly or indirectly.
    2. For purposes of the principle of equal treatment referred to in paragraph
1, indirect discrimination shall exist where an apparently neutral provision,
criterion or practice disadvantages a substantially higher proportion of the
members of one sex unless that provision, criterion or practice is appropriate and
necessary and can be justified by objective factors unrelated to sex.

Article 3   Scope

A-070   1. This Directive shall apply to:
    (a) the situations covered by Article 119 of the Treaty and by Directives 75/
         117/EEC, 76/207/EEC and, insofar as discrimination based on sex is
         concerned, 92/85/EEC and 96/34/EC;
    (b) any civil or administrative procedure concerning the public or private
         sector which provides for means of redress under national law pursuant
         to the measures referred to in (a) with the exception of out-of-court
         procedures of a voluntary nature or provided for in national law.
    2. This Directive shall not apply to criminal procedures, unless otherwise
provided by the Member States.

Article 4   Burden of proof

A-071   1. Member States shall take such measures as are necessary, in accordance
with their national judicial systems, to ensure that, when persons who consider
themselves wronged because the principle of equal treatment has not been
applied to them establish, before a court or other competent authority, facts from
which it may be presumed that there has been direct or indirect discrimination,
it shall be for the respondent to prove that there has been no breach of the
principle of equal treatment.

2. This Directive shall not prevent Member States from introducing rules of evidence which are more favourable to plaintiffs.

3. Member States need not apply paragraph 1 to proceedings in which it is for the court or competent body to investigate the facts of the case.

Article 5   Information

Member States shall ensure that measures taken pursuant to this Directive, **A-072** together with the provisions already in force, are brought to the attention of all the persons concerned by all appropriate means.

Article 6   Non-regression

Implementation of this Directive shall under no circumstances be sufficient **A-073** grounds for a reduction in the general level of protection of workers in the areas to which it applies, without prejudice to the Member States' right to respond to changes in the situation by introducing laws, regulations and administrative provisions which differ from those in force on the notification of this Directive, provided that the minimum requirements of this Directive are complied with.

Council Directive 98/59/EC of 20 July 1998 on the approximation of the laws of the Member States relating to collective redundancies

SECTION I DEFINITIONS AND SCOPE

Article 1

1. For the purposes of this Directive: **A-074**
    (a) 'collective redundancies' means dismissals effected by an employer for one or more reasons not related to the individual workers concerned where, according to the choice of the Member States, the number of redundancies is:
        (i) either, over a period of 30 days:
        –at least 10 in establishments normally employing more than 20 and less than 100 workers,
        –at least 10 % of the number of workers in establishments normally employing at least 100 but less than 300 workers,
        –at least 30 in establishments normally employing 300 workers or more,
        (ii) or, over a period of 90 days, at least 20, whatever the number of workers normally employed in the establishments in question;
    (b) 'workers' representatives' means the workers' representatives provided for by the laws or practices of the Member States.
    For the purpose of calculating the number of redundancies provided for in the first subparagraph of point (a), terminations of an employment contract which occur on the employer's initiative for one or more reasons not related to the individual workers concerned shall be assimilated to redundancies, provided that there are at least five redundancies.
2. This Directive shall not apply to:
    (a) collective redundancies effected under contracts of employment concluded for limited periods of time or for specific tasks except where such redundancies take place prior to the date of expiry or the completion of such contracts;

(b) workers employed by public administrative bodies or by establishments governed by public law (or, in Member States where this concept is unknown, by equivalent bodies);

(c) the crews of seagoing vessels.

SECTION II INFORMATION AND CONSULTATION

Article 2

A-075   1. Where an employer is contemplating collective redundancies, he shall begin consultations with the workers' representatives in good time with a view to reaching an agreement.

2. These consultations shall, at least, cover ways and means of avoiding collective redundancies or reducing the number of workers affected, and of mitigating the consequences by recourse to accompanying social measures aimed, inter alia, at aid for redeploying or retraining workers made redundant.

Member States may provide that the workers' representatives may call on the services of experts in accordance with national legislation and/or practice.

3. To enable workers' representatives to make constructive proposals, the employers shall in good time during the course of the consultations:

(a) supply them with all relevant information and

(b) in any event notify them in writing of:

(i) the reasons for the projected redundancies;

(ii) the number of categories of workers to be made redundant;

(iii) the number and categories of workers normally employed;

(iv) the period over which the projected redundancies are to be effected;

(v) the criteria proposed for the selection of the workers to be made redundant in so far as national legislation and/or practice confers the power therefor upon the employer;

(vi) the method for calculating any redundancy payments other than those arising out of national legislation and/or practice.

The employer shall forward to the competent public authority a copy of, at least, the elements of the written communication which are provided for in the first subparagraph, point (b), subpoints (i) to (v).

4. The obligations laid down in paragraphs 1, 2 and 3 shall apply irrespective of whether the decision regarding collective redundancies is being taken by the employer or by an undertaking controlling the employer.

In considering alleged breaches of the information, consultation and notification requirements laid down by this Directive, account shall not be taken of any defence on the part of the employer on the ground that the necessary information has not been provided to the employer by the undertaking which took the decision leading to collective redundancies.

SECTION III PROCEDURE FOR COLLECTIVE REDUNDANCIES

Article 3

A-076   1. Employers shall notify the competent public authority in writing of any projected collective redundancies.

However, Member States may provide that in the case of planned collective redundancies arising from termination of the establishment's activities as a result of a judicial decision, the employer shall be obliged to notify the competent public authority in writing only if the latter so requests.

This notification shall contain all relevant information concerning the projected collective redundancies and the consultations with workers' representatives provided for in Article 2, and particularly the reasons for the redundancies, the number of workers to be made redundant, the number of workers normally employed and the period over which the redundancies are to be effected.

2. Employers shall forward to the workers' representatives a copy of the notification provided for in paragraph 1.

The workers' representatives may send any comments they may have to the competent public authority.

Article 4

1. Projected collective redundancies notified to the competent public A-077 authority shall take effect not earlier than 30 days after the notification referred to in Article 3(1) without prejudice to any provisions governing individual rights with regard to notice of dismissal.

Member States may grant the competent public authority the power to reduce the period provided for in the preceding subparagraph.

2. The period provided for in paragraph 1 shall be used by the competent public authority to seek solutions to the problems raised by the projected collective redundancies.

3. Where the initial period provided for in paragraph 1 is shorter than 60 days, Member States may grant the competent public authority the power to extend the initial period to 60 days following notification where the problems raised by the projected collective redundancies are not likely to be solved within the initial period.

Member States may grant the competent public authority wider powers of extension.

The employer must be informed of the extension and the grounds for it before expiry of the initial period provided for in paragraph 1.

4. Member States need not apply this Article to collective redundancies arising from termination of the establishment's activities where this is the result of a judicial decision.

SECTION IV FINAL PROVISIONS

Article 5

This Directive shall not affect the right of Member States to apply or to A-078 introduce laws, regulations or administrative provisions which are more favourable to workers or to promote or to allow the application of collective agreements more favourable to workers.

Article 6

Member States shall ensure that judicial and/or administrative procedures for A-079 the enforcement of obligations under this Directive are available to the workers' representatives and/or workers.

Council Directive 2000/43/EC of 29 June 2000 implementing the principle of equal treatment between persons irrespective of racial or ethnic origin

Chapter I General Provisions

Article 1   Purpose

A-080   The purpose of this Directive is to lay down a framework for combating discrimination on the grounds of racial or ethnic origin, with a view to putting into effect in the Member States the principle of equal treatment.

Article 2   Concept of discrimination

A-081   1. For the purposes of this Directive, the principle of equal treatment shall mean that there shall be no direct or indirect discrimination based on racial or ethnic origin.

2. For the purposes of paragraph 1:
   (a) direct discrimination shall be taken to occur where one person is treated less favourably than another is, has been or would be treated in a comparable situation on grounds of racial or ethnic origin;
   (b) indirect discrimination shall be taken to occur where an apparently neutral provision, criterion or practice would put persons of a racial or ethnic origin at a particular disadvantage compared with other persons, unless that provision, criterion or practice is objectively justified by a legitimate aim and the means of achieving that aim are appropriate and necessary.

3. Harassment shall be deemed to be discrimination within the meaning of paragraph 1, when an unwanted conduct related to racial or ethnic origin takes place with the purpose or effect of violating the dignity of a person and of creating an intimidating, hostile, degrading, humiliating or offensive environment. In this context, the concept of harassment may be defined in accordance with the national laws and practice of the Member States.

4. An instruction to discriminate against persons on grounds of racial or ethnic origin shall be deemed to be discrimination within the meaning of paragraph 1.

Article 3   Scope

A-082   1. Within the limits of the powers conferred upon the Community, this Directive shall apply to all persons, as regards both the public and private sectors, including public bodies, in relation to:
   (a) conditions for access to employment, to self-employment and to occupation, including selection criteria and recruitment conditions, whatever the branch of activity and at all levels of the professional hierarchy, including promotion;
   (b) access to all types and to all levels of vocational guidance, vocational training, advanced vocational training and retraining, including practical work experience;
   (c) employment and working conditions, including dismissals and pay;
   (d) membership of and involvement in an organisation of workers or employers, or any organisation whose members carry on a particular profession, including the benefits provided for by such organisations;
   (e) social protection, including social security and healthcare;
   (f) social advantages;

(g) education;

(h) access to and supply of goods and services which are available to the public, including housing.

2. This Directive does not cover difference of treatment based on nationality and is without prejudice to provisions and conditions relating to the entry into and residence of third-country nationals and stateless persons on the territory of Member States, and to any treatment which arises from the legal status of the third-country nationals and stateless persons concerned.

Article 4   Genuine and determining occupational requirements

Notwithstanding Article 2(1) and (2), Member States may provide that a **A-083** difference of treatment which is based on a characteristic related to racial or ethnic origin shall not constitute discrimination where, by reason of the nature of the particular occupational activities concerned or of the context in which they are carried out, such a characteristic constitutes a genuine and determining occupational requirement, provided that the objective is legitimate and the requirement is proportionate.

Article 5   Positive action

With a view to ensuring full equality in practice, the principle of equal **A-084** treatment shall not prevent any Member State from maintaining or adopting specific measures to prevent or compensate for disadvantages linked to racial or ethnic origin.

Article 6   Minimum requirements

1. Member States may introduce or maintain provisions which are more **A-085** favourable to the protection of the principle of equal treatment than those laid down in this Directive.

2. The implementation of this Directive shall under no circumstances constitute grounds for a reduction in the level of protection against discrimination already afforded by Member States in the fields covered by this Directive.

Chapter II Remedies and Enforcement

Article 7   Defence of rights

1. Member States shall ensure that judicial and/or administrative procedures, **A-086** including where they deem it appropriate conciliation procedures, for the enforcement of obligations under this Directive are available to all persons who consider themselves wronged by failure to apply the principle of equal treatment to them, even after the relationship in which the discrimination is alleged to have occurred has ended.

2. Member States shall ensure that associations, organisations or other legal entities, which have, in accordance with the criteria laid down by their national law, a legitimate interest in ensuring that the provisions of this Directive are complied with, may engage, either on behalf or in support of the complainant, with his or her approval, in any judicial and/or administrative procedure provided for the enforcement of obligations under this Directive.

3. Paragraphs 1 and 2 are without prejudice to national rules relating to time limits for bringing actions as regards the principle of equality of treatment.

Article 8   Burden of proof

A-087   1. Member States shall take such measures as are necessary, in accordance with their national judicial systems, to ensure that, when persons who consider themselves wronged because the principle of equal treatment has not been applied to them establish, before a court or other competent authority, facts from which it may be presumed that there has been direct or indirect discrimination, it shall be for the respondent to prove that there has been no breach of the principle of equal treatment.

2. Paragraph 1 shall not prevent Member States from introducing rules of evidence which are more favourable to plaintiffs.

3. Paragraph 1 shall not apply to criminal procedures.

4. Paragraphs 1, 2 and 3 shall also apply to any proceedings brought in accordance with Article 7(2).

5. Member States need not apply paragraph 1 to proceedings in which it is for the court or competent body to investigate the facts of the case.

Article 9   Victimisation

A-088   Member States shall introduce into their national legal systems such measures as are necessary to protect individuals from any adverse treatment or adverse consequence as a reaction to a complaint or to proceedings aimed at enforcing compliance with the principle of equal treatment.

Article 10   Dissemination of information

A-089   Member States shall take care that the provisions adopted pursuant to this Directive, together with the relevant provisions already in force, are brought to the attention of the persons concerned by all appropriate means throughout their territory.

Article 11   Social dialogue

A-090   1. Member States shall, in accordance with national traditions and practice, take adequate measures to promote the social dialogue between the two sides of industry with a view to fostering equal treatment, including through the monitoring of workplace practices, collective agreements, codes of conduct, research or exchange of experiences and good practices.

2. Where consistent with national traditions and practice, Member States shall encourage the two sides of the industry without prejudice to their autonomy to conclude, at the appropriate level, agreements laying down anti-discrimination rules in the fields referred to in Article 3 which fall within the scope of collective bargaining. These agreements shall respect the minimum requirements laid down by this Directive and the relevant national implementing measures.

Article 12   Dialogue with non-governmental organisations

A-091   Member States shall encourage dialogue with appropriate non-governmental organisations which have, in accordance with their national law and practice, a legitimate interest in contributing to the fight against discrimination on grounds of racial and ethnic origin with a view to promoting the principle of equal treatment.

Chapter III Bodies For The Promotion Of Equal Treatment

Article 13

1. Member States shall designate a body or bodies for the promotion of equal A-092 treatment of all persons without discrimination on the grounds of racial or ethnic origin. These bodies may form part of agencies charged at national level with the defence of human rights or the safeguard of individuals' rights.

2. Member States shall ensure that the competences of these bodies include:
   - without prejudice to the right of victims and of associations, organisations or other legal entities referred to in Article 7(2), providing independent assistance to victims of discrimination in pursuing their complaints about discrimination,
   - conducting independent surveys concerning discrimination,
   - publishing independent reports and making recommendations on any issue relating to such discrimination.

Chapter IV Final Provisions

Article 14   Compliance

Member States shall take the necessary measures to ensure that: A-093
   (a) any laws, regulations and administrative provisions contrary to the principle of equal treatment are abolished;
   (b) any provisions contrary to the principle of equal treatment which are included in individual or collective contracts or agreements, internal rules of undertakings, rules governing profit-making or non-profit-making associations, and rules governing the independent professions and workers' and employers' organisations, are or may be declared, null and void or are amended.

Article 15   Sanctions

Member States shall lay down the rules on sanctions applicable to infringe- A-094 ments of the national provisions adopted pursuant to this Directive and shall take all measures necessary to ensure that they are applied. The sanctions, which may comprise the payment of compensation to the victim, must be effective, proportionate and dissuasive. The Member States shall notify those provisions to the Commission by 19 July 2003 at the latest and shall notify it without delay of any subsequent amendment affecting them.

Council Directive 2000/78/EC of 27 November 2000 establishing a general framework for equal treatment in employment and occupation

Chapter I General Provisions

Article 1   Purpose

The purpose of this Directive is to lay down a general framework for A-095 combating discrimination on the grounds of religion or belief, disability, age or sexual orientation as regards employment and occupation, with a view to putting into effect in the Member States the principle of equal treatment.

Article 2   Concept of discrimination

A-096   1. For the purposes of this Directive, the ιprinciple of equal treatmentι shall mean that there shall be no direct or indirect discrimination whatsoever on any of the grounds referred to in Article 1.

2. For the purposes of paragraph 1:
   (a) direct discrimination shall be taken to occur where one person is treated less favourably than another is, has been or would be treated in a comparable situation, on any of the grounds referred to in Article 1;
   (b) indirect discrimination shall be taken to occur where an apparently neutral provision, criterion or practice would put persons having a particular religion or belief, a particular disability, a particular age, or a particular sexual orientation at a particular disadvantage compared with other persons unless:
      (i) that provision, criterion or practice is objectively justified by a legitimate aim and the means of achieving that aim are appropriate and necessary, or
      (ii) as regards persons with a particular disability, the employer or any person or organisation to whom this Directive applies, is obliged, under national legislation, to take appropriate measures in line with the principles contained in Article 5 in order to eliminate disadvantages entailed by such provision, criterion or practice.

3. Harassment shall be deemed to be a form of discrimination within the meaning of paragraph 1, when unwanted conduct related to any of the grounds referred to in Article 1 takes place with the purpose or effect of violating the dignity of a person and of creating an intimidating, hostile, degrading, humiliating or offensive environment. In this context, the concept of harassment may be defined in accordance with the national laws and practice of the Member States.

4. An instruction to discriminate against persons on any of the grounds referred to in Article 1 shall be deemed to be discrimination within the meaning of paragraph 1.

5. This Directive shall be without prejudice to measures laid down by national law which, in a democratic society, are necessary for public security, for the maintenance of public order and the prevention of criminal offences, for the protection of health and for the protection of the rights and freedoms of others.

Article 3   Scope

A-097   1. Within the limits of the areas of competence conferred on the Community, this Directive shall apply to all persons, as regards both the public and private sectors, including public bodies, in relation to:
   (a) conditions for access to employment, to self-employment or to occupation, including selection criteria and recruitment conditions, whatever the branch of activity and at all levels of the professional hierarchy, including promotion;
   (b) access to all types and to all levels of vocational guidance, vocational training, advanced vocational training and retraining, including practical work experience;
   (c) employment and working conditions, including dismissals and pay;
   (d) membership of, and involvement in, an organisation of workers or employers, or any organisation whose members carry on a particular profession, including the benefits provided for by such organisations.

2. This Directive does not cover differences of treatment based on nationality and is without prejudice to provisions and conditions relating to the entry into and residence of third-country nationals and stateless persons in the territory of Member States, and to any treatment which arises from the legal status of the third-country nationals and stateless persons concerned.

3. This Directive does not apply to payments of any kind made by state schemes or similar, including state social security or social protection schemes.

4. Member States may provide that this Directive, in so far as it relates to discrimination on the grounds of disability and age, shall not apply to the armed forces.

Article 4   Occupational requirements

1. Notwithstanding Article 2(1) and (2), Member States may provide that a **A-098** difference of treatment which is based on a characteristic related to any of the grounds referred to in Article 1 shall not constitute discrimination where, by reason of the nature of the particular occupational activities concerned or of the context in which they are carried out, such a characteristic constitutes a genuine and determining occupational requirement, provided that the objective is legitimate and the requirement is proportionate.

2. Member States may maintain national legislation in force at the date of adoption of this Directive or provide for future legislation incorporating national practices existing at the date of adoption of this Directive pursuant to which, in the case of occupational activities within churches and other public or private organisations the ethos of which is based on religion or belief, a difference of treatment based on a person's religion or belief shall not constitute discrimination where, by reason of the nature of these activities or of the context in which they are carried out, a person's religion or belief constitute a genuine, legitimate and justified occupational requirement, having regard to the organisation's ethos. This difference of treatment shall be implemented taking account of Member States' constitutional provisions and principles, as well as the general principles of Community law, and should not justify discrimination on another ground.

Provided that its provisions are otherwise complied with, this Directive shall thus not prejudice the right of churches and other public or private organisations, the ethos of which is based on religion or belief, acting in conformity with national constitutions and laws, to require individuals working for them to act in good faith and with loyalty to the organisation's ethos.

Article 5   Reasonable accommodation for disabled persons

In order to guarantee compliance with the principle of equal treatment in **A-099** relation to persons with disabilities, reasonable accommodation shall be provided. This means that employers shall take appropriate measures, where needed in a particular case, to enable a person with a disability to have access to, participate in, or advance in employment, or to undergo training, unless such measures would impose a disproportionate burden on the employer. This burden shall not be disproportionate when it is sufficiently remedied by measures existing within the framework of the disability policy of the Member State concerned.

Article 6   Justification of differences of treatment on grounds of age

1. Notwithstanding Article 2(2), Member States may provide that differences **A-100** of treatment on grounds of age shall not constitute discrimination, if, within the context of national law, they are objectively and reasonably justified by a

legitimate aim, including legitimate employment policy, labour market and vocational training objectives, and if the means of achieving that aim are appropriate and necessary. Such differences of treatment may include, among others:

(a) the setting of special conditions on access to employment and vocational training, employment and occupation, including dismissal and remuneration conditions, for young people, older workers and persons with caring responsibilities in order to promote their vocational integration or ensure their protection;

(b) the fixing of minimum conditions of age, professional experience or seniority in service for access to employment or to certain advantages linked to employment;

(c) the fixing of a maximum age for recruitment which is based on the training requirements of the post in question or the need for a reasonable period of employment before retirement.

2. Notwithstanding Article 2(2), Member States may provide that the fixing for occupational social security schemes of ages for admission or entitlement to retirement or invalidity benefits, including the fixing under those schemes of different ages for employees or groups or categories of employees, and the use, in the context of such schemes, of age criteria in actuarial calculations, does not constitute discrimination on the grounds of age, provided this does not result in discrimination on the grounds of sex.

Article 7   Positive action

A-101   1. With a view to ensuring full equality in practice, the principle of equal treatment shall not prevent any Member State from maintaining or adopting specific measures to prevent or compensate for disadvantages linked to any of the grounds referred to in Article 1.

2. With regard to disabled persons, the principle of equal treatment shall be without prejudice to the right of Member States to maintain or adopt provisions on the protection of health and safety at work or to measures aimed at creating or maintaining provisions or facilities for safeguarding or promoting their integration into the working environment.

Article 8   Minimum requirements

A-102   1. Member States may introduce or maintain provisions which are more favourable to the protection of the principle of equal treatment than those laid down in this Directive.

2. The implementation of this Directive shall under no circumstances constitute grounds for a reduction in the level of protection against discrimination already afforded by Member States in the fields covered by this Directive.

Chapter II Remedies And Enforcement

Article 9   Defence of rights

A-103   1. Member States shall ensure that judicial and/or administrative procedures, including where they deem it appropriate conciliation procedures, for the enforcement of obligations under this Directive are available to all persons who consider themselves wronged by failure to apply the principle of equal treatment to them, even after the relationship in which the discrimination is alleged to have occurred has ended.

2. Member States shall ensure that associations, organisations or other legal entities which have, in accordance with the criteria laid down by their national

law, a legitimate interest in ensuring that the provisions of this Directive are complied with, may engage, either on behalf or in support of the complainant, with his or her approval, in any judicial and/or administrative procedure provided for the enforcement of obligations under this Directive.

3. Paragraphs 1 and 2 are without prejudice to national rules relating to time limits for bringing actions as regards the principle of equality of treatment.

Article 10   Burden of proof

1. Member States shall take such measures as are necessary, in accordance **A-104** with their national judicial systems, to ensure that, when persons who consider themselves wronged because the principle of equal treatment has not been applied to them establish, before a court or other competent authority, facts from which it may be presumed that there has been direct or indirect discrimination, it shall be for the respondent to prove that there has been no breach of the principle of equal treatment.

2. Paragraph 1 shall not prevent Member States from introducing rules of evidence which are more favourable to plaintiffs.

3. Paragraph 1 shall not apply to criminal procedures.

4. Paragraphs 1, 2 and 3 shall also apply to any legal proceedings commenced in accordance with Article 9(2).

5. Member States need not apply paragraph 1 to proceedings in which it is for the court or competent body to investigate the facts of the case.

Article 11   Victimisation

Member States shall introduce into their national legal systems such **A-105** measures as are necessary to protect employees against dismissal or other adverse treatment by the employer as a reaction to a complaint within the undertaking or to any legal proceedings aimed at enforcing compliance with the principle of equal treatment.

Article 12   Dissemination of information

Member States shall take care that the provisions adopted pursuant to this **A-106** Directive, together with the relevant provisions already in force in this field, are brought to the attention of the persons concerned by all appropriate means, for example at the workplace, throughout their territory.

Article 13   Social dialogue

1. Member States shall, in accordance with their national traditions and **A-107** practice, take adequate measures to promote dialogue between the social partners with a view to fostering equal treatment, including through the monitoring of workplace practices, collective agreements, codes of conduct and through research or exchange of experiences and good practices.

2. Where consistent with their national traditions and practice, Member States shall encourage the social partners, without prejudice to their autonomy, to conclude at the appropriate level agreements laying down anti-discrimination rules in the fields referred to in Article 3 which fall within the scope of collective bargaining. These agreements shall respect the minimum requirements laid down by this Directive and by the relevant national implementing measures.

Article 14   Dialogue with non-governmental organisations

Member States shall encourage dialogue with appropriate non-governmental **A-108** organisations which have, in accordance with their national law and practice, a legitimate interest in contributing to the fight against discrimination on any of the grounds referred to in Article 1 with a view to promoting the principle of equal treatment.

Chapter III Particular Provisions

Article 15   Northern Ireland

A-109   1. In order to tackle the under-representation of one of the major religious communities in the police service of Northern Ireland, differences in treatment regarding recruitment into that service, including its support staff, shall not constitute discrimination insofar as those differences in treatment are expressly authorised by national legislation.

2. In order to maintain a balance of opportunity in employment for teachers in Northern Ireland while furthering the reconciliation of historical divisions between the major religious communities there, the provisions on religion or belief in this Directive shall not apply to the recruitment of teachers in schools in Northern Ireland in so far as this is expressly authorised by national legislation.

Chapter IV Final Provisions

Article 16   Compliance

A-110   Member States shall take the necessary measures to ensure that:
  (a) any laws, regulations and administrative provisions contrary to the principle of equal treatment are abolished;
  (b) any provisions contrary to the principle of equal treatment which are included in contracts or collective agreements, internal rules of undertakings or rules governing the independent occupations and professions and workers' and employers' organisations are, or may be, declared null and void or are amended.

Article 17   Sanctions

A-111   Member States shall lay down the rules on sanctions applicable to infringements of the national provisions adopted pursuant to this Directive and shall take all measures necessary to ensure that they are applied. The sanctions, which may comprise the payment of compensation to the victim, must be effective, proportionate and dissuasive. Member States shall notify those provisions to the Commission by 2 December 2003 at the latest and shall notify it without delay of any subsequent amendment affecting them.

Council Directive 2001/23/EC of 12 March 2001 on the approximation of the laws of the Member States relating to the safeguarding of employees' rights in the event of transfers of undertakings, businesses or parts of undertakings or businesses

Chapter I Scope And Definitions

Article 1

A-112   1. (a) This Directive shall apply to any transfer of an undertaking, business, or part of an undertaking or business to another employer as a result of a legal transfer or merger.

(b) Subject to subparagraph (a) and the following provisions of this Article, there is a transfer within the meaning of this Directive where there is a transfer of an economic entity which retains its identity, meaning an organised grouping of resources which has the objective of pursuing an economic activity, whether or not that activity is central or ancillary.

(c) This Directive shall apply to public and private undertakings engaged in economic activities whether or not they are operating for gain. An administrative reorganisation of public administrative authorities, or the transfer of administrative functions between public administrative authorities, is not a transfer within the meaning of this Directive.

2. This Directive shall apply where and in so far as the undertaking, business or part of the undertaking or business to be transferred is situated within the territorial scope of the Treaty.

3. This Directive shall not apply to seagoing vessels.

Article 2

For the purposes of this Directive: A-113

(a) "transferor" shall mean any natural or legal person who, by reason of a transfer within the meaning of Article 1(1), ceases to be the employer in respect of the undertaking, business or part of the undertaking or business;

(b) "transferee" shall mean any natural or legal person who, by reason of a transfer within the meaning of Article 1(1), becomes the employer in respect of the undertaking, business or part of the undertaking or business;

(c) "representatives of employees" and related expressions shall mean the representatives of the employees provided for by the laws or practices of the Member States;

(d) "employee" shall mean any person who, in the Member State concerned, is protected as an employee under national employment law.

2. This Directive shall be without prejudice to national law as regards the definition of contract of employment or employment relationship.

However, Member States shall not exclude from the scope of this Directive contracts of employment or employment relationships solely because:

(a) of the number of working hours performed or to be performed,

(b) they are employment relationships governed by a fixed-duration contract of employment within the meaning of Article 1(1) of Council Directive 91/383/EEC of 25 June 1991 supplementing the measures to encourage improvements in the safety and health at work of workers with a fixed-duration employment relationship or a tempory employment relationship(6), or

(c) they are temporary employment relationships within the meaning of Article 1(2) of Directive 91/383/EEC, and the undertaking, business or part of the undertaking or business transferred is, or is part of, the temporary employment business which is the employer.

Chapter II Safeguarding of employees' rights

Article 3

A-114 1. The transferor's rights and obligations arising from a contract of employment or from an employment relationship existing on the date of a transfer shall, by reason of such transfer, be transferred to the transferee.

Member States may provide that, after the date of transfer, the transferor and the transferee shall be jointly and severally liable in respect of obligations which arose before the date of transfer from a contract of employment or an employment relationship existing on the date of the transfer.

2. Member States may adopt appropriate measures to ensure that the transferor notifies the transferee of all the rights and obligations which will be transferred to the transferee under this Article, so far as those rights and obligations are or ought to have been known to the transferor at the time of the transfer. A failure by the transferor to notify the transferee of any such right or obligation shall not affect the transfer of that right or obligation and the rights of any employees against the transferee and/or transferor in respect of that right or obligation.

3. Following the transfer, the transferee shall continue to observe the terms and conditions agreed in any collective agreement on the same terms applicable to the transferor under that agreement, until the date of termination or expiry of the collective agreement or the entry into force or application of another collective agreement.

Member States may limit the period for observing such terms and conditions with the proviso that it shall not be less than one year.

4. (a) Unless Member States provide otherwise, paragraphs 1 and 3 shall not apply in relation to employees' rights to old-age, invalidity or survivors' benefits under supplementary company or intercompany pension schemes outside the statutory social security schemes in Member States.

(b) Even where they do not provide in accordance with subparagraph (a) that paragraphs 1 and 3 apply in relation to such rights, Member States shall adopt the measures necessary to protect the interests of employees and of persons no longer employed in the transferor's business at the time of the transfer in respect of rights conferring on them immediate or prospective entitlement to old age benefits, including survivors' benefits, under supplementary schemes referred to in subparagraph (a).

Article 4

A-115 1. The transfer of the undertaking, business or part of the undertaking or business shall not in itself constitute grounds for dismissal by the transferor or the transferee. This provision shall not stand in the way of dismissals that may take place for economic, technical or organisational reasons entailing changes in the workforce.

Member States may provide that the first subparagraph shall not apply to certain specific categories of employees who are not covered by the laws or practice of the Member States in respect of protection against dismissal.

2. If the contract of employment or the employment relationship is terminated because the transfer involves a substantial change in working conditions to the detriment of the employee, the employer shall be regarded as having been responsible for termination of the contract of employment or of the employment relationship.

Article 5

1. Unless Member States provide otherwise, Articles 3 and 4 shall not apply **A-116** to any transfer of an undertaking, business or part of an undertaking or business where the transferor is the subject of bankruptcy proceedings or any analogous insolvency proceedings which have been instituted with a view to the liquidation of the assets of the transferor and are under the supervision of a competent public authority (which may be an insolvency practioner authorised by a competent public authority).

2. Where Articles 3 and 4 apply to a transfer during insolvency proceedings which have been opened in relation to a transferor (whether or not those proceedings have been instituted with a view to the liquidation of the assets of the transferor) and provided that such proceedings are under the supervision of a competent public authority (which may be an insolvency practioner determined by national law) a Member State may provide that:

(a) notwithstanding Article 3(1), the transferor's debts arising from any contracts of employment or employment relationships and payable before the transfer or before the opening of the insolvency proceedings shall not be transferred to the transferee, provided that such proceedings give rise, under the law of that Member State, to protection at least equivalent to that provided for in situations covered by Council Directive 80/987/EEC of 20 October 1980 on the approximation of the laws of the Member States relating to the protection of employees in the event of the insolvency of their employer(7), and, or alternatively, that,

(b) the transferee, transferor or person or persons exercising the transferor's functions, on the one hand, and the representatives of the employees on the other hand may agree alterations, in so far as current law or practice permits, to the employees' terms and conditions of employment designed to safeguard employment opportunities by ensuring the survival of the undertaking, business or part of the undertaking or business.

3. A Member State may apply paragraph 20(b) to any transfers where the transferor is in a situation of serious economic crisis, as defined by national law, provided that the situation is declared by a competent public authority and open to judicial supervision, on condition that such provisions already existed in national law on 17 July 1998.

The Commission shall present a report on the effects of this provision before 17 July 2003 and shall submit any appropriate proposals to the Council.

4. Member States shall take appropriate measures with a view to preventing misuse of insolvency proceedings in such a way as to deprive employees of the rights provided for in this Directive.

Article 6

1. If the undertaking, business or part of an undertaking or business **A-117** preserves its autonomy, the status and function of the representatives or of the representation of the employees affected by the transfer shall be preserved on the same terms and subject to the same conditions as existed before the date of the transfer by virtue of law, regulation, administrative provision or agreement, provided that the conditions necessary for the constitution of the employee's representation are fulfilled.

The first subparagraph shall not supply if, under the laws, regulations, administrative provisions or practice in the Member States, or by agreement with the representatives of the employees, the conditions necessary for the reappointment of the representatives of the employees or for the reconstitution of the representation of the employees are fulfilled.

Where the transferor is the subject of bankruptcy proceedings or any analoguous insolvency proceedings which have been instituted with a view to the liquidation of the assets of the transferor and are under the supervision of a competent public authority (which may be an insolvency practitioner authorised by a competent public authority), Member States may take the necessary measures to ensure that the transferred employees are properly represented until the new election or designation of representatives of the employees.

If the undertaking, business or part of an undertaking or business does not preserve its autonomy, the Member States shall take the necessary measures to ensure that the employees transferred who were represented before the transfer continue to be properly represented during the period necessary for the reconstitution or reappointment of the representation of employees in accordance with national law or practice.

2. If the term of office of the representatives of the employees affected by the transfer expires as a result of the transfer, the representatives shall continue to enjoy the protection provided by the laws, regulations, administrative provisions or practice of the Member States.

Chapter III Information And Consultation

Article 7

A-118   1. The transferor and transferee shall be required to inform the representatives of their respective employees affected by the transfer of the following:
   –the date or proposed date of the transfer,
   –the reasons for the transfer,
   –the legal, economic and social implications of the transfer for the employees,
   –any measures envisaged in relation to the employees.

The transferor must give such information to the representatives of his employees in good time, before the transfer is carried out.

The transferee must give such information to the representatives of his employees in good time, and in any event before his employees are directly affected by the transfer as regards their conditions of work and employment.

2. Where the transferor or the transferee envisages measures in relation to his employees, he shall consult the representatives of this employees in good time on such measures with a view to reaching an agreement.

3. Member States whose laws, regulations or administrative provisions provide that represenatives of the employees may have recourse to an arbitration board to obtain a decision on the measures to be taken in relation to employees may limit the obligations laid down in paragraphs 1 and 2 to cases where the transfer carried out gives rise to a change in the business likely to entail serious disadvantages for a considerable number of the employees.

The information and consultations shall cover at least the measures envisaged in relation to the employees.

The information must be provided and consultations take place in good time before the change in the business as referred to in the first subparagraph is effected.

4. The obligations laid down in this Article shall apply irrespective of whether the decision resulting in the transfer is taken by the employer or an undertaking controlling the employer.

In considering alleged breaches of the information and consultation requirements laid down by this Directive, the argument that such a breach occurred because the information was not provided by an undertaking controlling the employer shall not be accepted as an excuse.

5. Member States may limit the obligations laid down in paragraphs 1, 2 and 3 to undertakings or businesses which, in terms of the number of employees, meet the conditions for the election or nomination of a collegiate body representing the employees.

6. Member States shall provide that, where there are no representatives of the employees in an undertaking or business through no fault of their own, the employees concerned must be informed in advance of:
   –the date or proposed date of the transfer,
   –the reasons for the transfer,
   –the legal, economic and social implications of the transfer for the employees,
   –any measures envisaged in relation to the employees.

Chapter IV Final provisions

Article 8

This Directive shall not affect the right of Member States to apply or **A-119** introduce laws, regulations or administrative provisions which are more favourable to employees or to promote or permit collective agreements or agreements between social partners more favourable to employees.

Article 9

Member States shall introduce into their national legal systems such **A-120** measures as are necessary to enable all employees and representatives of employees who consider themselves wronged by failure to comply with the obligations arising from this Directive to pursue their claims by judicial process after possible recourse to other competent authorities.

Directive 2002/14/EC of the European Parliament and of the Council of 11 March 2002 establishing a general framework for informing and consulting employees in the European Community

Article 1   Object and principles

1. The purpose of this Directive is to establish a general framework setting **A-121** out minimum requirements for the right to information and consultation of employees in undertakings or establishments within the Community.

2. The practical arrangements for information and consultation shall be defined and implemented in accordance with national law and industrial relations practices in individual Member States in such a way as to ensure their effectiveness.

3. When defining or implementing practical arrangements for information and consultation, the employer and the employees' representatives shall work in a spirit of cooperation and with due regard for their reciprocal rights and obliga-

tions, taking into account the interests both of the undertaking or establishment and of the employees.

Article 2   Definitions

A-122   For the purposes of this Directive:

(a) "undertaking" means a public or private undertaking carrying out an economic activity, whether or not operating for gain, which is located within the territory of the Member States;

(b) "establishment" means a unit of business defined in accordance with national law and practice, and located within the territory of a Member State, where an economic activity is carried out on an ongoing basis with human and material resources;

(c) "employer" means the natural or legal person party to employment contracts or employment relationships with employees, in accordance with national law and practice;

(d) "employee" means any person who, in the Member State concerned, is protected as an employee under national employment law and in accordance with national practice;

(e) "employees' representatives" means the employees' representatives provided for by national laws and/or practices;

(f) "information" means transmission by the employer to the employees' representatives of data in order to enable them to acquaint themselves with the subject matter and to examine it;

(g) "consultation" means the exchange of views and establishment of dialogue between the employees' representatives and the employer.

Article 3   Scope

A-123   1. This Directive shall apply, according to the choice made by Member States, to:

(a) undertakings employing at least 50 employees in any one Member State, or

(b) establishments employing at least 20 employees in any one Member State.

Member States shall determine the method for calculating the thresholds of employees employed.

2. In conformity with the principles and objectives of this Directive, Member States may lay down particular provisions applicable to undertakings or establishments which pursue directly and essentially political, professional organisational, religious, charitable, educational, scientific or artistic aims, as well as aims involving information and the expression of opinions, on condition that, at the date of entry into force of this Directive, provisions of that nature already exist in national legislation.

3. Member States may derogate from this Directive through particular provisions applicable to the crews of vessels plying the high seas.

Article 4   Practical arrangements for information and consultation

A-124   1. In accordance with the principles set out in Article 1 and without prejudice to any provisions and/or practices in force more favourable to employees, the Member States shall determine the practical arrangements for exercising the right to information and consultation at the appropriate level in accordance with this Article.

2. Information and consultation shall cover:

(a) information on the recent and probable development of the undertaking's or the establishment's activities and economic situation;
(b) information and consultation on the situation, structure and probable development of employment within the undertaking or establishment and on any anticipatory measures envisaged, in particular where there is a threat to employment;
(c) information and consultation on decisions likely to lead to substantial changes in work organisation or in contractual relations, including those covered by the Community provisions referred to in Article 9(1).

3. Information shall be given at such time, in such fashion and with such content as are appropriate to enable, in particular, employees' representatives to conduct an adequate study and, where necessary, prepare for consultation.

4. Consultation shall take place:
(a) while ensuring that the timing, method and content thereof are appropriate;
(b) at the relevant level of management and representation, depending on the subject under discussion;
(c) on the basis of information supplied by the employer in accordance with Article 2(f) and of the opinion which the employees' representatives are entitled to formulate;
(d) in such a way as to enable employees' representatives to meet the employer and obtain a response, and the reasons for that response, to any opinion they might formulate;
(e) with a view to reaching an agreement on decisions within the scope of the employer's powers referred to in paragraph 2(c).

Article 5   Information and consultation deriving from an agreement

Member States may entrust management and labour at the appropriate level, **A-125** including at undertaking or establishment level, with defining freely and at any time through negotiated agreement the practical arrangements for informing and consulting employees. These agreements, and agreements existing on the date laid down in Article 11, as well as any subsequent renewals of such agreements, may establish, while respecting the principles set out in Article 1 and subject to conditions and limitations laid down by the Member States, provisions which are different from those referred to in Article 4.

Article 6   Confidential information

1. Member States shall provide that, within the conditions and limits laid **A-126** down by national legislation, the employees' representatives, and any experts who assist them, are not authorised to reveal to employees or to third parties, any information which, in the legitimate interest of the undertaking or establishment, has expressly been provided to them in confidence. This obligation shall continue to apply, wherever the said representatives or experts are, even after expiry of their terms of office. However, a Member State may authorise the employees' representatives and anyone assisting them to pass on confidential information to employees and to third parties bound by an obligation of confidentiality.

2. Member States shall provide, in specific cases and within the conditions and limits laid down by national legislation, that the employer is not obliged to communicate information or undertake consultation when the nature of that information or consultation is such that, according to objective criteria, it would

seriously harm the functioning of the undertaking or establishment or would be prejudicial to it.

3. Without prejudice to existing national procedures, Member States shall provide for administrative or judicial review procedures for the case where the employer requires confidentiality or does not provide the information in accordance with paragraphs 1 and 2. They may also provide for procedures intended to safeguard the confidentiality of the information in question.

Article 7   Protection of employees' representatives

A-127   Member States shall ensure that employees' representatives, when carrying out their functions, enjoy adequate protection and guarantees to enable them to perform properly the duties which have been assigned to them.

Article 8   Protection of rights

A-128   1. Member States shall provide for appropriate measures in the event of non-compliance with this Directive by the employer or the employees' representatives. In particular, they shall ensure that adequate administrative or judicial procedures are available to enable the obligations deriving from this Directive to be enforced.

2. Member States shall provide for adequate sanctions to be applicable in the event of infringement of this Directive by the employer or the employees' representatives. These sanctions must be effective, proportionate and dissuasive.

Article 9   Link between this Directive and other Community and national provisions

A-129   1. This Directive shall be without prejudice to the specific information and consultation procedures set out in Article 2 of Directive 98/59/EC and Article 7 of Directive 2001/23/EC.

2. This Directive shall be without prejudice to provisions adopted in accordance with Directives 94/45/EC and 97/74/EC.

3. This Directive shall be without prejudice to other rights to information, consultation and participation under national law.

4. Implementation of this Directive shall not be sufficient grounds for any regression in relation to the situation which already prevails in each Member State and in relation to the general level of protection of workers in the areas to which it applies.

Article 10   Transitional provisions

A-130   Notwithstanding Article 3, a Member State in which there is, at the date of entry into force of this Directive, no general, permanent and statutory system of information and consultation of employees, nor a general, permanent and statutory system of employee representation at the workplace allowing employees to be represented for that purpose, may limit the application of the national provisions implementing this Directive to:

(a) undertakings employing at least 150 employees or establishments employing at least 100 employees until 23 March 2007, and

(b) undertakings employing at least 100 employees or establishments employing at least 50 employees during the year following the date in point (a).

Article 11   Transposition

1. Member States shall adopt the laws, regulations and administrative **A-131** provisions necessary to comply with this Directive not later than 23 March 2005 or shall ensure that management and labour introduce by that date the required provisions by way of agreement, the Member States being obliged to take all necessary steps enabling them to guarantee the results imposed by this Directive at all times. They shall forthwith inform the Commission thereof.

2. Where Member States adopt these measures, they shall contain a reference to this Directive or shall be accompanied by such reference on the occasion of their official publication. The methods of making such reference shall be laid down by the Member States.

Article 12   Review by the Commission

Not later than 23 March 2007, the Commission shall, in consultation with **A-132** the Member States and the social partners at Community level, review the application of this Directive with a view to proposing any necessary amendments.

ACAS Code of Practice on Disciplinary and Grievance Procedures

Laid in Parliament on 17 June 2004 and subject to Parliamentary approval, is due to come into effect on 1 October 2004

CONTENTS

Section 1 – Disciplinary practice and procedures in employment

At a glance

Drawing up disciplinary rules and procedures
- Involve management, employees and their representatives where appropriate. Paragraph 52)
- Make rules clear and brief and explain their purpose (Paragraph 53)
- Explain rules and procedures to employees and make sure they have a copy or ready access to a copy of them. (Paragraph 55)

Operating disciplinary procedures
- Establish facts before taking action (Paragraph 8)
- Deal with cases of minor misconduct or unsatisfactory performanceinformally (Paragraphs 11 – 12).

- For more serious cases, follow formal procedures, including informing the employee of the alleged misconduct or unsatisfactory performance (Paragraph 13).
- Invite the employee to a meeting and inform them of the right to be accompanied. (Paragraph 14 –16).
- Where performance is unsatisfactory explain to the employee the improvement required, the support that will be given and when and how performance will be reviewed. (Paragraphs 19 –20)
- If giving a warning, tell the employee why and how they need to change, the consequences of failing to improve and that they have a right to appeal (Paragraphs 21 –22).
- If dismissing an employee, tell them why, when their contract will end and that they can appeal (Paragraph 25).
- Before dismissing or taking disciplinary action other than issuing a warning, always follow the statutory dismissal and disciplinary procedure (Paragraphs 26 –32).
- When dealing with absences from work, find out the reasons for the absence before deciding on what action to take (Paragraph 37).

Holding appeals
- If the employee wishes to appeal invite them to a meeting and inform the employee of their right to be accompanied (Paragraphs 44 –48).
- Where possible, arrange for the appeal to be dealt with by a more senior manager not involved with the earlier decision (Paragraph 46).
- Inform the employee about the appeal decision and the reasons for it (Paragraph 48).

Records
- Keep written records for future reference (Paragraph 49).

Guidance

Why have disciplinary rules and procedures?

1. Disciplinary rules and procedures help to promote orderly employment **A-133** relations as well as fairness and consistency in the treatment of individuals. Disciplinary procedures are also a legal requirement in certain circumstances (see paragraph 6).

2. *Disciplinary rules* tell employees what behaviour employers expect from them. If an employee breaks specific rules about behaviour, this is often called misconduct. Employers use disciplinary procedures and actions to deal with situations where employees allegedly break disciplinary rules. Disciplinary procedures may also be used where employees don't meet their employer's expectations in the way they do their job. These cases, often known as *unsatisfactory performance* (or capability), may require different treatment from misconduct, and disciplinary procedures should allow for this.

3. Guidance on how to draw up disciplinary rules and procedures is contained in paragraphs 52 –62.

4. When dealing with disciplinary cases, employers need to be aware both of the law on unfair dismissal and the statutory minimum procedure contained in the Employment Act 2002 for dismissing or taking disciplinary action against an employee. Employers must also be careful not to discriminate on the grounds of

gender, race (including colour, nationality and ethnic or national origins), disability, age, sexual orientation or religion.

The law on unfair dismissal

A-134   5. The law on unfair dismissal requires employers to act reasonably when dealing with disciplinary issues. What is classed as reasonable behaviour will depend on the circumstances of each case, and is ultimately a matter for employment tribunals to decide. However, the core principles employers should work to are set out in the box overleaf. Drawing up and referring to a procedure can help employers deal with disciplinary issues in a fair and consistent manner.

The statutory minimum procedure

A-135   6. Employers are also required to follow a specific statutory minimum procedure if they are contemplating dismissing an employee or imposing some other disciplinary penalty that isn't suspension on full pay or a warning. Guidance on this statutory procedure is provided in paragraphs 26 – 32. If an employee is dismissed without the employer following this statutory procedure, and makes a claim to an employment tribunal, providing they have the necessary qualifying service and providing they are not prevented from claiming unfair dismissal by virtue of their age, the dismissal will automatically be ruled unfair. The statutory procedure is a minimum requirement and even where the relevant procedure is followed the dismissal may still be unfair if the employer has not acted reasonably in all the circumstances.

What about small businesses?

A-136   7. In small organisations it may not be practicable to adopt all the detailed good practice guidance set out in this Code. Employment tribunals will take account of an employer's size and administrative resources when deciding if it acted reasonably. However, all organisations regardless of size must follow the minimum statutory dismissal and disciplinary procedures.

Core principles of reasonable behaviour

A-137   • procedures primarily to help and encourage employees to improve rather than just as a way of imposing a punishment.
   • Inform the employee of the complaint against them, and provide them with an opportunity to state their case before decisions are reached.
   • Allow employees to be accompanied at disciplinary meetings.
   • Make sure that disciplinary action is not taken until the facts of the case have been established and that the action is reasonable in the circumstances.
   • Never dismiss an employee for a first disciplinary offence, unless it is a case of gross misconduct.
   • Give the employee a written explanation for any disciplinary action taken and make sure they know what improvement is expected.
   • Give the employee an opportunity to appeal.
   • Deal with issues as thoroughly and promptly as possible.
   • Act consistently

Dealing with disciplinary issues in the workplace

A-138   8. When a potential disciplinary matter arises, the employer should make necessary investigations to establish the facts promptly before memories of events fade. It is important to keep a written record for later reference. Having established the facts, the employer should decide whether to drop the matter, deal with it informally or arrange for it to be handled formally. Where an investigatory meeting is held solely to establish the facts of a case, it should be made clear to the employee involved that it is not a disciplinary meeting.

9. In certain cases, for example in cases involving gross misconduct, where relationships have broken down or there are risks to an employer's property or responsibilities to other parties, consideration should be given to a brief period of suspension with full pay whilst unhindered investigation is conducted. Such a suspension should only be imposed after careful consideration and should be reviewed to ensure it is not unnecessarily protracted. It should be made clear that the suspension is not considered a disciplinary action.

10. When dealing with disciplinary issues in the workplace employers should bear in mind that they are required under the Disability Discrimination Act 1995 to make reasonable adjustments to cater for employees who have a disability, for example providing for wheelchair access if necessary.

Informal action

11. Cases of minor misconduct or unsatisfactory performance are usually **A-139** best dealt with informally. A quiet word is often all that is required to improve an employee's conduct or performance. The informal approach may be particularly helpful in small firms, where problems can be dealt with quickly and confidentially. There will, however, be situations where matters are more serious or where an informal approach has been tried but isn't working.

12. If informal action doesn't bring about an improvement, or the misconduct or unsatisfactory performance is considered to be too serious to be classed as minor, employers should provide employees with a clear signal of their dissatisfaction by taking formal action.

Formal action

Inform the employee of the problem

13. The first step in any formal process is to let the employee know in writing **A-140** what it is they are alleged to have done wrong. The letter or note should contain enough information for the individual to be able to understand both what it is they are alleged to have done wrong and the reasons why this is not acceptable. If the employee has difficulty reading, or if English is not their first language, the employer should explain the content of the letter or note to them orally. The letter or note should also invite the individual to a meeting at which the problem can be discussed, and it should inform the individual of their right to be accompanied at the meeting (see section three). The employee should be given copies of any documents that will be produced at the meeting.

Hold a meeting to discuss the problem

14. Where possible, the timing and location of the meeting should be agreed **A-141** with the employee. The length of time between the written notification and the meeting should be long enough to allow the employee to prepare but not so long that memories fade. The employer should hold the meeting in a private location and ensure there will be no interruptions.

15. At the meeting, the employer should explain the complaint against the employee and go through the evidence that has been gathered. The employee should be allowed to set out their case and answer any allegations that have been made. The employee should also be allowed to ask questions, present evidence,

call witnesses and be given an opportunity to raise points about any information provided by witnesses.

16. An employee who cannot attend a meeting should inform the employer in advance whenever possible. If the employee fails to attend through circumstances outside their control and unforeseeable at the time the meeting was arranged (e.g. illness) the employer should arrange another meeting. A decision may be taken in the employee's absence if they fail to attend the rearranged meeting without good reason. If an employee's companion cannot attend on a proposed date, the employee can suggest another date so long as it is reasonable and is not more than five working days after the date originally proposed by the employer. This five day time limit may be extended by mutual agreement.

Decide on outcome and action

A-142 17. Following the meeting the employer must decide whether disciplinary action is justified or not. Where it is decided that no action is justified the employee should be informed. Where it is decided that disciplinary action is justified the employer will need to consider what form this should take. Before making any decision the employer should take account of the employee's disciplinary and general record, length of service, actions taken in any previous similar case, the explanations given by the employee and most important of all whether the intended disciplinary action is reasonable under the circumstances.

18. Examples of actions the employer might choose to take are set out in paragraphs 19 – 25. It is normally good practice to give employees at least one chance to improve their conduct or performance before they are issued with a final written warning. However, if an employee's misconduct or unsatisfactory performance or its continuance is sufficiently serious, for example because it is having, or is likely to have, a serious harmful effect on the organisation, it may be appropriate to move directly to a final written warning. In cases of gross misconduct, the employer may decide to dismiss even though the employee has not previously received a warning for misconduct. (Further guidance on dealing with gross misconduct is set out at paragraphs 36 –37)

First formal action –unsatisfactory performance

A-143 19. Following the meeting, an employee who is found to be performing unsatisfactorily should be given a written note setting out:
- the performance problem;
- the improvement that is required;
- the timescale for achieving this improvement;
- a review date; and
- any support the employer will provide to assist the employee.

20. The employee should be informed that the note represents the first stage of a formal procedure and that failure to improve could lead to a final written warning and, ultimately, dismissal. A copy of the note should be kept and used as the basis for monitoring and reviewing performance over a specified period (e.g. six months).

First formal action –misconduct

A-144 21. Where, following a disciplinary meeting, an employee is found guilty of misconduct, the usual first step would be to give them a written warning setting out the nature of the misconduct and the change in behaviour required.

22. The employee should be informed that the warning is part of the formal disciplinary process and what the consequences will be of a failure to change

behaviour. The consequences could be a final written warning and ultimately, dismissal. The employee should also be informed that they may appeal against the decision. A record of the warning should be kept, but it should be disregarded for disciplinary purposes after a specified period (e.g. six months).

23. Guidance on dealing with cases of gross misconduct is provided in paragraphs 35 –36.

Final written warning

24. Where there is a failure to improve or change behaviour in the timescale **A-145** set at the first formal stage, or where the offence is sufficiently serious, the employee should normally be issued with a final written warning but only after they have been given a chance to present their case at a meeting. The final written warning should give details of, and grounds for, the complaint. It should warn the employee that failure to improve or modify behaviour may lead to dismissal or to some other penalty, and refer to the right of appeal. The final written warning should normally be disregarded for disciplinary purposes after a specified period (for example 12 months).

Dismissal or other penalty

25. If the employee's conduct or performance still fails to improve, the final **A-146** stage in the disciplinary process might be dismissal or (if the employee's contract allows it or it is mutually agreed) some other penalty such as demotion, disciplinary transfer, or loss of seniority/pay. A decision to dismiss should only be taken by a manager who has the authority to do so. The employee should be informed as soon as possible of the reasons for the dismissal, the date on which the employment contract will terminate, the appropriate period of notice and their right of appeal.

26. It is important for employers to bear in mind that before they dismiss an employee or impose a sanction such as demotion, loss of seniority or loss of pay, they must as a minimum have followed the statutory dismissal and disciplinary procedures. The standard statutory procedure to be used in almost all cases requires the employer to:

> **Step 1**
> Write to the employee notifying them of the allegations against them and the basis of the allegations and invite them to a meeting to discuss the matter;
>
> **Step 2**
> Hold a meeting to discuss the allegations – at which the employee has the right to be accompanied –and notify the employee of the decision;
>
> **Step 3**
> If the employee wishes to appeal, hold an appeal meeting at which the employee has the right to be accompanied – and inform the employee of the final decision.

27. More detail on the statutory standard procedure is set out at Annex A. There is a modified two step procedure for use in special circumstances involving gross misconduct and details of this are set out at Annex B. Guidance on the modified procedure is contained in paragraph 36. There are a number of situations in which it is not necessary for employers to use the statutory procedures or where they will have been deemed to be completed and these are described in Annex E.

28. If the employer fails to follow this statutory procedure (where it applies), and an employee who is qualified to do so makes a claim for unfair dismissal, the

employment tribunal will automatically find the dismissal unfair. The tribunal will normally increase the compensation awarded by 10 per cent, or, where it feels it is just and equitable to do so, up to 50 percent. Equally, if the employment tribunal finds that an employee has been dismissed unfairly but has failed to follow the procedure (for instance they have failed to attend the disciplinary meeting without good cause), compensation will be reduced by, normally, 10 per cent, or, if the tribunal considers it just and equitable to do so, up to 50 per cent.

29. If the tribunal considers there are exceptional circumstances, compensation may be adjusted (up or down) by less than 10 per cent or not at all.

30. Employers and employees will normally be expected to go through the statutory dismissal and disciplinary procedure unless they have reasonable grounds to believe that by doing so they might be exposed to a significant threat, such as violent, abusive or intimidating behaviour, or they will be harassed. There will always be a certain amount of stress and anxiety for both parties when dealing with any disciplinary case, but this exemption will only apply where the employer or employee reasonably believes that they would come to some serious physical or mental harm; their property or some third party is threatened or the other party has harassed them and this may continue.

31. Equally, the statutory procedure does not need to be followed if circumstances beyond the control of either party prevent one or more steps being followed within a reasonable period. This will sometimes be the case where there is a long–term illness or a long period of absence abroad but, in the case of employers, wherever possible they should consider appointing another manager to deal with the procedure.

32. Where an employee fails to attend a meeting held as part of the statutory discipline procedure without good reason the statutory procedure comes to an end. In those circumstances the employee's compensation may be reduced if they bring a successful complaint before an employment tribunal. If the employee does have a good reason for non-attendance, the employer must re–arrange the meeting. If the employee does not attend the second meeting for good reason the employer need not arrange a third meeting but there will be no adjustment of compensation.

What if a grievance is raised during a disciplinary case?

A-147

33. In the course of a disciplinary process, an employee might raise a grievance that is related to the case. If this happens, the employer should consider suspending the disciplinary procedure for a short period while the grievance is dealt with. Depending on the nature of the grievance, the employer may need to consider bringing in another manager to deal with the disciplinary process. In small organisations this may not be possible, and the existing manager should deal with the case as impartially as possible.

34. Where the action taken or contemplated by the employer is dismissal the statutory grievance procedure does not apply. Where the action taken or contemplated is paid suspension or a warning the statutory grievance procedure and not the dismissal and disciplinary procedure applies to any grievance. However, where the employer takes, or is contemplating other action short of dismissal and asserts that the reason for the action is conduct or capability related, the statutory grievance procedure does not apply unless the grievance is that the action amounts, or would amount, to unlawful discrimination, or that the true reason for the action is not the reason given by the employer. In those cases the employee must have raised a written grievance in accordance with the statutory grievance procedure before presenting any complaint to an employment tribunal

about the issue raised by the grievance. However, if the written grievance is raised before any disciplinary appeal meeting, the rest of the grievance procedure does not have to be followed, although the employer may use the appeal meeting to discuss the grievance.

Dealing with gross misconduct

35. If an employer considers an employee guilty of gross misconduct, and **A-148** thus potentially liable for summary dismissal, it is still important to establish the facts before taking any action. A short period of suspension with full pay may be helpful or necessary, although it should only be imposed after careful consideration and should be kept under review. It should be made clear to the employee that the suspension is not a disciplinary action and does not involve any prejudgement.

36. It is a core principle of reasonable behaviour that employers should give employees the opportunity of putting their case at a disciplinary meeting before deciding whether to take action. This principle applies as much to cases of gross misconduct as it does to ordinary cases of misconduct or unsatisfactory performance. There may however be some very limited cases where despite the fact that an employer has dismissed an employee immediately without a meeting an employment tribunal will, very exceptionally, find the dismissal to be fair To allow for these cases there is a statutory modified procedure under which the employer is required to write to the employee after the dismissal setting out the reasons for the dismissal and to hold an appeal meeting, if the employee wants one. The statutory procedure that must be followed by employers in such cases is set out in Annex B. If an employer fails to follow this procedure and the case goes to tribunal, the dismissal will be found to be automatically unfair.

Dealing with absence from work

37. When dealing with absence from work, it is important to determine the **A-149** reasons why the employee has not been at work. If there is no acceptable reason, the matter should be treated as a conduct issue and dealt with as a disciplinary matter.

38. If the absence is due to genuine (including medically certified) illness, the issue becomes one of capability, and the employer should take a sympathetic and considerate approach. When thinking about how to handle these cases, it is helpful to consider:
- how soon the employee's health and attendance will improve;
- whether alternative work is available;
- the effect of the absence on the organisation;
- how similar situations have been handled in the past; and
- whether the illness is a result of disability in which case the provisions of the Disability Discrimination Act 1995 will apply.

39. whether the illness is a result of disability in which case the provisions of the Disability Discrimination Act 1995 will apply.

40. In cases of extended sick leave both statutory and contractual issues will need to be addressed and specialist advice may be necessary.

Dealing with special situations

If the full procedure is not immediately available

41. Special arrangements might be required for handling disciplinary matters **A-150** among nightshift employees, employees in isolated locations or depots, or others

who may be difficult to reach. Nevertheless the appropriate statutory procedure must be followed where it applies.

Trade union representatives

A-151   42. Disciplinary action against a trade union representative can lead to a serious dispute if it is seen as an attack on the union's functions. Normal standards apply but, if disciplinary action is considered, the case should be discussed, after obtaining the employee's agreement, with a senior trade union representative or permanent union official.

Criminal charges or convictions not related to employment

A-152   43. If an employee is charged with, or convicted of, a criminal offence not related to work, this is not in itself reason for disciplinary action. The employer should establish the facts of the case and consider whether the matter is serious enough to warrant starting the disciplinary procedure. The main consideration should be whether the offence, or alleged offence, is one that makes the employee unsuitable for their type of work. Similarly, an employee should not be dismissed solely because they are absent from work as a result of being remanded in custody.

Appeals

A-153   44. who have had disciplinary action taken against them should be given the opportunity to appeal. It is useful to set a time limit for asking for an appeal five working days is usually enough.

  45. An employee may choose to appeal for example because:

- they think a finding or penalty is unfair;
- new evidence comes to light; or
- they think the disciplinary procedure wasn't used correctly.

It should be noted that the appeal stage is part of the statutory procedure and if the employee pursues an employment tribunal claim the tribunal may reduce any award of compensation if the employee did not exercise the right of appeal46. As far as is reasonably practicable a more senior manager not involved with the case should hear the appeal. In small organisations, even if a more senior manager is not available, another manager should hear the appeal, if possible. If that is not an option, the person overseeing the case should act as impartially as possible. Records and notes of the original disciplinary meeting should be made available to the person hearing the appeal.

  47. The employers should contact the employee with appeal arrangements as soon as possible, and inform them of their statutory right to be accompanied at the appeal meeting.

  48. The manager must inform the employee about the appeal decision, and the reasons for it, as soon as possible. They should also confirm the decision in writing. If the decision is the final stage of the organisation's appeals procedure, the manager should make this clear to the employee.

Keeping records

A-154   49. It is important, and in the interests of both employers and employees, to keep written records during the disciplinary process. Records should include:

- the complaint against the employee;
- the employee's defence;
- findings made and actions taken;
- the reason for actions taken;

- whether an appeal was lodged;
- the outcome of the appeal;
- any grievances raised during the disciplinary procedure; and
- subsequent developments.

50. Records should be treated as confidential and be kept no longer than necessary in accordance with the Data Protection Act 1998. This Act gives individuals the right to request and have access to certain personal data.

51. Copies of meeting records should be given to the employee including copies of any formal minutes that may have been taken. In certain circumstances (for example to protect a witness) the employer might withhold some information.

Drawing up disciplinary rules and procedures

52. Management is responsible for maintaining and setting standards of performance in an organisation and for ensuring that disciplinary rules and procedures are in place. Employers are legally required to have disciplinary procedures. It is good practice to involve employees (and, where appropriate, their representatives) when making or changing rules and procedures, so that everyone affected by them understands them. **A-155**

Rules

53. When making rules, the aim should be to specify those that are necessary for ensuring a safe and efficient workplace and for maintaining good employment relations. **A-156**

54. It is unlikely that any set of rules will cover all possible disciplinary issues, but rules normally cover:
- bad behaviour, such as fighting or drunkenness;
- unsatisfactory work performance;
- harassment or victimisation;
- misuse of company facilities (for example e-mail and internet);
- poor timekeeping;
- unauthorised absences; and
- repeated or serious failure to follow instructions.

55. Rules should be specific, clear and recorded in writing. They also need to be readily available to employees, for instance on a noticeboard or, in larger organisations, in a staff handbook or on the Intranet. Management should do all they can to ensure that every employee knows and understands the rules, including those employees whose first language is not English or who have trouble reading. This is often best done as part of an induction process.

56. Employers should inform employees of the likely consequences of breaking disciplinary rules. In particular, they should list examples of acts of gross misconduct that may warrant summary dismissal.

57. Acts which constitute gross misconduct are those resulting in a serious breach of contractual terms and are best decided by organisations in the light of their own particular circumstances. However, examples of gross misconduct might include:
- theft or fraud;
- physical violence or bullying;
- deliberate and serious damage to property;
- serious misuse of an organisation's property or name;
- deliberately accessing internet sites containing pornographic, offensive or obscene material;

- serious insubordination;
- unlawful discrimination or harassment;
- bringing the organisation into serious disrepute;
- serious incapability at work brought on by alcohol or illegal drugs;
- causing loss, damage or injury through serious negligence;
- a serious breach of health and safety rules; and
- a serious breach of confidence.

Procedures

A-157   58. Disciplinary procedures should not be seen primarily as a means of imposing sanctions but rather as a way of encouraging improvement amongst employees whose conduct or performance is unsatisfactory. Some organisations may prefer to have separate procedures for dealing with issues of conduct and capability. Large organisations may also have separate procedures to deal with other issues such as harassment and bullying.

59. When drawing up and applying procedures employers should always bear in mind the requirements of natural justice. This means that employees should be given the opportunity of a meeting with someone who has not been involved in the matter. They should be informed of the allegations against them, together with the supporting evidence, in advance of the meeting. Employees should be given the opportunity to challenge the allegations before decisions are reached and should be provided with a right of appeal.

60. Good disciplinary procedures should:
- be put in writing;
- say to whom they apply;
- be non-discriminatory;
- allow for matters to be dealt without undue delay;
- allow for information to be kept confidential;
- tell employees what disciplinary action might be taken;
- say what levels of management have the authority to take disciplinary action;
- require employees to be informed of the complaints against them and supporting evidence, before a meeting;
- give employees a chance to have their say before management reaches a decision;
- provide employees with the right to be accompanied;
- provide that no employee is dismissed for a first breach of discipline, except in cases of gross misconduct;
- require management to investigate fully before any disciplinary action is taken;
- ensure that employees are given an explanation for any sanction; and
- allow employees to appeal against a decision.

61. It is important to ensure that everyone in an organisation understands the disciplinary procedures including the statutory requirements. In small firms this is best done by making sure all employees have access to a copy of the procedures, for instance on a noticeboard, and by taking a few moments to run through the procedures with the employee. In large organisations formal training for those who use and operate the procedures may be appropriate.

Further action

A-158   62. It is sensible to keep rules and procedures under review to make sure they are always relevant and effective. New or additional rules should only be introduced after reasonable notice has been given to all employees and any employee representatives have been consulted.

Section 2 – Grievance procedures

At a glance

Drawing up grievance procedures
- Involve management, employees and their representatives where appropriate. (Paragraph 90)
- Explain procedures to employees and make sure they have a copy or ready access to a copy of them. (Paragraph 94)

Operating grievance procedures
- Many grievances can be settled informally with line managers (Paragraph 67).
- Employees should raise formal grievances with management (Paragraph 73).
- Invite the employee to a meeting and inform them about the right to be accompanied (Paragraph 77).
- Give the employee an opportunity to have their say at the meeting (Paragraph 78).
- Write with a response within a reasonable time and inform the employee of their right to appeal (Paragraph 81).

Appeals
- If possible, a more senior manager should handle the appeal (Paragraph 82).
- Tell the employee they have the right to be accompanied (Paragraph 82).
- The senior manager should respond to the grievance in writing after the appeal and tell the employee if it is the final stage in the grievance procedure (Paragraph 83).

Records
- Written records should be kept for future reference (Paragraph 87).

Guidance

Why have grievance procedures?

63. *Grievances* are concerns, problems or complaints that employees raise **A-159** with their employers.

64. *Grievance procedures* are used by employers to deal with employees' grievances.

65. Grievance procedures allow employers to deal with grievances fairly, consistently and speedily. Employers must have procedures available to employees so that their grievances can be properly considered.

66. Guidance on drawing up grievance procedures is set out in paragraphs 90 –95.

Dealing with grievances in the workplace

67. Employees should aim to resolve most grievances informally with their **A-160** line manager. This has advantages for all workplaces, particularly where there

might be a close personal relationship between a manager and an employee. It also allows for problems to be resolved quickly.

68. If a grievance cannot be settled informally, the employee should raise it formally with management. There is a statutory grievance procedure that employees must invoke if they wish subsequently to use the grievance as the basis of certain applications to an employment tribunal.

69. Under the standard statutory procedure, employees must:

Step 1

Inform the employer of their grievance in writing;

Step 2

Be invited by the employer to a meeting to discuss the grievance where the right to be accompanied will apply and be notified in writing of the decision. The employee must take all reasonable steps to attend this meeting

Step 3

Be given the right to an appeal meeting if they feel the grievance has not been satisfactorily resolved and be notified of the final decision.

More detail on the standard statutory procedure is set out in Annex C.

70. There are certain occasions when it is not necessary to follow the statutory procedure for example, if the employee is raising a concern in compliance with the Public Interest Disclosure Act or a grievance is raised on behalf of at least two employees by an appropriate representative such as an official of an independent trade union. A full list of exemptions is set out in Annex E.

71. It is important that employers and employees follow the statutory grievance procedure where it applies. The employee should (subject to the exemptions described in Annex E) at least have raised the grievance in writing and waited 28 days before presenting any tribunal claim relating to the matter. A premature claim will be automatically rejected by the tribunal although (subject to special time limit rules) it may be presented again once the written grievance has been raised. Furthermore if a grievance comes before an employment tribunal and either party has failed to follow the procedure then the tribunal will normally adjust any award by 10 per cent or, where it feels it just and equitable to do so, by up to 50 per cent, depending on which party has failed to follow the procedure. In exceptional cases compensation can be adjusted by less than 10 per cent or not at all.

72. Wherever possible a grievance should be dealt with before an employee leaves employment. A statutory grievance procedure ("the modified grievance procedure" described in Annex D), however, applies where an employee has already left employment, the standard procedure has not been commenced or completed before the employee left employment and both parties agree in writing that it should be used instead of the standard statutory procedure. Under the modified procedure the employee should write to the employer setting out the grievance as soon as possible after leaving employment and the employer must write back setting out its response.

Raising a grievance

A-161   73. Employees should normally raise a grievance with their line manager unless someone else is specified in the organisation's procedure. If the complaint is against the person with whom the grievance would normally be raised the employee can approach that person's manager or another manager in the organisation. In small businesses where this isn't possible, the line manager should hear the grievance and deal with it as impartially as possible.

74. Managers should deal with all grievances raised, whether or not the grievance is presented in writing. However, employees need to be aware that if the statutory procedure applies, they will not subsequently be able to take the case to an employment tribunal unless they have first raised a grievance in writing and waited a further 28 days before presenting the tribunal claim.

75. Setting out a grievance in writing is not easy especially for those employees whose first language is not English or who have difficulty expressing themselves on paper. In these circumstances the employee should be encouraged to seek help for example from a work colleague, a trade union or other employee representative. Under the Disability Discrimination Act 1995 employers are required to make reasonable adjustments which may include assisting employees to formulate a written grievance if they are unable to do so themselves because of a disability.

76. In circumstances where a grievance may apply to more than one person and where a trade union is recognised it may be appropriate for the problem to be resolved through collective agreements between the trade union(s) and the employer.

Grievance meetings

77. On receiving a formal grievance, a manager should invite the employee to **A-162** a meeting as soon as possible and inform them that they have the right to be accompanied. It is good practice to agree a time and place for the meeting with the employee. Small organisations might not have private meeting rooms, but it is important that the meeting is not interrupted and that the employee feels their grievance is being treated confidentially. If an employee's companion cannot attend on a proposed date, the employee can suggest another date so long as it is reasonable and is not more than five working days after the date originally proposed by the employer. This five day time limit may be extended by mutual agreement.

78. The employee should be allowed to explain their complaint and say how they think it should be settled. If the employer reaches a point in the meeting where they are not sure how to deal with the grievance or feel that further investigation is necessary the meeting should be adjourned to get advice or make further investigation. This might be particularly useful in small organisations that lack experience of dealing with formal grievances. The employer should give the grievance careful consideration before responding.

79. Employers and employees will normally be expected to go through the statutory grievance procedures unless they have reasonable grounds to believe that by doing so they might be exposed to a significant threat, such as violent, abusive or intimidating behaviour, or they will be harassed. There will always be a certain amount of stress and anxiety for both parties when dealing with grievance cases, but this exemption will only apply where the employer or employee reasonably believes that they would come to some serious physical or mental harm; their property or some third party is threatened or the other party has harassed them and this may continue.

80. Equally, the statutory procedure does not need to be followed if circumstances beyond the control of either party prevent one or more steps being followed within a reasonable period. This will sometimes be the case where there is a long-term illness or a long period of absence abroad but wherever possible

the employer should consider appointing another manager to deal with the procedure.

81. The employer should respond in writing to the employee's grievance within a reasonable time and should let the employee know that they can appeal against the employer's decision if they are not satisfied with it. What is considered reasonable will vary from organisation to organisation, but five working days is normally long enough. If it is not possible to respond within five working days the employee should be given an explanation for the delay and told when a response can be expected.

Appeals

A-163   82. If an employee informs the employer that they are unhappy with the decision after a grievance meeting, the employer should arrange an appeal. It should be noted that the appeal stage is part of the statutory procedure and if the employee pursues a n employment tribunal claim the tribunal may reduce any award of compensation if the employee did not exercise the right of appeal. As far as is reasonably practicable the appeal should be with a more senior manager than the one who dealt with the original grievance. In small organisations, even if there is no more senior manager available, another manager should, if possible, hear the appeal. If that is not an option, the person overseeing the case should act as impartially as possible. At the same time as inviting the employee to attend the appeal, the employer should remind them of their right to be accompanied at the appeal meeting.

83. As with the first meeting, the employer should write to the employee with a decision on their grievance as soon as possible. They should also tell the employee if the appeal meeting is the final stage of the grievance procedure.

84. In large organisations it is good practice to allow a further appeal to a higher level of management, such as a director. However, in smaller firms the first appeal will usually mark the end of the grievance procedure.

Special considerations

A-164   85. Complaints about discrimination, bullying and harassment in the workplace are sensitive issues, and large organisations often have separate grievance procedures for dealing with these. It is important that these procedures meet the statutory minimum requirements.

86. Organisations may also wish to consider whether they need a whistleblow-ing procedure in the light of the Public Interest Disclosure Act 1998. This Act provides protection to employees who raise concerns about certain kinds of wrongdoing in accordance with its procedures.

Keeping records

A-165   87. It is important, and in the interests of both employer and employee, to keep written records during the grievance process. Records should include:
- the nature of the grievance raised;
- a copy of the written grievance
- the employer's response;
- action taken;
- reasons for action taken;
- whether there was an appeal and, if so, the outcome; and
- Subsequent developments

88. Records should be treated as confidential and kept in accordance with the Data Protection Act 1998, which gives individuals the right to request and have access to certain personal data.

89. Copies of meeting records should be given to the employee including any formal minutes that may have been taken. In certain circumstances (for example to protect a witness) the employer might withhold some information.

Drawing up grievance procedures

90. When employers draw up grievance procedures, it pays to involve **A-166** everybody they will affect, including managers, employees and, where appropriate, their representatives.

91. Grievance procedures should make it easy for employees to raise issues with management and should:
- be simple and put in writing;
- enable an employee's line manager to deal informally with a grievance, if possible;
- keep proceedings confidential; and
- allow the employee to have a companion at meetings.

92. Issues that may cause grievances include:
- terms and conditions of employment;
- health and safety;
- work relations;
- bullying and harassment;
- new working practices;
- working environment;
- organisational change; and
- equal opportunities.

93. Where separate procedures exist for dealing with grievances on particular issues (for example, harassment and bullying) these should be used instead of the normal grievance procedure.

94. It's important to ensure that everyone in the organisation understands the grievance procedures including the statutory requirements and that, if necessary, supervisors, managers and employee representatives are trained in their use. Employees must be given a copy of the procedures or have ready access to them, for instance on a noticeboard. Large organisations can include them with disciplinary procedures as part of an induction process.

95. Take the time to explain the detail of grievance procedures to employees. This is particularly useful for people who don't speak English very well or who have difficulty with reading.

Section 3 – A worker's right to be accompanied

At a glance

The right to be accompanied
- All workers have the right to be accompanied at a disciplinary or grievance hearing (Paragraph 96).
- Workers must make a reasonable request to the employer if they want to be accompanied (Paragraph 96).
- Disciplinary hearings, for these purposes, include meetings where either disciplinary actions or some other actions might be taken against the worker. Appeal hearings are also covered (Paragraphs 97–99).

- Grievance hearings are defined as meetings where an employer deals with a worker's complaint about a duty owed to them by the employer (Paragraphs 100–102).

The companion
- The companion can be a fellow worker or a union official (Paragraph 104).
- Nobody has to accept an invitation to act as a companion (Paragraph 107).
- Fellow workers who are acting as companions can take paid time off to prepare for and go to a hearing (Paragraph 109).

Applying the right
- Agree a suitable date with the worker and the companion (Paragraph 110).
- The worker should tell the employer who the chosen companion is (Paragraph 112).
- The companion can have a say at the hearing but can't answer questions for the worker (Paragraph 113–114).
- Don't disadvantage workers who have applied the right, or their companions (Paragraph 116).

Guidance

What is the right to be accompanied?

A-167   96. Workers have a statutory right to be accompanied by a fellow worker or trade union official where they are required or invited by their employer to attend certain disciplinary or grievance hearings. They must make a reasonable request to their employer to be accompanied. Further guidance on what is a reasonable request and who can accompany a worker appears at paragraphs 103–109.

What is a disciplinary hearing?

A-168   97. For the purposes of this right, disciplinary hearings are defined as meetings that could result in:
- a formal warning being issued to a worker (i.e. a warning that will be placed on the worker's record);
- the taking of some other disciplinary action (such as suspension without pay, demotion or dismissal) or other action; or
- the confirmation of a warning or some other disciplinary action (such as an appeal hearing).

98. The right to be accompanied will also apply to any disciplinary meetings held as part of the statutory dismissal and disciplinary procedures. This includes any meetings held after an employee has left employment.

99. Informal discussions or counselling sessions do not attract the right to be accompanied unless they could result in formal warnings or other actions. Meetings to investigate an issue are not disciplinary hearings. If it becomes clear during the course of such a meeting that disciplinary action is called for, the meeting should be ended and a formal hearing arranged at which the worker will have the right to be accompanied.

What is a grievance hearing?

A-169   100. For the purposes of this right, a grievance hearing is a meeting at which an employer deals with a complaint about a duty owed by them to a worker, whether the duty arises from statute or common law (for example contractual commitments).

101. For instance, an individual s request for a pay rise is unlikely to fall within the definition, unless a right to an increase is specifically provided for in the contract or the request raises an issue about equal pay. Equally, most employers will be under no legal duty to provide their workers with car parking facilities, and a grievance about such facilities would carry no right to be accompanied at a hearing by a companion. However, if a worker were disabled and needed a car to get to and from work, they probably would be entitled to a companion at a grievance hearing, as an issue might arise as to whether the employer was meeting its obligations under the Disability Discrimination Act 1995.

102. The right to be accompanied will also apply to any meetings held as part of the statutory grievance procedures. This includes any meetings after the employee has left employment.

What is a reasonable request?

103. Whether a request for a companion is reasonable will depend on the circumstances of the individual case and, ultimately, it is a matter for the courts and tribunals to decide. However, when workers are choosing a companion, they should bear in mind that it would not be reasonable to insist on being accompanied by a colleague whose presence would prejudice the hearing or who might have a conflict of interest. Nor would it be reasonable for a worker to ask to be accompanied by a colleague from a geographically remote location when someone suitably qualified was available on site. The request to be accompanied does not have to be in writing. **A-170**

The companion

104. The companion may be: **A-171**
- a fellow worker (ie another of the employer's workers);
- an official employed by a trade union, or a lay trade union official, as long as they have been reasonably certified in writing by their union as having experience of, or having received training in, acting as a worker's companion at disciplinary or grievance hearings. Certification may take the form of a card or letter.

105. Some workers may, however, have additional contractual rights to be accompanied by persons other than those listed above (for instance a partner, spouse or legal representative). If workers are disabled, employers should consider whether it might be reasonable to allow them to be accompanied because of their disability.

106. Workers may ask an official from any trade union to accompany them at a disciplinary or grievance hearing, regardless of whether the union is recognised or not. However, where a union is recognised in a workplace, it is good practice for workers to ask an official from that union to accompany them.

107. Fellow workers or trade union officials do not have to accept a request to accompany a worker, and they should not be pressurised to do so.

108. Trade unions should ensure that their officials are trained in the role of acting as a worker's companion. Even when a trade union official has experience of acting in the role, there may still be a need for periodic refresher training.

109. A worker who has agreed to accompany a colleague employed by the same employer is entitled to take a reasonable amount of paid time off to fulfil that responsibility. This should cover the hearing and it is also good practice to allow time for the companion to familiarise themselves with the case and confer with the worker before and after the hearing. A lay trade union official is

permitted to take a reasonable amount of paid time off to accompany a worker at a hearing, as long as the worker is employed by the same employer. In cases where a lay official agrees to accompany a worker employed by another organisation, time off is a matter for agreement by the parties concerned.

Applying the right

A-172   110. Where possible, the employer should allow a companion to have a say in the date and time of a hearing. If the companion can't attend on a proposed date, the worker can suggest an alternative time and date so long as it is reasonable and it is not be more than five working days after the original date.

111. In the same way that employers should cater for a worker's disability at a disciplinary or grievance hearing, they should also cater for a companion's disability, for example providing for wheelchair access if necessary.

112. Before the hearing takes place, the worker should tell the employer who they have chosen as a companion. In certain circumstances (for instance when the companion is an official of a non-recognised trade union) it can be helpful for the companion and employer to make contact before the hearing.

113. The companion should be allowed to address the hearing in order to:
- put the worker's case
- sum up the worker's case
- respond on the worker's behalf to any view expressed at the hearing.

114. The companion can also confer with the worker during the hearing. It is good practice to allow the companion to participate as fully as possible in the hearing, including asking witnesses questions. The companion has no right to answer questions on the worker's behalf, or to address the hearing if the worker does not wish it, or to prevent the employer from explaining their case.

115. Workers whose employers fail to comply with a reasonable request to be accompanied may present a complaint to an employment tribunal. Workers may also complain to a tribunal if employers fail to re-arrange a hearing to a reasonable date proposed by the worker when a companion cannot attend on the date originally proposed. The tribunal may order compensation of up to two weeks' pay. This could be increased if, in addition, the tribunal finds that the worker has been unfairly dismissed.

116. Employers should be careful not to disadvantage workers for using their right to be accompanied or for being companions, as this is against the law and could lead to a claim to an employment tribunal.

Section 4 – Annexes

Annex A

A-173   **Standard statutory dismissal and disciplinary procedure**
(This is a summary of the statutory procedure which is set out in full in Schedule 2 to the Employment Act 2002)

This procedure applies to disciplinary action short of dismissal (excluding oral and written warnings and suspension on full pay) based on either conduct or capability. It also applies to dismissals (except for constructive dismissals) including dismissals on the basis of conduct, capability, expiry of a fixed term contract, redundancy and retirement. However, it does not apply in certain kinds of excepted cases that are described in Annex E.

Step 1

Statement of grounds for action and invitation to meeting

- The employer must set out in writing the employee's alleged conduct or characteristics, or other circumstances, which lead them to contemplate dismissing or taking disciplinary action against the employee.
- The employer must send the statement or a copy of it to the employee and invite the employee to attend a meeting to discuss the matter.

Step 2

The meeting

- The meeting must take place before action is taken, except in the case where the disciplinary action consists of suspension.
- The meeting must not take place unless:
    - i) the employer has informed the employee what the basis was for including in the statement under Step 1 the ground or grounds given in it; and
    - ii) the employee has had a reasonable opportunity to consider their response to that information.
- The employee must take all reasonable steps to attend the meeting.
- After the meeting, the employer must inform the employee of their decision and notify them of the right to appeal against the decision if they are not satisfied with it.
- Employees have the right to be accompanied at the meeting (see section 3)

Step 3

Appeal

- If the employee wishes to appeal, they must inform the employer.
- If the employee informs the employer of their wish to appeal, the employer must invite them to attend a further meeting.
- The employee must take all reasonable steps to attend the meeting.
- The appeal meeting need not take place before the dismissal or disciplinary action takes effect.
- Where reasonably practicable, the appeal should be dealt with by a more senior manager than attended the first meeting (unless the most senior manager attended that meeting).
- After the appeal meeting, the employer must inform the employee of their final decision.
- Employees have the right to be accompanied at the appeal meeting (see section 3).

Annex B

Modified statutory dismissal and disciplinary procedure   A-174

(This is a summary of the statutory procedure which is set out in full in Schedule 2 to the Employment Act 2002)

Step 1

Statement of grounds for action

- The employer must set out in writing:
    - i) the employee's alleged misconduct which has led to the dismissal;

ii) the reasons for thinking at the time of the dismissal that the employee was guilty of the alleged misconduct; and

iii) the employee's right of appeal against dismissal.

- The employer must send the statement or a copy of it to the employee.

Step 2

Appeal

- If the employee does wish to appeal, they must inform the employer.
- If the employee informs the employer of their wish to appeal, the employer must invite them to attend a meeting.
- The employee must take all reasonable steps to attend the meeting.
- After the appeal meeting, the employer must inform the employee of their final decision.
- Where reasonably practicable the appeal should be dealt with by a more senior manager not involved in the earlier decision to dismiss.
- Employees have the right to be accompanied at the appeal meeting (see section 3).

Annex C

A-175 Standard statutory grievance procedure

(This is a summary of the statutory procedure which is set out in full in Schedule 2 to the Employment Act 2002)

Step 1

Statement of grievance

- The employee must set out the grievance in writing and send the statement or a copy of it to the employer

Step 2

Meeting

- The employer must invite the employee to attend a meeting to discuss the grievance.
- The meeting must not take place unless:
- the employee has informed the employer what the basis for the grievance was when they made the statement under Step 1; and
- the employer has had a reasonable opportunity to consider their response to that information.
- The employee must take all reasonable steps to attend the meeting.
- After the meeting, the employer must inform the employee of their decision as to their response to the grievance and notify them of the right of appeal against the decision if they are not satisfied with it.
- Employees have the right to be accompanied at the meeting (see section 3) (25)

Step 3

Appeal

- If the employee does wish to appeal, they must inform the employer.
- If the employee informs the employer of their wish to appeal, the employer must invite them to attend a further meeting.
- The employee must take all reasonable steps to attend the meeting.

- After the appeal meeting, the employer must inform the employee of their final decision.
- Where reasonably practicable, the appeal should be dealt with by a more senior manager than attended the first meeting (unless the most senior manager attended that meeting).
- Employees have the right to be accompanied at the appeal meeting (see section 3)

Annex D

Modified statutory grievance procedure   A-176
(This is a summary of the statutory procedure which is set out in full in Schedule 2 to the Employment Act 2002)

Step 1

Statement of grievance
- The employee must set out in writing:
- the grievance; and
- the basis for it.
- The employee must send the statement or a copy of it to the employer.

Step 2

Response
- The employer must set out their response in writing and send the statement or a copy of it to the employee.

Annex E

Statutory Procedures: Exemptions and Deemed Compliance   A-177
The Employment Act 2002 (Dispute Resolution) Regulations 2004 contain detailed provisions about the application of the Statutory Dispute Resolution Procedures. This Annex summarises the particular provisions of the 2004 Regulations which describe:
- (a) certain situations in which the statutory procedures will not apply at all; and
- (b) other situations in which a party who has not completed the applicable procedure will nevertheless be treated as though they had done so.

Where a statutory procedure applies and one of the conditions for extending time limits contained in the 2004 Regulations has been met, then the normal time limit for presenting an employment tribunal claim will be extended by three months. The guidance notes accompanying tribunal application forms describe those conditions. However, in cases where the procedures do not apply at all, there can be no such extension.

(a) Situations in which the Statutory Procedures do not apply at all

The Disciplinary and Dismissal Procedures do not apply where:
- Factors beyond the control of either party make it impracticable to carry out or complete the procedure for the foreseeable future; or

- The employee is dismissed in circumstances covered by the modified dismissal procedure and presents a tribunal complaint before the employer has taken step 1; or
- All of the employees of the same description or category are dismissed and offered re-engagement either before or upon termination of their contract; or
- The dismissal is one of a group of redundancies covered by the duty of collective consultation of worker representatives under the Trade Union and Labour Relations (Consolidation) Act 1992; or
- The employee is dismissed while taking part in unofficial industrial action, or other industrial action which is not "protected action" under the 1992 Act, unless the employment tribunal has jurisdiction to hear a claim of unfair dismissal; or
- The employee is unfairly dismissed for taking part in industrial action which is "protected action" under the 1992 Act; or
- The employer's business suddenly and unexpectedly ceases to function and it becomes impractical to employee any employees; or
- The employee cannot continue in the particular position without contravening a statutory requirement; or
- The employee is one to whom a dismissal procedure agreement designated under section 110 of the Employment Relations Act 1996 applies.

The Grievance Procedures do not apply where:

- The employee is no longer employed, and it is no longer practicable for the employee to take step 1 of the procedure; or
- The employee wishes to complain about an actual or threatened dismissal; or
- The employee raises a concern as a "protected disclosure" in compliance with the public interest disclosure provisions of the 1996 Act;
- The employee wishes to complain about (actual or threatened) action short of dismissal to which the standard disciplinary procedure applies, unless the grievance is that this involves unlawful discrimination (including under the Equal Pay Act) or is not genuinely on grounds of capability or conduct.

In addition, neither party need comply with an applicable statutory procedure where to do so would be contrary to the interests of national security.

(b) Situations in which the Statutory Procedures have not been completed but are treated as having been complied with.

The Disciplinary and Dismissal Procedures are treated as having been complied with where all stages of the procedure have been completed, other than the right of appeal, and:

- The employee then applies to the employment tribunal for interim relief; or
- A collective agreement provides for a right of appeal, which the employee exercises.

The Grievance Procedures are treated as having been complied with where:

- The employee is complaining that action short of dismissal to which the standard disciplinary procedure applies is not genuinely on grounds of conduct or capability, or involves unlawful discrimination, and the employee has raised that complaint as a written grievance before any appeal hearing under a statutory procedure or, if none is being followed, before presenting a tribunal complaint; or

- The employment has ended and the employee has raised a written grievance, but it has become not reasonably practical to have a meeting or an appeal. However, the employer must still give the employee a written answer to the grievance; or
- An official of a recognised independent union or other appropriate representative has raised the grievance on behalf of two or more named employees. Employees sharing the grievance may choose one of their number to act as a representative; or
- The employee pursues the grievance using a procedure available under an industry-level collective agreement.

(c) Other Special Circumstances in which the Statutory Procedures need not be begun or completed

In addition, neither the employer nor employee need begin a procedure (which will then be treated as not applying), or comply with a particular requirement of it (but will still be deemed to have complied) if the reason for not beginning or not complying is:

- The reasonable belief that doing so would result in a significant threat to themselves, any other person, or their or any other persons' property;
- Because they have been subjected to harassment and reasonably believe that doing so would result in further harassment; or
- Because it is not practicable to do so within a reasonable period.

INDEX

650 Index